THE
HIDDEN
DIMENSION

THE HIDDEN DIMENSION

Psychodynamics in Compulsive Drug Use

Leon Wurmser, M.D.

NEW YORK • JASON ARONSON • LONDON

*To my family: Zdenka, Daniel, David, Yoram, and to my mother; to all
friends, loyal in adversity*

Meglio e la piccola certezza che la gran bugia.

The little truth is better than the big lie.

—Leonardo da Vinci

CONTENTS

PREFACE

This book will raise more questions than it answers and arouse more controversies than it reconciles. It will look at drug abuse in an unaccustomed, strange light, go against popular opinion, and touch on a number of social and legal taboos. Its major ideas can be summarized in the following five points.

1. The focus of inquiry and intervention is shifted from drugs to personality, from drug use as a social phenomenon— which might with relative ease be manipulated, deterred, or cured by such external means as counseling or the law—to drug use as a symptom of a depth dimension which has up to now been only rarely investigated or treated. Psychoanalysis and psychotherapy have much to contribute to the study and treatment of this dimension.

At a time when both psychoanalysis and psychiatry are under fire as irrelevant, moribund, or dead, this book asserts its firm grounding in the psychoanalytic process of inquiry in regard to both observation and abstraction. It will refuse to join the current stampede to get "imperial gallons of facts"—the flight from theoretical construction and hierarchies of abstraction. Nor will it take any such theory itself as dogma, as anything more than a form of symbolic representation.

Symbols are not facts, but ways to order them—indispensable, but on a different plane of understanding.

2. Since psychoanalysis as theory may in turn benefit from the new observations gained in this field, the present exploration tries, above all, to examine in depth a considerable number of individual cases, and thus question and enlarge some common, and a few less common, psychoanalytic and psychiatric concepts, especially narcissism and aggression; the defense mechanisms of denial and externalization; and the problem of splitting. In the case of simple defense mechanisms, added investigation may lead to a deeper understanding of their actually quite complex nature and eventually to their hierarchical ordering. They must, at the same time, be viewed as patterns of drive gratification, as cognitive forms and basic elements of symbolization, and as fundamental action patterns. Perhaps most important, this book reexamines the concept of boundaries and limits—a notion crucial for an understanding of these patients—and integrates it more solidly with current psychoanalytic theory. Consideration of the affects of guilt and shame and their archaic precursors will be of special help in attaining this deeper understanding.

3. Differentiating nonintensive from heavy drug use shows that sociolegal definitions are woefully inadequate for a rational approach. The concept of compulsiveness is chosen instead as most operationally meaningful, both in this particular field and in psychopathology in general. As a criterion, it serves to establish single mental acts, rather than whole persons, as emotionally sick (see Kubie 1954), and as such proves especially useful, fruitful, and elucidating. This specific "elementary particle" which fulfills the criteria for scientific knowledge as set down by Cassirer (1921, p. 428 and 1923a, p. 76), has many practical, theoretical, and even value philosophical implications.

Compulsiveness is a *relative* property of mental processes and may vary from person to person or within an individual from one time to another. Mental processes felt to be absolutely compulsive or absolutely free either do not occur at all or are very rare. Finally, since it is to a large extent observable, this criterion may prove particularly helpful for research.

4. Since drug abuse always involves pharmacological and social factors, it is strategically placed at the crossroads of psychoanalysis and pharmacology, of somatic medicine and general psychiatry, of sociology and politics, of history and philosophy, even of literature and anthropology.

No look at the hidden dimension can fail to notice the connections between the main underlying problems in the individual and sociocultural and philosophical antitheses, conflicts, and contradictions. Connecting lines must be drawn from the individual to the surrounding circles of etiology, no matter how unspecific they remain.

Drawing connections, for example, between various aspects of the superego and of value philosophy displays the pathology of the formation ideals in compulsive drug users against the backdrop of a deeper, more general betrayal of philosophy and is both psychoanalytically and philosophically illuminating. The experiences garnered in psychoanalytic and psychotherapeutic work cast new light on questions central to value philosophy and philosophy of law, and hence on legislation and law enforcement as well.

The psychoanalyst is in a delicate position: he cannot advocate concrete ethical values but must remain, even in his clinical work, a scientist primarily beholden to the value system inherent in every scientific method. Yet, as it applies to his field (integration, freedom from compulsions, integrity and honesty, etc.), this value system has an ineluctable effect upon his material decisions; his central value is beyond ethics in a narrow sense, but not beyond value philosophy which, as implemented in psychoanalysis, influences general ethics perhaps more profoundly than does any other area of scientific inquiry.

5. Obviously there are no simple or quick solutions to be found, at any level. The answers to many questions still lie out of reach, and glib, either/or reactions inevitably founder on this complexity.

In no case of severe drug use does one form of treatment suffice. As with severe chronic physical illnesses, like leukemia or tuberculosis, one method of therapy is not enough; many modalities may have to be employed, concomitantly or sequentially. It is not at all rare that a therapeutic advance becomes possible only when, for example, individual, group, and family therapy are combined and then supported by medication and vocational counseling.

The one-track mentality is common, a cardinal part of the usual bureaucratic requirements imposed on drug treatment programs. A single modality orientation does not do justice to the complexity of the problem and quite often proves disastrous. Not only may it impede the tackling of severe inner problems, but it may also contribute to a severe pathology in entire programs and systems. A special study is therefore devoted to "insolence of office" as witnessed in the administration of such programs—a reflection and support of particularly noxious features of this type of illness by the people expected to treat it. Very often treatment comes down to the widespread policy of penny wise and pound foolish—by saving in the short run, the long-run expenditures grow most outrageously. One thinks of the enormous costs of criminality committed by compulsive drug users engendered for the most part by society's irrational approaches to their problems.

Even individual psychotherapy needs new methods, new parameters, to cope with the peculiar problems of this important group of patients. Psychotherapeutic work as usual quickly runs into insurmountable difficulties. At the same time some of the basic conditions of psychoanalysis (analysis of transference, countertransference, resistance) remain indispensable.

To present a balanced view of depth and surface, of inner suffering and outer pressures and temptations, will be one of the goals of this book. Out of it, however, arises a second, more important goal: to formulate more rational approaches to the major problems in this field. Not far away is a third, for me central aim: to view severe drug use, particularly addictions of various types, in a more human, humane and sympathetic light, to enlighten the public (lay and professional) about the severity of the plight underlying the compulsive drug use, a plight which is then in turn inflicted by the user on his immediate surroundings and on society at large and thus evokes rage, revenge, bitterness and disdain from many. Thus the drug problem will become not only a problems of personalities, but because of that change in focus, will be connected with some of the relevant issues of culture and philosophy in general.

What numbers are for statistical research studies, case descriptions are for an inquiry like this, a particular form of painstaking research over many years, resembling the research a historian undertakes. Just as one picture can express what a thousand words cannot, these case presentations, though highly condensed, can give the reader a feel for the point I will work out more systematically in the theoretical chapters, thus trying to avoid what Clifford Yorke criticized with much justification: "that too many papers fail to supply convincing clinical evidence to support their assertions" (1970, p. 156). Moreover, many descriptions of drug patients suffer from a patronizing, dehumanizing narrowing of the focus on the symptom and immediately adjacent pathology, in stark contrast, for example, to the full human pictures drawn by Freud in his case histories, even in vignettes. What we tend to forget is that even in severe impairment (whether of neurologic or of psychopathologic nature) the mind functions as a whole, the personality appears as a new, often strange whole whose deeper unity and meaning we need to grasp, despite and including its distortions and lacunae. As trite as it may sound: a drug addict is not primarily a drug addict, but a severely damaged human being with reestablished unity, fullness and reintegration, though in a narrower form, a unity which nevertheless remains remarkable. S. Langer (1972, pp. 322–324) speaks, in regard to similar organic reintegration, of the "law of concentrical reduction" (Börnstein); we may—glancingly—apply it to the psychosocial reintegration on a lower level which we witness.

The focus will be on two dozen individual cases, most of them studied in great detail and over many years by myself, material collected over nearly two decades (a dozen years of which were spent mainly in work with these patients). Several very impressive cases or vignettes were contributed, very much at the end of writing this book and as illustrations for some of its major points, by a number of co-workers at University of Maryland Hospital or by colleagues from the outside.

These patient studies teach us more graphically how to order the bewildering amount of data, the more stunning emotional reactions in the surroundings, and help us to arrive at more satisfactory conceptualizations.

But there are several major problems connected with such case descriptions: The first and most important by far, is that of confidentiality. These revelations were given mostly in the doctor-patient relationship, a setting of the highest privilege for protection from public knowledge. The ways how I try to solve the conflict between this right for confidentiality and the need to make this book a living, convincing document, had to be varied. In a number of most detailed cases, I was able, early on, or during or after treatment, to get an explicit permission from the patient to publish, in disguised form, the relevant aspects of our work.

In other cases—due to the peculiar combination of this form of socially, so massively shame-laden pathology, the intimacy of revelations, the defiant flight from treatment into renewed illegality, or the advance into a life totally respectable—it was neither easily possible nor advisable to contact the patients; in some instances a decade or more had elapsed. In these cases, I tried to disguise the material as much as humanly possible, without infringing on the quality of the notes; sometimes I tried to give a composite picture from two patients—to attain both protection and relevance.

And then there were unhappy instances where I contacted former patients and was told off in no uncertain words.

A second problem is that of all research of this type: what appears relevant in psychotherapy—to patient and to me—points up what Cassirer called (in regard to historical science) the "paradox of an objective anthropomorphism" (1944, p. 191): I cannot *prove* my point in the sense of the natural sciences, but I can *present* a strong case for the meaningful connections of innumerable observations and for the hierarchical structure of abstractions I build on them. The reader will have to believe me, trusting my professional integrity and honesty, that what I can give him only in small, fragmentary evidence—here a few sentences and generalizations out of several hundreds of therapy hours with one patient, there one life history standing for dozens of others which I came to know—is in fact truly representative for my overall findings.

To enhance the authenticity and vividness as well as to allow the reader to some extent his own evaluation and critique, unfettered by the abstractions presented by me, I included, whenever feasible, nearly verbatim although condensed notes from the sessions (taken in shorthand). I am very cognizant that, as in all research in psychoanalysis and psychotherapy, the quandary is what Merton Gill so aptly called "the dilemma between the significant and the exact," a dilemma faced but not solved by our current attempts.

Perhaps we have to resign ourselves in this field to what Aristotle in the Nicomachean Ethics (Bk. 1, Ch. III) wrote—namely, that the same exactness cannot be expected in all departments of science and that it is part of wisdom to expect merely that amount of precision which the nature of the field admits (see Wallerstein 1963, 1964, 1974, Wallerstein and Sampson 1971).

Thirdly, several commentators of my work have felt that what I observed may be quite valid for white middle class drug users, but not, e.g., for lower class or black users. I cannot go along with this. It is true that most of the patients I have worked with intensively over long periods of time, were white (although I offered my services to many black compulsive drug users); but all my findings were corroborated in shorter therapies with non-white patients as well. The patients came from all social classes. Some of the cases actually presented here were very poor and of lower class background, many of middle class, a few of upper class origin.

I also cannot agree that what holds true for a very intelligent, introspective, articulate patient (and again the vast majority of patients seen in psychotherapy by me fall into this category) needs not also be true for less articulate people. Again, I have seen—it is true, mostly for shorter periods—too many compulsive drug users who were dimwitted and even a few outright retarded to presume that the old adage "Natura non facit saltus" (nature does not make jumps) suddenly would be cancelled in this realm. The dumb addict shows the same dynamics as the highly intelligent one—just as the feeble-minded hysteric, obsessive, or schizophrenic shows the same basic symptoms as the genius in the same category.

The very same holds true for yet another objection: "You see only those who seek psychiatric help." To begin with, I have worked with many who were compelled to sit in groups or to enter programs. Several of the patients presented were on probation under the condition to be seen in psychotherapy. I also have interviewed quite a few who did not see their compulsive drug use as a problem. However, I am unable to perceive any really basic difference in underlying pathology between them and those who were highly motivated to come to psychotherapy. If anything, the psychopathology appears more striking and extensive precisely in those who seek their help by the means of drugs and a vast array of other external actions, rather than in those who stick to long-term therapy. I can boldly make such an extrapolation because I have interviewed so many who came at the time of a drug panic from the street and just wanted methadone to tie them over, or who were sitting in jail because they were caught—or students whose parents dragged them in to see me. It just does not make any decisive difference as to the central issue raised here!

However, two restrictions may have to be mentioned now:

Unfortunately I shall not be able to cover sufficiently an area which clinically, psychologically, even logically, definitively belongs under the title given to this book: alcohol abuse and its psychology. Although

I have treated in psychotherapy several alcoholics and more superficially many dozens more, I am able only up to a point to integrate all those findings into the picture gained in my work with the other compulsive drug users. Moreover there is such a vast literature in the field of alcoholism the scanning of which I leave to those better equipped. It will become rather clear, however, that most of the findings of this book can indeed rather easily be translated into those with compulsive alcohol (and perhaps even nicotine) abuse.

With even stronger reason I leave out all references to neurophysiology and brain chemistry. It is not my kettle of fish, nor do I consider it particularly relevant for the purpose of this book, which does not study primarily the effects of drugs or the imputed neurophysiological basis of psychopathology, but merely the psychology of the drug consumer, his motivation, and his personality.

Ample use will be made of metaphors—both in clinical descriptions and in theory formation. Unlike many today I hold that metaphor is the warp and woof of developing a science; only at late stages of research can symbolic representations reach higher levels of abstraction. We are still very far from such a stage in psychoanalysis and psychiatry—if it is attainable at all. Wherever practical I have signified the use of what I consider metaphorical notions and constructs with quotation marks, for example "energies," "mechanisms."

Part of this approach perforce is the frequent use of formulations by great poets or philosophers of the past. I hold with Freud that it is granted to them "to haul up without too much effort from the whirlpool of their own feelings the deepest truths, towards which the rest of us have to find our way through tormenting uncertainty and with restless groping" (1930, p. 133). Wherever possible, I have tried to put the often foreign experiences of my patients in the context of literary and shared human tradition and formulation.

In several appendices supportive material, in the form of test observations, phenomenological studies, and studies of approaches to severe psychopathology, is added so that the interested reader can check on some of the major assertions in the book itself. This was done to leave the main flow of the argument uninterrupted.

The entire book, however, has one central focus: the hidden, often stridently negated, slyly circumvented core issue of drug abuse—the *severe inner problems* underlying the compulsive use of mind-altering drugs, the use of drugs to prop up *defective defenses*, the interplay between individual psychopathology, severe family disorders, and sociocultural conflicts ("collective pathology"). Drugs are not the problem. Even drug abuse is not really the core but solely the symptom hiding what it proclaims to reveal. Cautious recommendations will be made concerning how to cope more rationally with individual and social conflicts and how to resolve some of the most glaring inconsistencies and antitheses in the origin of, and in the response to, compulsive drug use.

Still some of the insights as well as the recommendations may strike many as revolutionary, as outlandish, as puzzling—many who have not struggled themselves with these patients' problems for years, who have not been burned many times trying to build up programs dealing with them, and who have not been called to help by the desperate families of these patients and subsequently vilified and cursed.

Yet I consider this type of effort very important. A considerable proportion of the population in our culture is involved in mild or severe forms of substance abuse; dependent on definition it may be less than one fourth or more than half of the population. And a very large group undoubtedly is involved in compulsive forms of drug use (at least between 5 and 10 percent of the population in Western countries), if we include, as we must, alcohol abuse. Drug abuse probably involves more people than schizophrenia or most forms of somatic illness; therefore, systematic in-depth studies must be considered with the seriousness a social and health problem of such magnitude demands.

In addition the social consequences of this symptom are fantastic— yet another partially hidden dimension, usually dealt with at best either cavalierly or irrationally, always inconsistently, and mostly by the dreadnaught of the legal system which is as suited to deal with this problem as with plague, cholera or depressions.

I hear already and again exclamations sounding loud and protestingly: "You use here a medical model; how inappropriate!" My answer: "Yes, it is a problem of illness and with that of medicine, and more specifically, it is a problem of psychopathology and therefore of psychiatry and psychoanalysis. I shall defend why logically and historically this makes more sense than any other currently fashionable claims. It is the only approach which is humane, seeing and treating this illness like all others, as part of the human condition and its tragic dimensions, and still taking it very seriously—neither, as a social and legal deviance, put down with levity or vindictiveness, nor, as a part of politics and economics, dehumanized to some statistics, nor, as a part of physiology, magically overcome by some enzyme repairs and powerful potions."

The time has long come when we ought to act and condemn less and try to understand more.

Acknowledgments

Thanks are due to very many persons who have made this study possible. Above all my gratitude goes out to the people at the University of Maryland Hospital and Medical School who have given me the latitude and support without which this work would not have been possible. Special thanks go to John M. Dennis, Dean of the Medical School and Vice-Chancellor.

Then particularly hearty thanks are due to Dr. Peter Bourne, now the President's Special Assistant on Health Issues and the former Assistant Director of the Special Action Office for Drug Abuse in the White House, who originally, in 1974, commissioned the study out of which this book eventually grew, and to his co-workers at Metcor, Joseph P. Kane and Yonica Homiller.

I feel no less appreciation toward Dr. Jason Aronson who, merely on the basis of the first study, allowed me to write this current book without undue restriction.

But then again it appears a little unfair not having started off thanking the co-workers who have contributed directly in discussions, help, and write-ups to this work: above all Stanley L. Rodbell, Lucy Kirkman, Cloe Sojit Madanes, Drs. Ari Gerson, Ellen McDaniel, Melvin M. Kayce, Antonio Wood, Leon Levin, Jay Phillips, Henry Harbin, Rochelle Herman, Edward Khantzian, the secretaries (especially Ruth Aaronson), and the patients who were gracious enough to lend me their permission to use often very painful, sensitive material. Special thanks go to R. McLaughlin, who helped unceasingly with the logistics of this study, and to J. Whitehill, who helped me with some crucial earlier efforts of getting my thoughts published.

Then I ought to give tribute to the Drug Abuse Administration of the State of Maryland, especially Mrs. Hubertine Marshall and Irvin

Desser, who have in great fairness and understanding supported the buildup of the program and helped us through many more difficult times, and to some of the earlier proponents of the treatment efforts I was involved in, especially Drs. A.A. Kurland, Herzl Spiro and J. Elkes.

But then—how could this book have been written without the thoughtful teaching and comments from within the Baltimore–District of Columbia Institute of Psychoanalysis, above all by Drs. Jenny Waelder Hall, Paul Gray, James Bing, Francis McLaughlin, S. Tower, and R. Marburg, and, from without, by Drs. David Beres, H. Kohut, and O. Kernberg, as well as the deep and steady friendship of my peers, both within the Institute, especially Drs. Alan Zients, Cibeles Vidaud, Ellen Mc Daniel, Deha and George Owen, William Arnold, and Hazen Kniffin; and within the psychoanalytic community at large: Drs. Helm Stierlin, Henry Krystal, Henry Rosett, and André Haynal. Many stimulating discussions with all of them have contributed in a more hidden form to the shaping of the thoughts presented here. So did my close working relationship with Dr. Joseph Berman, Chief of Community Medicine at Sinai Hospital and, for a number of years, the continuous encouragement, support, and constructive criticism by two other faithful friends: Dr. Edward J. Khantzian in Cambridge, Mass. and Dr. Ellen Feer Devereux in Honolulu, Hawaii. All these friends were not deterred when the gales of political storms were threatening to destroy the chances of finishing the endeavors described in these pages.

Since I presume that quite a bit in this book will be controversial, that some may be misunderstood and misconstrued and other considerations refuted or refined, it is particularly important to stress that I alone am fully responsible for the ideas, findings, and conclusions. They cannot reflect in any way the opinions of the scientists and clinicians who have stimulated my thinking; this is especially applicable to the philosophical considerations.

THE
HIDDEN
DIMENSION

Chapter 1

INTRODUCTION

*Non ridere, non lugere, neque detestari, sed
intelligere*
(Not to deride, not to grieve, not to detest, but
to comprehend)
—Spinoza

The Neglect of Psychological Factors

I open this book with an admission of profound, mixed feelings which have gripped me untold times over the many years as I have worked with addicts of all forms. At first I was hit by the provocative nature of their habits and attitudes—a feeling that I was indeed dealing with the scum of mankind; anger about being lied to and manipulated; and scorn about their flaunting of being high and their flouting of all efforts to help them and of all the rules we live by.

Yet the more I got to know them, anger, disdain, and frustration vanished, and a deep sense of despair and pity broke through—often a sense of helplessness, a wish to help, and an ignorance of how to help. The problems of drugs, drug effects, and drug prohibition receded before the overwhelming problems posed by these patients who sought help, were forced to be treated, fled from help, died.

When I followed the literature, the discussions at scientific conventions, the opinions expressed by friends, in audiences, by lawyers, no suggestions, no help were offered. A vast terra incognita was lying before me, covered by such expressions as: "They are just sociopaths!" or "They were not motivated," "the living dead," "the dope fiends." Thus the problem posed itself with glaring sharpness: How could drug abuse be understood from the context of the individual's life experience, his wishes and fears, his deficiencies and efficiencies, his conflicts in past and present—in short, from a psychological point of view. How could these deeper problems be treated? We have a realtive plethora of pharmacological studies and sociological inquiries. I certainly do not imply a redundancy; much more work in these fields should be done. The politics and the legal aspects of illegal drug use fill the columns of our newspapers ad nauseam; many deal seriously and compassionately with the problems, many others exploit them, but most just skim the surface.

Drug abuse has remained off the beaten psychiatric and psychologi-cal track. There are good reasons: one being precisely the complexity of this problem, namely that psychological factors are so tightly interwoven with sociological, economic, and legal factors. More importantly, the field has been ruled by law enforcement bureaucrats and has traditionally been off limits to the core troup of psychological investigators. When the values of power, expediency, public success, and cost efficiency are uppermost, and the required strategies of manipulation and control become so intermingled with therapeutic considerations, then the value of insight, inner change and control, and with them the methods of introspection and empathy, must take a backseat. Yet, during twelve years that I have consistently devoted a large part of my professional work to nearly all types of problems connected with the broad area of drug abuse, I have been struck more than anything else by the overriding impression that severe psycho-pathology was the warp and woof in those people for whom drug abuse had become a real problem and that these inner problems were indeed of crucial explanatory importance—the hidden dimension.

At the same time, I noticed waves of resistance against this view. Medical colleagues frowned upon it. Psychiatrists doubted it. Even some psychoanalytic friends felt I exaggerated the role of intrapsychic and family problems as compared with social, cultural, and political influences. My coworkers in the drug abuse programs were often quite negative about recognizing the psychological problems and emphasized instead—sometimes with some derision—the value of manipulation and exhortation in the form of counseling. The patients themselves very often—though by no means always—put their problems on friends, "bad environment", "curiosity", and "society". Their families regularly did the same—nearly without fail.

A large role in this negation is played by an antipsychiatric bias on many levels, a prejudice against looking at one's inner life, at times so strong that we might call it "psychophobia". It reflects a deepseated fear of taking emotional factors seriously and leads to the *denial of the importance of emotional conflict*. This denial, as we shall see, haunts drug abusers as well as those dealing with it.

Thus I decided to try to collate as much evidence for the importance of psychopathology as I could muster and put it in a reasonable perspective.

Definition of Major Terms

Ỷ Drug abuse is clearly a social, legal and political term with strong derogatory, judgmental explicitness (not just connotations). Therefore I would have liked to avoid this term altogether; yet, as I shall state shortly, simply to change names and their connotations does not deal with either problem: the one with hanging a depreciating label on some behavior, and the more important one that there is in fact a group of persons who are *clinically, psychiatrically* and *medically* "patients," suffering—not because society proclaims their symptom as "drug abuse" but because they use pharmaca for unknown inner reasons and with often deleterious effects, and continue using them in spite of the knowledge that the drugs not only help but also interfere, often massively, with daily life and reaching for their life goals. They themselves see it as "abuse"—often, not always. Thus "drug abuse" has a psychological significance as well—besides the odious and noxious sociolegal meaning. For that reason I shall continue using it, but occasionally replace it with terms which do, I believe, more justice to the psychiatric issues involved.

The ancient use of drugs is interwoven with mythology. Intoxication was sanctioned and restricted to the religious ritual. It magically lifted the faithful over the boundaries of time, space and individuality, and let him forget the limitations of reality. Thus drugs were considered a gift of the gods—those ancient guardians of regression.

But can we consider such use "drug abuse"? Some authors would deny it and define drug abuse as any use of a drug for reasons which are medically not accepted and are against the prevailing social and legal standards (e.g. Jaffe 1965). I suggest that it is more consistent with medical tradition, logically and practically, to define as drug abuse proper the use of any mind-altering drug for the purpose of inner change if it leads to any transient or long range interference with social, cognitive or motor functioning or with physical health, regardless of the legal standing of the drug.

Again this puts the focus on the person instead of arbitrary societal standards. Why should, for example, the drunkenness of a physician at a party or driving under the influence of alcohol not be drug abuse, whereas the often ineffective smoking of one marijuana cigarette would be? Or why should compulsive smoking be any less a form of drug abuse than heroin addiction?

There are some alternate, less burdened words.

A term which lacks all sociolegal connotations is the one typically used in Europe: *toxicomania*—the craving for toxic substances. Thus I find this term by far preferable to "drug abuse" and plan to use it at times for a very significant segment out of the area covered by "drug abuse" as I defined it—but still the latter remains the broader term, as we shall note very shortly.

A third term, even less devaluing in meaning, is the one used by Radó: *pharmacothymia*, in a narrow sense denoting a mood disorder, akin to manic-depressive illness, but marked by the use of drugs. In a broader sense this term can mean: the use of drugs for emotional reasons without any relationship to cyclothymic illness; in this sense the concept is eminently useful and rich in meaning, as we shall discover in the course of the systematic exploration to follow.

The term most frequently used by me, because of its psychodynamically most telling import, will be *compulsive drug use*—obviously again covering a narrower area than the broad field marked out by the definition of drug abuse given.

In the sweeping sociolegal considerations and the political pronouncements (as well as the fears of parents or physicians) one crucial fact is obliterated: the clear and quite radical distinction between experimental and occasional users on the one side, and intensive and compulsive users on the other side. The first group rarely presents problems—with the exception of bad trips or accidental overdose—but they represent the vast majority of the so-called drug problem. All the energy—medical, social, legal, and otherwise—devoted to the casual user is drawn away from the real problem that needs infinitely more attention: the compulsive drug user. In him the drug use is solely the tip of the iceberg, an indicator of all the deeper troubles besetting him, and which we will study in detail. Only those relatively few casual or experimental users proceed to predominantly compulsive use who carry a set of rather specific predispositions. We have to spot early and treat this much smaller category. If we equate the two—and both popular prejudice and our legal system do just this—we do the same as if we treated any and every elevation of body temperature in every person with broad spectrum antibiotics and isolation.

A derivative myth is the frequently heard belief that "once heroin, always heroin," that to take it once or a few times already hooks the person. In reality there are very many heroin users who, for years, take it irregularly, occasionally (the so-called chippers) or in binges.

All these thoughts can be applied equally well to alcohol consumption.

This carries us to a far more sophisticated classification, the one used in the Second Report of the National Commission on Marijuana and Drug Abuse (Shafer 1972, pp. 95–97); here five groups of use are distinguished: *Experimental use* is a self-limited trial of drugs, primarily motivated by curiosity or the desire to experience new feeling or mood states. *Social or recreational use* occurs in social settings among friends or acquaintances who desire to share an experience perceived by them as both acceptable and pleasurable, usually on a more frequent basis than experimental use. *Circumstantial-situational use* is task-specific and is motivated by the wish to cope with a specific, sometimes recurrent, situation or condition of a personal or vocational nature. *Intensified use* is defined as the regular, long-term, patterned use of drugs at a minimum level of at least once daily while still compatible with social and economic integration and apparent compensation. "*Compulsive use* is patterned at both high frequency and high intensity levels of relatively long duration, producing physiological or psychological dependence such that the individual cannot at will discontinue such use without experiencing physiological discomfort or psychological disruption. It is characterized primarily by significantly reduced individual and social functioning."

For practical purposes the first of these two groups (experimental and social users) appear not to be particularly associated with serious pre-existing psychopathology, whereas the latter two most definitely are, and very many of class 3 as well. Obviously, we deal here with a continuum, a curve of compulsiveness steeply inclining between classes 2 and 4.

However, since this division is based on external behavior we are led into a semantic quandary, because compulsiveness, drivenness in a psychological, subjective, and psychoanalytically relevant sense is present wherever we find significant psychopathology (the exact correlation of compulsion and emotional illness will be studied in chapter 4). Therefore, the nomenclature will have to be changed here. The fifth group should rather be called *psychologically or physically addicted* ("enslaved").

After this revision the continuum can be put into the following (admittedly oversimplified and overgeneralized) graph—estimated solely from very long and broad clinical experience:

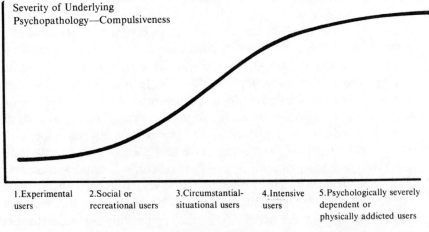

Type of Drug Abuse

This simple curve has to be modified: accessibility, legality, and acceptability by the immediate surrounding tend to flatten it. Good examples are the use of nicotine and alcohol throughout society, the use of cannabis among graduates of the "youth culture," heroin among the youngsters in some particularly degraded areas of the ghetto. How far this flattening of the curve actually goes I do not know.

Of course the reverse is equally true: the more inaccessible a drug is and the more laden with social and legal opprobrium, the more severe usually is the psychopathology of the users. In other words: *a compulsive alcohol or nicotine abuser shows far less preexisting psychopathology than a compulsive (or even casual) user of heroin, LSD or cocaine.* I suggest that the reason lies in the inner resistance against jumping over the hurdles of illegality and massive social disapproval: this hurdle appears lower the more severe the inner pressure for relief, the drivenness, and the extent of pathology.

I gladly also would admit exceptions; no curve is true for every individual. It is an average. But I have not yet been convinced by many self-styled "exceptions" which proclaim their well controlled, intensive use of cannabis, amphetamines or alcohol, and their total lack of any psychopathology or of interference with good functioning. One becomes modest and undogmatic in this clinical work, but still I meet these loud claims with considerable skepsis and puzzlement. I keep wondering: am I fooled, or are they?

Two Illustrations

CASE 1: HEINRICH

When I presented the Shafer Commission's grouping and my curve to a group of second year medical students, one twenty-three-year-old white man protested. During college he had used marijuana and hashish two to four times a day, studied with amphetamines for exams, and sampled all the other major drugs short of heroin. He still quite often used cannabis as relaxant at bedtime or on weekends. He felt that driving a car, playing his guitar, tasting food—all were enhanced by the use of marijuana. He denied ever having had perceptual distortions with it, but ascribed to his extensive cannabis use not only quite severe interference with his short term memory and attention, but also an overall decrease in his memory. He had for this reason reduced his drug use and took the drug only when he did not have to learn, and sometimes, before finals, went without it altogether. Since, he stated, all his friends, as a matter of fact, his whole dorm, engaged in similar drug use, he felt he was "using, not abusing" the drug, that its use was partly recreational and social and partly situational. He felt no psychological "compulsion" to use it. He was, he felt, completely able to take it or leave it according to his rational judgment.

Since I felt this case both typical (in phenomenology) and yet bewildering (as to claimed and overt absence of psychopathology), I sat together with him for an hour alone and for another hour together with a black student who, it turned out, had never experimented with any drug—not even alcohol or aspirin. During the first hour, Heinrich denied all psychopathology: family life was usually happy; he had had several steady girlfriends over the years; his only problem was a very irascible younger sister, a typical problem child. My first conclusion was that, as is often the case, statistical and general findings do not have to encompass the individual case. When the third participant joined us, however, Heinrich started needling both of us: we were not curious enough; we had not explored all the beauty life has, all the great variety of experience, including the religious and mystical realities he discovered with psychedelic drugs. I started wondering again. It turned out that he had always toyed with fate through such activities as sky diving and, of course (predictably), gambling.

He finally agreed that this constant need, not just to experience various stimuli but to gamble with mind and life contained many compulsive elements. Pathology became even more evident when he interjected that for five years he had not watched or listened to any news nor read any newspapers. "Why should I care about something I cannot control anyway?" In short, all his extracurricular activity was intended either to gain control against all odds over what he experienced or to avoid it altogether. Even his reckless curiosity and drivenness to discover new experiences seemed part of this *counter-phobic activity*—the effort, frantic at times, to prove he was in control. Characteristically, when challenged in exams, for example, he reduced his counterphobic activities. Why should he need them? After all, the exam was, like skydiving and getting high, a test of whether he was indeed in control of fate and his life. The counterphobic theme in this vignette was a reckless, audacious stand against death and insanity, against losing ultimate control. Each challenge became an ultimate proof. This will be seen as one of the important features of clearly compulsive drug use. (See cases 4, 12, and 15)

CASE 2: BLACK ROSE

As a counterexample, I present now the brief history of the second case typical of severely compulsive drug users. Black Rose was a twenty-one-year-old girl—unskilled, but rather intelligent, not unattractive, black-haired, pale, acne-scarred—who came for temporary methadone maintenance and detoxification from heroin and Dilaudid. I saw her intermittently in psychotherapy for about half a year—intermittently because, as soon as she was withdrawn from methadone, she dropped out of treatment, came back, stayed perhaps two or three months, and left again. Here are excerpts from what she told me:

At sixteen I started off with LSD, then smoked grass, then hash, then took amphetamines and barbiturates. About four years ago, I started taking heroin on weekends, out of curiosity, I guess. I was raped about the same time, when drunk with a boy, and got pregnant, but got an abortion. I really have no sexual desires. My mother hates sex; she sees it as a bad thing. It makes her sad when someone is pregnant. She did not want me to be born [the patient is the middle of three girls]. She tried to kill herself when she was pregnant with me. I was always taught that sex is a bad thing. She now keeps me all the time at home and locks me up. She is overprotective; she loves me too much. She threatened to beat me up if I had sex with a boy. She said if I did not shape up—with sex or drugs—she would shoot me and herself. She slit up my clothes, so that I cannot leave the house. She is afraid of losing me. I would like to have a baby [she thought she was pregnant again] even if it is only to spite my mother. I never fought her. I was a good girl. She favored me, but she has to understand that one day she will have to let go of me. I tried to kill myself before with barbiturates, after fights with my mother about going out. Once I threw a mirror at her and cut her leg. I kicked her once. If you had to live with her you would also try to kill yourself to get away from her.

After an interruption in treatment and, after an additional suicidal attempt with Tuinal, she mentioned that she was back on Dilaudid. "When I got off methadone, I felt sick. Father went and bought me dope. I hate him. He tried to molest me, his own daughter, when he bought me the dope. He tried it once before, after the abortion. I hit him and was screaming and crying. My mother threatened to kill him. Then I forgave him. Mother and father always yelled at each other. He used to whip us with a belt. When he was walking by, we all would duck, scared he'd hit us. If he tried again to sleep with me I'd kill him with a butcher knife; I have it ready. I do not go near him, do not talk to him. Mother threatened again to shoot me if I took drugs again. If I'd die she would bury me the same day. She has already bought three burial plots, one for herself, one for father, one for me."

All these ghastly stories were told with flatness—not a schizophrenic flatness, but a depressed, sad, apathetic one. She occasionally mentioned "hurt." A few weeks later: "I visited a boy. He has a $300 a day habit. I gave him all the money I had in the bank, $42. I helped him a little bit, but my mother slapped me for it." She reminisced with loathing about her earlier LSD experience: "I felt very dirty. My teeth felt like they had a coating, my hands as if they were made of rubber. My face looked horrible in the mirror." She unsuccessfully tried to find a job and live with an aunt, but was not accepted because of her drug history. In order to get away from the stifling presence of her mother, she wanted again to get off methadone, and go far away, traveling with a girlfriend. Her request for withdrawal could not be refused (because of the regulations). Two weeks later she was brought back by her mother who protested to me: " *You* told her to move out. She was not yet ready. She kept taking sleeping pills, fell and busted her head open. I want to see her institutionalized rather than dead. My love is all for her." It was at that encounter that her mother confirmed father's seductions, her own threats to kill Rose, and the grave plots. The patient was hospitalized, but continued the psychotherapy with a perceptive, warm female medical student who had sat in during some of the previous therapy sessions. Half a year later, on leave of absence from the state hospital, the girl killed herself with an overdose of barbiturates. It surely takes no psychoanalyst nor any explicit abstract concepts to recognize the connections in this life history.

The Challenge of the Central Questions

In this book the focus of inquiry and emphasis is different than in most other studies, and that dictates a whole set of new questions. I do not pretend that I shall come up with equally clear new answers; much will be left hanging in the air, but this stance still seems to me at least preferable to the attempt so commonly, though implicitly, made to find answers before the questions are known.

What then are the main questions raised by drug abuse?—drug abuse, as I have experienced it, not luridly fascinating, not heroic, not decadent or depraved, but drug abuse as a profound problem of inner conflict, haunting the patient, psychotherapist, and environment, a symptom fraught with compulsiveness and drivenness.

What are the extent and nature of severe psychopathology in compulsive drug users, as reflected by phenomenological and psychodiagnostic assessments (Appendix A) and observed in psychotherapy and psychoanalysis (chapters 3, 5–9)? What defines psychopathology and normality anyway (chapter 4)?

How do the current treatment modalities tackle serious psychopathology, including psychoses (Appendix B and C)? How can we understand some psychopathology as a consequence of drug use (chapter 10)? What influence does the family have (chapter 11)? What role do society, culture, and philosophical problems play (chapter 14) and what is the observed impact of ineffectively treated drug abuse on society at large (Appendix D)?

Then we turn to a series of more practical problems: What about the denial of psychopathology by the treating professions and the more general problems of psychophobia and anti-psychiatry (chapter 12)? We must examine the darkest, most sordid side—the collusion, in deviant action, between patients, staff and public officials, the abuse of power, the extrusion of such programs by the establishment, and some of the major psychological problems faced in running drug abuse programs (chapters 13, 15). Finally, we have to look into the future and search for ideas and ways how to explore, manage, and treat this massive psychopathology and which conclusions can be drawn in regard to prevention, law and education (chapters 16–19).

Since the leading idea of this book—that psychopathology is the central issue of all problems of compulsive drug use—is, in Schiller's beautiful expression, "von der Parteien Gunst and Hass verwirrt" (confused and threatened because of the parties' favor and hatred), I shall have to be as circumspect and comprehensive as one person can be and present as much detailed material as possible.

This is of necessity a personal study. I try to bring together vividly a long series of personal, often traumatic experiences, consistently attempting theoretical formulation, drawing on a vast array of metaphors, as well as on the higher level abstractions used in the one theory which allows me to order such an immense amount of material: psychoanalysis,

Methods Used

Naturally I cannot claim complete coverage of the entire literature and knowledge of all the existing programs which try to focus attention on these questions and problem areas. A synthesis from the following four sources was undertaken:

Direct personal observation during twelve years (1964-1976) of clinical work in various modalities of drug abuse programs: compulsory abstinence, short and long term detoxification, methadone maintenance; direct work in intensive individual psychotherapy (three to five hours a week and occasionally more per patient, often over three or four years) with about forty-five patients (taking near verbatim notes), group therapy (for about five years); family therapy (sporadic), and shorter as well as extensive evaluations of about one thousand additional patients. The first methods applied obviously almost exclusively to narcotics addicts with or without polydrug use in addition. Individual and family therapy applied to all types of drug abuse (narcotics, psychedelics, sedatives, stimulants) as well as to varied intensity (casual as well as compulsive drug users). In addition, in the preceding years of work as a psychiatrist and psychotherapist I have seen a number of toxicomanic patients, a few in long intensive treatment; actually several of the cases presented here stem from that time (1956-1964). Also, in order not to be blinded by the intensity of work with these patients against the rest of pathology and to remain able to compare, I saw and continue seeing many other types of patients in intensive psychotherapy and in classical psychoanalysis. I hope this prevented me from a practical one-sidedness and a theoretical narrow-mindedness.

A systematic review of the entire caseload of the program I am currently in charge of, a methadone maintenance program which places particular emphasis on *temporary maintenance*, six months to two years, and encourages continued attendance in the clinic after very slow, very cautious detoxification. I reviewed, together with the counselors, about three hundred cases.

A systematic review of the pertinent older and recent literature, correlating drug abuse with such topics as psychopathology, psychotherapy, psychoanalysis, psychosis, as given by various reference sources. This review yielded only relatively little of pertinence. Particularly the works of Chein and co-workers, of Krystal and Raskin, the papers of Wieder and Kaplan, and of Khantzian, were of outstanding value. Some of the old studies—by Radó, Simmel, Glover and Rosenfeld—are still very valuable reading and often raise new questions where complacency has closed our minds or give old but interesting answers to, and comments about, only seemingly new questions. Still, in much they are evidently outdated.

The direct *systematic perusal of the prominent journals* in the fields of psychiatry, psychoanalysis and drug abuse, covering mainly the last five or six years, but also going back to the twenties; hundreds of articles were studied in the hope of finding more information in regard to any of the problem areas to be covered. The yield was impressive only in reply to a very few of the questions posed, but practically zero as to the overwhelming remainder.

As always in such an ambitious undertaking, the nagging feeling remains that some crucial document or some exhaustive system of research and retrieval may have escaped attention—hopefully though not to the detriment of the overall picture and the conclusions reached.

Still, this worry has one added dimension anyway: In July 1975, after the first version of this book had been finished, a flash flood destroyed my office at University Hospital and with that a large portion of the resource material. I hope that most of the gaps caused by this were noticed and filled during the reworking of the book; where not, I hope for kind understanding and future supplementation from my readers.

Chapter 2

SOME POPULAR MISCONCEPTIONS

AND

SOME LESS POPULAR CLARIFICATIONS

"Man's most valuable trait is a judicious sense
of what not to believe"
  —Euripides, *Helen,* translated by R. Lattimore

The "Drug Epidemic" and the "Drug Problem"

This first set of myths can be summarized as follows: "Drugs and
pushers are an epidemic, a plague, a contagious disease which needs to
be stamped out with equal ruthlessness as it attacks society. If we could
get rid of the dangerous drugs of those retailing them—by plugging the
sources and by shooting the pushers—the problem would be largely
solved."

I remember meeting, early in my work with narcotics addicts, the
chief of the Narcotics Squad of a large city, a veteran of decades in the
field, who bluntly told me: "There is just one answer to dope: to line up
the junkies against a wall and shoot them, all of them. You waste your
time!"

This chapter is a revised and expanded version of "Drug Abuse: Nemesis of Psychiatry," which
appeared in *American Scholar* volume 41:393–407.

Some examples are taken from Szasz's thought-provoking *Ceremonial Chemistry* (1973). Nelson Rockefeller: "We, the citizens, are imprisoned by pushers. I want to put the pushers in prison so we can come out." And in a macabre one-upmanship William F. Buckley: "But it is not ... inappropriate to suggest that a condign means of ridding the world of convicted heroin pushers, is to prescribe an overdose" (p. 14).

In contrast to these attitudes, which Szasz rightly compares to witch hunts, many also eagerly concede that drug abuse is really a "people problem," not a "drug problem." In reality, this nearly always just remains lip service.

As Szasz points out, the labeling of drugs, sellers of drugs and users of drugs as illegal, as murderous and deviant serves moralistic, pseudoreligious purposes. The focus is shifted from the question "Why do people take drugs which often are noxious to them?" to the superficial command "Let's find the drugs, the pushers, and the users and quarantine or eliminate them."

I also am quite uncomfortable with the metaphor of the "epidemic." Not only does it lend itself quite easily to abuse by concretization and literalness, as just exemplified; more important, it also diverts the attention to the "agent" (the drug) and the "carrier" (the pusher), from the major focus where it belongs: the person who allegedly is "susceptible." Even if put in this milder form, we overlook that that person is not "infected" from the outside, but actively grasps drugs for inner reasons which will be explored in this inquiry. Here indeed the metaphor not only becomes more and more concrete in its application, but perforce leads in the wrong direction. Decades ago Radó had to deal with the same metaphor. In his still very valuable paper of 1933 he commented on how little fruit its use had borne, and asked: "How did it happen, then, that psychiatry became so wedded to this idea? The obvious answer is that the idea was developed because infectious diseases were used as paradigms."

Radó strongly objected in these classical, often cited, and still eminently valid words: "The psychoanalytic study of the problem of addiction begins... with the recognition of the fact that not the toxic agent, but the impulse to use it, makes an addict of a given individual ....The drug addictions are seen to be psychically determined, artificially induced illnesses; they can exist because drugs exist; and they are brought into being for psychic reasons."

Drug Use as "Ceremonial Chemistry"

This myth is Szasz's opinion: "Dangerous drugs, pushers and addicts are scapegoats of society. Their persecution is a ritual akin to the purification in primitive societies by stoning scapegoats. Drug abuse is not a chemical, but a ceremonial distinction." In Szasz's own words: "Heroin and marijuana are approached and avoided not because they are more 'addictive' or more 'dangerous' than alcohol and tobacco, but because they are more 'holy' or 'unholy'—as the case may be" (1973, p. 3). He goes beyond that and asserts that *phármakos* means "the person sacrificed as a scapegoat": "The root of modern terms such as pharmacology and pharmacopeia is therefore not 'medicine,' 'drugs,' and 'poison,' as most dictionaries erroneously state, but 'scapegoat'!"

As always with Thomas Szasz, whose thoughts are brilliant and provocative even when stretching a partial truth into the whole truth, he points out one important aspect of the problem.

It has been my own view for many years that the often hysterical concern about drugs, which actually was even more marked at the times of the narcotics legislation of 1914 and the Marijuana Tax Act of 1937 (see the outstanding book of David Musto, 1973), has a very strong ring of *projection*: an emotional outrage about an outer target, a "scapegoat," as Szasz remarks, instead of a more rational approach to a condemned part of oneself, with all the falsifications and exaggerations, the rage and collusion going with such a projection. Whoever has worked intensively and for a long time with the problem cannot help but feel that the concern and worry is mostly shifted away from the *persons* who take drugs and the *families* which breed them, to the *drugs*, that the anger is displaced from deeper personal and social problems to the superficial level of the drug effects, and that the practical response follows the lead of these displacements. Thus Szasz is quite right in depicting social policy as vendetta, where the drug is treated as the concretized evil, a demon to be exorcized by the most concrete, brute measures of persecution. (Actually the model of a mass phobia would probably be more apposite dynamically.)

When we pierce this veil of projection, externalization, and displacement, we discover that drug abuse is a problem, but it is more of a problem for what it hides than for what it shows.

But that is as far as I can accept Szasz's thoughts. I disagree with him and hold that "emotional illness" is not just a semantic error, or a misuse of metaphor, as Szasz postulates. For him "medical values have replaced religious values, medical rituals have taken the place of religious rituals...." He regards "the entire mental health movement as a gigantic pseudomedical ritual: that which is considered good is defined as mentally healthy and is embraced; that which is considered bad is defined as mentally sick and repudiated" (1973, p. 27).

The whole construction of Szasz is elegant and impressive, somewhat like the Eiffel Tower. But one of its pylons has been placed on a faulty premise and thus the entire tower with its flawless logic stands on muddled thinking. The faulty premise is that all values are ethical, that "healthy" perforce equals "good" and "legal," socially "acceptable," and "holy," whereas "ill" must equal "bad" and "illegal," "deviant" and "unholy." From this value muddle emerges the philosophical statement that, since we use a combination of game-analytic, sign-using, and rule-following models (Szasz 1961, p. 15), we deal in what is called mental illness or emotional disorders with ethical, sociopolitical, and economic violations of communication, or of rules, or with a mixing of various game plans, with special types of game playing behavior (p. 90). Szasz views the concept of mental illness as an illicit expansion of the medical model of illness to hysteria and hence to mental illness. According to him, the medical model is defined as "a state of disordered structure or function of the human body as a physicochemical machine"; thereafter the "new" criteria of disability and suffering were added, and eventually "any sign of malfunctioning" was declared ill. Therefore, the concept of mental illness is a myth: "we shall be compelled to regard psychiatry as dealing with communications or sign-using behavior, not with 'mental illness' " (p. 51).

Actually, as we shall examine in more detail in chapter 4, it was precisely the supposedly superadded criterion of "suffering" which was the starting point of delineating sickness or illness. Although the notions "ill" and "sick" were and are in many cultures mixed up with morally evil and bad, their ancient and original meanings have been and remain the foundation of all medicine: "causing harm, pain or disaster" (a thirteenth centure definition of the English word ill). Similarly the Latin words *aeger* and *aegrotus*, and Greek *nosos* and *nosein* meant "pained," physically or mentally suffering (see also Plato, *Laws* 929). The German *siech* (English "sick") means suffering, usually physically; the word is of very ancient, Indo-European origin and meaning and probably related to weak (*schwach*). Its derivative *Sucht* is physical and emotional suffering and actually has become in modern times and secondarily an equivalent to passionate greed; today *Sucht* is almost synonymous with "addiction," to drug dependency.

Thus emotional or mental illness has always been considered a special form of suffering and pain. It is the latter which served as a starting point to classify first somatic *together* with mental illness, then to find more precise criteria defining the origins of pain, and, with that, to move beyond this original criterion of suffering to the also already very ancient (Greek) concept of "disordered functioning" as a criterion of illness.

How compulsive drug use (*Sucht*) will fit into such a classification without illicit stretching of metaphor, will become clearer in chapter 4.

It is also relevant to note here that, most recently, the still fashionable sociological definition of mental illness and its use as primary criterion, the so-called labeling thesis, has been quite unhinged by Jane M. Murphy's (1976) important research. This, too, will be taken up in chapter 4.

Moreover, I very much question Szasz's etymology and his ensuing conclusions: that *phármakon* originally meant "scapegoat." From all sources it is convincing that *phármakon* and many related terms signify a "means," a "measure" to help, a "remedy"—whether by medication, by purification, or by poison. Sacrificial purification (with the help of a *phármakos*, a scapegoat) appears to be only one special, derivative form. Even in Homeric times, *pharmakon* clearly meant "drug, remedy, an herb."

In short, Szasz is right in criticizing the sociopolitical abuse of the concepts of illness and addiction in the form of scapegoating. He is wrong, however, in his logical premise that mental illness is basically a social judgment, a secondary wrong classification, a metaphorical mislabeling. Addiction is not just a ritual, a ceremonial activity, although occasionally it has become just that; it is a *Sucht*, an illness.

Drug Dependency as a Sociolegal Problem

This myth is really just an expansion and generalization of the second myth. It can be stated briefly: "Drug abuse and drug dependency are simply social deviancies created by the mores of a society."

Since, as we saw, "drug abuse" is viewed by and large as a sociolegal term and based in most publications on just such superficial criteria (as any use that contradicts legal, social or medical standards) it is often reduced to a solely sociolegal problem—in a process of "pars pro toto" reasoning. We met the extreme form of this antipsychological reductionism in Szasz. Drug abuse, compulsive drug use, mental illness, somatic illness—all these have important sociolegal implications. Among other attributes, man is also, but not only, a *zoon politikón*, as Aristotle called him—a "social animal"; and thus, whatever his other activities and problems are, they usually have a social and with that also often a legal and political aspect. But man is also, in Cassirer's words, an *animal symbolicum*, a symbol creating animal (1944). And we may add: he is also an *animal in conflictu*, an *animal dialecticum*, a conflicted living being, conflicted internally, not socially, a knowledge stressed by Freud, but going back to Plato. (Jaeger 1943, Simon 1973). In short: drug abuse is also an intrapsychic problem, not simply a sociolegal one.

"Society Is To Blame"

This—in contrast to most other myths—is one promulgated by the "insiders"—by the drug users themselves who turn the tables. Instead of being scapegoated and vilified they proclaim: "Drug use is primarily a problem of society. If the ills of society were cured, there would not be any problems of addiction." Some are more specific and say: The Vietnam war and the reaction to it, the depersonalization caused by technological society, the hypocrisy of the Establishment, racism, unemployment, the values prevailing in the ghetto's subculture, are *the* factors responsible for the tide of drug abuse. There is indeed again much truth to this—yet once more only partial truth (chapter 14). Even in countries and continents without these problems we encounter the same or other forms of massive drug abuse. Many of the drug abuse problems we have witnessed in the U.S. have started with at least comparable fury, especially in the last decade, in such sedate countries as Switzerland or Sweden—not to speak of West Germany or France. As I shall explain later on, I grew convinced that whatever impact society has works via the small groups in school and friendship, goes via the family, and is transformed by the individual's own stability or lability. For example, western society may create far more instability in family life than was the case in the past or is still in more cohesive societies; this in turn shakes the foundations of the personality's development.

More specifically we witness in our days a *neo-romantic movement*, which rebels against materialism and authority, against rationalism and science, against injustice and inequality in one swipe. Yet, there is little new even about that. Much of history has shown such a dialectic between the opposite trends of romanticism and enlightenment, between mysticism and rationalism, We find it in ancient Greece between the mysteria of Eleusis, the Bacchic rites versus the high rationalism of the Ionic thinkers, and of Socrates and Aristotle. A supreme synthesis of both was reached by such different men as Plato and the tragedians Aeschylus, Sophocles, and Euripides. In Rome, the romanticism of mystical cults of all varieties was opposed by rationalists like Cicero, the Stoics Seneca and Marcus Aurelius, or the Epicurean Lucretius. Or we may view the Renaissance spirit of clarity and lucidity of minds like Leonardo Da Vinci, Cusanus, and lastly Galileo, against the sublime romanticism of a Giordano Bruno or the far less sublime ones of Paracelsus and Cellini. Even during the century of the Enlightenment itself, we find a strong current of a romantic view of world and life—in Rousseau, even in the early periods of Kant, Goethe, and Schiller (*Sturm und Drang*); while the nineteenth century, the culmination of romanticism, was also a period of highest scientific, technological, and philosophical rationalism (Cassirer 1927, 1932 a, b, 1945). Our own century is no different. It is true: presently we witness a further discrepancy between the two extremes (see for example Bendix 1970), but I believe only transiently. The real question is: How can we achieve a synthesis of these two trends in our culture?

The Value of Drugs for Creativity and "Being Oneself"

"The use of psychedelics (or other drugs) enhances creativity, mystical insights, or is a help to psychotherapy." This leads back to the just described over-valuation of unreflective experience, of submersion in feelings and of unrestrained pleasure or aggression in any romantic movement, and is equally reflected and often paralleled by some current "therapeutic" fads: sensitivity training, encounter groups, primal scream, sexual promiscuity to enhance "expressiveness," "experience," "to overcome alienation," etc. Again there are many forerunners of these movements—De Quincey, Coleridge, Gautier, Rimbaud, Verlaine, and, particularly, Baudelaire.

Alfred Kazin (1976) has published an excellent article about a similar mythically sought role of alcohol: "in twentieth century America the booze has been not just a lifelong 'problem' and a killer. It has come to seem a natural accompaniment of the literary life—of its loneliness, its creative aspirations and its frenzies, its 'specialness,' its hazards in a society where values are constantly put in money terms" (p. 44). He emphasizes the terribly destructive impact, not just on the lives, but often on the very creativity which alcohol is supposed to enhance.

Creativity and lack of rational control have in reality very little in common. It takes little cultural or clinical acumen to see that neither "pot" nor "acid" has liberated any bound soul or given birth to any genius. Only if we equate blind effusion of dreams and preconscious flights of ideas with creation or psychotherapy and if we call unstructured chaos art—may we come to such a conclusion.

The same holds true for the breakthrough to the "real self," to the "real feelings." The sudden collapse of many defenses, the plunge into very deep perceptual and emotional regression, may indeed unmask deep layers which usually are well hidden. But are the higher layers of the personality, are the defenses, are the integrative cognitive functions really bad, and outside of the self? Does that not imply a rather curious valuation of being human, of being in meaningful contact with the world of values, and with one's own and the collective history and culture? Does it not willfully, though transiently, destroy the most human of all human attributes, the capacity to develop, use, integrate symbols, to develop an immensely rich structure of abstractions, of symbolic meanings and connections, of hierarchical layers of felt, though symbolic significance? What does it tell us if a person sees a profound cleavage between his self, a large part of his feelings, and this dome of symbolic forms and the feelings connected with the values expressed in that dome?

The answer to these rhetorical questions is provisional and will be given in full in the pertinent chapters (chapter 6, 10). Now we can say that it reflects a crucial inner split of very archaic nature, a wish to regress to that image and feel of the self which can do and be everything, wants everything, gets everything and disregards boundaries and frustrations—yet merely in illusion. It is a solution to archaic narcissistic conflicts, not to problems of creativity and identity. It is a regression in the *disservice* of the ego, freed of the controls of the ego, an illusory form of control and mastery.

The Doctor's Sanction

This bias brings us back to far more mundane and familiar regions and is really just a variant of the third myth: "Drug abuse is any use of a drug not prescribed by a physician." Much unwarranted and harmful drug use occurs with tranquilizers (currently, expecially Valium and Librium), amphetamines, sedatives, even narcotics, though prescribed by physicians. These medications may be used to quiet a complaining or conniving patient, and they can serve to cover up serious emotional problems in patient and family. As a matter of fact, the often promiscuous prescribing of potent drugs by physicians to disturbed patients has often provided their children with an alibi for their own type of drug use. By the same token some of these drugs are invaluable parts of the medical art. The really difficult question for all of us is, where to draw the line.

Another rebuke to this myth is that much drug abuse occurs with potent mind altering substances which are not even considered drugs at all and therefore not prescribed—the .cutely interfering or chronically damaging use of alcohol, of nicotine, of over-the-counter analgesics. As already mentioned I consider all that not very different from other types of drug abuse, except that our laws do not reflect our clinical knowledge and rational judgment. Here the real question is: where can we draw the boundary between safe and recreational use of a drug or medically necessary use and those uses of legal or illegal mind altering substances where interference outweighs benefit?

The Dangerousness of Narcotics

In particular this myth states: "Narcotics are far more dangerous than all other drugs." This myth is one of the most widely believed and most deeply engrained. Again, there is partial truth to it. Narcotics, whether opiates or synthetic narcotics like methadone, are more likely to lead to physical dependence than any other class of drugs, and the therapeutic range (between pharmacological efficacy and lethal dosage) is far narrower than with all other substances (unless tolerance has been established). But these are the only properties which make them more dangerous than, let us say, barbiturates or alcohol. All the other devastations caused by narcotics are mainly due to their illegal status. Acute intoxication, overdose with narcotics, is so dangerous and frequent mainly because of the unknown dosage in illegal drugs. And psychologically, psychedelics (even the stronger forms of cannabis) or amphetamines are far more disruptive, far more dangerous to life and society than the narcotics. Again the question is: how should our laws reflect this knowledge?

Although this is not a book about drug effects, a few additional remarks are in order here because of the rampant misconceptions, even among physicians. Often when I bring up this point in public I raise howls of ire and disbelief.

It is an error to assume that addiction to narcotics causes, by itself, physical damage. It does not. To quote Kolb, one of the leading experts in the field of drug addiction: "I have seen addicts who have remained healthy despite their use of 3 to 40 grains of morphine daily for as long as 20 to 65 years" (1962, p. 117). This does not imply that there may be no long-lasting or enduring *physiologic changes*. Rather, there are indications that following a state of addiction and withdrawal proper, some physiologic functions remain mildly changed at least for a number of months, but it is more and more dubious that the continued craving has anything to do with these minute physiologic alterations.

Much more important are the indirect consequences, due mainly to the illegal status of narcotics use (overdose, infections, secondary criminality). Here is not the place to expatiate on these widely known effects (see for example Wurmser 1968a, Brecher 1972, Kolb 1962).

Withdrawal from opiates, "cold turkey," without substitution by methadone, is quite unpleasant, like a strong flu, but usually not life threatening, except in cases of congestive heart failure or other serious disease.

Sedatives (barbiturates, other hypnotics, like Doriden) and alcohol are truly addictive as narcotics. The intoxication with barbiturates leads, as with most of the other depressant substances, to sleepiness, and, with that, to impaired functioning. The speech is slurred, the gait atactic, staggering; the driving of a car is very hazardous. It is most important to know, however, that withdrawal (in contrast to that from narcotics) is highly dangerous. If barbiturates are withdrawn suddenly or too rapidly, epileptic seizures and delirium occur; these withdrawal symptoms lead in a high percentage to death, unless treated properly. During tolerance the ledge between euphoriant and lethal dosage becomes narrower and narrower. What has been said about the barbiturates is valid also for meprobamate and other "minor tranquilizers" (Valium, Librium) although to a much lesser degree— there is psychological as well as physical dependence with epileptic seizures as withdrawal symptoms and, in higher doses, severe interference with psychomotor functioning.

CASE 3

A clinical case may serve as frightening illustration. Several years ago I was consulted by a professional for severe anxiety attacks and depression. He mentioned in passing that he suffered from severe insomnia, and despite moderate use of Placidyl (ethchlorvynol), one or two capsules of 500 mg, had an almost total day-night reversal. He asked for psychotherapy and withdrawal from the drug. Overconfidence on my part let me assume only a mild and relatively harmless form of drug dependency. I slowly reduced the dosage from two to one capsule and then stopped. After total withdrawal, he felt fine for about three days, then began to hear music in the air conditioner and car and to suffer from increasingly severe anxiety attacks. In the light of the rest of his psychopathology, I ascribed these symptoms to the overreaction of an extremely anxious man who was terrified about the loss of his artificial prop. Twenty-four hours later he had two epileptic seizures (one in the bath tub), was injured, unconscious, and developed in the hospital a most severe psychotic episode of a clearly exogenous type (withdrawal delirium) which lasted about three days.

Few words need be added in regard to alcohol. As Lemere (1968) stated, "alcohol outranks all other dangerous drugs by a wide margin in its total damaging effect on millions of people and society in general. After all, alcoholism is our fourth largest public health problem."

The Myth of Abstinence

"The only acceptable goal of treatment of drug abusers, in particular narcotics addicts, is cure, meaning abstinence. Methadone is just another addiction." It would be exceedingly desirable indeed if we could attain this goal. It would also be nice if we could wean all our schizophrenics off phenothiazines, all our neurotics off psychotherapy, and all our cardiac patients off digitalis drugs. Clinical reality dictates to us to allow a patient, through a combination of methods, to live as comfortable, as rich and fulfilled, as socially useful and law-abiding a life as possible. In some, it may be psychotherapy alone, in others combined with active counseling, in some with tranquilizers, in a few a sheltered environment in form of a therapeutic community that affords such social and emotional rehabilitation. Still others, who are not able to profit from psychotherapy, the combination of well-supervised additiction to a narcotic—most practically to methadone—with social and vocational counseling has proven to be the method of choice. Unfortunately, it still holds often true what was found by Simmel in his psychoanalytic sanitarium, the Tegel Clinic, half a century ago (as quoted in Crowley 1939): "Treatment of abstinence (alone) is regarded as leaving the patient with a crippling neurosis which may drive him to suicide."

Many questions remain unsolved: what to do with the failures in such a combination program? What with the adolescent narcotics addict? How to expand the needed psychotherapeutic services? These important questions will keep emerging in the course of our study.

The Myth of the "Sick Healer"

The saying goes: "One has to have been a drug user himself, an ex-addict, in order really to be effective in the treatment of drug abusers." This myth is particularly and multiply pernicious: It has dictated the staffing pattern of programs all over the country, has imposed funding schemes which demand the most crucial treatment functions being carried by ill-trained, ill-equipped, often ill-suited people, and has established a new selfrighteous pseudo-elite which looks sneeringly at both professionals and patients. In turn, many patients gleefully or painfully participate in this myth, become "buddies," even intimately involved in secret and impenetrable liaisons of bribery, "fencing," and sexual favors in exchange for "getting away" with their own shady dealings. A tight and terror-laden conspiracy of silence surrounds this web of underground threads and intrigues. More will be said about this sinister subject when we turn to the description of the history of some programs (chapter 13).

Here the rhetorical question may be allowed: Would we expect a ward of in-patient schizophrenics to be run, staffed, directed, according to their own secret rules, by "ex-schizophrenics"?

This can of worms has to be opened audaciously and fearlessly. I shall deal with it from two angles—in chapter 10, from some direct personal experience, in chapter 13, from observations with ex-addict counselors.

The Cry for Funds

An adjunct myth is: "The more money is pumped into treatment and/or law enforcement, the closer we get to the elimination of the drug abuse problem."

The sad truth is that we have only very limited answers to some segments of the problem, that we are not able to reach the vast majority, even if we were funded maximally, and that we very often cannot hold those in treatment who sought help and seemed motivated for a while.

We simply lack the theoretical knowledge and practical techniques to help all or even most compulsive drug users. *No quantity makes up for lacking quality—no money substitutes for missing know-what and know-how.*

We "experts" have, at best, only partial answers.

At the same time, it is nefarious not to allot the necessary funds to do as well as possible, where we have such partial answers; and it is humanly, socioeconomically and criminologically shortsighted and narrow-minded not to allocate sufficient funds to pertinent research.

The Marijuana Myths

"Marijuana leads to other drugs, to violence, to irreversible brain damage, etc." These myths have lost most of their virulence with the recent fantastic spread of cannabis use. Still some comments are in order.

In a study carried out about six years ago we found that only 18 percent of our heroin addicts had used cannabis as their first illegal drug. In turn, and this is a guess, about 20 percent of intensive cannabis users may proceed to the use of other drugs, not because of marijuana, but because of the underlying problems which had prompted them in the first place to get deeply involved with marijuana use.

The fallacy consists in making a temporal sequence into a causal consequence. This leaves out not only the severe psychological, familial and social problems underlying most instances of heroin addiction, but also the state of multihabituation preceding and often paralleling the use of opiates. In most cases we find an intense search for relief and pleasure antedating and encompassing the more specific use of narcotics. Use of barbiturates and alcohol as well as sexual promiscuity reflect this basic orientation no less than the smoking of marijuana. In other words, there is not a causal link between marijuana and opiate use, but both are a reflection of the same basic psychological orientation.

The only point which may be conceded is that socially the involvement with one illegal drug facilitates the experimentation with any other illegal drug. Thus the market for marijuana may at times overlap with the market for heroin.

The Myth of "Drug Abuse Education"

"Drug abuse education is the best prevention." There is not the slightest factual evidence for this, and some clinical experience and now even statistical evidence against it (see chapter 18). I do not want to be misunderstood: I am very much for education in drug abuse, because knowledge of any kind allows a deeper and clearer understanding and is, I deeply believe, a value in its own right; but I think we again underestimate the effect of irrational factors in drug abuse if we ascribe to this education any preventive value.

As will be explained in chapter 18, I presume that the line of true prevention will have to be sought on the one side in spotting early those disturbed families and children which are the breeding ground of drug abuse. On the other side, I gained more and more the impression that education at home, in elementary and secondary school, and through TV and radio, can indeed gain a preventive effect if it is enriched and broadened in a very different way and much earlier than just in regard to drugs. For example, I think the almost exclusive emphasis on technology, science, and physical education is one-sided and needs complementation from the humanities in a deep and inspiring sense, from elementary school on. Perhaps an even more important problem is the pervasive boredom of high school and college students. I seriously wonder whether the setting up of higher education, particuarly of college, as a precondition for most jobs, has rendered us much service. Yet, the question is whether and how this pressure on badly motivated youths, expecially to go to college, could be vastly reduced without at the same time undermining the rational functioning of a highly technological society.

The Myth of Deterrence

The last myth is: "Criminal justice is the main answer." Not only has our legal system, employed now predominantly for about sixty years vis-á-vis drug abuse, massively failed; it is indeed in many regards counterproductive: death and injury caused by illegal drugs, massive corruption, the enormous overloading of police courts and jails, and the fantastic burden on the economy in form of property crimes. At the same time we know that some forms of controls, of regulation, and in some regards even controls through criminal justice have to be maintained. I suggest, however, a shifting of emphasis from penal controls to a combined system of medical controls, tax regulations, civil commitment, and, only peripherally, of criminal justice (chapter 18).

On a deeper level we may raise also a crucial question of legal philosophy: should laws create "crimes without victims" (E. Schur 1965, Lindesmith 1965) which are by definition unenforceable, or should they completely restrict themselves to postulate as crimes only what interferes with the rights and safety, the integrity and health of others?

Yet there is a more psychodynamically relevant question implicit in this: How effective is any form of deterrence with a "compulsive" disorder like the more malignant forms of drug abuse? Here we have of course the help of experience with many other forms of compulsions, since the severity of the underlying drivenness in compulsive drug users is in actuality quite akin to that of severely suicidally depressed patients or to schizophrenics. Deterrence is, as a patient stated in another context, "like a storm on the surface of the ocean; the waves do not touch the depths of the waters."

Now a case will be presented which illustrates particularly well this last point—the inefficacy of deterrence—but which also may serve to give us a feel for the depth and severity of inner problems compared with which the questions of legality or illegality appear trivial.

CASE 4: PATPET

I saw a young man twenty-five years old in psychotherapy. He was very intelligent and attractive, had a thriving hectic business which he himself built up. He was an incessant, compulsive talker, hiding behind a flood of bragging, unnecessary details, and tangential answers, the deep shakiness of his self-esteem. He walked around in flamboyant, expensive dress: one of his outfits included a blue velvet sports coat with gold buttons and patchwork leather shoes.

From his background: The father was very strict, stubborn, irascible, vehemently objecting to his son's ostentatiousness and his wife's extravagant purchases. The mother had the motto: "Make most of what we yet may spend/ before we too in the dust descend." She asked Patpet not to tell his father about all the jewelry she bought on a brief vacation trip. She always hid and continued to hide the son's wrongdoing or problems from the father, in order not to upset him. Much more generally, she covered all her son's problems. For example, she berated the father for having told me about some of Patpet's most recent excesses and legal muddles. She covered all difficulties with a beaming, "Let us all be happy." In her view her son was not sick, but just had some minor problems because of some earlier peer associations. About the crisis leading up to drug use we know only that he felt sexually inferior to his peers when he was arounds 16: "They bragged about their sexual exploits. I had not matured as yet. So I wanted to show them that I was a 'man' by my exploits with drugs and my success with people. I looked at a peer-group of rowdies for approval, threw Molotov cocktails at cars from a hill, grabbed smaller kids and ridiculed their little penises, threw an egg from the sixth floor at a car, etc." On a deeper level he felt himself to be a rebel against his overbearing, stubborn, power-hungry father whose highest value was "victory"—success—and a mother who treated him and still deals with him as a "baby," always intruding on his life ("she is the world's best spy"). Moreover, he had to outclass his very successful, very straight older sister. He felt this rebellion had begun around age eight. It became an overt crisis in middle adolescence. Drugs became part of it at its peak and have remained its focus since.

Every narcissistic injury, even every lonely moment or hour of idleness, of not hectically running around, of not feeling important, being successful and likeable, rekindle the desire to take drugs. An alternate solution was sexual exploitation, "just for sex' sake," which, as we shall see, led to near disaster. Thus even the narcissistic crisis with its pseudo-solution, the drug, is only an episodic expression of a much deeper "addictive career," i.e. of a malignant narcissistic disorder.

Since about age seventeen he had used all types of drugs, being at times addicted to narcotics, repeatedly kicked out of Methadone programs, and arrested. Still when faced with a frustration at work or with the emptiness of an unstructured weekend—once the fast pace of his week's routine had slackened—he managed to get a wild variety of drugs: preferentially Valium and Methadone, but also Quaalude, Cocaine, and sometimes alcohol. Almost every second or third Saturday for several months he had had serious car accidents. He was on probation for a moderately long jail sentence; he knew from his own experience the devastating effects of drug use; all his professional and social successes hung in the balance, and yet—no deterrence! The psychotherapeutic sessions were filled with empty prattle about how well he was doing during the week, how the coming weekend he would certainly resist the temptations because "I have so much going for me" or had gained so many new interests. He talked about his glorious experiences on a trip all through Europe and Asia when on the run from a previous trial; he chatted engagingly about the philanthropical work on which he was spending his surplus money. He bragged about his intellectual interests, his business success, his reputation as a charitable, respected, up-and-coming young man in a community which knew nothing of the dark sides of his life. He emphasized the wonderful relationship he had with his parents and his older, quite successful sister.

Where did deterrence function in this man? Neither law nor jail, neither the loss of great success nor the collapse of respect had any such influence. None of his car wrecks had had such an impact.

I had rather the impression that a combination of most massive *denial*, by him as well as his family, of the dark, depressive, tragic aspects of life (of aggressions? of a shameful family secret? of the pain connected with much strife and competition in the parents' families?) with a continued need both to *prove himself* a splendid, impressive success and to *punish himself* for it by wrecking it, drove him on from debacle to disaster. While an outpatient, hardly a glimmer of insight broke this spell, and the external punishments he received made no dent whatsoever in the compulsion.

Two and a half months after beginning of psychotherapy the following reports filtered in, first from his mother, then him: He had taken (as usual on a Saturday evening) a large amount of Valium and methadone, driven hours later into the back of a car at a red light, had been arrested, released on bail, and then remained, watched over by his parents, at their home. But a day thereafter he managed to get from a relative, a physician, one hundred tablets of Valium and in his Valium induced stupor put fire to a newspaper. The following day, still very intoxicated, he appeared in court, had his driver's license revoked, managed to overdose himself once more, practically under his parents' eyes, and was finally brought to a hospital, admitted, but signed himself out within twelve hours, thus risking both the termination of psychotherapy with me and court commitment. Both would have come to pass if the "real" story of the preceding weekend had not been revealed by his mother to me and the legal authorities.

On that previous Saturday he allegedly was called by Perle, a former girl friend of his, and wooed to come to her house. Since he felt lonely—and sexually aroused, he went there. When he arrived there—he said—he was attacked by this woman and her boyfriend, bound, threatened first that they were going to cut his penis off, then that they were going to kill him. They stuck a needle in his arm, and he was, after a tremendous "rush," knocked unconscious. He awoke after a while, still high, and heard his two companions deliberate on how to dispose of his body. He climbed out through a window, got in his car, fled, still very high, though he was chased by them and had then the car accident. The following days the pair kept calling either the parents or the patient, threatened him with the Mafia's revenge if he told anyone what had happened.

After denouncing all his connnections with criminals in utmost detail to the State's Attorney—including this last, most menacing affair—he let parent, police and me know that he saw several armed men approach his living place and slid out; he fled to another city, but returned after a few days. However, not much later he admitted to me that he had made up the story in order to avoid the consequences of yet another car accident.

He had decided, however, to break off therapy with me—since I had described psychotherapy as a long, arduous, painful process, since I had moved to have him committed and taken a firm stand against his drug taking, and since I had declared him "severely disturbed." Instead he had arranged to see a lenient psychiatrist, "a soft cookie" who catered to the whims of his junkie friends.

I pointed to the foolishness of leaving therapy with me just at the point where we had gotten to an apparent clearing in the thicket of dishonesty, conniving and drug use, when as he said he had finally "made a clean breast" and "put all the cards on the table at the risk of my life." I openly expressed my honest respect and liking for him and my disappointment of "getting the boot" when we could really start working. Not hiding, however, that I considered his emotional problems grave, I added that anyone telling him he could help him to change and solve his problems without pain was a liar, that I believe in Aeschylus' *páthei máthos*—that one learns in a deep sense only through suffering. I also repeated that he would have to be hospitalized if he started again on the drug-taking cycle and asked him to draft himself in writing for the next session the treatment contract which we had orally discussed three months before.

For a few weeks a genuine improvement seemed to occur, but soon the fears of external threat were once again outweighed by the internal factors. The "microscopic" analysis of one very typical mini-crisis will help us to refine our observations.

After his "total break" with the drug culture, he had one of his many relapses. Again, it was a weekend. He was furious about a co-worker who had not shown up for two days and thus forced him to do her work on the weekend. His rage simmered down, especially after he interviewed a potential replacement. When he came to his apartment building he ran into a youth whom he did not know, but who apparently knew him as a "leader of the drug culture." The young man offered Patpet a shot of heroin for free; and Patpet, despite all good resolutions, promises, accomplishments, accepted.

And here he **was**—accepting it again. Why? It took one hour of constant probing, beyond a barrage of evasive answers, anent his co-worker, the respect he has earned in the community, his financial success, anent the wonderful relationships with his parents, to get to the following reasons:

1. The first reaction was, "*I deserve it:* people have taken advantage of me. *I am most dangerous when I feel cheated.* I get very angry, and instead of punching them in the mouth, I punch myself in the arm and destroy myself"

2. "I could forget about my problems, *escape* everything. It is the strongest antidote against problems." This was too vague. In the therapy we could tackle problems without his feeling tempted to take drugs—even when he had laid them out on the desk in front of me (as two days before).

3. "What I can discern is the role his (the youth's) building me up as a *superhero* played. I felt I belonged to these people. Suddenly I was again the drug guru." This played a role, especially at a moment of loneliness and let-down.

4. "It was the *euphoria* which put me thousands of miles away from the current environment. I saw all the details of my experiences in India."

5. And he immediately added, and, I think, came to the core: "It removed me from my *disappointment*. That was it, much more than the rage. It was my *pride*: I was mostly disappointed with myself, that I could not control my employees, the business. And the euphoria removed me from that—to Amritsar, to the Taj Mahal. If my mother had not caught me, I would probably again have continued, day after day." I believe he was right: It was the narcissistic injury and mostly the feelings associated with it which prompted him to resort to the "cure": heroin.

Only about five weeks after the most threatening crisis he was back taking almost daily high doses of Valium (up to 200 mg at a time) and methadone, and missed appointments. He started seeing a psychiatrist who had him paint mandalas, used "music therapy" and medication, while, as Patpet told me later, he, the patient, was "high as a kite." I was informed only ex post facto by patient and psychotherapist of this parallel treatment. On the way home from one of these sessions with this "collega mysticus," Patpet had a hit-and-run accident and was arrested by the police. At 4 A.M. and with difficulties (posting considerable bail once more) the parents got him out of jail, about seventy miles away from their domicile, and brought him home; but he, still massively drugged, cursed them out at home, hailed a cab, went to the ghetto, got heroin, and retired to his apartment to sleep. A few hours later, in a borrowed car, he repaired again downtown to get drugs, was arrested yet a second time within twenty-four hours. On my urging he went to a hospital for admission—while high on ten bags of heroin, but left, staggering, under the wings of his mother. The next morning he called me—very lucid, full of insight and determination: "I must enter the hospital today. I am so weak now that I would continue what I have been doing (despite being on probation). I have spent $4,000 in the last four weeks on drugs, and thousands more on flamboyant clothes. I do not know what to do with them—I have not even the space for them! Despite my huge income I am deep in debt." In order to facilitate and speed up admission and to prevent yet another bolting when he felt confronted with his inner problems I insisted this time on a judicial commitment which was promptly, once one of the hospitals had reluctantly agreed to accept him on an emergency basis, objected to by the family, especially the mother. He commented himself how emasculating she really was with all her "support," protection and lying in his behalf; with her pervasive denial of his most threatening illness, in short, how destructive her spoiling and overweening care really was. I added that even now when he himself recognized the severity of his problems she did not grant him that one honor badge he deserved—to be *taken seriously* when he admitted and felt to be sick and at the edge of compulsive self-destruction.

And yet, even at this juncture, the family succeeded in averting court commitment. The probation officer had become a business associate of the patient!

A few additional insights emerged while he was hospitalized: "Only now, that I am free of drugs, I realize how severe my problems are. I refused to admit them—not only by taking drugs, but I avoided them by spending enormous sums of money. It was a feeling that the money would never stop, that I am so great that I would have ever more customers and more money."

But the revealed deceptions were far more serious. The story about Perle was made up. No threat of any kind had been involved—and yet he had accused her and her boyfriend of heinous crimes not simply to his family and to me, but to the legal authorities as well (which in itself was a serious offense). "Lying has become such a habit. It is very

painful for me to admit the truth. And soon I start believing the lies
myself. They give *me* an alibi from how I am. I actually wanted to
believe these stories, and thought they were true. If I had not believed
in it, everything else would have collapsed—e.g., why I left the first
hospital. And it was revenge on Perle. I always felt exploited by her
(financially and emotionally). So I told myself: Now I have control
over her. I did everything to destroy her. With these madeup stories I
refused to remember also how degraded I felt by the way I had met her:
not on my own, but by a friend (yet another probation officer, drug
abuser and pimp), that she was a whore, and that she saw me just for
my money. This conning is still going on in me."

We probed his childhood. Very little was remembered which could
explain the whole severity of his problems, foremost this systematic
self inflation and self deception. "I remember I had a deep sense of
rejection and rebellion—very far back, certainly at age eight, but why?
I remember they always praised me and only rarely disciplined me. Yet
I remember when my father (a landlord in the inner city) kicked a guy
who was intoxicated on his property, strewn on the steps of one of his
houses, with the bottom of his shoe against the head. The man got up. I
was frightened he might hurt us. We were always afraid for father's
safety. And my mother, who was prominent in the community, was
often away; I remember crying when she left, although I was already in
school. I was Mama's boy. But she had always loved and spoiled me so
much. She and my sister literally kissed my feet. She was always proud
of everything I did, and both parents praised me for how much smarter
I was than my sister. Just like I have now a compelling desire that
everyone must like me. I had and have a compulsive need for levity, like
my mother. Everything painful I laugh off after one minute. Even what
is vital concerns me just for a fleeting moment, and it is forgotten again.
This escape must go very far back. When I was four I dug a very deep
hole in our back yard thinking that I could escape to China, right
through the globe."

He keeps coming back to mother's overindulgence and infatuation
with him. "Even now in the hospital she is bragging that a nurse called
me a 'charm'. She tells me: 'Everybody likes you, you are such a
likeable person.' She always blamed all the others when something
went wrong. She pushed always the best food on me and served me
first—and I ate with compulsion (up to now). I also always tried to split
my parents—to have mother on my side. Father seemed to win out

over mother." The last I presume to be only partly true. In a deep sense mother's collusion in denial, in projection, in shared narcissistic glory with our patient, remained triumphant over father's more austere, disciplinarian attitude. In a yet deeper sense, however, father was and remained the winner in the oedipal situation—regardless of all the shared lies and seductions between mother and son. We had some inkling of this profound conflict. He remembered as a child having overheard their intercourse: "It would upset me. I used to stay up and put the ear to the wall and wanted to hear what they were doing and saying. I was upset by what my father was doing to my mother. Her sounds were, for me, sounds of pain. And then mother again told me, as always, that I was the prettiest baby that the stork ever brought. It was very confusing!"

Still deeper he remembered mother's endless preoccupation not only with food, but with enemas. Both were cure-alls, as he remembers them, for all ills. (His masturbation, from early on, was also partly anal).

How ambivalent, powerful and multifaceted the oedipal triangle really may have been and still was was shown in the Perle story: in reality, it was a tale of seduction by a woman, then his finding a rival there, engaging in a peaceful game of drugs, but being eventually excluded, and finally taking revenge by lies. In fantasy it was a plot of murder and horrible retribution—a fantasy lived out in the *grand lie*. Was this not all a powerful symbol for the oedipal story?

Even when the family met with me these layers could be discerned: a superficial alliance between both parents and me to take decisive action. Underneath, and after the session, an angry alliance between mother and Patpet against the father for having told the truth, and father's ultimate giving in and going along. And all, of course, based on a yet deeper deception, a split: that the merger between son and mother was feasible without disturbing the "devotedness" of mother to father. And as foil behind that: a family torn apart by strife and ambition, unempathic, unresponsive, overstimulating. The mother had not talked with her siblings for years, allegedly because of their jealousy and envy. The father knew only one value: financial success; money was not a means, but an end in itself. His philosophy: "Money is only a tool to make more money, and if you do not take risks, you do not improve yourself." The mother's top value was "happiness"—built on the sandy ground of deception. The son's value certainly was not truth either, but partly a rebellion against father's money orientation, partly a bragging with his own huge success with it; more importantly it was partly to prove mother right. "I am the most loveable person on earth", partly a direct rebellion against this in endless actions of self-defeat, because "she never allowed me my own individuality, to stand on my own feet; it was (and is) so confusing and suffocating."

"The drugs give me self importance; I do not have to deal with the confusion, the feeling of rejection, the fears to be manipulated, the anger."

He was in the hospital and wanted to continue seeing me, but had not paid for the psychotherapy for months—and his parents balked in making the necessary arrangements (now he was confined) to put this debt in order (in contrast to other debts), because as they persuaded him: "He has not helped you in these months up to now—why should he be paid? Why should you continue seeing him? There is nothing wrong with you basically; just stay in the hospital until all your trials are over. You do not have any deeper problems."

Reluctantly the family had agreed to come to family counseling with a social worker. Soon thereafter, he broke off treatment with me and exchanged his drug career for one in homosexual promiscuity.

*

The questions are posed with particular acuity in this case, as in many comparable ones: What motivates a man who is gifted, intelligent, handsome, successful, surrounded by devotion and admiration—from family, friends, both male and female, and the community at large—to take on innumerable occasions huge, potentially suicidal doses of all kinds of illegal drugs? What drives him to destroy whatever he has built up: his reputation, his self esteem, his business, his human relationships, including those with his various therapists, and eventually his freedom? Why is a chain of sentences (though their full impact has not yet hit him) no deterrent? Is it simply the pleasure of getting "high," of blurring all boundaries to power and self esteem, that outweighs everything else—every threat and price to pay?

His own answer: "I know I am sick; I know I destroy myself. I want help." But immediately the condition is added: it must be at his convenience, under circumstances compatible with his "self-infatuation," as he calls it, at no sacrifice to his dignity and limitless self-determination. In this situation, this amounts to total control, to boundless manipulation of everyone around him. So we are faced with his own paradox: "I want to live out my *self-infatuation*," versus: "I know I *destroy myself*." In somewhat different terms this paradox recurs with nearly all compulsive drug users. It is that paradox which makes psychotherapy nearly impossible, makes the patients flee, evade, circumvent by absences, lies, omissions, and makes self-deception equally as grave a problem as overt lying.

The questions recur: how can we understand this combination of self-overvaluation and demandingness ("I want what I want when I want it"), of massive self-destructiveness, wrecking of success, and disregard of actual threats to life and health, and of broad distortion and contradictoriness of how reality is seen and resolutions are kept? How can we understand and thus conceptualize this asking for external structures and limitsetting, and yet the violent breaking down of all such barriers, the wild revolting, like the horse prancing up and bolting against its harness?

And here, too, a difficult ethical question raises its head: How can we reconcile the use of power in the interest of therapy and rescue, the imperative need for external structure and constraint to make treatment possible, a use of power in the service of the needs of both the sick individual and society, with the civil rights and the needs for confidentiality in such a case? (see chapters 16, 18).

Thus we are caught in a continuing double paradox, a double conflict in this and in many similar cases: The first paradox is the one formed on the one side by adult *freedom* and responsibility which is claimed in excess, beyond society's and nature's bounds, and thus leads to ever more extreme confinement, enslavement, and destruction. Its counterpoint is *structure*, limitsetting, the guard e.g. by parents (or by society's delegates, like police, probation officer, judge, hospital) over every step of self-determination and self-assertion; equally naturally the patient rebels with virulent vehemence, with violence or passive resistance against this encasing. The second paradox is the one already described: between self-love, self-infatuation, the incessant narcissistic parading: "look, what a great, good, powerful man I am," and the continued actions of self-destruction, "self-abuse" as several patients aptly called it—by drugs, crimes and other potentially suicidal acts.

Superficially it is this "*quadrangle of fire*," of licentious freedom versus encasing structures against which only revolt appears possible, of self-infatuation and self-destruction, within which the psychotherapist has to move with greatest care and caution. I get the feeling that it is the combination of these four superficial factors which give us an understanding of the utter unreliability (as to time, to commitments and responsibility, as to money, and as to truth) which almost all compulsive drug users show and which makes them so inaccessible to psychotherapy unless they hit the rock-bottom of despair.

I hope that a deeper understanding of these phenomena will be opened up in the course of this treatise.

What all this means beyond individual and by-and-large phenomenological impressions will now be examined in detail.

Chapter 3

PSYCHOTHERAPEUTIC AND

PSYCHOANALYTIC OBSERVATIONS

OF PSYCHOPATHOLOGY:

A REVIEW OF THE LITERATURE

A Survey of the Older Literature

I base the following mainly on the excellent surveys first by R. Crowley (1940), then by H. Rosenfeld (1964), and most recently by C. Yorke (1970). I put their main points in a summary form; for a more careful study of the literature, the reader should refer to these reviews and to the still most helpful and instructive papers by Lévy (1925), Radó (1926, 1933, 1963), Glover (1932) and Simmel (1929). Instead of following the main writers I shall order the material by examining briefly some of the main points of theoretical understanding and controversy.

REGRESSIVE WISH FULFILLMENT

Throughout the literature much emphasis has been laid on the wish fulfilling nature of drugs. This follows the popular opinion that drug use is but an "expensive search for a cheap pleasure." In analytic theory the focus merely shifted from conscious to unconscious wishes.

What these earlier explorers found, however, is by and large not outdated or wrong, but one-sided—at times rather irrelevant or entangled in semantic sophistry, yet often brilliant and still valid.

At first the emphasis was naturally on the fulfillment of libidinous wishes. Freud called very early *masturbation* the "primal addiction" (1897, Yorke, p. 142), but also mentioned the use of the drug as a *love object* (1912, p. 188), and based on constitutionally heightened orality (1905a, p. 182). By a basic change in mood ("Stimmungslage") and the ensuing removal of inhibitions and undoing of sublimation alcohol allows regressive wish fulfillment in general (1905b, p. 127). A connection between alcoholism and homosexuality is inferred.

✓ Radó stressed the "orgastic effect of intoxicants": "In comparison with the abrupt curve of genital orgasm, the course followed by pharmacotoxic or pharmacogenic orgasm is generally a long drawn-out one" (1926, p.401). "The whole peripheral sexual apparatus is left on one side as in a 'short circuit,'" a phenomenon he calls "metaerotism" (p. 402). The loosening of relationships to reality is secondary to this abandonment of object-directed sexual love and of the particular erotogenic zones. Although orality is an important way station on this course of regression, even that appears too structured: "The whole mental personality, together with the drug, then represents an autoerotic pleasure-apparatus. The ego is completely subjugated and devastated by the libido of the id—one might almost say that it is converted back into the id; the outside world is ignored and the conscience disintegrated" (p. 405). The crucial orgastic gratification lies not in the oral zone per se, but in a "hidden and mysterious pleasure," brought about by sucking: the "alimentary orgasm," "the agreeable feeling of a full stomach (repletion) and by a general diffused feeling of well-being which extends far beyond that of repletion, the whole organism here again taking its share" (p. 408). Thus he implies, as Yorke rightly infers, that oral experience is just a forepleasure. This orgasm underlies the sequence: oral impregnation—abdominal pregnancy—anal birth (Radó 1926, p. 409, Yorke 1970, p. 148). Radó's central postulate is: "It is in alimentary orgasm with its psychic ✓ superstructure as outlined here that we shall find the specific fixation-point disposing the subject to morbid craving. Pharmacotoxic orgasm is seen to be a new edition of alimentary orgasm" (p. 410), though far surpassing it in pleasure. He makes two additional equations: intoxication — alimentary orgasm — mania; the depressing aftermath — long-continued, paralyzing hunger — melancholia. Yorke criticizes, among other points, the entire concept of the "alimentary orgasm"; I have not found it useful myself.

In his 1933 paper Radó, however, states what is indeed crucial and replicable: Especially the initial pharmacogenic pleasure-effect lifts the patient suddenly out of a state of chronically painful, "tense depression," the response to any of life's frustrations, and provides him with a sharp rise in self regard and an elevation of mood (1933, p. 5). He adds the important point that this pleasure effect "is brought about by the ego itself. A magical movement of the hand introduces a magical substance, and behold, pain and suffering are exorcized, the sense of misery disappears and the body is suffused by waves of pleasure ....The ego is, after all, the omnipotent giant it had always fundamentally thought it was. In the pharmacogenic elation the ego regains its original narcissistic stature ....It is not only an infantile wish but an ancient dream of mankind which finds fulfillment in the state of elation" (pp. 7–8). He rightly describes it as "a narcissistic disorder, a destruction through artificial means of the natural ego organization .... Objects of love are no longer needed"(pp. 9,11). The elation reactivates a narcissistic belief in invulnerability: "*Nothing* can happen to *me*" (p. 13)—until this elation collapses in pharmacothymic crisis and most profound depression whence there are three exits: flight into a drug free interval (in order to "rehabilitate the depreciated value of the poison" or in a "masochistic orgy"), into suicide ("to dispel the depression for good by an elation which will last *forever*"), or into psychosis ("the latent *wish* fantasies of masochism are transformed into the manifest *terror* fantasies of the ego") (pp. 14–15).

Simmel (1929, p. 84) is the first, as far as I can see, to emphasize the role the fulfillment of aggressive wishes plays: "Ultimately the person whom the toxin poisons in these patients is the person from whom the threat of castration emanates, i.e., in the deepest stratum the introjected object longed for, yet hated: the mother, the great castrator of the past on the anal and oral levels.... The victim of a craving is a melancholic who makes his guardian superego drunk with the poison with which he murders the object in the ego."

Glover (1932) calls the addictions "circumscribed narcissistic neuroses" and further stresses the importance of aggression. One element in his views is particularly striking: the symbolic importance of the drug itself, besides and over that of the drug effect; the drugs represent in concrete form

repressed aggressive or sadistic interest.... This would suggest that in the choice of a noxious habit the element of sadism is decisive. The drug would then be a substance with sadistic properties which can exist both in the outer world and within the body, but which exercises its sadistic powers only when inside. The situation would represent a transition between the menacing externalized sadism of a paranoid system and the actual internalized sadism of a melancholic system. The addiction would represent a peculiar compound of psychic danger and reassurance. [pp. 206–207].

✓ Drugs represent sadistically used "ejecta" of the body, not just milk and semen, but more importantly urine and feces (p. 203). They are both destructive and restitutive, instruments of hatred and of reassurance, bad and good. Most importantly, "the drug symbolizes excretory substances which in turn represent a primitive and almost uncontrollable form of excretory sadism" (p. 213). The drug is used to *cure sadism* with sadism:

> the individual's own hate impulses, together with identifications with objects towards whom he is ambivalent, constitute a dangerous psychic state. This state is symbolized as an internal concrete substance. The drug is then in the last resort an external counter- ✓ substance which cures by destruction. In this sense drug addiction might be considered an improvement on paranoia: the paranoidal element is limited to the drug substance which is then used as a therapeutic agent to deal with intrapsychic conflict of a melancholic pattern. In the sense of *localizing paranoid anxiety* and enabling external adaptation to proceed, this may be one of the specific functions of drug addition. [p. 208]

Fenichel (1945, pp. 375–382) again emphasizes the libidinal aspects. ✓In his view "addicts represent the most clear-cut type of 'impulsives.'" They use the pharmacological effects "to satisfy the archaic oral longing which is sexual longing, a need for security and a need for the maintenance of self-esteem simultaneously .... During the drug elation, erotic and narcissistic satisfactions visibly coincide again." Also: "Erogenously, the leading zones are the oral zone and the skin; self-esteem, even existence, are dependent on getting food and warmth." They are fixated to "a passive-narcissistic aim .... Objects are nothing else for them but deliverers of supplies." Like Glover, he adds interesting comparisons to eating-, reading-, and love-addictions ("addictions without drugs").

In a vein similar to Glover, Rosenfeld (1960) states that "the pharmacotoxic effect is used to increase the omnipotent power of the destructive drive," and compares this "omnipotent destructive drugging" to mania (p. 130) and explains it as "primary oral envy" (p. 131). He also sees in the withdrawal a masochistic self-punishment akin to depression, but also equates the drug itself with an ill or dead object (p. 131) (as in depressive states). However, most of his considerations are devoted to a combined explanation of defense and wish fulfillment.

DRUG USE AS DEFENSE

Yorke remarks: "It is the instinctual side of addiction which has received the lion's share of attention" (1970, p. 156). Nevertheless, some interesting crumbs fell from the table on the defense side too.

Lévy (1925; see also Crowley 1940, p. 41) clearly described the effects of "dissociation of personality" with denial and projection, brought about by "morphia" in organically fatally ill patients.

Freud (1930, p. 78) saw in narcotics a means of coping with pain and disillusionment ("keeping misery at a distance"). Glover was more explicit in regard to "drug addiction" (referring to cocaine, paraldehyde and presumably also to opiate addictions): "Its defensive function is to control sadistic charges, which, though less violent than those associated with paranoia, are more severe than the sadistic charges met with in obsessional formations"; "Drug addiction acts as a protection against psychotic reaction in states of regression ..." (pp. 202–203). In turn, he saw in unconscious homosexual fantasy systems "a restitutive or defensive system ...acting as a protection against anxieties of the addiction type."

It was also Glover who most emphatically and in considerable detail studied the "compromise character" of drug addiction, in the earlier mentioned statements ("exploitation of sadism to cure sadism") and in descriptions of drug use (and homosexuality) as a compromise-mechanism between regressive and progressive elements: "there appears to be no question that noxious addictions represent the reaction to a more acute state of anxiety; that the destructive properties of drugs lend themselves to symbolic and actual expression of sadism,, nevertheless that the restitutive and neutralizing effect even of noxious drugs cannot be excluded" (p. 212). In yet another formulation this concept proved useful when he saw in drug use the "exploitation of later and more genital elements as a reassurance against earlier anxieties of menacing external substances..." (p. 210). The addictions can be "the beginnings of an expanding reassurance system ... due to contributions from later libidinal stages" (p. 211). Finally, he alludes to drug addiction being "a compromise between projective and introjective processes" (p. 213); the drug cuts off, kills, cures, punishes self and external world. The extreme compulsion "is specially marked √ in cases where both 'self' and 'introjected objects' are felt to be bad and dangerous, and the only chance of preserving a good self lies in isolating it in the external world in the form of a good object" (p. 214).

√ Radó is also quite explicit: "**Drugs supply exactly that which the mental organization lacks—namely, a shield against stimulation from within.** This artificial shield functions centrally, at the sensory approaches to the mental apparatus, and acts, as we may say, as a second line of defense" (1926, p. 397). It is a help against suffering, √ against frustration—what he later (1963) came to call "narcotic riddance": "they allay and prevent 'pain'" (1933, p. 4). More specifically, the drugs overcome the earlier mentioned "tense depression."

Similarly, Fenichel writes: "When the addiction can be looked upon as a last means to avoid a depressive breakdown it is understandable that the breakdown occurs when the addiction becomes definitely insufficient" (1945, p. 380).

√ Unfortunately, none of these authors describe how these defensive functions, exerted by the drug, actually work—except in most general terms: as redistribution of libidinal energy or as use of sadism against sadism, fire against fire.

Rosenfeld (1960) is more specific. His emphasis is definitely on the side of defenses. He first describes, what he calls (with M. Klein) "manic mechanisms," used by the addict (mainly the barbiturate addict) "to control paranoid anxieties, such as idealization, identification with an ideal object, and the omnipotent control of the objects which may be part or whole objects" (1960, pp. 129–130); "....all frustration, anxiety, particularly iersecutory anxiety, is *denied,* and the bad aggressive part of the self is split off. The drug symbolizes an ideal object, which can be concretely incorporated, and the pharmacotoxic effect is used to reinforce the omnipotence of the mechanisms of denial and splitting" (p. 130). Self and objects are excessively split into idealized and denigrated entities (e.g. "as if he were two or more different people"). Also the drug effect increases "the omnipotence of the mechanism of projection and the omnipotence of the destructive drives which are directed against the analysis" (p. 132), thus leading to massive crises of a negative therapeutic reaction (p. 138) and acting out (p. 143).

SUPEREGO

Radó (1926) describes, as part of the regression, a "defusion of the instincts and liberation of the destructive component" and adds: "The destructive force, once let loose, finds a second stronghold within the superego," thus leading to "a strong need for punishment" and a vicious circle of increased craving (p. 406; see also Radó 1933, p. 9). Instead of guilt or castration anxiety, the fear is more and more "a dread of pharmacogenic failure" or (pharmacothymic) impotence (1933, p. 12). Eventually "sadism is rushed to the rescue of imperiled masculinity, to shout down, by its vehemence, fear of castration and masochistic temptation" (p. 20). Thus he assigns guilt only a small role.

Glover only passingly refers to this problem; in these patients only "primitive objects are introjected"; projection of a massive type endures (1932, p. 213). Apparently he presumes that the action of the drug is exploited by the addict to blunt both projection and introjection of bad self and object. In his earlier paper about alcoholism (1928) he sees the latter as "a disastrous attempt to cure the abnormalities of primitive conscience" (p. 88). All these considerations of superego pathology appear now rather crude and unsatisfactory.

NOSOLOGICAL CONSIDERATIONS

Radó considers all types of drug cravings as one single disease which he calls "pharmacothymia," one special form of severe narcissistic disorders, parallel to melancholia and schizophrenia.

Glover, in an article about perversion-formation (1932), states: "I would place the average drug addiction as transitional between the paranoias and obsessional character formations, the reason being that in drug addictions the projection mechanisms are more localized and disguised than in the paranoias, yet stronger than in obsessional disorders. In drug addictions the projection mechanisms are focused (localized) on the noxious drugs; in obsessional states the need for projection is lessened by the existence of restitutive reaction formations" (p. 222). They are neither neuroses nor psychoses, but "transitional states." Neither can they be classed with psychopathy, since the conflict resolution occurs autoplastically, whereas those in "psychopaths" are alloplastic.

Very interestingly he views addiction as the companion problem of fetishism. Fetish and drug are "external dangerous objects" with which the patient attempts to establish friendly relations and originally are projections of the "sadistic penis of the father which the child has stolen from the mother." During abstinence a corresponding contamination phobia or fear of fetishes (clothes) may appear.

As already mentioned, Fenichel, emphasizing the pleasure aspects, puts drug addictions in the grouping of "perversions and impulse neuroses"; Rosenfeld describes them as "closely related to the manic-depressive illness, but not identical with it" (1960, p. 142).

√ I have to agree fully with Yorke when he criticizes the above literature for not defining "addictions" or differentiating between various forms more carefully, for a nosological confusion (specifically by equating "depressive affect and its relief with manic-depressive states"), and for a lack of more careful metapsychological scrutiny.

From newer studies, I select only the most relevant ones.

Modern In-Depth Explorations

The following studies (except for the book by Chein) are special insofar as they combine two of my major foci in this book: They are not simply studies of deep massive psychopathology in compulsive drug users, but they employ intensive psychoanalytically oriented psychotherapy as a specific treatment tool for this exploration. In this regard, they not only belong in the current section about the gap in the perception of psychopathology, but also form the nucleus of the later section on what is actually being done to cope with severe psychopathology.

ISOLATED (CASE) DESCRIPTIONS

Before I turn to the major and more systematic studies I briefly mention a few relevant modern psychoanalytic examinations which touch on our topic. Despite the small number of cases, they are of great clinical and theoretical value.

Phyllis Greenacre (1960) describes a "pseudo addiction" to sleeping pills with dependency not on the pharmacological nature of the drug, but on its mere appearance. It is considered by her a form of fetishism serving to "support and reinforce phallic (or clitoral) value as part of a general body safety and so defend against bodily separation anxiety" (pp. 184, 195). In other contexts she describes "addiction" to anxiety driven tantrums, to provocative, nagging attacks, as forms of acting out in analysis (1963, pp. 702, 703; 1970, p. 781).

Anna Freud addresses herself repeatedly to the problem of addictions. In her book *Normality and Pathology In Childhood: Assessments of Development* (1965), she contrasts the overwhelming craving for sweets used "as an antidote against anxiety, deprivation, frustration, depression" in children (which indeed may go over into fullfledged addictions at a later age) with addictions in adulthood:

A true addiction in the adult sense of the term is a more complex structure in which the action of passive-feminine and self-destructive tendencies is added to the oral wishes. For the adult addict the craved-for substance represents not only an object or matter which is good, helpful, and strengthening, as the sweet is for the child, but one which is simultaneously also felt to be injurious, overpowering, weakening, emasculating, castrating, as excessive alcohol or drugs actually are. It is the blending of the two opposing drives, of the desire for strength and weakness, activity and passivity, masculinity and femininity which ties the adult addict to the object of his habit in a manner which has no parallel with what happens in the more benign and positively directed craving of the child. [p. 202]

Her very important reference to the importance of externalization as defense will be taken up later on.

At Hampstead, Radford, Wiseberg and Yorke present two cases of "mainline" heroin addiction (1972), using Anna Freud's Diagnostic Profile for a more thorough metapsychological diagnosis. A few of their findings: "We are impressed by a lack of uniformity in the diagnostic status of the patients .... Drugs appeared to reduce aggressive impulses and thus afford better control." The externalization of the superego, its "double sidedness" and the impaired reality sense are striking in their first case. For our own future inquiry their concluding comment about that case is highly remarkable: "Conflicts which at first sight appear external have generally proved to be re-externalizations of internalized struggles." Strong sadomasochistic and narcissistic components were noticed—both in relationships to people and in her drug use. The other patient, a mixed heroin and methedrine (amphetamine) dependent man, emphasized the narcissistic value of the latter drug's effect: "on 'meth' I was the me I wanted to be." The drugs also alleviated his sexual anxieties and mitigated the strictness of his superego. Thus in the first case, heroin reduced aggression, in the second heroin and amphetamines decreased inhibitions both against loving and aggressive feelings.

Leon E. Berman gives a very instructive analytic report about the role of compulsive amphetamine use in a case of hysteria (1972); I have treated a patient whose symptoms and dynamics were nearly identical, but whom I cannot present in this book.

From Berman's case description: "Relinquishing the amphetamines—her masculine defense—threatened her with the emergence of her feared femininity," meaning "intense feelings of shame and revulsion." The reduction in dosage evoked the fear of becoming "weak, lifeless, intellectually dull." In the transference, depression and hopelessness took over: "She had wanted me to replace the pill with my love, and now she felt with me as she used to feel with her mother: disappointed, frustrated, and empty." Without the pill she feared that she would feel absolutely unlovable. The outer layer of phallic symptoms (including the amphetamine-induced strength and the pill-phallus equation) served as a defense against the deeper oral-depressive ones.

We turn now to the large scale investigations. Again, in all excerpts the emphases are usually my own.

The monumental work of Chein, Gerard, Lee, and Rosenfeld, *The Road To H* (1964), is still, after more than a decade, a very relevant and enriching study. It is impossible to do justice to the breadth and depth of observation and conceptualization and to the methodological thoroughness of this work.

Some of its major findings as they pertain to our subject are the following:

In regard to causation, the authors state that at the inception of their studies, they did not ask (as they came to later)

how much drug-taking behavior would not take place were it not for the challenge of the risk; the attractiveness of the forbidden; the glamour of defying authority; the power of self-destructive needs given a socially validated channel of expression; the drawing power of illicit subsociety to *lonely* individuals alienated from the main stream and the lure of its ability to confer a sense of belonging, inter-dependence of fate, and common purpose to individuals who would otherwise feel themselves to be standing alone in a hostile world . . . . [pp. 6–7]

On the road into narcotics use, the historical antecedents are relevant: "Already by the eighth grade, about a fifth of the boys in highly deprived areas give evidence of having acquired what we have characterized as a 'delinquent' orientation to life. This orientation consists of moods of pessimism, unhappiness, a sense of futility, mistrust, negativism, defiance, and a manipulative and 'devil-may-care' attitude on the way to get something out of life" (p. 12).

Farther back, the alarm signals are up in regard to their family life:

Relations between parents are far from ideal, as evidenced by separation, divorce, overt hostility, or lack of warmth. In almost half the cases, there was no father and no other adult male in the household during a significant portion of the boy's early childhood. As children, they tended to be over-indulged or harshly frustrated. The parents were often unclear about the standards of behavior they wanted their sons to adhere to and tended to be inconsistent in their application of disciplining measures. Their ambitions for their sons were typically unrealistically low, but in other instances, they were unrealistically high.

They stress "that all addicts suffer from deep-rooted, major personality disorders . . . . Contrary to common belief, the drug does not contribute rich positive pleasures, it merely offers relief from misery" (p. 14). "Heroin is a tranquillizer—perhaps the most effective tranquillizer known—but it comes in expensive doses." (p. 64). And: "The addiction of the adolescents we have studied was adaptive, functional, and dynamic" (p. 194).

Fitting to this picture is the very ambivalent relationship to the mothers—clinging, dependent and mutually destructive—a relationship where the mothers appear as pathogenic as the child pathological (pp. 212–216).

Another characteristic is the "role-diffusion," the "role playing," the "influenceability" of many addicts; "these youths present various aspects of themselves to various observers in a bewilderingly luxurious variety of roles" (p. 224). This trait and their vanity and preoccupation with their bodies let the authors suspect profound problems about sexual identity (p. 225).

The adaptive functional use of narcotics in the *suppression of anxiety* is emphasized (p. 229). "It is an enjoyment of negatives" (p. 232), due to the "opiate's capacity to inhibit or blunt the perception of inner anxiety and outer strain." The "degree of positive evaluation of opiate intoxication" is therefore expected "to be highly correlated with the initial level of distress" (p. 241). "In this sense, the drug itself is a diffuse pharmacological defense" (p. 233). *Road to H* describes a "melange of projection, rationalization, and denial": "Not I, but the drug in me does these things. I am not responsible; it is the monkey on my back" (pp. 233–234). These are all findings confirmed and amplified by what I am going to present; the correlation of their remarks with my own observations was surprising to me. This is particularly true for the connection of craving with crisis in the form of acute anxiety, bewilderment, incipient panic, increasing despair, and unhappiness born of a sequence of failures and disappointments and "a state of longing, a distressing condition of unfulfillment, pervasive of all the experience which is alleviated by opiate intoxication and may be conducive to craving" (p. 243). To this pharmacogenic relief Chein et al. add the narcissistic gain of beating life's debacles with an "esoteric, illegal, and dangerous nostrum": "When self-esteem is meager, any satisfying experience may be a source of enhanced self-esteem, as well as of pleasure" (pp. 244–245).

Drug Dependence: Aspects of Ego Functions, by H. Krystal and H.A. Raskin is another excellent in-depth probing of the personality structure of compulsive drug users. The convergence of some of their findings with my own is again so striking, that these concurrent, but independently arrived at, conclusions seem at least partly a mutual verification. They maintain that the etiology of drug use "resides in the psychological structure and functioning of the human being, rather than in the pharmacological effect of the drug," that "the drug is not the problem but is an attempt at a self-help that fails" and "that drug dependence represented a manifestation of ego function, a mode of adaptation, perhaps the sole adjustive mechanism to living problems the person has available to himself at the moment" (pp. 10–12). They direct the focus of their exploration to three areas of drug-personality interaction: affect, object representation, and modification of consciousness.

Regarding affect, they write: "In many drug dependent persons we find an affect combining depression and anxiety, a disturbance in which the de-differentiation of anxiety and depression takes place or a state in which the differentiation was never successfully accomplished .... The affect seemed to approximate the infantile 'total' and somatic distress pattern rather than a clear-cut adult affect pattern" (p. 22). This "total", archaic affect precursor shows another aspect of its primitivization, besides the already mentioned resomatization, namely "deverbalization" (p. 20)—a point I, too, will take up, under the label hyposymbolization. Because of the overwhelming, "traumatic" nature of affects in such persons, "drugs are used to avoid impending psychic trauma in circumstances which would not be potentially traumatic to other people" (p. 31). The drug serves either to raise the stimulus threshold (e.g. with opiates) or to evoke alternate stimuli to ward off threatening perceptions (e.g. with amphetamines): "This is a selective 'numbing' and blocking" (p. 34). They again refer to drug use as a "defense against affects" (p. 73) and even stress the specificity of drug effect for the relief sought.

Krystal and Raskin's thoughts on the aspects of the object relation (the ambivalence, especially the combination of intense oral dependency and inordinate guilt, of craving for union and need for separation) are fascinating elaborations of concepts mentioned elsewhere, (especially by Chein and Radó). They describe the alteration of consciousness, especially disorientation and dissociation, as major defenses, "as a block against confrontation or for carrying out a dangerous impulse" (p. 79): e.g., "the hyper-attention to the minimal stimuli acts as a distraction and protection against painful affects and threatening ideas" (p. 83); this is true mainly for psychedelics and stimulants.

D. Hartman (1969) stresses the defense aspect of drug use—"the wish to avoid painful affects (depression)"—and "the need to replace a lost object" (p. 389). The personalities of compulsively drug using adolescents are seen as mostly "orally fixated (or regressed)," whereas occasional drug users use the symptom simply as a form of transient, rebellious acting out. Structurally, compulsive users are either inhibited ("very passive") in regard to aggression or, at times, have uncontrolled outbursts of aggression. They show crumbling of superego and ego functions under the drug's influence. Most have been depressed prior to drug use and feel less depressed when on drugs (pp. 388–389).

In Wieder and Kaplan's outstanding essay, "Drug Use in Adolescents: Psychodynamic Meaning and Pharmacogenic Effect" (1969), we find a penetrating study of the psychodynamic substrate and meaning of drug use within the texture of the whole development.

They open the presentation of their own concepts with the statement that "chronic drug use, which we believe always occurs as a consequence of ego pathology, serves in a circular fashion to add to this pathology through an induced but unconsciously sought ego regression" (p. 403). Again, they see the dominant conscious motive for drug use not in the seeking of "kicks," but in "the wish to produce pharmacologically a reduction in distress that the individual cannot achieve by his own psychic efforts" (p. 403). But they go a crucial step farther: "We believe that different drugs produce different regressive states that resemble specific phases of early childhood development. Drugs act as an energic modifier and redistributor, and as a structural prosthesis .... When an individual finds an agent that chemically facilitates his pre-existing, preferential mode of conflict solution, it becomes his drug of choice" (pp. 28–29). How Wieder and Kaplan correlate specific choice of drugs with specific dynamic conflicts and thus with developmental fixation will be presented in chapter 7.

In 1974 the same authors published a book with the telling title *Drugs Don't Take People, People Take Drugs*. The book is excellent and reflects about two decades of intensive psychotherapeutic work with all types of drug abusers. It deserves much wider recognition than it has received. In popular, clear style, with many case presentations, the authors make a most convincing case for a shift of emphasis from drugs, drug abuse treatment, and drug abuse programs, to personality problems, psychopathology, and psychotherapy.

A few salient quotes will make the point. "'Drug use,' 'abuse,' and 'addiction,' describe increasingly severe forms of self-medicating behavior. This behavior is an attempt to fulfill the wish for a magically altered state of mind. Abuse and addiction reflect the urgency of a pathological need—a compulsion—to create and perpetuate altered mind states" (p. 22). The importance of magical self-alteration in its psychoanalytic and culture-philosophical implications will be further investigated later.

Drugs do not cause dropping out. Rather the long-standing personality disorders produce the painful ego states which lead to both drug use and dropping out (p. 139). I could not agree more.

"The pharmacological key, the special regression induced by the specific drug, fits the psychological lock, the drug taker's private (and usually unconscious) wish for a particular regressive state. This crucial specific meshing of pharmacology and psychology propels the individual into severe abuse and addiction. Each repetition of the special satisfaction from the intoxication engraves itself deeper into the user's memory. Soon there is a yearning to recapture that intoxicated ego state and a craving for the particular drug that produces it. A drug of choice is established" (pp. 54–55).

This self-confirming, self-perpetuating circular process, a kind of vicious spiral, can be seen not only in decompensation, due to mind altering drugs, but also in neurotic and psychotic states, where depression, masochistic (self-tormenting) acting out, phobic behavior, and schizophrenic withdrawal very clearly feed on themselves. This seems to be a general law in nature (see Langer 1967, 1972). Shakespeare, writing of another "addiction," that to a sexual partner, has Antony say of Cleopatra: "Other women cloy/the appetites they feed, but she makes hungry,/ where most she satisfies" (II, 11). No scientist can find better words for this universal, physiologically and psychologically overwhelmingly important process.

As to the drug effects sought by various types of drug abusers, Kaplan and Wieder use the genetic model to differentiate; we shall return to their concepts later on.

Another series of very valuable contributions concerning the severity and nature of psychopathology and its treatment has been published by Edward J. Khantzian and some of his co-workers (Mark, Corman, Schatzberg) in Boston. He worked exclusively with narcotic addicts and has studied the interrelation between narcotic use as self-medication and the patients' underlying problems centering mainly around aggression. The main point of this thesis is that the major motivation for drug use is not the search for pleasure, but the suppression, the muting, of various forms of severe unpleasure.

From his 1973 paper we can glean some salient formulations:

> On the basis of my clinical experience and observation, I hope to show how a significant number of individuals become addicted to opiates because they learn that the drug helps to cope by relieving dysphoric states associated with rage and aggression and by counteracting the disorganizing influences of unmitigated aggression on the ego. [p. 60].

> More specifically, observations of narcotic addicts treated with methadone maintenance have led the author to hypothesize that a significant portion of these individuals become addicted to opiates because they discover that the drug acts specifically to reverse regressive states by attenuating, and making more bearable, dysphoric feeling involving aggressions, rage, and depression .... Repeatedly I observed histories of physical violence, accidents and physical trauma dating back to childhood among a large percentage of our patients. I was surprised to discover how many patients spontaneously reported physical beatings by cruel, sadistic, and impulsive parents. Similarly, these same patients gave histories of impulsive and delinquent behavior in school, and much antisocial and violent behavior that predated their addictions. [pp. 64–65]

Khantzian notes that failure to consider adequately that the psychopharmacologic action of narcotics helps with coping and adaptation which may explain in part why results with conventional psychotherapeutic approaches have been so uniformly poor: "In the author's experience, psychotherapists tend to concern themselves prematurely with the maladaptive aspects of drugs when they first engage the patient rather than first trying to understand why the addict so desperately feels he needs his drug" (pp. 66–67).

He castigates some of the current "self-help approaches" for the effect they actually have on the patients' problems about aggression:

> Forced work and some of the more humiliating tasks and activities to which the addict is subjected are effective because these

exercises are in part successful manipulations of the addict's sadomasochistic tendencies. What is probably underestimated by the proponents of such an approach is how they merely play into the addict's sadomasochism and thereby offer little toward producing permanent change. To the extent that this is not appreciated, there exists the constant danger that the "treatment" becomes just a symptom of the illness. [p. 67]

Similarly he considers the effect of encounter groups: "Many of these encounter approaches grossly underestimate many addicts' limited capacity to deal with intense affect, particularly aggressive feelings" (pp. 67–68).

Again I have to lend much support to these statements. Often it is presumed that a narcotics addict's functions are reduced because of the drug; the reverse is often true—even in illegal drug use. Narcotics use indeed has potent adaptive aspects—besides its severe maladaptive, self-destructive sides. Khantzian emphasizes the use of heroin as an adaptive measure: "In the clinical material presented, we noted an absence of the more usual mechanisms of defense and of attempts at conflict resolution. Instead, the opiates have been used by addicts as a costly form of adaptation, a kind of total solution to a variety of conflicts within the individual and in his interpersonal and work areas," (Khantzian et al. 1974, pp. 162–163).

The role of methadone is viewed in a similar psychodynamic context (Khantzian 1972): "What is proposed in this formulation is that methadone maintenance is effective not only by compensating for what is believed to be a metabolic defect induced by narcotics, but that it is also effective because it has a stabilizing anti-aggression action in the central nervous system" (p. 373).

These last remarks will have to be taken up later when we ponder the theoretical implications of these findings.

H. Hendin of Columbia University has just published two excellent articles, one dealing with the psychopathology of students on heroin, the other with that of students on amphetamines (1974). Both papers contain particularly valuable case descriptions.

He views the heroin use more as a buffer against anxiety about closeness and sexual and emotional intimacy, stemming from a very disturbed relationship with the patients' mothers, but he also adds the dampening effect on rage (they "hide their rage behind a passive facade"—p. 248).

He writes: "Heroin is essentially a drug of despair. It has the effect of putting people—even oneself—in parentheses, of making everyone unimportant, of turning human involvements into an only ancillary experience. No group of students I have seen, with the exception of severly suicidal students, have been hurt so deeply and so early in life .... In using heroin to achieve this withdrawal, these students achieve the illusory freedom and illusory invulnerability of the isolate and the emotionally dead" (p. 255).

In his paper on compulsive amphetamine users Hendin writes: "The study indicates the ways in which amphetamines are used by students to drive themselves toward goals they did not desire, but felt they had to pursue. These students have learned early to ignore their own feelings and sacrifice themselves to please someone else. Amphetamines permit them to function in an automatic, unfeeling way while ignoring their own frustration" (p. 256). "Amphetamines permit them to control their feelings and achieve both the energy and detachment that permit them to 'get control' of themselves and 'function efficiently'" (p. 265).

Stephen Proskauer and R.S. Rolland (Roxbury Court Clinic in Boston) reiterate what we have now heard from many observers (1973): "Drug taking is more usefully described, in our experience, as an adaptive and defensive choice made by a young person for a combination of intrapsychic, familial, and social reasons ..." (p. 33). Their recommendations for treatment based on their psychotherapeutic findings will be cited in chapter 20.

More Cursory Inquiries

A group of psychiatrists at Hillside Hospital in Glen Oaks, New York, offer an interesting set of observations about a specific type of compulsive users of sedatives (Quitkin et al. 1972): "We have observed the association of severe drug abuse and the phobic anxiety syndrome, characterized by panic attacks, subsequent development of anticipatory anxiety, and consequent emergence of phobias" (p. 159). Many of these patients appear to respond very well to therapy with the antidepressant drug imipramine (Tofranil).

Of course anxiety is such an unspecific, broad, vague sign of deeper psychopathology that the correlation between compulsive drug use and anxiety would add little to what we have already noted. It is their specific emphasis on the phobic type of anxiety and the response to Tofranil which make their findings intriguing. I have noticed phobias in drug users of all varieties, as part and parcel of much more complicated psychopathologies. I have not observed the specific sequence: phobic anxiety—drug use—response to anti-depressants. Yet this thesis should indeed be systematically tested.

Many other authors emphasize the connection between severe psychopathology and compulsive drug use, among them Charles R. Shearn and D.J. Fitzgibbons (1973):

> Our findings point to an association between drug use and psychiatric hospitalization that is in excess of the association between drug use and student status, but the findings do not bear on the issue of cause and effect. We believe that the association can be most usefully interpreted as one currently popular manifestation of psychosocial deviance.
>
> One hypothesis to consider is that drug use is, for the adolescent and young adult, a readily available technique for attempting to cope with life difficulties and intrapsychic stress. [p. 1387]

Several writers, like Proskauer and the NIMH group of Frederick, Resnick, and Wittlin (Appendix A), emphasize the role of depression. H. Wishnie (1971) calls the addiction "a masked depression"and E. Harms (1973) sees in depressions the most extensive problem in drug abuse. He adds: "In many cases, depression haunts the individual prior to the addiction. In many cases, this is the direct motivation for the actual abuse."

Robert A. Kramer reports that the clinical record of 48 twelve- to sixteen-year-old drug dependent adolescents showed that 98 percent were failing in school or had dropped out. Eighty-one percent had major parent-child conflict, 40 percent had made suicidal gestures or were clinically depressed, and 40 percent were characterized as having very poor self-image." In all of the patients the pain of poor parent-child relations, the feelings of worthlessness and general lack of success had been uniformly relieved by their drug experiences. Recidivism occurred with every major stress and particularly on threat of a separation experience ..." (p. 7).

Even in occasional heroin users the same psychodynamic factors seem to play their fateful roles. D.H. Powell studied occasional heroin

users and reported these interesting findings about the so-called
chippers, a little known yet widespread socioclinical phenomenon:

> Some of the subjects use heroin because it is a form of self-
> medication and it enables the user to tolerate what is for him an
> intolerable world. Subject 11 is the best example. Not able to find
> work, not able to find anything else which interests him,
> supporting himself by trafficking in drugs, he loathes himself and
> his world. Occasional heroin use helps him deal with the
> depression and anger he feels in a world that, in his view, is not
> treating him justly. [p. 591]

Besides depression he observed one social anxiety as motivating
factor: "For some, heroin is a facilitator of emotion. The majority of
the sample would agree in part with s2 and s3 who said that when they
used heroin they felt less shy, less self-conscious, and able to relate to
others more easily" (p. 591).
More generally it is observed:

> The scores of the OHUs [occasional heroin users] for both state and
> trait anxiety were higher than the undergraduate population at
> large. In fact, only two of the subjects scored below the 50th
> percentile in current anxiety state. Two-thirds of the OHUs scored
> beyond the 75th percentile in trait anxiety. This means that these
> subjects live daily with a good deal more anxiety than most young
> people do....[p. 593]

Others put more emphasis on the character disorders, especially of
massive denial as part of their character. It would be redundant to
excerpt a number of similar studies (Poze 1972, Brown et al. 1973,
Halikas and Rimmer 1974). They present a transition to the
phenomenological works summarized in Appendix A.

Extent of Psychopathology as Observed in a
Methadone Maintenance Program

A brief digression into observational data may serve to illuminate
our review of the literature. The following observations and facts were
gleaned from a methodical survey of our own clinic, which falls now
into what critics rightfully call a "silted up" program: It is a program

which runs more or less smoothly, cost efficiently, now with a stable population of about two hundred patients, only about three to four admissions a week (sometimes less), and a very small attrition rate.

This was very different at the beginning: not only did we have a rapid turnover rate during the first year (perhaps 50 percent) but we had to turn away nine out of ten applicants because they did not fit the standards set down for a methadone maintenance program. Some of these criteria are: absence of massive polydrug abuse, verified two years or more of narcotics addiction, verified attempts at detoxification, etc. We helped many of these rejects by transporting them to other facilities (scarce though these were for such cases) or did whatever crisis intervention we could render under these circumstances.

But now: what do we find in our "stable" program? Careful clinical observation shows that very many patients in our progam suffer from moderate to very severe emotional problems which come more to the foreground once the hectic up and down of intoxication, withdrawal, hustling, and imprisonment has been replaced by the calm stable atmosphere of a well-run and well-structured methadone program. My impression has become deeper that *all* patients have at least moderate disorders which an experienced clinician can quickly discover, although a good many patients appear at first blush "normal."

This first category of patients can cover up the signs rather well as long as they are supported on the one side with the help of a high dose and the tranquilizing effect of methadone, on the other side with the active assistance of the paraprofessional counselor. They "get along," despite the underlying, potentially serious psychopathology. I would estimate that about 30 percent of the methadone maintained patients coast along "without any problems": they work, they are "clean," they present no major problems to their counselors, they are "good, reliable" patients. Even in situations of emotional stress (divorce, loss of work) they hold up quite well. Yet, the careful clinician who studies their life histories or who witnesses their attempts to "go it alone," by withdrawing from drug or counselor, sees with concern how the aforementioned serious psychopathology reemerges and is quickly covered up once more when the "compensation level" of methadone is crossed upward again (20–40 mg in most cases) (see below).

Then there are another 30 percent, who are episodically "good" patients, "make it" for a while, then decompensate, and then again, with much, often heroic help from the side of the counselor, pull

themselves together again. They may take drugs a few times, have some
rather serious run-ins with the law or their family, are depressed or very
angry and unhappy, lose jobs, do not work, passively drift, "lose" their
bottles of take-home medication, are caught in lies or deception, but
after a few weeks or months are all right once again.

Then there is a third complement of yet another approximate 30
percent: those with whom the counselors begin to feel helpless. The
counselors ask for psychiatric evaluations of these patients, describing
them as having "gone to pieces," "crazy," "clearly sick": "unless you
help him, we cannot keep him in the program." They are usually
patients with severe, often potentially suicidal depressions, with
paranoid misperceptions, suspicions and accusations, threats to kill
family members, "weird," bizarre utterances or actions, often with very
marked use of other drugs (barbiturates and related sedatives, like
Quaalude, Doriden, Valium; alcohol; amphetamines and cocaine). Or
they fail to come in and absent themselves for several days, often "lose"
or sell their medications, do not work anymore and have unexpected,
severe conflicts with the law. Unless energetically treated, these
patients are soon lost: killed, incarcerated, back in the underworld, or
ending up in some hospital.

Finally, there are a few, perhaps 10 percent, who are blatantly
schizophrenic or suffer from some epilepsy-related psychosis.
Untreated they are like all chronic schizophrenics with a variety of
prominent psychotic symptoms: They show either a bland bizarreness
and talk gibberish, are maybe frightening, though really not much of a
menace, are unreliable drifters in and out of the program. Or they burst
out in sudden wild rages, shocking in their acts of violence, like
breaking through a wall with their fist—or into a sudden homicide. Or
they ramble on in disjointed fragmented statements of vague suicidal
despair or homicidal menace, cut themselves up in bizarre arm, throat,
and head-slashing, provoke others into stabbings, go into hiding, flee
suddenly from some clinic office and disappear with the implicit threat
"that something is going to happen," drop and nearly kill their
newborn baby, etc.

A new survey in the spring of 1976 by Mr. Rodbell gave the
following astonishing data. From the slightly more than 200 currently
and very stably ensconced patients on our methadone maintenance
program, 40 to 50 are alcoholics, about half of them severe alcoholics
with very serious somatic pathology; four of them are described "at

death's door." In addition 56 are on Valium, a few more on Placidyl. Thus, roughly half of our 200 patients continue using "drugs."

Beyond that, the vast majority (perhaps 90 percent) of our methadone maintained patients are depressed—mildly to severely, but clinically observably so to non-psychiatrists.

Program structure and funding are not geared to deal with any of the four types of psychopathology discerned above, which we may now characterize as: (a) the submerged moderate character pathology; (b) serious character pathology with episodic alarming, but eventually manageable decompensation in form of rages, depression or terror; (c) the chronic, severe, decompensated, à la longue unmanageable character pathology with severe affect storms, but of the same types as above; and, (d) overt schizophrenic or organically caused psychoses.

I tend to avoid the term *borderline,* although I cannot quite circumvent it altogether. I have become convinced with David Beres (1974) that this wastebasket term has little explanatory value, and that we are far better off examining the full range of moderate to very severe pathology (except for those of florid psychoses) as to various types of deep character disorders with varied affective pathology. Their classification is very difficult. Quick descriptions of character pathology (impulsive, infantile, explosive, unstable, chaotic, narcissistic, masochistic, depressive characters), descriptions which seem to fit best the superficial phenomenology, are usually just that: quick superficial labels. Only in-depth studies can reveal the true nature of the character pathology. No research of any breadth or depth into this has yet been possible, but pioneer work is proceeding on many fronts (in respect to character pathology in general: e.g. Beres, Greenacre, Kernberg, Kohut, Dickes; in respect to drug abusers in particular: Wieder and Kaplan, Krystal, Khantzian, Berman, Savitt).

Zinberg's Tripartite Model

An original, intriguing contribution comes from a researcher and psychoanalyst, N. Zinberg, whose conclusions are, though not irreconcilable with the whole tenet of this book, quite at variance in emphasis. In his 1974 monograph he states:

The most important single concept about drug induced states to emerge in the last decade is this—to understand the subject's

response one must consider drug, set, and setting as a basic whole.
"Set" refers to the person's attitude toward the experience and
includes his personality structure. "Setting" refers to the influence of
the physical and social environment in which the drug use takes
place. ... My insistence on the set/setting interaction means that I
place less emphasis on the irremediable basic influence of early
psychic development. While I do not ignore this early aspect of set, I
see the effects of persistent social attitudes, particularly when
magnified by the mass media and accepted by the public as a social
crisis, as a factor influencing the continuing personality development of the individual. [p. 2]

The weight is placed entirely on the "current reality," therapy oriented
fully toward an "awareness of the crucial role of the social setting in the
current ego state of the addict," a shift away from the "focus on
motivations and unconscious conflicts. ... It was the social setting that
got out of hand" (1975, pp. 567–586).

He states "that the decision to try a drug in certain situations of set
and setting need not have deep, complex, or emotionally disturbed
motivationed structures behind the decision." Obviously not! But then
he continues, sliding imperceptibly over from experimenters to those
who use drugs intensively, compulsively:

Once defined as deviant, removed from usual social supports, thrust
into an increasingly less diverse group for social stimuli, drawn into
constant real and imagined conflict with the police and the law,
personality changes occur. When all this is aided by the persistent
use of a drug that, at least in the United States of 1974, furthers this
social process, is it a surprise that heroin users can be diagnosed as
severe narcissistic character disorders?

For Zinber, then, both compulsive use and psychopathology are
largely effects of the environment.

I cannot follow him in this; my in-depth work with compulsive drug
users leads me to lend much more weight to what he calls the "set,"
although I do not deny the importance of "the setting." Both—
combined with the drug effect—become indeed very complex, and
their interaction most intricate and variable. The "setting," which I
describe as "concurrent causes," is examined in as much detail as

possible in chapter 14; the "set," which I consider far more relevant because it transcends the drug history (before and after), encompasses the complex interaction of predispositional factors and the heptad of the specific cause (see chapters 6–8, 11).

Another correlation can be seen in the curves of psychopathology described in the introduction: the more acceptable a drug (the more conducive the setting), the less severe the psychopathology (the less important the set); e.g., the Vietnam example.

A third application concerns the effects of psychedelics (see chapter 10): in my experience again far more interest has to be paid to "set" than to "setting."

Thus, all in all, his tripartite model seems to me far too simple and not to do justice to vast amounts of observation; Zinberg vastly overstates his case (e.g. "the most important single concept, etc."). Along with the proponents of the sociological label thesis in regard to all types of deviance (especially mental illness) he assigns society's reactions the main etiological significance, comparable to Szasz, Laing, and Rosenhan (see Murphy 1976). How unsatisfactory such a one-sided approach is, will become clearer in the next chapter.

Summary

If we look back over this chapter we find that there is ample, but chaotic, unsystematic, scattered evidence for the clinical adage that heavy drug use is the consequence of, not the origin for, severe psychopathology. The particular roles of depression and self-destructive behavior prior to and independent of drug use have been seen time and again.

There is an urgent need for a coordinated, large scale, well-planned study, structured and guided by both experienced clinicians (especially psychotherapists and psychoanalysts) plus methodologically well-trained research strategists to study in depth and in a systematic way the underlying psychopathology of various types of drug users—of the narcotics users and addicts, of sedative users and addicts, of psychedelic users, and of stimulant users. The focus obviously should be on categories 4 and 5 of the Shafer classification ("intensive" and "severely dependent" users).

Chapter 4

THE CRITERION OF
PSYCHOPATHOLOGY: COMPULSIVENESS

> Mephistopheles: "Du glaubst zu schieben, und
> du wirst geschoben.
> (You think you shove, and you are shoved.)
> —Goethe, *Faust*

Before we turn to an in-depth study we have to ponder the whole problem of compulsiveness, of drivenness, and its theoretical importance.

The Compulsive Need for a Substitute Solution

At first we have to broach our question phenomenologically. Already from the fundamental opposition of the two ends of the continuum (occasional versus compulsive users), as described in chapter 1, the significance of compulsiveness for the problem we study becomes obvious.

Glasscote and co-authors (1972) stress this factor of compulsiveness:

By contrast [to the term *psychological dependence*], *compulsion* is a more specific term that connotes one of the greatest obstacles in successfully treating people who have abused drugs. *Compulsivity* can be manifested in practically any aspect of behavior.... Compulsivity is believed to commonly underlie any number of widespread behavior problems, such as overeating, heavy use of alcohol, gambling, and so on. It seems certain that some portion of those who use illegal drugs do so out of compulsion. The significance is this: compulsions are notably resistant to presently known methods of treatment; the long-term success rate is low, the relapse rate is high.

Now, of course, the question is immediately raised: how far is this compulsiveness of a physical nature? Is that not just the point which led to the prohibition of these drugs in the first place—that they induce inevitably or at least very often a physiologic dependence which henceforth cannot be broken? Is it not like the contagion of an epidemic disease?

If we carefully study on the one side history and treatment experience, and on the other side the interesting observations in medically and psychiatrically induced addictions (e.g., when opiates were used to treat melancholics), we are forced to assign very little valence in the long range to this factor of physical dependence. The crux is that "the readiness is all."

Everyone who works closely and personally with a compulsive drug user has time and again the experience that if his drug of predilection is taken away he desperately tries to substitute another symptom. We see this in successful clampdowns by the police. A kind of natural experiment occurred during the dock strike in 1971 which lasted 59 days and led to a shutdown of imports, including of opiates. Although the underworld had apparently enough stockpiles, these were held back in order to drive up the price. The result was a severe shortage of narcotics. Those addicts who could not get methadone from unscrupulous physicians, from programs, or illegally, turned mainly to barbiturates and related sedatives (e.g. Quaalude). We find the same phenomenon of drug or symptom substitution in the host of symptoms preceding and accompanying compulsive drug use. Most frequently other symptoms have a similar compulsive quality: use of alcohol and hypnotics, stealing and running away, occasionally violence or suicidal depression. A particularly valuable set of observations is offered in compulsory abstinence. Finally drugs available nowadays often do not suffice to induce actual physiologic addiction since they are so diluted or expensive.

To demonstrate this point I select two impressive cases from the time when I was in charge of a program of compulsory abstinence (1964-1968), but similar observations can be made as well in methadone maintenance and other modalities of treatment (appendix B).

CASE 5: SHAKY

This was a tall, usually quite neglected looking, beardy and haggard man, age 36; because of his apprehensiveness and trembling he was called Shaky. He started taking drugs after his wife had left him about four years prior to his conviction and had soon become dependent upon them. He was sentenced to two years for selling narcotics. His father, a minister, was described as very harsh. He would "get carried away with temper. This was the only unpleasant thing about him." The patient said: "I loved him. He was not unjust" yet added that he was punished by being beaten with a belt until he was about fifteen years of age. The mother was nagging and semi-illiterate. The parents were divorced when the patient was twenty-two. The patient, youngest of three children, completed an eighth grade education. He had frequently changing sexual relationships since age sixteen. After twenty months in the Army, where he was honorably discharged, he went at age twenty-one to work on the railroad as a trainman; he was a very hard worker, frequently working one shift on and one off. About his wife whom he married shortly thereafter he said "I had her on a pedestal. I had a guilt complex. She was perfect; everything had to be my fault." He bought her a house and practically lived on the railroad to earn money to support his family.

When the marriage broke up after seven years, he stopped working, started drinking and soon was introduced by a girlfriend to the use of opiates. He financed the habit mainly by transporting and selling drugs. During his stay in the program of compulsory abstinence he got increasingly depressed, talked about suicide and used narcotics in the first months not infrequently, though still sporadically; he had to be warned several times that he would be returned to jail if he did not stop taking drugs. While he took narcotics less and less often, his depression became so marked that he was put on Elavil. His depression was mainly motivated by the loss of his wife and his son—the monotonousness of the lowly jobs open to him. He felt everyone disliked him. About eight months after his admission to the program, he stopped violating the rules of the clinic, came in quite regularly and no longer showed any positive urine specimens. Often, however, he came unkempt, disheveled, unshaved and obviously inebriated to the meetings. He admitted freely that he could stay away from drugs only when he took to alcohol and, as he added the day when he left our program because parole expired (he stayed in it for 545 days), also to marijuana: "How did you think I was able to stay away from drugs? I have to have some escape." And he explained: "The threat has been a help more than anything else—I wish I still had it." He indicated he probably would return to drugs once he was off the program.

The impression is that this extremely passive, orally dependent man had exchanged the relief and gratification by opiates with that by alcohol and cannabis. He suffered from a severe neurotic depression which had become manifest by the break of the apparently symbiotic relationship with his former wife, a symbiosis which he felt constrained to reestablish within the drug experience.

CASE 6: BREATH OF MORPHEUS

A twenty-four-year-old white man will appear next. We might call him the "Breath of Morpheus," both because he used this corny metaphor himself and because of a surface fatuousness and vacuousness expressed in his glib, "sociopathic" behavior. He had been involved for about seven years in the use of narcotics and concomitant crimes (including an armed holdup), was sentenced to one and one-half years in prison, but he had earlier sentences of several years for which he was presently on probation, in addition to and beyond the current time on parole. He was a very intelligent rather handsome young man, with a particular gift to verbalize his experience but also to manipulate other people.

He came from a broken home and was the older of two children; his sister was married to a drug addict. The father, a soldier in the Army, left the family early. The boy was placed in an orphanage so that his mother could go to work. At age ten, he started to drink—whiskey, wine and beer. On weekends he would come home and return to the orphanage with bottles of alcoholic beverages; this resulted in his expulsion. At thirteen he joined a gang and soon started smoking marijuana; at fourteen he began having sexual relationships and, at seventeen, shooting drugs. At home there was no discipline and no consistency. At eighteen he married a girl who was a drug user and an alcoholic herself. A few days after she gave birth to a baby she left him and the child and disappeared for good.

The feelings he derived from the use of drugs, he wrote in an autobiographical essay, were utterly indescribable:

> The first thing I experienced was an overwhelming, gratifying experience. Every cell in my body would be screaming out to be fed, and after taking the drug everything would be all better—no anxiety or tension—I felt completely at ease. I inhaled the breath of Morpheus and began to feel the warmth and comfort, and then she went down and kissed me upon the lips, and I realized that the Greeks and the Romans were in error. Morpheus was a woman. Time passed, and she suddenly disappeared—my surroundings were pale, sickening vomit green.

There were fantasies of grandeur, of power, of being above the law, of torturing and killing his enemies, of being invisible, able to read the mind, to overcome the limits of time and space and physical size. "Frankly, doctor, I do not think I'll ever stop taking drugs. I can't find any substitute." So he took opiates sporadically, every two to three weeks for the first four months. When offered an evening off, he preferred to continue coming in every night. When he changed from a rather menial type of work to a job in a bookstore, which was more suitable to his intellectual interests (though not to his schooling) he stopped taking drugs entirely. He was enthusiastic about his work. This did not last more than about two months and the patient came in inebriated more and more frequently. Again, several months later, he took to opiates again, allegedly after one of his several girlfriends tried to force him into marriage by pretending she was pregnant. He succeeded in hiding his drug use for several weeks (at that time he had to come in only three nights a week) by taking the drug right after his clinic visits, by drinking excessive amounts of liquids and by injecting saline solutions. When he got a warning letter from the clinic, he stopped taking drugs from one day to the other; but he was increasingly alarmed about his boundless and obviously severely destructive alcohol excesses. He stated that it had become a matter of course, when he got off from work, to get a couple of whiskeys, followed by a quart of beer. He said that, because it was the end of his work day, he had nothing to do and nothing that interested him. "I have never drunk like this before. Every other day I crave to get drunk, and if my money holds out, I will. True—I am keeping away from drugs. I think I am by far one of the more fortunate members because I could make this transition." He asked to be treated with LSD in order to overcome his alcoholism, and when this did not seem feasible, he again resorted to illegal drugs, this time to an assortment of cocaine, methadone and heroin. When this spree was stopped, an even severer and more dangerous crisis developed; he started making extended and obviously desperate phone calls to me, explaining that he had two of his girlfriends in his apartment. The relationship with both girls seemed to have deteriorated to one of sexual and financial demands and exploitation. In the following days he picked several serious fights on the street (hitting other drivers and pedestrians over the head with a baseball bat), had two car accidents, stopped working and was almost constantly drunk. He increased his daily alcohol consumption to two-fifths of a gallon of rum, came severely drunk to that week's group session; had afterwards, on the way to a friend's apartment, two more car collisions, got away from both of them (hit-and-run) and was impatient to carry through his resolution that night, to kill himself with an overdose of alcohol and drugs. In the apartment of a friend(who incidently was arrested the day thereafter for attempted murder and robbery), he injected five grains of Dolophine directly into his blood stream. "I was very disappointed to wake up and discover that I had 'killed' myself only for six hours." So he injected seven grains more—again without the desired effect. Leaving the apartment he ran into other close friends who told him that they just had shot and killed someone.

After these events our patient decided to commit himself to a state hospital, in order not only to undergo a cure for his alcoholism, but mainly to protect himself against his own overwhelming urge to kill someone. In the first two weeks in the hospital, he still was very much afraid of his own murderous aggressivity and of the actual and possible legal implications of the two cases of homicide he had been peripherally involved in on the few days prior to his commitment. It also became obvious that not a small part of his vehement hostility was directed against me in the group sessions. At the beginning he had been filled "with a profound sense of hope" and "confidence in you as a doctor, as my doctor....I just do not know how to show my gratitude.... I wish to help you to succeed....That is why, when I turn in a positive specimen, that I am falling down on my part of the project." Once he wrote: "After each time that my specimen is exposed as positive, I am filled with fear and shame, fear that by violating this condition of the program I may be sent back to a place that was a veritable horror, and shame, for exposing myself as such a weakling." The disguised hostility towards the therapist and diffuse rage resulted from a total sense of disappointment: for our not having provided him with a sense of fulfillment, for not having taken away the constant feeling of emptiness, for not treating him as a unique, special, admirable being, infinitely better than the other patients. To quote him in this *narcissistic entitlement*: "What I refuse to be is just a face in the crowd. I think the world owes me something. I did not ask to be here."

It is obvious that this patient tried to find gratification of his limitless wishes for power, dependency, adoration and total acceptance: in alcohol, various drugs, girlfriends, fantasies, music—and if these were not met in their whole insatiable extent, the equally total primitive rage broke through in form of a suicidal and self-destructive spree, or of a homicidal and ruthlessly violent outburst. The closing of the narcotics exit brought this conflict much sharper and in much more extreme and dangerous form into focus. In many ways he still was an adolescent faced with the necessity to accept the limitations of reality, yet unable to submit to this necessity.

Catamnestically it was learned that after repeated stays on compulsory abstinence and revocations of parole (with return to jail) he joined a local methadone program. Later on he participated in a bank hold-up, injured a policeman critically in the following shoot-out and is now spending a long sentence in prison.

A deeper understanding of some of these extremely important self-observations will become possible when we study in a detailed way the question of narcissistic wishes and the problems of limit and boundary formation in these patients. But already with these two patients the function of the narcotic in coping with low self-esteem and rage (case 6) and loneliness and despair (case 5) is rather evident. Before we go on we should now organize our observations.

THREE LAYERS OF COMPULSION

In the life history and the direct experience of every patient dependent upon physically addicting drugs, we may discern three layers of compulsion: (a) the compulsiveness of physical dependency based entirely on processes on the level of the cells; (b) the compulsiveness of protracted withdrawal, a gray area in theory; and (c) the emotional compulsiveness leading first to start drug use and then to continue the search for the effect. Only this third form will be encountered in compulsive users of drugs which are not also physically addictive, like psychedelics or stimulants.

The most superficial layer of compulsion is that of the physical dependency—the compulsive need to continue with the drug to avoid the very uncomfortable feelings of acute withdrawal. This is a strictly physical problem; the compulsion in this situation is analogous to the one in an acute bout of flu with high fever when most people would confess to a compelling need to go to bed and to take aspirin. Similarly the addicted person faced with acute withdrawal would require a considerable effort to go through abrupt withdrawal on his own; and even slow withdrawal by his own effort is quite difficult, since he cannot know the right dose of drug he receives on the black market. In contrast, we know from our experience that slow withdrawal over a period of a few weeks with known dosages in a well supervised program is not only feasible, but actually requested and well tolerated by many patients. But to expect self-weaning or abrupt withdrawal on the street is unrealistic, because it presumes qualities of self-discipline and self-abnegation our addicts commonly do not possess.

Addicts who have been withdrawn and are not physically dependent anymore, typically show a persistent longing to return to the drug. This urge or desire is known to endure years, even decades, of enforced abstinence. How to explain this is a matter of theoretical dispute; but its existence cannot be doubted. The interpretation may be—as Dole assumes—that the addiction has led to an irreversible metabolic change. Some support for this hypothesis has been seen in the observations that a number of basic physiological mechanisms remain altered at least for many months after withdrawal. Dole and Nyswander postulate, mainly on the basis of their clinical observation, a "metabolic lesion" of unknown nature in the nervous system which would explain this lasting narotics hunger.

An alternate interpretation was proffered by the theory of conditioning. This second hypothesis can be summarized so: if an action consistently leads to reward and thus causes a reinforcement to occur, this action is strongly encouraged; such a learned response is difficult to extinguish.

I am inclined to interpret it still differently, namely, the way any other kind of gratified neurotic impulse is explained in psychoanalytic theory and as basically identical with the third layer. As will be explained later, every neurotic compulsion is viewed as outcome of a conflict of several incompatible wishes and fears, a conflict which is forcibly pushed out, and kept out, of consciousness. It is characteristic of such compulsions that the more they are lived out in outer reality, the more insatiable they become (they "feed on themselves"); it is as if they were continually searching for their real, though unconscious, aim without ever being able to attain it—precisely because the real aim of the wish is buried.

This leads us directly to the third and most important layer of compulsion, the conflicts preceding and underlying the use of drugs.

It is valid to adduce several analogies: A first one is the really compulsive smoker. He knows (and denies!) that he might be "punished" by a number of physical illnesses and even possible premature death if he continues. Actually he may already have had a heart attack and knows by now that in all probability his continued smoking hastens the day of a fatal attack. He may have seen relatives of his die because of smoking related diseases, or he may have had to undergo operation after operation...and yet, no outer warning can stop him. In this instance we have practically only this layer of psychological compulsiveness, because there are merely mild physical withdrawal symptoms with nicotine; and yet the craving can be well-nigh irresistible—regardless of the known consequences.

Another example is the food addict, e.g., an obese woman weighing three-hundred or four-hundred pounds. Again we deal just with the clearly psychological layer of compulsiveness. The punishment is glaringly obvious: low self-esteem because of the gross deformity and ugliness, fatigue and shortness of breath, heart and other health problems, physicians' warning about an early death, clear knowledge of what diet would help. And yet even prominent men and women are subject to this psychological compulsion.

Yet another analogue is a handwashing compulsion. No threat stops this. Similarly, hysterical and schizophrenic symptoms, which are of the same emotional compulsiveness as the ones just described, have never ceded to coercion, even death penalties. Most witches who were burned in the seventeenth century were actually hysterical, schizophrenic, or melancholic people. No threat deterred them. If anything it may actually have supported precisely their compulsive self-destructiveness. This was, e.g., the view of one of the few enlightened men of the time, Johann Weyer (1563; see Trevor-Roper 1956, p. 146). Despite the new insights gained by anthropology, e.g., by Jane Murphy, it appears likely that this statement is still valid. And this is really the crucial point: every addicted or otherwise compulsive drug user I have known is determined, almost destined, by this irresistible, emotional compulsion to seek relief or meaning with the help of a drug or of another symptom. Addiction can most convincingly be compared to phobic neurosis—as a kind of negative of the latter. While the phobic neurotic compulsively avoids the condensed and projected symbol for his anxiety, the toxicomanic compulsively seeks the condensed and projected symbol of protection against uncontrollable, overwhelming affects and mobilizes with its help a transient and lastly spurious counterforce.

If we study the three types of compulsiveness described before, (acute withdrawal, protracted "withdrawal" whose existence as separate entity I questioned, and emotional need) the latter two show typical fluctuations. Under any psychological or physiological stress the compulsion to take drugs (or to show other forms of symptoms) increases. In turn it can be observed that the emotional dependency on the drug is overcome if the psychological dependency and commitment is displaced onto other objects, e. g., to a concrete community (as Synanon), to a cause (Black Muslims), or to a therapist (positive transference). In other words, *potent meaning-giving factors can replace in highly motivated individuals the compelling role the drug exerts.*

This implies a most important fact: that there is a continuum of compulsiveness—ranging from zero to total; it is not a strict either-or. Compulsiveness is a relative, not an absolute concept; it represents a more or less. Most importantly, when we speak about compulsive drug users we have not a clearly defined group in mind, but simply one where the extent of compulsion most of the time is very prominent.

Many of the analogies we were adducing do not lie at the extreme of complete compulsion, but at a high degree. We have observed before that the more some form of behavior is carried out regardless of the legal and physical consequences (the more, in other words, it has to break down the barriers of prohibition and is likely to be found out), the closer it will have to be placed toward the 100 percent end of this spectrum. Compulsive smoking, e.g., would not qualify for such an extreme position nor would the abuse of alcohol or even of sleeping medication, but the illegal use of narcotics would. This correlation is complicated much more by group pressures, group standards and expectations, but as a thumbnail rule it is valid.

We may add now that what we saw before as fluctuations means that the emotional compulsion to resort to drugs may move up or down considerably on this continuum dependent upon external and internal stress.

Some objected to this as circular reasoning: because these particular forms of drug abuse are compulsive, the users must be particularly emotionally disturbed to begin with; but to be emotionally disturbed means to show compulsive behavior. In fact compulsive drug use is but one striking example for a general observation: that compulsiveness is the most useful criterion for any and all forms of psychopathology. The more striking the former, the more blatant the latter.

Thus compulsive drug use is eo ipso and observably a sign of emotional illness and, as in the case of the positive tubercle culture, we are well advised to scout for other signs, for other symptoms, and usually are not embarassed in this search. If we were, we would have to doubt whether the basic criterion is valid anymore; it would, in my estimation, force us to a revolutionary search for a new paradigm. I see no such need at this moment.

In this view compulsion is not the language of the unconscious (that is rather a complex system of symbolic equivalences with its proper rules), but it is the sign that unconscious functions have usurped the controls. It is a sign, not a symbol.

To pose now the problem yet more explicitly: Compulsiveness may be used as that quality of any mental process (and behavioral characteristic) which is theoretically and practically the best operational criterion of "psychologically ill." Obviously, this is one crucial problem which psychiatry should urgently tackle in a more systematic fashion: is the use of this observable quality as basic criterion justified or not? This equation was postulated not only by Waelder and Kubie but actually goes back to Socrates, Plato and Aristotle. Or should we rather use social qualities, like maladjustment, the inability to work and love, as criteria for illness (e.g. Freud)? Is it the quality of inner harmony instead, as employed by the late Plato and by Hartmann? Or should it be a complex definition of all these? Ought it to be abolished altogether, as Szasz demands?

The moment has arrived when I cannot evade this central question. I take compulsiveness of any kind, including the compulsiveness of drug use, in and by itself as the criterion of emotional disturbance, but, even without accepting this premise, we have in all cases of severe ("compulsive") drug use a history of other serious symptoms, usually complying with any other definition of emtional disturbance to back up my original statement.

By no stretch of the imagination can we postulate these people to be considered healthy, were it not for their one problem of drug use. No one who knows them well and has learned the rudiments of psychiatry would declare them well even if the drug problem was magically wiped out. Theoretically I allow for exceptions: perhaps there are some compulsive drug users who have not shown any other symptoms of severe psychopathology. They have eluded me however.

Still I am not off the hook. My statement, equating psychopathology with compulsiveness, remains a bold assertion which I must justify. "Hic Rhodus, hic salta," as the Latin proverb says (about the one who, bragging about his feats of high jumps on the Isle of Rhodes, was challenged: "Here is now Rhodes, jump here!") What follows is a metascientific, in a deep sense "metapsychological" section, a philosophical choice of a criterion, of a value, around which our entire science and method revolves.

Are Suffering or Social Deviance Scientifically Useful Criteria?

The definition of the twin concepts of psychic normality versus psychopathology is a task both exceedingly difficult and yet of critical importance for theory and practice, not only of psychiatry in general, but also of all types of psychotherapy, of social work, sociology and anthropology, of law and even of politics.

To begin with, the concept of normality is equivocal and should be avoided, were it not so ubiquitous. On the one side it means conforming to a standard, to a relative rule and pattern (as its etymology indicates), on the other side it has become inseparably tied to health. In the following the notion of normality is equated with that of health.

The problem is easy, though even there not entirely without controversy, in regard to the gross forms of pathology: unmistakable massive schizophrenia, manic-depressive psychosis, or severe brain damage. Still, there are a few authors, e.g., R.D. Laing, who would claim that it is not the individual but society that is sick, or, with Szasz, that to use the concepts of illness, sickness, pathology for mental phenomena is employing an illicit metaphor, a carryover from somatic medicine misapplied to social deviance—that there is indeed no such phenomenon as "mental illness" but merely a breaking of set social rules, norms, standards, that the label of "mental illness" has been created by society to condemn, scapegoat and destroy whoever does not fit into these artificially defined structures. For the proponents of this thesis mental illness is equated with, and superseded by, social expulsion and persecution. Szasz goes even so far to compare and even equate the witch hunts of the past, the Nazi persecution of the Jews, and the treatment of the mentally ill, particularly of the user of again arbitrarily illegal drugs. I have, in a provisional way, refuted some of these contentions. Here we cannot content ourselves with such a provisional response but must deal far more thoroughly with this pivotal problem.

There is just no doubt that there is an urgent practical and theoretical need to abstract a pair of concepts (psychic normality versus psychic illness) from the very concrete, often obtrusive problems presented either by psychotic and neurotic suffering, or by socially disturbing behavior. These can serve merely as starting points for conceptualization. Contrary to Szasz's opinion, there is good reason not to equate the abstract concepts with ethical judgments, since the notions of illness, sickness, and pathology actually originated in the basic phenomenon of suffering, not in that of social unacceptability; this is as true for psychiatry as for somatic medicine. Still, history shows that these two criteria were mixed up time and again. A combination of this criterion of suffering with the sociocultural one is historically well documented. Thus the Egyptologist Weeks writes in a most recent review of a book about Egyptian medicine:

So much of medicine is culturally determined. Indeed, about the only way one can define the concept of 'health', which is what medicine seeks to maintain, is to say that it is the physical and psychological state of an organism that allows it to participate normally in its culture and society. Obviously, such a definition is a culturebound one, and it is often culture that dictates what a physician should study and what he should ignore. [Weeks 1976, p. 44]

Is this statement indeed entirely accurate? Is the definition of health and illness in fact so culturally determined?

In the last two or three decades this presumption has gained more and more credence—almost the status of a scientific truth. Particularly in regard to *mental* health and illness this sociocultural relativism has assumed nearly dogmatic certainty—outside of the small circles of traditional psychoanalysts and psychiatrists. I have reviewed the "extreme" positions of people like Szasz and Laing, positions which logically flow from such a relativistic point of view.

Recently, Jane Murphy's article (1976) appeared and cleared the air. She summarizes the sociological thesis very well. "Labeling theory proposes that the concept of mental illness is a cultural stereotype referring to a residue of deviance which each society arbitrarily defines in a distinct way....the primary deviations of mental illness are held to be for the most part insignificant, and societal reactions become the main etiological factor." Referring to Scheff, she quotes him on how the environment responds to a deviant in "stereotypes of insanity": "his amorphous and unstructured rule breaking tends to crystallize in conformity to these expectations." Thus for the labeling theorists the influence of societal reactions is considered genuinely causative: "For mental illness the labeling theorists have tended to use the 'pure case' model rather than the more complex model represented by blindness, where lack or loss of sight is primary deviance and the role of blind mind is secondary deviance." Even beyond that, these label theorists "share the view that in our society the appellation 'mentally ill' is a 'stigmatizing' and brutalizing assessment. It robs the individual of identity through profound 'mortification' and suggests that he is a 'nonperson.'" Moreover the concepts of "inner life" and "mind" are viewed as late concepts of Western society (often considered and devalued as Cartesian; see Ryle, Schafer).

It is truly fascinating in the subsequent study of this Harvard-based anthropologist that in three different cultures (Eskimos, Yorubas in Nigeria, and the Zapotec in Mexico) the usual descriptions and even partially the labeling of psychosis, neurosis and psychopathy are encountered as well. In regard to psychoses there are also labels in the various languages and culturally different, but distinct, healing practices.

The symptoms of neuroses are recognized and treated as illnesses, by shaman and witchdoctor, although no comprehensive label is used; "the phenomena exist independently of labels." Vis-à-vis neurotics and psychotics there is a similar ambivalence as in our culture, a mixture of strong compassion and rejection.

Moreover specific labels are reserved for those who transgress against social standards, who break many rules (lying, cheating, stealing, excessive use of drugs), but this category is not believed to be subject to the healing powers of shamans and healers, but it is presumed that in turn such transgressions may cause physical or mental disease.

In contrast to these three categoreis, the shamans and witchdoctors which Western observers used to see filling "a social niche in which psychopathology is socially useful and...therefore mental disorder is positively valued" are clearly different: "One Eskimo summarized the distinction this way: 'When the shaman is healing he is out of his mind, but he is not crazy.'" Thus, according to these findings, the distinction lies in the degree to which the symptoms are controlled and utilized for a specific social function: "The inability to control these processes is what is meant by a mind out of order; when a mind is out of order it will not only fail to control sensory perception but will also fail to control behavior."

In the words of an Eskimo, if "the mind does not control the person, he is crazy."

It is indeed the crux of Murphy's (and my) argument that, though explicit labels for insanity exist in these cultures, they "refer to beliefs, feelings, and actions that are thought to emanate from the mind or inner state of an individual and to be essentially beyond his control." We conclude, therefore, that "rather than being simply violations of the social norms of particular groups, as labeling theory suggests, symptoms of mental illness are manifestations of a type of affliction shared by virtually all mankind." It is very clear from this that social deviance as criterion for psychopathology, though now usually employed by the sociologically oriented version of antipsychiatry (e.g., Szasz, Laing, Dumont), is at best marginal in anthropologically or historically explored cultures.

If we return now to the criterion of suffering which originally defined illness (somatic or mental), it becomes rapidly evident that this central phenomenon of suffering can serve us at best as a starting point, not as an abstract concept which any systematic theory can use as its cornerstone. If we take the analogy from physics: the free fall of heavy bodies was one of the starting points for Aristotle's and Galileo's constructs of physical models, but it could not, without crucial abstractions and alterations, be used to build a theoretical system: the concepts of force, energy, and velocity are abstractions from the various phenomena of free fall. With Galileo, a rationalistic grid, an inner vision of a mathematically conceived ordering principle was superimposed on the empirical data. Theory based on reason became more important than sensory truth (in contrast to Aristotle's stringent empiricism).

The much greater difficulty arises not with this starting point and basic justification but with the choice of an enduringly valid criterion to use in the building of such a theory. And here the philosophical problem enters that, no matter how scientific we try to be, such a choice would entail a value judgment. This is so, not withstanding the old and persistent conviction that science must be free of values, and that, insofar as psychiatry and psychoanalysis attempt to be scientific, they ought to be free of values. (A similar and parallel prejudice is directed against the use of metaphor in theory formation. Torrents of print are spent to eradicate metaphors, just as an obsessional patient tries to exorcize his hidden masturbation; see Wurmser 1977.) The fallacy here lies once more in the equation of value with moral judgment.

Obviously the various sciences as such are free of ethical values as far as their theoretical constructs go although very many of their practical applications indeed lend themselves to moral implications and overt judgments. But we have to pose the rhetorical question: Are the four criteria which Cassirer (1906) used for physical theory—clarity, lack of contradiction, absence of equivocation in the description, and fruitfulness—not all expressions of scientific or theoretical truth, and, with that, are they not quite explicitly forms of value statements?

Thus we ought not to be too squeamish to use a value as theoretical cornerstone. This means that our field, too, is not value-free but has to become far more explicit, conscious, even conscientious, about the constant and legitimate use of value concepts.

If after this initial justification we turn to the task itself we may use two major roads—roads which may intersect here or there, but lead to a different destination. The first road is the one commonly used: to define a whole person as normal or healthy—or as pathological or sick. The second road, however, has been barely used, and yet it might well be far superior: to define inner processes and functions as free of, or fraught with, pathology, as normal or as abnormal.

The Totalistic Approach

If we want to explore the first well-trodden path, we can use the excellent exposition in the book *Normality* (Offer and Sabshin 1966)—the most modern, complete and thoughtful examination of this approach. They differentiate four possible, equally justified perspectives whose usefulness varies dependent on vantage-point and aim.

In a modified form we may define the four approaches suggested by Offer and Sabshin as: (1) emotional normality or health as absence of gross symptoms; (2) health as an ideal or Utopia; (3) normality (or health) as statistical average; and (4) health as time adequate and culturally appropriate adaptation or adjustment. Throughout I will try to relate them to compulsive drug use.

1. *Health or normality as absence of gross symptoms:* This concept is the one still prevalently used in somatic medicine and, often somewhat awkwardly, imposed upon psychiatry. Basically it is a biophysiological model which is more and more recognized as too confining even for somatic medicine. In this view health is an almost universal phenomenon. "Concentration is then focused upon definitions of pathology, leaving the large residue as 'normal' or 'healthy.'" This accords with the general medical model in which the lack of unfavorable symptoms indicates health: "Health in this context refers to a reasonable rather than an optimal state of functioning. The psychiatrist subscribing to such an approach is interested in the prevention of disease; for him, prevention implies the treatment of the

symptoms that overtly interfere with the adequate functioning of the patient" (pp. 99–100).

In this perspective "a healthy person is one who is reasonably free of undue pain, discomfort, and disability" (p. 100).

Obviously this approach uses the starting point of suffering also by and large as the theoretical criterion and thus follows closely an early version of the health model of somatic medicine.

Applied to compulsive drug users this criterion would declare them ill for two reasons: the drug use in and of itself would be considered a most serious symptom, disabling and interfering in most instances; plus the gamut of other symptoms mentioned before cannot be negated even if the lead symptom were "healed" by medical withdrawal or incarceration.

2. If we follow our scheme farther and turn to the second functional perspective, *normality or health as utopia or ideal,* we find it best typified in psychoanalytic writings; it "conceives of normality as that harmonious and optimal blending of the diverse elements of the mental apparatus that culminates in optimal functioning, or self-actualization....Dating from Freud's conception of normality as an ideal fiction, the Normality as Utopia view almost has become the trademark of the psychoanalyst" (pp. 102–103). He seeks accordingly to facilitate the patient's development of a healthier character structure and to help the patient to utilize effectively all the resources with which he is endowed. "The 'Normality as Utopia' perspective makes the normal man not only a person to be admired but also one who is seldom, if ever, seen in flesh and blood."

In line with this concept of normality which actually reaches back to Socrates we find the criterion of harmony—as expressed by, for example, Hartmann (1947). In connection with the pathogenetic role of "disharmonious precocity in the development of certain tendencies" he concludes: "Facts like these and some others mentioned before make me inclined to formulate conditions of health in terms of the equilibrium that exists between the substructures of personality on the one hand, and between these and the environment on the other hand" (p. 60).

The school of Hippocrates already asserted that "the doctor's duty is to restore the secret proportion when it is disturbed by disease"; normal health is for the Hippocratic school as well as for Plato the "symmetry of parts or forces" (Jaeger 1943b, pp. 27,45), the "harmony of elements" (Plato, Symposium 186; Philebus 31, 65–67). This ideal is "destroyed by excess or deficiency," and "preserved by the observance of the mean" (Aristotle, *Nicomachean Ethics* II, 2). This "golden mean" was, as "aurea mediocritas," a central value of antiquity and is of such relevance (though often hidden) in all our psychotherapeutic efforts, that some want to eliminate psychiatry or psychoanalysis altogether and let them be dissolved into a vaguely propounded "art of living"; i.e., into some sort of value philosophy or sociology. Clinically again there is no compulsive drug user who would not fall very far indeed from that mark of ideality, of harmony and balance.

3. *The statistical view:* Here we are closest to the original meaning of "normality." Patients in treatment use this perspective not infrequently as a defense. It is the attitude: since "everyone else" or many other people have this problem or that attitude also, it is thereby self-evident, right and in no need of exploration. Offer and Sabshin call it "normality as average": "This approach is based on the mathematical principle of the Bell-shaped curve and its applicability to physical, psychological and sociological data....Norms have been established and pathology defined according to strict statistical criteria" (pp. 105–106). "One striking result of such an application of statistics to behavioral data has been the idealization of the average, or the middle, since both ends of the scale denote pathology" (p. 107). When I referred to labeling theories before, I implied that "sociologists begin with the central values of the society, labeling them normal, and then judge deviancy by its differentiation from these norms" (p. 108).

In an analogy with somatic medicine, an epidemic of flu or the almost ubiquitous presence of caries would have to be adjudged "normal," if this statistical concept of normality were used as crucial criterion. This criterion is indeed vastly deployed in order to declare some, most, or all compulsive drug use "normal" for a given subculture or an entire culture. I will deal with this argument shortly.

4. Finally we turn to the fourth perspective, *health (or normality) as adjustment (or adaptation).* Offer and Sabshin speak of "normality as transactional systems."

This view "stresses that normal behavior is the end result of interacting systems that change over time." Thus it stresses changes of processes rather than a cross-sectional definition of normality (pp. 108–109).

Best known is Erikson's version of this criterion.

So far we have traveled on the first road—that of defining persons as normal, using a great variety of criteria. It is clear that even when we now turn to a quite different approach, we cannot entirely relinquish the gains made with this first group of methods. It even seems likely that all four models or frameworks have to be employed dependent on the practical aim pursued. None is wrong; each is of use though limited and relative.

The Part Approach

When we abandon the attempt to call an entire person normal or sick and instead begin by judging single or complex mental phenomena or processes with these concepts and consider the judgment about entire person only as a border event, an extreme on a continuum, we immediately realize that we have made a radical departure. One of the best analogies can be found in physics where Newtonian mechanics becomes a theory covering merely the endpoints on a continuum which itself is more satisfactorily explained by the theories of Einstein and Planck.

The real merit of Kubie's theory, which I favor as a basis for a discussion of this problem, lies in this leap, best expounded in his exceptionally valuable and succinct article of 1954 "The Fundamental Nature of the Distinction Between Normality and Neurosis."

Although Kubie's arguments are ostensibly restricted to those pertinent to neurosis it is clear that they cover the entire problem of health versus psychopathology (including organic psychoses and, of course, drug abuse). His major points can be summarized as follows:

The first point has already been stated: "We should limit ourselves to an effort to characterize the state of health of a single act or moment of life, and not the normality of neurosis of an entire personality" (p. 179). "Every human act, thought, feeling, and impulse can under appropriate circumstances be normal or it can be neurotic" (p. 182).

The second point is that of the essential nature of the concepts. We have to ask "not what are all the differences between sick and healthy human behavior, but which among these is the essential difference, the quality of the presence of which is the *sine qua non* of health, and that absence or distortion of which is the *sine qua non* of illness" (p. 168).

Thirdly, we need a clear description which sets down unmistakably the phenomena: "Not one of the qualities popularly associated with the idea of neurosis is an invariable concomitant or cause or result of the neurotic process. One quality however is constant and sets a normal act apart from one that is a manifestation of the neurotic process." This trait is observable, descriptively and clinically derived; it is "the freedom and flexibility to learn through experience, to change, and to adapt to changing external circumstances." This stands in contrast to the freezing of behavior into patterns of unalterability that characterizes every manifestation of the neurotic process. *"No moment of behavior can be looked upon as neurotic unless the processes that have set it in motion predetermine its automatic repetition irrespective of the situation, the utility, or the consequences of the act..."* (pp. 182–183; italics in original). This holds true, whatever the culture or circumstances.

A fourth step is an analysis in depth, going beyond the phenomena to an explanatory, theoretical construct. Here Kubie advances an hypothesis based on Freud's early model of differentiating conscious, preconscious, and unconscious: "wherever an alliance of the conscious and preconscious systems predominates in the production of behavior, the resultant behavior will come to rest either when its goal is achieved and satiety is attained, or when the goal is found to be unattainable or ungratifying or both, whereupon the effort ceases. Thus such behavior never becomes either insatiable or stereotyped. It can be altered by the experience of success and failure, of rewards and punishments, or pleasure and pain." In contrast, "whenever the unconscious system (or perhaps an alliance between the preconscious and unconscious systems) predominates, the resultant action must be repeated endlessly. This occurs because its goals are predominantly unconscious symbols, and unconscious symbolic goals are never attainable....Since the predominant forces are unconscious, they will not be responsive to the experience of pleasure or of pain, or to rewards and punishments, or to logical argument—neither to the logic of events, nor to any appeals to mind or heart" (pp. 183-184).

Obviously this fourth point is hypothetical—indeed the central hypothesis of Kubie's theory. In contrast to Kubie some may advance a parallel hypothesis, based on Freud's later model, that of the three bundles of functions or "structures" (ego, id and superego), and the idea that wherever the id and superego functions dominate, processes show the characteristics described on the third step; but this substitution does not satisfy.

Kubie's hypothesis appears in this particular context more explanatory and fruitful. A similar conclusion has been reached by Sandler (1974).

Only in border concepts, in extrapolations, we move on a continuum of quantitative preponderances to whole patterns and personalities: "a state of greater health is achieved whenever those areas of life that are dominated by inaccessibly unconscious forces are shrunk, so that a larger area of life is dominated by conscious or preconscious forces, which can come to awareness when necessary" (Kubie 1954, p. 184). More descriptively, a preponderance of inner freedom, flexibility and control versus a preponderance of inner compulsion, restrictedness in thought, feeling and action mark the distinction between healthy and sick persons.

The operational, pragmatic nature of this definition is emphasized: on pragmatic grounds we are justified in calling normal any act in the determination of which the alliance of conscious and preconscious forces play the dominant role, that is, forces that are accessible on need; whereas on the same grounds we are justified in calling abnormal or unhealthy or neurotic any act in the determination of which unconscious processes are dominant (whether alone or in an alliance with the preconscious), because such forces will predetermine its automatic repetition irrespective of its suitability to the immediate situation or its immediate or remote consequences.

The quantitative nature of this hypothesis is pointed out: "The hypothesis does not assume a homogeneous determination of any moment of behavior. For instance, it allows for the observable fact that even when anyone is functioning under the domination of unconscious forces, conscious and preconscious processes are helping to shape many of the seconday symptomatic manifestations of the neurosis. It recognizes similarly that when conscious processes alone or a conscious-preconscious alliance dominates, unconscious processes play a significant subsidiary role in the energizing shaping of behavior" (p. 187). This means that unconscious forces become destructive only when they play a preponderant role in the determination of behavior. What Kubie unfortuantely omits here is clearly most pertinent to his entire proposal (as well as to our own considerations): Freud's eminently useful model of the complementary series and the continuous spectrum (see Freud 1905a, Rangell 1972).

The ideal of normality as pertinent to the whole personality and its Utopian nature is expressed when Kubie acknowledges the impossibility of ever fully knowing one's own unconscious:

> The implicit ideal of normality that emerges from this hypothesis is an individual in whom the creative alliance between the conscious and preconscious systems is not constantly subjected to blocking and distortion by the counterplay of preponderant unconscious forces, whether in the prosaic affairs of daily life, in human relations, or in creative activity. Here is no unreal fantasy of a "normal" individual out of whom all the salty seasoning of secondary unconscious motivations has been dissolved. [p. 187]

This also means that "the healthy integration of psychological processes requires that they should be accessible to self-inspection on need, and not that they should be continuously in the center and forefront of consciousness." Thus it is an ideal which can be approached but never reached. Therefore the acquisition of insight, like education, is a process never finished. Insight is a point on a continuous, never-ending scale; it is relative and not absolute (p. 188).

One may argue—with Offer and Sabshin—that Kubie's theory is merely a special form of the common psychoanalytic perspective of "normality as utopia." It seems, however, that there is a crucial theoretical difference in changing the vantage point from person to inner process, from a complex, total phenomenon to a small, separable unit. It is the step which—to use another historical analogy from natural science—was taken in chemistry when the focus turned from metaphysical, global concepts of matter and its major variants (as fire, water, earth and air) to the study of specific quantifiable processes and functions, and lastly to the identification of the smallest differentiating units as atoms and molecules.

Here I focus only on its application to drug abuse. In another publication (Wurmser 1978) it is also applied to homosexuality and other sexual deviations. Just as in regard to these others areas the crucial point here is that we have to distinguish most strictly and clearly between political or sociological criteria and the criterion of psychopathology employed here.

The psychiatric relevance of drug abuse lies primarily in its compulsive forms. The means (drugs, needle, television, even books and work) are indeed less important than the "addictive" nature of the use of such external means to attain the aim of transient resolution of the unbearable tension.

Thus the use of illegal drugs is in and of itself neither normal nor pathological; the compulsive, insatiable, driven nature bespeaks its pathology. Environmental influences are of course very important precipitants, but they are usually embedded in the context of prior, not drug related forms of compulsive ("addictive") behavior, or (more rarely) they unmask a previously hidden, massive pathogenic conflict and trigger a kind of snowball effect, just as a first sexual experience or rejection may spread into a massive complex of repetitive, severely disruptive symptoms (ideas of reference, outright delusions and hallucinations, or a severe neurotic depression). But there is yet another implication in this concept which is of great practical importance.

Compulsiveness is, even in the categories we are concerned with, still relative. Kubie used to say: there is no one who is always and fully psychotic, and no one who is always and entirely free of psychotic or neurotic processes. All compulsive drug users have controls—some more, some less. In this context Zinberg's suggestion, as quoted by Judson (1973), is certainly meaningful: "even heroin, and it's a very powerful drug, can really, under the right circumstances, be brought under the control of certain rituals....People get a lot of control over highs—marijuana, LSD, even some junkies over heroin highs." He sees one of the values of the British clinics precisely in their using "the formalized and very sustaining social rituals of the doctor-patient relationship, the weekly visit and discussion, and the subsidiary informal relationships with the rest of the clinic, as a way to subject the heroin use to viable, accepted controls" (pp. 143–144).

In the dynamic interplay between compelling forces and self controls the balance can be tipped in favor of the latter by a number of procedures—ritualization being one, other forms of gratification and especially boosting of self-esteem presenting a second, insight-oriented psychotherapy a third possibility.

This discussion has to deal, if only briefly, with the criminalization of drug use. Right away it is clear that any wholesale criminalization of compulsive behavior is a mixing of criteria, a blurring of distinctions between scientific values and ethical values.

Criminality is based on a criterion totally divorced from that of psychopathology, namely on that of the transgression of officially set legal limits. They are often arbitrary, which really means irrational. In a more general and deeper philosophical sense the core of this postulated criterion must lie in the violation of the functioning and integrity of one or several other persons, as well as of the functioning and order of society as a whole. In simpler terms criminality is what violates the rights of others and the needs of the state. In an ideal sense this criterion would express a compromise between the maximum of liberty for the individual and the fulfillment of the richest potential of the entire sum of individuals comprised in a political entity. It is at best highly questionable whether compulsive drug use per se violates this latter criterion.

Nearly all criminal actions also fulfill our criteria for psychopathology: they are of a compulsive, driven, insatiable quality, heedless of consequence, unconscious as to their deeper dictating significance. Of course, the fact that one action fulfills two such criteria does not invalidate one of them: the fact that nearly all criminal actions can be judged sick does not wipe away their criminal nature. But it may force the question upon us: what then would be the most rational way of dealing with them? From clinical practice we know very well that punishment has usually neither a profound influence nor much of a deterrent, preventive effect upon such compulsive behavior. At the same time we also know that society, for the sake of its own further orderly existence, cannot tolerate acts which create "victims" (in contrast to the so-called "crimes without victims," e.g., adultery, homosexuality, drug abuse, abortion, the creation of which category by legal fiat is basically irrational). Thus unrestrained freedom for most of those we regard as criminals would rapidly lead to social anarchy without bringing about that inner change in the individual which would entail less psychopathology. Furthermore, and disappointingly, psychotherapy, psychoanalysis, behavior modification, and medication have so far all been only most modestly successful in the treatment of these so-called criminals.

At this point confinement without vindictiveness combined with the individually most useful form of treatment appears to be the most rational approach, taking account of both criteria—the sociolegal and the psychological.

Since most drug abusers are by legal fiat (I think unfairly) criminals, but more importantly, since a large proportion of them are before and beyond their compulsive drug use also compulsive criminals (shoplifters, thieves, robbers, even murderers; see chapter 6), these thoughts are very relevant for the population studied.

It is also important to note that compulsion in a psychopathological sense does not eo ipso entail reduced legal responsibility. We have to separate very clearly the two sets of criteria. As Fingarette (1975, 1976) explains, legal culpability is based on "the community standard of response-ability" and with that on the capability of response to the "background-nexus" of shared values, the "practical capacity to take the relevance of the law in account...to respond relevantly to the issue." Thus its determination requires a "creative application of tacit social values, and not merely of expertise as to facts." He adds (1976): "These are all factual-normative concepts...not concepts within a scientific theory." In my own words: moral-legal value criteria have to be sharply distinguished from scientific ones. A similar way of arguing applies to the following issue.

Much observable psychopathology in the socially deprived and discriminated population (including narcotics addiction) is dismissed and denied because allegedly such a judgment is based on middle class values and prejudices or seen as a form of adaptation to an unbearable external reality and thus as "healthy." If we use our criterion, this is a particularly patent nonsequitur. Are tuberculosis, gunshot wounds, exorbitant obesity, and chronic lead damage any less pathological because they are caused or contributed to by slum conditions? Implicit in this objection is what Kubie described as "the clichés of those hostile to psychiatry, who express that hostility by looking down their noses at all who suffer from neurotic disabilities" (Kubie 1954, p. 173). The fact that many or most people in such a subculture show these traits does not make them any less pathological. "Cavities in the teeth and colds in the head are universal, but they are not therefore normal; nor is health itself abnormal because it is rare" (p. 172). The criterion of cultural acceptance and ubiquitousness is entirely separate and irrelevant to the criterion used to distinguish mental health and pathology. No general statement can be made, but any attitude, character trait, or action showing the signs of pathology described above is sick, regardless of origin and ambiance. What is understandable, justifiable, even unavoidable under certain circumstances is not any less sick. To take an extreme paradigm: the severe, unavoidable, largely irremediable aftereffects withnessed in concentration camp victims are fully understandable, were unavoidable, but are a particularly horrifying, crushing form of psychopathology.

The operational heuristic use of the criterion as suggested here is, as Kubie emphasized, provisional, pragmatic and based on a plausible hypothetical construct. It is a value judgment of a nonmoralistic, noncondemning nature. It is practically the simplest and clearest, theoretically the most fruitful, and the least equivocal of all the clusters of criteria suggested, and thus fulfills Cassirer's postulates for a scientific theory quoted above. It is of course not perfect and may be superseded by better distinctions.

Chapter 5

TOPOGRAPHY AND

HIERARCHY OF ETIOLOGY

Felix qui potuit rerum cognoscere causas.
(Fortunate is he who has been able to recognize
the causes of things.)
—Vergil, *Georgica* 11.490

Scientia et potentia humana in idem coincidunt
quia ignoratio causae destituit effectum.
(Human knowledge and power coincide in
that ignorance of cause prevents effective
intervention.)
—Bacon, *Novum Organum* 1.3

It has been obvious since the beginning of science that only an exact
understanding and knowledge of causes can lead to effective rational
forms of intervention—to bring about desired change.

This and the following two chapters are an enlarged and revised version of "Psychoanalytic Considerations of the Etiology of Compulsive Drug Use," which appeared in the *Journal of the American Psychoanalytic Association,* volume 22, pp. 820–843.

Causality in Psychology

This is not the place to enter the controversy about causality in psychology. I disagree with Roy Schafer's debunking of this among many other theoretical concepts.

Psychological understanding which by definition is based on introspection and empathy (Kohut 1959) indeed operates with meaning and reasons as part of the stream of inner experience, not with causation and forces in a physical sense.

However, this entire differentiation is one of the hoariest, most entangled problems of epistemology. Causation in its modern, sharp meaning was first formulated by Galilei: It is the "comprehensive concept of all conditions and of all external and internal relations whose positing includes a certain effect by necessity" (*causa:* "la qual posta seque sempre l'effetto, e rimossa si rimuove") (Cassirer 1906, Vol. 1, p. 396). Reason (*ratio*), in contrast to cause (*causa, causatio*) was at first, with Descartes and Spinoza, the connection in our mind, contrasted by the connection in Being. According to Cassirer (1907, Vol. 11, pp. 91–92), Spinoza saw them as identical, Descartes as sharply different. One hundred years later the German philosopher Crusius made it an absolute opposition: *reason* (principium cognoscendi, Erkenntnisgrund — a psychological condition for our understanding), versus *cause* (principium essendi vel fiendi, Realgrund, Ursache — a cause in reality determining an effect). Again, seventy years later, Schopenhauer (1813) in his doctoral dissertation, *The Fourfold Root of the Principle of Sufficient Reason,* follows Crusius almost without change (see Cassirer 1907, Vol. 11, p. 550).

In this, I follow the usage in critical philosophy (and, with that, common psychoanalytic parlance). Causality is, according to the Kantian tradition, "a knowledge of orderliness according to law" (see Cassirer 1936, pp. 62, 82, 114–115). Langer writes: "It is not only as 'causation of the psychical,' but as this and more, that I would use the term 'motivation': as 'causation of acts'.... This indirect causation of acts via the prevailing dynamic situation is 'motivation'" (1967, Vol. 1, pp. 281 and 283). All this belongs in an urgently needed epistemology of psychoanalysis which transcends the Procrustean mold of positivistic curtailment of theory.

Henceforth I shall use, quite unabashedly, the broad concept of causes, and the narrower one of reasons, i.e., in the old intellectual tradition of Western philosophy, as the formers' reflection or recreation in our understanding. Even more narrowly, motivation or motive is causation applied to objectively studied or subjectively experienced acts (including of course mental processes of human beings, conscious or unconscious).

We have to differentiate in a study of causes (etiology) the *origin* of influence, the *hierarchy* of specificity, and finally the *strength* of these causes.

In the following, a novel approach to the intricate puzzle of etiology is sought.

In a first, rather provisional step, we seem to be looking at the problem from inside out: from the individual and his inner history to the circles of influence surrounding him. It is a kind of "topographical" approach describing place of influence on the subject, one of course not to be confused with the "topographic model" in psychoanalysis.

In a second, far more relevant step, however, we try to discern logical-historical layers in a hierarchy of specificity. This problem of specificity is most intricate and difficult. The question which I kept asking myself was a double one: (1) What do I find dynamically powerful in *all* cases with the symptom of compulsive drug use, especially if examined "microscopically"—what is *necessary* and indispensable in all of them? (2) Which, however, among these factors distinguishes these patients, by its existence or at least intensity, from the many other patients which share a majority or all other features, yet without my resorting withal to circular reasoning? This then would be a *sufficient* reason.

In contrast to physics this model lacks absoluteness and with that the elegance and convincing beauty of a model in natural science. The specific reason or common final pathway will reveal itself to have more *and* less specific factors, and the underlying precondition, the personality structure, shows the same—relatively more specific factors, besides others which are necessary, but far less specific.

To be now more explicit: A circular model of at least seven separable (though often partly confluent) phenomena will be proposed. These phenomena are all part of the specific constellation historically immediately preceding compulsive drug use. But even on that level we can differentiate particularly specific elements, nearly completely absent in patients without this problem, versus less specific elements, always present in this necessary constellation, but very frequent also in other forms of severe pathology. Their very intensity and strength is part of their relative specificity, but this does not suffice; it is a necessary, not a sufficient cause.

In turn even in the lower levels of the hierarchy, in the predisposition and the overall enveloping cultural matrix, we can distinguish more and less specific elements.

It is a tentative model; future observations and refinements at conceptualization will, I hope, lead to a more secure theory.

CONCENTRIC CIRCLES OF ETIOLOGY: A "TOPOGRAPHY OF CAUSATION"

When we approach this problem we can take at first a global view of the etiological factors in drug abuse and see them arranged in six concentrical circles. This arrangement conforms, as we shall see, already also to causative specificity.

The outermost circle are general problems of human existence—philosophical problems of accepting the limitations of human power, understanding and mortality and the general unwillingness of man to live within the confines set by nature, his unwillingness both about having to pay a price for any expansion of power, knowledge and life, and about the inability to fulfill his demands here and now into the infinite. Drugs lend support to these angry demands of irrationality.

The next inner circle is that of more specific *cultural* contributions. Here I only point again to vast cultural conflicts between rationality and enlightenment on the one side, irrationality, mysticism, romanticism on the other. As noted earlier, our time is by no means unusual in being beset by this archetypical conflict. It has accompanied much of human history. What is specific to our culture is the enormous expansion of technical power and material success which has not been matched by a corresponding growth of inner control and rationality. We can put this cultural conflict in terms of value conflicts: where should we set the priorities—in material gratification, affluence, technical power, or in inner integration, harmony and honesty? There is no question that most cultures have put their eggs in the first basket, though none as successfully as our Western culture. Some forms of drug abuse (e.g., compulsive use of psychedelics and of minor tranquilizers) are a misguided and fallacious attempt to escape from this priority—a magical, infantile way of establishing power over one's inner life and to shut out the din and haste of the race to power, possession and prestige.

The next and third circle is our society. We might contemplate the role that rebellion against powerful authority plays in young people, how they can use the forbidden fruit as a weapon to punish and flaunt parents and elders, at a time when sex has lost its function as such a symbol of assertion and defiance to drug use. We will also have to consider the role of the successful pusher as an ideal of economic success in the ghetto and at the enormous importance of the entire black market in "hot stuff" fueled by the need for illegal drugs for the slum economy (for these three circles, see chapter 14).

The fourth, already much narrower, more personalized circle is that of the peer group. Especially where the family is fluid, shattered and weak, the peer group assumes an important "educational" role. Drug use and drug traffic are symbols of belonging, of solidarity, of initiation. Where teachers and parents are deposed as inspiring authorities, the peer group prematurely takes over.

The fifth circle is the family and the sixth, last and central circle the individual and his intrapsychic conflicts. About them we have to speak in the following. Now I can only emphasize that whatever factors from the outer four circles contribute to drug abuse, they have to be mediated through family and intrapsychic constellation. There lies the core of the disposition. This still leaves the problem of etiology vague and unsatisfactory. From the material already accumulated in the preceding pages we get the distinct impression that we can do better than that. But how?

Indeed, there has been very little work exploring the etiology of "drug abuse" in a way which would be both systematic and appropriate to the problem. The situation is well-described in Glasscote et al. (1972, p. 19): "It may be fruitless to make the effort to identify a group of universal causes of susceptibility. In any case, while there has been some interest in determining what drug users are like, by means of interviews and standardized tests, there has been little systematic effort to delineate and quantify causes. On the other hand, there has been much hypothesizing about the conditions, events, and circumstances that lead to drug abuse, most of which fall into three categories: the physical, the internal or intrapsychic, and the social and environmental."

A study, at least to fulfill a first part of the postulate contained in this quotation, is envisioned here: namely, to delineate in a systematic way the etiology only of compulsive drug use, on the basis of large-scale clinical experience.

The Hierarchical Structure of Etiology

A PHENOMENOLOGICAL DISTINCTION

Even if we select an apparently homogeneous group, such as clearly compulsive narcotics addicts, we still are bewildered by the variety of causes and correspondingly the vast array of proferred, discussed and disputed cause-and-effect relationships. The logic of scientific discovery destroys all simple assertions, and we have to assent to the skeptical conclusions reached in the (quoted) book by Glasscote et al., (1972).

The problem, in any case, is that none of these characteristics or conditions, other than the metabolic alteration theory, predicts for us who will become a drug abuser. The young heroin user from the suburbs did not take up his habit because rats ran across his bedroom floor. Within the slums, where rats are plentiful, there are many more people who do *not* take up drugs than who do. And while some may take up drug use from boredom or rebellion, clearly there are many who are bored or rebellious but do not take up drugs. Most essentially, there are countless immature people who do not resort to illegal drugs. And so on. Among commonly cited causes of drug abuse, *none* predicts the inevitable use of drugs.

What we try to discern now is a logical layering of causes ordered according to causative specificity. By and large such a hierarchy, thus based on a logical criterion, also reflects a pyramid of historical layers, as we shall see, a hierarchy based on a temporal criterion. The two types of ordering will be for our practical purposes close enough to each other that they can be used nearly interchangeably, but their theoretical factual distinction has to be kept in mind; a more thorough method may allow a clearer factual distinction, too.

As methodological starting point we may use the differentiation between two factors which are supposedly always present: the psychological hunger or "craving," which might be described as the "addictive search," in form of the entire group of activities, predating, accompanying and following the compulsive drug use, which historically in the life of the individual were all employed to provide external relief for an internal urge of overpowering driveness— activities like irresistible violence, food addiction, gambling, alcohol use, indiscriminate, "driven" sexual activity, running away, etc. This is the final common pathway which precedes (historically and psychologically) the more or less contingent, even accidental entrance of various drugs, accidental both anent their accessibility and seduction. This second factor we can call the "adventitious entrance of drugs."

HIERARCHY OF CAUSES

This is a surface distinction. Behind this facade we can perceive a logical and historical structure of causes which we now analyze as a hierarchy of causes of various specificity.

Again what in this analysis is torn apart as various groups and layers appears in reality to be a continuum of causes, ranging from high to low specificity. As soon as we deal with any psychopathology, we find an early concept of Freud (1895) still very useful. He distinguished four types of causes for an emotional disorder: (a) precondition; (b) specific cause; (c) concurrent cause; and (d) precipitating cause.

As far as I could find out this distinction was an original contribution of Freud to the philosophy of causation. With this he tried to apply the basic concepts of accidental, necessary and sufficient causes which had originated in Aristotle, and had been developed by d'Alembert, Leibniz, and Schopenhauer, to the problems of motivation, in particular to the causation of emotional illness. He used a precursor of this four part model in Draft B (1893) and later on replaced it by the concept of the complementary series (see M. Sherwood 1969). I was not able to consider all the philosophical roots, merits or weaknesses of this model as a basic logical concept, but I feel it may serve us heuristically better than other models of causation. Each of the following layers will be explored more in detail later on.

A cardinal, indispensable, but broad layer of causation is the precondition. "The factors which may be described as *preconditions* are those in whose absence the effect would never come about, but which are incapable of producing the effect by themselves alone, no matter in what amount they may be present" (Freud 1895, p. 136). Applied to our problem, these inevitable preconditions can be located, e.g., in a life history of massive narcissistic disturbances and in a rather specific pattern of family pathology (see below).

"The *specific cause* is the one which is never missing in any case in which the effect takes place, and which moreover suffices, if present in the required quantity or intensity, to achieve the effect, provided only that the preconditions are also fulfilled" (Freud 1895, p. 136). In contradiction to this definition in its absoluteness (the "never" and "suffices") a more relativistic conception is envisaged, as was explained in the first chapter of this section. Despite this reduction in stringency to a probabilistic one, the definition is still of great value to us.

Most people would now be inclined to seek the specific cause of compulsive drug use in the temptations by peers or pushers. I believe this would be misleading; it is, though semantically correct, clinically and theoretically wrong. Instead, we differentiated before between "addictive illness" and "adventitious" appearance of the drug and now can repeat that we find an emotional illness brewing independently whether the drug enters or not. The specificity for its outbreak in manifest form lies in an experience of overwhelming crisis, accompanied by most intense emotions, like disillusionment and rage, depression or anxiety, by specific defenses and by other coping mechanisms. This crisis is an actuation of a lifelong massive conflict about omnipotence and grandiosity, meaning and trust—what will be described later on in more detail as a narcissistic conflict. This actuation nearly inevitably leads to emotional disruption and thus to the addictive search. In other words, if we focus on the illness "addictive syndrome," the specific cause is a more or less acute external and internal crisis bringing about an exacerbation of a narcissistic disturbance. We may call this a *narcissistic crisis*. In contrast, if we focus on the symptom "drug abuse," we are wiser to talk about precipitating, not specific causes, the category I will mention shortly. Even without the advent of the drug itself, we still have the characteristic seeking for a way out, for an escape, a driven desperate attempt to find a crutch outside of oneself.

Much vaguer and several steps removed are the "causes" which litter the literature and which we can all put in the next category. Their nature is very unspecific, broad, of little predictive value. They are shared by many who do not join in the illness, and vice versa. Yet they indeed are the only ones which can be found with epidemiological and sociological measures based on statistical studies.

"As *concurrent causes* we may regard such factors as are not necessarily present every time, nor able, whatever their amount, to produce the effect by themselves alone, but which operate alongside of the preconditions and the specific cause in satisfying the etiological equation." (Freud 1895, p.136).

The most general ones are widespread value conflicts in our culture, basic philosophical questions about the limitations of human existence, pervasive social conflicts like hypocrisy, overvaluation of, and disappointment about, technology and power, the influence of television, the changed role of sex and social degradation. To them we will turn in chapter 14.

Finally, we have to return to what I described phenomenologically as the "entrance of the drug" and labeled "adventitious":

"We may characterize as the *precipitating* or releasing cause the one which makes its appearance last in the equation so that it immediately precedes the emergence of the effect. It is this chronological factor alone which constitutes the essential nature of a precipitating cause" (Freud 1895, p. 135).

We would assign the previously mentioned easy availability of drugs and the seduction by peers to this category. The *advent* of the drug suddenly allows the previous desperate search to crystalize around the one object and activity which relieves the unbearable tension.

In sum: there is no compulsive drug use without this triggering factor; but there is still an overriding emotional compulsiveness directed toward other activities and objects without the specific substance. It can be assumed that only the latter two sets of factors (concurrent and precipitating ones) are identical for experimenters and compulsive users alike.

Chapter 6

SPECIFIC CAUSES OF

THE ADDICTIVE SYNDROME

To sink your shaft deep, and polish the plate
through which people look into it—that's what
your work consists of.
                    —Henry James, "The Author of Beltraffio"

When we start out with the observation that, even before the beginning of compulsive drug use itself, there are clear signs of a serious emotional disorder, one which was called in the previous section "the addictive illness" or the signs for an addictive career, we are confronted with the very difficult question how to analyze the complex of phenomena leading almost ineluctably to the overt outbreak of the illness, especially in form of compulsive drug use, but not always restricted to this symptom; a few equivalents to drug dependency which precede or replace this symptom have been mentioned here repeatedly. To facilitate our task, however, we have to focus now entirely on compulsive drug use.

The following issues emerge clearly—as problems or already as evident answers: (a) We have to distinguish the view on a quasi-horizontal plain ("what goes on in the here and now when I start taking drugs for inner needs") from the history, the depth dimension, the vertical perspective—the predisposition. (b) Even on this horizontal level, however, we clearly can discern that there are covert events which gradually emerge during detailed probing beneath the overt phenomena; these covert processes are partly preconscious and relatively easily retrievable, partly unconscious and, due to the particular difficulties of psychotherapy or psychoanalysis with these patients, almost inaccessible. (c) The conscious and preconscious processes can, without undue problems, be arranged in a fairly regular sequence, a vicious circle, which will be presently outlined. This vicious circle has, as all psychopathology to some extent, a particularly strong self-perpetuating quality, a feeding on itself. (d) When we explore the underlying dynamics of the single elements of such a cycle, we discover that all of them are themselves already compromise formations, partial conflict solutions. The entire vicious circle thus presents itself as a complex series of compromise solutions. (e) Proceeding from this we are plunged into difficulties of how to transcend the phenomena and to define clearly the underlying constituent components: What exactly are the unconscious impulses, wishes, drive components? What are the defenses? How do the defenses themselves reflect instinctual processes? And, what are structural defects—neither defense nor instinctual drive? (f) In answering some of these questions we get onto very slippery terrain and are in danger of drowning in too broad, pseudoexplanatory concepts. We come face to face with something which Roy Shafer (1968a) rightly complained about: "many of the familiar descriptive and explanatory terms of psychoanalysis are global terms, and, if used without further specification and qualification, they limit or distort perception and conceptualization of the phenomena." The notions of narcissism, denial, splitting, and aggression proved to become what was called by Szasz "panchrestas" (1957), catchall terms, too broad, playing into the need for complacence and a sense of knowledge, but becomming imprecise, even contradictory clichés. At the same time they could not be discarded by any means. They are, as the term *panchreston* connotes, overly useful, but they need further specifications, redefinitions, and, occasionally, new contents. At times the attempts to do that have to be carried out with profound uncertainty, first trials at putting into words, at differentiating, what seems well covered with the broad notions.

But to start out we have to examine this more overt, less arcane vicious circle which is accessible to any careful ("microscopic") inspection. As an illustration to develop this model, I use the near verbatim account of a patient (Andreas, case 19) of how he experienced his going to the Bowery at age nineteen and getting drunk; the same sequence occurred in many different contexts (drugs, homosexuality, fantasies within the sessions; see also case 4).

1. It starts out with "any big event whether I succeed or I fail; it has the same aftermath: sadness, letdown, loneliness." In all patients it is some form of disappointment—realistic or in fantasy, a letdown from an expectation which may be justified or, as it is mostly, vastly exaggerated, an expectation usually of one's own grandeur, far less importantly the disappointment about someone else. This sudden plummeting of self-esteem is best called a narcissistic crisis.

2. The next step is that the feelings become overwhelming, global, archaic, physically felt, can not be articulated in words. "I feel a foreign power in me which I cannot name; all barriers are gone." The patients describe an uncontrollable, intense sense of rage or shame or despair, etc. This is clearly an affect regression and, as that, a generalization and totalization of these very archaic, often preverbal affects (see Krystal and Raskin 1970). It is a breakdown of affect defense.

3. What happens then is least clear. The affect disappears; only a vague, but unbearable tension remains; there may be a longing, a frantic search for excitement and relief, a sense of aimless, intolerable restlessness, and craving (not unlike the one later seen in acute withdrawal). Instead of the prior feeling we hear (again Andreas): "I thought about myself as something else, as an object, as a character in a book, that I was creating the story about myself, a novel. I am not even actually aware of the pain anymore; it is not you, it is a character in a book you are creating. My whole life is so: a part who acts and a part who observes." The intellectual, observing part is not really alive, the acting one lives. Like Alexander the Great comparing Achilles with Homer, our patient states: "It is better to *be* the character than to *write* about him in a novel"—better to act than to observe. This points ahead, but what is important for us to notice is the split as observed in depersonalization. This splitting recurs in many forms in our patients. In the passage just quoted it is between observing (and controlling) versus acting of a particular kind which we study shortly. More typically it is between the most troublesome feelings suppressed, disregarded, the inner problems in general, and a facade, an illusion of

being all right. I believe the split necessitates above all a massive denial of inner reality, specifically of the overwhelming affects. Other defenses—negation, avoidance, repression and projection—seem to operate as well, but they pale besides the role of denial, taken in the exacting, not loose definition (as so frequently employed): "Disavowal or denial as originally described by Freud involves, not an absence or distortion of actual perception, but rather a failure to fully appreciate the significance or implications of what is perceived"—especially of affects (Trunnell and Holt 1974). Much more needs to be said later on about this issue. What is important for us is the phenomenological evidence for many forms of massive splits, accompanied by unconscious denial, by an "invalidating fantasy," and by partial acknowledgment. How splitting is related to isolation and dissociation is yet another problem to be taken up later on.

4. There follows a wild drivenness for action, for seeking an external concrete solution to the internal (and denied) conflict. "It was unbearable; I had to do something on the outside to change the situation—no matter what." Violence, being caught, drugs—the modus of this defense by externalization is not terribly relevant at the moment for the patient: the defense by concrete action on the outside which magically changes life is what counts.

5. "It was something fascinating when I went to the Bowery. The position was appealing: to destroy myself, to be a bum. It was sheer self-destructiveness." In other moments it was murderous anger. Again, as Anna Freud and many others observed: aggression, especially directed against the self, becomes an inevitable link in the chain. Andreas also notes: "I progress, and then suddenly I have the urge to break out, to destroy everything I have built up, and then I am completely down for a month and slowly build it (self-esteem, social accomplishment) up again." This fifth step is the involvement of aggression, usually by "breaking out," transgressing boundaries, violating social limits, attacking others, destroying oneself, hurting and being hurt, humiliating others and being shamed.

6. "When despair takes over, the question of honesty becomes ridiculous." The drowning man has commonly little regard for questions of integrity. Conscience becomes utterly irrelevant. Trustworthiness, reliability, commitments to others are acknowledged, and yet made meaningless, treated as if of absolutely no importance whatsoever. Again I believe there is a profound splitting of

the superego, usually accompanied above all by denial, but also by projection and externalization. No compulsive drug use (perhaps except for the one commonly not recognized as such, like compulsive smoking) goes without this superego split.

7. "When I have broken out, there is so much enjoyment and excitement, that everything appears okay. I am satisfied then: I feel sheltered. I am acknowledged: the world owes me a living. I get something for nothing, and I deserve it." It is pleasure of many forms—entitlement above all—which forms the end point of the cycle.

Let us summarize what we have found so far: It is a series of conflicts, actuated in an acute crisis, which forms the specific cause. This specific cause is the following circular constellation: It starts out (1) with the narcissistic crisis, leading (2) to overwhelming affects, to an affect regression, a totalization and radicalization of these feelings (due to underlying defects in the affect defense to be studied in the predisposition). (3) Simultaneously the closely related phenomena of splitting ("ego splits") and fragmentation and defense processes in form mainly of denial, but also of repression and other "mechanisms," ensue. These are carried out partly by psychological means alone, partly and secondarily by pharmacological propping up (pharmacogenic defense). (4) The latter requires an additional form of defense, the element most specific for this syndrome amongst this constellation of seven, i.e., the defense by externalization, by reasserting magical (narcissistic) power by external action—including magical "things." (5) This reassertion of power by externalization requires the use of archaic forms of aggression, of outwardly attacking and self-destructive forms of sadomasochism. (6) In most cases this is only possible by a sudden splitting of the superego and of defensive operations against superego functions. (7) The final point is the enormous pleasure and gratification which this complex of compromise solutions of various instinctual drives with various defenses brings about. Most importantly the acute narcissistic conflict appears resolved—for the moment, but, as Radó (1933) described, the patient is caught in a vicious circle: "The elation had augmented the ego" (now we would say the self) "to gigantic dimensions and had almost eliminated reality; now just the reverse state appears, sharpened by the contrast. The ego is shrunken, and reality appears exaggerated in its dimensions" (pp. 8-9). The patient is not merely back where he started, but on a yet much lower level of self-esteem.

The Heptad of Specificity in Compulsive Drug Use

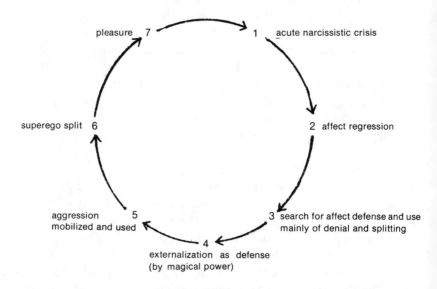

I was compelled to see these seven factors as of overriding etiologic significance and pursue them from specific causation through preconditions back to the culture. After the far more detailed exploration of this heptad, the major groups of compulsive drug use will be described, illustrated by a series of cases in almost every category. They will be distinguished mainly by the second factor—the overriding affect defended against. Before we venture into this study it is most important to consider the probability that each of these seven members of the heptad is already in itself a compromise formation, a derivative of impulse, defense and defect (or deficiency).

We will have to keep this in mind and try to analyze this unconscious substratum as well. As stated: that part will be most difficult and uncertain in its outcome. We also will have far less direct material from patients as evidence to support us in this.

Here still another objection will be raised: What is so specific about this League of Seven to make them the culprits in the problem posed? Do we not all undergo narcissistic crises, and are severe narcissistic disorders not even the daily bread of all psychiatrists and many psychoanalysts? Or, turning to the next: Aren't the internal and external structures safeguarding against these affects often very brittle in other people, just like the ground around a geyser—apparently firm but breaking in at smallest weights and letting the boiling water flood over? Isn't affect regression a very common occurrence? And thus we could march down the list together and eliminate all specificity. It appears to me, and I cannot be more than hypothetical about it, that the combination of defective affect defense (of inner structures channeling affects, eventually part of the predisposing personality structure), with the two most specific and most important factors: (a) deep-going and labile, rapidly shifting splits, largely resulting from the all-pervasive use of the defense mechanism of denial, especially against affects, and (b) the massive defensive use of externalization in its characteristic concreteness of action—that this combination in its severity and massivity marks these patients and sets them apart from all others. This bold claim is based on a careful comparison in my mind of a number of neurotic patients often showing amazingly similar problems, whom I see in analysis, but who have never developed any drug problems, with all the toxicomanic patients I have known. Whether this specification will hold up, however, only further comparative scrutiny will show.

But here I have rushed ahead of myself. First we have to explore the heptad in detail and mostly in theoretical terms.

The Narcissistic Crisis

THEORETICAL CONSIDERATIONS

This is obviously the starting point where the deeper conflicts about self-esteem and power get mobilized. Such a mobilization quite typically occurs at first during adolescence, rarely earlier, not too often later. Often the relapse from abstinence into drug use again is clearly marked by the recurrence of such a crisis. Most generally this crisis is the point in time where the conflicts and defects converge with a particular external situation and with the availability of the seeming means of solution: the drug.

By definition, a narcissistic crisis would have to entail a particularly intense disappointment in others, in oneself, or in both, so intense because of the exaggerated hopes and so malignant because its history reaches back to very early times.

Precipitating external events can typically be found in family crises coinciding with the maturational crisis of adolescence, or in being abandoned, betrayed, humiliated, disappointed in a love relationship, in school, at work, by friends.

In this narcissistic crisis the addictive search starts. It is the beginning of the common final pathway, of the cluster of specific reasons, which gets the entire wheel spinning, the circle designated as "heptad."

What is crucial is the centrality of the narcissistic frustration, the injured self-esteem, the sense of disappointment and disillusionment, as a starting point.

But with this we are right in the middle of a whirlpool of controversy; a clearer definition of this vague term *narcissism* becomes imperative. I do not know whether we can read any deeper meaning into the likely original linguistic connection between *narcotics* and *narcissism*. The stem for both is said to be the Greek verb "narkân," meaning "to become paralyzed or rigid, numbed." The flower "Nárkissos" is supposedly derived from it because of its intoxicating, numbing smell, although the ending -issos is typically pre-Greek. (Of course, the name of Narcissus and with that the myth underlying this central theoretical concept is correlated to, and presumably derived from, the flower.) Thus the concept of "pleasurable, numbing intoxication" would underlie historically both ideas: use and abuse of narcotics, and the myth and theoretical concept of Nárcissos. Or is it just an historical fluke and a matter of levity?

In shortest form, the term *narcissistic* is generally used as denoting a pathologic phenomenon: an archaic overvaluation of the self or of others, a host of grandiose expectations, and an abysmal sense of frustration and letdown if these hopes are shattered. Beyond this it denotes a number of normal developmental phases, experiences and abstractions. However, it is not employed as a pejorative term (although such vulgarization is now frequently encountered), connoting self-centeredness, egotism, having "a big ego," etc.

Freud's views appear deceptively clear and simple (see Bing, McLaughlin and Marburg 1959: narcissism = "libidinal investment of the self-representation"). This accords with Freud's well-known definition (1930, p. 118). What complicates matters, however, is that objects, other persons, are also chosen on a narcissistic basis:"in their later choice of love-objects they have taken as a model not their mother but their own selves. They are plainly seeking *themselves* as a love-object, and are exhibiting a type of object-choice which must be termed 'narcissistic' " (Freud 1914, p. 88). He calls overvaluation of the object (and of course of the self as well) the "narcissistic" stigma (1914, p. 91). This is not the place to give a thorough account of the by now bewilderingly broad and vague usage of the term (for this, see Pulver 1970, Jaffe and Sandler 1967, Moore and Fine 1967).

Specifically, Vann Spruiell (1975) subdivides what Freud encompassed under the one "umbrella" formulation (the one quoted initially above): (a) a phase, (b) a perversion, (c) a major part of the regulation of feelings of well-being, including self-esteem, (d) an aspect of self-love, (e) a type of object-choice, (f) omnipotence, and (g) secondary structures, especially the ego ideal. I shall come back to Spruiell's reformulations shortly.

Eisnitz (1974) suggests we distinguish between narcissistic conflict, narcissistic defenses, and narcissistic pathology (pp. 280, 283–285).

The focus on cathexis and boundedness of the self-representations allows the signally important contributions of Kohut and Kernberg to the notion "Narcissism" to remain integrated with the rest of the analytic theory. Kohut describes "narcissistic personality disturbances" as "suffering from specific disturbances in the realm of the self and of those archaic objects cathected with narcissistic libido (self-objects) which are still in intimate connection with the archaic self (i.e., objects which are not experienced as separate and independent from the self)" (1970, p.3). He stresses as the most important point about narcissism "its independent line of development, from the primitive to the most mature, adaptive and culturally valuable ... the side-by-side existence of separate developmental lines in the narcissistic and in the object instinctual realms in the child" (1972, pp. 362–363). The two cardinal narcissistic structures are "the grandiose self" and the "idealized parent imago," the first reactivated in therapy as "mirror transference," the latter as "idealizing transference" (1970, p. 97).

In narcissistic personality disturbances these archaic configurations retain cohesion, whereas in borderline and psychotic patients they become fragmented (1970, p. 97). The only two theoretical differences between Kohut and Kernberg, as far as can be made out, lie in the latter's view of the archaic structures just mentioned as pathological, and in his opinion, identical with Freud's original concept, that there are not separate developmental lines (Kernberg 1974, pp. 257–261).

Vann Spruiell (1974, 1975) singles out for special study three separate "strands," perhaps independent developmental lines (A. Freud 1963)—self-love, the regulation of self-esteem, and omnipotence—and traces these three "coherent themes of ego motivations" through the entire course of early development. For our purposes the last of the three turns out to be of cardinal significance: "The intention here is to separate omnipotence from the other forms of narcissism, following Pumpian-Mindlin (1969). Furthermore, the intention is to connect omnipotence to the broader issues of action psychology, and beyond action psychology to the even broader and more abstract issues of aggressive drive derivatives. If it seems reasonable to assume that self-love is predominantly a derivative of libido, it seems reasonable to regard issues of action and power as predominantly derivative of aggression—especially if aggression is thought of as consisting of more than simply destruction" (1975, p. 582). Thus he views narcissism partly as a vicissitude of aggression, not solely of libido.

The concept of omnipotence also entails that of the limits to power (p. 586) and thus opens up an entirely new theoretical area: the conceptualization of boundaries and limits in terms of the theory of narcissism and aggression; this will occupy us in a later section very centrally. But to return to Vann Spruiell's thoughts: Patients who have never been able to deal with "the progressive wilting of infantile omnipotence...retain it as a quasi-delusionary way of life. Such patients are preoccupied with power, exploitation, manipulation, deceit, and fear of overt dependence. They have little or no real concern for their objects. Behind their exterior masks of grandiosity, which they sometimes get the world to accept, they exist as lonely, hungry, and angry 'infants' whose defenses are exceedingly primitive." (p. 588).

It is this strand of narcissism which is centrally evident in all types of compulsive drug use.

All these are very difficult theoretical questions which cannot be resolved by the methods used in the study underlying this book. Nevertheless, it was impossible for me to avoid the concept of narcissism; on the contrary, it is a pillar of the entire book. I restrict its usage to the following meanings:

1. *Narcissism* refers to the investment of the self with psychological interest. I leave it undecided whether this is restricted to libidinous or extends also to aggressive investment, although I become more and more inclined to the broader version. Narcissism thus means anything pertaining to self-esteem, to the valuation of the self, high or low. It may be healthy or pathological (conforming to the criterion expounded in chapter 5).

2. Consequently, narcissistic conflicts mean conflicts about self-esteem and self-worth, about power and self-love. However, archaic narcissistic conflicts (the leading notion used in these considerations) refers to the two "structures" described by both Kohut and Kernberg, the grandiose self and the idealized other, since they originate in a time when there is no sharp demarcation between self and other. They mean the wishes for massive overvaluation of the self and the pertinent other, the inevitable disillusionment, the consequent overwhelming affects (rage, shame, envy, loneliness), and the usually primitive defenses against these affects. Thereby they always also involve conflicts about limits, limitations and boundaries.

3. I also concur with Kohut in his description of the complementary series of fragmentation and cohesion of the self and the crucial role both play in depth and severity of these narcissistic conflicts; the more regressive the latter are, the more fragmentation prevails over cohesiveness and boundedness of the self. I believe, too, that Kohut's concept of fragmentation refers clinically to the same as what Kernberg called "dissociative or splitting mechanisms."

Most of the patients presented cluster clearly toward the more regressive end of this continuum.

4. I leave it as yet undecided whether these two narcissistic "structures" are parts of a basically independent developmental line or an inseparable segment of the development of libido (let alone aggression!) with developmental interchangeability of object-directed and self-directed libido. This whole question is bound up with the problem of the, now so controversial, concept of psychic energy. In my opinion the latter is still a highly useful metaphor, but how far its applicability reaches is murky. Still a decision about its range of validity would have direct clinical consequences. Should we aim, as therapists and in our own lives, ideally at a "transmutation" of archaic narcissism into object concerns (Freud, Kernberg) or, on the contrary,

into "higher forms" of "normal narcissism" and more solid "inner structures" (Kohut)? If we cannot devise, at least, a clinical thought experiment (a prediction in regard to conceivable clinical observations) which would answer this question and the search for a possible verification or refutation in clinical experience, the question may remain unanswerable and hence specious: an overstretching, a too literal and concrete use of the metaphor. As I wrote in my metaphor paper (1977): Metaphors are essential for theory formation, but the limits to their applicability must be recognized. They are forms of abstractions, not concrete, observable entities or processes. I suspect, however, that in this issue, the answer, as so often, may eventually be found not in the either-or, but in the concepts of the complementary series and the continuous spectrum (Rangell 1972)—that there exist neither full independence nor full interchangeability, except as pathological extremes, that a partially separate line of development of narcissism is necessary for healthy functioning, and that in turn a partial developmental back-and-forth of self-interests and object-interests, of investment in self-images and of investment in the representations of others, is required in both development and therapy.

5. Even if we thus go part way with Kohut, by granting at least a partially separate line of development of narcissistic investments, and thus also admit the normality of the early development of these two narcissistic structures (against Kernberg), this still would not preclude their likely use also as defenses against the yet deeper conflicts of oral libidinous demands and aggressions, as Kernberg proposes. The feelings described above as outcome of narcissistic conflicts (shame, rage, envy, etc.) which they clearly are, may though be very typically multilayered, as Jones (1929) described in regard to fear, guilt, and hate: "If hate causes guilt, then only more hate, or rather hate otherwise exhibited, can remove the guilt" (p. 307). He talks about "a curious series of layer formations," and "a complex series of interactions" (p. 304). Clinically, both in psychoanalysis of less severely disturbed narcissistic personality disorders and in the psychotherapy of the patients presented here, both connections were found: loneliness and emptiness as outcome of the narcissistic conflicts; and the reverse—narcissistic conflicts of utmost pervasiveness as defense against yet more archaic states of fragmentation, annihilation, helplessness, and total frustration (what Jones described

as *aphánisis*), of most archaic envy, rage, shame, self-destruction ("guilt"?), of preverbal anxiety and loneliness. Again, the circle may be the better model than the line. Still, the question remains where this vicious circle started. In my opinion the answer transcends the theories of both Kernberg and Kohut. The origin, as far as I see in these patients at least, lies in the overwhelming sense of helplessness and powerlessness caused by real traumatization leading to global types of aggressive and narcissistic demands. The traumatization is severe, early, and mostly based in actuality (see Krystal 1975). Instead of the overused and diluted notion of trauma I follow Krystal's succinct and strict definition: "Trauma refers to an overwhelming, paralyzing psychic state which implies a loss of ego functions, regression, and obligatory psychopathology" (personal communication, 1976). Such trauma is caused by situations which put child or adult into positions of total helplessness.

Yet again, with these theoretical concepts we reach the limit of what we know now and perhaps of what is knowable by the means we have now. We can only state that we observe crucially important archaic narcissistic conflicts which on the one side lead to overwhelming affects and to aggressive and libidinous conflicts involving objects and, on the other side, serve to protect against yet more archaic states of overwhelming feeling and perhaps conflicts.

By and large, I shall restrict all following considerations to the fairly firm ground described under the first three points. I shall hardly employ the fourth and fifth points, but hope the material presented may lead others to attain more clarity about what I leave undecided. However, a very important additional consideration will be added in chapter 7, the problem of boundaries.

In conclusion, I agree that many of our concepts, especially narcissism and masochism, need to become subdivided into sharper and more specific categories, and that, wherever possible, we need to be more explicit, e.g., what type and form of narcissistic wish, gratification or frustration we actually refer to.

CLINICAL ANALYSIS

To return to the phenomenon at discussion, the narcissistic crisis, the one question which is of rather more interest to the psychoanalyst than the theoretical debates remains unanswered: Is this phenomenon already in and by itself a compromise formation of forces of more basic import?

This topic really deserves an extra study. In a broad encompassing sense the entire heptad could be considered and termed a *narcissistic crisis,* but it appears preferable to narrow the concept to the beginning point: the sudden breakdown of expectations about self-esteem, self-respect, power and control in the face usually of an outer and inner limitation. It is implied that this crisis—in our cases—needs to be massive. But narcissistic crises are commonplace. Each one of us has—in conscious memory—gone through mild or severe crises of this nature.

As so often it might be helpful to look at it "microscopically" once again. Many an effective interpretation or clarification triggers an acute narcissistic mini-crisis and can give us clues as to answering the question. A patient who lost his job and is looking in vain for a "stable, interesting, challenging, remunerative" replacement feels he cannot talk about some of his other problems: "Everything else just appears rarified and sanitized." For example, in regard to women "I feel like a powerless, castrated, unemployed bum; how can I effectively deal with my feelings about them as long as the job question is not resolved?" I: "So what you say is that you go through a kind of internal, external and analytic moratorium." He: "Exactly, but I wish you had not made it so clear and put it in these words. I ask you directly—what else?" I: "The magical expectation that I could end the moratorium." And then he started asking himself seriously about inner obstacles—for example a possibly inflated view of a job.

The sequence in this mini-crisis starts off with the gnawing loss in self-esteem. What is not related to it appears isolated, intellectualized, decathected. My more explicit words (not about the defense just employed, but in a very cautious way about his sense of narcissistic woundedness—"I want to wait") are wished away, consciously suppressed, as if he had said, "The truth hurts, I do not want to hear it," immediately followed by the fantasy that I could —magically—find a way out for him.

Another example: In the working through of an archaic, mostly shame-laden, often reexternalized superego, a patient opens the hour: "I realized at the end of yesterday's session that I had forgotten all about what I have known about the 'inner judge.' I could not remember it." I: "That it was warded off, defended against." On closer scrutiny the patient stated: "I am concerned how I look at myself without the inner judge—I'm afraid; I cannot imagine myself as still being me without it, of feeling still myself. If I try to think about its absence it is as if it had never existed; the memory is wiped out." Only gradually the real need for this forgetting emerged: "This inner judge protects me from the harsh reality of how I am. As long as I have this self-condemnation I really do not have to look at my faults objectively, but I can feel sorry for myself. I use it as a crutch and do not see which limitations I really have and do not deal with them: that I see myself as clinging, stupid, odd, deformed, and weak."

Here we have a double narcissistic injury within the analytic situation: the particular, very aggressive superego is narcissistically vested as an indispensable part of the identity: "I fear the loss of my identity"—it is a very important carrier of standards of perfection and idealization; but it also serves as a very real protection against a profound sense of shame, which otherwise would have to be dealt with on an ego level, in a rational weighing of what is the real self, as against a profoundly split, both idealized and deprecated, self-image. How does the patient respond to this two-layered problem within the hour? First by realizing the prior transient repression (or denial?), then by magical undoing in a comparison: "Just as it feels the world would cease to exist if I were dead," afterward by projecting it into the past (her always condemning father) and into current outside reality (a spouse fancied as dictatorial), finally by concretization: " 'He' protects me against what I feel most vulnerable about." As the end point, the "inner judge" is recognized itself as a defense against overwhelming feelings of inferiority, a defense which the patient cannot lightly part with.

From such well-studied small examples we can see what the more severe narcissistic crises entail. There is usually a sudden clash between a set of fantasies about oneself and radical inner and external limitations. As one patient said: "I felt substantial, now I feel empty." It is as if suddenly a gaping fissure opened up between two large areas of self-representations, e.g., between a grandiose, powerful, admired self-image, and that of an abysmal failure; this is followed by a quick succession of attempts to reconcile the contradiction, to build bridges, one after the other. These bridges, as we saw in the two little vignettes, consist of an almost limitless variety of ad hoc defenses, most prominently: conscious efforts of suppression, avoidance and "denial" (in the vernacular sense —see Trunnell and Holt 1974): "I do not want to think about it; I do not want to have it in words; I do not want to see it; I cannot bear to face up to it, I want to save my fantasy." Or it is negation: "It is not true; I cannot and won't accept and believe it." Thence ensues a rapid spiraling down; the gap grows broader and broader, the defenses become more and more archaic, the fantasies more and more imperative, expansive, the fears and anxieties stronger and deeper. Projection, idealization, more primitive and truly unconscious forms of denial are the preferred defenses. Another quite archaic form is a conscious mobilization of aggression, a "counterattack" to undo what is perceived as disgrace.

Very often the immediate reaction to the crisis is derealization (or depersonalization)—a stunned numbness, "everything seems untrue, unreal, dead, meaningless," obviously comprising a most radical form of denial and splitting.

Finally this stage merges into the next one, the affect regression. But to come back now to the original question: Is the narcissistic crisis a compromise formation? The answer is: It contains a huge variety of possible compromise solutions between a hypercathexis of inflated fantasies about the self ("a hypercathexis by the ego of the preloss self and self-object representations"—Altschul 1968) and the countercathectic activity ("a counter force to the reality recognition of loss") in the form of many conscious and unconscious defense efforts verging into most massive denial. This is the outcome in severely pathological persons. In less disturbed ones (obviously not to be found among compulsive drug users) this compromise solution is rapidly or gradually replaced by a realistic solution: the self-image is accepted with its new limitations, the wishes for negation, denial, etc., are replaced by resigned acceptance or determined efforts to bring about change, if possible; the gap is closed.

For our toxicomanics, however, the wheel keeps turning and the second part is on top.

Affect Regression and Breakdown of Affect Defense

This phenomenon which is shared by all toxicomanics and by many other "borderline" patients as well, can variously also be described as generalization, radicalization, totalization of affects, or, as Krystal and Raskin (1970) did, as dedifferentiation, resomatization, deverbalization. The terms are ponderous, the facts simple: the feelings become suddenly and irresistibly overwhelming, fearfully out of control. Words can not do justice to them, nor can they be clearly differentiated from each other: anxiety, anger, despair, pain, etc.—all flow into each other. Henry Krystal (1974) devoted a special and excellent article to this concept which had been developed by M. Schur (1953, 1966). In Krystal's description the two pathognomic signs of affect regression are: (1) the affects are expressed in a somatic way (mainly as psychosomatic symptoms) with very limited verbalization; the cognitive aspects are very difficult to discover, appearing, for example, in dream associations and metaphors; (2) the affects appear in a dedifferentiated way and are vague and "incomplete"; their nature is blurred and dimly perceived, not "mixed" as in ambivalence.

All compulsive drug users have the following affects in common which have to be warded off by all means (not only by drugs). All these feelings are the direct outcome of narcissistic frustration. Some of them are more prevalent in one type of drug use, others in another form, but basically they are all there. These basic moods and affects are: disappointment, disillusionment, rage, shame, loneliness, and a panicky mixture of terror and despair.

In a short preview we can survey the correlation of specific affects denied, the nature of the narcissistic wish fulfillment attained, and the preference for certain types of drugs.

1. The narcotics user has to cope with the emotional pain and anxiety flowing from the entire array of affects mentioned above. Among them rage, shame, and loneliness seem particularly prominent. What he attains on the side of wish fulfillment is a sense of protection, warmth, and union, of heightened self-esteem and self-control.

2. The user of barbiturates and other sedatives has to deal with nearly the same task. Perhaps the feelings of humiliation, shame and rage are particularly prominent and need the most powerful form of denial: that contained in estrangement (partial or total depersonalization and derealization). A study of the barbiturate addict will have to pay particular attention to that peculiar form of compromise formation; depersonalization is not simply a defense. The particular wish fulfillments are those contained in this symptom and will be

studied in depth. (However, this does not mean that we shall not meet in most other toxicomanics also hints of this very important symptom. It is solely most prominent in the user of hypnotics.)

3. In psychedelics users the major affects to be denied are the moods of boredom, emptiness, lack of meaning; from the primary list too it is mostly disillusionment and loneliness which is walled off with the drug's help. What is attained—as gratification—is a sense of meaning, of value, of admiration and of passive merger, concerning the self as well as ideals.

4. The users of stimulants—again beyond the primary list—fight against a particularly intense form of depression, despair, sadness, loss. Shame about weakness and vulnerability, boredom and emptiness, are quite prominent. The narcissistic gain lies in the feelings of strength, victory, triumph, invincibility and invulnerability, in some (but by far not all!) nearly a manic state. The importance of magical control, so ubiquitous in all categories, is particularly eminent and obtrusive in this group.

5. Alcoholics are less subject to the primary feelings listed above; the main feelings denied appear to be guilt and loneliness, also in many shyness, shame, social isolation. The narcissistic gratification lies in the expression, not in the denial, of anger which had been so long suppressed or repressed. In many there is also the feeling of company and togetherness, of shared regression and acceptance in a childlike status, the overcoming of being an outcast, when alcoholized.

These manifold negative affects break through with unrestrained force when archaic narcissistic demands are thwarted. Many of them are already expressions of aggression, the twin brother of narcissism (see Freud 1930, Eissler 1971, 1975, Rochlin 1973). Especially in the section about predisposition the connection of the two will be studied in a new light.

We have seriously to ask ourselves, however, whether this radicalization and totalization is simply a breakdown of deficient inner structures, of primitive defenses, or may be in itself a form of defense. Clinical experience with "borderline characters" (not solely compulsive drug users) leads me to presume that it can be both: manifestation of a structural defect as well as a defense.

This becomes clearer when we see how this affect regression leads to a generalization in perception and cognition. It is the exaggeration of a correct percept—for example, the generalization from one injustice, unfairness, or hurt to the whole life. This global spread, like oil on water, I have often witnessed during sessions. A patient gradually learned to catch herself when she was doing it, to recognize how a question of mine with an ironical undertone was enlarged to a total degradation by me of her as a woman, then generalized to all men being just out to deprecate her, and finally to the whole world (and fate) which treats women so abominably and thus is not worth being lived in. The world literally is to be shut out: no friend, no sunlight, no reading, no culture, no human values. This becomes clearly a form of defense: it is in a way so much easier to deal with total badness and blackness than to discriminate, to differentiate, and thus to tolerate ambivalent, conflicting feelings.

The global overinclusiveness in this brief example is of course typical for paranoid characters and schizophrenic patients, but it is a fairly common defense in many other severe character disturbances, especially in compulsive drug users. An ubiquitous weaker variant is the all-or-nothing, the either-or philosophy, which we find probably in all neurotics.

Affect regression is of central importance for the character structure of all patients with severe drug problems; and it is a totalization not restricted to some minor areas and choices; it permeates the whole view for certain periods, until they can relativize it again. If they do not anymore, I think we deal with a *paranoid* deepening of the character pathology already outlined. Very often it is experienced merely as a vague, but overwhelming physical tension and restlessness.

If we return to the totalization of affect we encounter two ancient concepts, expressing both affect and suffering: the Latin *passio* and the Greek *pathos*. This will be taken up again in more detail when I formulate the notion of the "tragic character," one of whose characteristics is precisely this phenomenon of totalization of affect. This entire phenomenon of affect regression is intertwined with a factor which will occupy us in the study of the underlying personality, the predisposition: the factor of hyposymbolization, the stunting of symbolic processes.

In regard to the question of compromise formation we can be brief: All this stormy boiling up of affects is an outlet of regressed instinctual drives, mainly many forms of aggression. Simultaneously we have already remarked how this "totalization" serves as a defense, a flight from all too painful, all too limiting, crushing reality.

The Search for an Affect Defense

This third step is the most difficult to conceptualize. The patient is, as we saw, overwhelmed and flooded with unmanageable affects and often also most intense wishes, mostly destructive ones. His usual defenses have proven deficient. It is here that the drug enters—as memory or fantasy, then as sought after means of solution, and finally as *found* help and protection, as a discovered coping mechanism (Khantzian et al. 1974).

When Dorian Gray recalled the murder of his (homosexual) admirer, mentor and father substitute, Basil Hallward, the morning after, he felt: "It was a thing to be driven out of the mind, to be drugged with poppies, to be strangled lest it might strangle one itself." Many observers have noted that all compulsive drug use is to be considered an attempt at self-treatment, and that the specific importance of the drug effect can be best explained as an artificial or surrogate defense against overwhelming affects, at least on a par with the aspect of wish fulfillment. Moreover it was already noted that there evidently exists some specificity in the choice of the drug for this purpose. But then the problems become so difficult and complex that one is tempted to exclaim with one of Dickens' characters: "'Tis a muddle, and that's aw." And yet it is perhaps the most crucial issue to be solved if we want to gain a deeper comprehension of compulsive drug use.

PHARMACOGENIC DEFENSE

Let us look at some clinical statements. Patpet described it as removing him, detaching him, as putting him thousands of miles away. Andreas describes it as a clear split: the experiencing, participating self is at some distance, separated from the observing self. Others describe it as being numbed, dulled, nonhuman, foggy, or, on the contrary, being a different, better, stronger, self—all expressions which are identical with those used for estrangement (depersonalization and/or derealization). Thus it becomes more and more likely that the pharmacogenic defense is really not a defense sui generis nor a specifically increased, particular defense mechanism nor even a welter of many defense mechanisms, but a very complex structure, showing several facets in a quite orderly, organized fashion.

The most prominent feature in it is that of a substitute affect defense, of an artificial inner barrier and structure, after the usual inner dams have burst. In this sense Kohut is very accurate when he states "The drug ... serves not as a substitute for loved or loving objects, or for a relationship with them, but as a replacement for a defect in the psychological structure" (1971, p. 46); or, in an important earlier paper (1959): "These addicts, therefore, have to rely on drugs, not, however, as a substitute for object relations but as a substitute for psychological structures" (p. 467). Though clinical experiences go beyond and indeed teach us also to acknowledge an object character in the drug used (as Anna Freud maintains), Kohut's notion is far more important. We also already had some occasion to note that when this attempt at self-treatment is taken away, when this artificial structure is removed without massive alternate support to the ego of the patient, most menacing forms of decompensation are likely to occur: violent, even homicidal rage in the narcotics addict, severe suicidal depression in the amphetamine user, a careless apathetic drifting in the psychedelics user.

This raises at once the question: What is the nature of this affect defense, of this barrier against such massive, intolerable feelings? Thus we have to study briefly the notion of affect defense.

DEFENSE AGAINST AFFECTS

It has often been observed that drugs, especially narcotics, dampen instinctual drives (see chapter 3). This may very well be the case. However, I have been much more impressed by their impact on affects, which, of course, are drive derivatives.

(Incidentally, I have encountered little evidence for pharmacogenically induced sexual impotence or increased potency either as motivation for use of various drugs or as side effect—except for an occasional complaint by methadone maintained men.)

The notion of *defense against affects* is a well-known analytic concept and has been elaborated by Jones, Anna Freud, Fenichel, and Rapaport. As mentioned, E. Jones described the stratification of affects in his 1929 paper, "Fear, Guilt and Hate," and elucidated how the hate-sadism reaction can be recognized as a defense or protest against inhibition and guilt (and vice versa); he also "called attention to the various layers of secondary defense that covered the three attitudes of fear, hate, and guilt, and pointed out that the defenses themselves constituted a sort of return of the repressed." Fenichel wrote a paper in 1934 under the expressive title, "Defense Against Anxiety, Particularly by Libidinization."

Anna Freud was particularly explicit (1936): "The ego is in conflict not only with those id derivatives which try to make their way into its territory in order to gain access to consciousness and to obtain gratification. It defends itself no less energetically and actively against the affects associated with these instinctual impulses. When repudiating the claims of instinct, its first task must always be to come to terms with these affects. . . ." She goes on to describe the clinical parallelism between defense against affects and instincts: "It is the same ego, and in all its conflicts it is more or less consistent in using every means which it has at its command. . . . We find the same constant connection between neurosis and defense mechanism when we study the modes of defense which a patient employs against his affects and the form of resistance adopted by his ego." She specifically names repression, displacement, reversal, suppression, denial, isolation and undoing (pp. 31–41).

Rapaport wrote in his 1953 essay, "On the Psychoanalytic Theory of Affects": "affect charges themselves also seem to become subject to defensive countercathecting, that is, to direct modification of their discharge threshold," and, even more precisely: "'Affect Charge' if discharged may arouse further tensions. To prevent the development of these the underlying drive as well as the 'affect charge' must be defended against. Thus affects (e.g. anxiety) become motives of defense."

But we have to broaden our view considerably. All defense mechanisms have some instinctual aspects as well (see Hartmann 1951, p. 150). Eissler worked out such connections for isolation (1959, pp. 44–46). Merton M. Gill (1963) is most explicit: "What is defense in one layer is impulse in relation to another layer." He quotes Fenichel (1941, p. 62): "In a certain sense it can be said that all defense is 'relative defense'; relative to one layer it is defense, and at the same time, relative to another layer it is that which is warded off." And he goes on: "In general a behavior is a defense in relation to a drive more primitive than itself, and a drive in relation to a defense more advanced than itself" (pp. 122–123). And he goes beyond that: "In this range of the continuum, behavior would be called 'id' in relation to behavior higher in the hierarchy but 'ego' in relation to behavior lower. This conception parallels that of the layering of impulse-defense units discussed earlier" (p. 146).

Thus a given process, say isolation or denial, may be viewed from one perspective ("from above") as a *defense mechanism*, from another perspective (and not merely developmentally, but within, for example, one psychoanalytic session or sequence in a case) as an expression of wishful activity, providing libidinal and aggressive *gratification* (Schafer 1968b), and, moreover, as a *cognitive regulatory structure* (Lichtenberg and Slap 1972): as a mechanism of perceiving, remembering, and, above all, of thinking (see also Freud 1926, Eissler 1958). If, parallel and supportive to cognition, this same process is also viewed as a *motor action* performed at times of low drive tension (following Piaget, see Wolff 1960, Lichtenberg and Slap 1972, Langer 1967, 1972), a fourth perspective emerges. In sum, then, what we describe as defense "mechanisms," can also serve as "mechanisms" of gratification; as processes needed for thinking and perceiving; and as basic action patterns. Such a comprehensive, fourfold view would not only integrate the psychoanalytic theory of defenses with experimental psychology but with many crucial insights gained in the philosophical theory of how we construct our "self-world concept" (*Weltanschauung*), the very "possibility of experiencing," (the basis of Kant's philosophical questioning).

After this hint at a vast theoretical expansion of psychoanalytic insight we have to revert to the narrow task at hand: What is the nature of the defenses employed in these patients and propped up or instituted with the help of the pharmacological effect? The answer to this question is difficult and complicated.

FOUR CONTINUA OF DEFENSES

Again when we examine the following continua of defense "mechanisms" we should keep in mind what has just been briefly touched upon, that these continua would then be identical or at least very similar to continua of instinctual drive derivatives, of controlling processes of perception and cognition, and of basic action patterns (beyond the drive-motivated).

The continua stretch from highly differentiated, subtle, usually mostly preconscious or conscious ones (called by Freud 1937, "ego syntonic controls"), to defenses operating on an archaic, undifferentiated level, functioning in a state of low integration, of global overinclusiveness, and, as processes, carried by a most peremptory, that is, unconscious force. As to the latter I again refer back to Kubie's (1954) and Sandler's (1969) hypothesis: the more peremptory, compelling, rigid, and inflexible, the more pushed by unconscious motivation (even if the process itself appears on the surface to be conscious).

Despite the current onslaught against the energy concept in psychoanalytic theory formation I find it, also in this context, to be most useful, albeit metaphorical. The defenses on the more mature end of the continua operate with "neutralized," sublimated "energies"; those toward the primitive end are, even experientially, of quite archaic instinctual, mainly directly aggressive quality. I propose to consider these defenses as lying on four continua:

1. A first continuum, the *avoidance* type of defenses, stretches from conscious and preconscious proclamations and wishes—"I do not want to know" (in Trunnell and Holt's paper, "denial" in the vernacular sense: "a 'declaring' not to be true")—over neurotic (unconscious) forms of denial (keeping the affective significance of perceptions and entire parts of percepts unconscious) and repression (directed against drive derivatives) to very regressive, much more global forms of denial (of psychotic or near-psychotic proportions). This first continuum is artificially instituted or, far more likely, massively reinforced by depressant drugs: narcotics, hypnotics, minor sedatives, and alcohol. The other two types (psychedelics and stimulants) sometimes support especially denial, sometimes *lift* these defenses; their major action lies in what follows. This first line follows the systematization proposed by W. A. Stewart (1970). In contrast to my earlier views I have now also to disagree with Jacobson's impressive formulation (1957, p. 76) which equated denial with keeping ideas preconscious and repression with making ideas unconscious and inhibiting the corresponding affects. Among all these defenses lying on the continuum, conscious "disavowal" and massive unconscious denial are by far the most prominent—immediately prior to drug use and then as part of the drug effect. In the cognitive realm, we find, among other

things, the same basic processes employed in the averting of attention as opposed to the focusing of attention.

2. The second continuum pertains to the *dissociation* type of defenses, the breaking of connections. It stretches again from conscious and preconscious versions, as described by Eissler (1959) and also in the Glossary (1968): conscious isolation in concentrated thinking, use of the conscious ego "split" and superego "split" in the psychoanalytic situation, the quite conscious split instituted by Andreas (quoted early in this section), to unconscious isolation, and the various forms of dissocation accompanying denial (denial of loss, of castration), to more regressive types (Kohut's "vertical" splitting and the limited, partial forms of fragmentation), to very severe, erratic labile forms of disjunction or dissociation in pervasive regression and to the two most extreme forms of what Kernberg describes as global splitting in all-good and all-bad, and of radical, psychotic fragmentation and disintegration. Its cognitive usefulness in concentration was commented upon by Freud (1926) and Eissler (1958).

In all compulsive drug users severe forms of disjunction and fragmentation can be encountered. The depressant drugs usually reduce these dissociations and indeed thus help to synthesize, whereas particularly the psychedelic drugs massively deepen the dissociation. Who prefers dissociation, chooses psychedelic drugs.

3. The third continuum pertains to the *action or fight* type of defenses: again from conscious, controlled use (alloplastic change, creative use of externalization, outright aggression as defense) to unconscious externalization, turning passive into active, possibly even identification with the attacker and reaction-formation, turning aggression against the self, and magical undoing, all on various levels of primitiveness. From all these, archaic forms of externalization will loom up as an omnipresent, massive form of defense in all compulsive drug users and will be treated separately. Stimulants are the one category of drugs which particularly supports the defenses on this continuum, especially externalization and the aggressive turning of passive into active, often in a very primitive form.

4. A fourth continuum of far more cognitive and action oriented significance than for defenses is the continuum of the *boundary and limitation* type of defenses, stretching again from highly differentiated and preconscious forms of boundary forming and limit-setting

"mechanisms," of boundary creation and breaking, to the most archaic forms of fusion, boundary and limit blurring and transgressing.

Instinctually the continuum reaches from extreme merger to full separateness, cognitively from the archaic syncretistic thinking (Werner 1948) to full differentiation and integration (Hartmann, Kris, and Loewenstein 1946, Wynne and Singer 1963; see also Cassirer 1923a, b, 1929), in action patterns in Piaget's sense, from "original reflex or global schemata" to schemata based on "generalizing assimilation" and differentiation (see Wolff 1960). In regard to the defenses on the one end we have largely preconscious identifying, learning and once again externalizing, also conscious detaching, separating and transgressing, whereas at the more primitive end we would encounter well-known archaic defenses like introjection and projection, radical idealizing and devaluing, primitive forms of externalization and identification.

I presume that the placing of one well-known defense mechanism (e.g., externalization) on several continua is quite justifiable, because the processes contained are often of multiple significance and thus multidetermining. I hold that in all drug abuse this fourth continuum of defenses (and beyond this, of gratification, cognition, and action) is used throughout and is of particular importance; it will be explored later on, in chapter 8. Since I presume that all four continua reach back into earliest childhood, I doubt whether any drug type by itself evokes a more or less regressive form of defense "mechanism" (and with that of conflict solution). Usually severity of preexisting pathology and massivity of drug effect (usually dependent upon the dosage) determines the depth of regression on each of the four continua.

I do not pretend that I have encompassed all defense "mechanisms." It is quite conceivable that more forms and different lines can be found. It appears to me too that, as Hartmann postulated, all defenses operate mostly with aggressive energies, often in very archaic, not "neutralized" versions (Hartmann, Kris, and Loewenstein 1949). "It is likely that defense against the drives (countercathexis) retains an element [fight] that allows of their description as being mostly fed by one mode of aggressive energy, and that this mode is not full neutralization" (1955, p. 232). This reference, including the indispensable energy metaphors, is amply supported by the observations in drug patients: the pharmacogenic deepening of a defense is blatantly aggressive in nature, the pharmacogenic lifting unleashes overt conscious forms of aggressive defense (e.g., conscious disavowal and invalidation, use of direct violence for defensive purposes).

Thus the very deepening of the major defenses (denial, splitting, externalization) with the help of drugs is an act of destructive aggression, albeit intense libidinous, especially narcissistic gains are also attained by the intensification of these defenses: the very muting of severly disruptive affects itself can lead to overwhelming feelings of joy, warmth, "good vibes," and, as we will see in due course, much heightened self-esteem. Patients often become more sociable, friendly, accepting, harmonious, and at peace, especially with depressant and psychedelic drugs. This then leads to the conclusion that again this step, the pharmacogenic defense, is in truth a compromise formation, in these patients, between their major affect defenses (denial, dissociation, and externalization) and gratifications of aggression and libido, in narcissistic and object-related forms.

DENIAL

Rather little needs to be added now to what has already been described and quoted at the beginning of this section and in the survey just completed.

In all compulsive drug users we find not only a massive denial of the affects, but additional devastatingly broad extensions of this denial. All these drugs to a greater or lesser extent obviously deepen the regression to merger experiences (as a defense, e.g., against loneliness)—a lifting of the boundaries between self and others, a detachment as defense against limiting, separating reality, that crucially also involves denial.

Patpet (case 4) when faced, in the hospital, with several pending court cases, enormous debts, a collapsing business, the reneging by the parents of their obligation toward both the family therapist and me, recognized the depth of his unconscious denial: "When I feel an emotion which is uncomfortable, I immediately search for this overwhelming self-importance or for excitement with people, and I am out of the depression at once....I am calm while talking about and recognizing all these great worries. It is a detachment from myself. I speak about these great crises in a glib grand way, as if it did not pertain to myself." Then he added that he had many times had intercourse with patients and visitors on the ward, clearly inviting punishment: "If they don't love me, at least they hate me." Action breaks through the lack of feeling. So does punishment: "I am a glutton for punishment."

In this brief statement we clearly see the whole complex defensive process: denial of the emotional impact, while acknowledging the percepts, thus the splitting, the feeling of detachment (depersonalization) and the cover-up by exciting action. The sequence is: unconscious denial (defense mechanism) and conscious acknowledgment → splitting (a functional discrepancy) → depersonalization (symptom) → exciting action–externalization (defense mechanism) → transgression and provoked punishment (symptom).

But now we focus on the first element in this sequence—the pervasive denial.

The particular denial of boundaries in cognition is of course mostly noticeable with psychedelics, but can be found in some milder, cognitively less striking forms in the other groups as well. Outer reality is very often "detached," depersonalized, just like inner reality. As another patient said: "It is like a fog," similar to the veil, the glass wall, the "waking screen" of depersonalized patients.

But another area of denial pertains to the limitations, boundaries, restrictions of social life and of nature. It is this denial which evokes so much outrage and counteraction in the surroundings. And yet a fourth area (besides affects, cognitive reality, social and natural limitations) is strangely denied—very much overlapping with the one just mentioned: the whole conscience, internally as well as, of course, expressed in continued actions. Some patients are widely known to be of utmost honesty, conscientiousness, integrity, industriousness, and reliability —especially by those who are ignorant of their drug history. Besides that, at other times, it appears as if the superego simply were deposed, put out of function, cut off like a dead limb. Suddenly, anything goes: lies, manipulation, inconsiderateness, transgression of all boundaries and standards, violence, ruthless exploitation of others. All three major functions of the superego: the prohibiting, the observing and the ideal-setting suffer this drastic fate of temporary cancellation. They often are not even projected or experienced as external anymore—they seem simply absent. Still every probing quickly reveals that they have not vanished altogether; they are temporarily split off, denied, "inoperative." This will be studied separately as "superego split."

Thus it is ineluctable that all denial immediately involves another process, derived from defensive mechanisms on the second continuum: a split.

However, before we turn our attention to it, another issue cannot be omitted here, although we have much more opportunity to study it later.

Trunnell and Holt (1974) hold:

The split in the ego in denial or disavowal is possibly regularly maintained by an invalidating fantasy. The person has some idea which allows him to disregard his accurate perceptions on the ground that for some reason they do not or need not apply to him. These fantasies of invulnerability and the need to be special may have their own importance, and consequently are retained along with the split in the ego they maintain.

I can confirm this from each case I got to know well. Patpet said when in the hospital: "No matter what happened, I put myself above shame or guilt. I *knew* I cannot get caught. And this was always confirmed by the family: do it, but don't let yourself be caught. I always felt I could get away with everything, that nothing would happen to me, that I would *never* have to go to jail, regardless of what I did." And: "I felt I deserved these extras because I was such a success and philanthropist."

But always in these patients, as if to say: "Nothing will happen to me. I can get something for nothing. The laws are for others, I do not have to pay the price for what I do. I am in total control of my life and will always find a way to retain it." When this control finally slips and the denial crumbles, the fall into depression can be hard and deep.

In summary: Denial and related defenses are magical controls.

SPLITTING

As enigmatic and secretive as the working and nature of all defense mechanisms is, splitting surpasses them all in the difficulties which it presents in defining it, in giving it clear, generally understandable and agreed-upon meaning, in understanding it in depth, in circumscribing its extent, and in separating out different forms. I leave it open for the moment whether it is a separate defense-mechanism or a quite different phenomenon. It is often, but not always, defense related. It has normal, neurotic, "borderline," and psychotic varieties—dependent on its extensiveness, its limited or its global, radical nature. It clearly also has cognitive equivalents which are not of any defensive portent and import, yet are indispensable for many achievements (e.g., in the "splitting up" of the author's inner life into the created persons of a novel or drama, into figures of a most powerful general symbolic significance), and valuable, for instance, in the analytic situation (see below). Moreover, there exists a very close connection with at least one defense "mechanism": denial. "Simultaneous denial and acknowledgment of the same observation constitute proof that the ego is split into two attitudes" (Katan 1964).

At first I give a theoretical exposé, followed by some brief concrete examples.

There is much talk in the current analytic literature about "splitting"; its use is manifold and often not too clear. For Freud, in his very late, incomplete works (1938a, b), the meaning is precise: "On the one hand they are *disavowing* the fact of their perception—the fact that they saw no penis in the female genitals; and on the other hand they are *recognizing* the fact that females have no penis and are drawing the correct conclusions from it. The two attitudes persist side by side throughout their lives without influencing each other" (S.E. XXIII, pp. 202–204). This unreconciled persistence of "disavowal of the perceptions" with "an acknowledgment" leads to a "rift" in the ego which never heals, but which increases as time goes on (S.E. XXIII, p. 276). In neurotics such a split is partial, limited. In psychotics it is far more extensive; at times the ego is, under the influence of the instinctual drives, entirely detached from reality (S.E. XXIII, p. 202).

We know of other ("normal") splits—e.g., the split in the analysis between the experiencing and the observing ego, or, as Paul Gray (pers. comm., 1973) stresses, the split between the suspended superego functions in regard to the feeling, thinking and talking processes within the analytic session versus the necessity for continued functioning of the superego outside of the analytic situation.

Many authors, under the influence of Melanie Klein and Kernberg, see the radical very archaic split between "all good" and "all bad" as the important effect of a supposed defense mechanism, that of splitting.

Kernberg defines splitting as an "active process of keeping apart introjections and identifications of opposite quality." He sees this defense mechanism as the "essential defensive operation of the borderline personality" and describes, as its best known manifestations the division of external objects into 'all good' and 'all bad' ones with the concomitant possibility of complete, abrupt shifts of an object from one extreme compartment to the other; that is, sudden and complete reversals of all feelings and conceptualizations about a particular person. Extreme and repetitive oscillation between contradictory self-concepts may also be the result of splitting. [1967, pp. 667–668]

While in the psychoses the differentiation of self from nonself and with that the *differentiation* of "ego boundaries" fails altogether, this is not so in "borderline" patients; however, the *task of integrating* libidinally determined and aggressively determined self and object images cannot be fulfilled mainly because of the pathological predominance of pregenital aggression:

The resulting lack of synthesis of contradictory self and object images interferes with the integration of the self-concept and with the establishment of "total" object relationships and object constancy. The need to preserve the good self and good object images, and good external objects in the presence of dangerous 'all bad' self and object images leads to a defensive division of the ego, in which what was at first a simple defect in integration is then used actively for keeping "good" and "bad" self and object images apart. [Kernberg 1970, p. 811]

The very careful analyses of the concept of defense mechanisms by Schafer (1968a, b), and by Lichtenberg and Slap (1971, 1973a, b, 1975) are particularly helpful for our considerations. Their distinction is most clearly expressed in the summary of their 1973 paper, devoted to "splitting of representations":

We would restrict the term "splitting" to the tendency in infantile life by which the organization of memory traces of the earliest experiences is based on the primordial quality of pleasurable–good or painful–bad. By the term "splitting of representations," we would designate a mechanism of defense which acts to separate the representations of self and of objects in instances in which two differing currents of strong feelings and urges would arouse anxiety if experienced simultaneously toward an object. The one affective current, and the self-representation related to it, is experienced toward one object while the opposite current is limited to a separate object representation.

They presume that this splitting of representations as defense mechanism may be an important factor in the formation of what Freud called "splitting of the ego" and which they, after Schafer, prefer to call a pathological intersystemic suborganization.

In the rest of this book when I use the term *splitting* I shall refer to it in three meanings, largely (though not fully) concordant with Lichtenberg and Slap's distinction: (a) as disjunction and fragmentation of representations, (b) in their extreme form as polarization into all-good and all-bad, and (c) very importantly, as "splits" in the entire personality organization, what Schafer, Lichtenberg and Slap called "pathological intersystemic suborganizations" = "persistent drive-defense–prohibition couplings".

Lichtenberg and Slap describe these couplings: "manifestations of *defensive* activity become connected with a specific *drive* and with *superego* structures ....Associated with such drive-defense-prohibition couplings are elaborate networks of memories and displacements. These networks are built around the ideational contents of the developmental disturbance" (1972, p. 786).

Since these latter theoretical expositions are very abstract and difficult to understand, I gradually try to put them into somewhat simpler and more observational language. In all forms I consider *splitting* not as a separate defense "mechanism," but at this point rather as a *phenomenological or descriptive* concept denoting the result of a number of defensive acts. Hence it has assumed too many meanings and its outcomes ("splits") are too varied and often too complex for us to see in it a simple explanatory element on the same level as defense mechanisms proper. This different nature does not make the concept of splitting useless, but it seems to me that we always have to specify what we mean by it. Probably its general meaning is that of a *functional inner disparity*, not necessarily restricted to the ego, but going through the entire personality. It is brought about by defense mechanisms, like denial, repression, regression and dissociation.

Dynamically this concept encompasses Freud's use: This functional inner disparity which always centrally affects cognition presupposes the side by side but unreconciled presence of disavowal (warding off, repudiation, etc.) and acknowledgment.

PARTIAL SPLITTING BY FRAGMENTATION AND DISJUNCTION

Perhaps a microanalysis of the phenomenon encountered in many patients will be of help here. This event is best described as a sense of scattering, fragmenting of thoughts, of turbulent feelings, of not connecting what is experienced, ending up in a state of "total confusion."

CASE 7: DOLOROSA

I try to demonstrate this from the analysis of a patient who is paradigmatic for what I described (1975b, c) as "tragic character"—a severely depressed woman with a pervasive negative therapeutic reaction. Every deeper insight was being followed year after year by a most radical self-condemnation. Her history was filled from earliest childhood on with violent traumata, abandonment by her real father and abuse by the stepfather, betrayal by mother and degradation as girl and woman. Her case history cannot be presented here; only one characteristic event in the analysis should be studied briefly because it is quite typical of what many other patients showed. This patient, however, is not a drug user, but a "borderline" patient being "addicted" to fantasy love relationships. She herself stated: "I am an addict in my own way," commenting on being totally dependent for many years and in suicidal despair on a man who had shown but scant, passing interest in her. All the other traits of the addictive personality are present (and recognizable to her). Why did she not resort to drugs? For two, mainly superego motivated reasons: she was horrified of those parts of herself—especially sexuality—which would become uncontrollable under the impact of drugs, and afraid of the illegality. In other aspects there were clear superego splits, e.g., compulsive lying—replicating mother's frequent warnings: "Do not tell your [step-] father!" (because of his fury).

One of the severe problems in her own life as well as in therapy was the interference by "pseudo-stupidity." In the treatment it manifested itself in the following disconcerting way: Many comments and experiences within and without the analysis evoked a sense of "tilt," that "my computer goes bananas," "the intake is shut off," "there is too much input." Dreams often ended in a similar state equated by the patient with this "tilt": "A sense of fainting," a "numbness coming down my forehead like molasses," a "blackout from which I always wake up and feel my heart racing." Was this "blackout" not a form of a dream within a dream? And was with that the numbing confusion not an actual historical memory? This blackout occurred usually at the end of dreams, e.g., in one where she "killed yellow jackets and bees" (with their stings) and had reduced the bald head of a terrifying car driver in the frontseat to a penis stump but who still raced down with her into disaster, dreams showing her "penis hatred," as she calls it (the "shaft is missing!"), her "killing revenge," then the terror of this menacing penetrating monster, and ending in blinding confusion, not knowing and numbness—just as Greenacre (1947) so beautifully described.

Her nearly daily attacks of *headache*, centered behind the eyeballs, seemed like the photographic positive to the numbness just described: "It hurts (and infuriates) so much what I have seen." The expression of "tilt" for confusion or perplexity was in itself an interesting metaphor: it is a signal on a pinball machine when the "system is overcharged," or the "ball goes in the wrong hole!"

Thus the "tilt" appears as a striking metaphor for repression and denial: not to hear, read, understand expressed not only her fear of succumbing passively to intrusion, of passive surrender and merger, but above all to be passively overwhelmed by the storms of primal scene (excitement, rage, terror) and the other traumata. "I want to see and hear and understand it, and I cannot and do not want to grasp it. It is too painful. I do not see what I see, I do not hear, what I hear"—just like mother's denial: "You could not have seen what you have seen." The result: perplexity, confusion. But there was another aspect: what she called "fragmenting" or "scattering," a "splitting up"—what we may describe as *disintegrating, disjunctive form of intellectualization,* an activity which was indeed a dismembering quality; it is a "cutting to pieces." An example: In session 673 the moment seemed finally to have arrived to pull together the various parts of her penis envy (which up to then had been scornfully denied as a Freudian fiction) when she stated how identified she felt with her castrated male cat. The strands were: (1) her bitterness, resentment, and anger about the mistreatment of women in general, of her and her mother in particular, (2) the expressed childhood wish in one of the early sessions of wanting to have a penis and her insistence of wanting to have power and prestige, (3) the pervasive feeling of envy, especially towards me, and (4) the intense castration wishes dominating very many of her dreams and her own use of phallic instruments of vindictiveness (guns, snakes, pointed splinters of glass).

Immediately—after the first "tilt" reaction against this comprehensive reconstruction of her penis envy—she started to quibble, about the cat, whether women in general might have penis envy, "and now I have forgotten the rest," etc. The defense of "divide et impera," of isolating and cutting into separate pieces and thus invalidating the central message of the interpretation was terribly important. It was not really isolation in the proper sense. Certainly, although she called it herself a "splitting up," it is not precisely what Freud sparingly, nor what some new authors abundantly describe as "splitting." Perhaps we should best use a new term for this defense, without all the ballast of reminiscences from psychoses or perversions: the defense of disjunction, an active process opposed to the synthetic function.

As in all defenses an instinctual charge is also contained: the cutting to pieces, the dismembering which I presume to be an active act of primitive (oral) aggression, as sadistic as a symptomatic act of her childhood when she tore out the legs and wings of insects. This form of sadistic dismembering has assumed the quality of a most effective and self-destructive defense. I think its origin may be triple.

One is her own memory of mutilations by operation and the abyssmal sense of pain of being castrated and therefore excluded and not taken seriously.

The second is derived from the primal scene and may be put in this form: "I perceive the violent sexual scenes between my parents—and yet I cannot see, hear, name, understand, and comprehend." (And perhaps too: "I cannot see them 'together'.") She generalizes this split into an overall learning inhibition and passivity, into a fragmenting up of all experience in bouts of "craziness." She chops up all comments, all interpretations, everything which is read, into unintelligible bits and pieces. Or she sees visual reality dissected and splintered up, the structures of space and objects fractured and confused. Thus, the defense by disjunction is one form of defense on the dissociation continuum.

The third root lies in the split identifications and thus truly in the realm of splitting of representations. The contradictory identifications are with the helpless, traumatized, castrated, or killed victim versus that with the murderous, all powerful parent and then applied to all objects and thoughts, and ending in a splitting up also of values and ideals. This will become much clearer in the case of Andreas (case 19).

I hesitate to restrict this phenomenon of splitting to the way Lichtenberg and Slap defined it: to a defense mechanism affecting representations, unless the latter term again becomes so all-encompassing that it loses its meaningfulness. It is a subjectively and objectively experienced splintering of thoughts and feelings, a radical disconnecting of what belongs together because it is too frightful and painladen to "understand," to "put it all together." It ends in confusion, but not in a fairly neat split of parts of the self- or object-images.

POLARIZING FORMS OF SPLITTING

By and large this fits quite well with what Lichtenberg and Slap defined as splitting of representations. One version was presented in the preview of the case of Andreas at the inception of this section: his splitting into an observing-creating and an acting-experiencing part. The attentive reader may have noticed that, in contrast to most other patients with depersonalization, in him the sense of reality was, at that moment at least, on the side of the acting-experiencing part, whereas usually, in other patients with similar splits, the sense of reality lies on the observing part. In most cases of this book, however, this polarization of self- and object-representations goes much farther, into a very regressive splitting into all-good and all-bad. The examples will speak for themselves. With this regressive form, we are very close to what was described in the previous chapter as totalization and radicalization. This regresive phenomeon of splitting of self and world in "all good" and "all bad" is a yet more archaic form than the split by disjunction and partial fragmentation.

Fragmentation and global, total splits in all good and all bad are, of course, particularly pronounced in transient psychotic episodes (e.g., in withdrawal, in acute panic, under psychedelics), although a total fragmentation as in schizophrenics is unusual in compulsive drug users—unless they indeed are also floridly schizophrenic. Even there the drug has an integrative effect.

THE "SPLIT" PERSONALITY

Almost every compulsive drug user sees himself as leading a double (or multiple) existence—as having, like Faust, two souls *("Zwei Seelen wohnen, ach, in meiner Brust"),* switching magically from one into the other. They live out two or more separate, well isolated, irreconcilable "intersystemic suborganizations", as we saw, e.g., in Patpet or will see in many of the cases to come.

The purpose of all these splits is to prevent or to heal narcissistic injury, to overcome the narcissistic crisis, to reestablish the collapsed defenses against affects and aggression in this magical and aggressive tearing apart of connections. Similar massive splits can be encountered in their families. Again, to illustrate these more massive personality splits (into "intersystemic suborganizations") I select a case vignette.

CASE 8: VAUTRIN

We shall encounter this man once again later on in chapter 13. Here only a brief, dynamic sketch: He was the ex-addict leader of a drug program, the "soul of the agency", concerned, honest, always, day and night, available to help, encouraging patients, counselors, nurses and physicians, holding all operations together, while establishing crucial support throughout the community. This was one side: a combination of most valuable attitudes and actions. High ideals (superego) were translated into a multiplicity of integrated ego activities, carried by strong defenses (repression, denial, reaction formation), and leading to great gratifications of narcissistic claims, (much heightened self-esteem), and constructive aggression (frantic, constructive activity, bulldozing through of resistances). Yet the narcissistic claims were also his undoing. They opened up the "split." He suddenly turned out to be also dishonest and in cahoots with criminals; his prior defenses collapsed and, instead, archaic projection, introjection and turning of aggression against the self (suicidality) took over.

The superego came to be seen outside: in a host of persecutors and condemnors. He went back on drugs and destroyed his position, his respectability, the integrity of others, and by a long chain of criminal acts, the rights and needs of many other persons. He ended up as a fugitive, a drug addict and pusher once more. Two basically "pathological intersystemic suborganizations," both encompassing drives, defenses and superego aspects are seen in a total split of life, personality and actions. Of course they both had existed before their sequential manifestation. This type of wholesale "splitting" is unfortunately most typical for all compulsive drug users I have known. The splitting pertains to all cognition, (denial and acknowledgement), to all attitudes and actions, to the life history as a whole, and very importantly as will be studied later, to the superego. I chose the pseudonym of Vautrin from Balzac's *Comédie Humaine* for a man who at one time was a cleric and benefactor, at another an abject evildoer and felon.

Another example of such a split would be Oscar Wilde's Dorian Gray: One is the idealized living out of all desires in limitless narcissism, the beautiful adored part who *acts* in the most villainous ways, following an ego ideal of absolute beauty and pleasure, ("form is absolutely essential"), the "worship of the senses," "enamoured of his own beauty, more and more interested in the corruption of his own soul." "Eternal youth, infinite passion, pleasures subtle and secret, wild joys and wild sins—he was to have all these things." On the other side his own portrait, the "inoperative" (denied) part of himself, "his soul", was to bear the burden of his shame, the hidden, secret "mask of his shame," "a visible symbol of the degradation of sin." It was veiled by a "purple-and-gold pall as a curtain," locked up from all eyes. He both "hated to be separated from the picture that was such a part of his life, and was also afraid that during his absence some one might gain access to the room, in spite of the elaborate bars that he had caused to be placed upon the door." The first part was the acting and observing sub-personality, a facade of being a somewhat dubious, though successful gentleman, an aristocrat of form, fame and wealth, a symbol of beauty, but a murderer of souls and bodies. The second part was the suffering, disfigured degradation, the canvas of horror and anxiety, the bearer of shame and guilt. The first was overt, the second secret. To a similar split I referred to in an earlier book (1959), the division in the creative, famous goldsmith Cardillac, who, at night, turned into a most secret assassin and robber (E. Th. A. Hoffmann's "Das Fräulein von Scudéri").

What is crucial in these "split" or "multiple" personalities is the sudden total flip-flop, a global lability with no mediation and no perspective. It is a picture of "peripéteia," of total turnabouts, which one might call the *about-face syndrome.* I suspect that this type of "splitting" actually is composed of the defenses of repression (or denial), regression, projection, disjunctive type of dissociation, combined with a deep structural deficit. In less severely ill patients such "splits" are clearly due to isolation and repression, as I hope to demonstrate in a separate study.

When we now return to the three radical forms of splitting encountered in all compulsive drug users, three features stand out: What I am most impressed with is the lability of these splits, the steady shifting of them, the sudden flipflops. Now there is synthesis—now there is a split.

This pertains to feelings, to external limits, to self-image, the value of others, to ideals and to the conscience (see Kirkman's test results, Appendix A). The cases will make this utter unreliability of structures, the iridescence of denials and of splits yet more evident.

Secondly, these are very often covered over by depressants, exacerbated by stimulants and psychedelics. In the former instance (use of narcotics, hypnotics, alcohol) they become particularly evident during withdrawal and abstinence. Thirdly these splits always involve cognition. At the least it is what Freud described, the rending of the ego between two functions: e.g., the acknowledgment of the standing structures of the object world and the largely unconscious disavowal of such cognitive entities. Beyond this, in much broader terms, these splits profoundly affect the cognition of objects and self, of time and space, of all representations of self and object world, of one large part of the personality versus another massive part.

If we look back over what we have found, especially the prominence of denial and splitting, we are not surprised about the frequency with which these patients describe phenomena of depersonalization and derealization. These twin symptoms occur either spontaneously or pharmacogenically. The more I study the material the stronger my suspicion becomes that if we only observed carefully enough we would find at least bits and pieces, if not the panoply, of the estrangement syndrome in these patients.

Drug abuse thus seems like an artificial depersonalization state coupled with the next defense, externalization, which is so characteristic for "sociopaths."

Thus, at least as seen from an ego psychological point of view, one may pose the question: Are they perhaps nosologically a group uniting near psychotic estrangement with "sociopathy"? I am much inclined to answer it in the affirmative, but will elaborate later.

If we try to sum up this entire section we can see that this third step represents a search for an affect defense in various severity of regression: conscious avoidance and unconscious denial, splits in forms of labile dissociations, archaic isolation and disjunction, splits in several forms of fragmenting of self, of thinking and feeling, splitting finally as polarization and psychotic, global fragmenting up; eventually these defenses verge in all patients into a kind of restitution: concrete action, externalization, which needs to be studied now.

Externalization: The Neglected Defense

I set externalization apart, because it does not only function as a direct pharmacogenic affect defense (e.g., in stimulants, alcohol), but it has an overriding importance in all drug users in the form of seeking the solution to an inner problem on the outside, by action and in concrete form, quite apart from the eventually successful or failing function of the drug effect as affect defense.

MAGICAL ACTION

This critically important defense of externalization is the action of taking magical, omnipotent control over the uncontrollable. Everything else appears less specific compared with this peculiar and I think rather novel form of defense, valid for all compulsive drug taking. The anxiety is always there: "The various feelings, like rage and depression, are going to overwhelm me." This fear of the traumatic state is powerfully warded off by the potent substance which is eaten, injected, snorted, or smoked: "I have the power—via this magical substance—to master the rage, the pain, the boredom, etc." It is a specialized form of defense by acting—just as many analytic patients feel they solve an inner problem by an outer action (or avoidance of action), instead of by exploring, understanding and remembering. Moreover, since the Archimedean standpoint we have to take in psychoanalytic theorizing is, after all, always the inner stream of feeling and thought, any such act as utilizing an external help to "cope" with the frightening feeling is a form of externalization—just like the picking of a fight by a guilt laden patient or the carrying around of the powerful protecting lion by the boy who is afraid of his own aggression.

Now all the rest falls into place too. Of course who magically externalizes as a defense against being overpowered by frightening affects uses the same defense in form of "concretization": "It's not me who feels, it's society or the body which makes me suffer from this unnamable tension", what was already referred to as *hyposymbolization,* the inability to articulate feelings in symbolic expressions (words, images, music, etc.). Who thus externalizes by massive action cannot form the guiding values and ideals—again abstract, symbolic versions of early feelings toward persons; instead the drug is a concrete, external, sought after vehicle of action. It stands in the place of the group of the most potent symbols: values and ideals. The powerful drug effect replaces the power which values have for us, thus the chemical mythology!

Archaic guilt and shame are all over the place anyhow in these patients; the drug is both a magical protection, a talisman against them—from the outside, and an implementation of this double Nemesis—again from the outside. In other words: It tries to ward off (mostly) externalized (not yet internalized) retribution and humiliation (the original double meaning of the Greek "Nemesis"), but simultaneously it functions itself as a punishment and as a shaming, a shameful proof of weakness and failure. The drug dependency is both a matter for boasting—the conquest of shame, and a cause for shame— an obvious weakness and failure, exposed for all to see, though anxiously hidden. The same interpretation holds for the archaic dependency, thus tying together Kohut's and Anna Freud's view which seemed to contradict each other: the defect in inner structures leads the patient to seek an external object of magical power to depend on for this all pervasive control. Again it is defense by externalization.

Externalization thus proves the magical key for understanding not only all the proposed predispositions, but also so much of the external bluster. I spoke—in connection with Patpet (case 4)—of the "Quadrangle of Fire" as a metaphor: all four "corners" are forms of externalization! It was the yearning for total unbound freedom, yet fatally abused; it was the need for security lending structures, sought even as jail, but violently fought and rebelled against; it was the continuous search for adoration, the external confirmation of self-infatuation, the parading of phallic self-glorification. And it was the self-destruction by external means, the continuous arrangement of life that he had to flee like a hunted animal from police, mafia, vindictive whores—or imaginary enemies.

In contrast to paranoid states the crucial "mechanism" of defense is not projection, it is externalization. And of course "society" falls in with it: "they"—police, politicians, physicians, parents, public (these five external powers)—go right along with the compulsive drug user's demand for externalization: they punish, prosecute, shame, hunt, prohibit, set up structures—and fall in the trap they set up themselves—they, the non-addicts, are victims nevertheless.

In a sense the addict, like the paranoid, has been most successful in making the world serve his inner defense. Just as paranoid leaders influence world history by their terror-ridden projections, the addicts influence social history by their incessant demand for externalization. The success of both lies in forcing their surroundings near and far to play their necessary roles in what is originally an internal conflict. The world goes along in this game of externalization, just as it does all too often with the projections of the totalitarian terrorists (whose concrete ideologies are but icing on the cake!). Why? These games of projection and externalization must have a potent lure for the "masses" to fall in so willingly. But that is an issue to be taken up at its place: when we talk about the sociopolitical psychology of drug abuse. But to return to the defense of externalization: That is surely not restricted to compulsive drug users. Do we not find it in many other patients (and non-patients!)? What then is specific for the form externalization assumes in the addicted person (even in its extensions—the TV addict, the gambler, the food addict, the compulsive smoker, and of course the alcoholic)? It is the magical power invested in a thing; the "thing" is endowed with control over the self, over the inner life, over the feelings. The solution for any inner problem is sought in this one magical thing or type of things. The parallel case of endowing a person with such a magical power—very akin to the addictions—is the symbiotic surrender (and domination) in very regressed, often paranoid (distrustful, suspicious), but not necessarily psychotic patients. On the other, healthier side are those neurotics who externalize all over the place, but do not endow *one* thing (or type of thing) with any of this exclusive, magical power.

But aren't we suddenly placing the main emphasis on the symbolic meaning of the drug (as an external problem solver) and forgetting about the direct pharmacologic, psychotropic effect as the crucial impact of the drug? Is there not a contradiction: on the one side I have said the drug effect is really what matters psychodynamically; on the other side I say now it is externalization by use of a magically powerful thing? The solution to this quandary lies in the fact that the effect of the drug is indeed still extrinsic to the flow of the inner process (see Gray 1973). The "magical self-control" is really not exerted and attained by the person ("the ego"), but by an external agent introduced into the mind. The crucial wish is still: "I want to ward off, deny, split off, rage, shame, boredom, etc., with the effect of the drug which I can procure only from the outside—not with the help of my inner resources." Thus the reliance on the pharmacologic effect is still identical with the defense by externalization in the form of the magically powerful substance. Kazin (1976) put this dynamic fact excellently: "the addict to alcohol, like the addict to anything else, believes that he can will a change within himself by ingesting some material substance. Like so many of the things we do to ourselves in this pill-happy culture, drinking is a form of technology.... Drinking cuts the connections that keep us anxious" (1976, p. 45).

It is also blatantly obvious that externalization is thus not solely a defense mechanism, but also a wish fulfillment, above all the wish for magical power, the subcategory of narcissism stressed earlier—and so again a compromise formation. Still this leaves out another typical feature of the compulsive drug user: his "unreliability." Perhaps the key may be found once more in the same "mechanism," the defense by externalization, although it would clearly be a different mode.

EXTERNALIZATION BY DECEPTION AND UNRELIABILITY

The deep meaning of lying, conning, manipulating, of not showing up for appointments (a particularly distressing and disastrous obstacle on the road to attempt psychotherapy), in short of the general unreliability, is not yet fully clear to me, although I suspect that it is also another expression of the pervasive lability cited above. It clearly antedates the drug use, is independent from it, and is multidetermined.

As we shall note, there is not a "lack of superego," but a very archaic, external, splintered, strongly shame-oriented bundle of massive superego fears, commands and ideals. But there are many patients around with such forms of superego without showing this propensity for lying and evading.

Then there is the problem of narcissistic power: other people are made into things, are dehumanized by manipulation and conniving; an exhilarating sense of self-importance, of narcissistic grandeur and independence ensues.

The not showing up is almost like a disdainful signal: "I do not need you. You wait for me while I have my fun. Once I waited in vain for a meaningful other person, I am not fooled a second time. You mean nothing to me." The subsequent threats—by physician, court, etc.— trying to establish the "structure," feed into the vicious cycle of the patient's rebellion and invited retaliation from the outside—and thus into a lifelong power struggle: the more retribution, the more need for magical power.

There is yet another side to the mendacity: much lying by commission and omission is done out of shame, i.e., to preserve the self-esteem, to avoid criticism, and disapproval, even to prove to the therapist that the patient is not sick at all, has no problems, is in control of the situation, and thus defeats the therapist's intent and claim. "I am well; I do not need you. I am in control of the situation. What temerity on your part to declare me in need of treatment?"

Still deeper is another aspect of narcissism, expressed in this syndrome of lying and general unreliability: It is the split within congnition, between rational, secondary process insight into truth, and the fantasy, the irrational, primary process command: "I dictate that what was false be true. Truth is what *I* declare to be correct." It is indeed, as indicated at another place, a real rending of the ego, similar to the one described by Freud in fetishism though it appears of pregenital, far more archaic, truly narcissistic nature—very close to the "double registry" *(doppelte Buchfuehrung)* of schizophrenics. Again this ego split is lived out all over the place: it is externalized.

THE NATURE OF EXTERNALIZATION

Most analytic authors equate externalization with projection: e.g., the glossary by Moore and Fine (1968): "A term used to refer in general to the tendency to project into the external world one's instinctual wishes, conflicts, moods, and ways of thinking (cognitive styles)...."

Rapaport (1952) opposes the defense mechanism of projection to externalization as projection in a very broad and nondefensive sense: "the organization of perception and production in terms of intrapsychic organizing principles," forming a continuum or hierarchy of externalizations and including the expression of strains and stresses.

Eissler (1950) did not use the term, but described the process in regard to delinquents:

> The delinquent's deficiency in developing awareness of internal processes, his constant preoccupation—almost like an addiction—with sectors of external reality, his inability to tear himself away from external reality and to direct his attention towards himself, make me believe that genetically part of his psychopathology is rooted in that early transition period between the time when the child was mainly occupied in taking possession of reality and the time when he discovered his own ego. [p. 113]

I employed the notion in the meaning given to it in great lucidity by Anna Freud (1965):

> Since all children tend to externalize their inner conflicts in the form of battles with the environment, they look for environmental solutions in preference to internal change. When this defense predominates, the child shows total unwillingness to undergo analysis, an attitude which is frequently mistaken for 'negative transference' and (unsuccessfully) interpreted as such. [pp. 35–36]

In the transference, externalizations are "processes in which the person of the analyst is used to represent one or the other part of the patient's personality structure.... The child thus restages his internal (intersystemic) conflicts as external battles with the analyst, a process which provides useful material...." She even states: "In the analysis of drug addicts, the analyst represents at the same time or in quick alternation either the object of the craving, i.e., the drug itself, or an auxiliary ego called upon to help in the fight against the drug" (pp. 41–42).

And most explicitly and beyond the transference situation:

> In the preoedipal, oedipal, and latency periods, this habitual lack of perceptivity for the inner world also serves the child's reluctance to experience any conflict consistently as intrapsychic. This is where

the mechanism of externalization, not only onto the analyst, comes to play. It is well known that many children, after transgressing in one way or another against their own inner standards, escape the resulting guilt feeling by provoking the parents to assume the role of critical or punishing authority, an externalization of conflict with the superego which is responsible for many of the child's otherwise unexplained acts of disobedience. [p. 222]

The crucial emphasis lies in changing internal conflict into external action: "by displacement and externalization, the whole internal battleground is changed into an external one" (p. 223). It presupposes the "denial of the intrapsychic nature of conflict" (p. 224).

Certainly it is very difficult to separate cleanly and clearly externalization from projection. The way how I conceive of the difference is that the emphasis in externalization as a defense lies on action (including and especially provocation), whereas in the case of projection as defense the emphasis is put on emotionally distorted perception. Obviously both very often go hand in glove together.

MODES OF EXTERNALIZATION

We can now look back and distinguish various modes of defensive externalization:

a. by use of a magically powerful, mind altering, especially self-esteem increasing and effect dampening substance or thing
b. by use of another impersonal agent as internal problem solver, like television, gambling, money, food
c. by use of an all-powerful, all-giving personal agent in symbiotic bonds or by fight against a totally evil enemy (here the projections are particularly prominent)
d. by lying, manipulating and evading all personal commitments
e. by transgressing in grandiose "acting out" the limits set by nature and society (in what the Greeks called "Hybris," a specific characteristic of the "tragic character")
f. by provoking retaliation in form of shaming, of angry punishment or of diffuse attack
g. by outright violence: to destroy a symbolic representative of part of oneself, or, as in the just described mode, to bring about punishment

We saw also (h) how very typically affect regression is experienced as a vague, but broadest, all-permeating tension, a drivenness and restlessness, a longing for risk and excitement; action as exciting risk, especially, if forbidden and dangerous, is an attempt to get rid of this almost somatic uneasiness and pressure, felt as primitive "discharge", a breaking out of being closed in and trapped with this undifferentiated, but deeply frightening tension within. (This is perhaps the prototype for all other modes of externalization.)

In all these examples an external conflict situation and action ward off the internal conflict and the archaic overwhelming affects stemming from it. It is a very primitive group of defense modes. Also in all patients, this defense is combined with other defenses, above all—as we saw already—with disjunction, regression and of course most massive denial, often with projection. All compulsive drug users show all or most of the eight modes of externalization described, concomitantly or alternatively.

As a general characteristic of all defensive externalization, we discern its dehumanizing quality. With the defensive use of action, this action itself is relevant, not the needs, qualities, properties of the persons "used", unless these happen to fit totally into this activity serving denial. It is mainly this dehumanizing use of others which strikes us as so infuriating in all "sociopaths."

Another aspect of it has been described again by Eissler (1950): "their tendency to accept only the concrete part of external reality as valid and valuable." He adds that, "the tendency toward concreteness is mainly based on oral fixation and is also the result of the comparative deficiency in the ability to sublimate, which is significant of so many delinquents." This last remark, however, would lead us clearly into the question of predisposition and will be taken up there.

But it is important that this fourth state in our sequence is marked by the predominance of a magical, global form of externalization directed towards impersonal, concrete, dehumanized objects and action for action's sake.

It should be added for clarification that there is, of course, also the broad spectrum of externalizations which have no defense function: it would lead to an absurd solipsism to consider all needs for external action—for work, creativity, object relationships, etc.—as a form of defense and on a par with the eight modes described above.

The crucial difference lies not only in the use of the latter as defense, but in two additional elements accompanying them: aggression and superego split or collapse.

Before we examine these, an important aspect of externalization, in these patients at least, is so obvious that it is almost omitted. The defense of externalization reestablishes the illusion of narcissistic power and control. Most prominently in compulsive amphetamine users, but to an only slightly lesser extent in all toxicomanics we find fulfilled a feverish wish for autonomy, for being in control, an escape from the panicky fear of not being in charge of one's destiny, especially the most ominous "ghosts," the haunting representatives of one's inner life.

And since it is action, frenetic action, it always must perforce use aggression in the service of this narcissism. Externalization is obviously the exact opposite of inhibition: the blocking of the feared and wished action. Thus again this state can be comprehended as a compromise formation.

Aggression

The more I study the material, the more persuaded I become that the just described defense by various forms of externalization needs to be carried by an intense aggressive—outwardly or self-destructive— charge. All eight, nearly interchangeable modes of defensive externalization outlined require intense sadistic or, even far more importantly, masochistic "energies," conscious or unconscious impulses, for their implementation.

In other people there may also be some intensely defensive use of externalization, but one which turns out to be constructive; I believe the difference lies in the lack of intense, native ("deneutralized") aggressive drive components. Such additional modes may underlie compulsive work or, often amazingly, compulsive creativity.

In contrast, all eight modes outlined before emphatically operate destructively. Thus we cannot get around assigning aggression a very important, indispensable role: in the service of externalization, but also of its antecedents: denial and the affects of the narcissistic conflicts, and even far beyond the scheme already outlined.

In going over the cases the reader will himself be able to judge how important the derivatives of aggression in form of affects and direct wishes and actions are: as rage, anger, depression, as impulses to provoke revenge and humiliation, as envy and jealousy, self-degradation and self-devaluation, as direct acts of murderous destruction. We may notice also how the relationship with others, with society, with the therapist, has a very sadistic note, often with a manifest masochistic counterpoint: The incessant wishes to transgress, to exploit, to attack. Thus, as already clear, all the forms of externalization are not simply a defense; they are to an enormous extent a living out of aggression, often even with the declared, conscious intent of letting the other suffer, to take blind revenge, or to destroy the other and society as a whole. The drug use is also in that regard a compromise: most drugs mute aggressive affects, while at the same time their use is in itself an attack, a living out of aggression, towards the outside as well as against the self. And this last points ahead to the superego and its main two affects: shame and guilt. These affects, too, operate with two different forms of aggression, contempt versus hatred.

An altogether different question is: how much do we truly deal here with primary conflicts about aggression, or how far is this aggression secondary to the primary problem of narcissism and the inevitable thwarting of narcissistic demands. Narcissism and aggression are so intimately intertwined (see Kohut 1972, Rochlin 1973, Eissler 1975) that I found it difficult in many cases (drug users as well as other types of patients) to come to convincing clarity myself. It is more of a vicious cycle where one feeds upon the other. One thing I can declare with some conviction: that narcissism in form of narcissistic conflicts appears as a crucial, indispensable, starting element of the vicious circle in specific cause (and predisposition), whereas aggression— though omnipresent—appears to enter as a secondary instrument. There is scant doubt: where we see the horrible traumata, the violence and humiliation these patients typically, but not always suffered as children, are involved in as adolescents, and bring about as adults, we are at times hard pressed if we assign aggression a second place behind narcissistic problems. Still if we listen to the material gained in many thousands of hours of psychotherapy, problems of self-esteem, of wounded pride, of ruthless ambition, of helplessness and hopelessness are like Goethe's metaphor: a "red thread," running unmistakably through and through as leading theme.

In short: generally aggression is narcissistically motivated, but is rooted in most cases in severe, overtly violent traumata throughout all of growing up, in a minority in a more covert atmosphere of extreme narcissistic spoiling and seduction. The defenses employed, with and without drugs, to cope with these massive, varied aggressions, are mostly turning against the self, turning passive into active (of suffered violence), undoing in many forms of magical actions, projection— besides the leading contenders already put in the center: denial, disjunction, and externalization. Repression, as a more advanced form of defense, is conspicuous by its diminutive role.

Split in the Superego

What we find is a split (more than just a conflict), again a functional inner disparity, within the superego, with often most rapid vacillations between acknowledgment and acceptance of some standards and abrupt (conscious and unconscious) denial and disregard of them; I encountered such flipflops in all toxicomanics. A case I shall describe later in this book (The Seeker) will demonstrate the honesty and integrity of a co-worker whose history is filled with evidence of the opposite of these values. Some most intensive amphetamine users (not presented), Andreas, described in particular detail in a separate section (chapter 9), Vautrin (case 8), the glorious and decompensated leader of a program also described in chapter 13—all show this strange phenomenon of even eminent trustworthiness, integrity, reliability, honesty—and, after years, the sudden breach of promise, the blatant criminal violation, lying, betrayal of trust, brazen or subtle. Most frequently it appears that all values have simply collapsed, have become "inoperative"—a global denial of all superego contents— under onslaught of intense narcissistic demands or needs. Here the split is seemingly not within the superego, but between ego interests and the superego as a whole.

In truth, however, some archaic forms of superego functions often remain—usually in the service of narcissism: above all the wish to hide, to conceal out of massive, externalized shame (see Lowenfeld 1976). The trustworthy, honest person does not tolerate his or her humiliation of having engaged impulsively in the breach of confidence, in homosexual acts, in renewed drug taking, and disappears in fright, lies, even deceives himself about what he has done. In short, the split in the superego (again in a phenomenological sense, not in that of a defense mechanism) is that between a relatively reality adjusted, socially conformistic, guilt directed superego part and one which is largely narcissistically oriented, regressive, shame directed.

I suspect too, that one form of this split is also apparent in the few patients whom I have seen in the past in very intensive psychotherapy over arduous years, who have overcome nearly fatal forms of compulsive drug use and become very respected people in their fields, but for whom, despite all possible suggested disguises which would have made them fully unrecognizable to all but themselves and me, their shame was too strong to permit me to publish here even brief excerpts from their past. An archaic, unresolved piece of the shame part of the superego stood tall and strong against the other values they not only professed, but lived in their professions: loyality, scientific interest, a recognition of the clinical and theoretical value of such case illustrations.

To some extent smaller splits, unrecognized, though lived out, probably play a role in most, perhaps all of us; in these patients, however, they are huge, bewildering, embittering, infuriating to those who suddenly are faced with such a flipflop. They make us wonder about our own judgment, let us doubt our own ability to trust anyone ("If I cannot trust him, how can I trust anyone?").

These splits mirror similar somersaults and most radical inconsistencies in the families of these patients, as we shall see later on.

Even here we see complex compromise solutions or at least combinations: the wish to have the protection by an intact conscience inside and the security of self-respect and respect by others on the one side of the ledger, the narcissistic and aggressive gratifications after the collapse of the conscience on the other, replicating both strength and weakness, threat and protection, control and cowardice of the parents (or their substitutes).

It should be added that this is the one factor in the heptad which may be minimal or absent in those forms of compulsive drug use which are socially fully sanctioned (nicotine, much alcohol abuse, drug use legally covered by physicians, possibly in societies where, e.g., opium use is an integral part of social life, as among the Meos in Laos).

Pleasure—Regressive Wish Fulfillment

If we look into the background of these patients, drug use has been in most the last and noisiest series of compromise formations. The components on the side of instinctual drives have proclaimed themselves as loud and insistent participants in their lives for a very, very long time before, just as the defenses have.

This particular side both of the aim of compulsive drug use and also of the predisposition has been studied most extensively during the history, as can be seen in chapter 3 and Appendix A.

ORAL GRATIFICATION

The literature is replete about oral fixation and oral traits in these patients. The very premise "I want what I want when I want it", the demandingness and low frustration tolerance, the use of archaic defenses, especially of denial, externalization, projection, and turning passive into active are telltale signs for such an early (oral) fixation. Often drugs, food, sexual partners are greedily "consummated" and discarded again. Ravenousness towards food ("food addiction") or money were frequently expressed in the cases presented.

VARIOUS LAYERS

As we saw, Wieder and Kaplan (1969) provide us with a balanced and exemplary description. They attempt to correlate psychopathology with drug of choice, and try to see such a correspondence between "preferential mode of conflict solution" and drug effect; with that they balance defensive and wish-fulfilling aspects and correlate the regressive states attained with the drugs with developmental stages as conceptualized by Margaret S. Mahler, although their emphasis lies on the side of the fulfillment of regressive wishes. In detail, they state that the effect of LSD and related drugs "facilitates the fantasy fulfillment of wishes for union, reunion, and fusion with lost or yearned for objects. The regressive ego state achieved is suggestive of the transitional period from autism to symbiosis." Narcotics evoke fantasies of "omnipotence, magical wish fulfillment and self-sufficiency," reminiscent of the "narcissistic regressive phenomenon" during the symbiotic period (here the term *narcissistic* is far narrower than used in the rest of this book). Stimulants provide feelings of magic omnipotence, of heightened self-esteem and denial of passivity, similar to the toddler's "practicing period." Cannabis and alcohol finally "lessen defenses against drive and impulse discharge" of later developmental states.

This correlation of attained gratification with four distinct genetic layers is most impressive and persuasive. Many of my own observations fit well into this genetic grid. Still I keep wondering whether it is not oversimplified: Is not the nature of pleasure gained much more dependent upon severity and qualitative nature of affect-, impulse-, and defense-regression to be coped with than upon the type of drug? And in turn: Is the drug chosen not so much in regard to the depth of these regressions, but the qualitatively different nature of these affects, impulses and the four continua of defenses?

NARCISSISTIC PLEASURE

From all the forms of regressive gratifications attained with the help of all types of drugs, it appears that the increase in self-esteem, the recreation of a regressive narcissistic state of self-satisfaction is the most consistent one. As we saw and shall observe the most important narcissistic gains pertain to the overcoming of boundaries and limits on many levels, in many forms, to the transcending and breaching of the limitations of the self, of the object world, between fantasy and reality, between wishing and action.

This narcissistic pleasure obtained with the help of drugs and other forms of externalization, especially lying and conning, is basically a magical transformation of the self and the world. One form of it is a hiding in a mask of numbness and blindness, almost a magical cloak of invisibility (in the Germanic sagas, the *Tarnkappe*), either not to be seen, or not to see; it is a power of secrecy which we will reencounter later on. A second version appears to be its opposite, but actually only an often concomitant counterpart: the power displayed by fascination and awe, by impressing others, by flamboyance. A third is the power of lying and making the other and oneself believe the lies, the power of the imposter. In Hardy's words it is the "image of an arch-deceiver." A fourth form is: to grow into a giant, to feel like a unique demi-god and to be accepted as a grandiose spectacle, loved and admired by everyone as this totally likeable "charm."

All four (partly overlapping) forms of narcissistic grandiosity and violation of boundaries we encountered most clearly in case 4, Patpet, the Gabber (see also case 6, The Breath of Morpheus, and case 13, Shakran). But alas, in all cases this pleasure ends like the life of Hardy's "Mayor of Casterbridge": "his attempts to replace ambition by love

had been as fully foiled as his ambition itself.... He stood like a dark
ruin, obscured by the shade from his own soul upthrown ."

ARCHAIC OBJECT DEPENDENCY

Up to now, we have examined the eventual psychodynamic role of
the various pharmacological effects of these drugs. There is a further
dynamic implication which is also important and generally known:
"Among the unconscious motivations (in addition to oral gratification
and passive identification with a parent), the need to replace a lost
object seemed to play a very important role" (Dora Hartmann 1969).
Many patients talk about their drug, the paraphernalia and
circumstances surrounding it, with a tenderness usually reserved for a
love partner. Obviously, it is more the object character of the drug
which here assumes a central motivating power, less its pharmacological nature. Actually, the very phrase drug dependency reminds us of
what we are dealing with, namely an archaic passive dependency on an
all-giving, hugely inflated object, as evident in the singleminded
devotedness and frenzy of the chase after the beloved, in the
incorporative greed, the masturbatory and orgastic aspects of the use,
and in the mixture of ecstatic idealization and deprecation vis-à-vis the
drug ("star dust," "blue heavens," "white lady" versus "shit," "scag").
Just recently, one of our patients made the following revealing slip of
tongue (quickly corrected) when he requested his methadone dosage:
"Give me my woman!" The similarity to fetishism (as to the split in the
object image) has been already duely noted and commented upon.

In a deeper sense, all depressant drugs (narcotics, barbiturates,
minor tranquilizers, even in higher doses alcohol) function as a
maternal claustrum, as the fantasized interior of mother, as much as it
is very often extremely feared in conscious life; many patients describe
a lifelong claustrophobia. A particular aspect in this claustrophobia is
the terror of the devouring mother and, far more importantly, the
terror or the patient's own devouring, consuming aggressions. To be
entrapped, enclosed, and to be in a state of blind rage become very
often identical, as if the outer caging left them helplessly exposed to the
uncontrollable inner aggressions: instead of incessant action and
running around they are alone with this inner adversary: rage.

Far beyond the dependency on the drug, there exists a deep passive
dependency on others, often quite impersonal others. S. Rodbell

(personal communication, 1976) describes it: "They are just 'not connected.' They would like to go through life without being hassled; they want to avoid the tasks of life and fear any responsibility. They blame everyone else for their own lack of responsibility. They need a very structured environment besides the 'magic potion' of methadone." This dependency on outer structures (as exemplified, e.g., by the relief felt in jail) is not only a superego defect, not only expression of the general passive dependency on objects, but, as Kohut emphasized, a need to make up on the outside for what they lack in inner structures (1959, p. 476).

At the same time there is, as in other severely disturbed patients, a fear of closeness and intimacy, a turning passive into active: "I want to reject first before I am rejected." Closeness is frightening (the claustrophobia!), and the patient provokes rejection—mainly by his many ways of externalization. Nonhuman structures appear safer than human relations (with their built-in boundary conflicts). The walls of a jail, the invisible walls of a drug, of a program, represent security.

One question remains to be answered in this context: Is this phenomenon of pleasure itself, as all the prior ones, also a compromise solution? Again if we look back to the case material already presented this appears rather likely: On the one side and most obviously we have the gratifications just described. But these gratifications depend upon a continued successful exclusion, elimination, denial of perceptions which do not fit, upon the removal of all limits to narcissistic grandeur, expansion and often open belligerency. In other words the re-establishment of the more or less "purified pleasure ego" (Freud, 1915), regardless of the nature of the drug, is always connected with very archaic forms of defense mechanisms or perhaps precursors of them: ejection, extrusion, negation of all that is unpleasurable, and projection. The split temporarily appears successful between a massively altered, but totally good sense of self, and everything else which does not fit. Thus even here the law of forming a compromise, albeit on a most archaic, most deeply regressed level, holds true.

Summary

When we summarize now the material of this section and ask ourselves, What is now the specific constellation, the final common pathway, immediately preceding acute beginning or resumption of compulsive drug use? What is essential and present every time?—it is the following group of indispensable phenomena:

We noticed the externally precipitated, internally strongly experienced crisis in self-esteem, the severe narcissistic crisis, the collapse of expectations and valuations of the self and of others, and the reactivation of archaic narcissistic conflicts in an acute form. Their contents vary, from one case to another, one time to another, appear isolated or in combination; but the acute precipitation of a conflict about self-esteem, valuation, meaning, in other words of an acute narcissistic conflict remains.

This is followed by affect-regression, a totalization and radicalization of feelings. The narcissistic conflict is either accompanied by overwhelming feelings of anger and rage, of shame and guilt, of boredom and emptiness, of loneliness and depression, or by a vague sense of wanting "excitement," adventure, to feel alive, oneself, awake, not estranged any more, a broad ill-defined tension, and sense of emptiness. This totalization serves at least partly defensive functions.

The third component is the urgent, again acute, need to defend against these overflooding, overbearing affects—above all by denial and dissociation; these two are the major affect defenses, now pharmacogenically supported, because insufficient in their own right. They affect not solely the emotional life and the underlying instinctual drives, mobilized in the crisis (most prominently intense sado-masochistic impulses, often of uncontrollable intensity), but all of reality testing. It manifests itself as an acute, pervasive, and characteristically labile, but very destructive ego split. This splitting up may be of varied severity: as in fetishism a narrow one, more extensive disjunctions and partial fragmentations, or an overall polarization into all-good and all-bad. The combination of denial and splitting very often leads to typical states of depersonalization and derealization, without and with drugs.

The fourth, most specific, most intense component is the use of externalization as defense: "I have to find an external solution for the unbearable internal problem which I do not want to see, cannot cope with, and yet am not able to avoid entirely either. I have several ways of external action: If I cannot find the magical substance, I choose one of the other avenues"—one of the other seven modes described. They are initially interchangeable and typically combined. The crux is: action, "excitement," risk—as a lightening rod for what is mobilized and denied.

This defense by externalization carries intense sadomasochistic impulses with it; very often these aggressive intents are most vehemently repressed and denied, feared to the extreme, and yet palpably and indispensably present.

There is not merely an ego split; there is a characteristic sudden "inoperativeness," a collapse of the superego, and an appearance of much more primitive forms of superego functions, a surprising, abrupt change from more mature, more integrated functioning of conscience, responsibility, ideals, to a much more primitive one, very often even a side by side existence of the two forms of superego. This superego with a suddenly unmasked Janus head is the split in the superego. This sixth constituent, ineluctable part of the specific cause: the acute splitting of the superego (or superego regression) occurs under the onslaught of the urge for externalization, for impetuous, impulsive, seemingly redeeming action to heal the narcissistic wound.

Finally, the end goal is getting "high" or at least finding relief—the euphoria, the regressive pleasure, usually of a combined narcissistic, oral, object-dependent nature, and, as part of the narcissistic fulfillment, a sense of being a cohesive, bounded self again. Furthermore, claustrophilia wins out over claustrophobia.

This is the *heptad of compulsive drug use,* psychoanalytically a series of complex compromise formations, appearing in this order, in this sequence, the next dependent upon the former, a vicious circle of mutual reinforcement and malignancy.

One problem was deferred and needs to be taken up now, although only briefly. The question was raised before in connection with the concept of the pharmacogenic affect defense: May we not be dealing here with a group uniting the major characteristics of neurotic depersonalization, i.e., denial and ego split, and those of the impulse neuroses or "sociopathy," i.e., externalization and superego split? I thought this to be the case but insufficient. A much neglected dynamic constellation can, at least very often, be discovered as exerting a powerful, though typically well disguised effect; that of a severe, largely pregenital phobic neurosis. In most of the case descriptions to be presented, sooner or later pervasive archaic phobias can be detected whose secret effectiveness for symptom and character formation endures. As it is typical, phobias and the entire phobic syndrome are peculiarly shame laden and thus often reveal their centrality only after years in treatment. One may well wonder whether the entire panoply of compulsive drug use, depersonalization, sociopathic acting out and even of the often noticeable depressive and paranoid states are not secondary, mostly regressive constellations defending against the primacy and massivity of such archaic phobic constellations (typically entailing the well known defense "mechanisms" of repression, projection, reversal, displacement, regression and condensation). Such a phobic core state may be particularly easily misperceived as of paranoid nature, because of the common features; distinguishing is the prevalence of undisguised, unrepressed aggression in the latter while anxiety prevails in the phobic state. Especially the case of Andreas (case 19) will allow a more careful study of these problems.

Chapter 7

SPECIFICITY OF NEED FOR

AFFECT DEFENSE AND

CHOICE OF DRUGS

This section will give us a further opportunity to study in depth the material collected and see in practice how applicable the elements of the heptad just outlined are. I shall use few intrusions by theory, but let the material speak for itself, as illustration of what has been postulated hitherto and as deepened later on when we examine the predisposition.

Narcotics Addiction as Compromise Formation

From the primary list of affects narcotics calm above all intense feelings of rage, shame, and loneliness and the pain and anxiety evoked by these overwhelming feelings. These affects are usually derivatives of pervasive conflicts about the limitations of life: rage and shame are reactions to the massive disappointment and disillusionment in regard to their own grandeur; the intolerable sense of loneliness and hurt is the result of a longing for a symbiotic bond with a need-fulfilling, powerful other person who would give in to all demands. Theoretically there are several possibilities of how that pharmacogenic effect comes about: Either the drug increases the thresholds of decompensation from narcissistic conflicts; or it decreases the intensity of these conflicts by elevating the sense of omnipotence and self esteem; or it functions directly as an artificial dampener on overwhelming affects, as denial. Or the effect may consist of all three. I reached the conclusion that the second and third possibility together give us the key to unlock this riddle. The cases presented will show us how and why. Among the four continua of defenses, the avoidance type is particularly enforced by the drugs; those of the dissociation type are very strongly and frighteningly present in the personality, but soothed, covered by the drug of choice. Pleasure consists mostly in vastly increased self-esteem and physical warmth and orgastic union. There is an easy exchange, because of similarity of effects particularly on the defense side, between narcotics, all sedatives and hypnotics, and alcohol.

These effects can be witnessed with particularly striking clarity in patients who are put on methadone maintenance—especially if they are followed in psychotherapy both in periods of abstinence and while on the narcotic. I have seen by now about two dozen such patients in intensive psychotherapy, many of them for a prolonged period (several months to several years). Before I summarize these observations, I would like to present two very characteristic cases—the first unusual only for his articulateness and the outcome, the second very typical.

CASE 9: THE MELANCHOLY PRINCE

In light of this patient's life Hamlet's word about Polonius, "thou wretched, rash, intruding fool," could well lend itself to symbolize for us this unhappy man and his family relations. Reflecting about his own words though, the pseudonym given above appears more justified. I saw him for about one year in intermittent psychotherapy, at least twice a week. He was at the time in his early twenties, from a middle-class background. He had been on narcotics for five years but had also taken barbiturates. Although he had used stimulants and psychedelics, he currently refrained from them: "Under hash I'm thinking about my situation, I am too aware of myself. I am even very afraid of pot: I feel others can look into me then." He is concerned about his isolation from others, which at times approaches feelinglessness: "Nothing fazes me. I cannot give myself—also not in sex. And still—I cannot stand the loneliness either. With methadone" (his main drug of abuse) "I'd flow with it, though still feeling alone." He supported his habits by burglaries (specializing in TV's and tape decks) and was never arrested.

His father died when the patient was nine. The father's brother, who had not been on speaking terms with the father, divorced his own wife, moved in a few years later, and married the patient's mother. "I hate him, and I am afraid of him. He wanted to impose discipline, for instance by sending me away to camp and military school." He had absolutely no memories of his own father, who, in contrast to the stepfather, had been rather unsuccessful. It was actually his mother who had talked his father into not seeing his brother. She thought he had stolen money from her." She is very weird. She has but two ways of talking to me: either it's a demand-question or a command-statement. One is either the best for her, Jesus in person—or a devil. When I was overseas, I felt at ease talking with strangers—without dope, but I am so uptight around her. Now it drives me crazy to be with people, but when I am not with them, I am lonely and depressed." He saw everyone as being superior to him; he was on the stone bottom. "They had the answers, I did not. Now I hit back, tear the masks off their faces. The same with mother: for so long I felt weak, inferior, afraid, and she was strong and knew all the answers. But in a way I now do the same as she does: Everything in my life has to have its peak. I cannot accept things for what they are. The actual happening is a let down compared to the anticipation." It is this feeling of disillusionment which he tries to relieve: "It seems then as if all of life comes down on me—in a sense of total despair. Then my first reaction is to get me some dope—not to forget, but to put me farther away from the loneliness and estrangement and emptiness. I still feel empty and lonely, when I am on dope, but it does not seem to matter as much. All is foggy then and mixed up."

Thus heroin was for him a cure of disillusionment by explicit derealization and depersonalization. He goes so far to say: "Heroin saved my life. I would have jumped out of the window—I felt so lonely." Besides this use as affect defense, he wants to recreate in the drug use the feeling of full acceptance and union, a fantasy whose reality he postulates in early childhood: "I was given everything. My parents were my protectors. Later I realized I did not have them any more: no protector, no shield—only myself. In this world you need a shield. Everybody needs it." Whatever is not complete union, he takes as rejection and abandonment; whatever is not total fulfillment, he takes as bitter disappointment. Whenever he is not the greatest and best himself, ' e feels abysmal shame. "Everyday is the crisis of my life; everything may have a critical bearing for the rest of my life. Then with dope: it becomes very irrelevant, my mother's expectations, my own fears—all look minor." Thus life is a constant flight from disappointment or feared disappointment, from expectation and aspiration, from emptiness, loneliness and anger, a flight into numbness, boredom, and detachment, eventually into a narcotics-induced "optimism" and abolition of superego pressures. His family life had been an unending chain of arguments. The patient's later childhood and adolescence were filled with violent outbursts of rage, attacks on cars, attempts to run away. "I did it because I was either angry or stone bored." One time, about 6 years ago, he threw the old stepfather against the wall and grabbed him at the throat until the old man went down. "I grit my teeth even now; but it's not worth killing him and going to jail."

He felt he was like a prince with mother: "She has given me everything I wanted, and now I expect the world to do the same. But she also has expected the ultimate from me. I let her down, I let myself down in all what I do. So she bugs me all the time. She does not get along with anyone." She had paid a lot of money to get him out of legal problems, into the Army reserves instead of the war, etc.

His drug use had started when he had been dropped, after one and a half years, by his girlfriend while he was in the service—the narcissistic crisis. "She called me too possessive. I had built her up in my fantasies. I felt so let down. It was like mother's remarriage. The past is like a friend who has died; I dream about it. That is what the future always is: the past. It is the sadism of Nature: to give us the power to remember, but not to experience again. The past was security and protection. The world is cold. No matter how beautiful it is, how I fantasize and daydream: it is very cold. I wanted the girlfriend to treat me like a very little kid; I wanted and needed her, but even in intercourse I felt: I was still thrown back upon myself, always by myself, alone. That flipped me out. It was a let down; I could not accept for her being her and me being me. It was insane! I needed her so much, like a little kid. I pushed her away and wanted her back everyday. I am not able to dig this separateness. When I don't have complete control I feel rejected. I am just like my mother. Then the dope comes into my body; it is like oneness, flowing in my body. You are never rejected by dope." The phobic quality of human relations, as traced back to the image of an aggressive, smothering, castrating mother, became clearer; he remembered terror of witches as a child, when he was by himself in darkness. "When eleven or twelve I felt ashamed of admitting my anxiety of being by myself. But at night—and even still later, while in the military—I had nightmares, jumped up and would crawl in a corner." In dreams and reality he feared to be closed in and tried to flee, then saw himself followed by enemies and driven into a corner. Or he was hit by a group and could not hit back. This maternal claustrum, so much part of all depersonalization (see Slap 1974), is both extremely dreaded and desired. But so are separation, structure, discipline.

"Mother put me in a summer camp as a kid. I forced them to send me home by going out at midnight to the loudspeaker and calling through the whole camp: Fuck you!"

Rage remained one of the huge problems—even when he felt sedated and dazed with methadone and while on the program, especially when he suffered injured pride, humiliation, shame. His fantasy was often: "Everybody is looking at me and sees me as inferior. When I gave a speech in class, people were looking at me; their eyes—that was the main thing—that everyone is disillusioned with me. That's projecting: it fits in with my expectations, and their eyes said exactly what I thought." Or: "When things are not under control—when I do not have everything pat in my calendar—I completely fall apart. When things overwhelmed me, I took dope." He pointed to school, tests, competition, to jobs and tensions with superiors—or at home. In society he felt an outsider, someone apart. All of this shows the external, mainly shame-oriented functioning of his superego and of the pervasively phobic character traits.

The crucial role of the "eyes " will be studied in depth later on.

How his pathology was an intricate web of depression and estrangement, covering up for intense claustrophobia (and claustrophilic wishes) and murderous aggression, becomes clearer from the primary data. So does its narcissistic quality.

When starting on methadone, he stated that he felt "more able to tolerate the empty feelings, the sense of letdown without becoming foggy." He still felt a sense of the void, though, and was bored, depressed: "no meaning, no goal, no dreams, no feelings, not even despair." But without medication, he would feel as if he completely fell apart—the deep fragmentation. He resumed his studies, lived an orderly though bored life, neither "chipped" nor stole nor tried to get high on other drugs. After five months he requested gradual withdrawal.

A few days after the request, he came in: "A crazy thing happened with my stepfather. My mother called for dinner while I was in the bathroom; she had to call three times. When I came, his face was red. He jumped up; mother was crying. I flipped out, felt frantic, uptight, tried to control it, wanted to talk him down. He screamed I was taking dope. That was enough! I was furious. My mother defended me. He picked up the phone and came with it at me. I could have killed him, but I caught myself. Mother stepped between us. Then he took up a lamp; I threw the lamp down. I wanted to kill him. I thought he had hit my mother (which turned out to be a diversion maneuver of mother). I threw him against the wall. Then he broke down. The next time I'll throw him out of the window. I am crazy enough to put him away— just like putting a needle in my arm. *I am afraid of my rage.* Seven or eight years ago, when I was still a child, he threw me against the wall; my older brother called the police to protect me. He always called me 'hey, ugly!' He had all these rages. I do not need a father like that, he is nuts. At times my mother had to hide me. I have only one emotion with him over which I have no control: my rage when mother is crying because he hurt her." Eventually he talked it out with his stepfather, and they reconciled themselves once more.

During detoxification his depression at times felt unbearable. He resorted to incessant TV or movie watching as "an emergency escape— an escape from me as I am. When I sit there I forget everything, how time is going by. I keep myself from realizing that I am in the stream. Time is just hot air; when I fought with my stepfather, for a moment I felt, I was living, the depression was less."

Most of the time he felt at best a "hair strand away" from depression and depersonalization. The alternatives were: giving in to most regressive murderous aggression, to turning it against himself as depression, or to denial and splitting in form of depersonalization. TV addiction functioned, like the drugs, to foster the third option. He saw in methadone just a crutch—in itself yet another cause of shame and dependency. Thus he insisted on going all the way (to abstinence) while continuing psychotherapy. He yearned for a regular life—defying the overwhelming anxiety. Despite severe depression and estrangement he did not take illicit drugs. Physically he felt alright—except for some insomnia. Sometimes an almost orgastic pleasure of exultation overcame him: "to be so special, to be the exception" (when he was intensely working at night, when everybody else was sleeping, making the best of insomnia and abstinence).

One month after the end of detoxification he felt his inner tension intensely: "That's my whole life: to be bored, angry and depressed. I feel an emptiness, like a big hole in my life; I have no substitute for it." He mentioned how he once came close to killing some addicts whom he suspected of taking advantage of him, of "treating me as an idiot." It was again more the humiliation than the cheating itself. He wanted to "kill time," had a sense of enclosure and entrapment, wanted to travel (again the claustrophobic side!).

Thus he went on vacation "in order not to flip out"—returned three weeks later, got various drugs (barbiturates, heroin, alcohol) immediately and threatened to shoot some relatives and former friends. But the overwhelming feeling was again loneliness. He promptly recompensated when put back on methadone. The violent rage disappeared within one day. He compared the two states, off and on narcotics: "Methadone has kept me from a showdown with myself—from the dilemma either to destroy myself completely or to move in a new direction without the aid of anything. When I stop methadone, I cannot put up with my frustration. I get frantic about every problem. I face the reality that I need people, and it hits me directly and puts me very uptight. I do not know how to survive the next five minutes, and I cannot function. I let everything hassle me and I blow up over nothing." The narcotic serves as a protection against the fear of loneliness: "I had to face myself again. The main thing is: I have no friends whom to relate to. I am desperate for companionship, and methadone shields me from the realization that I have no companions. Methadone is a house of warmth. When I stepped out of it, I saw how miserable everything was. I clammed up and ran back into the house. I do not like to be back on methadone, but at least I do not feel that superlonely and excluded; I feel more at ease. The difference is: with methadone I can cope with not being with people, but I still cannot be with people. Without it, I am hassled, with it I am bored. I build it as a shield. It is my protector."

Shame—besides rage and loneliness—was the dominant feeling; he viewed it as a disgrace to be back on the program, feeling trapped in his anger, ashamed towards mother and sister, guilty towards his stepfather—just wanting to get out, get away. Drug and program were claustra! He saw himself as very small, inferior, rejected, weak. The shame around mother and sister had strong sexual undercurrents—quite consciously. "This feeling strips me down, makes me feel very bare, especially when I am alone around them." If he killed the stepfather he would have mother all to himself—"that is exactly what I fear." But there was also shame about mother's and stepfather's living together before their marriage. All the while he successfully went through college—while living a Hamlet drama on the inner stage, a most intense, nearly real enactment of the Oedipal fantasy, with the frequent collusion of mother.

About four months later he took an extra dose of methadone and some "speed," decided to get detoxified and terminate the psychotherapy with me: "I was leaning on you. You were a crutch, too. I have to live my own life. I want to do it, no matter how it hurts." Again the breaking out of the claustrum.

I ascribe this abrupt change to a massive disappointment in me (in the "idealizing transference") because at that time I went myself through one of the severe crises (described in chapter 13), one I unfortunately was not able to share with him. I realized too late that this may have been the major reason for his sudden "independence."

Very soon he went back on illegal drugs, was arrested and accepted in another methadone program. Many years later I learned that he had entirely renounced drugs, finished university successfully and was living as a professional in another state.

To look back: Without the drug, this patient was overwhelmed by his intense feelings of loneliness, disillusionment, emptiness and rage; with the drug he still had these feelings but was not overwhelmed by them and felt bored and depersonalized instead. Life seemed a desperate running back and forth between claustrophilia and claustrophobia, regression to mother and flight from mother, being alive, but enraged, and being calmed, but bored and depersonalized.

CASE 10: SEAN

Another case, really only a vignette, a patient I saw once a week or every two weeks for seven months in superficial psychotherapy while he was on a methadone program. He was twenty-five years old at the time of intake, of lower class background.

Again I use his own words: "I started taking drugs when I was fourteen. For three years I was deep into barbiturates and alcohol. I was often heavily intoxicated with drugs or got drunk. I rarely had marijuana or LSD; I did not like them. When I was seventeen, I switched to heroin and later on to dilaudid. It took me two and a half years to get addicted; I did not take it regularly at first. When I began, the drug addicts were looked at as folk heroes in the neighborhood, the addicts against the cops. I discovered that I had an easier time talking with people when I was on narcotics; I could converse freely. I was always extremely shy and had a hard time talking. Heroin took away my inhibitions, I could joke and talk, even make a fool of myself, without feeling ashamed. That was the main reason why I used drugs: *they helped me to overcome my extreme shyness.* Without drugs, I was withdrawn, would stay in the house, did nothing, was moody, had outbursts of *anger.* I was always arguing; I was a headache for my parents. I didn't want to talk to anybody, just to be left alone. Also when firing, I did it alone. Since I am on narcotics, I do not drink anymore. Drug addicts look down on alcoholics, the 'juicers.' Drug addicts are more peaceful. At first I financed my habit by stealing money at a bank where I was a teller; then I had a job at a large drug store and was stealing there. Later and most of it, I stole from a ship for Vietnam. Again often I was a 'runner,' a go-between, bought, carried and sold drugs. Now I work at a newspaper; I do not want to steal and have not done so for a while. Why am I so easily embarra ed? First you have to understand: My mother and I always were very close— whereas my father is an alcoholic and extremely brutal. I was very embarrassed about him. Then my sister was older, and her girlfriends always teased me. People and my family treated her as an adult, me as a baby. Mother even used to introduce me: 'This is the baby'—even when I was 13! Later on, in parochial school, I was poorly dressed, known to be the child of an alcoholic, shunned, not the smartest, not very popular. I got in a lot of fights. Up to now I feel somewhat ashamed about sex—but that is both because the girls might see the 'tracks,' and I usually was impotent due to the drugs. Later on the drug taking was itself a means of being accepted by a group in the area where I live. I also took cocaine and Methedrine, but basically it was a one drug thing for me." He kept returning to the correlation of shyness and taking heroin. Even while on methadone he felt rather "normal" and not beset by embarrassment, although somewhat cut adrift from his usual associations and suspected, as he said, by his former friends to be an undercover agent. Gradually he found new associations, new friends, who were not drug users. "Now at times I am bored and would like to take some drug, alcohol or heroin. I refuse pot: it makes me paranoid and so nervous." Again as in many other instances, he found an "outlet" in music, but, when with his band, shunned even alcohol. Eventually he became abstinent and is now a successful professional.

Here the use of narcotics functioned as an affect defense mainly against shame, to a lesser extent also against anger and aggressive impulses. Again the Oedipal constellation, lived out in reality was remarkable.

Now back to the more general picture with a summary of the observations made in stabilized methadone addiction plus psychotherapy, observations which can be extrapolated to apply to all stabilized addictions to narcotics.

All of the patients on methadone described feelings of loneliness, emptiness, and depression, of meaninglessness and pervasive boredom preceding drug use and following withdrawal. In all of them any disappointment always was massive and triggered very intense feelings of murderous rage and vengefulness, or of profound shame, embarrassment, injured pride, and almost paranoid shyness, or of hurt, rejection and abandonment. As soon as they were put on methadone these feelings of disappointment, rage, shame and hurt were reduced. In a few of them they disappeared altogether; in some they still occurred occasionally, but had a less overwhelming quality. Some of them simply stated the drug made them feel normal and relaxed—implying that they felt those pervasive feeling states to be abnormal, sick, intolerable. Others said it helped them "not to think of the depression." Several stated that they felt bored, but that they preferred this over the overwhelming feelings before.

It was obvious that in none of these patients the underlying inner problems were resolved, but that the dampening of the mood disorder brought about by methadone was experienced as a great relief. Both the resulting boredom and the insufficient relief from the underlying conflicts led most of them to occasional or habitual use of other drugs while on methadone: mainly cocaine, Ritalin, alcohol or Valium (see below).

In fantasies or with the narcotics' help they tried to reestablish an omnipotent position where either their self was grandiose and without limitations, or where the other person ("the archaic self-object" of

Kohut) could be treated as all-giving and was demanded to live up to the highest ideals. As soon as limitations were imposed, very archaic emotions emerged; they were uncontrollable, reminding us much of those in psychotics. Disappointment was the first, but most elusive and transient, rage the most prominent affect. Typically this narcissistic rage was close to murderous or suicidal dimensions. When the ideal self or the ideal world had collapsed, only total devastation remained. Shame was the third, as outcome of the conflict between the limited, disappointing self and the grandiose ideal self. Hurt (loneliness, rejection, abandonment), the fourth basic emotion in these patients, was the outcome of the experience that the other person (mother, father, girlfriend, boyfriend) proved not to be as great and redeeming, as all-giving as expected; the experience that anything short of total union with this person was total isolation and rejection, the shattering of the symbiotic illusion which was sought and often found and confirmed externally and concretely. Many manifested most intense terror about the collapse of these grandiose illusions; however, few put it in words.

The importance of narcotics, including methadone, lay in their effect of reducing or even eliminating these basic five affects.

All patients described states of craving after past or current withdrawal. In all of them, it became more and more obvious that the real content of the craving (after the physiologic symptoms had subsided) consisted precisely in the upsurge of these most disturbing affects. Their craving can be equated to a rapid narcissistic decompensation and the breakthrough of those archaic feelings evoked by a most massive sense of narcissistic frustration. In most, this breakthrough was experienced as fragmentation ("going to pieces, falling apart"). The reinstatement of methadone led to a prompt recompensation.

Addiction to Barbiturates and Other Hypnotics and the Role of Depersonalization

When I survey my notes and also just my memory, a very large number of patients whom I saw also took at one time or another barbiturates and related sedatives rather intensively besides narcotics or other drugs. Then there is a much smaller number of barbiturate addicts who whizzed by in my experience—whom I saw very few times, had hospitalized, was consulted about, but never really got to know. There is only a miniscule number, half a dozen perhaps, whom I treated myself for a significant length of time plus a number whom I supervised residents about, so that I can claim only a very limited knowledge about their pathology.

But one type sticks out as a recurrent constellation which certainly seems only one type, but not *the* type of barbiturate addiction: a woman, late adolescent to middle aged, with severe eating disorders independent of, usually preceding the intensive barbiturate abuse, massive depersonalization and often suicidal depression, brief hallucinatory episodes (independent of barbiturate use), most intense conscious rage and underlying carefully hidden, all-pervasive shame. The latter covers both an overriding demand to be in control, very domineering, and the panicky fear of ever losing control, of appearing weak and exposed. About a decade ago I called this particular syndrome in its extreme and full picture "the shame psychosis" (1968), but it would perhaps better be described as the *archaic* shame *syndrome*, because, though most incapacitating, it rarely and at most only very transiently reaches psychotic proportions. Psychodynamically the central importance lies in very primitive forms of shame: in fears of and unconscious wishes for magically killing or devouring *eyes,* and fascinating by gestures (and generally by all forms of appearance); it symbolically displays the aim of shame: to be turned into stone and to become non-human, to disappear and to become invisible, lastly to be dead and nothing in order to evade humiliation and mortification.

Thus the hypnotics in particular are functioning as "Tarnkappe," deadening, hiding, numbing the self; thus they lend themselves to an enormous deepening of the estrangement syndrome. There is such a deep truth in what Arthur Miller lets Maggie say before her suicide with barbiturates and alcohol: "But Quentin—you should look at me, like I existed or something. Like you used to look—out of your self ... I'm fighting all the time to make you *see*. You're like a little boy, you don't see the knives people hide." Quentin: "I saw your eyes that way— betrayed, screaming that I'd made you feel you didn't exist." And later Maggie: "And you were ashamed of me. Don't lie now! You're still playing God! That's what killed me, Quentin!"

Behind this battle of killing eyes and shame is the conflict of total union and total destruction: "It's that if there is love, it must be limitless; a love not even of persons but blind, blind to insult, blind to the spear in the flesh, like justice blind, like...." And later on, again Quentin: "Something in you has been setting me up for a murder .... Whoever goes to save another person with the lie of limitless love throws a shadow on the face of God ....Always in your own blood-covered name you turn your back."

Still the similarities with the narcotics addicts in regard to the main affects defended against with the help of barbiturates is striking. Basically in both, conflicts about grandiosity, about boundless union and total destruction, rule supreme and lead primarily to rage and shame and often massive depression. Loneliness and feeling hurt, rank closely behind. Even the defenses preferentially used are the same. Since depersonalization, its components and cognate phenomena are particularly prominent in this group of compulsive drug use, this is the place to study them much more in detail.

I shall present three examples, two very sketchy ones (one whom I saw only a few months, another vignette kindly given to me by Dr. A. Wood), and then a patient whom I treated for two and a half years and over five hundred fifty hours most intensively. In her, however, compulsive barbiturate (or any drug) abuse remained a short episode embedded in a history of massive psychopathology.

CASE 11: KATHARINA

An upper class woman in her thirties with severe addiction to barbiturates (1200 mg) and alcohol. From her childhood: an early crippling disease made her fiercely try to cover her weakness, to cling to the pride not to appear flawed and damaged, and to keep up with everyone else. Later great fear of sex and marriage. Throughout adolescence an alternation of greedy devouring of sweets and fasting, followed by severe depressions about being a "greedy pig." There were horrible fights between the parents throughout adolescence. The mother made the patient pretend she, Katharina, was having a nervous breakdown, in order to keep father from leaving with another woman. When this failed the mother accused the girl of having betrayed her because she had visited the father. The father eventually killed himself with alcohol and drugs, and so did a younger brother. The mother's terrible tantrums cast a shadow over all of the patient's life.

Katharina was torn between hatred, pity and disdain towards her mother. Her profound physical and emotional pain and hurt was covered by a rough shell of: "I don't need you; I am strong on my own, desperately strong. I do not want to be trapped by anyone!" An attitude: If "I be waspish, best beware my sting."

She had, unsuccessfully, tried to protect her younger brother who later killed himself, from the agony and anguish of family life, took the worst on herself, periodically stopped eating and became very emaciated.

Underneath a crust of haughty disdain and will to dominate, the patient was very sensitive, creative, but self-depreciating, suffering from a terrible fear of failing and of not being in control. A long chain of severe physical and psychosomatic ailments led to her being put on barbiturates which she then abused for about ten years. She is full of scorn and anger at psychiatry and just "played the game," presenting the front of a cooperative patient, but ridiculing her therapist. She ostensibly used barbiturates and alcohol to "fend off her past from consciousness and her compulsive eating."

It is a fair assumption that the sedatives mainly defended her against intense feelings of weakness, of losing power and control, of being a humiliated, abused, hurt child, and the helpless rage shown in her entire behavior. But the wall of resistance against therapy maintained the double defense so typical for addicts of all stripes: denial of the inner conflicts which tear her apart and externalization.

The similarity with what was observed in the narcotics addicts is striking.

The next case vignette has been kindly contributed by Dr. Antonio Woods from our Department. The case shows with particular clarity some of the points I will work out.

CASE 12: MAYA

Maya was a twenty-nine year old single woman, with a history of compulsive drug use that started at age fourteen.

The patient was the youngest of three children in a low middle class family. There was abundant pathology in all the members, the father being described as a "withdrawn provider" who would become real to the patient only during episodes when he exploded in rage. The mother, a weak, always sick and complaining woman was represented in the patient's memories as never having had physical contact with her, and as always being afraid of her husband. A brother three years older than the patient was suspected to be mentally retarded and lived a solitary life in his parents' house. The sister, a very significant figure in the patient's life, was ten years older than she and represented the opposite characteristics of those in the rest of the family. She was described by the patient as "the strong one in the family," assertive, outgoing, attractive, dominant and very successful in her professional life. She was also partially an external representation of the patient's idealized self; it is significant that the compulsive drug use of Maya started just a few months after this sister became engaged and left the paternal house.

Maya's earliest memory is of being extremely scared of one of her father's rage episodes, and running to her mother for protection. Mother, however, was just as scared as she was, and she was rejected. The father laughed at this, and the patient started running from one to the other looking for comfort, but now both were laughing at her; she felt extremely ashamed, lonely and feared she would die. Other memories depict the patient sitting between her parents on the front seat of their car, while driving to a swimming pool. They didn't talk to each other nor did they look at each other or at her. She looked up at them thinking "who are they?...what am I doing here?...." Throughout childhood until puberty, all the memories, brought back in therapy, talked of fear, loneliness, withdrawal, an almost paranoid shame and also murderous rage which appeared in some of the patient's fantasies. She recalled being at a family party at age seven: "so many people, so much noise ... my sister was not there ... I was so scared, everybody looking at me, I had gorgeous long blonde hair ... I ran to my mother, I wanted to be protected, to be embraced, but she pushed me away ... I ran and ran ... I was so scared and lonely...."

School was an academically successful experience, but also painful and difficult.

At age fourteen, the patient's sister married; and for the first time she started experimenting with drugs, at first with alcohol and marijuana—"Everybody was doing it"—and then minor tranquilizers, barbiturates and other hypnotics. Despite her heavy drug use, she finished high school and had several jobs as a secretary or clerk, which she was able to maintain for periods of several months to one year, when her drug abuse was less intensive. During these working periods the patient would leave the paternal home, only to return when her drug use increased and she had to abandon her employment. Relations with men were always of a masochistic nature. It is important to note that when she developed a close relationship with one man, her drug use decreased until the affair was terminated—always by the man.

At twenty-six, while using barbiturates at a dosis of one gram daily, she had a withdrawal syndrome after having been unable to obtain the drug. She developed delirium and convulsions which required hospitalization at a general hospital. After being discharged she ill-advisedly was placed on Dilantin and Phenobarbital "for the convulsions" and Seconal h.s. for "sleeping problems" by her family physician. She also started seeing a psychiatrist on a very irregular basis; he eventually recommended psychiatric hospitalization after two severe car accidents under the influence of barbiturates and alcohol. She was admitted to the facility where Dr. Wood was a psychiatric resident. Anticonvulsant medication was discontinued, and the patient was detoxified from barbiturates in a period of three weeks. She developed a severe symptomatic depression, and at times she seemed to be at the verge of a psychotic break: "I feel miserable, like being in a hole. There is nothing that I can do. Nobody can. I am ugly, awful ... I want to disappear ... I feel that everybody looks at me ... I don't want them to see me [other patients and staff] ... everything is so confusing. I sit here for days and days ... nothing...." She gradually improved while becoming more deeply engaged in psychotherapy, which can be characterized as a cathartic experience with great release of affect and an incipient development of insight into her relationships, mainly with the members of her family and also into her drug use. A psychological study done one month after her admission stressed the role of denial and self-directed aggressions: "There is a paucity of responses to the Rorschach with a general sense of inertia, and inability to generate much enthusiasm for her own creative responses, and a noticeable lack of commitment to the tasks. When anxiety or emotion was aroused by test stimuli or interview the patient almost automatically became avoidant through the use of *denial* mechanisms or in the refusal to stay with the situation. There appears to be a deeply ingrained character structure in which almost any emotion, whether it be love, affection, sex or anger, will automatically trigger off the denial mechanisms. Maya quickly retreats into a posture of not perceiving the full implications of the situation, physically withdrawing, and emotionally blocking or 'turning off' her feelings. Perhaps her long term addiction to drugs is but the more extreme manifestation of this defensive pattern. Moreover, this appears to be accompanied by an equally ingrained attitude on her part which is generalized to almost every aspect of her life; an attitude of 'what's the use,' 'why try, nothing is worthwhile,' 'I can't do it,' or 'there is no sense in getting involved.' In addition, the patient's situation is even more difficult in that she seems to have also developed a pattern best described as 'cutting off her nose to spite her face.' Here there is a tendency before she even begins a task to tell herself that she is unable to do it. If she should somehow be able to start a project and she is doing an adequate job, thus disproving the initial attitude, she is likely to sabotage her efforts and even destroy what little has been accomplished. Rather than look at what is causing a problem, how an error came about, or what even constituted a failure, Maya will discount the entire effort and thus hinder any resolution of a problem. She then blames herself and turns anger against herself. Thus, her denial and avoidance behaviors not only serve to reduce easily triggered off anxiety responses but also simultaneously act in a self-destructive manner. In brief, such behaviors are utilized in a guilt ridden manner to punish herself and to undercut over and over again any possibility of moving toward a life satisfaction. This also seems true of the impulsive behaviors. Maya seems prone to heedless, apparently meaningless acting out behavior which brings no real pleasure, let alone long-term satisfactions. However, it is our impression that this cannot be attributed to poor impulse control per se. Rather, it is counterphobic in nature and as such becomes part of the tendency to punish or to spite herself. When it is oppositional in nature it can best be understood as 'I'll do this to spite you even though it spites myself."

After six months of hospitalization she was discharged, and started very successfully college level studies. She was in psychotherapy as an outpatient for a period of four months, until she terminated "to dedicate all her energy to school."

Two months later the patient contacted Dr. Woods, expressing her desire of starting psychotherapy again; she complained about feeling "lonely, bored, like dull, a numbness all over. I don't have bad times. I don't suffer, but I seem unable to enjoy anything." Psychotherapy was started again on a biweekly basis, and the feeling of boredom and loneliness was related by the patient as "exactly the same feeling I had before getting into drugs...." (The patient had not used drugs nor medication since she was detoxified during her hospitalization.)

From the beginning of therapy the contrast was striking between what the patient reported to experience in her daily life, i.e., "boredom, numbness, dullness," and her at times overwhelming anxiety which she experienced during the sessions together with memories of loneliness, shame and also rage directed towards her parents and sister.

This rage was also turned against herself: she recalled the long years of her addiction with the severe depressions and self-destructive behavior which motivated her last hospitalization. She recalled a very vivid fantasy which started about age five: "I had a doll or a girl. At times it was almost real for me. She was beautiful, and about my own age. I hated her. I used to beat her and at times kill her. Also everybody else, my parents and sister, used to beat her. I did this to the girl when I was so angry at them [relatives]." Quoting her from another session, where she talked about shame and loneliness and also about her narcissistic disturbance: "I always wanted to be perfect. I can not stand my faults. I hate them. Everything I do is imperfect. Clothes, I have millions. I don't wear them. They are not perfect. They don't fit me at perfection. I think my parents wanted me to be perfect. If I wasn't they laughed at me. They always laughed at me. I was the youngest in the family, and everybody laughed at me. I felt so dumb. Like two inches big...."

Even when her therapy was still at its beginning, it seemed likely that the barbiturates, alcohol and tranquilizers, the drugs mainly used by the patient in the past, acted in its effect as a "pharmacological" defense against these feelings. In the words of the patient: "Barbiturates allowed me to turn people off. I don't feel anything for them. I don't care. I can be with my parents, and I don't get angry, they don't exist. I can be with people, and I don't get nervous and shaky. I can talk to them but I don't care...." Also she elaborated on a fantasy that she had since age twenty-three where she was a twenty-year-old girl, beautiful, perfect, without faults. This perfect woman had a relationship with a man: "He is sadistic. He humiliates her mentally. This is what turns her on." In her fantasy, the couple had no relationship with the world: "They don't care about anybody...everybody else is boring for them. They don't count...."

This fantasy seemed to serve the same purpose as the barbiturates, which made her oblivious to the world and her own feelings.

In sum: throughout her life the patient was torn between grandiose wishes for pefection and abysmal, family supported shame and derision. She had two ways of coping with these feelings of shame, rejection, loneliness and concomitant helpless rage and pain: Either she had to deny the emotional significance of self and world, leading inevitably to a split between engrossing fantasies and far reaching depersonalization and derealization. Or she achieved the same aim with the help of hypnotic drugs, an artificial denial and split, a pharmacogenic syndrome of estrangement. The pseudonym was chosen by the resident; he compared the veil of illusion in Indian philosophy (*maya*) with that in his patient.

The next case will show this process yet more illustratively.

CASE 13: ALEXA

Alexa was twenty when she was admitted for the first time to a psychiatric instituition because of severe anxiety, estrangement and stuporous depression. She was diagnosed as schizophrenic, mainly because of her frozen emotions and complete inability to cope with any tasks of her external life. She usually did not show any fragmentation of thinking but a tendency to concretization and particularly severe inhibition of action and expression. I definitely disagreed and disagree still with this diagnosis.

A few years before, she had been treated in a general hospital with the diagnosis of anorexia nervosa. At that time she had weighed only eighty pounds. Somatic treatment with hormones and tranquilizers had not influenced her anorexia; rather, a "spontaneous remission" intervened in the meantime, so that, at the time of her admission to the psychiatric hospital, she had regained her former weight of 130–140 pounds. Actually, the "remission" had been due to frequent gorging spells which made up for the weight loss due to her anorexia. It became known only passingly that there was a longer period (probably several months) where she was in a continued stupor induced by high doses of barbiturates. Also during her stay in the hospital she at times secretly took sleeping medication.

In the mental hospital she usually sat in her chair, blocked and mute, with a pale, waxy face like a statue. Occasionally she had some contacts with other patients and was apparently much more outgoing and responsive. Treatment with chlorpromazine only increased her symptoms, especially depression and estrangement, with the exception

of the sleeplessness; under anti-depressants (imipramine, chlorpro-
thixene) she started hallucinating. After ten months of hospitalization
and a short time after the beginning of psychotherapy with me she
made a very serious suicidal attempt with two hundred pills of different
sedatives. Intensive psychotherapy, (about five times a week for one to
two hours), lasted for the following two and a half years. There were in
between innumerable phonecalls, usually deep in the night or on
weekends where she called on the verge of killing herself: "I am on the
bank of the river," or "I am under the watertower." Hours were spent
on such magical rescue missions over the phone. In hindsight I am not
sure whether my own acting out of fantasies of omnipotence saved her
life (see Eissler 1950) or were merely signs of inexperience and
ineptness. I am inclined to the latter: other, more rational measures are
possible without such extreme masochistic and heroic acts of being a
savior.

All in all Alexa responded well to the treatment. About half a year
after beginning the therapy, she was discharged from the hospital and
started studying medicine. At last report, many years ago, she had
successfully finished her studies and was doing well.

More details from her past history reveal that her father was a
teacher and the leader of an extremist party. Because of his political
views, he and the whole family were ostracized and despised. His very
remarkable artistic abilities were stymied, as he felt, by the sticky
narrowness of his bourgeois environment; but in reality it is more likely
that they fell victim to his own devouring hatred, directed originally at
his father, but spread out to society in general.

As deeply as he hated his father, he idealized his mother; he revered
her as a saint leading the life of a martyr at the side of her cruel and
alcoholic husband. Yet, he himself was just as cruel and nagging
toward his own wife as his father had been; he humiliated her
constantly. Once, when Alexa was twelve, he attacked his wife with a
chair screaming he wanted to kill her. He adored Alexa as a child, but
hated and despised her when she entered puberty and started making
herself attractive. He derided her dresses and her makeup and forbade
her to join her girlfriends in outings. When she disobeyed some of his
demands he threw dishes at her or refused for weeks to talk to her.
Another very important element, besides this constantly threatening
paranoid rage, was that the father used to walk around in the family
home entirely naked, obviously again protesting in this way against

bourgeois conventions. A similar exhibitionistic practice was followed by her mother. This woman, her mother, made a very rigid, sour, unhappy impression. Although she had been an accomplished pianist, the pursuit of her artistic career had been foiled by her husband's jealousy. She submitted to all his violence and contempt with the attitude of self-sacrifice—"like a beaten dog." Often she cried about her unhappiness in front of the children, but never felt free to express warm feelings towards them except in sudden outbursts of tenderness.

Alexa was the oldest of three children, (the youngest of whom, a girl, became much later, after Alexa's treatment was terminated, overtly psychotic).

Since the age of two (the time her brother was born), Alexa had a severe stool retention so that she continually needed enemas. A pediatrician threatened to cut her belly open! There already was much overt anxiety: when she met a stranger she "turned into a pillar of salt." At the age of four, she discovered her mother's bloody sanitary napkins and hid them, full of shame and rage. The last pregnancy of her mother Alexa explained to herself (then three and a half) as being caused by kissing. She was convinced the abdomen had to be slit open with a knife for delivery. From age five until puberty, she was very scared she would be made pregnant by her father through touching, bathing in the same tub he had used, sitting on the chair her father had sat on, or simply through thoughts; so she avoided his presence scrupulously. Another phobia from early years on was that pigeons and other birds would pick out her eyes.

When she was approximately six, she was seduced by an older boy to undress herself in front of him. Subsequently there were similar episodes of mutual looking and touching of the naked body with some girlfriends. She was convinced her parents would reject her forever if they discovered these games. When they actually did, she was severely scolded and threatened by her mother. Until the time of therapy she remained extremely ashamed for these incidents, as much as they may *seem* paradoxical in view of the parental exhibitionism.

Following a seduction attempt by a stranger when she was seventeen, she became amenorrhoeic; her menstruation returned, very dramatically, only the evening after her first psychotherapy session, three years later.

Before I go over the history of her breakdown, I have to add that Alexa always had been a brilliant, highly gifted youngster. Her fantasy life was very vivid and productive. In school she was outstanding and managed at the age of eighteen to give language courses herself at a highly respected university—this at the same time that she spent her nights on the cold veranda and pressed her grandfather's gun against her temple or running with the head violently against the wall, thus punishing herself for her sexual feelings.

When she was nineteen, while studying in another country, a brief platonic relationship with a boy broke up. She felt deeply rejected and humiliated, lonely and desperate. For a few days she *hallucinated* being choked and persecuted by men. Everything seemed distorted: the buses flat and long, like sardines; the movies showed scattered, disjointed grimaces. After her precipitous flight home she withdrew more and more. Since the objects of her vision seemed remote and blurred, she went to see an opthalmologist. It was then that she doped herself massively with sedatives; depersonalization, depression and anxiety increased to such a degree that she had to be hospitalized.

The depersonalization was prevailing: "All voices come from far away and hurt me. I do not see things right any more; it is like cotton between me and the world. I cannot consciously perceive them anymore. I reject even my own world; it is a chaos. I feel total apathy, no feelings. It is as if all life had ceased. I do not know where I am and whether I exist. I feel I become insane. My will is sick, I hardly can get up. It is a diffuse dreaming without objects." She felt her body as immovable, head and abdomen as swollen, her own hand as far away, strange, frightening. The voices and looks of others were perceived as piercing knives; people were faceless. She felt as if physically crushed by a steamroller. The nurses were seen as gravediggers; she vividly imagined (or hallucinated?), and felt terrified about, her own interment. She had brief hallucinations of intercourse with shapeless men or of flying through beautiful palaces. Death and darkness were of overpowering fascination; hatred and love were intertwined; death meant union and love, and sexual merger was total destruction. Everything else seemed unreal, freakish, phony. She saw how much she had suppressed her own personality in order to please the ambitions of her father whom she adored as well as detested: "All my life I played a role. They branded me as a model student. Everything now seems unessential, played." She felt extremely excluded and despicable. These fears of rejection increased to semi-delusional ideas. It was as if the eyes of her girlfriends hypnotized and persecuted her. Her fright was indescribable; it seemed that the whole community was uniting against her, that something unspeakable was approaching. Horrifying dreams and fantasies, which all through her life, since early childhood, had occurred, now assumed more and more the character of reality; giant ogres with large, staring, punishing eyes, closed in on her; a devouring blaze leaped after her. Her anxiety took on the almost real dream figure of a huge black owl throwing sand in her eyes and slitting her up. In nightmares she was drowning, or dogs attacked her and tore the flesh in pieces from her. She felt herself being dismembered. Eating, gorging herself, remained the only tie binding her to reality and counteracting the overwhelming fears—but only to lead to ever more pervasive self-condemnation. A plate was like a battlefield. She felt extremely ashamed about her gorging.

How dominant her shame in general was is evident from the fact that in therapy it took weeks until she could mention any names of persons or name any feelings beyond those of extreme estrangement and self-condemnation; it was several months until she could express in words any sexual feelings. Many hours she sat in therapy, in stony impenetrable silence, only occasionally whispering: "I do not know what to do." Her shame for her strongly sadistic sexuality was so intense, the fear of rejection and condemnation from the outside and from her conscience were so unbearable that she limited and froze her movements and her speech as if she were a puppet.

She was ashamed of her "electrifying" sexual feelings for her father and for other men, ashamed really for her lack of autonomy and control over her feelings and desire, but also ashamed of and detesting her mother's lack of pride and her state of humiliation, ashamed of her own femininity. In her shame she was convinced that she was to be condemned to an existence of extreme and lasting loneliness.

The conflict between exposure and condemnation was evident in the dream preceding her suicidal attempt. She was paraded in full pomp to a place in front of the cathedral. While her father and all the dignitaries of the town were looking on, she was led to the stake. When the flames rose from the pyre and reached her she felt indescribable bliss and love. The suicidal attempt one day later appeared to her like a wedding, a final, total acceptance, lastly by father, and thus a transcending of the unbearable self-condemnation. Oedipal victory was total union and death in one.

In short, in her symptomatology we met besides the transient compulsion to take sedatives, persistent depersonalization, suicidal depression, gorging expiated by fasting (in a true sense a "food addiction"), panic with persecutory ideas leading to severe motor inhibition, and states of terror culminating in brief periods of stupor and accompanied by something at least nearing hallucinations. This syndrome was quite obviously rooted mainly in oral-sadistic conflicts with a predominance of the factor of shame, conflicts of union, murder and atonement lived out mostly in the field of perception and expression, of looking and being looked at, of magical expressiveness and vanishing.

All symptoms, but estrangement more than all others, expressed these and related conflicts.

Since in very many cases the use of various sedatives and even of narcotics and psychedelics serves precisely the purpose of artificially achieving this state of estrangement, of depersonalization and derealization, it is incumbent on us to give this very important phenomenon more thought, based on experiences not solely with compulsive drug users, but with about a dozen other patients seen in intensive psychotherapy in whom depersonalization reached near-psychotic or psychotic dimensions (see Wurmser 1962, 1966a, b, 1968 b, c, d).

As a starting point, we might use the inner contradiction in this experience, the split between acknowledgement of the perception, "It is true," and the emotional conviction: "It cannot be true; it is not true!" (see Arlow 1966). Our patient said: "It is as if I were living in two worlds." This split between recognition and denial is caused by repressed conflicts involving perceptions of oneself and of the outside world. These leading conflicts are: (1) total union and fusion versus separateness and total isolation; (2) exposure versus contemptuous rejection; and (3) idealized versus devalued identifications.

On all three levels Arlow's statements hold true: "Stated in terms of ego function, this state represents a sudden, dramatic dissociation of two functions of the ego which ordinarily operate in a harmonious and unified fashion.... Expressed in terms of self-representations, depersonalization may be said to constitute a split between the participating self and the observing self. In depersonalization the sense of estrangement applies particularly to the participating self, and there is a concomitant accentuation of the function of the observing self .... Both wish fulfillment and defense contribute to the phenomena of depersonalization and derealization" (1966, pp. 456, 457).

The major difference between his view and mine is that he sees the split due to a broader range of anxieties than the ones specifically tied to the three levels just mentioned, e.g., also castration anxiety and guilty fears. Due to the central role of "observing and being observed" I still believe the common final pathway needs to lie eventually in various forms of shame or at least of perceptual fusion and detachment. Jacobson (1959) focuses mainly on level three, Bradlow (1973) on level two, and Slap (1974) on level one.

The first conflict, union versus separateness, is the broadest and most encompassing, the most diffuse and least specific conflict, representing chiefly some of the most archaic id derivatives. The ego functions, too, assume those archaic global qualities which characterize the warring factions of the basic conflict. The conflict is chiefly an heir of the *oral* or undifferentiated stage.

First we consider the (unconscious and preconscious) denial of the wishes for union. We can put it into words: "The object has not hurt (rejected, left, or overwhelmed) me, I do not need to overpower and destroy it. It is already dead and inanimate, a harmless thing which I can control" (derealization). And similarly the feelings of anguish, rage, and self-destruction evoked by the frustrations of these impulses are muted by the robot-like emptiness: "I do not want total satisfaction, I am not hurt, I do not need to be enraged or guilty. If I am a lifeless thing, nothing can happen to me" (depersonalization). In this connection, the prevention of separation anxiety by denial of the wishes for union seems to me of particular practical importance: "If I am already detached, no separation can hurt me any more." It is as if to say: "I have cut the ties myself; I have isolated myself." And since separation is equated with death: "I am already dead and in the Nothingness—no abandonment can destroy me anymore." And similarly for the outside world: "The object is already distant and unreal; I cannot lose it anymore." This can be viewed as a kind of counter-phobic defense against a symbiotic bond, anticipating and preventing the dread of (passive) abandonment.

Now let us examine the other side—the denial of isolation and separation with the positive aim inherent in this type of estrangement: "If I am away from reality, I am close to the object with whom I want a symbiotic unity. If I destroy the world, I am alone with mother. I am not separated, I am merging and losing myself in her." If the patient (e.g., Maya) degrades reality to a meaningless puppet play, her imagination can assume the role of reality: "I am fused with mother, hidden, veiled," within the claustrum, the glass wall, the caul, the cotton (see Slap 1974).

To summarize this first conflict: Estrangement expresses and veils both drive and defense. This double denial hides both the positive hallucinatory wish fulfillment in the union with loss of the self and the negative hallucinatory wish fulfillment in the total isolation and destruction with loss of the object. These two opposites break through to consciousness in extreme regression (the brief psychotic and dream states), when only global delusions and hallucinations of world redemption with unending gratification and cosmic cataclysm with boundless hatred appear real: the whole rest of reality is covered by detachment. In short, everything that is not total is denied in its *emotional relevance;* it is perceived but not accepted.

Again the barbiturate induced stupor supports both aspects, union and detachment of this first conflict—by denial and partial acknowledgment.

The second and in my opinion central conflict, namely that between perceiving and exposure versus shame anxiety, is essentially the conflict between certain superego functions and id-derivatives. Besides its anal and phallic sources, this conflict, too, has strong oral roots: looking, hearing, as well as self-exposure and self-expression have a devouring quality. The ego follows suit by summarily veiling vast areas of self-and world perception.

The goal inherent in the feeling of shame is: "I do not want to be seen; I want the person that I present to the world to disappear." Or simpler, "I want to be (seen) different than I am." Correspondingly, in depersonalization, the patient indicates: "I am not this, this is someone else, not I."

This "being different" or "being looked at as a different person" is thus a direct fulfillment of the demands of the superego or the expectations of the surroundings inherent in shame. In the context of Alexa's life: "All my life I have held my feelings and fantasies back; I had to force myself in and to hold a mask in front of me; I have bluffed as if I had played in a theater. Everything is played, unreal, just a role." Again the final, most radical aim of shame is to hide, to disappear and eventually to turn into stone, into a lifeless, inanimate statue—and she and many others turned symbolically into this, into lifeless masks, "petrified," like marble.

At the same time, however, part of the underlying, warded-off wish to be seen or to be exposed (on the pyre!) may force its way through: the compulsive self-observation and the frequently resulting ideas of reference constitute one of the cardinal symptoms of the typical state of depersonalization.

We can infer that that part of which the patient is most ashamed appears also as most estranged, as unreal, as lost and dead, whereas the "eye" of the (otherwise hidden) conscience may remain open and unrelentingly staring. In several cases it was clearly the castration shame which was lying at the core of this symptom.

Can we understand derealization also on this level of shame conflicts? One possibility is suggested by several patients' comments: "People do not look real to me. They look as if they did not have eyes or faces. If they were real, they would hurt me by humiliating me." In this form derealization can be seen as the denial of the shame anxiety directed against exhibitionistic wishes.

Its counterpart (in form of the fears underneath the denial) was also described by Alexa: "I cannot tolerate my looking or hearing or touching; I would feel ashamed of it." And: "I feel haunted by the eyes of my friends, eyes which hypnotize and persecute me." The oldest dreams and fears were: "Huge cannibals come with gas masks and trunks who have wide, gaping, murderous eyes—like the disapproving eyes of my mother" (see also the bird phobia). Here it is the perceptual processes which, because of their devouring or exciting quality, are warded off by shame anxiety: "I do not want to see and hear or to be seen and heard" and covered by estrangement. It is evident that repeated watching of the primal scene or the nakedly parading parents burdened all perceptions with unbearable shame.

In short, we see how estrangement (as psychogenic or pharmacotoxically sought symptom) fulfills the aim of shame: It symbolically hides oneself and the world, like a magic hood or magical looks: either one is not seen anymore or one makes the world unreal, invisible. Yet it also reflects the fears connected with these magical actions: that one may turn into lifeless stone or into a non-human creature; and on the other hand, there is the fear of becoming blind. It would lead us too far afield to pursue this line further at this time; I only add that the fear of total abandonment inherent in shame reappears in the symptom in form of the most painful detachment and remoteness.

We may sum up our observations about the correlations between shame conflicts and estrangement as follows: The acceptance of the wish to be recognized appears as: "I am observed by everyone, I am seen as a fake, I am observing myself." Its denial: "I am not visible, I am numb, I am different." Or, "I am not looking and hearing; everything is blurred or far away—there is a curtain between the world and me."

The third, the intra-identificatory conflict, the deep split into devalued and idealized aspects of the identificatory object, involves primarily *ego*-functions of relatively high order of symbolization and differentiation. This conflict with its delimited identifications and counter-identifications appears to originate largely from Oedipal sources. These patients fight against living on borrowed identities.

It is well known that pathological identifications play a decisive role in the genesis of depersonalization (Jacobson 1959). In Alexa's case, the patient tried to achieve such an idealized fantasy identity in long stories which she shared with her brother who was part of the story and the sister who was permitted only to be an outsider. "It became reality for us, it was so persuasive. Every night a dream carriage brought us to a fairy land with an all-good and all-powerful king. We could forget all problems with him. He invited us. We were not asked who we were; we should really not have belonged into that kingdom. We wore different dresses, I had 'souliers à pas de bruits', soundless shoes. I was mother, and my brother was father, but gender played really no role anymore. The king was neither man nor woman."

In reality she complied partly with the ideal her father (whom she also had infinitely adored) harboured of her: to be the very best in all— in school, in propriety, in creativity. As long as she complied with this ideal image, she was accepted by father, admired as perfect and good; but she felt like a robot and despised herself for it. On the other hand, hidden in her, was the "real self"—separated by an abyss from that "ideal self": "I feel that there is a gap between this world which is nice and orderly and calm, and that archaic world with those ugly, horrible, overwhelmingly terrifying, uncanny feelings, visions, and thoughts." Whenever this abyss between the ideal and the real self widened, the feeling of emptiness and meaninglessness, of aloneness and coldness grows. It crystallized into the conviction: "If they really knew me, they would reject and hate me forever."

This conflict between an ideal godlike image and a concealed angry destructive reality actually was her inner replica of the family picture:

copy and response at the same time. There was a facade of highest moral self-righteousness and being the fighter against "the compact majority", for the rights of the opppressed and suffering, a facade with quite overt claims of grandiosity, but also of ruthless honesty. And there was the other side: a virulent rage and resentment, a disappointment which seeped through everything in the tone of voice, the lack of warmth, the punishing glances, the twitching lip and the violent screams and fights. No matter what one did, the certitude of falling short of the expectations remained. What was concealed was this vast stream of silent anger and, even more painfully, of contempt. Each person in the family with whom the girl identified and the family scene as a whole were radically split into an absolutely good family ideal which was demonstrated as a showpiece of perfection, "an idol on a pedestal" with emphasis on appearance to be absolutely good and to suffer for this fight for a dogmatically upheld value, and a totally tabooed and concealed side of angry demands, unfulfilled yearnings for tenderness and trust, and bitter disappointments. It was shameful and guilt provoking to rebel; yet, it was equally shameful to conform and not to be oneself and spontaneous. When she identified with the family ideal, she felt that she was a phony because she submitted to the "family lie." On the other hand, when she angrily tried to break through the stifling mask of compliance, thereby identifying with the hidden rage and yearnings, she saw within herself an ogre, a devouring lion. In both identities, she felt extremely cut-off, isolated, not herself.

Thus, we can see how identification forms a bridge between the as-if of the family and the as-if of the estrangement of our patients. The whole family is permeated by this air of as-if. Everything which does not fit into the family's ideal image of moral rectitude and martyrdom (in other cases, of self-sacrifice and unselfishness) is considered unreal. One has to identify with a standard of insincerity and double communication, with a basic lie and deception which leaves the whole rest of the self out of cognition.

These are not conflicts between identifications with different objects, but the split is within the identification with one and each object, perpetuating the ambivalence of the whole relationship. Quite typically, this intra-identificatory conflict leads to an exaggeration of the ideal into an ethereal image ("counter-identification") (Binswanger 1957), accompanied by a demonization of the hated identification with the devalued aspect of the parent.

On this level the compromise character of depersonalization is again obvious. The fulfillment of identification and unity by similarity is expressed as: "I am not myself, but a puppet of my father. I have no will and identity of my own." Its denial is: "I am not dirty like my parents, I am not feminine like my mother, or angry like my father. I am pure and ascetic, though feelingless" (E. Jacobson, personal communication, 1965).

It is decisive that these three conflicts involve the perceptual processes and this to a various extent. The first and broadest type of conflicts—union versus separateness—affects the basic perception of the boundary between self and world. The shame conflicts are more circumscript and involve in particular visual perception and exposure. The third type, the intra-identificatory conflicts, are still more differentiated: certain character traits or patterns of behavior of oneself are perceived, compared with the ideal, and devalued, disowned, despised.

What is the central theme of these three types of conflict? It is what Murray (1964) called the "narcissistic entitlement," the grandiosity— in form of her demands on others, on herself, and of the demands expressed by the entire family. This narcissistic entitlement can be put into words like: "I want to *have* something special; I want to *be* admirable; and I *have to be* adorable if I want to be accepted by my family."

As another similarly conflicted patient admitted late in therapy: "If I cannot be especially good, I feel I have to be especially bad. And because of my grandiose wishes I can not see people as real—if I saw them I would have to realize how small I really am."

When we started out with the phenomenology of estrangement, we noticed in passing the peculiar "*Aktcharakter der Widersprochenheit*" (Hartmann 1922), the contradictoriness inherent in the act of experience, the split: "It is real" and "It is not real." More specifically, we have the acknowledgment of reality as a perceptual fact; we have the denial of reality as an emotional fact (see S. Freud 1938 a, b, B.D. Lewin 1950, E. Jacobson 1957, S. Altschul 1969, W.A. Stewart 1970, Siegman 1970, Bradlow 1973, Trunnell and Holt 1974). The denial prevents certain emotions which are unconscious from becoming conscious (Stewart 1970, Trunnell and Holt 1974). The affects denied are those accompanying the perceptions and are derived from the three conflicts. Denied are fright and helplessness, rage and all encompassing self-condemnation derived from the conflict of total union versus isolation; they are consciously experienced in the symptom as detachment and deadness, as discontinuity or blurring. The emotions of profoundest disillusionment and mortification, of massive shame and of feeling exposed as unworthy, again are denied. These unconscious derivatives of the shame conflicts emerge into consciousness in the form of the veil, the phoniness and self-consciousness. The denied emotion of being similar to a devalued object appears as being changed and strange.

Underneath this split are the conflicts themselves: Repressed are the conflicts between desires for extreme closeness and those for the development of boundaries between self and surroundings; repressed, in particular, is the role which perceptions and self-expression play in this process of self-delimitation. Repressed are the wishes for self-exposure (exhibition) and incorporation by perceptions and the concomitant shame anxiety. Repressed is the wish and the fear to be like the loved, but degraded object. Repressed, moreover, are all the specific memories connected with these conflicts and their ideational representations.

From this examination of the dynamically double aspect of the symptom of estrangement, symbolizing instinctual drive as well as fear, we have to conclude that depersonalization (pharmacogenic or spontaneous matters little) is not a defense mechanism, but the result of a compromise between partial wish fulfillment and defense mechanisms (denial and repression). It is not the place here to describe how to resolve in therapy the three basic fallacies in the lives of these patients, which we can summarize now into these words: "I have to isolate myself, in order to retain my identity. I have to avoid exposing myself or looking, in order not to be despised and abandoned. I have to conform, in order to be related at all." Nor can I discuss here how we have to go through many crises of silent withdrawal and often suicidal rage in which, gradually and bit for bit, their lives are brought back into human relationships—lives experienced now not as being devoured by others, but lives which are accepted in closeness and trust and thus felt as real again.

The only additional role which the drug plays is the same as the function of food (in the typically concomitant "food addiction"): to seek an external means to achieve this compromise formation. In other words, the crucial, additional factor is defense by externalization.

To summarize the importance hypnotics and sedatives have as affect defense we can state: they help to deny above all pervasive shame anxiety, a general feeling of terror about helplessness and abandonment, and intensive rage and sado-masochistic impulses (fears and wishes); they very often deepen or create massive estrangement.

Compulsive Use of Psychedelics

Psychedelic drugs potently counteract the emotional state of emptiness, boredom and meaninglessness. The drug-induced illusion that the self is mystically boundless and grandiose and that the world becomes endowed with unlimited meaning seems to be a direct antidote to the pervasive sense of disillusionment in the ideal other person and of loneliness. It artificially recreates ideals and values, when they have been irreparably shattered inside and outside. Not only does this illusion outweigh the disillusionment; it resurrects or supports the collapsing defenses against overwhelming shame and against aggressions. It is important that this artificial ideal formation has a peculiarly passive-receptive ring, most like the identification with a hero in a movie or on TV. Indeed, there seems to be a remarkable similarity between the psychedelic experience and the turning on and tuning in to TV; several patients actually compared it with an inner movie.

The wish fulfillment, besides the artificial erection of ideals, lies in admiration and adoration, and in passive surrender, fusion, union, especially through the senses.

Besides this affect defense of denial and the wish fulfillments, especially of idealization, grandiosity, and union, we shall notice the drug enforced deepening of all forms of dissociation and splitting—of self and others, the polarization, the split in personality organization, and, of course, in cognition.

It appears to me that here the intensified mechanisms on the dissociation continuum work particularly strongly against terrifying, mostly repressed aggressions.

Furthermore the mystical tranquility is not only a denial of all the troublesome affects, but also truly an increased reaction formation, in form of gentleness, kindness, passivity, patience, against very intense aggressions. Reaction formation is probably part of the third continuum of defenses (the action-type); however, I am not yet sure whether dissociation, the second type, might not enter into it as well. The case to follow will illustrate this point quite well.

Finally the blurring of all boundaries and limits in the service mainly of magical omnipotence has also deep significance as a defense, a defense by de-differentiation and aggression, working against guilt, shame and separateness, and supporting archaic versions of projection, introjection and idealization.

New boundaries of secret, magical power appear established—but they are fluid, like "writing in water and building in wind," transient, dreamlike, "clouds of secret significance and cosmic meaning."

CASE 14: BOHEMIAN

In the following I present a rather detailed history of the psychotherapy of a compulsive user of psychedelics. This young man, twenty, shaggy, disheveled, dirty in appearance, but with a sweet, gentle smile—when visible behind his long hair—conforming to a style of non-conformity which was quite in vogue at that time, opened his first session of psychotherapy, which was going to last without major interruption and rather intensively (two to three hours a week) for one year, with these words: "I have a general fear in different situations; I feel inhibited. I started two summers ago with drugs, and it changed me; I gained a lot, but I lost also. I have a kind of paranoia because of the drugs—grass, hash, acid, mescaline. Speed I took only during exams. I am looking for new ideas and values. If I can apply these I would have a sense of fulfillment. At times I attained a clearer sight with LSD, despite the fears with it and the warping of perceptions. It showed me the goal I later could strive to reach in straight consciousness. Thus it helped me to recognize a lot about myself; but when I am not true to myself—and that is most of the time—I feel guilty and depressed, because I am not how I want to be." Not only did he doubt himself—while fighting off the ridicule from brother and friends—but he was "down on the ills of society, very down on the emphasis on money and success" (his parents were successful business people). "I am very critical of everything. Acid changes that: I think more about good things instead of criticizing, about the spiritual, mystical values: If I do not love myself, I do not love the others. Thus I try to appreciate myself while I take acid."

Without drugs he felt in isolation, found it hard to talk to people, was very self-conscious, open to ridicule, while with drugs his thoughts scattered: "My thoughts are all over the place; I have no place to run and to hide, to crawl into a hole. But still things are then very relevant, and when I come out of the drug state, I just cannot engage in irrelevant conversations. Nothing comes to mind to say, and then I feel very uneasy that I am unable to talk. What I feel—my union with others—I just cannot put in words. I have 'vibes,' and I don't need words; they are only symbols anyway. My problem is in talking: to rap with people— whereas I *feel* all this. And I am uptight because of the silence."

So he sought help because of the superficial embarrassment and shame about not talking, but felt that psychedelic experience had helped him adequately and appropriately to broach his deeper problem, namely to come to his true self, to his true feelings, which were ideal, beautiful, good, never disappointing if they were just retained in continued consciousness without drugs: "But then I am often not true to myself or am obnoxious to others, and I don't know why. And this gives me guilt." He referred to counterattacks when ridiculed or when disappointed by the cynicism and dogmatism of a close friend or his brother: "I feel let down; he deflated the little bit of ego that I had."

His main interest and "material tangible work" was rock music: "There I get very good 'vibes.' Even without drugs I had spiritual feelings. The others are not playing ego games there, they are honest like little kids. Now I am insecure, self-conscious, at a loss for words with you. I feel: if I do sow, I shall reap. The goodness wells up in me, and I can give and take—the 'vibes,' an ecstasy in the rhythm. I lost my self-consciousness; I could pop out of myself, out of the ego games. Now it's sorrow that life is not all this spiritual pleasure, to be all good." He opposed the evil, greedy, hostile, material world to the spiritual, immortal, good world of God and universal truths: "I am longing to return to where I came from: the ether, heaven. I have read: 'The best thought is no thought. In not knowing you know!'" He referred to the Buddhist and Hindu concept of "Avidya," of "not knowing," which historically actually had very antithetical valuations.

This concept took on a critical significance in his life: "I am not sure whether people outside, the whole external world, really exist." His psychological brooding was an intellectual version of annihilating people and world. We shall see later how this Yoga concept served itself as a veil for a deep conflict from his childhood.

His drug taking was preceded by disappointments in emotional and physical intimacy. "In high school we got hold of a prostitute; it was a 'gang bang,' thirty standing in line for one girl, five dollars for five minutes. It was a status thing, a knock game, to put people down. I was afraid of impotence. And I was impotent. A little later I had a girl friend. I wanted her to respond to my feelings, to me—but she didn't show her feelings; she was not giving of herself. She looked at me as a knight in white armor, but found me immature and unsure of myself. I was, and I am. We measured each other by our expectations." The relationship broke up in painful mutual disillusionment. He remained very frightened of sex and was often impotent. So the lofty ideals could be considered a regressive flight from the challenge and fright of sex, which he was "scared to death" of. In his more general shame: "It is a complete loss of self, of identity. I doubt myself totally and lose all sense of acting in a natural way" (after "coming down" from hash). "These downs destroy what the drug has built up: to be superior, to see you as superior. When the doubts start, I am spiraling down."

He talked about a religious neighbor who always gave him "a spiritual uplifting" and whom he admired and felt in an instant "union and communication" with: "I would speak about LSD, and she about Jesus. For me the two came together in the same mystical experience." He was profoundly attracted by Eastern religions. Every session he talked about seeking to transcend self-consciousness, doubt, self-centeredness and lack of faith in spiritual values. External reality, like school, family, the impounding of his car, (he failed to get tags), appeared irrelevant: "I am not disciplined about external technical things because I am so concerned about my inner reality." So external life with its requirements and limitations "slaps me in the face" (the same about sessions with me: often he was one or two hours early or late!). A first glimpse of the family reality: "Mother puts great emphasis on accomplishing things, not just in regard to money, but just on doing something—in external reality." This was the first detail about his parents—after one month of psychotherapy! And only two months into therapy some relevant aspects of the past emerged: that his vicious cycle of fear and shame, of self-doubt and ruminating, had started much earlier, that at age twelve he saw a psychiatrist because of a number of severe compulsions: "I was putting pencils pointing at me away and separating them evenly, as if they were guns or knives. Or when a book was lying over the edge of the table, I put it right; it was as if the edge were cutting it. Shoes had to be parallel. Or I 'regurgitated' the number seven—the same number as there are people in the family; I had to touch or brush everything seven times." This was accompanied with obsessive fantasies about the death of father, mother, or of one of the siblings, accompanied by severe guilt. He still had some of these "habits" (while he talked about this he kept smacking his lips); because of this "analyzing and doubting compulsion" he had problems studying; he added that the same symptom, in form of a compulsion to ask "what?," went back far into childhood and had been annoying to his mother. How much better indeed were "these ideals which I have for the immediate presence; I experience these ideals with 'acid': love, truth and honesty; they are so tremendously fulfilling"—in contrast to digging into the past, to working in psychotherapy, where he had to face up, e.g., to his passive submission to a most unnecessary advice of his brother to forge a signature and thus to his stumbling into all the ugly consequences of a serious law violation! The drug served the denial of external humiliating, disappointing, limited reality as well as the denial of his deeper problems: the conflicts about aggression and disappointment, mainly vis-à-vis his angry, ridiculing, aloof father and his equally un-ideal, unfeeling, at times rather sadistic brother. At the same time it helped him to flee from his deep sense of degradation, loneliness and alienation ("who am I?") into "unification," the "good vibes," "telepathic communication," the "reality of God," into a state of union and ideality. Fortified by these idealizations he was enabled to break out of his oppressive silence and the "agony of estrangement." A sequence emerged, true both for relationships with people and for the drug experience: "First I am high, see all of the beautiful things of love and union come true. Once I've gotten into it, my high does not stay. Then comes all this anxiety, and I back away. And I end up again very inhibited, lonely, and alienated, unable to rap, very self-conscious." (He referred to both boys and girls.) Of course no jealousy was permitted in his life—about his "ideal love" partner living with another man—"to feel jealous would mean to be possessive and selfish; that would be *my* hang-up, just part of my insecurity." As it is of course typical for obsessive-compulsive neurotics we find a whole array of reaction formations: instead of being murderously aggressive or at least angry, he was passive-submissive and brooding within himself (with his brother: "I was submissive so he would not beat me"); instead of feeling jealous and sexually possessive, he retreated into a state of ideal bliss, love, union and unselfishness; while being beset with the feeling of embarrassment and being ridiculed and laughed at, he did not realize how much his entire attire, his grubby, unkempt, neglected, shabby, often smelly appearance was (unconsciously) a defiant, rebellious invitation of scorn and anger (denied by the rationalization: "It is hypocrisy to judge people from what they look like"—of course! But one thinks of Romeo's "Hang up philosophy!"). And last, but not least: he had to observe (and humiliate) himself incessantly as a reaction formation against wanting to observe and humble others (probably originally his haughty, grand older brothers and father, and, on a deeper level, inferentially, perhaps the primal scene and thus the origin of the repeated pregnancies of mother.)

All forms of aggression and reaction formation were mirrored in a haunting conscience, a constant sense of guilt and shame, which was then externalized (e.g., in his bungling of a minor legal matter or "getting on the nerves of the parents") to bring about the condemnation of all sorts from the outside.

In his first dream in therapy, about two months after the beginning: "It was a fight of two groups. I had a sword. I plunged it in one of the enemies. But then the people on my side ridiculed me, condemned me and decided to hang me. I tried to appeal to their sympathy. I was not hanged."

All these insights, achieved within about ten weeks, brought about a general sense of freedom, of being able to talk and even to elicit a friendly, happy response from his rigidly constrained father, and a vast reduction of the need to use drugs. This sequence in its simplest form was: (1) I am angry at father; (2) I feel guilty; (3) father is angry at me; (4) I do something to be punished by him (and an entirely parallel sequence of ridiculing and shame). Only the end result of these repressed conflicts: feeling inhibited, blocked, excluded, above all very empty, was overcome with the psychedelics; ideals, Love and Strength (almost concrete personalized entities), filled out the gaping emptiness and shame- and guilt-laden loneliness and weakness; they endowed him with meaning and reality, where estrangement and depersonalization had taken over: "I feel so free, so intensely conscious that there is a place where there are no problems, where I can realize my full potentiality and appreciate myself. I feel so strong and can be my own man."

And yet, as always, it is a pseudo-solution—bought with more depersonalization and social isolation, with a sense of "confusion", expressing the permeating shame anxiety and guilty fears, and leading back to the need to be beaten and hooted out by laughter.

"When I am tripping, often others appear as robots. Then to provoke at least means to relate"; so anger provides another exit from isolation, instead of the drug induced union! But again this "inner demon" has forcibly to be moved into the background by the "drug high": "On LSD I can laugh at him and my own suffering and ridiculousness—as if it were someone else." Thus "tripping" equaled a depersonalization both of a haunting superego and the everyday self and a deepening of the split between both.

Aggression of any kind was denied and condemned as a selfish, vain search for glory and praise (here a superficial version of narcissism was clearly used as a form of denial in the service of defending against rage): "I do it only for my ego." On a deeper level, however, he was undoubtedly right as to the narcissistic meaning of his anger, e.g., in a childhood dream, he was fighting his older brother, who was just laughing at him. "I punched him, but nothing happened, it was like jello." As an eight year old he actually wanted to kill the big brother with a can opener, after the older one had spit at him. There was still an enormous amount of narcissistic rage about his own smallness, timidity, weakness and frustration, in front of his laughing, older brother or his replicas in roommates. Verbal and physical fighting—just like the drug—counteracted philosophically embellished pervasive depersonalization which he called "skepticism": that he himself and the world were worthless, condemned, nothing.

With the unfolding of all these connections, he indeed was freer to be aggressive and thus felt much better, abstained from drugs, and was able to overcome his fear of an emotionally and physically intimate relationship with a girl.

The transference shame which had at the beginning made it almost impossible to talk with me had nearly completely vanished; he felt only rarely exposed, watched and inadequate anymore, when with me. He found it hard, but necessary to accept that he could not maintain the "highest level of power" which he sensed when "tripping," but that there were "lows." "At least I can strive for the high level; there is a constructive way in confronting the weakness instead of escaping from it. Still I am so drawn to the perfection, and I hate and detest myself for all my fears."

When describing the sense of omnipotence and invincibility with LSD he suddenly remembered: "That's exactly how I felt when I was four or five: that I was God, and all the others were just catering to me. And if people were hurting me, it was all a big plan. I was like Christ. I felt all eyes were centered on me, adoring me as king, and they were my servants. On acid I am like an uncorrupted fresh kid—strong, admired, yet not using my power." The fall from this greatness most naturally must have led to abysmal and continuous shame, while the very idea of grandiosity, to be in the center of the world evoked profoundest guilt; it is so counter to his conscious yearning for love, unselfishness, and union. He now got very angry at me: "My entire inner search for all the things truthful is all being disillusioned. If that is so—where do I turn?" Every relationship was seen either "as admiration or bullshit." With tears he recognized that his whole pride in his own humility, of "not being on the same tremendous ego trip like everyone else," was itself a continuation of this wish for admiration. In his ecstatic dancing, while on LSD, he felt hit from behind on his head by a revelation: that the rest of life was a mere playing of foolish games; he suddenly felt one with God and with other people. "You are right; it is mutual admiration, that we are all superstars; but it is glorious!" He felt very conflicted and furious at me: "It shook my foundations. All my own questioning suddenly seems to be only a clothing for the fact that it is all a search for admiration. No—I want to love. The admiration is exactly what I am fighting against." He feared his own insight and memory, quoted back to him by me, as a supreme threat to all his beliefs and ideals. He was torn by a tremendous conflict between emerging wishes to be strong, invulnerable, perfect, and his ideals of love and union, a conflict leading to the massive fear of the "watching eyes" who were seeing him as weak, exposed, and hurt. "This is now my main conflict: wanting to go toward this goal of having no limitations, and the other side which has been introduced in the last two months: that I do have limitations." (This was four and a half months into therapy.)

He dealt with the conflict by studying more Yoga and the Tibetan Book of the Dead. "I am not tripping anymore: I am searching the oneness by other means, by meditation." He was disappointed in me: that I could not with magic words relieve him totally of his "inhibitedness," his hurt, without also confronting him with his human limitations. Gradually he recognized his constant need for idealization of himself and others, and how the drugs (and Eastern mysticism) protected him against disappointment and disillusionment; but he was very angry about this recognition and wavered back and forth between acknowledgment and denial: "My anger defends the ideal; I have to defend it with passion. When I trip my ideal is clear: to be free—to be strong and capable—or completely loving, passive, not angry."

He started questioning the hypocrisy in all religions, the outer humility of Jesus and Gandhi and their inner arrogance, compared it with his own secret arrogance in his spirituality and wish for perfection.

He still used "speed" to get through exams and suffered from depression when he "crashed" afterwards, felt also ashamed about his boisterousness and talkativeness during the "speed-high." A new round followed: disappointment about the childishness of his girlfriend, then feeling humiliated himself, disgusted about her and himself, anxious, depressed, sad about the transience of fulfilling his highest potential in music and sex—but no drugs! "It is so painful that the sexual union does not last. It got me down. And I am ashamed that I had to resort to sex to maintain this closeness." He could not love a girl with her weaknesses and faults; the idealization of the other person turned rapidly into disgust, then anger, then depression, and guilt about his negative feelings. And again the painful, angering facing of limitations to the ideals! Anew, music and meditation provided him "with the magical connection" and carried him over the gloom about her problems; but then he also considered Western philosophy, felt attracted and repelled by a friend's Socratic "elenchus" (proof or refutation), compared it with my method of treatment, the relentless questioning. (This was about five months into treatment.) He felt far more rational, disciplined, orderly, recognized his own jealousy and anger, even sadistic feelings, rejected his regressed, drug-using girlfriend, perceiving in his initial idealization of her the deeper wish "of looking for my mother who always unconditionally accepts me." He had always been close to her, yet far from father. Being alone again he felt like after "dope": exposed and looked into, full of shame, tongue tied. "Dope had opened up my repressed shame." Again the recurrent childhood dream: "I was the center of the world," but with the important addition: "My mother made me feel like the center. She fulfilled all my wishes and demands. And then I was angry—as now with the girlfriend—when she couldn't gratify me anymore. Then I squeezed my dog almost to death." Memories of temper tantrums, past and present, became accessible—despite the shame. For the first time—after an earlier cautious inquiry by me—he listened to classical music—and felt "high," "my head expanding"—without drugs: "I was flowing along with it, the whole range of feelings. I got into the harmony; I could feel every note almost physically." He compared it with "trips" and mantras in meditation: "to return to the source, to the creative intelligence." It was another idealization (tied to me). Music and speed (before tests) gave him "flashbacks" of the trips: distortions, strange colors and fears of a "confused bummer state." Despite that, he felt very good and powerful, combining the insights gained in psychotherapy with those in meditation. Still: "Acid was for me the real reality"—more than these insights which have given him, though, "a sense of control over my actions." He felt he had overcome with this his problems of shame and inhibition; in a fight with friends his rage became very conscious, though under control, after having been covered up for so long; he compared it with the helpless, demoralized rage toward his brother, the latter's tormenting and ridiculing, "you can't do anything," his own hurt and crying as a child. Using more "speed" he lost some of the controls again, stayed up all night, came to therapy with a huge ice cone, soiling the chair with its drippings, feeling chaotic and irritable—but caught himself again. The reason: the anxiety about a new relationship with a girl, again shame, not feeling to be masculine enough for her.

He reminisced about the "mirror experiences" while tripping: "When I was tripping my 'roles' appeared so very much magnified. I watched myself in the mirror as if it were a different person. I had a kind of silent dialogue: 'You are playing games, you little bastard. I caught you.' It was just funny. 'Whom are you fooling?' I gave an insane laugh. I had a fun time with myself looking at these games. I do not have that with grass or hash; with that, you totally lose control, the mind speeds up, it's like fainting. I do not like it (in contrast to LSD). Acid opens up so clearly the dichotomy between your outer presentation and your inner self. I can notice and laugh at my self-consciousness. It is like seeing a monkey in the cage who bites himself!" He clearly described various levels of splitting.

But he stayed completely off drugs, felt at times depersonalized, but regained inner control, worked hard in his studies (ancient cultures), though still struggling with omnipotence (disregarding any fatigue), felt a deep split between the goals of meditation ("cosmic conscious-ness, getting into God") and our psychotherapy ("accepting limitations and boundaries"). More and more he used the broad boundless generalizations of "transcendental meditation" and slid out of our work: "Only the universal aspects count; we should forget our individual, personal problems." I interpreted it as a resistance against looking at his own problems, and compared his metaphysical systems with his ancient counting compulsion and other intellectualizations. He poundered it and agreed: "It is a big farce!" That was though just paying lip service. He felt free, floating, clean, thanks to meditation; "the mantras overcome my aggressions, I feel growing." But I felt helpless! He: "I feel conflicted between the two methods. I cannot straddle the middle of the road." I heartily agreed (we were by now six and a half months into therapy).

He wanted to have the cake and eat it too. He felt how lonely he really remained. I interpreted his meditations as a desperate attempt to avoid his loneliness and the very painful, conflicted feelings about a girl who was very "cool," being successful at work, free in her erotic favors, but also deep into drugs and into stealing as protest against society; they also served to avoid the conflicts in the relationship with me. I compared the meditative efforts with the drug high. He genuinely agreed this time, saw his (conscious) avoidance and (largely unconscious) denial. He broke with the "flippy, shifty, spaced-out chicks" and saw his own "hang-ups" clearly again, feeling productive in his work and honest with himself, fully drug free. "All my energies are in creative activities and studying." He respected himself, reconciling the more useful parts of meditation with the analytic introspection with me. He felt happy, calm, in control—instead of either being ecstatic or mortified. For the first time (after seven months) he could speak about how his father did not listen to any of the children, did not hear what they said. "He is so closed off, withdrawn, even inappropriate; no one knows what he wants; he is so very inward, impervious. I had no masculine figure in him; so I turned to my oldest brother, and he was sadistic to people below him. That's the gist of my problems: the conflict between wanting to be Jesus Christ and to be just a man, between being like a three year old and an adult." He criticized both the "drug world" (and the whole counterculture) and the "straight society, the whole technology, the establishment culture. Both are traps. I feel less and less limited; the barriers are falling away." It was music, meditation, study—not drugs—which helped, and to express anger to his friends instead of turning it inward: "Just that is a tremendous release. I see how restricted my life was, and that I am beginning to open up." He studied music, literature, history, archeology—and felt very enriched. And he talked to others—a lot. He learned in order to grow, not to get a degree. Time and again he made a step forward by distancing himself, contrasting himself against a boy or a girl who showed his own past in caricature, "freaks," "pseudo-humble," troubled people. He did it without hostility, but set limits to others and himself. His outer appearance too had radically changed: long hair, dirty clothes and stinky mocassins gradually had lost their symbolic value for him.

He kept coming back to the mixture of shame and rage at his oldest brother in childhood, and worked it through in steadily new connections from the present. And more: "It was father who did not protect me against him; he favored him. My mother told me so. I had not seen *that* before." Father's fury, violence and tyrannical not-understanding versus mother's protection reached back to memories from age three. He identified with her orderliness and industriousness, instead of fleeing into a fantasy world of godliness and martyrdom. "Father is still today not present as a person. He comes home, flicks on the TV and falls asleep. Whenever I see him, he is asleep, or he bursts upon the scene in a wild rage, not in control of himself. There is such a discrepancy between how I feel he should have been and how he was. Since age three I have disrespect for his opinion. For the whole time of my growing up he was nonexistent or exploding. His not caring was just as painful as the brother's bullying. He treats my mother with the same neglect; in a way he is content through and through, but makes all the others feel bad." These feelings towards father and brother were relived and recognized in the transference relationship with me, especially in the form of anger against a dogmatic, self-righteous, not-listening bully he saw in me; he was feeling confused, frustrated and was confusing me too in a labyrinth of statements and counter-statements. He was still profoundly troubled about his identity, felt a lot of embarrassment about his passivity, his feminine traits, feared to appear homosexual: "When I was tripping, there was no difference between female and male, no polarity, no conflict, only Me." All siblings had severe problems—with sexual identity, drugs, aggression. "For me my mother was the greatest thing in the world; that was my idealization. My sister hates her and says she has castrated us all, including my father. I disagree with her, but now I can see also my mother's faults. Yet, she had to take over, because my father was so withdrawn, but she is not really dominant or bossy. She was put by default into a masculine, leading position." Still she had been and remained his major model for identification.

After one year and a longer interruption during the summer vacation, he decided to break off treatment. He felt he understood now most of his problems and could live with all of them with the help of meditation. The only symptom he recognized was still the fear of talking in front of people, but felt this would not warrant continuation of therapy. And in a triumphant flourish he stated that learning to live with limitations meant to say that man is inherently weak; he had arrived, thanks to transcendental nedictation, at the exact opposite conclusion: that all limitations could be dissolved by ever more meditation. He wanted to go fully into art and contemplation. No drugs ever anymore! And he assured me that he was not admiring himself anymore; he knew now that that had been based on fantasy.

I saw him one year later once more when he requested a psychiatric deferment from the draft. He was moderately good in school, still doubtful about his goals, still feeling passive, self-conscious, paralyzed in front of a group, bored by life, though all in all far more confident than in the past, apparently drug free.

I have not heard from him in quite a few years.

A summary of the dynamic findings in this case appears redundant. All that was stated at the introduction of the case was demonstrated in many forms.

The crucial role of the drug in deepening the defense mechanisms of denial and reaction formation, and various modes of isolation, undoing, of dissociation, and of wiping out many forms of boundaries and limits, as well as the wishful aspects intrinsic in all these defenses (narcissistic aggrandizement, magical omnipotence and symbiotic fusion) is very evident. The splits (in the sense of functional disparities) were strongly reinforced by the drugs. Unfortunately, "transcendental meditation" simply took over all these functions of the psychedelics. A true working through of the conflicts was impossible.

CASE 15: OBLOMOV

Here only a vignette of a twenty-year-old man who was brought by his parents for treatment because of intensive cannabis use; perhaps more importantly he also came because he wanted to avoid the draft. I saw him for half a year, once a week.

"I smoke hash, because I am bored. I am not interested in college. I have bad grades, do not work, have no plans; it is an aimless drifting. The only things I enjoy are the band and my girlfriend." He goes to school because his father insists. "I cannot find anything I am interested in. At home the parents were and are constantly yelling at me. I do not like to argue. My smoking is the direct outcome of my boredom. I do not know what to do; I live more for the moment than for the future. I cannot get motivated. So are my friends. I know it is a false sense of alleviating boredom, and I am depressed about it. But I don't know what the answer is. I look out for something more exciting. I do not like reading. The Army is the only thing that pushes me to stay in school. The parents ridicule me: how would you support yourself, were it not for us?"

The parents had tended to be very permissive, and he bitterly resented their sudden assumption of authority: "I had not many restrictions placed on me, was always free to come and go, whom to see, to have money. And now suddenly I am to be a slave; it's hard to adjust." It has to be added that about two years earlier he had made his girlfriend pregnant; the child was given away for adoption.

Discipline and limitations were equated with punishment and unfair curtailment of liberty. "I want to have money, but I am not going to prostitute myself to have it: to be nobody and to lose my individuality." His orientation was passive: "I want opportunities to be given to me, something meaningful," and: "I want tangible rewards for my work. I am lazy; everything has been given to me up to now. I do not want to work. I visit women, smoke pot and hash, go to movies and rock concerts—a whole lifestyle of relaxation and pleasure seeking—no ideals, no values." The psychedelic drugs had only one function: "to escape boredom."

He asked me where to begin with his inner problems. "Do you have any idea where my problems lie?" This "give me" wish was repeated over and over again. "I do not understand the purpose of therapy. Just to sit here and grope for answers? I have talked myself out, but you have not given me enough—just some ideas, but not where my real problem lies. It is true: I want to take, not to give." But whenever I started saying something, he interrupted me; he could not listen, except to himself. I presumed that what he had to offer himself must have been rather glorious. He denied it. Then he accused his friends; they were to blame for his rut: "It rubs off on me." Despite the inner self-glorification and the outer demandingness he was worried: "My whole environment is bad; all my friends want immediate gratification. It is difficult to break out. All my friends at school look down at those who have a goal."

Then he was thrown out of school—only to be readmitted on probation at his father's insistence. "Constant arguments and fights, especially incessant harping from my mother. I yell back at them" (confirmed by my own observations).

After about two months in therapy everything seemed to improve. He became interested in his courses, got good grades, worked a lot in his father's business' and reduced his cannabis use to perhaps once or twice a day (before he had been "stoned" continually). On his own he called his drug taking "a compulsion to relieve boredom"; as boredom diminished, this compulsion dwindled. "It is like masturbation. Drugs are a substitute for deeper meaning." But this goal, this meaning eluded him; the old boredom grew once again. He left home, moved in with some friends. "We all have had bad relationships with our parents. We are less goal oriented, do not plan for the future. We are alienated from society. They take LSD openly in the high school now! It's unbelievable. It's a complete breakdown in discipline." Slowly he slid back into the old passivity: drugs, little work, terrible boredom, rebellion against dependence on his parents coupled with total reliance on their succor. Arguments and threats grew to ugly proportions—and so did the drug taking. Finally he flunked out of school; the fights at home became punching matches. He kicked a hole in the door and destroyed some furniture. He was suspected by the parents of selling cannabis and taking also methaqualone (Quaalude). I met with the whole family. The patient professed a profound compulsion both not to work and to take hash, and, rightly, viewed psychotherapy as an exercise in futility! Very soon all three were screaming at each other; no sentence could be finished. The parents felt they had been too permissive and inconsistent; they had even massively bribed the judges whenever the son had gotten into trouble. They had saved him whenever he had to face the consequences of his actions.

Therapy was broken off. I was convinced: (a) that he was very deeply disturbed and had a dismal prognosis, and (b) that he would be motivated only to work on himself and change, once he had hit "rock bottom," once he had to suffer severely for his lifestyle.

Fortunately, and to my profound surprise, my prognosis proved to be wrong. About two or three years later, I was contacted by the parents: their son had successfully finished college, had become a pilot, wanted to enter the Armed Forces as a flier, and had totally stopped all drug taking. They asked me to write a letter to the draftboard rescinding my first one ... which I gladly did!

In retrospect, I still believe that Oblomov—like his literary prototype, whose name I chose as pseudonym—suffered from a very severe adolescent crisis, a combination of his own overweaning wish for passive dependency, a back and forth of furious rage and temper tantrums, of revenge and revolt in the entire family, and underneath a most permissive, indulgent behavior on the side of the parents. Boredom was the lead affect, hiding both passivity and anger; it was dealt with nearly exclusively with the help of compulsive marijuana and hashish use (using the defenses of denial and externalization) until the thrill of getting high in a literal sense broke through the stifling pall of apathy, passivity, meaninglessness and boredom.

Compulsive Use of Stimulants

Superficially, amphetamines and cocaine have much in common with what I just described. They also eliminate boredom and emptiness. But these more or less conscious affects appear to be caused predominantly by repression of feelings of rage and shame whereas in the previous group, these moods seem primarily motivated by the collapse of ideals. Accordingly these stimulants provide a sense of aggressive mastery, control, invincibility and grandeur, whereas the psychedelics impart a sense of passive merger through the senses and a reestablishment of the union with a concrete, personalized ideal.

But there is more to it: The amphetamine effect serves most importantly as a defense against a massive depression or general feelings of unworth and weakness. In the about half a dozen cases of compulsive amphetamine abuse which I was able to treat in intensive psychotherapy, and the many more I have seen more superficially, the long term abstinence was typically accompanied by intense self-directed aggression, in some by suicidal rage and despair, in others by lethargy and self-degradation. Thus, amphetamine abuse can at least in some patients be called an artificial normalizing or even manic defense against the underlying affect of depression.

For reasons of confidentiality I unfortunately cannot present any case histories here; for better presentations I have to refer the readers to the excellent studies of Berman and Hendin. Instead, I describe a *type* of patient I have seen repeatedly: On one side their lives appear strangely split, chaotic, tumultuous, regressive, full of lies, rages, suicidal attempts, paranoid fears. On the other they are often very gifted, successful, charming, and through wide areas of their lives very honest and of high integrity! I have watched similar splits in superego and ego in other types of drug abusers, but have found them rarely anywhere as profound as in the amphetamine users.

Often their drug use appears already in early or middle adolescence—ostensibly either because of overweight or exam pressures, a stimulant not rarely being provided at first by a careless physician or by an obese mother. In girls (and most I have seen were women) this is promoted both by a deeply ambivalent, split attitude toward the mother; the intense hatred of femininity is one part, the craving to be taken care of by the obtrusive or just overprotective mother is the second part.

The relationship to the father figure is equally conflicted and split. In some cases the father had left the family very early and only vague memories, but overpowering yearnings for the all-good, beautiful, seductive father remained, coupled with intense hatred for the stepfather and an angry blaming of mother. In another case the father was weak, the mother a nagging shrew who massively mistreated and beat the eighteen-year-old child. Severe conflicts between the parents and their in-laws were hidden with shame and lies by them, but furiously and gleefully pulled out into the open by the ostracized, scapegoated, drug taking youth. In one case there was a secret erotically tinged alliance between father and daughter which the mother tried to destroy in intense jealousy. As soon as the three were together, though, the father switched sides, right in front of me, and gave in to the spell of the massive mother and first meekly betrayed the daughter, then turned with hollow paternal authority against her. The intrigues of all against all were striking.

What is perhaps most impressive in the patients themselves, is, as already mentioned, the severity of the underlying depression.

Dynamically speaking it is again—as in the cases described under sedative addicts—a depression more filled with shame than with guilt. It is typical that severe depressive episodes, including suicidal attempts, preceded the amphetamine dependency, often by many years. Some were seen as hyperactive children long before any self-treatment with stimulants started.

After withdrawal, I have accompanied several patients through episode after episode of most intense, paralyzing depression, up to a year or more, after total abstinence, with intermittent hospitalization for suicidality. Anti-depressants were usually ineffective, whereas very intensive psychotherapy—as described in chapter 16—led to a gradual resolution of the most severe pathology.

This frenzied, terrorizing depression has essentially the following underlying motivations:

a. Deep down, but often not unconscious at all, are intense *murderous* feelings, originally against both parents. The pervasive fright is that if the drug (or a substitute, like prestige, a relationship) were taken away, the patient would feel confronted and alone with this murderous rage, mostly against himself or herself.

b. In common with other food addicts there is a devouring, gluttonous (some called it "ravenous") greed for food and people, an escape from the terrifying sense of loneliness and abandonment. The stimulants are of course a direct antidote against the attacks of bulimia, and often physicians faced with patients who alternate between anorexia and gorging give into the urgings of the (usually young female) patient. I have described this syndrome in my thoughts about "the archaic shame syndrome." Of course, because of the cannibalistic nature of the devouring, it is just a variant of the already mentioned murderous, sadistic rage and destructiveness and therefore accompanied by *guilt*. More importantly, however, it is a "filling" of a profound narcissistic weakness and emptiness ("I am all bad") and, therefore, accompanied with most intense shame. Greed, jealousy, envy, in their very archaic nature, are far more often accompanied by shame than guilt, at least in the more severely ill patients. Again, Alexa comes to mind: already as a child she hid her gorging attacks (directed mainly at sweets). As she said: "The shame was too overwhelming."

c. Especially in women it is a dread, again, of shame-laden weakness, of looking at herself as castrated and inferior—as Leon Berman (1972) so well described: the amphetamine possession and effect are means to cope with the immense, repressed (and lastly, in my experience, intractable) penis envy of these patients. A parallel castration shame I observed in some male amphetamine users. In both, the drug gives a direct sense of overwhelming, triumphant magical power, of masculinity, of invincible grandeur, of surpassing everyone else (especially the rival parent and sibling). Part of it is that they are sadistic teasers—men and women alike, sexually and more generally; and the drug is a powerful support in turning passive into active, masochism into sadism, thus particularly reinforcing the defenses on the "action fight continuum." Also the denial with the help of the drug is a loud protest: "I am not a weak, castrated, lonely, passive dependent child anymore! Now I want the power and worth and repute which have been taken away from me."

Another aspect of this narcissistic theme is the conflict between helpless dependency on a powerful object and the wish for defiant independence, for instance in the form of running away.

In addition, they all have what was already described for the other types of drug users: the massive archaic narcissistic conflicts, the ego split and a particularly pernicious split in the superego: a facade of great honesty, loyalty, charm and sincerity, but one which crumbles with special swiftness and painfulness to others under the onslaught of narcissism. In no other type of patient I have found this insistence on their integrity, their respect, their freedom from their past, their absolute conquest of shame, but at the same time the equal demand on being in control, in power, not to appear in any way weak and stained and getting their "pound of flesh," their due reward, "my absolute right." Of course, as Rangell (1976) so well wrote, integrity and narcissism are not compatible. The collapse of the illusion of reconciling the two again is part of the severe depression.

e. *Idealization:* On the one side, there is an intense wish to idealize other people, usually male figures, especially authorities and therapists and to see in them, and to do everything in their power to make them into, omnipotent rescuers and saviors. This archaic appeal for an omnipotent role is quite taxing on the therapist and can easily lead to various countertransference actions, such as giving in to insatiable demands for attention, for mothering, for drugs. Often, there is a marked sexualization of this idealization. The other side of the narcissistic problem is the intense wish for grandiosity and admiration, for praise and, as already mentioned, for actual extreme, magical control and power.

As soon as either of these two archaic narcissistic wishes (grandiosity and idealization) is thwarted, the patients act with massive rage and with a plummeting of self-esteem. The next step is that this whole rage is directed against themselves, that they start "wallowing in dirt" and engage in intensely self-destructive actions.

The suicidality is motivated both by rage directed against themselves and the defiant revenge on the other, a kind of radical flight from the other persons who have disappointed and betrayed them, usually a lover, originally the parent, now the therapist.

Again tied up with these narcissistic problems, are intense wishes for phallic exposure and exhibition and of course again the hidden, but powerful role shame plays in that connection.

In women, the most intense anger is usually reserved for the mother, however, who is intruder, tormenter and rival in reality, and the origin of all evil: of father's betrayal, the girl's "castration" and inadequacy in fantasy. Again, as in the barbiturate addicts, castration shame and penis envy are very intense; but whereas the former deal with it by retreat from reality into pharmacotoxic depersonalization, and a displacement to and living out of envy and greed in the oral area (by gorging, fasting, vomiting), the amphetamine using patient throws himself or herself into reality, into frenzied activity; instead of depersonalization and derealization there is a hyperacuity of reality perception. Instead of bulimia, the drug helps to keep abstemious, slim and trim—in control! Achievement, success, sexual frenzy, prestige, have to make up for the profound shame about being incomplete, flawed, unacceptable to the parent, for the massive narcissistic injury suffered early and repeated over and over again.

These patients are also peculiarly prone to hide their psychopathology, their drug abuse problem, their weakness—because of the particularly profound vulnerability of their self-esteem. Still, the similarity to barbiturate using patients (nearly two sides of the same coin) is so striking that the combination of both abuse forms is, not surprisingly, frequent. The main difference between these two (often alternating or simultaneous) forms of drug dependencies lies in the choice of the main defense: in hypnotic users it is above all the use of the avoidance type of defense, especially denial, a form of hiding, a retreat into the unreality, numbness, dreaminess of depersonalization;

in stimulant users it is the action and fight type of defenses which take the spotlight. Both use very massive splitting (in our redefined sense). One finds magical power in hiding, the other in aggressive self-exposure. One flees into the claustrum, the other flees from it into a spurious, hectic autonomy and independency.

Clinically the main point bears repeating: the defense is mostly against the affect of depression. Among all toxicomanics they are most likely to kill themselves when deprived of their drug.

A brief history of a male stimulant user, though of a much more complex nature, is added here and will illustrate at least some of these points.

CASE 16: SHAKRAN, THE LIAR, 23 YEARS OLD

His was a particularly tragic fate and at the same time a most provocative, even outrageous behavior demonstrating particularly graphically the various modes of externalization and its dynamic underpinnings: the intensity of grandiosity and aggression, supported particularly by cocaine.

First a superficial summary: Shakran, while seen in intensive psychotherapy and on the methadone program kept using cocaine. It gave him a triumphant sense of mastery and omnipotence, of invincibility and superiority, and time and again confirmed his magical conviction that reality had to bend before his lies and demands. As long as he took cocaine, he was not willing to admit to himself that he had limitations, that his claims for power ruined his life and that his lying created for him a hell of distrust, utter loneliness, and icy isolation, that in reality he had nobody he could trust. While hospitalized and weaned off narcotics as well as other drugs, he was able to face up to his intensive narcissistic demands, his craving for admiration, his wish to overcome all limitations of reality. But it took him only a few weeks outside of the hospital—a few weeks of all the frustrations of daily life and unskilled labor, of a psychotic and utterly dishonest mother and a ruthless, faraway, very rich father who refused to pay for hospital or psychotherapy—for him to drop out of therapy and start on drugs again.

As so often happens, the manifest "sociopath" has turned a history of being a helpless and tragically abused victim, of passive suffering, into the illusion of triumphant power and ruling over truth by lies and cons.

His massive use of cocaine occurred or was revealed only several months after the beginning of psychotherapy and methadone maintenance. I saw him for about one year, twice to three times a week for an hour. His parents were divorced when he was a little child. He spent some time with his father: "When I was twelve or thirteen, I stole some money from him and gave it to friends. When it was discovered, my father beat me up with a stick and made me eat a pack of cigarettes. My mother is just crazy. She steals and sells furniture and pictures of my stepfather. They scream all the time at each other. She is either raving about a person or feels persecuted. She is always conniving. I am like her. I want the world, but do not know where to begin. I am frustrated and depressed. Mother pampers and spoils me." Although extremely intelligent, he didn't finish college. "Why study, if I can cheat?" He got drugs mainly by flimflam. "Mother just has no pride. She tells all her girlfriends that I am sticking needles in my arm. I am her business—all that I do. Or she suddenly—out of the blue—starts screaming and yelling (in one of her rages), or she speaks gibberish. She was a spoiled child too. When I was an infant, she left me alone when the baby sitter did not show up."

Most of this information proved to be correct when I had repeated contacts with his mother where she also tried to ensnarl me with a web of raving praise, rage, meaningless chatter, trying to con me into forging some insurance forms, etc.

Shakran had a lot of problems with embarrassment and shame (e.g., to be watched while urinating or sitting face to face to me). "It is very difficult for me to look somebody in the eyes or to be looked at. I am afraid they look through me, or I look through them, that they know I am not honest." He was selling drugs of all kinds and was arrested a number of times. Narcissistic (shame oriented) aspects of the superego prevailed when its claims were felt at all: "It is kind of a *split*: I know I have feelings and a conscience—and yet often nothing seems to faze me. Other times I care a lot, am very depressed and worried, and often ashamed of mother's interference." Also in regard to psychotherapy he felt always "in power, special, exempt from agreements"; all limit setting was seen as a sadistic attack. "I place my self-esteem and my greed first. I want to get something for nothing. Drugs take the place of people. I am alone, sorry for myself; I cry when I listen to music. But I always want to 'beat' people; even my best friends do the same to me. So I turn the tables."

About two months into treatment he came out directly: "I pulled the wool over your eyes; I wasn't truthful. For three weeks I have been using cocaine, and I owe many people money. I forged checks, pawned TVs, or got it from relatives." He had spent $1500 during this brief period. But he immediately engaged in grandiose ideas: he wanted to be a writer or "I could work with addicts," go into psychology or into law. He saw drugs in general as "a way of avoiding sadness," was crying a lot without knowing why. "It is always a feeling of sadness about myself, the reality of me. After I cried I feel joy that I can overcome this and stand alone. Yet every time I succeed and things go better—when my debts are paid or I get a job—I do something stupid, an impulsive self-destruction."

Eventually because of suicidal depression he was hospitalized, but still felt unable to get close to anyone—compelled to exploit every person and yet not wanting to hurt anyone either, deprecated himself as a slimy, slippery con man, but obviously was abysmally unhappy and alone. "I am too much like my mother." Criminality, especially violence, gave him the same satisfaction as drugs: to be "on top of the world, king of the world, fantastic—the same when I have *power* over a beautiful chick. Always I am playing games to be in control of people and situations, playing out one against the other." Cocaine and methedrine had given him this intense feeling of control and power—just for a few minutes; it had to be repeated very often. And girls were just objects of conquest. Or he got that feeling of power by gambling. When he did not get his way, he became very frightened and depressed. He put the same power play with me into scene, tried to "out-psychiatrize" me with pseudo insights and a heap of well-applied psychiatric knowledge. It was clear that he defended himself in many ways by the feeling of omnipotence and invincibility against an overwhelming sense of helplessness and despair—these ways being (all the modes of externalization outlined in chapter 6): conning, lying, daydreams of his future greatness, the drug "high,", especially with cocaine, conquest of money and women, outright violence and criminal transgression of any bounds, or a minor thing like enjoying to drive through a red light.

In dreams he went to war, strangled and knifed people, especially women ("I stuck it in her back, got to her heart and was grinding it in"), or he had to avoid awakening sleeping lions at home. When he was depressed, he yearned for cocaine (while still hospitalized). All of life was seen as testing fate, trying to win, never to live within limits—as he could do with his very seductive mother. She had fondled his penis when he was a child, and was always adoring his appearance; even at the time of treatment she still paraded in front of him half naked. Mother admired his capabilities, clothes, etc., excessively, and in turn gave him everything he desired when he flattered her. He tested the staff on the ward, sold some medical students LSD and was indignant that they "broke the confidentiality" and reported it. He then tried for a month to seduce a female medical student right on the ward; yet he also felt guilty and upset about it, but could not see why the Hippocratic code should interfere with his wishes. He got drunk (on the ward) on alcohol as a substitute for other drugs to get over his depression. Then he threw out all guilt, was determined to continue that particular affair and was angry at me for disapproving of it: "It's a battle with you and my conscience. But you are the only real obstacle. She also has a few scruples; she thinks you hate her. I won't give her up." Finally he got the female intern to masturbate him; but then she did not look perfect enough to him. Still he continued having nearly daily sexual relations with her; he didn't miss her, however, but still enjoyed being with her, especially feeling equal with a physician. "But I feel incapable of love or loyalty. I am sorry for her; she felt very guilty and ashamed. I care about her. She is very upset about it. I was just playing a game with her. The whole thing was just a challenge. I planned it that we would end up so: it was a search and destroy mission. But when she started crying, feeling used and abused by me, I felt shot down and began crying too. It is the same craving to get what I want with girls as with drugs." In this particular liason the violation of professional standards gave him a special "high": "I get pleasure out of breaking the rules." Having a good time meant transgressing limits. He then discarded her, after leaving the hospital. (This was six weeks after his suicidal depression, close to a year after the beginning of therapy.) He stayed off drugs while continuing therapy and working on his enormous narcissistic wishes and his absolute compulsion to find pleasures everywhere. He worked though and had quite helpful plans to get involved with some theatre group, playing or writing drama—thus getting some of the more destructive urges under control and lived out in a useful form. But naught came of such plans. He yearned for drugs when he felt low: lonely, depressed, hurt, frustrated. Every slight was a deep hurt—and the drug (heroin, cocaine) would make up for it. He was telling himself: "Now I deserve it"—the entitlement. "When I feel hurt, I want either food or women or alcohol or drugs."

About six weeks after discharge from the ward he again started with heroin and cocaine. The ostensible reason: he missed one of his girlfriends, was rejected by a second one, felt "hurting, crying, craving, very depressed;" "it was mostly the humiliation that I was turned down." The depression deepened and thus the drug use increased. "All that I feel is pain. I feel lonely; I want to have somebody all the time, twenty-four hours a day. I want too much." He again became addicted to narcotics, was angry at me for not seeing him often enough (projection: he frequently missed the thrice a week session), felt like a little child that should be spanked—always testing fate, but feeling defeated, insignificant. He pointedly said "My shadow ran fast." He promised a married woman marriage if she divorced her husband and lived with him; but he knew his promises were about as firm as those of both his parents.

He knew that his problems, especially his narcissism, his cravings, had not diminished, and wanted to flee from drugs, from therapy, and from all the legal and personal entanglements to the Southwest, but professed sadness about leaving his mother and me.

A few months later he was back in town, on another program, studying at a university but still deeply in debt because of his prior addiction. He admitted that he had lied to me for the last three months of treatment—when and how much he was back into drugs and debts. He requested resumption of therapy; I agreed only under the condition that he would first pay up all of his debts. I did not see him again until many years later when he enrolled in another methadone program which I was in charge of. This patient showed particularly clearly the layering of defenses and wishes. On the surface he appeared simply as a sociopath, enjoying rule breaking and all kinds of illicit pleasures. On the next level the prevalence of the defense by externalization in all its modes is striking. One may be tempted to see in its manifestations a naked living out of archaic aggressive, object libidinous, and narcissistic wishes. However, it is more apropos to see in these "drive manifestations" defensive maneuvers (by externalization), attempts to protect him against the gaping emptiness he called "depression," a lack of feeling, of meaning, of contact. This "gaping hole" represents the third layer—the residue of massive traumatization and lack of warmth and responsiveness throughout childhood. All externalization is used to cover over this festering narcissistic wound—alas, without success: "My shadow ran fast."

Compulsive Alcohol Use

As mentioned in the preface, I cannot deal with this group as thoroughly as with the others.

The most consistent comment I have heard from alcohol abusing patients is something like this: "It becomes a pacifier emotionally, a guilt releaser; I can allow myself pleasure. And it alleviates the tension about separation, loss, betrayal....I need an hour of complete oblivion. ...I feel no violence then; it is an anesthetic. I feel the pain less of having to deal with reality, with being betrayed and lonely. Drinking is a substitute for the creative process: it brings about visual changes." These are some of the thoughts of an often severely depressed, very gifted artist who, through a number of severely self-destructive actions, is leading a very tragic, extremely impoverished life. (She will be described more in detail in the next chapter, case 18; Razit.)

Pete Hamill, as quoted by Kazin, put it in these words: "Drink was the great loosener, the killer of shyness, the maker of dreams and courage..." (1976, p. 49).

Alcoholics are in general far more socialized, have much better inner structures (controls, capabilities to adapt) than most other compulsive drug users. Their conscience is more stable, less archaic. The affect defense seems primarily directed against guilt, secondarily against painful loneliness and "feeling betrayed," sometimes also against shame. Their narcissistic conflicts, though remarkable, are far less prominent than in the groups hitherto described. It is very important that the dampening of guilt goes along with a lowering of inhibitions against aggression, and with that opens wide the horrendous problem of the alcoholic's rage and violence.

I am very grateful to Dr. Jay Phillips for having made the following case history available to me. He has seen this patient in intensive psychotherapy for about one year, under my supervision. I quote him directly.

CASE 17: CASSANDRA

She is a woman in her thirties first seen for psychiatric help at age nineteen for difficulty in her studies.

The patient was the younger of two children, there being a brother three years her senior. Her earliest memory is of being beaten by her mother in a deliberate and systematic fashion such that the entire rear surface of her body was covered with horizontal welts. Another early memory is of details from a hospitalization for tonsillectomy, of not crying when her mother left her, of being punitively treated by nurses prior to and after the operation. She remembers her mother praising her to others for angrily throwing stuffed animals and blankets out of her crib and playpen. (She was "such a big girl.") Beatings from her mother were severe and frequent, occurring during her father's frequent business trips.

At about age five, while visiting family friends with her mother, the patient became frightened and screamed. Her mother, in her haste to get to the child, fell down a flight of steps near the bottom of which was a table where a meat cleaver lay. Her mother's face was horribly lacerated, a large area nearly removed by the instrument. In the turmoil of blood and screaming, the patient remembers her mother's friend shouting at her, "this is your fault."

By late latency, the patient was struggling with overt sadistic behavior. She recalls going to her mother, crying, to tell her that she had beaten a four-year-old cousin and had locked her in the closet. Her mother had all of them agree to tell no one else.

School was a consistently frustrating experience. She had great difficulty sitting still and was dyslexic. These conditions were never evaluated professionally; instead they were considered willful disobedience and harshly responded to. She related frustration such that on the playground she would "just run and run" until exhausted. Academic achievement was highly valued in the home, and she responded to school with compulsive copying as the necessary compensation to meet expectations. She had, all along, difficulty remembering words (naming aphasia) and compensated by learning many synonyms, building an impressive vocabulary. After failing the ninth grade, she changed schools and completed the four years of high school in three.

She began college, but was unable to use her usual methods for the increased volume of work, and became so noticeably depressed that she was referred to student health. Her parents were notified, and began a series of therapist changes, allowing therapy to progress until the therapist insisted on confidentiality; then they would remove her. (She recalled with contempt and bitterness one of these therapists telling her how "attractive and charming" she was and that she "should be enjoying life.") Eventually, she was identified as suicidal and admitted to the psychiatric ward of a general hospital. After a visit from her mother on the first hospital night, she picked up a blunt metal object and beat her entire body, bruising most of it. She reported a certain satisfaction at the expression of horror from the nurse who first saw her and again when her mother screamed at the sight of her. Characteristically, the satisfied feelings were fleeting, followed by massive guilt and the idea that she was responsible for her mother's suffering. Over the next week, she secretly beat the bruised regions nightly with her roommate's hairbrush, until the ward staff realized that she needed constant observation.

She was sent to a long-term hospital, where she stayed two and a half years, a course punctuated by interference from her parents, who threatened to take her out, and frequently insisted on the organic etiology of her troubles. This was complicated when neurologic dysfunction was inferred from a pathognomic response to phenothiazine. It should also be stated that this experience in the hospital left her very sophisticated as a patient. It also gave concrete expression to several forms of self-destruction through fellow patients, several of whom committed suicide.

Approximately six years after discharge, she was admitted to another facility, where I was her therapist. She had been referred by her current out-patient therapist, who felt the patient had become dangerously suicidal. The major precipitant seemed to be an evening writing course that the patient was taking: she was getting A's and praise from the kindly young male teacher. After he read one of her papers to the class, she began talking about her eventual suicide in such a convincingly hinting fashion that the therapist recommended hospitalization.

Relations with men have been of two rigidly separated types: friendship with "nice guys" she "couldn't ever find attractive," and painful affairs with distant, rejecting men. Similarly with women, she has maintained some friendships with warm, "feminine" women—when with them she feels normal and "wants a man." In the presence of a more aggressive, "bitchy woman," she frequently feels sexual attraction and has had a homosexual affair.

The details of Cassandra's course since we began working together would be unnecessarily lengthy, adding little besides the documentation of the negative therapeutic reaction that could be predicted from the history. Her relentless sabotage of every positive aspect of her life, including, of course, therapy, as well as her life itself, is ongoing. She provokes abuse and rejection, pulls together briefly, only to fall victim to crippling guilt and humiliation. In her desperate attempts to subdue these intolerable affects with drinking, she directly threatens her life and others (she picks these times to drive) and has serious falls.

This, then, is her masochism: the patient peruses suffering, both passively and actively; the object is an amorphous amalgam of a torturing mother and a collusive rejecting father.

We know that the ego is first a body ego. It is clear that for Cassandra this body was all over its surface a source of pain, and that she was nearly incapable of experiencing pleasure beyond the relief of pain.

She is anorgasmic in heterosexual intercourse, and does not often masturbate. She is occasionally orgasmic in rare homosexual intercourse, but only with a "bitchy woman," and it is always followed by merciless humiliation and self-castigation.

Cassandra began out-patient treatment with me about three months after discharge from the hospitalization during which we met. She had terminated with her previous therapist during the hospitalization abruptly, distorting her therapist's communication during a phone conversation into a rejection, which the therapist assured me was not the case. The patient saw this distortion and its meaning somewhat spontaneously a year later.

Our work began on a once weekly basis, and was increased to twice weekly at her request. Together we progessively illuminated her self-defeating behavior with others, after which she began living out these behaviors in the therapy itself: missing sessions, quitting by phone in a rage, only to return a week later wanting me to continue with her. As the months went by, and our work moved closer to very painful childhood memories, this reliving in the therapy escalated, unresponsive to clarification.

After about one month of work, the patient first mentioned her drinking. I did not focus on it at first, and this may have contributed to her rage at me and assertions that I was incompetent. Two months later she was already reporting drinking heavily and falling down steps or driving while intoxicated, at the same time saying in one session, "I wanted you to be more harsh." She complained of an uncomfortable feeling state, angry that her neurologist and I had not relieved it: "My head is in the clouds, it has been for weeks. Ten years of therapy and I'm still nowhere. Maybe I'm hopeless. If I get angry, I'm afraid I'll black out. Then I'd be on the floor and they'd be laughing."

The danger in her drinking emerged starkly as time went by: "I was at my parents' home, we were all drinking...I drove back...I wasn't scared I'd black out. I know what that means—that I want to have a wreck."

Two months later, "I was angry at you and angry at therapy. Nothing is changing and I'm still fucked up. I don't let myself feel relief, there are too many recriminations from my mother and father, when I was getting punishment I didn't deserve." In the same period, regarding therapy, "I feel like you're trying to engage me, chasing after me, and I'm running away, even though I want to stand still, it's embarrassing." And, after beating her dog and forgetting the circumstances, (I: In some ways it's harder to understand than to hurt) "I know what you mean—that I'm comfortable feeling guilty, I've felt guilty all my life."

The meaning of drinking sketchily emerged: "I feel I can be friendly, say hello. Otherwise I feel weird, like people don't like me...that they're staring at me, not because I'm pretty but because I'm weird." (Confirming then my interpretation that these attitudes derived from punitive adults—ultimately her parents.) And as the reliving began to escalate, "I hope I don't drink tonight. I have a friend coming over. I will think: I'll feel weird, the apartment's a mess." (I: Then the alcohol is to soften the embarrassment—and feeling exposed) "That's it."

Soon after this, another brief, "termination" was carried out, in the work with which it emerged that Cassandra has an imaginary companion, a "little girl inside me, and she won't let me talk, it's not a feeling, it's real," psychically real. "I know she's inside me, not a separate body...she has her own soul; you have to be careful how you talk about her or I'll get it—be tactful. She does a lot, she's the bright one. When I go out she takes over and I meet a lot of men. Sometimes I feel mad and she takes over. Like she says you talk too much...."

Her self-destructive drinking increased markedly after the emergence of the companion. "I've got to stop drinking, I'll kill myself. I can't stop, and I'm really worried."

In this increasingly chaotic period, more feelings emerged related to drinking and its consequences. "Someone looks at me and smiles. I can only look for a little while, then I have to look away. I get scared that they'll stop—or hurt me. (It comes from) experience I guess, that I was hurt a lot. I can't help it." Some friends were "kidding me, and I got hurt. I know I'll feel hurt again when they start kidding me." In another episode, "I felt hurt, rejected. I went out, drank too much, met a man on the street. I'm gonna need a VDRL." This pattern in turn related to genetic hurts which were difficult to discuss, but needed to be understood if the pattern described was to stop: hurt and shame, attempt at relief through drinking, self-destructive behavior while drunk, then crippling shame and guilt for those actions, with suicidal ideas and more drinking to relieve the pain. After some missed appointments and some near fatal accidents, a one A.M. phone call: "This has got to stop. I'm scared now—I'm out of control. My mother was here. She doesn't want to know how fucked up I am. She never did." Later that week: "I've been mad all day, just feel mad, that's all. I know I'm going to go home and get drunk, and find a man to spend the night with." In response to my wondering about having a man in bed, "that I'm attractive...but it's just superficial—men just like me for my body." And she agreed this indicated she felt herself to be utterly without worth. Earlier it emerged that she only found a man attractive when he confirmed her view of herself and treated her as worthless. The next week, a phone call during time for the session: "I'm drunk and I'm calling to say it's time for me to go in the hospital for a while." Although hospitalization was arranged and the patient admitted, she reenacted these provocations and self-defeating behavior in that setting, and was continuing to do so in another hospital at last contact.

More from Dr. Phillips' report—about the treatment—will be presented in chapter 21.

Pain as affect, pain as sexual masochism, pain as sadistic inflictions on others, pain as self-destruction and self-punishment appear central:

she wants to cry out in pain, as a hurt, humiliated, wounded child—and mutes it by drinking. She has a symbiotic tie to her huge female dog whom she needs in bed as part of herself, really as a transitional object, but whom she also beats so mercilessly (with or without alcohol) that concerned neighbors have had to step in. When the dog is sick or constipated, it is "done on purpose"; the dog is attacked and punished. The dog indeed is she as the tormented child, while Cassandra abuses her, turning her own passive suffering into brutal, raging revenge. All forms of pain: physical and emotional, including anxiety, guilt and shame, are at first mitigated, but subsequently deepened by alcohol, *her* drug.

There is a profound sense of doom hanging over this patient. Therefore the pseudonym—reminding us of Cassandra's desperate, nonverbal outcry in Aeschylus' *Agamemnon* (1072: "Otototototoi póppoi dâ," a meaningless scream of wild pain and anxiety, her sense of catastrophe: "Is it some net of death?... Ruin is near and swift") and Schiller's beautiful poem about her: "Joyless in the abundance of joy,/ Withdrawn and alone.... My youth was only crying / And I only knew the pain...." She is a "tragic character."

Multihabitual Drug Users

It is fashionable today to use the Greek adjective and to call these individuals "poly drug users."

They use nearly indiscriminately sedatives and narcotics plus psychedelics plus stimulants and alcohol. But still most of them prefer either one category—say, narcotics—or combined with a stimulant (heroin plus cocaine, barbiturate plus dexedrine.) Most stay far away from a psychiatrist and, even if seen in psychotherapy, drop out after a few visits; they are the most unstable, the most disturbed type of personalities among all six groups.

It is my impression that they have an overriding desire to show themselves great, to be in control of their lives, to "put one over"—a profound fear of being vulnerable, weak, inferior, not in control, embarrassed. The affect fended off by this omnipotent range of pharmaca may indeed be the fear of vulnerability, of shame, injury, dependence, of being exposed and not masters of every situation.

Since I have had no chance of seeing a true indiscriminate user for any length of time, but already described in nearly all my cases "poly drug use,"[1] though with preference for one type of drugs, I refrain from a further pondering of this group.

[1] e.g. case 4, Patpet: Narcotics plus Valium as preferential combination; case 16, Shakran: heroin and cocaine; case 19: Andreas: narcotics and alcohol. An additional case of true poly drug use: barbiturates, analgesics, narcotics, sedatives and amphetamines will, however, be presented in chapter 15, primarily because of the fascinating implications for treatment; that case is generously being contributed by Dr. Ellen McDaniel.

Chapter 8

PRECONDITONS AND

THE ETIOLOGIC EQUATION

As befits a psychoanalytic inquiry we have to add to the perspective on a *horizontal* plain, which encompassed mainly a microanalysis of the structural, dynamic, topographic and some economic and adaptational factors as they are needed to understand the historically closest and logically most specific antecedents directly leading up to the addictive syndrome, a *vertical* perspective—a look into the historical depth of the personality, an attempt to see the aforementioned factors in their genesis and unfolding.

The aim would be to evolve out of history the ability to predict, in Shakespeare's words:

There is a history in all men's lives,
Figuring the nature of the time deceased.
The which observed, a man may prophesy,
With a near aim, of the main chance of things
As yet not come to life, which in their seeds
And weak beginnings lie intreasured.
Such things become the hatch and brood of time....

[*Henry IV, Part II,* Act III, Sc. i]

We are very far away from such an ideal.

What follows is a sketchy outline, a beginning attempt "to gather up the scarlet threads of life and to weave them into a pattern," fully conscious that "history is *one* tapestry. No eye can venture to compass more than a hand's-breadth" (Wilder).

This skepticism is particularly justified in our field. What Eissler (1969) wrote in regard to treatment holds true no less for theory:

> Strangely enough, psychoanalysis is not able to provide the tools with which to combat the majority of forms in which drug addiction is now making its appearance among the younger generation in the United States. It seems that, just as psychoanalysis is, with few exceptions, not the method of choice in acute conditions, so it is not prepared to stem the tide of that form of psychopathology that is provoked by *anomie*. The dissolution of societal structures does not travel solely the path of lessening the strength of institutions and finally abolishing them entirely (at least for the time being), but also the path of reducing structure in individuals. The structure of the ensuing psychopathology seems to be quite different from the psychopathology whose treatment led to the evolvement of psychoanalysis. [p. 463,]

Thus we face the following obstacles to a genetic exploration:

a. The methods of psychoanalytic inquiry have to be modified to such an extent in the treatment of these patients that the observations gained do not lend themselves easily to simple and minor modifications of the theoretical abstractions gained by the classical method.

b. Very few patients stick to psychotherapy long enough to allow us sufficient genetic reconstructions which would give us the security of empirical probability rather than imbuing us with the complacency of well worn, empty clichés.

c. As Eissler noted there is such an intertwining of intrapsychic with familial, societal, cultural pathology that we can not investigate and understand one without at least trying to do this for the other.

d. The drug user himself is crippled by his very symptom in some of the core processes of judgment and self-recognition. Retrospective falsification is an ever looming danger.

e. The main tool of recognition in psychoanalysis, the transference neurosis, only rarely becomes clear enough in treatment. The therapist has to assume so much of a reality role, the patient is so intolerant of deprivation, that very little indeed remains of the "as-if" nature needed to explore in a systematic way the transference aspects (Tarachow 1963)—no matter how hard a good, conscientious therapist and analyst tries to keep parameters to a minimum. Very often the choice becomes between keeping the patient in treatment or even alive versus maintaining a therapeutic relationship that would allow a maximum of theoretic insight.

So all in all I feel very humbled when discussing the genetics of these patients with my friends, because I have chanced upon so little that is really reliable and firm, and all simple schemata suggested by my most respected friends (e.g., the very convincing genetic grid given by Kaplan and Wieder in their outstanding studies) leave me with a lingering doubt: are they not oversimplified?

In favor of our efforts are, however, a few clear insights:

a. The heptad described in chapter 6 gives us plentiful clues to tie very many processes, seen in our patients as an ensemble, together with similar processes in other patients where they may appear "in single file."

b. There is no question that these patients all suffered very massive traumatization throughout their childhoods, mostly in form of grossest violence and crassest seduction and indulgence. What neurotics show mainly as intrapsychic conflicts with preponderance of fantasy, these patients experienced as massive external conflicts of overwhelming dimensions, and going on from early childhood right through adolescence.

c. Thus drug use is not simply an adolescent crisis gone awry (as the parents regularly wants us to believe).

There is no doubt that all compulsive drug users whom I ever got to know show that severity of pathology nowadays often subsumed under "borderline personality organization" (Kernberg 1967, 1970a,b, 1971, 1975). The only probable exceptions were a number of alcoholics and certainly the majority of compulsive cigarette addicts whose psychodynamics appear to be of an entirely different nature (see Marcovitz 1969).

The toxicomanic patient allows us a detailed study of some of the traits shared by all "borderline" patients—especially regressive splits of many variants, denial and idealization—but also permits us to gain rather novel insights into the role of manifold externalizations, the problems of affect tolerance and affect regression in general (not just anxiety), the important role of depersonalization, and especially the broad spectrum of various forms of boundaries and limits.

d. As Eissler and Kohut in particular emphasized: these archaic personality organizations reflect a lack of inner structures which early damage, family and societal pathology conspire to bring about. A fourth aspect, usually omitted, may play a very important role in this lack of inner structures: heredity. How important a role, we have no way of knowing today, but this is a scientific problem open to experimental solution.

e. The seven factors enumerated in the heptad all point to very archaic fixations—to problems in the first two to three years of life, to severe damage suffered at the time when these inner structures need to be built, when the child has to come to terms with frustrations to his omnipotence, to oral gratification, when boundaries between self and others are established, when he gradually learns to establish his own regulations of self-esteem, and, most importantly, when his affects become differentiated, put into symbols (including words, but not restricted to them) and slowly manageable (see Schur 1953, 1966, especially Krystal 1974). There is no question that the severest damages in our patients lie in these early, largely preverbal times, though perpetuated on and on. They express themselves as massive narcissistic conflicts and primitive aggressions, directed with little differentiation against others and the self, as a general problem about boundaries and limitations, as archaic forms of defenses, as structural deficiencies of manifold nature.

Yet here we need far more specificity than our current theory provides us with.

The following is merely a first, by no means complete account. Speculation will be held to a minimum.

The case histories already presented have taught us that the "specific constellation" as detailed in the heptad does not strike out of the blue. As we have noted in all case histories, most severe problems existed inside and outside of the person, long before crisis and compulsive drug use entered the stage.

Ego Defects

DEFECT IN AFFECT DEFENSE

The general tendencies to externalize, to deny and to dissociate, were prevalent throughout the life history. No further documentation appears needed. We have merely to remind ourselves of the antisocial acts, of the many forms of split in all-good and all-bad in others and the self, into various subpersonalities, etc., of the experiences of overwhelming feelings in inarticulate, pervasive form, denied, "acted out," and particularly of the described "flipflops," the "about-face syndrome."

The archaic, primitive, unmanageable nature of these feelings is, as Schur, Kohut and Krystal described, a deficiency in the structural makeup of these patients. They have not become "transmuted," "channeled," sublimated; they remain at the ancient level of pervasive narcissistic conflicts. The defect in the affect defense is thus pervasive, and denial alone does not suffice to describe this particular part of the predisposition. Besides the overall, lifelong propensity for externalization as defense, it appears most likely that this profound defect in the defense against affects is at least one of the most specific elements in the predisposition.

HYPOSYMBOLIZATION

Hyposymbolization is a special aspect of the ego defect just alluded to. With this, I refer to the frequent observation of a general degradation, contraction, or rudimental development of the processes of symbolization and, with that, of verbal expression, of creativity, of sublimation of all kinds, and of the fantasy life. This curtailed ability to symbolize pertains particularly to the patient's inner life, his emotions, his self-references. One example of this is the inability of most of these patients to articulate the most important, most bothersome feelings. Many, if not all, relevant affects are translated, really projected, into somatic complaints, e.g., about craving and physical discomfort or into social accusations: "It's all society's fault." They remain preverbal as affects. I quote Krystal: "in certain types of alcoholics and other drug-dependent patients the emotions, for the relief of which the drugs are taken, are virtually without exception unverbalizable and perceived only dimly and vaguely.... In fact, Raskin and I searched in vain for a drug-dependent patient who could verbalize his 'bad feelings'.... It thus appears that perhaps *verbalization* is too specific a term: the very translation of the affect into any type of symbols or image may already permit its desomatization" (1974, pp. 102, 115). This goes far beyond the "lack of developed sublimatory channels," noted by Kernberg (1967) for "borderline personalities."

The same constriction seems to hold true for much of the fantasy life. Among others it is this lacuna which makes psychotherapy so particularly difficult and frustrating. After all, psychotherapy employs as its instrument precisely the verbal band out of the spectrum of symbolic processes. It seems most logical therefore to dub this defect "hyposymbolization"; I consider it close to what I found in Blos's (1971) concept of "concretization" which he defines as "the engagement of the action system in problem solving and the use of the environment as tension regulator" (pp. 679-68), a point already hinted at by Eissler in 1950. When one goes over the material already presented (and yet to be offered), the concreteness of expressions, the literalness of metaphors, the immediate translation of thought and feeling into concrete action is often striking.

The drug is utilized, not to substitute for the lacking symbolization proper (although Louis Lewin suggested this by using in 1924 the term *Phantastica* for some of these drugs), but rather to remove that vague discomfort and tension, which is only dimly, preconsciously, perceived as an affect, and rather projected as an untoward somatic or outer reality instead. The drug alters body image and world image into a less unpleasant or more meaningful one. In other words, it modifies the projection, without removing it or the more basic defenses (denial, repression, affect regression).

A second example is the inability of most to make use of leisure time and capabilities in *creativity;* even very gifted toxicomanic patients abrogate their earlier creative efforts, complain about "having nothing to do" and use drugs to fill the emptiness (e.g., cases 4, 13, 19—Patpet, Alexa, Andreas, and some of the amphetamine users not presented as case histories).

How can we understand this problem psychoanalytically?

I believe it can be best seen as part and parcel of some knowledge already gained. Above all: archaic, overwhelming affects which are not of "signal" nature, but of original, traumatic intensity or threaten to become so at relatively minor provocations, must interfere with the development of symbolization and abstraction in whatever area they irrupt into. In some patients, as in case 13 (Alexa), particularly the perceptual processes, especially seeing and being seen, are flooded with these primitive affects, and the patient, whose symbolic capabilities outside of this area were phenomenal, precocious and of near genius level, was not able to put the affects which were most pathogenic into higher level forms of symbolization (into names, concepts, creativity).

Moreover the denial employed against these affects blocks inner perception, the internal pole of the symbolic process (see Kubie 1934, 1953, a, b, 1956); to put feelings into words or other symbolic means (pictures, music) means at least their partial acknowledgment, the antithesis of denial. In other words: defensive hyposymbolization is just one special form of denial.

Beyond this there may be a genuine deficiency: many people have never gained much mastery of symbolization. This may be due to inborn shortcomings: the ability to symbolize (including "sublimation," a special form of symbolization) is probably based partly on inborn givens (see Sifneos's "alexithymia"). We still know terribly little about the weight of constitutional, inherited factors in almost all emotional disorders, weaknesses, *and* fortes! Freud often pointed to the importance of the complementary series and the continuum of constitutional and environmental factors in the etiology of neuroses.

I believe the consideration of inherited factors in the entire predisposition of compulsive drug use (e.g., propensity to externalization and action, besides the problems with symbolization) can not be dismissed out of hand. In many, such factors are very unlikely to play a role, specifically in this area of hyposymbolization; in many they are indeed very likely to be significant.

But then we have to pay particular attention to the deficiency in the upbringing, the lack of learning of symbolic activities from very early on. Often the lack of stimulation of, and attention to these processes within the family is a striking phenomenon. This, of course, is usually paired with another enemy of symbolization and an ally of the first factor (overwhelming affects): massive, repeated traumatization from the outside, by violence and sexual overstimulation, which interferes with the secondary autonomy needed for the growth of this most human and most complex activity. This has a very important implication: one of the major fixations of these patients lies not in the stage of omnipotence of words, but in the earlier one when magical omnipotence is attributed to action, to looks, to things; it is a preverbal omnipotence as manifested in the eight described modes of externalization and the concrete, dehumanized nature of all object relationships (cf. Pumpian-Mindlin 1969, p. 217, regarding obsessive-compulsive characters, etc.).

Finally, and rather superficially, I cannot absolve the abuse of television from all responsibility in this regard. We are not only living in a culture which is "shameless," "permissive," and prone to "compromise of integrity" (we shall come back to these very important concepts developed by Leo Rangell and Yela and Henry Lowenfeld)—we participate in a culture where symbols have become degraded and, like money, deflated. And here television, especially used as a baby sitter and parent substitute and with its incessant nonsymbolic, usually rather primitive overload, fosters and deepens this onslaught of a pervasive, massive anti-symbolism and anti-intellectualism. But more about this later.

EGO SPLIT

This issue can lead us easily into circular reasoning: Because the defense mechanisms of denial and dissociation are so prominent in these patients, they must preexist. Do we have independent corroboration that indeed there was an "ego split" prior to onset of "crisis" and drug use? Do we find an "ego split" expressed in a feeling like: "There was always this other part in me which I feared very much, an unnatural, overwhelming Me which I could keep under wraps most of the time, but which always threatened to break through—a foreign part, very strange, and still part of me, known and yet not known?" In many patients I have encountered such an observation—but only some of them had the other defense as well: a magical mode of externalization, and with that were compulsive drug users (e.g., cases 9, 13 and 19, the Prince, Alexa, and Andreas). And in the other cases such a radical denial–split has to be presumed to preexist, but we have no certain evidence.

The very specific concept of split in the way Freud originally described it as valid for the fetishist: the acknowledgment plus denial of perception and cognition, I have already amply demonstrated. Still the damage in toxicomanics seems much earlier, the pathology much more severe, the disrupted instinctual drives far more archaic, and hence the defenses (including denial-split and externalization) far more global, encompassing and of magical-regressive nature than if splitting were limited to this more specific form; enough has already been stated, except that these splits can be remembered back into rather early childhood (see Maya, case 12; Alexa, case 13, Cassandra, case 17; Andreas, case 19). It appears indeed quite common to find, once one gets to know these patients very well, these expressions of splitting and its sequelae.

They felt since childhood split up into different persons, mostly into a secret person inside, who either was observing, condemning, ridiculing, commanding—or being admired, loved, omnipotent, absolutely beautiful—or being killed, beaten, mercilessly destroyed. This part very often was the only felt reality that counted. At first blush it appears that it represents just one small portion: an ego function, a superego activity, the helpless early self-image which was now at the pitiless mercy of the older self which is identified with a cruel parent. At deeper inquiry this other, inner person, which is so real and yet such a consuming fantasy, represents far more and probably is an entire "intersystemic suborganization" in the sense specified by Schafer, Lichtenberg, and Slap.

Parallel with this deep immersion in the fantasy, the rest of self- and object-representations are estranged: the world is dull, unreal, far away, small, behind a veil or cotton; the self, outside of the split off "other part," is unreal, full of shame, pain and burdened with loneliness, scorn and ugliness. The "other part" may be perfect, or at least may be filled with life, with exciting action, albeit guilty one. We have various forms of depersonalization and derealization since very early times (ages five to seven).

Thus the whole area of *feelings* is split—into regressed, archaic, but denied, depersonalized affects, and also archaic affects accompanying triumph, goodness and idealization.

The same holds true for the area of *action:* all through life they give a split appearance to themselves and to others—Dr. Jekyll and Mr. Hyde, the outer appearance of Dorian Gray and his secret image. Again the split may vary very much. To use Jung's metaphor: the "persona" may be affable, amiable, easy going, successful, responsible, honest, the "shadow" a monster, a killer, a wild animal, one who transgresses every limit and betrays every trust. Or the reverse holds true: for a long time the "persona" is the self-destructive, self-punishing, irascible or withdrawn "bum," "junkie"; degraded, loathed, full of self-contempt; the "shadow" is that fantasy of perfection, the angel, totally good. The flipflops, as mentioned, can be most disconcerting—both to their environment and often most surprising and shocking to themselves.

The enormous role of magical fantasy, and with that of omnipotence, is implicit in what just has been outlined. It was Pumpian-Mindlin (1969) who was wondering whether not all fantasy is a derivative of this very early omnipotence (largely reaching back before age two). The later drug use is just one form of living out such fantasy, of taking on an enormous magical power. All the disconnecting is a form of magic (self- and world transformation), all the denial is, all the lifting of boundaries, limits and limitations is.

In short, as far as ego defects are concerned, these patients impressively resemble psychotic patients, and one can well understand that Glover assigned them to a "transitional group" between neurosis and psychosis, and that they usually are called "borderline." As far as their ego functions are concerned, the major differences, if compared with overt psychosis, lie in the preponderance and intensity of both psychogenic and pharmacogenically massively re-enforced denial, the liability and shiftiness of the splits, and particularly in the broad spectrum of modes of externalizaton available. I suspect that mainly thanks to the prevalence of the two defense mechanisms of externalization and denial and perhaps the somewhat less thorough versions of disconnecting, the cognitive functions remain largely protected against the telltale schizophrenic thought disorders. Occasionally I have observed the breaking down of these defenses and the breakthrough of overt schizophrenic processes, particularly as triggered by abstention from drugs.

SELF-CARE

This aspect of ego pathology is very striking and impressive. I quote from a seminal paper by E. Khantzian (in press):

I have been impressed with an apparent disregard that drug dependent individuals show to a whole range of real or possible dangers to their well-being, including their substance involvement. I believe this type of self-disregard is associated with impairments of a generic or global ego-function that I have chosen to designate as *self-care and self-regulation*. I say "generic or global" because I suspect such functions and their impairments are related to component ego functions and various mechanisms of defense. It is probably related to ego functions such as signal anxiety, reality testing, judgment, control, and synthesis, and when impaired, to such defenses as denial, justification, projection, etc.

He explicates that

much of the addict's self-disregard is not so much consciously or unconsciously motivated, but more a reflection of defects in self-care functions as a result of failures to adopt and internalize these functions from the caring parents in early and subsequent phases of development. The overdetermined and defensive forms of self-destructive behavior among addicts do not adequately account for all the terribly dangerous and destructive activity, including death, that such people get into. In such cases danger is not so much consciously or unconsciously welcomed, or counterphobically denied, but rather is never anticipated, perceived and/ or appreciated. These are problems that I consider to be related to self-care (ego) functions, that are impaired, deficient and/ or absent in so many of the addicts we see.

We may add here Anna Freud's comment, in her paper on "developmental lines" (1963), that very often adolescents still uphold their claim and right to endanger their health until remarkably late, and she wondered whether this lack of self-care and risk-taking "may represent the last residue of the original symbiosis between child and mother" (p. 256). There is no possibility to know at this time how far the defect in self-care in these patients may be due to early neglect and deprivation in mothering, how far it may reflect the excessive upholding of the fantasies of omnipotence and symbiotic union with an idealized, but spoiling, mother "who always will take care of me."

Looking into the background of these patients we can find both extremes: utter deprivation as well as maintenance of a symbiotic unity throughout life. In both extremes the outcome may, even dynamically, be the same: "I need the fantasy of a magical unknown force to take care of me; I do not have to do it myself." The fantasy of such a guardian angel I have occasionally encountered in these patients, regardless of whether they had been deprived or overgratified. I suppose that this leads right back into our considerations about splitting and the fantasies of magical omnipotence.

Superego Pathology

What I have noticed most strikingly—not only in this particular group of denying and externalizing patients, but in "sociopaths" in general (who basically use prevalently the same defense mechanisms to cope with narcissism—except that their mode of externalization differs), is not at all the absence of a superego altogether, but what Rangell and the Lowenfelds have described so masterfully: the conflict between ego and superego and the major defenses successfully directed against the latter in form of "the syndrome of compromise of integrity."

THE DEFENSES AGAINST THE SUPEREGO

"Nowadays one can say, though this is oversimplifying, that the decisive repressions do not concern the id, but the superego," wrote Henry and Yela Lowenfeld in 1970. Rangell in two important papers (1974, 1976) postulates a separate entity of disorders:

> In the neuroses the id is sacrificed; in psychosis, reality; in compromise of integrity, the superego gives....Narcissism is the unbridled enemy of integrity....New mechanisms, or combinations of mechanisms, of defense or adaptation may need to be defined in this area of ego-superego, or ego–external world operations, at the border between individual and group action....[1974, p. 8]

In this syndrome "the virtue of consistency is gradually excluded from the armamentarium of moral values. As a final move in this cynical process, the value of living up to one's values, a superego value intrinsic to all the others, is abandoned, by an unconscious mutual pact and common consent. But a price is paid for these appeasement processes and temporary gains. With the loss of integration comes an erosion of integrity, of the unity and cohesion of the human self" (1976, p. 49). One defense, originally suggested by Arlow and taken up by Rangell, is "irrationalization," the "covering of an irrational act by a cover which was itself irrational" (p. 50); others are tentatively suggested to be "a combined mechanism of distortion, denial, rationalization, deception of the self and others, and bridges across unconscious—preconscious—and conscious" (1974, p. 9). There may be intrasystemic conflicts between ego goals (e.g., personal versus rational interests) and between superego values themselves (personal loyality versus truth) (1976, p. 55). Rangell proposes that "the syndrome of compromise of integrity is on a par with neuroses in the life of the human mind" (p. 53).

I add here a few notes from a most important, though little noticed paper: Henry and Yela Lowenfeld's "Our Permissive Society and the Superego" (1970): "today we have the following problem: the inhibiting, controlling, and guiding function of the superego, which largely merges with the ego, is weakened through the weakness of the parents, through indulgent education which fails to train the ego, and through the general social climate of permissiveness. The sexual and aggressive instinctual drives are much less under the guidance of rules. But the severe superego of early childhood still lives in the individual. The result is restlessness, discontent, depressive moods, craving for substitute satisfactions" (p. 596). With the disappointment in the weak, deserting parents goes both a search for "the organizing strength of an ideology" and the "contempt of history," of tradition, of cultural ideas. "The ethical rules lose their power in the fatherless society." Hence "the individual also gains no narcissistic gratification from his ego ideal" and shows the typical symptoms of narcissistic character disorders.

About the societal implications of Rangell's "Compromise of Identity" and Lowenfeld's concept of a prevalence of shamelessness in our culture we shall talk in the chapter on society and culture.

Here we deal with individual pathology of this nature which is of particular intensity and breadth.

Clifford Yorke (1970) noted in addicts "the combination of an externalization of the superego with an impaired reality sense," the "double-sidedness of the superego," and quotes Simmel's observation of a "two-faced superego" as both extremely seductive and severely punitive (1970, p. 153). It appears to me that compulsive drug users may give us a better opportunity to study in detail the defenses against the superego than most other groups of patients (except for other classes of "sociopaths").

In the intrapsychic (and intrafamilial) pathology of drug users the vast syndrome of the compromise of integrity can be studied in depth, in its various facets and variants.

I cannot suggest specific new defense mechanisms. What I find most prominent are:(a) the split within the superego described above, (b) faulty value and ideal formation and (c) archaic, largely external forms of shame anxiety and guilty fears.

SUPEREGO SPLIT

Obviously this phenomenon is merely mobilized in the "heptad of specific cause," but preexists as part of the predisposition, and without difficulties can be discovered prior to any drug use or any other "addictive" activities. How this splitting of standards and precepts is preformed in and continually upheld by the family will be studied later (see also case 4, Patpet).

FAULTY IDEAL FORMATION

Another aspect in the superego pathology is the lack of meaning giving, life determining and guiding values and ideals, or, in their personified form, all powerful myths. The affects described in the "narcissistic crisis" typically emerge when such central values have been shattered or when the need for such an ideal has become particularly painful. (A good example is our Bohemian, case 14).

And here again the family pathology enters. Parents who did not provide a minimum of consistency and of reliability, to the child, especially during his crises of growing up, are not usable as inner beacons, but as targets of rebellious rage and disdain. Such parents, unless replaced in their crucial functions by capable substitutes, make it hard for their children to internalize them as inner guardians against transgressions.

The "high", the relief and pleasure sought with help of the drug is a surrogate ideal, a substitute value, a chemical mythology, which normally would be supplied by the internal sense of meaning, goal directedness and valuation.

EXTERNAL SUPEREGO
FUNCTIONS AND SELF-PUNISHMENT

Part of the externalization or non-internalization of the superego manifests itself as fear of responsibility and commitment. It is part of the passive object dependency instead of an internal directedness by the superego.

As has been noted by nearly all authors writing about alcoholism and other compulsive drug use, the self-destructive, self-punitive aspects of drug abuse are extremely prominent. In some cases, we may observe the direct equivalency of drug use with suicide (cases 5, 6, 19— Shaky, Morpheus, and Andreas). If we take the first away, the second may become the menace. Drug abuse in itself can often (not always) be considered a tamed and protracted suicidal attempt, though we have to be cautious not to fall into the pitfall of the teleological fallacy (post hoc ergo propter hoc). In line with the other aspects of superego pathology described above, we may now add the important role of archaic forms of shame and guilt experienced by all toxicomanics. Moreover their inner need for opprobrium is reflected also outside: in society's disdain, in most of our legislation, in much of the vindictive measures in Synanon and other therapeutic communities. There is no question that very primitive and global fears of humiliation and revenge play a dominant role in the social interaction of these patients. They are usually not simply the consequence of society's reaction, but part of the patient's make-up to begin with.

The vindictiveness and corruptibility of the archaic superego is well known—and this fact is easily observed among our patients, too. Yet this dynamic datum is so frequent and general that we have to assign it low specificity in the predisposition to compulsive drug use.

Again—as throughout—the preponderance of external shame (over guilt) is noteworthy. The difficult question is: is this a reexternalizing of guilt and shame, or is it rather the lack of internalization and introjection to begin with? I cannot give a definitive answer but I have the impression that again we deal with a complementary series, with great individual variations: In some patients we deal mainly with only partial, relatively small scale reexternalization; on the other extreme we find patients who have never internalized much of any shame or guilt.

The extent of remaining islands of solid functioning of the superego—despite splits, defects in ideal formation and externalization—largely determines the prognosis: whether they are treatable, e.g., in psychotherapy, whether they can change in any deeper sense, whether they stick to commitments of any kind—in short whether eventually the toxicomania or other forms of damaging externalization remain master over their lives—or whether the patients themselves become masters over their compulsive drug use.

This makes it necessary to give here a brief comparison of shame and guilt, one which will form, in more extensive shape, part of another study (see Wurmser 1968c).

a. In shame we compare actions, feelings, thoughts, wishes and other aspects of ourselves with an image we want to have of ourselves and we want others to have of us. This comparison is basically a comparison of qualities.

In guilt we compare similar aspects of ourselves, but with a code of ideal actions (demands) and feared counteractions (prohibitions) what we ought or ought not to do. This comparison is basically a comparison of actions.

Thus, we confront the basic quality character of shame with the basic action character of guilt.

b. The next point is the global character of shame, the delimited character of guilt. This difference again does *not* lie on the side of for what we feel guilty or ashamed, but with which we compare it. In shame it is a wishful self-image, the image of a whole person with ideal features, which we use as a yardstick of measure and against which we hold the (delimited) aspects of ourselves. In guilt it is a complex system of ideal actions which we use as measure; this code is delimited and additive, not global.

These two points of differentiation are based on functions of the ego ideal. In contrast, the following two use different aspects of the self-criticizing, self-punishing agency, the conscience.

c. The affect tone in the two types of feared and anticipated condemnation is different: Shame is a form of self-contempt, guilt is a form of self-hatred. Hatred is a type of aggression which wants to mutilate, to hurt and to kill. Contempt wants to eliminate like dirt; it is a more global, less personal type of aggression.

d. Shame has an expressive-perceptual, guilt a motor-aggressive nature. Shame blocks wishes for active exhibition (active fascination) and active looking (curiosity), for being exposed to the looks of others (passive exhibition) and to the exhibition of others (being fascinated). Guilt blocks wishes for attacking, for causing physical pain and penetrating the skin of the other. The aspects of exposure, condemnation and rejection by scorn, and atonement by hiding are the typical steps in the original shame experience. Attack, retaliation by physical punishment and atonement by pain are characteristic for guilt.

Correspondingly, in shame, the censor uses looks (the "eye" of the conscience), in guilt, primarily physical pain ("remorse," "beating"), secondarily the inner voice (the "voice" of the conscience).

e. Shame entails the time element of suddenness, of surprise (of discovery), guilt only the regular sequence of action and counteraction (in its most primitive model).

f. Both have protective functions: they protect the separate, private self with its boundaries and prevent intrusion and merger; thus, they protect in fact the human relationship and prevent complete isolation and rejection. *Shame is the basic protection mechanism in the field of expressive and perceptual interchange* (touching, looking/exhibiting, hearing/talking); guilt fulfills a similar function in the motor active and aggressive field, protecting the physical integrity against hurts (biting, lacerating, castrating, killing).

g. Logically, there is an important difference between shame and guilt experiences. Shame shows two logical levels, the level of the conflict itself and the level of the expressed content of the condemned activity. A similar structure can not be found in guilt; there we have only the conflict itself and a further specification of the condemned activity.

Specifically, in shame, the conflict is between the wishes to expose and express oneself and the anticipated rejection for these wishes; the content of what would be exposed to the expecting or condemning "eyes" of the inner or external censors can reach through the whole developmental spectrum of qualities: oral dependency (exposed weakness), anal or urethral lack of control (exposed dirtiness), phallic mutilation (castration shame) and oedipal exclusion. The only precondition is that these qualities (or actions, etc.) are subjected to the erotized (or destructive) activities of perceptions and expressions.

On the side of guilt, the conflict is clearly that between wishes to hurt and the anticipated painful retaliation. The hurting itself does not, however, have any "content," as opposed to the exposing (*what* to expose), but can only show further specification (*how* to hurt).

After this short exposé of the differentiation between shame and guilt it should be added that in the later developmental stages where all emotions assume a higher symbolic quality and express predominantly internalized and thus structuralized tensions, the original qualities of guilt and shame, as just described, may be transformed and disappear to some extent; but they reappear in the different types of regression. And obviously those are the levels we are concerned with here. These thoughts about guilt and shame have yet other, very relevant sequelae to be taken up in the next two chapters (dealing with narcissism and aggression).

Narcissism and the Concept of Boundaries and Limits

Turning now to one of the towering pillars of predisposition, we have already alluded to the problem of severe and deep narcissistic conflicts as so prominent and wide ranging in our patients: they are archaic conflicts about self-esteem and grandiose expectations, about exaggerated demands and a sense of entitlement, disregard for limits and limitations, the profound wishes for merger or power fears of disillusionment, the painfulness of any structure that embodies a No—we have seen all this overtly in the examples already presented, and all through their lives. We also noted how "narcissistic crises" bring about a regression to earlier, much more archaic forms of narcissistic conflicts. To some extent these phenomena are part of adolescence anyway, e.g., in Pumpian-Mindlin's words: "He knows no limits in fantasy, and accepts grudgingly any limits in reality." Only later (in the early twenties) "the step from omnipotentiality to commitment" is done. However, "if the individual finds the conflict too great to be more or less successfully resolved, he may retreat into fantasy, often regressing to the level of infantile omnipotence and magical thinking" where no limitations need to be recognized (1969, pp. 222, 223). This is always the case in compulsive drug users.

Unfortunately, we do not yet know whether there is any further specification about these conflicts which in their archaic and massive form are certainly not restricted to this category of pathology (see Kernberg 1975, Kohut 1971). Therefore, there is quite low specificity (though particular massivity) to this part of the precondition, in contrast to the earlier aspects. (In this, the distinction between specificity and strength in the etiological consideration is helpful.) Here, however, might lie the reason for the peculiar breakdown in reality testing so often encountered in these patients. Reality has to bend to their wishes. Denials, omissions and lies are so often in the service of the magical omnipotence of wish and thought, leading, as described, to the many types of "splitting." All reality has to be stretched, altered, (really "over-stretched and broken"), to accomodate the grandiose self. And yet it is not a psychotic break with reality. The limits are known—acknowledged and denied.

It is also important that the massivity of narcissistic demands squarely rests on the "grandiose self," often various, contradictory nuclei of this narcissistic structure; the "idealized self-object" is far less important.

The counterpart to these intrapsychic narcissistic demands and defenses against them is the family pathology. We shall return to that shortly. But the more we ponder these problems, the deeper we find ourselves mired in new questions which are barely mentioned in the literature.

If we accept the definition of narcissism as investment of the self with psychological interest, we immediately recognize that we can subdivide in many ways such a vast "investment." Even when we add to this the important two "structures" worked out by Kohut and their various developmental stages we are still faced with a continent of vast uncharted territories.

Where we deal with narcissism we resort above all to concepts of power (and their extremes: omnipotence and helplessness), and with that to borders, to limits of power. I.e., we have to contemplate expansion and contraction of this power and with that the many plains on which the self claims or abrogates rights, and where his rights are confirmed or violated. Then we have to deal with knowing and its extremes: omniscience and ignorance. Also we would have to be concerned about what we are permitted or allow ourselves in claiming pleasures and in renouncing them, where to set limits and accept limitations. We have huge gaps between what we value very highly and what we despise—in ourselves as well as in others, in society, in culture, in history: we claim traditions or national solidarity as ours (within some imaginary border), and we perceive others as violently foreign, strange, "outside." (Freud and Eissler wrote about such cultural and national narcissism.) Perhaps most importantly and most primitively there is the boundary between self and others.

Thus the whole concept of boundaries and limits turns out to become crucial for the study of narcissism. (The following is a shortened and much revised version of Wurmser 1968d; I am very grateful for the comments and suggestions which I received from Dr. A. H. Modell.) All the boundaries are starting to shift, waive, become blurred in the use of drugs. Typically, toxicomanic and even less compulsive types of drug abusers, have a profound problem with these boundaries on many levels, in many areas—long before they ever touched their first drug. To some extent, some blurring of boundaries occurs in the conscious and preconscious thinking and feeling also in neurotics, and is probably an integral part of the human condition. In drug abusers it is far more massive, extant also in areas which usually are spared in others.

In the following I can give only a very abbreviated study of this most complicated, vastly neglected field. My thoughts are very tentative and cautious. In this chapter about narcissism and in the following about aggression—in both of which I arrive at novel formulations—I feel I am groping in an overgrown, dark thicket, trying to find a lost path. I believe the best glimpses of light were lent by the patients. What it eventually all will mean theoretically (e.g., for our metapsychology, especially the drive theory) will have to accommodate the vast range of new phenomena shown to us by these experiences.

THE PUZZLE OF BOUNDARIES

When we try to be more specific and clearer, we might think first of the border between inner life and outer reality, the one implied in Heraclitus' words: "Those who are awake have one and a common world; each one, however, of those who sleep turns to his own private world." Yet where is this line between inner and outer reality, between private and common?

Moreover, even in the shared outer world many boundaries are drawn and may assume psychopathological relevance. It becomes a fascinating task to examine where to draw these lines. Where, for instance, is the line of intimacy? What do we mean if we do not recognize the borders between private and public, between what belongs in an intimate relationship, and what belongs in a mere acquaintance? What if we feel distant and aloof from another person, when we say we cannot reach him, that, in a sense, he is off limits to us, or that we would be out of bounds if we intruded? What line do we overstep when we demand something unreasonable? What if we do not draw the line between what was and what is, what belongs to me and what is your possession, what if we violate someone's honor or dignity?

There is something very intriguing, yet barely explored, in this connotational realm of limits, boundaries, lines. But what makes it especially relevant for a psychotherapist is not its theoretical import, but how precisely charged this cluster of connotations is in psychotherapy. We know how painful it is for our patients "to realize that they have to accept their limitations." We also know what a central role, particularly in the therapy of "borderline" patients (including all compulsive drug users), that type of interpretation plays in which we make the patient aware of the limits of reality, that limit where shared reality ends and where his fantasy begins, or—in the area of superego prohibitions and ideals—where the limits of his rights are and where those of the other person begin.

What makes this theme even more bewildering is the fact that both self and object world do not cover simply a territory on one plain of functions, but a range of interconnected areas. Moreover, the experience of self and object world is often not even coherent and self-consistent. Just as after a number of conquests, the old borders, like the Roman "Limes," remain still noticeable, so the old boundaries of the self and of the realms of objects endure to a certain degree throughout life. (Freud used a similar metaphor in *Civilization and Its Discontents*, comparing the persistence of inner structures with the walls and buildings of the various historical layers of Rome.)

DEMARCATIONS

Plainly, these topographic terms are of limited usefulness. Whereas affects, wishes and defense, and ideation can be experienced and thus are observable, boundaries can be concrete or on various levels of abstraction. The concept of boundaries where it is psychologically most relevant is a strictly metaphorical, therefore theoretical model, based often more on metapsychological inference than on direct subjective experience. The basic metaphor employed in the boundary concept is, of course, that of spatial relationships. However, since only structures can have boundaries, this (version of a "topographic") model can be considered an expansion of the structural point of view. However, all three structures, id, ego, superego, participate and conflict in these complex narcissistic constructs, although all boundary setting, -keeping, -recognizing, and -changing are part of ego functions (or a separate ego function by itself?).

Not all boundaries are *ego boundaries* as Federn originally described them, but we may start out with them. This term is usually used to describe how far the feelings of the *unity of the self* are extended—both as a continuity of the self in time, as a cohesion of functions in the present and as a bounded unit vis-à-vis others (Kohut). It appears preferable to designate them as self-boundaries. What is enclosed by them is experienced as identical with and part of the self.

A second form of boundaries is recognized as limits in our relationships to objects. We may designate them as *boundaries of our activities and passivities*. These limits to our power of relating have a most relevant narcissistic aspect which will be studied in the rest of this chapter in detail.

A third form are *intrapsychic boundaries* between different macro- or microstructures in our mind (also studied in still very illuminating papers by Paul Federn and his student, Eduardo Weiss), e.g., various states of our self, past and present self-images, between ego and drives, between various ego functions, between different percepts, affects and thoughts, between thinking and acting, (and, not to forget, the inner lines set by our conscience—actually just an internalization of the second form of boundaries). That the delimiting of these inner structures depends largely on the narcissistic equilibrium became clear when we studied narcissistic decompensation in chapter 6. In the collapse of self-esteem all these structures either regress or disappear. Ego and superego become rent and torn, a sense of fragmentation is directly expressed by very perceptive patients. (Andreas, to be presented, will be a particularly good example.)

A particular instance of blurring of this type of boundaries is encountered in some neurotic patients, again where there is a prevalence of shame. The equation has four parts: all thoughts, feelings and desires (as emerging in analysis in form of words) = actions = the whole self = the consciously identified with, but contemned and condemned, parent. This includes, of course, the most frequent magical equation of words and actions.

The fourth form of boundaries are the *boundaries between different objects* as we see them, not only people, but things as well, also boundaries between illusion and real world, between how we would like to see objects and how we have to distinguish them. Especially psychedelic drugs are of course famous for the blurring of these boundaries.

One patient who, in a very self-sabotaging way, changed every work situation into a "cocoon," a shelter, a replication of a very dependent, but also extremely ambivalent relationship with both parents (and obviously originally mother, the great "betrayer"), found that the critical step in his treatment occurred when he drew the line between reality and fantasy: "Again it is a question of boundaries; I distorted the whole situation into one where I was special, where I was given something for nothing, where I was protected—not one where I actually used the given opportunity and factually worked. Instead I saw it as a shimmering screen, obscuring the reality." It was the insight into the clear boundary between a persistent (and still present) fantasy and the real circumstance, which he found the turning point of maturation. What this boundary drawing entailed was indeed a kind of adaptive splitting: the cleavage obtained between clinging to (and gradual dissolution of) a regressive fantasy and a clear recognition of reality—a therapeutic cleavage within an illusion which had merged both.

The fifth and final form of *boundaries* is set up *between different areas of functioning*—e.g., the boundary between the private and the public domain, or the boundary between concrete material functioning and symbolic functions. A typical example is the one so frequent in neurotic patients: the mixing up of professional, social, sexual, and business interests in one relationship. A doctor-patient or a co-worker relationship becomes also sexual (without a real deepening into a true emotional intimacy) and, in addition, turns into a partnership in some "get rich quick" game. Moreover a goodly dosage of psychotherapeutic one-upmanship (e.g., misusing psychoanalytic terms, using notions from transactional analysis, etc.) may be thrown in for good measure. All boundaries are dissolved; everything goes.

In all this a much deeper dialectic becomes apparent: All forms of growth mean expansion, transcending of boundaries, merging, deepening of relations regardless of limits—and yet even that has to be within confines. Expansion without crucial boundaries and limits turns into outer anarchy and inner disintegration, whereas too strict observance of boundaries of all forms turns into an obsessional rigidity, a conservative fixity, stifling creativity and growth, openness and spontaneity. The synthesis necessary is a delicate, constantly changing balance.

This entire problem of boundary formation has been theoretically and practically neglected. It is usually simply equated with self/non-self boundaries, and yet the concept transcends that particular differentiation by far.

Although the boundary theory is crucial in the understanding of psychotics, ubiquitous in neurotics, it is of particularly broad significance for compulsive drug users—theoretically and, even more importantly, practically: if we do not help the patients to accept limits, "structures," borders (all special forms of boundaries), if we do not draw clear lines in all areas just described, we are lost in quicksand where no foothold is possible.

Since the drawing of all such demarcations is basically nothing but a form of separation, the formation of all these boundaries has to be profoundly affected by conflicts attending the separation and individuation process.

Furthermore, the formation and recognition of boundaries of the kinds described is an inherent aspect of various ego functions, above all that of reality testing—but also of defensive mechanisms (referred to above as a special continuum, e.g. projection and introjection), of perception and of symbol formation. An examination of boundary formation implies thus a change of vantage point and helps to comprise a considerable number of observations and clinical theories in one model whose core still remains the concept of *narcissism*, but will also shed new light on the development of aggression.

All five types of boundaries are certainly part of the representational world, but, like the notions of identity or symbols, they also always have a referent in outside reality. The boundaries as seen by the individual, that is the boundaries in his representations, may or may not coincide with the boundaries as seen by and shared with his surroundings. The attempt to attain congruence of these two referents is known to us as reality testing.

This double function of boundaries—as inner representation and as outer referent—is particularly clear when there is a discrepancy, as in the well known clinical situation when the subject's view of the boundaries of his self, his self-representations, do not coincide with the boundaries assigned to him from the outside, by his family or his peers. For the study of the overtly psychotic patient and the "psychotic character," this first form of boundaries, namely the boundaries of the self, appears, as emphasized by numerous authors, to be most relevant.

In this chapter, however, I propose to explore the boundary formation of the second kind in particular, an inquiry which can be understood only if we see it as a small segment of a much larger inquiry. This second form of boundaries consists of the limits set to our activities.

For this study I select two affects as starting line, which may help us on the way to understand and to formulate this more clearly. Since we had occasion already to use them in regard to the superego, but more importantly, because they seem to be peculiarly relevant for this topic of boundary formation and its narcissistic libidinous and aggressive aspects, I again refer to the affects of guilt and shame, which in one formulation or another are of cardinal importance in every psychoanalytic and psychotherapeutic situation.

BETWEEN SCYLLA AND CHARYBDIS: THE GUILT-SHAME DILEMMA

Among the tragedies, it is probably the drama of Antigone, Oedipus's daughter, which describes the double dialectic of shame and guilt on both sides of the conflict in the most gripping way.

Antigone decides, against the tyrant Creon's decree, to render to her traitor brother Polyneices the honor of the burial rites instead of the exposure of his body to dogs and birds, "a ghastly sight of shame." She consider herself without guilt: "For me who is going to do this, it's noble to die; for I owe a longer allegiance to the dead than to the living." Defiantly she transgresses man-made laws to honor "the unwritten and stable laws of heaven." For Creon her deed is both a "grave guilt" and a shame for acting apart from "all these Thebans" and "of rendering a grace" to the traitor. Thus she accepts the guilt of breaking Creon's law in order not to be guilty of breaking the laws of the Gods. She accepts the shame of being an outlaw in order not to partake in the shame of dishonoring her dead brother.

Creon, however, sees in this attitude "hybris," arrogant pride: "But know that too rigid spirits fall deepest. It does not behoove him to think in pride who is the neighbor's slave. Yet this one understood herself in arrogance (hybris) perfectly when she overstepped the existing laws." Antigone accuses him of the same arrogance: "And if you think my acts are foolishness, the foolishness may be in a fool's eyes." But he maintains his guiltful stand of strength to avoid the shame of weakness: "Therefore I must support the cause of order, and not let myself be beaten by a woman. Better to fall from power, if we must, by a man's hand; then we should not be called weaker than a woman .... While I live, no woman will rule me." His own son, Haemon, tries to shake him in his false pride: "No, though a man be wise, it is no shame for him to learn many things, and to bend in season ... think not that your mind, and your alone, must be right." Stubbornly avoiding humiliation and shame, Creon is crushed by guilt for having by his arrogant pride brought death to his whole family.

Leaving aside the complexities and the fineness of the texture of the Sophoclean tragedies, we may recognize in "Antigone," as in all the others, in both protagonists, a double conflict between two extreme stands for two values, resulting in double defeat: In Creon it is an overriding and stubborn emphasis on honor, pride, and power; thus he tries to avoid the curse of shame (the shame-pride conflict). Yet ineluctably he thus transgresses the laws of ethical order and incurs guilt (the guilt-triumph conflict) - and at the end he still falls into abysmal shame and humiliation, into an ultimate doom of disgrace and weakness. Both parts: the affirmation of excessive pride and the violation of the ethical postulates are narcissistic phenomena, although we can discern in both also intensely aggressive elements. On the other side we find in Antigone an extreme stand of defending the higher laws and avoiding a higher order of guilt—but thus incurring shame and disgrace (and even lower order guilt as well); it is an absolute defense of an object libidinal value, but in its very excess and overvaluation again, paradoxically, assumes narcissistic qualities and ends in at least one form of narcissistic defeat.

A similar dialectic may emerge in clinical situations: A typical example of this conflict I have seen in an agoraphobic woman in intensive psychotherapy who reacted to the interpretation of her transference feelings by the words: "It made me so uncomfortable; it was like you were looking through me. It was weird. I thought, what I think is my business, you do not have to know about it. But when I came home I felt guilty of not having told you." She was ashamed to talk or hear about her feelings and ashamed of the feelings themselves yet felt guilty afterwards of having hidden them. "There is a tremendous difference between guilt and shame. Guilt feelings bring material into the interview, shame keeps it out" (Tarachow 1963, p. 171).

Another shame-guilt dilemma can be seen in a woman, just separated from her husband, who requests a therapeutic abortion: she is ashamed of being pregnant and having people know about it; so she wants to eliminate the disgrace and to conceal the fact from everybody. But she feels guilty of "killing the baby." As intolerable the shame may have appeared before, as deep is the guilt felt afterwards.

CASE 18: RAZIT

This woman, at the time I started seeing her, was in her mid-twenties. I saw her first in a chronic state of suicidal depression and depersonalization, where the conflict between these two categories led to a near psychotic break. Much later on she developed a problem of compulsive alcohol abuse. This woman, an excellent painter and photographer, but living in severe poverty, is the older of two daughters of an alcoholic, cruel father and an overbearing, nagging mother; the parents separated on and off during the childhood, while the patient was left mainly under the care of an embittered, but indulgent grandmother. As a child she hated her father with a vengeance because of his very frequent outbursts of devastating rage; at times she even believed that he tried to poison her. In school, the patient was treated with a curious mixture of open contempt and hidden admiration: she was avoided as an outcast because of her drunkard and promiscuous father, but praised for her exceptional gifts as a little artist. As an adolescent she finally succeeded in pushing her despised father out of the household (and having mother and grandmother all to herself), but soon got married herself to a paranoid man who later turned out to be a transvestite. With him she reestablished the home situation: the dependency on, and the clinging to, a weak and ineffectual, but also tyrannical and demanding partner whom she could not forgive the failure to support and protect her, and with whom she got into incessant quarreling and murderous fights.

Despite the advent of two children, she continued both her training as an artist and her work as the main provider for the family until the third pregnancy made both economically and emotionally impossible. The birth of this third child thus became the cataclysmic event which sealed her breakdown: it was immediately followed by a sense of physical sickness and utter weakness, ineluctably to be paid for by death. At the same time, she was bare of any of the usual feelings; she could not sense the colors, but, instead, felt noise and light to stab her as with knives and an all-pervasive horror. It was a vacillation between a state of severe depersonalization and a state of almost hallucinatory hyperperception of aggression, very similar to Alexa (case 13).

In an oversimplified synopsis of her life history we see the following texture: From early childhood she lived in a world without trust and warmth, full of rage and power demands. On a deeper layer of consciousness she tried to re-establish a symbiotic union with her mother and to kill her intruding father. This conflict on the level of oral-sadistic incorporation and symbiotic merger was a revival of early fixation in the oral phase, and had followed the regression from traumatic events on the oedipal level, mainly from central fantasies of oral impregnation.

Important for us is that her (highly narcissistic) ideal was to become a powerful, essentially bisexual person, a savior of mother and grandmother, invincible and invulnerable, superhuman and dependent upon no one, of sovereign creativity and godly mastery. "Actually I was God. Feelings could not penetrate. It was the same apartness (as now), but I was superior, I was in control of everything and never upset. I want to have this power back." Her artistic gift provided her with the tool to maintain this fiction of omnipotence which outweighed her outward humiliation. It was only when this image was effectively shattered and the fiction became untenable that the fall into humiliation and helpless dependency became irreparable. This crucial moment occurred when, overwhelmed by pain during labor, she broke out into crying and screaming; this was proof to her that she had lost control over herself and over her whole life. "From this moment on, the world was not the same anymore." Then, the panic of loneliness and the rage of hunger took over. She wanted to give this third child away for adoption; "I cannot accept the baby; it is destroying me. The baby is my depression. It wants everything I eat." She wanted to eliminate it because it reflected her own oral demands and rages. Shortly before this climax, the long overdue separation from her schizophrenic husband evoked deep rage against herself, so aptly described by Modell as "separation guilt" (1965). "Like some voice told me I have no right to live. If I did feel better, it would be only temporary—I should die anyway." Unable to separate from outside persons, she cannot divorce herself from her own raging inner demon, her superego, either; it is more powerful than she is, like a heavy black weight in the head, an inevitable, pervasive sense of guilt. As part of this "separation guilt" she blames herself for having inflicted something horrible on her children because she has deprived them of their father. Deep down, separation appears as a mutual and murderous betrayal, punishable by death.

Yet, in turn, now more than ever, any contact, any pleasure leads to new guilt; it is not only undeserved; it is evil in itself because it consummates again the devouring destructive union where she may reassert her control and power. Thus, the dilemma appears to be: not to separate, to be fused with the object in a union, which is incompatible with outer reality—or to withdraw totally into extreme isolation—which is incompatible with inner reality. Both paths lead to archaic rage and destruction.

Creativity as a painter presented her with a way out from this lifelong conflict: she was mastering the outside reality, she was independent, yet not separated from it. Again in this context we have just to bypass the central equation between her creative activity and her fantasy that she—not mother—had a baby from her father, and the guilt brought about by this transgression. We focus now only upon that function of creativity which helped her to gratify her exorbitant wish for power without her being overwhelmed by psychotic demands for omnipotence. As she expressed it succinctly: "The painted things become very real, I have a sense of reality in the painting. If I did not succeed in it, I would not exist either." Already as a child, she astounded everyone with her creations. "They were almost like visions. I felt kind of supernatural—that no one could enter into these visions and these types of expressions."

Yet this way out into creativity meant also guilt: "When I started drawing, when I could see visual images different from other children, I felt guilty about having this talent; it was like witchcraft because of the way the world perceived me: 'how could this wretched kid with a drunken father possibly have this talent.' The more I felt the power, the stronger I felt it was an evil power—to draw. The deeper the feeling, the sense of creativity, the more it was godly, magical. If I could reach this godlike feeling, I had thought it would protect me from guilt and shame. But the fulfillment was never enough. I was riding on the crest of a wave until I crashed. Creativity and destruction were equal. What I put into my drawings is not what I see. I break it up and put it together again. This impending of destructiveness must have seeped through. No matter how much I tried to build and rebuild, some kind of horror was tearing it down. Now that I broke down I can never make up for this sense of failure."

This leads to the second point: "I am denied the sense to be like another human being; I feel a separation between you and me. It is my weakness. If people found this out, I would be disgraced, I would be lost. I had the feeling something was after me, as if people were staring at me, closing in on me. I felt I was going to disappear; everything became disorganized, chaotic. It is mankind's betrayal, the humiliation in my childhood which set me apart. And that I screamed (during the childbirth) was such a humiliating defeat. That changed everything; suddenly something was terribly wrong, my world had collapsed. Underneath is now always this horror: that I did collapse, physically and mentally, and could collapse again."

Thus the alternative can be reformulated: to be omnipotent but to feel guilty both for overstepping her boundaries and for the destruction inherent in power, particularly inherent in the power of creation—or to be weak, but to accept the abysmal humiliation and shame of failure, of not having made up for the ignominy of the family.

We may vary this formulation and also say: she is torn (split) by an identity conflict—one identity (actually again an entire "intersystemic suborganization"), that of the creative, but inherently omnipotent, artist is guilt-ridden and leads to depression; the opposite identity (suborganization), that of the Pariah, the helplessly dependent girl, and parasite on human society, greedily dependent upon the scornful pity of charitable agencies, is inherently shame-ridden and leads first to massive depersonalization, then to near psychotic states of persecutory anxiety. Both identities reflect her archaic narcissistic conflict, one her grandiose self, the second the omnipotent (and dangerous) other. In passing we can notice once again the prominence of varied phenomena of splitting in life and personality organization of this woman.

The consequences of the two types of conflict are different: Beset by guilt, she hurts herself in a number of severe physical ailments and pains. She sentences herself to death and sees the world either as lifeless or as attacking her with its cruel glaring and loudness.

Beset by shame, she wants to disappear, to hide from the contemptuous eyes of the world; she veils the outside reality with the curtain of estrangement and mutes all her emotions with the cover of depersonalization. Yet, the result of shame is deepest loneliness and separation, accompanied by wild violence by looks and words from the outside, and thus again leads back to an omnipresent devouring rage and with that back to guilt.

What we have found so far we may now translate into the boundary concept: What she tries to achieve is a complete trustful union and intimacy where she can give up all boundaries but those of respect. Since she is unable to attain this basic goal of trust, she tries on two alternative routes to find a replacement: One is the route of superiority, grandeur and dignity, but leading to grandiosity and arrogance, to the hybris of the Greek heroes, and ending in a catastrophic sense of guilt. The other is the route of submission and weakness, but leading to a sucking dependency, to self loss in symbiotic merger and desperate helplessness, and ending in a catastrophic sense of shame (Erikson 1968, p. 168, 183, Grinker 1955). Thus, after the breakdown of her illusions, the boundaries, defended by guilt and shame, collapse; and panic and aggression, bound in these two affects, break through (Fenichel 1945, pp. 132-140)—as traumatic guilt anxiety: the fear of being mutilated and dismembered; and as traumatic shame anxiety: the overwhelming sense of being stared at and of dissolving into a nothing, of vanishing under punishing, stabbing looks into unreality, lifelessness, stoniness, indeed appearing like a mask.

SHAME AND GUILT BOUNDARIES

Both guilt and shame are complexly structured affects arising only after the formation of the superego; but each one is built around a cluster of preoedipal precursors, above all guilt anxiety and shame anxiety. As we have already seen, there is a core experience for each one. In guilt it is: If I *hurt* the love object, it turns against me and hurts me—physically or emotionally (Jacobson 1964, p. 146, Levin 1967, p. 274). In shame it is: If I *expose* myself to the object and show that I am weak, it stares at me in contempt (Piers and Singer 1953, Lynd 1961,

Levin, 1967, p. 268), feeling, e.g., as Hester Prynne in *The Scarlet Letter*, "the heavy weight of a thousand unrelenting eyes," or it burns, as in Conrad's *Lord Jim:* "to burn a man to ashes with shame," and, "the shame that made you burn, the attentive eyes whose glance stabbed." The extreme threat in guilt is to be mutilated, beaten and bitten to pieces, to be dismembered, e.g. as the totem victim. The extreme threat in shame is to be separated, isolated, rejected, excluded forever, an icy sense of not being human anymore, of becoming stonelike, of being treated with that scorn which a German expression puts well:—"to treat like air."

In this context, however, the spotlight shifts onto one particular aspect: i.e., preceding both feelings there is a movement or action of the subject, of us, which, when a certain line is reached, may lead to this specific anxiety. If we examine the different lines guarded by guilt and by shame, we come to the following antithesis: If we violate the physical integrity of the object or his social prestige and power we hurt him. The object feels pain and hurt. We feel guilt, we have transgressed a moral boundary. Victor Hugo had the same boundary in mind—though on a higher level of abstraction—when he said that "despotism violates the moral frontier, as invasion violates the geographical frontier" *(Les Miserables).*

If we violate another form of limit around the object, namely, if we intrude into his privacy, the object feels shame. This form of intrusion has a different quality: "Never look a horse or a dog or a child in the eye for longer than a few seconds; it shames them" (Thornton Wilder, *The Eighth Day*)—whereas "in love it is the dissolution of pride and separateness; it is surrender."

We can rephrase this same social observation in different pairs: *Guilt prevents our power from infringing upon the sphere of the other; shame prevents the other from infringing upon the private sphere of ourselves.* In Hawthorne's words: it "keeps the inmost Me behind its veil." Or in Conrad: "A single word had stripped him of his discretion—of that discretion which is more necessary to the decencies of our inner being than clothing is to the decorum of our body" *(Lord Jim.) Guilt limits strength; shame protects weakness—it is caused by, and stops, the reduction of power.* Guilt protects the object relationship from the narcissistic claims and its aggressive "henchmen"; shame protects one's own narcissistic integrity. These terms have a double meaning: both affects prevent violation of these boundaries, as anticipatory signals; but they also arise after these boundaries have been violated. They are guardians and helmsmen, protecting the borders in peacetime and defending them, once war has broken out.

If there are exalted claims and we fail, our territory of power shrinks, and we feel shame; if the same claims succeed infringing upon the rights of the other person, we feel guilt. Two examples: any attempt to show power, to impress, to force, to attack—sexually or socially—in regard to an object, who is valued as a separate and loved person, and which leads to hurt of the partner, causes guilt. If this attempt, however, fails to arouse any response or leads to defeat and rejection, it engenders shame. Our showing of emotions and giving of ourselves which is responded to and accepted does cause neither guilt nor shame, but if it is an aggressive move to overpower the object, it can evoke guilt in us. If it is turned down, it leads to shame in us.

The movement covered by guilt is that of hurting and harming the other; the movement watched over by shame is the intrusion by the other into the sphere of my privacy. Both movements are object related; and yet, both are expressions of crucially important narcissistic wishes as well: of the sense of power, of self-esteem, self-expansion and self-protection. The direction is different, however; in guilt it is an outward movement—towards the objects; in shame it is an inward movement, quasi an invitation, an opening up, by the subject.

The two fears thus delimit the range of power: Both shame and guilt are topically different forms of anxiety and have characteristic signal functions. Shame marks the boundary beyond which no object may intrude, a form of inner boundary which we may call the *boundary of privacy*. Guilt, on the other side, signifies the limits beyond which the subject may not step, a kind of outer boundary, which could be called the *boundary of power expansion*.

Whenever this signal function totally fails and the boundary collapses, massive traumatic guilt—or shame anxiety occurs.

But there is a second essential difference: These movements have a predilection for certain aspects of the body and for certain relationships ("areas") with the outside world, and use radically different forms of aggression. To this point I shall return later on.

Applied to our patient Razit we recognize these two boundaries. She felt guilty whenever she expanded her power. Her creativity was a kind of hybris violating the social rules and the laws of nature. She stepped with temerity "out of her place." Her separation from her husband (she threw him out in a fight as she had fought off her father) was guiltful mainly because she assumed she had hurt her children irreparably— since "separation is the worst thing that can happen." She had really "destroyed" the father of her children. In her spiteful suicidal rages against her friends or her therapist, she expected "to be put back in her place"—by angry retorts which would relieve her of her guilt and reestablish the old balance, the old frontier.

In contrast, she felt humiliated beyond endurance, filled with shame, when she saw herself as weak and without the magic power and complete self-control. "The scorn of a whole lifetime now suddenly got through to me." The looks of people, the glares of light, seemed to penetrate into the core of herself, without any protection by the boundary of privacy.

Shame is not just the shattering of the ideal; it requires the element of exposure; it is felt only when one is seen in ignominy—by the eyes of the world or by the inner eye of the conscience (Erikson 1959, pp. 142-143, 1968, p. 280). For Razit, to be vulnerable meant to be now without any defense; she would not have any boundary left, she would disappear under the looks of people.

We need to pursue this difficult line of inquiry yet further, to still more meaningful "lines," boundaries, limits, of still broader applicability.

THE TERRITORIALITY OF THE SCHIZOPHRENIC: PRIVACY AND OBJECT LOSS

Up to now we have talked in a metaphorical way about an outer boundary limiting some of our activities, and about an inner boundary limiting some of our passive, receiving patterns. We may now ask ourselves whether we cannot place this one group of observations into a larger picture. Perhaps these two types of boundaries—the guilt and the shame boundary—are merely particular instances of a more general rule and really perhaps derivatives of an archaic inheritance of territoriality in man. To answer this question we may turn to a curious phenomenon observed with many regressed schizophrenics. Like animals, these patients maintain a safe distance from any other person. If someone tries to enter their territory they attack the intruder with furious rage. In less regressed schizophrenics this territoriality is not so much in form of physical distance as in that of aloofness, unapproachability and narcissistic haughtiness. The imprudent penetration of the boundary leads to violent rage, mostly in form of self-destruction. It is as if there existed an inner boundary the violation of which is frightening to the utmost and equated with the annihilation of the self. We see too that this boundary is not metaphorical at all anymore, but very often very concrete.

In turn, in most of these patients there emerges an outer geographic boundary. The patient may appear shy, withdrawn and angrily seclusive yet he has a quality of yearning, as if waiting for the distant other to move closer. While maintaining all the safeguards of unassailability, he still tries also to prevent the separation from the other. If he pushes the other beyond this border, the object appears lost to him, dead, not existing anymore. Again the consequence is fright and rage, the attempt to coerce the object back to the boundary and thus to retain it under his power and influence.

What makes life so intolerable *to* these persons and often indeed *with* them, is their incapability to reconcile the needs for these two boundaries. Their demand for fusion with the object has to violate the inner boundary of narcissistic self-preservation, whereas their demand for isolation from the object has to push the other far beyond the outer boundary, thus disrupting the relationship. It is simpler to state this in terms of the two abundantly known conflicting basic impulses: the impulse to merge with the object totally, and its opposite, the wish to isolate the self from the object equally totally; but this simple formulation clearly shows the problem of the "self-boundaries" while neglecting the deep impact this conflict has on boundary and limit formation in the entire *field of action*—in regard to human relations as well as to non-human objects, even just action per se.

THE INNER AND THE OUTER BOUNDARY

We can now go yet one step further in our inquiry and outline in a few strokes a more general interpretation of what we have found. The appearance of these two boundaries is restricted neither to schizophrenics nor to guilt and shame experiences. This duplicity of boundaries is a common and normal phenomenon, occurring in all areas of human relationships: the inner is guarding privacy and narcissistic integrity against the intrusion by others; the outer is guarding the object relationship against one's own narcissistic-aggressive claims. The inner is maintaining the intactness of the self, the outer the intactness of the object; the inner prevents total merger and dissolution of the self, the outer prevents total separation and destruction of the object. The inner boundary decides how far I may allow the outside world to intrude into my domain ("the right of your fist ends where my nose begins"); the outer boundary determines how far *my* claims may reach. Thus, we realize that guilt is merely a specific type of the outer boundary, namely in the specific area of force, whereas shame is one example of the inner frontier, namely in the area of self-expression and communication.

It is the mutually recognized range of activity between these two boundaries which, I believe, constitutes what Erikson designated as "identity." If the inner line breaks, we lose (in that area) our identity, and have a sense of disintegration and self-loss, partially, temporally— or more radically. If the outer limits are partly or fully disbanded, often a very similar feeling of self-loss, of flowing out and merging with strangers, of diffusion and anarchy occurs. This loss of the object's boundary is really just as frightening as the loss of the self-boundary. If we transgress these established outer boundaries, we try to delimit our identity anew, perhaps by violence or by our own new claims for laws. If the lines in different areas are too discrepant, too inconsistent, we struggle between disparate identities of ourselves.

Although in the cases of Razit (case 18) and Andreas (case 19) these boundaries are particularly important, playing on many levels, reflecting a precarious balance between aggression in the service of narcissism and protection of object libidinal ties, I have to reemphasize that this entire comparison of guilt and shame boundaries is merely one small example of the bewildering intrapsychic and interpersonal problem of boundary and limit formation. The boundary problem is a narcissistic topic insofar as it is always narcissism which tries to expand the self's territory outward with its power, its prestige, its wish to exploit, to know and explore, to pry, to unveil, to garner admiration and fascinated acclaim, etc. It is a problem of aggression insofar as it destroys the boundaries and claims and rights, even survival of others. It is object-libidinal only insofar as and when it respects these boundaries, these manifold, subtle lines which demarcate the other's needs, rights, claims, weaknesses and when the limits are lifted by mutual consent (e.g., in sexual merger and loving trust).

I feel that with these thoughts I have only scratched the surface of an as yet barely considered problem of extreme complexity which, if pursued further, could elucidate much about the nature of narcissism and the optimal treatment for narcissistic, "borderline," and even psychotic personalities (see chapter 16 and Appendix E). As stated, this entire problem needs above all urgent theoretical attention in psychoanalysis.

But what has this to do with the predisposition of compulsive drug use? A lot—and yet most of it also is unknown, unexplored. I already mentioned that not one of the conceivable inner or outer boundaries remains firm and stable in these patients. Their exorbitant narcissism plus their massive splits of ego and superego derived from the all-pervasive denials, repressions and regressions, plus, on top of everything else, the direct pharmacotoxic effect (let alone the very illicitness of most of these drugs)—all lend to these boundaries a curious fluidity. Yet this lability and flux indeed precedes the inception of drug use. The question has to remain open: How is it that the narcissistic problems affect all these initially mentioned boundaries and limits to such an enormous extent, I would say, far more than in any other category of illness (including very many schizophrenics)?

A most striking counterpoise to this narcissistic dissolution of boundaries is the yearning many of these patients have for external structure, even confinement in jail. Yes, even the hustling after drugs, the drug rituals themselves, the drugs and their effects, all of them provide these weakly bounded selves, these boundary-dissolving personalities, with some semblance of external structure, form, shape. We shall return in the sections about therapy to this curious need for external boundary, even rigidity. Here though we may take up a thread from earlier on and refer to one other consequence: the fear of being limited by boundaries is one form of claustrophobia, and the wish to be protected by them its opposite (a counterphobic attitude? or claustrophilia?). Together with the profound ambivalence these patients have about all limits, they show a typical vacillation between a frenetic bursting out and running away from everything that hems them in (rules, deadlines, laws, structures, human closeness) and a rueful return to confinement, an oscillation between claustrophobic and agoraphobic character traits. As hinted at in the discussion of the heptad and repeatedly seen in the case presentations, we can conclude that at least part of the core disturbance in these patients consists of a very archaic (pregenital) phobic neurosis, with features of claustro- and agoraphobia, and referring to all types of external boundaries. Accordingly the defenses entering into the phobic constellation— repression, projection, displacement, reversal, regression, and condensation—all are to be sought in their core of pathology.

In psychotics these boundaries collapse primarily in regard to perception; in compulsive drug users and perhaps in "sociopaths" generally they are destroyed primarily in action. Both types eventually meet in the field of cognition where inner fragmentation and massive misjudgments reflect a similar breakdown of boundaries in both categories of illness. It deserves noting too that I postulated earlier a fourth continuum of defenses: setting and breaking boundaries and limits.

The double character (drive and fear invoked defense) is particularly clear in the many (almost countless) forms of violating, blurring, disregarding boundaries, as described in chapter 6, and carried out both consciously and, more often, unconsciously. Every session with a compulsive drug user is likely to give examples for the defensive use of creating distance or, to the contrary, of near-fusion, of disrespect for the outer and inner boundaries just described. These include massive transgressions, blurring of the borders separating fantasy and illusion from reality testing, mixing up of public and private domains and other areas of functioning, and refusion of inner structures. The prevalence lies by far on lifting of boundaries (with all types of drugs) as defense, but the artificial detachment and self-removal is an important opposite phenomenon. Of course the most primitive forms on this continuum: projection (as, e.g., in the phobic character traits), introjection, primary identification and union, are well-known defenses. Classically all these forms are again used as defenses against narcissistic disappointments.

A few examples from the material already presented: Patpet (case 4) and Andreas (case 19) felt removed, detached after letdowns, the former thousands of miles away. This is quite an extreme form of boundary creation, of separation and distancing.

Skakran (case 16) was particularly explicit: every rejection and state of feeling low and disappointed had to be warded off by a breaking of all limits, a violating of boundaries for the transgression's sake—as violence, seduction of women, lying, drugs, fraud. In him this effort was largely preconscious.

All psychedelics users, including many noncompulsive pot smokers, or even alcohol drinkers, want to break down the "barriers" of their loneliness and social isolation in the sense of partial union with the trusted, idealized other. The affect defense in these cases is less the denial than the removal of inhibitions and with that really of all the separations and limitations—very reminiscent of Schiller's "Ode to Joy." What Schiller attributed to the overwhelming power of joy, sympathy, and all-forgiveness, the transcending of all boundaries, our patients seek not just as pleasure effect of the drugs, but indeed as defense against despair, aloneness, guilt and shame. And it is no coincidence that Schiller's poem appeals to the elimination of anger, revenge, remorse, despair, strife, and guilt and ends with a glorification of wine. The lifting of all boundaries is indeed a most massive, radical, global repudiation of everything painful—human!

To return to more mundane spheres: similar and other archaic forms of boundary elimination we saw in our patients: the Bohemian (case 14) found union in "tripping", and in music a glorious antidote against shame, whereas many others use projections galore and tend to blame everyone but themselves for all their ills. Finally, Cassandra showed, in her mistreatment of her dog, a nearly psychotic mélange of introjection, projection, and identification.

In short a book could be written just about the topic dealt with in this chapter.

As I expressed in my metaphor essay (1977) all scientific theory rests upon the consistent use of metaphorical analogies. Whereas in the natural sciences the move to high level abstractions, mainly in form of mathematical formulas has gradually been possible, no such avenue has opened up in the type of science and scientific theory to which psychoanalysis belongs. I shall have a few additional thoughts about this at the end of the book. Right now I only look back over these last few pages and want to note that we deal here on the one side with very frequent clinical observations and practical needs in handling these patients; on the other side we use several well-known metaphorical constructs and a novel one.

The well-known metaphorical system is above all the one of structures, in its gross form the id- ego- superego configuration, a most powerfully persuasive, helpful tool in theory formation. Its usefulness has been so evident that all attempts to scuttle it have in my opinion utterly failed (see for example Kubie, Schafer). But we need to be clear:

even if we use concrete language, we deal with abstractions, with very necessary metaphors, not with "facts" or "things." Finer microstructures such as defense "mechanisms," instinctual drive derivatives, the often mentioned suborganizations—are all part of this metaphor. When we use, rather loosely, the "need for or lack of inner structures or controls" we basically employ this metaphor. Its prototype is that of authorities (*Instanzen* in Freud's writings), government agencies—and with that a hierarchical model. Several other metaphors (conflicting forces, use of energies) I skip here; they were clearly used.

The novel one I introduced is the metaphor of territoriality: of borders, boundaries, limits, limitations. The structural, hierarchical metaphor covers many, but not all phenomena dealt with clinically. At least for me the switch to an entirely different model, particularly with these patients (though not quite restricted to them), has proven its operational usefulness. More of the how and why will become clearer in chapter 16 and Appendix E, both on treatment. Again it is important to see that patients may put these experiences concretely, as we saw with schizophrenics; for our theory they fit solely into a low level abstraction, a metaphorical system. We have to guard against taking the metaphor literally—with one exception: phylogenetically and perhaps also ontogenetically the boundary concept, the notion of territoriality, may have concrete predecessors to what we now put into psychological abstractions. But what follows is speculation, not part of the theory itself. We may ask ourselves whether the metaphor does not contain a symbolic truth pointing beyond to a concrete substratum— that is, this phenomenon may be compared with that observed with animals where we not only hear of a basic drive for relationship, closeness, and association, and of a hierarchical order (e.g., the "pecking order"), but of an equally fundamental drive for territorial separation, delimitation and dissociation. It has even been stated in view of this second motive "that density regulation, and through this, control of numbers, is the main function of all forms of social organization in animals." Tinbergen sets forth the hypothesis "that man still carries with him the animal heritage of group territoriality," and a number of other ethologists conclude "that the function of a great deal of conflict was the control of food and reproduction through the control of territory and the maintenance of a hierarchy within groups" (Washburn, Collins, Wynne-Edwards). If the territory is intruded upon, or if the hierarchical structure of social organization is interfered with, fighting ensues (Leyhausen 1966).

However, the drawing of analogies between animals and human beings is very treacherous, as both the philosopher S. Langer (1972), and the psychoanalyst G. Rochlin (1973) stress. Hence I simply point to the fascinating similarities without claiming any phylogenetic connection.

Finally, one may object and call this model not intrapsychic but "relational, transactional, interpersonal." It is not. As with all psychoanalytic metaphors its core meaning is intrapsychic, at the center of the six concentrical circles, depicted in chapter 5; the applicability of intrapsychic concepts outward is as evident as the reverse, though the relevance may change for a given posed problem. I have no doubt that intrapsychic and family theories complement each other to such an extent that in many severer forms of emotional illness one alone cannot be fully theoretically explanatory nor helpful in clinical strategy unless complemented by the other. Here, though, I restrict myself to a psychoanalytic, centrally intrapsychic theory.

Let us now examine whether this metaphorical system of boundaries may yet have additional usefulness—in regard to a more careful, subdividing theory of aggression.

Aggression

SADOMASOCHISM

Again this aspect has been already noted in the heptad; and the cases in their turn have convinced us that this problem of massive aggression preceded by far the onset of that vicious circle. Undoubtedly this drive pair and its conflicts form part of the precondition as well. Finally, a lot of ground has already been covered when I discussed the role of self-destructiveness and self-punishment as part of the superego pathology.

But again we have to venture into new territory (in two meanings of the term!).

THE ROLE OF AGGRESSION IN THE ESTABLISHMENT AND DEFENSE OF BOUNDARIES

Thornton Wilder writes in *The Eighth Day:* "Family life is like that of nations: each member battles for his measure of air and light, of

270 THE HIDDEN DIMENSION

nourishment and territory, and particularly for that measure of admiration and attention which is called 'glory'" (1967,p. 357).

It is my theoretical inference that the expansion of an area of ego actitivies as such is predominantly of narcissistic nature, and that only if this expansion runs into resistance, mainly the limits set by objects, aggression is mobilized and either put in the service of the expansion or of the defense of the already conquered "territory."

We have noted the analogy between a concrete (literal) concept of territoriality (in phylo- and ontogeny) and the (metaphorical) psychological concept of boundaries. From the thoughts set forth in the previous chapters it is clear that the setting up and defense of all these boundaries is carried out by aggressive investment '("energies"), commonly in the behest of narcissistic demands and needs. This is in line with what G. Bychowski wrote:

"The role of the aggressive drive in the delineation of personality deserves our special attention. Observation shows that in the course of his development the child must use a certain amount of the aggressive energy in order to set up the boundaries between himself and the mother (or other parental figures). Important turning points in the process of individuation are characterized by outbursts of hostility in a child otherwise pleasant and easy to manage."[1968, p. 28]

If we consider how decisive aggression is for the establishment of boundaries, we may indeed postulate: *the history of aggression is the history of the boundaries of ourselves and the boundaries limiting and structuring our social functions.*

We may thus conceive of the whole process of psychological life as an unending dialectic between the narcissistic drive to expand, to overwhelm or to merge on one level or another, with an object, and the (aggressive) drive to establish limits—to defend them, to constrict them, or to enlarge them "by force into enemy territory." (These two archaic drives—to merge and to establish limits—were personified and described by Nietzsche as the dialectic between Dionysus and Apollo.) If we examine cases like our paradigm (Razit, case 18) or Andreas, case 19, the violation or contesting of either boundary (the "inner" or the "outer" causes an outburst of archaic rage, of devastating, destructive anger and fury as if the aggression bound up in the establishment of the frontier were explosively set free.

But this already moves us beyond yet another frontier of knowledge, into a new area.

VARIOUS TYPES OF AGGRESSION

If we continue this train of thought, we are suddenly surprised that the aggressions set free in the violation of different boundaries vary.

We saw already in passing how the object reacts with *contempt* to me if I open myself up in degradation, in shameful exposure, and how the object reacts with *hatred* and revenge if I try to step into his territory. From other observations we have already learned that contempt is the aggression inherent in shame, hatred, the aggression bound in guilt. This is still noticeable when the whole process is internalized and the superego uses these different types of aggression.

The collapse of any boundary—in the present context the line of defense represented by self-determination and strength and the line of defense represented by self-respect and dignity—is accompanied by overwhelming panic: traumatic guilt anxiety in the first, traumatic shame anxiety in the second. Now we can add that the aggression following this panic is an equally diffuse, general, undifferentiated form: *rage*. And it is this rage which lures always and ubiquitously in the psychotic and "borderline" patient. A history of the development of aggression ought to start out with this most primitive type of aggression (Hartmann, Kris, and Loewenstein 1948, pp. 23, 27), but would have to proceed through different stages of the genesis of boundaries. However, the most intriguing and promising conclusion from this postulate, namely that the genesis of boundaries and with that the development of aggression may follow only to a limited degree the development of object libido, but that we may indeed design on the basis of narcissistic expansion and boundary formation an independent series of developmental stages for aggression, cannot be pursued within the limits of this inquiry. But what we notice is that there are at least two very different types of more differentiated aggression: contempt (and similar feelings: disdain, scorn, wishes to humiliate, to despise, to discard, to embarrass) and hatred (or wishes to hurt, to pain, to torment); the first dehumanizes, the second recognizes (and hurts) the other as a person. And then we have the undifferentiated third form of aggression: wild, undirected, apparently aimless rage—or, more exactly, rage just aiming at destruction per se, at revenge, redress and gratification by destruction, at "discharge," usually even disregarding the boundary between self and nonself. In "borderline" and psychotic patients, including of course all toxicomanics, it is hard to see suicidal depression as rage turned from the object onto the self. Only on a more differentiated level within the same patient this becomes true. Deeper down, on a more primitive layer, the distinction "feelingly" just does not exist. Rage to the other is also rage against oneself, inseparably, identically. All else appears, within the therapeutic situation, as a superficial ratiocination.

This third form, rage, is relatively easy to understand. As Kohut (1972) so convincingly described: it is the direct reaction to massive narcissistic injury. "The need for revenge, for righting a wrong, for undoing a hurt by whatever means, and a deeply anchored, unrelenting compulsion in the pursuit of all these aims which gives no rest to those who have suffered a narcissistic injury—these are features which are characteristic for the phenomenon of narcissistic rage in all its forms and which set it apart from other kinds of aggression" (p. 380). "In its typical forms there is utter disregard for reasonable limitation and a boundless wish to redress an injury and to obtain revenge" (p. 382). He calls "chronic narcissistic rage one of the most pernicious afflictions of the human psyche—either, in its still endogenous and preliminary form as grudge and spite; or, externalized and acted out, in disconnected vengeful acts or in a cunningly plotted vendetta."

But then—what about hatred? What about contempt? For the first let us look again to our original guidepost, which sent us on our scouting mission: guilt. We have discovered that the category of hurting, leading up to guilt, appears to originate in body areas with a dominance of muscular action: biting with jaws and teeth, beating and grasping and holding with the hands, kicking and stamping, piercing the ears with screaming. On higher symbolic levels this hurtful action may be displaced away from the physical arena to hurtful words, gestures, even of course to thoughts, fantasies, feelings. All these activities occur on one plain, in the area of direct forcing power.

This is not all. The hatred is directed against delimited objects— against individuals, nations, things. It is aggression directed against objects which are acknowledged, even respected in the very attack, as persons or personified enemies. The direct forcing and hurting power in hatred is grounded in object relation; it is an object related aggression.

Let us turn to the other form. De Gaulle wrote about Marshal Petain, his erstwhile revered model and later enemy, that he was a

> master who...has disdained the fate of servants—thus showing the greatness of independence, which receives orders, seizes advice, but closes itself to influences—the prestige of secrecy, preserved by deliberate coldness, vigilant irony, and even by the pride in which his loneliness is wrapped.... Too proud for intrigue, too strong for mediocrity, too ambitious for careerism, [he] nourished in his solitude the passion to dominate, hardened by his awareness of his own merit, by the obstacles he had met, the contempt he had for others. [Hoffman, 1968]

Narcissism sole and simple? No. Also, no word about force, but a lot about disdain and contempt. The boundary of the narcissistically aggrandized self is defended against personal relationships by this form of aggression. It is not object related aggression, it is the aggression protecting the magically exalted, overly proud, arrogant self (whereas rage tries to undo the wound of the injured self). The boundary around the state of pride, regardless whether we talk now about haughtiness or dignity, is defended by the forces of contempt against the outside. It is a directly and originally narcissistic form of aggression. In case of narcissistic downfall it is directed inward as self-contempt, as shame.

Whereas hatred wants to inflict hurt and pain and to destroy right and integrity of the other, contempt devalues the being, the self of the other. It attacks centrally the object's narcissism, his self-esteem, his self-value.

In this sense I seriously wonder whether we cannot distinguish between object-aggression and narcissistic aggression in the same sense as we talk about object libido and narcissistic libido, with a clear difference in the nature of the "energies" involved. The type of energy or investment lastly makes the difference. Just as in the case of libido the narcissistic stigma is overvaluation, in the case of aggression the narcissistic stigma would be devaluation, destruction of value.

But we know more about this. We have heard before, again returning to our second guidepost, shame, that the category of exposing, leading up to shame, seems centered in entirely different areas of body and social interaction. There appears one basic activity—or really a pair of activities—the importance of which has been greatly underestimated. It is the very early arising attempt to achieve magical powers through expression, to impress, to fascinate, through gesture, sign, look, on the one side, and on the other, its counterpart: the interest, the wish to be attentive, to be impressed and fascinated, the wish to grasp the world with the eyes and thus to control it (Langer 1942, p. 110).

This is not just an oral devouring, it has a different quality—as much as it may be colored by oral-incorporative tendencies. From Piaget's and Wolff's studies it is evident how early this double activity starts—the active perceptions in the first weeks of life, the magic gesturing and expressing around the eigth month. In their observations, however, there is no reference to conflicts. It is in our schizophrenic patients or in other severely disturbed cases that we see that the conflicts appear to be as focally localized in this archaic area of expression and perception as the different neuroses in the respective erogenous zones. It is the area which on higher levels is known as exhibitionism and scoptophilia.

In many variations, on many layers of development, from very early to adulthood we find these magical wishes to look and to be looked at, later on, more broadly, to be perceived, approved in understanding, and to perceive and adjudge in knowing—and the corresponding equally magical fears: to fail, to be punished, scorned for these wishes and what they entail (their content, the second logical level mentioned above), all fears falling under terms like *shame, embarrassment, disgrace, narcissistic mortification,* with the most primitive aim—to turn invisible.

When we examine this affect of shame even more in detail within the boundary metaphor we may state, in a variation of Tolkien's nice phrase ("The wide world is all about you: you can fence yourselves in, but you cannot forever fence it out.") that we have just noted how the "fencing out" is done: by contempt. We may now wonder whether we could not find a similar parallel to the second function of the boundary: to "protect what is behind"—the integrity and, in the case of the grandiose person, the glory of the self. The historians Stanley and Inge Hoffman wrote in regard to De Gaulle himself:

The leader is the man who owes his power to no one but himself— who imposes himself, who is propelled by what is in him, not by other people's doctrines.... When De Gaulle tries to describe the craft that must shape the gift, again it is not to techniques of action nor to ideas that he turns, but to psychological traits; *secrecy, mystery, distance, silence, and protectiveness*—all summarized as "the contrast between inner strength and self mastery".... [1968, p. 846]

As in the art of the actor the skill consists in the prudent and controlled use of two opposite devices: exhibition and hiding, a basic polarity in the assertion of the grandiose self. This skill to control in a balanced way revelation and secrecy is the precondition to reach the pinnacle in this area of expressive-perceptual interchange, the aim of fascination and awe, the highest form of narcissistic power, present in political leaders, in the most creative artists, and in saints. I presume that this balance composes much of what is commonly described as "charisma," known in anthropology as "mana," sometimes felt as something uncanny, casting a spell on all.

Thus, both exhibition and hiding appear to be ploys in the service of "the fencing in," using primarily narcissistic energies—I believe both of libidinous and aggressive nature. What we notice also, of course, is that what is clearly of instinctual nature in one perspective, is equally blatantly serving as defense from another vantage point.

The logical punishment for this supreme narcissism is, of course, the echo of his own aggression. It is contempt in response, "the indifference or hostility of the led"; lastly it is humiliation and ends in the shameful collapse of the grandiose self.

But this led us far afield and would give enough stuff for another book. We have to break these considerations off and sum up what we have found.

We discovered two basic forms of aggression, an object related one, hatred, and a totally narcissistic one, contempt, in which the other person is annihilated, made into dirt, into vermin, totally deprived of his worth as a person. And then we have a third form, rage: the undifferentiated response to the massively wounded narcissism. We also noticed that the counterpoint to contempt in the protection of the self lies in both: exhibition and hiding, both as wishful assertions of the grandiose self. The basic conflict is omnipotence, especially by magic looking and showing, versus total powerlessness and disappearance in that archaic mortification, called "aphanisis" by Ernest Jones, and recreated to a very large extent in shame conflicts on very many layers.

To return to our patients now: In line with their basic narcissistic orientation we are not surprised to find that the leading forms of aggression are haughty contempt and vindictive rage—much directed against others, even more directed against the self. And often there is a direct sexual connotation especially to the contempt: the wallowing in dirt, the masochistic pleasure. Sadomasochism is not restricted to hatred and pain, but refers even more to humiliation and scorn, thus to both types of differentiated aggression. It is likely that at least one crucial, original, pathogenic conflict in compulsive drug users (and probably also in schizophrenics) lies on this very archaic level—a fixation during the oral stage, but more specifically, in the areas of perception and expression of most primitive, magical, omnipotent, self and world-creating wishes and of boundary forming defenses.

How relevant this differentiation is will be more noticeable when we study Andreas, our next case. But ere we turn to him, the scene changes; we inquire for a brief moment into the family pathology in this context.

The Family as Part of Predisposition

Another main pillar of the precondition lies in the family pathology. Due to its signal importance a separate and systematic section, written by two specialists, will be devoted to it. Here I present only a summary of my own observations. Clinically I have been struck by the impression that there is hardly any compulsive drug user who does not hail from a family with massive problems. Not only do we see very often *broken families,* but this fact in and by itself is less of a problem than the overall family atmosphere, the life style in which the child grew up.

The most constant family features are the absence of consistency in setting and enforcing of, and sticking to limits, and the undermining, undercutting, the power struggle between the parents. In other words, it is the lack of structure, and the amount of overt or covert aggression which is striking in these families.

One very frequent constellation (and a special variant of the inconsistency) is the vacillation between seduction and vindictiveness. On the one side, there are virtually no limits to the living out of material gratifications, in form of eating, drinking, and sex, in providing money, cars, and luxury. Even in many slum families we can see this type of spoiling, a permissive granting of wishes, a curious lack of discipline. On the other side, the parents engage in wild temper tantrums including physical violence, to enforce a particular limit. They like to justify their outbursts or rage as "discipline," but we see clearly that they are rather the opposite.

In the same or other families, the conflict is between an intrusive form of pseudo-love and overprotective "care" and a complete disregard for the individuality of the child and his real emotional needs.

Particularly in upper (middle) class families, the self-centered preoccupation with success and prestige on the parent's part is matched by the self-centered retreat into a drug induced dream world by the child, and supported by the parent's guilt-ridden giving-in to all demands of the child.

Very often the parents themselves are deeply involved in using prescribed or not prescribed drugs and alcohol to sustain their own versions of what Ibsen called the "lifelie," and other attempts to cover over, to deny, the tragic dimensions of their own entanglements, their sense of being lost. Often we sense, as if shrouded in a mist, but cannot perceive clearly, profound family secrets, forms of family shame and family guilt, of rifts and broken loyalties putting an almost unbearable burden on the parents, on the children, on the family as a unit.

Occasionally it was noted in the literature (Chein et al.) how severely neglected and deprived many drug users were. Going over the cases in our own methadone program it is striking how many patients were illegitimate, and/or scapegoats, always outcasts, degraded in their own immediate surrounding which hardly can be called "family" anymore—so much of a parody it is. The sheer amount of criminality, mayhem and murder, alcoholism and just all-pervasive neglect, is staggering, the result in the child horrifying and disastrous.

Perhaps we might come closest to the clinical truth if we say: by and large the symptom of drug taking on the child's side is a derivative of the whole family's attitude of inconsistency, self-centeredness, and, most importantly, of inner and outer dishonesty. The deceptiveness and wiliness of many drug abusers is a reflection of their parents' denial or deviousness and power-hungry manipulations, or it is a frantic escape from disillusionment and anger about the unavailability of their parents as persons during the crises of growing up. The hierarchical structure and authority within the family is split up, broken, blurred, subverted and overthrown. All the limits and boundaries shift, are unreliable, get blurred, are transgressed.

Thus we see in the families the crucial features of the major problems of these patients performed: narcissism (self-centeredness, no limitations to freedom, inconsistency of hierarchy and boundaries), denial and splits (inner dishonesty, the "life lie"), externalization (revenge and pleasure, in action, unrestrained, without structures), and superego splits (the secret shame, the silent guilt, the broken loyalty, vacillation between vindictiveness and indulgence, and most importantly, conscious lying and manipulating while maintaining a sham respectability, a Tartuffe-like piousness, a facade of integrity). This allows the pretense of maintaining magical powers, of omnipotence and self-glorification (supreme narcissistic gratifications), to stand. The circle of the heptad is closed in them, as in their offspring.

Some of these observations were strikingly and independently confirmed by careful interactional research, as chapter 11 will demonstrate.

The Etiological Equation

If we look back over all factors which form the underpinnings of the hierarchy of etiology and try to disentangle the interweaving of predisposition and specific reasons, we have to start out with what is truly specific about the compulsive drug user, what we find in all of them, and what would give us a clue to predict future toxicomania.

1. I think our task is somewhat simpler now. As *specific reason* we found a constellation of seven phenomena as final common pathway to manifest addictive illness; all of them are typically present and indispensable. But from among the seven factors highest specificity was assigned to the combination of denial/splitting and externalization as leading defenses to cope with the overwhelming affects mobilized in the narcissistic crises. All seven factors, particularly the peculiar splitting of the superego, are most pronounced in illicit, oppressed drug use, are mitigated in the half-tolerated ones (alcohol and cannabis addiction), and probably either minimal or absent in fully accepted compulsive drug use (nicotine, coffee). The latter blends over into the "pathology of everyday life"; the drugs used in these latter instances are of course also of minimal or no manifest short-term interference.

2. If I try to select the one train in the personality of the compulsive drug user which is most specific, it is again the tendency to deny, with that to "split" (in the various meanings given, especially as "the about-face syndrome") and hence the overall lability of inner structures and of boundaries. Not only are the emotions inconsistent and overwhelming, but so are the defenses, the boundaries between self and other, generally the perceptual boundaries, and the limitations and boundaries watched over by the superego. Clinical experience, social and administrative observations and the test findings described especially by L. Kirkman (Appendix A)—all converge on that one point: the inner *anomia,* lawlessness, the lack of consistency, structure, boundaries. As Kohut so rightly remarks: this is the expression of a profound narcissistic defect. On the one side it is the outcome of acute and chronic narcissistic conflicts; therefore, the archaic, peculiarly narcissistic affects are overwhelming and unrestrained. But on the other side there is also a profound deficit in structures to cope in any consistent way, with the help of a reliable defense constellation, with such conflicts and ensuing affects. Withal, we encounter this peculiar shiftiness of boundaries and limits of all sorts, concretely and metaphorically.

What I state comes down to this circle in regard to structure formation:

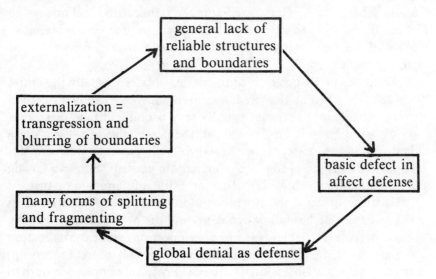

One may separate these five into different defenses or defects; it is perhaps more approximate to view them as different parts of the same phenomenon which appear as defenses and as defects. When we look at it as denial we emphasize the defensive aspect; when we stress splitting, we view the double nature of disavowal or denial and acceptance or acknowledgment, especially from a cognitive point of view; and finally when we focus on the boundaries, structures, and lack of effective affect defense, we see mainly the "defect" nature of the phenomenon.

Again, as on the level of the immediate antecedents, we see the entire constellation of the *predisposition* as necessary preconditions. Among them I consider this element of an inner anomia, this peculiar lability in structures, as the most specific one.

The pathogenic conflicts probably reach, as in schizophrenics, very far back: to most archaic conflicts in perception and expression and, with that, to the original forming of any boundaries and self-nuclei. These conflicts are postulated to form a specific part of what is too loosely and broadly known as the oral stage.

The immensity of other (though closely related and overlapping) problems, especially of severe and archaic narcissistic conflicts in the patient and the gravity of inconsistency, aggression and promotion of externalization and deception in the family, are indispensable. To summarize the other necessary parts of the precondition: hyposymbolization, labile, often externalized superego, defect in ideal and value formation, lack of self-care, prevalence of shame, massive aggression, mainly of the rage and contempt type, and more self-directed than against others.

Even in the predisposition of the patient himself usually the entire "heptad" described as the "final common pathway" can be discerned throughout life and becomes usually very prominent in adolescence.

If we compare this predisposition, the personality, the "set," with other nosological categories, the work with patients who are not compulsive durg users (e.g., psychoanalytic patients) allows a strong contradistinction: Above all, the intensity and archaic nature of narcissistic conflicts is usually much more pronounced in toxicomanics. The extent of boundary problems and the prevalence of the very archaic defenses of denial, various disconnections and externalization are most striking. Neurotics use, instead, much more repression, introjection, or the obsessional defenses. Projection appears in both to a moderate extent. The superego pathology is far deeper in addicts than in all types of neurosis. Finally, a strong case can be made that the peculiar form of aggression which is evident in shame, namely contempt, disdain, scorn, plus undifferentiated rage, but less anger and hatred, are the ones which are particularly prominently used in the service of externalization in these patients, and this even more in a self-directed, masochistic version, than against the outer world.

In contrast to the various psychoses the extent of ego split and superego split and, more generally, of fragmentation of cognition and perception is less strong in addicts. Projection, dehumanization, depersonalization are much stronger in psychotics during the acute phase than in addicts. Recompensated psychotics have much in common with recompensated addicts: if anything, the propensity to the characteristic splits, fragmentation, denial and externalization, even projection, the extent and massivity of narcissistic and sadomasochistic problems may even be more manifest and conspicuous in the addictive than the latently psychotic personality.

3. The *precipitating* cause is the entrance of the drug. It is hardly an understatement if I add that the drug's advent on stage functions merely like the crucial, though irrelevant messenger, in the antique tragedy, a hapless catalyst: "I that do bring the news made not the match."

The reader may interject and point here to the allegedly crucial role of the pusher. Yet, very rarely can he indeed be dignified by such a title; he is at most merely the precipitator, usually just a supporter of a habit, not a causative agent.

If we view now this etiologic structure in the terms of Leibnitz, we may say: All of the seven specific elements (the heptad) and those described under precondition are necessary causes. Only the combination of the entire heptad, as mobilized by its first member, the acute narcissistic crisis, with the precipitating factor, namely the adventitious entrance of the drug, represents the sufficient cause.

The theoretical conclusions presented here could serve us as a starting point to go into three directions—for one, into systematic research of the hypotheses presented here, secondly into a more thorough metapsychological exploration of these clinical observations, and thirdly into applications to prevention and treatment which would go beyond the present mad rush into action before thinking.

Research would have to proceed from this nodal point of the etiological equation in several directions. Of course, one road would lead simply toward confirmation (or refutation) and deepening of these findings. Another even less paved road would be a genetic exploration tying the described defects and conflicts together with developmental disturbances and family pathology. On another path, one would have to study the constitutional factors involved; at this point, we have no way of knowing how much of the underlying problems are of hereditary nature. Yet study beyond speculation is particularly tantalizing in this area. Still another route goes into an altogether different direction: the defects in ideal formation may open a deeper understanding for value psychological and value philosophical questions; thus such a study would assist us in a more thorough theoretical superego analysis than has been known hitherto.

All this has large practical significance, which will guide us through the rest of this book.

Only a few very brief observations can be added here as to prognosis. It is not so much the malignancy of the past history which gives us an indicator for the future course in treatment, as the following aspects:

1. We can distinguish two extreme types among compulsive drug users: On the one side there are those in whom the heptad described is most massive, or where one of its seven constituent parts is particularly prevalent (especially the defense of externalization and the extent of dissociations, or the collapse or external nature of the superego): with them treatment is not adhered to, and the patient ends up shattered, his life destroyed by the vehemence of the illness. On the other side we have patients where all this is much milder, and where in particular there is detectable a quite solid core of responsibility and commitment (to work or marriage), and where a much less profound "fissure" in the superego keeps opening up. They turn out to be far more treatable.

2. Another indicator is the extent of the collaboration of the immediate family with the heptad: where especially the mother keeps upholding the defense of denial, assists in externalization as defense and has the same corrupt, vacillating conscience, the prognosis is very dim.

3. Lastly, a solid relationship to a spouse who has no problems with drugs or alcohol (never mind the masochism necessary to put up with the horrors experienced with the patient) is a most propitious omen for therapy; in turn a spouse devoted to some form of compulsive substance abuse is a miserable augury. Of equal, if not yet greater

importance, is the combined and continued presence of children (together with the spouse).

Our best successes (including withdrawal from methadone) were with patients who had a spouse, one or several children, a deep sense of commitment to them, and a challenging, fulfilling type of work.

Chapter 9

ANDREAS: SOCIOPATH OR

TRAGIC CHARACTER?

In the following I try to build a bridge between the theoretical insights we have gained so far and the practical sections which will follow later. At the same time it should further serve to "humanize" the picture of the compulsive drug user, to make it come alive and weaken the hold vacuous clichés have on us, by presenting a patient who might appear particularly frightening, ominous and enigmatic. On the way I hope also to cast some deep shadows of doubt on the derogatory and, I believe, not very useful concept "sociopath," and some light on a character constellation which, for a number of reasons, I came to call a "tragic character." I have already interjected brief examples from his experiences here and there, particularly when introducing the concept of the heptad. The following extensive case history was contributed by Dr. Ari Gerson who treated the patient in New York in the 1960s.

Case 19: Andreas

I (Dr. Gerson) saw this man, at the time in his early thirties, for four years in psychotherapy; at the beginning it was very sporadic, in the final two years psychotherapy gained momentum and intensity.

He entered our methadone program when the doctor who for a few years had prescribed liberal doses of narcotic to him was closed down by the authorities. At that time he said he was maintained on one to two hundred mg methadone a day. He wanted to see me because he suffered from severe anxiety attacks and insomnia when starting on our program: "I am afraid of dying—or that something was going to happen to me. Still more frightening are thoughts that I might harm my wife and my two boys. These feelings of near-insanity and panic come over me several times a day and particularly at night. Some time ago, I tried to be withdrawn from methadone in a mental hospital, but they put me on Thorazine. I started hallucinating, was overwhelmed with fear, and had convulsions. Yet the more frightened I became, the more Thorazine they gave me, once four hundred mg for the night alone! Since then I feel most frightened of myself. I was never as close to killing myself as then. That was far worse than any withdrawal, so I signed myself out. I felt I couldn't communicate, was suffocating, drowning, the worst torture."

As to his immediate history: "I have never stolen. Either I got my drugs from a physician or I worked in construction or in the shipyard. Before that I was in college, but broke it off, worked a while as a computer programmer." Then he added: "I have to tell you something which still haunts me, and my life has never been right since—nor really before. When I was nineteen, I killed a man."

Then in bits and pieces he wrote or told me his life history over the next few weeks:

I am the younger of two: my sister is ten years older than I am. I doubt if my father was ever different than unhappy, discontent and chronically ill and crippled. However, a nagging wife and a job he completely loathed kept him from dwelling on his other misfortunes. Although my parents never physically hit each other, they either argued violently, or they sulked in silence. The fights were always for silly or no reasons. They never went to church, but I vividly remember being very young, attending church with my sister and praying that my mother and father would stop fighting. I was never emotionally very close to my father. I didn't hate him or even dislike him; I just was not close to him, nor did I respect him. We occasionally would go places together (such as to ball games and movies) but we never did things together (such as playing cards or going fishing). I cannot remember having an extended meaningful conversation with my father at any time in my life. I felt that my father loved me; I was able to sense that on a nonverbal level. But we were unable to communicate. To a large measure this may have been the result of my being unreceptive. I was emotionally close to my mother but I honestly believe the element of love was a small fraction of the total emotional relationship. There was a degree of competition between my mother and me. For example: during the period when I was learning to play chess and checkers my mother would have never considered losing for my benefit. My mother went to all extremes to provide good meals, clean clothing, educational equipment and the other material goods concomitant with American motherhood. I was close and found comfort in my sister who seemed to me to be able to stand stalwart in times of confusion. When I was four or five my next-door-neighbor and playmate was killed before my eyes as a truck ran over him while we were playing in front of my house. I had no real conception of death; I ran down the street thrilled that something important and exciting had happened. I may have felt badly about the incident later, but at this point in time I do not recall.

An early play experience stands out in my mind as being rather odd, if not bizarre. While playing with toy soldiers I would fantasize that I had been captured by the enemies and was tortured until I would give up the secrets. The fantasizing pleasure was from two sources: the physical pain itself and the concept of bravery resulting from withstanding the pain in a manly fashion. I would also pretend that the lady across the street was my mother. I visualized her as a cruel, sadistic woman who would administer spankings.

When I was six I stole a bottle from a Coca Cola truck, was caught and undoubtedly punished. I can still recall the fear and shame associated with the scene.

At a preschool age I had several sexual experiences with two girls about my age or a little older. Among other things we acted out sexual intercourse. We knew, I suppose instinctively, that what "I had" should go into what "she had." Of course I didn't have an erection; actual intercourse was not taking place. I had no shame or guilt feelings; it seemed like a natural thing to do. We were finally discovered and made to feel what we had been doing was very wrong. I don't remember who discovered us, but our parents knew because I was not allowed to play with these particular girls again unless under supervision.

From the age four or five until my teenage years I was very thin. I would never be able to finish a full meal. When I would begin to eat I would be obsessed by sickening thoughts such as dead animals and insects (I dislike waterbugs almost to the degree that it could be considered a phobia). I would take a few bites and be unable to go on. This upset my mother very much. When she would give me a bath, she would sometimes break into tears because I was so skinny.

Still I was a very tough child; I would never be caught crying if any of my peers were around. I hated school and felt the teachers were utterly incompetent and "old maid man-haters"; they never would ask me a question regardless of how actively I would raise my hand in response. I devised a devious plan: when I would want to answer an important question I would idly gaze out the classroom window pretending not to be paying attention. One time she called upon me, hoping to catch me unprepared so she would be able to criticize me. I answered correctly; she responded sarcastically: "You really think you're smart, don't you?" Obviously this absurd relationship with my teachers did nothing for my scholastic achievements. It was not until high school that I learned to read effectively. And only then because several male teachers took an active interest in my education. I responded by making all A's in my senior year in high school.

In the first or second grade, I became aware of the word *claustrophobia*, or, if not the word itself, the concept. I would panic if I were closed in a small space and was unable to get out, or if I were held and unable to break the hold in a wrestling match.

Thus, he loved to "run others over" in football, but became so terrified and enraged if he was "run over" that he gave up all sports— afraid he might blindly attack the one who pinned him to the ground.

He noted that from age eight to fifteen was a good period in his life:

I had several interesting hobbies (collecting stampes, etc.); I played sports and games; and in general I interacted well with other children. Almost all of my friends were two or three years older. I would lie about my age (making myself out to be a year or two older), and this didn't create a problem until my early teens when my friends developed what I thought to be an inordinate obsession with girls. For a year or two I would tag along with my friends as they sought out girls and when a mixed group was formed I would stay in the background, bored and shy.

When I was eleven I joined the Boy Scouts; and I very much enjoyed hiking, camping and belonging to an organization. I appeared to be what is generally referred to as an All-American Boy. However, somewhere in the back of my mind was the nagging thought that I was somewhat mentally deranged, as with fears of being trapped, masochistic fantasies and a haunting sense of sadness and doom which, though, was also very attractive to me.

I have on occasion day dreamed about having a scarred face. I've wished to be uglier on the surface since deep down inside I know I'm not as good looking as I appear to be. When I started taking drugs, I somewhat enjoyed the fact that I was bringing myself down to my rightful level of ugliness.

I started going to dances when I was fourteen. Almost from the first dance I would drink before the dance. I felt uncomfortable with dating, dances, and girls in general. Drinking served not only to relax me but to engender an older more mature self-image.

In the crowd of associates I cultivated during my teens, being a good fist fighter was a prerequisite for manliness. I treated fighting as a sport and during this period participated in numerous fights. In retrospect, these fights were really not that vicious (one didn't kick an opponent if he was down, etc.—rules, just like in any other sport), and no one was really seriously injured.

At a very early age, perhaps three, I have a recollection of an experience that evoked feelings of fascination and excitement. I remember the first time I became aware of the radio that was in my parents' bedroom. The radio had always been in the room, and I am sure I had heard it play before; but I had never previously made the connection between the radio and something alive. I was convinced that there was a small person inside. I can recall feelings of excitement. This feeling of excitement, as I remember it, was something akin to what I would identify now as sexual excitement. I'm sure if I could have gotten my hands on the little man in the radio I would have brought pain to him. The picture of a cat toying with a mouse comes to mind.

What's really odd here is that the thought of an animal being hurt—even a mouse—is repulsive and upsetting whereas the thought of human pain brings about an emotional response somewhere between indifference and perverse curiosity. Of course, I'm referring to an abstract situation. If the person in pain is a friend or relative my response, I'm sure, would be typical.

Of course, I was thwarted in my efforts to capture the little man in the radio; however, for several years to come I would generate the fantasy of capturing little men and keeping them confined in bird cages.

However, during the same time, Sundays and often weekdays, too, were filled with a mood of meaninglessness, sadness and forlornness. Much later he described it so: "I experience life only in tragic situations—as if I created a novel. I do not know how many young children feel that. But already at eight or ten when I was walking all by myself on a Saturday or Sunday morning, I had that lonely, haunting feeling. And that it was appealing to me was crucial—otherwise I would have avoided it. It is a perverse fascination: to walk through the ghetto, seeing people drunk, whiskey bottles in alleys, hearing the blues. It sounds sentimental, but there was a heartache, something odd, haunting, a pain and sadness that permeated the air. It was insane, but at age fifteen I became in my free time a bill collector for a jeweler in the ghetto and had a provision of 40 percent, because the money had already been written off as bad debts anyway. When I walked around I was yielding to that sadness. It attracted me—it drew me to alcohol and drugs. That was definitely one of the reasons why I eventually became an addict. If anyone tells you there is *one* reason why somebody takes drugs, he is stupid. We have found perhaps eight or more, and each was part of it and true."

Anyway, around that same time he was close to a roaming gang of rather wild "friends." When they were attacked with snowballs, one of them, the Whelp, got out and stabbed two of the "attackers" to death. Andreas was not with them, but came upon the scene shortly thereafter. The Whelp was sent to jail for four years. A little later, Andreas had improved very much in school—emulating the first consciously remembered ideal he had: his sister's husband, a scientist. Tragically, however, shortly thereafter this young man died of a malignancy, and Andreas, who was now in college, good, but not outstanding, lost all interest in studying.

Before, at sixteen and seventeen he had earned some money by serving as a homosexual "hitchhiker," being "sucked" by men of respectable standing: policemen, physicians, etc.: "It screwed me up a lot with adult males, not having much respect for my father to begin with." He suddenly dropped out of school, "because I was not the best anymore," engaged in several homosexual adventures, and got in with the same group of friends, including eventually again the Whelp. By then the patient was nineteen. One evening three of them had group sex with a girl in a club room. She taunted them that one of them had not been a "good lover." The Whelp felt ridiculed, played the threatened and humiliated one, tried to pick a fight with our patient and finally spat in his face because Andreas would not give him a ride home. "He wanted to think that I was afraid of him, that he should get the respect he felt he deserved after he had already killed two people. That I did not fight back right then and there when he spat on me, was because I felt stunned by shame, like paralyzed: that was the only motive to what followed." About a week later when they ran into each other again, the Whelp told Andreas: "You are okay, I am sorry; I did not mean what I said." Strangely enough this semi-apology was the crisis point which led up to the conviction in Andreas: "Now he has shown himself to me to be weak—now you can get back at him! His brief sign of weakness was so repulsive." Thus repulsion and scorn were added in Andreas to the long accumulated shame and rage. One week later his foe challenged Andreas again into fighting him and taunted him as a coward. The patient refused, but went home, got a gun and eight bullets, drove around throughout the night afraid of coming upon his enemy and scared of his own anger, even consciously avoiding places where he might run into the Whelp. Finally, in early dawn, he came, as he wants at least to see it, almost by chance, upon his antagonist, when the latter, after yet another brawl, tumbled out of a bar room. I give him the word to tell the event as he recounted it only four years into psychotherapy:

The Whelp and his adversary were just coming out, ready to fight. I was not upset, not trembling; I had convinced myself that I had allowed myself to be as insane as I could be. I shot him twice through the chest. It came as a surprise to me. It was unbelievable. In any such emotional situation, the time element changes, seems to pass at a different rate. It was like a slow motion movie, frame after frame, but ten seconds appeared like a lifetime. My first feeling was humor, surprise; it sounds terrible. I thought he was just play acting. He began to stagger, appeared to make it seem worse than it was, overly dramatic. And every moment was strobe-like. I still see every scene separately. [Question: Fragmented?] Right. And the time was very stretched out. At first it was humorous. Then he was falling towards me. I had the fear that he was falling on me, and I wanted to fight him off and tried to shoot again, but I did not have any more bullets. I was puzzled: I had had eight bullets and had shot only two. So I went to the car looking for the additional bullets but could not find them. Then I went straight home for more bullets. I did not assume at all that he was dead. It was a complete feeling of unreality when I was driving home—no sorrow, not one emotion, nothing. The only thing on my mind was to get more bullets. I ran to the kitchen, took a big butcher knife and stuck it in the belt. I was definitely going now for all out war—that "it" was about to happen, not that "it" had already happened. The thing that changed it completely and got me suddenly stuck in the tracks was: my mother had left food out for me with a note. It made me sick! I suddenly realized—it put it back in proportions: "Someone loves me, shows me human kindness! What the fuck have I done!" That was reality for me: leaving the food out, and I realized what I had done. I went back with the car and looked at what had happened. There was a lot of police there. I rode by. No one noticed me. I did not know where to go. I had no desire to run away. Then I told myself: "You have not done anything wrong—but something justifiable." I got myself more and more convinced of that. Then I thought I needed to hire a good lawyer and might have to go to jail for eight, nine years and could get a lot of reading done. But then this fear began, to be locked up, my old claustrophobia. That kept me running. Then I said: "What the hell, I can handle it. Or I always can kill myself when it becomes too bad. That's no problem!" I felt completely fearless and had nothing to worry about. Dying had absolutely no meaning. I went to the police station after driving around several hours and told them I had shot that guy. At first they did not want to believe me. They had already arrested someone for it! It was the guy with whom the Whelp had been fighting and who had run away after I had shot the Whelp. If I had not given myself up, he and the police would have been in trouble. When I came in that room where that guy was sitting—I never saw anybody so relieved. He shouted: "That's him, that's him!" It was like a movie. He might have been convicted for it. [Question: Had you been drinking before?] A good deal, but not more than it was typical for the time. Spread over the night it was half a pint of whiskey perhaps and several beers. But that was a normal amount. Why did I do it? He had tried to torment me for about two weeks. One element was that that girl had left with me. But also: I was afraid of him, and I did not want him to know it. And he wanted to see himself as this underworld hitman and respected as a killer, that who did not bow to his wishes was doomed. And I believed him.

I commented that the murder was out of proportion with the torment. "Definitely—except that he was a killer. I felt the streets were unsafe with him walking on them; he was a looming presence, a menace." I asked, still wondering, whether this was not partly displaced, from his own history. He: "That's possible—my father?"

Acquitted because of "temporary insanity" a year later, while adjudged sane in an institution for the criminally insane, Andreas was—paradoxically—set free after one year in jail and went back to college. But soon his moods of emptiness, boredom, dullness, loneliness and sadness took over again. He also felt very much an outsider, out of place, ill at ease with the "normal" students. During that dark time he got married.

In that period there were two adventuresome things which made life interesting and worthwhile again: a homosexual liaison and the turning to narcotics. These two, by their very "wrongness," broke through the empty, sad mood. He dropped out of college. Some of the conscious reasons for leaving college were not so much the feelings about his crime, but that he was deeply involved in a homosexual relationship and other "excitements." Part of it was that he felt profound shame about it. A similarly conflicted issue was to be a drug user: At first it was a triumph; to break society's laws was partly experienced as a victorious feat: "Heroin was the cement of a secret group of people, like a conspiracy. It added spice to my life. I was not alone, but could socialize, be friendly; I suddenly felt very special and in control." But this triumph soon turned into a humiliating dependency. The narcotics had many functions, besides the vague breaking of society's laws in spiteful challenge. They muted the shame about his homosexual propensities, his social defeat, his passive dependent drifting. They soothed his despair and loneliness in his guilt. But most of all they calmed the attacks of terror and anxiety, lure and temptation, and forestalled the welling up of murderous rage and guilt-fed self-wrecking, all of which appeared puzzling and out of control. Whenever he withdrew from narcotics, anxiety and violent anger became unmanageable.

For the next eight years, he was on illegal heroin and dilaudid, then methadone, working only irregularly as an unskilled laborer.

After entering the program and becoming stabilized on methadone, the initial attacks of anxiety rapidly ceased; he stopped seeing me altogether after about seven weeks, I presume, mostly out of embarrassment because he did not work, but lived from his wife's income and some unemployment compensation. About half a year later and without consulting me, he withdrew himself from metha-done, went to Lexington, could not stand the regimentation and structure there, hurried back, and wanted to see me to be readmitted to the program. I happened to be not available just then, and he was told to return the next day. He felt he could not wait and got some drugs on the street, broke into a drugstore in a most inept and self-sabotaging way and was arrested. For the following fifteen months he lived under the thundercloud of the trial, worked a little, but mostly sat just passively around, came to see me regularly, though without much active psychotherapeutic work: all was fear, hopelessness, despair, passivity, feeling low about not working, but unable to start anything as long as he was waiting for the trial. A lot of drinking, ruminating about his self-destructiveness, his fears of being closed in, a conviction: "Whenever I take control, I almost purposely punish myself. This self-destructive part is very embarrassing to me. I do not understand it, yet it was equally embarrassing for me to do well in school." Success was always followed by a need to fail, a sense of disgust and depression. But it was also embarrassing to him to speak about his problem with me. "I am good at being a failure. I can't be an average person. I can't deserve to have a good time." Then, about four months after resumption of therapy and a brief period of work in the dry docks, his murderous and tragic fate nearly repeated itself a second time: During a period of unemployment he gave late one night a co-worker of his, Sleazy, and some others a ride home from a tavern. The other reviled the old homosexual friend of his. Andreas finally burst out in verbal anger and was in turn slapped in the face by Sleazy. Again the jump from humiliation to blind rage was instantaneous. He got out of the car, knocked out his foe with such force that he broke his own hand. He fled. The hostilities escalated. The windows of Andreas's car were smashed. A few nights later it went up in flames. A warrant was issued for Andreas's arrest for the assault on his foe. Sleazy was said to be out to shoot him, but eventually stole away and did not appear before the magistrate to press charges against Andreas. Thus our patient went free once more.

A few days after this, he was called back to work and congratulated for his manly deed against a generally disliked, provocative "bastard." He found, on his return, that one of his closest friends had died of an overdose of drugs in the meantime. His former co-worker and now foe, Sleazy, had not shown up, thus showing to the patient that "he was afraid of me." This meant, "I have crossed the thin line from respect to fear. I do not want him to fear me, only to respect me."

He ate his lunch alone, thought—or rather brooded—about death with great sadness, loneliness and anxiety: the death of his friends, of himself, of his earlier homicide. The sense of anxiety, of fear of losing his mind, of losing control, of killing himself, set in, and, as he saw someone else peeling an apple with a knife, this became so "symbolic for death and violence," that he ran away. He had a knife in his pocket, went to the water to throw it in, but was afraid that he might jump in himself. And yet in all that, he was neither angry, nor enraged, nor even "aggressive"—just terribly afraid of an unknown force within himself. He finally landed in a friend's house and took a Valium. His disastrous aggression was experienced as an outside force, mobilized by humiliation or loneliness, split off, unrecognized in its emotional content (denied and repressed), and yet breaking through with unmanageable, "meaningless" force and violence. Suicide and homicide were bloody realities for this man.

Brooding, idleness, gambling and betting, playing mathematical games and chess in his head filled the following year till his trial for the break-in. He recognized the pervasiveness of shame in his life—especially about his homosexual impulses. "I picture myself as masculine, and at the same time I have these homosexual feelings. Before the homicide I had an episode of homosexuality; before I was starting to use drugs, I had a homosexual episode. And with Sleazy again it was about homosexuality; he touched on my most sensitive spot; in all these situations my rage becomes uncontrollable. I am ashamed of these still present wishes and acts (fellatio on boys about eighteen years old); I cannot reconcile them with my self-image as a man. The boy is like me when I was at that age; *it's like a split in me—a big brother and another kid which is in trouble.*" He compared himself to his father who also had been passive, inactive, had given up on life, defeated, humiliated.

The homosexual escapades were exciting, forbidden, very shame-ridden and led to severe anxiety attacks and a lot of guilt; and so did his childlike dependency and passivity towards his wife, his wish to be treated as special, as he remembered he was as a child with mother: the center of the universe. And time and again: "There is like a wild animal closed up in me. And when I am closed up, there is a panic that 'it' would break out of me, that I have nowhere to turn."

Then the trial came. I testified for him and suggested to the judge continuation of psychotherapy and methadone maintenance as the only hope for this man; a long jail sentence would do no good and probably finish off most chances for rehabilitation. As usual I found the judge very insightful and glad to grab any opportunity to provide drug addicts with a more promising alternative than the signal of capitulation: the jail sentence. It was only then, a little more than two years after inception of treatment, that psychotherapy started in earnest. I gave him a near-ultimatum: that I was going to continue working with him only under one condition—that he would resume his studies, some studies anyway, thus make use of his very high intelligence, and add skills to gifts in a field where he would really find inner satisfaction. With a stipend from a state's agency he resumed his studies in a scientific field and within a few months became an honor student, enthusiastic about his new life, "happier than ever," but also fearing that "what is so good cannot last, something might happen—a disaster, a catastrophe."

Considerable work on his narcissism and his fear of success had already been done in the year of passivity and waiting: "I was spoiled. My mother showered me with attention—not so much out of love, but because she tried to get me to dislike my father—when I was still very young." But time and again—remembrance of claustrophobia, fears of being closed in, the past flights into drinking, aggression, grandiose fantasies. "The opiates made me less shameful, less withdrawn. I could be for the first time friendly, easy going, pleasant. Without them my ego gets easily bruised." Then memories of his father throwing dishes around, his mother's provocative silence or packing and threatening to leave, fifty times! "It was so horrible—on Christmas morning they would fight—when everything was supposed to be good. It's like my feelings now: when things are good they aren't going to last. It's even so at the race tracks: When I lose I am in a relaxed state of misery; when I win, I am nervous and have more of a feeling that I did something wrong than when I lost. The losing is the lesser of two evils. The same in life in general."

But gradually the deeper meanings opened up and started illuminating the puzzling history. The puzzle was an extremely bright, attractive, honest, searching man with a very nice wife and two children—living a history of nightmare after nightmare: one homicide, another near murder, ten years of narcotics addiction, episodes of homosexual escapades followed by shame, depression, rage, a life filled with a sense of foreboding and doom, of despair and grandiosity, of long "lazy" passivity and destructive frenzy.

As in a detective story the puzzles started to solve themselves— slowly, but with a shared sense of discovery in him and in me. Hereafter I follow the slow pace of revelations in the therapy step by step in his own words. Some repetitions will be unavoidable: known facts in new contexts, thus assuming their deeper significance and compelling force. During the most productive period of therapy I saw him only once a week (roughly the third year of treatment).

When I think about myself, my life, everything seems meaning-less. As long as I can lose myself in work and school I do not feel it; things go quite well. When I start thinking, I start feeling guilty. As long as I can see the taking of drugs as a separate part of my life no one knows about, nothing is wrong with it. Only if you are caught, it's wrong. Then suddenly I want to do everything anew and right and am upset about how my life is. But this depression was long before I messed up my life, before the drugs, before the homicide. Already as a kid I was saddened by no particular external fact, but just by how life was in general. [I asked him for specifics.] Now I do the same as in school. When I should talk I block my thoughts. I cannot talk about a mathematical problem. I become nervous and am failing or freezing under the desire to do right. And when I think about the sadness as a child, it is impossible to think of an image. It is now as if a part of me is working against me, stops me from thinking. I have been working against myself, over and over. It is like the part in me who wants to see me fail in everything, to be a miserable failure, even in talking. Or that makes me feel things go too well. Similarly I had always the feeling during sex: that I was not able to perform—or in the program with the urine samples, that I cannot give it. It reminds me of feeling embarrassed with my parents when I succeeded in school. I did not want them to watch me. They were complimenting me too much—that I was the tallest, or was good in sports. Whenever I get the advantage, like this morning when I stood in line in the bank and suddenly a window opened and I was right there, I feel it's undeserved and I feel embarrassed, as if I had been too aggressive. It has to be something completely unconscious, I was never aware enough to head it off. This self-destructive thing always had sexual overtones. It's difficult to explain. Now it is largely suppressed by the methadone. I only feel these two somehow go together: to be self-destructive and this sexual feeling. Although now I am like a prisoner in the program I do not fear this destruction so much; it is controlled by the drug.

When I was in withdrawal, before I came on the program, while under Thorazine, I had the most horrifying nightmare, similar to an experience I had under LSD: "I'm not sure about my identity, but I think I was first either a mad scientist or his assistant who found a new drug. Whoever took it would lose touch with reality so that the other person looks like a roach or a bug, or even as a reptile. It was most vivid, the brown shiny armor. My part was to combat—but I am not sure whether I was the one who made the medicine or fought the mad scientist." How I interpreted it then was that it was my fear of losing touch with reality and going crazy. It reminds me of dreams from childhood where I was drowning. This unknown force in me which always destroys what I built up entered time and again: when I started college it was such a happy point in my life—but I felt it had to change. And all collapsed. And when I left jail it was the same: I was back in college and married—and both times there was this combination of sex (homosexuality) and self-destruction. Precisely because it was wrong, it was sexually exciting. I feel it right now: to let go, completely to allow me to be taken over by this part, an excitement, adventure, to break the chains. The same with heroin. School was no excitement; homosexuality and drugs were—the very wrongness of it and destructiveness of it was exciting. And still I could not enjoy it either (the breaking out of school and conventions) because of this unknown underlying thing. Each time sadness and despair took over. When I was about to kill the Whelp, I was so disgusted by myself that I wanted to commit suicide. *It was almost an accident that I killed him, not me.*

I remember already when I was four or five I thought of suicide. When mother was hanging up clothes on the roof I wanted to jump off the roof. Suicide has accompanied me throughout life. Life was and is so dark. My parents were always fighting, my father screaming and throwing things. An image: a bowl of spaghetti on the floor. Mother would not clean it up for how long, although for her cleanliness was next to godliness. At night I always wanted a pillow over my head—not to hear the arguments. I sided mostly with my mother. It was fear and sadness; I was crying, was hurt, more than upset. I remember too that the parents were spanking me, but I always refused to cry, so they gave up in frustration.

[In the next session he was furious because of having been delayed in traffic.] I justify my rage by telling myself that I am in the right; really everything becomes an insult to me. And still—when I feel angry, at least I feel awake and alive, almost a good feeling, to be powerful; I feel myself and ready to fight. The anger is exciting. I don't understand it. The image of my mother appears; she seemed all powerful when I was a child, but my refuge was with my sister. When mother and father were arguing, she would comfort me that everything would be all right. I am still so ashamed in front of her because of all my troubles, that I shun her. She was so proud of me when I was a freshman—and now I have been such a failure! [One may note again the contrast between depersonalization and rage, as in many other cases.]

We came close to the unknown "inner demon" who always *wrecks:* "I remember my earliest dream, a very frightening dream; perhaps I was five. 'A monster was looking in through the second story window where I slept. I saw his very long legs from the ground. Then I was looking down from a bridge and saw a very large, big, teddybear-like animal running, or a lamb; it was monstrous.' I only remember the terror and the feeling of death. The first time that I was in contact with death was when the neighbor next door who had been very fond of me and treated me like a son, and whom I liked very much, was very sick in the hospital. He jumped out of the window and killed himself. All that was when I was less than six." Here I reminded him of the child which was crushed to death. He immediately responded: "But there was nothing emotional. I was too young to understand it. I was not upset, only excited. I could not wait to tell my friends when they came from school what an exciting thing I had experienced. I still see the image: he was black and blue, the wheel was on top of him. It was a Coca Cola bottle truck on a construction site" (in contrast now to the first version where it was in front of his house). I asked him directly whether he might not have repressed another part—the intense anxiety and ensuing rage—which later on emerged in the claustrophobia (being pinned to the ground) whose importance he kept emphasizing. "That's a very good point. It's also the feeling crushed—and especially in sports, that I am run over and crushed to the ground. I was a tremendous football player, because I could run over people; it was a relief for my aggression." I suggested that he did to others what the truck had done to his playmate. He came to the next session very depressed. There was a mood of loneliness and emptiness with vague danger and irritation—"as if I were avoiding something."

In the following session he talked more about this demonic force in him which kept condemning and sabotaging him: as soon as he felt insulted it broke out in murderous rage. "Therefore I killed. When I was insulted, I was so stunned that I was not able to have a repartee. I was stunned and afterwards enraged about the most minor thing—all through my life; for instance when my parents were critical of me, I smashed a mirror and injured my hand. Later I wanted people to be afraid of me. I always thought of myself as such a majesty, so special, that every little thing enraged me. I felt I was very important to my parents. I always hoped they would die first so that they would not have to suffer my loss. I did not wish them dead; it was out of concern for them." I wondered whether this feeling of *self-importance* was not indeed a *protection,* that it may have been just the other way around. After all that was also the time when he felt utterly helpless, unprotected, hurt and thinking of suicide. I asked whether this fantasy might not have given him a sense of importance precisely in his helplessness; we should also not forget that in reality he wanted to kill himself in order to punish the surviving parents. He immediately recognized the connection: "I was so helpless, hurt and angry that I could only go in two directions: either kill myself and have them suffering, or be all important and have them dead."

After his first startling successes at his resumed studies and following an interruption in psychotherapy: "Every week I feel I am growing, I am becoming something, but the problem is still the underlying anxiety that I will ruin things, that there is something about me that is uncontrollable. Just under the surface the animal is working, under a thin veneer of civility, the part which shot the Whelp. The worst now is that I have that feeling precisely with those people I am closest to and I care for most, my family, some friends, you: to strike out where there is no justification, to hit, to kill, for no reason at all. This is the most horrible thing for a person to have. It feels good to be physically injured [he was, just then!] and weakened—so I don't feel as dangerous." He talked about his narcissistic rage in the present as well as in his childhood—how he "got away with murder" with his very inconsistent, spoiling, materially massively indulging parents which only increased his deep sense of guilt.

Then he mentioned that until age eight he slept in his parents' bedroom and vaguely remembered having witnessed their intercourse: "I thought that mother was crushed by father. There was never any privacy. This sounds crazy: as a child I felt as if there were hidden microphones or concealed cameras so that the parents always knew what I did. It was my fantasy that the parents had only the best in mind for me and never would harm me." (thus dealing by reversals with frightening looking, exhibition, and attacking).

The following hour he returned to the "crushed boy": "I spoke the other day with my mother about that memory. She told me that I was so upset at the time when I came home that I was unable to talk. It is odd how differently I remembered it. And it also occurred to me that I stole the Coke bottle from the same type of truck at the same place and in such a way that I was caught at once. I expected to be punished, but the response was not as severe as I expected. There must be a connection to all that. I remember the boy who died was a very good kid. We played a lot together. He shared his toys, but I did not want to share my things with him. I have never thought about that before, but he was my best friend and best enemy; I competed so much with him and was jealous. I wonder whether I felt responsible for his death? We were not allowed to go on the street, but I went with him anyway. I turned around and saw the truck behind me. If I could have given him a warning? I wonder what really happened." I: "So that you may have felt guilty?" He: "Right!" I: "Especially because you had felt aggressive towards him anyway." He: "Exactly. And I understand the stealing of the Coke now too: that I was getting back at the people who killed him." I: "Or to provoke punishment." He agreed. He then said how deceptive his memory was and how he started to look at that event in the last few days as if it had happened just recently. His repressed feelings were welling up. I added that I believe the crux lay in his guilt feelings: that his murderous wishes could indeed become true— towards that boy and perhaps also towards his parents, and that we can understand now the anxiety in his early dream, too. The monster staring in was his bad conscience for his murderous wish: "He sees it and is going to get you." He: "That dream was so real. And then this weird shaped animal, like a giraffe, running below, a funny animal, that was movement, but in the monster part there was no action, only staring; it was static, and the fear he would do something, I don't know what. His face was as big as the window. The animal below was polka dotted, or a strange color, perhaps purple." I intervened: "Was that not perhaps the purple, distorted form of the crushed boy, but running again? And then came the monster, the guilt; in the dream you were partly undoing the terror by making the animal, the boy, funny and running again." I tied it in with his lifelong need to repeat both aggression and self-punishment, with his never getting the punishment he expected from the monster: not for the boy's death, not for his stealing the bottle, not for his outbursts with the parents nor for his murder, and that he was still haunted by the fear that the monster was catching up with him. He was almost stunned by the connections, then added: "After the homicide I wanted to go to jail and expected seven to ten years, and did not get it. Instead the following ten years were as if I had been in jail, wasted, on drugs." He mentioned friends who killed themselves, his own wishes to commit suicide, a lot of shame situations (impotence with women, welfare, urine rituals). Nightmares came where he was killed by a firing squad, again thoughts of suicide, then the insight: "I wonder whether I pushed the boy or argued with him. Perhaps it's not real, but I feel the guilt." He mentioned murderous impulses towards his own sons, the exact opposite of what he consciously felt. I added: "The unconscious guilt not to deserve to feel good, and then the attack to prove why you feel guilty."

Then he returned to the still extreme phobia of waterbugs and roaches, how he burned one as a three year old, how in the Thorazine nightmare he changed people into these bugs. "It was especially their long legs and the thin long antennas, and that they came out of nowhere. It feels very important. It has something to do with my parents or sex." Again he thinks of self-destruction, sees the firing squad, wishes to pick fights, and his homosexual fellatio: "It is bittersweet like drugs or drinking. I remember when I was about eight I was forced by a fifteen- or sixteen-year-old guy to perform fellatio on him. I was not a willing participant. He forced me down; I was crying. There all came together—sex, to be forced, the wrongness." He went farther back: the bug phobia was preceded by a hair phobia (in the bath tub or on plates), and he equated fast moving hair and legs with the parental intercourse and the later forced fellatio. I noted a similar split of his feelings regarding the "crushed boy." In the latter he remembered only the excitement but had repressed his horror and guilt; with the "hair" he remembered disgust and horror but had repressed the excitement. Yet both repressed parts were repeated in actions—the first in his compulsive self-destruction, the haunting sense of Furies following him, of impending doom, the latter in the compulsive repetition of a masochistic, homosexual act. Thereupon a clear very early memory suddenly emerged: "I was still in the crib, it's a flash of a memory—no details. I had a terrible taste in my mouth and felt very constrained. It was an inky smell, like an old piece of celery or something like that. It's an overwhelming memory. It was before words. It has no substance, only this smell and taste and the feeling of being constrained. I must have been two years old. It was as if I were choking." Its deep meaning was not revealed though I suspect it expressed the earliest version of a primal scene experience: the bitterness of helpless rage, jealousy, exclusion, confinement—perhaps, within the context, a sight of fellatio? He immediately returned to the memory and split in feelings regarding the dying boy, his haunting feelings afterwards: "I should have prevented it—but I did not have anything to do with it. There was no fault on my side, certainly not! But he had been nice to me, and I was a rotten kid; I was jealous and angry as hell that mother made me share things with him." Thus the memory of the crushed boy may have been the nodal point in which all his primal scene feelings converged: rage, anxiety, guilt, excitement, jealousy, shame, helplessness, a sense of betrayal by mother, the ambiguous meaning of watching. And was the crib memory a similar, far earlier nodal point and screen memory?

He added that a girl told him years later that he had not warned the boy, though he protested his innocence. I maintained that the intensity of the guilt feelings which had haunted him ever since spoke for more than just fantasy. Even his "happiness" and "excitement," retained in memory, could have caused guilt. Here again he switched right back to the primal scene: "The bugs suddenly appear out of nowhere, at night, and it is like the parents at night when they had sex." And he also remembered how seductive his mother was: "She had only a slip on when she was washing me; her breasts were hanging right in my face. My father was mad about it." (As far as is known, he had been bottlefed.) He also remembered that many of the fights between the parents revolved around his father thinking his mother was flirting with makebelieve lovers. Andreas expressed increasing hatred and disdain for father: he was a gambler, a bookmaker, squandering money, slobbering all his food over his face, "a gluttonous pig." Then a "horrible memory": "He chewed cigars and spat them out all over the apartment. It's the same disgust as with the bugs." He shuddered and went on: "He was farting, had foul language and was cursing, but his nastiest habit was that he rubbed his balls and then smelled his fingers." So it appears likely that hair and water bugs came to stand for the disgusting, hated, anal sadistic father—but also for the opposite (positive) feeling lived out now in homosexual humiliations. And both the "crushed boy" and his own compulsive, for him ununderstandable crying at his father's funeral expressed the overwhelming guilt for his murderous rage against father. He stressed that he had no male image to look up to, none he liked to identify with—until, transiently, his brother-in-law. Every depression, every haunting sense of impending doom was henceforth reducible either to yet another piece of unconscious guilt, leading always back to the crushed boy, to hatred against father and primal scene, or to unconscious shame, leading back to the forced fellatio, the masochistic submission to the anal sadistic father and emasculation.

It became clear that he had a strange feeling after he killed the Whelp. "It took me two months until I felt really sorry. I had never felt so calm in my whole life [as after the murder]; it was as if the whole burden of the world had been lifted off from me. It was the only time in my life that I had any real power." I believe this, too, was a compromise: the murder gave substance and reason to the unconscious guilt and led at first to real punishment and real expiation; it was a symbolic parricide-fulfilling rage, jealousy, revenge; it wiped out the shame of his helplessness and submission to his father as a homosexual but detested seducer. It gave him the self-righteous rationalization: "I rid the world of a pest"—really, as we heard earlier, rather an "irrationalization."

He realized the extreme ambivalence toward both parents. Probably as expression of his idealizing, nearly symbiotic, but also profoundly ambivalent transference to me, he responded to a chain of crises I went through which must have been perceived by him in form of my covert depression and anxiety, with a reappearance of the "haunting, ominous feelings," a sense of strangeness, of not fitting, of going to fail, of destroying himself. A dream of a haunted house, a boy defecating in the bathroom, Andreas screaming of fright. He could not tell me something he was most ashamed about, but didn't know what he was hiding. It concerned most likely the anal-masochistic, homosexual impulses which he soon enough started to live out again. Once more it was externalizing—the homosexual gratification for an unknown reason, followed by extreme gloominess and guilt, "the excitement to do something that was wrong, without getting in trouble, and then feeling so guilty and ashamed that I could not mention it to you for two weeks. And I just felt miserable, that I would be caught, that Fate will destroy me, that I'd fail in school." A flash image: "Nausea about my father—never wanting to be like him, but like these young boys whom I pick up at night and perform fellatio on." He questioned his sanity and self-control. He feels a close connection between homosexual and murderous impulses, but does not understand it. The tie-in is "masochism." He feels sexually excited about hearing children beaten up with belts by a woman which leads to a microanalysis of a very important part of acting out: "It is the same sexual feeling with homosexual wishes—that I am punished, that it is wrong, that I am completely controlled by someone else, that he has total power over me. It is like looking in a mirror: that I am ultimately in control. I only play-act, as if I were controlled and exploited, and have him push my head down to his penis. If I really lost control, it would turn into something unpleasant. I want to be masochistic, but I want to dominate the situation. If I lose control, if a girl or man really takes the whip out, I get furious. It is paradoxical. I enjoy a homosexual act where I pretend that the person has me under control and forces me to fellatio, that I am subjugated by someone stronger than me, but as soon as they really believe it, it turns my mood off." It is indeed a very precarious balance between two nearly equally strong parts, which were not really in conflict with each other but coexisted in a curious split with most abrupt flipflops: the illusion of total power/the illusion of masochistic subjugation. Socially it was no different.

He added that this whole area of homosexuality-masochism (and the two were for him almost identical) was deeply frightening and attractive, full of fear and pain. It reminded him vividly of the childhood fantasy of the cruel, spanking neighbor and the torturing enemies: "It was sex, not bravery: I wished my parents were more cruel to me." He remembered their vicious fights. Would physical violence have been a relief from this unending yelling and pouting? His mother took sex as martyrdom, too—just as he took his first forced fellatio at age eight: "He so overpoweringly forced me; it was there that masochism and homosexuality merged."

Dreams emerged where he witnessed his wife being raped, remembered his jealousy when he first was dating his wife and on his own added: "Part of that jealousy was my own homosexuality, that she was doing something that I was barred from doing legally." Nearly four years into therapy, he asked whether he could lie on the couch to associate and talk more freely—obviously partly to avoid the shame these most painful problems gave him. (I saw him at the time two to three hours a week, and the method started resembling more that of an analysis proper.) A lot of transference shame emerged: "That you cannot help but think of me as a very childlike person—just as I think about myself, that I am foolish. I respect you and want to impress you—I care about these things." Another dream: "That my wife was having relations with someone else; it was bittersweet agony, a masochistic feeling, the pleasure about pain, agony, torment." He added: "I was observing her as when father was on top of mother. It was painful and yet curiously pleasurable, like a sore in the mouth you keep touching. My father was very large, two hundred forty pounds, like a whale, and in the dreams I reexperience that fascination.

Another fantasy as child: to be tied down where I could not move and to be beaten with a whip, but to have only just that much pain that it was pleasurable, to be subjected to someone else's complete domination by power—or perhaps rather, that I am using the other person so that I have the power—to use him as an intermediary so that I have complete control over myself. At the same time I am both completely helpless and have total mastery of myself. And what is so self-destructive is that I allow this bittersweet pleasure to affect my life." He thinks of self-flagellation in art and of Cellini's autobiography. The present homosexual acts appear like an attempt to master the trauma of the forced fellatio.

My feeling was that these acts were both turning passive into active and archaic repression with splitting. The mixed wish-fear scenes of parental intercourse and fights, of the crushed boy, and of forced fellatio were turned from situations of extreme passivity, helplessness and powerlessness into situations of a merely feigned subjugation, but real, complete control and power. It combined sexual excitement and fascination with a curiously split experience of brute force and violence, masochistically replayed and reenacted, but secretly controlled and mastered by him, followed by a sense of guilt, repentance and shame, while feeling relaxed and freed of his boisterous anger and combativeness, and able to work! The shame part, I suspect, was the reaction to the replay of the early scene in its masochistic version (identification with the mastered and castrated mother); guilt, relaxation and freedom of anger were the response to his own sense of force and power (the identification with the controlling, castrating father). So the split reflected the repressed double identification with the sadistic father and the masochistic mother in the primal scene. His lifelong, most destructive sense of self-punishment in the many forms of humiliation and self-murderousness repeated these three original traumata in split, double form. And so did his drug addiction: It gave him a sense of power and specialness, accompanied by guilt, and a sense of dependency, weakness, enslavement, filling him with shame. Thus his life was like a constant dangerous journey between the Scylla of shameful defeat and humiliation, leading to blind rage and murder, and the Charybdis of guilty success, triumph and self-sabotage.

Then new facets of the rage-guilt relationship with his father surfaced: In a dream he first strangles "the old man"—who only laughs at him, and then he kills himself by jumping from a high board. He does not recognize at all that the old man referred to father. When I make him aware of the defense, he laughs out and suddenly recalls a temper tantrum against his father at age eight, where father only laughed, and the sense of helpless rage and ridicule. "I really wanted to kill him," but the rage, hatred and scorn were turned directly against himself as suicide and shame. (The transference implications were bypassed.) New memories surfaced when he mentioned the fear welling up that "I might go insane and do something over which I have no control and do not want to do." He remembered when he was about nine being run over in a fighting game by a very heavy boy, who pinned him to the ground and literally crushed and splintered his elbow. He was in the hospital for a long time. "Two years later the same kid was climbing over a high fence. I pushed him, and he broke his arm, too." He continued tying together this (claustrophobic) fear of being pinned to the ground, crushed, locked up, with the panic about being possessed by a foreign part of himself, losing control, drowning. He contrasted it with the homicide where no such feeling existed. Then the following memory: "When I was about seven my father took me to the beach one evening. He went to see a friend of his, a bookmaker. He only told me not to go out too far in the water and left me alone. I went in. But the ground suddenly dropped, and I was drowning. A girl jumped in and rescued me. I had never been to the beach before and could not swim. Afterwards my father made me feel guilty, that I had done something wrong, and I was yelled at. I doubt whether my mother ever learned about what had happened."

He concurred with me how the very negligence and unconcern of father in that episode had a murderous quality. This aspect had not occurred to Andreas before, but was both surprising and convincing, and he himself connected the mutual murderousness between father and him with that between the Whelp and him. He then remembered how his father used to reproach him for every minor infraction, like coming home fifteen minutes late, that Andreas was "killing" him. Later on he yet added, if Andreas took drugs, this would be the worst thing he could do and would kill him. It was indeed only about one year before father's death that Andreas started taking narcotics—evidently a magical means to finish once and for all father's blackmail in form of these death threats.

Knowing all this, the following statement is reminiscent of Joseph Conrad's words: "a tragic and familiar Shade,...stretching bare brown

arms over the glitter of the infernal stream, the stream of darkness."
Andreas said, more prosaically: "Often everything is such a tragedy for
me, so dark and gloomy, despite all the insight. Then I feel I am living a
tragedy, and that people are aware of it; then I use homosexuality,
violence or drugs to boost my self-esteem and remove the pain. I am
leading a double life—tragedy and success."

Unfortunately Andreas's psychotherapy came to a sudden and
unexpected end: More than four years after the beginning and one and
a half years into his most successful professional studies, he felt ready
to be detoxified (withdrawn)—very slowly, with increase of psychotherapy (from two to four or five hours a week). Despite greatest care
he felt worse and worse: very depressed, unable to do anything, empty,
lonely, vaguely nervous, uneasy, and apprehensive. "The depression is
like a weight on my stomach. I am not interested in anything. I don't
like anything, and get irritated about the slightest thing. I am almost
sleepwalking. It is a total blackness, completely enclosing me." From
this deepening depression with clear anhedonia, depersonalization and
all the physical signs of a somatically felt depression (psychomotor
inhibition), he went, when the medication was down to ten mg of
methadone, into violent despair: he threatened to kill his wife, himself,
his therapist, to rob a bank (just to break out of the depression).
Neither Valium nor Librium helped. He took to heroin, methadone,
and methamphetamine. Only the latter seemed to help the
depression—and then only for a few hours. He got drunk every
afternoon, but to no avail. Eventually his methadone dosage was
increased, in steps, back to forty mg. Still the severe depression
continued. Thereupon it was decided to put him on a tricyclic
antidepressant—Elavil. Ten days went by without change and then,
almost overnight, the depression went, to his complete surprise. "I feel
completely different. I have never felt so good in my whole life, even
not with drugs. Now I can start working and have hope for my future.
It is like I have a new lease on life. I have confidence even to make it
without methadone."

After the interruption for my summer vacation, Andreas did not
return to therapy, broke off Elavil treatment as well, but continued on
methadone maintenance. When I by chance encountered him he was
furious at me for having "forced" him into detoxification for what he
saw as my own vanity.

I am fairly certain that he terminated therapy with me because of massive—partly justified—disappointment with me (and himself) and the ensuing rage and guilt. Facing up to his past and the inner problems flowing from it proved to be an unending narcissistic injury: "Now I want to look only into the future and to external questions." I wonder if therapy (especially on the couch) was another situation repeating the claustrum, where he was pinned to the ground and laid low, against which he had only two options: fight or flight.

At last report he had been taken off Elavil because of tachycardia, was on low-level methadone, and employed in a very responsible position. In light of the good response to amitriptyline it is likely that an endogenous element markedly contributed to his chronic depression.

(This concludes Dr. Gerson's summary of the case.)

Psychoanalytic Evaluation of the Patient

If we try to use the scaffolding of metapsychological abstractions it is important to start out with some genetic understanding of this still profoundly enigmatic man. Very clearly he has been massively and continuously traumatized throughout his childhood—faced with overwhelming external occurrences and hence with unmanageable internal conflicts and ensuing affects.

There were, between ages five and nine, several very traumatic memories—the "crushed boy," the "drowning," the "forced fellatio," the "crushed arm"—which had a multiplicity of consequences.

All of these served as very drastic confirmations of the fantasies connected with earlier traumata and their fears. Symbolically, the "crushed boy" in particular can be presumed to stand as a most powerful confirmation of castration anxiety and, more deeply, of punishment by narcissistic dissolution, fragmentation, and dismemberment.

The "crushed boy" trauma also can serve as a very important screen memory for the nearly forgotten, but at least equally traumatic, earlier and later primal scene experiences. In both the characteristic ego split ("I do not see, feel, understand—and yet I do") is based on "It is frightening and exciting to observe!" This ego split had been a problem all through his life, and was still very obtrusive during therapy. The screen memory had to be taken together with one of the earliest memories: the excitement about the little man in the radio in the parents' bedroom and his wish to get his hands on him and to bring him pain. I suspect (and this remains speculation) that it covered three, perhaps even four, simultaneous inner realities. One was his own masturbation, stimulated by his observations of the parental intercourse. In the light of the general suffusion of his entire early life by aggression, especially by a sadistic form of it, his own masturbation must have been equally bound up with pain.

The second supposition is that he wished to attack and castrate his father: that the little man he wanted to get hold of and sadistically wrench off was father's penis; another slightly different version is the erotically *sadistic* (not castrating) use in fantasy of father's penis. After all, even at the time of therapy he devoted an important part of his sexual life to a masochistic replay of such a homosexual act. In between, in his adolescence, it was even closer to the original: he had older, "respected" men suck his penis, had them humiliated, was himself more in a directly sexual sadistic position whereas later this was reversed. We will come back to this later.

A third and no less likely interpretation of the "little man in the radio" is mother's phallus whose nonexistence would of course be such a threat to his own that excitedly, fascinatedly, he had to look "within" and engage in a "perverse curiosity"—again in a very sadomasochistic form.

Finally—in the light of the depth and severity of his narcissistic conflicts—I wonder whether the aliveness of the hidden little man who could be uncovered only "with pain and hurt" represented himself; we know that even now he feels only in the excitements of narcissistic rage or of his masochistic, "self-seeking," risk-taking escapades really alive, instead of being depersonalized. Was the little man an image of the alive self under the bug armors (seen in hallucinations, dreams and phobias), a picture of the deeply wounded, narcissistically most vulnerable, but also magically powerful, speaking, exhibiting or observing self, surrounded by a mechanical hulk, a protective armor, a frightfully constraining claustrum, a self which was constantly and painfully shattered? Was it an early version of the depersonalizing splits which run all through his life?

All four interpretations would apply much more traumatically and massively to the later memory as screen—to that of the crushed boy:

not as "discovery" now, but as destruction of these four equivalents. I pose this as hypothesis.

Particularly the "crushed boy" event, not as screen memory, and also to a lesser extent the later traumata, must have served as a powerful force to regress from open and still largely conscious manifestations of the Oedipus complex: the remembered murderousness against his father, and the inferred murderousness from father, the equally remembered sexual and emotional seductiveness of his mother. The regression went to strong fixations on earlier levels: to anal sadistic and masochistic interpretations of all his life, which were constantly reenacted and sought, as mentioned, in the incessant chase after "excitement." The disgust towards the father's open masturbation thinly veiled his own masochistic wishes to submit to him; in turn he abruptly switched into the murderous, sadistic role (killing of father, his adolescent homosexuality, the two murderous assaults, the threat to attack, in case his masochistic "play" gets out of "total control"). I suspect the bug phobia is partly a derivative of this very early sadomasochistic relationship to his father (and perhaps to his phallic mother?).

But the regression, under the onslaught of all traumata (not solely that of the "crushed boy"), went farther to an oral-narcissistic position. There is no need to repeat the most massive evidence for this orientation. But I agree with Stolorow that even the sadomasochistic acts and attitudes can be understood as *also* serving narcissistic needs. Stolorow (1975) quotes Keiser (1949) "that in the masochistic perversion the masochist achieves a sense of 'complete control' over his punishment and his sadistic partner." He concludes, using Kohut's helpful concepts, that "the compensated masochist typically seeks narcissistic reparation by resurrecting the idealized parent image. The structurally deficient overt sadist most commonly strives for self-cohesion, self-identity and self-esteem by attempting to reactivate and validate his grandiose wishful self" (pp. 445–446). In a case the same author describes (1973 and 1975), a masochistic patient had also a preoccupation with bugs; in contrast to our patient it was a sexual perversion: the squashing of a bug by a woman equaled squashing of the penis equaled having a bounded and cohesive self in pain equaled masochistic pleasure and narcissistic restoration. In Andreas it was a bug phobia. This is presumably so because the excitement in the given equation was too murderous for it to be acceptable, but we do not really know.

This regression to an oral-narcissistic fixation was supported by the parents' own narcissism and their spoiling of the boy. He indeed got his narcissistic entitlement just as strongly fed as his narcissistic helplessness and powerlessness.

The earliest memory, the "flash" of the crib memory, is unclear in its meaning. Since its hallmarks are "bittersweet," "being tied down," and "speechless," Dr. Gerson suggested that this might be a very early primal scene, in a mixed oral and masochistic experience of overwhelming nature and repeated in the "bittersweet" homosexual-masochistic dreams and acts of the present. Was the taste in the mouth milk, semen, urine, father's fecal smell?

Last, but surely not least, all traumata described and the regression to sadomasochism and archaic narcissism just outlined lived on in the haunting sense of shame and guilt, the continually enacted self-humiliation and self-destruction, the foreboding of doom. The superego functions expressed very archaic, very sadistic and very grandiose expectations, and they were easily (not always, by any means) re-externalized.

As to the structural point of view much has already been stated: the ego split and superego split under the double-barrelled attack of narcissism and aggression, the double identification with sadistic father and crushed mother and hence his split, bisexual identity, the sudden jumps from shameful, eroticized passivity to guiltful, also eroticized, but murderous triumph and activity.

A few additional connections to the previous chapters (specific cause and predisposition) can be added here:

There is a lack of internal structure, as observed by Kohut and Kernberg in narcissistic personalities. One expression of it is the proclivity for affect regression. No further evidence needs to be added. Here we can focus on the two forms of defense, which are typical for all such patients, but particularly clear in Andreas: externalization and denial, as well as various forms of the phenomenon of splitting.

Externalization in form of drugs, masochism, violence, and just search for risk and excitement, has to provide the sense of self as bounded and cohesive entity; without it he said: "I go crazy"—and he had indeed a number of experiences where he was fragmented (for example, the mad scientist dream) or the continued fear that he would go insane and kill the persons closest to him. The feeling was "I would do something I do not want to do consciously, that I'm possessed by a power that is foreign to me, that all barriers are broken down, that it would be not me, as I am now. What now appears meaningless, would then become frighteningly real." Outside action, externalization, thus is autotherapy for this lack of inner structure. Even in therapy life was not conceivable for him without "excitement," meaning dangerous, potentially very destructive forms of risk taking. It had become the search for a hazardous, masochistic adventure—e.g.,, a sadistic prostitute with a steel whip, or at 2 A.M. picking up a homosexual hitch hiker, etc. This yearning for excitement was part of an aimless flight from the inner conflicts, a search for discharge and relief in blind outward action. Even guilt and shame in their excessive weight and externality were additional props, a kind of second line of defense by externalization, a defense again not only against aggression and object-libidinous regression, but most centrally against loss of the self and its boundaries and cohesion.

The "pendant" to these forms of externalization is the defense by denial against overwhelming affects. Of course these archaic feelings and moods were so prominent precisely because of the lack of inner structure. The most prominent in Andreas were—on the negative side—depression, rage, shame, loneliness and—on the positive side—excitement, fascination, a grandiose feeling, a sense of recklessness and triumph. All were ecstatic (also in the negative sense, of transcending the self) and called for artificial help in form of the affect defense by narcotically reinforced denial.

Thus, it is easy to see how the leading defense in his archaic, mainly narcissistic conflicts had been for most of his life history precisely this magical form of externalization, of control by action, the search for conflict solution by a magical thing and magical force, not in personal relations.

Parallel with the denial, the ego split was evident: "It is not me, it is a foreign power which I fear might take over." This split off part, conscious, disowned, of terrorizing force, muted by narcotics, reached back in his life history to the time of the traumata: being pinned to the ground, closed in, crushed, drowning. This leads over to the next defense.

There is no need to repeat how crucial the pervasive phenomenon of splitting—as outcome of defenses, occasionally as defect ("going to pieces" when overwhelmed by affects)—is in this case history. We have several markedly different forms of it.

A first one was the defense by disjunction, by partial fragmentation of thoughts and feelings, the inability to connect. I believe an outstanding example was his experience and memory of the murder where each second seemed to be totally divorced from the other, a deep sense of discontinuity.

A second one was just alluded to: going "insane," losing all inner cohesion under the onslaught of affect regression.

A third form is particularly interesting, the one he often described: the nearly artistic split between the observing-creating self and acting-experiencing self (see chapter 6). Although he ascribed the sense of reality to the latter, I wonder whether there was not a back-and-forth shifting of reality feeling, a much deeper, less solid split as in common states of depersonalization: that at times indeed the observing poetic functions of the ego are experienced as the truly alive self, looking with thrilled amazement and a smile at the "other" one—a foreign one, "just a figure in a novel," whereas at other times the active, really very aggressive and destructive self which risks his life in adventures and wild acts of fury and entitlement, forgetful of all commitments, becomes really "alive," breaking out of the cage of detachment and unreality. In other words, depersonalization was a shifting, almost tumbling form of symptom in this patient. As I mentioned I suspect that the "little man in the radio," a hidden "observing, talking," though encased, self-figure, may be a forerunner of that part of the split represented now by the enchained "poet."

This third split probably leads over to the fourth, the most important split of all, one which I think we can call a splitting into "intersystemic suborganizations," two massive parts of his personality, comprising drive-, ego-, and superego-functions. This quite archaic version of splitting is the one already exactingly described: On the one side there was the responsible, honest, successful, heterosexual, hard-working man in control of his outer life, but with a gnawing sense of guilt and impending punishment, and an underlying claim for entitlement, specialness, fame, a constant egging on to transgress limits, not wanting to be restricted as other mortals, feeling confined by society and nature. His opposite number was the homosexual-masochistic, castrated, weak, irresponsible counterpart, the one who indeed suddenly succumbed to the haunting sense of sadness, despair, loneliness, and sought relief in the secret acts described—the one who remained attracted to drive through the areas of drug traffic, who glumly gave up his school efforts for weeks, lounged around passively, overwhelmed with a sense of disgrace, shame, and masochistic wallowing in his hopelessness and despair. We saw this split as a double identification with father and mother, as derived above all from the primal scene observations. Again in both parts pain played an important role: to be a tormentor and to suffer and enjoy pain—quite similarly to Cassandra (case 17).

But there is yet a fifth and a far more regressed version of splitting:that between robot and monster. Frequently, Andreas came back to the deep seated, at times overwhelming, fear that there was a *wild beast* caged within him, ready to break out and to torture and kill—particularly the persons he loved most. The beast's counterpart was the totally, psychotically depersonalized *bug,* without feeling, without any life (a Kafkaesque metamorphosis). Again in this most regressive form of the two opposite suborganizations the figures appeared to be nearly unifunctional. The monster ("the wild animal") is just blind rage, uncontrolled aggression; the robot ("the bug"), a total denial of all feelings, and a radical separation and isolation from anything human (as on the deepest layer, discerned in depersonalization, when we studied Alexa, case 13). The horrifying aspect is that in Andreas this most archaic split did not always remain dreaded fantasy or dream. It became terrible reality during withdrawal and in his two homicidal assaults. I suspect that these two parts were not as simple and unifunctional as they appeared, but basically the "wild animal which is entrapped" is the rage fighting off the most terrifying original union with mother, the furor against the (unconsciously desired) return to the claustrum, whereas the "bug armor," all levels of depersonalization, represents not only a defense against this rage by absolute, total separateness, but also a return of the repressed (of the wish for union with mother), though in form of a lifeless, encasing claustrum. Thus even these most archaic figures were already compromise solutions.

If we look back over these five forms of splitting in sequence, each one becomes more encompassing and deep reaching, more archaic and regressed, and also spanning much longer time periods than the prior one. The fifth has a psychotic quality. The five seem, however, ranged on a continuum.

As with all types of splitting the various drugs have a radically different impact; clearly narcotics decrease very much the process and effect of splitting, whereas withdrawal from them, psychedelic drugs and, very interestingly, the major tranquilizers, like Thorazine or Mellaril, shift the scale very dramatically—from a controlled, conscious use of this mechanism (concentrated work)—to the most regressed end of the spectrum. That tranquilizers have this traumatic impact may be ascribable to some suspected paroxysmal or episodic substratum (EEG showed some possible hints of psychomotor epilepsy).

Alcohol, too, had a curious impact: in small doses it helped against the splitting; in larger dosages it increased it massively. The worst forms, where the split-off parts broke through and took over (without full disappearance of the opposing side), occurred when Andreas was under the influence of a lot of alcohol; however, there was no amnesia, no pathological intoxication. It is likely that alcohol in these high quantities actually eliminated the defense by denial and repression, simply removing the restraining counterparts and allowing the other part of the person to rule supreme. Suddenly a reversal occurred of which part was in command, a reversal dictating all three: action, dominating self-image, and sense of reality. Sadist and masochist, murderer and victim, beast and bug, guilt and shame, observer and actor, homosexual and heterosexual changed very rapidly, back and forth—each one being real now, ruling supreme now, and suddenly turning into the unreal and repudiated part (the "about face syndrome").

The cognitive disconnections and fragmentations were derived from these conflict generated splits, really from all five levels.

What is fascinating, however, is how much cognitive functioning, including excellent self-observation and self-expression, and with that highest achievements at work and therapeutic accomplishments, remained preserved, despite these most massive processes of splitting. Other expressions of this intactness are the use of humor, including self-irony, of course the basic stability of his marriage, and also the solidity of the working alliance with Dr. Gerson.

This man was not schizophrenic, regardless of the severity of the processes described! Only on the fifth level of regression, which really was experienced only in brief moments of actuality, though feared throughout life, the conflict reached psychotic dimensions: the fears and wishes of dissolving the boundaries between self and mother, countered by blind, fatal rage. But this points ahead to the boundary problem which will have to be taken up separately.

As to hyposymbolization: On the one side this man was eminently capable of using the most abstract forms of symbols; it is also astonishing how capable he gradually turned out to be over these years of putting his introspective observations into words. On the other side it was very difficult for him to articulate some of the most overwhelming archaic feelings; he acted—without clearly knowing what he felt. Another example was the inability for many years to engage in any activity of higher symbolization: literature, philosophy, art, mathematics, science—all fields which only gradually opened up again.

In this case I do not doubt that the "hyposymbolization" was secondary to the severity of conflicts and traumatization and the archaic nature of the affects involved. "Truly one of the things I stifled most in my whole life is art. When I drew, I was criticized, and I never tried it again. Anything where I was not immediately good at, I never attempted again, out of fear of criticism. The same with writing. My sensitivity stifled everything. Therefore I like mathematics: It is either perfect or not done, wrong, but beyond criticism."

Thus a deeper understanding of this blocking of sublimation and use of symbols leads us to the massive investment of raw "energies," especially of narcissistic and aggressive nature, in action (as defense)— leaving little to the processes of symbolization, but also to the lack of ideals throughout his life—our next point.

He had only two conscious, passing male ideals: the old neighbor who killed himself and the first brother-in-law who died at a crucial time in his life. The transference was for four years clearly an idealizing one which, I believe, made it possible for him to return to transpersonal ideals: to values—in this instance scientific truth, at least partial loyalty to wife and children, and much of the time a ruthless honesty towards himself and, within psychotherapy, vis-à-vis Dr. Gerson. Suddenly this transference, unanalyzable, "flip-flopped" to a demonizing negative one, while the therapist proved fallible. For most of his life drugs and adventure were a kind of "countervalue," something which gave meaning to an empty, boring life, an artificial excitement, a fleeting boost to self-esteem, which ordinarily (and persistently) only the intense pursuit of values would engender, a "countervalue" consciously mostly repudiated.

Archaic guilt, shame and superego split were, of course, central themes in his life. The amount of self-punishment, of expected catastrophe and retribution by fate was a single thread through life and therapy. The enormous sensitivity to imagined or real shame was evidenced by the one homicide and several near murderous events.

The split in the superego was preeminent—a very honest man of great integrity versus an impulsive man acting out perversion, murder and deception: "When despair takes over, the question of honesty becomes irrelevant, ridiculous to think about. If you're on the brink of survival, do you care about integrity? Often I felt when I was on drugs that I had only one week to live, because the drug supply would run out. Or I hoped the drug would be strong enough to kill me. Then it was ludicrous to think about honesty. This was not a matter of degree anymore, but a quantum jump, a totally different state of mind. Once I really stole a radio from a store after I had gotten 'beat' for the money and did not get the drug. I was so mad and sick. It would have been easy for me to kill the person, but, in contrast, it was very difficult to steal the radio; that was the most traumatic thing, much more than the killing of the Whelp. I walked out of the store with the radio under my arm, trembling. It was unbearable. I had to do something external to change the situation. If I got caught, fine; if not, I would have the money for the drug. Either way it would have eased the tension." In contrast to that one theft, he had no conscious guilt (at least for a long time) about his violence.

From the dynamic point of view we can be rather brief. The prevalence of most intense conflicts about narcissism and aggression was striking. But here we have an opportunity to look at the compromise character of some of his major symptoms.

His "homosexual-masochistic adventures" show compromise formation in object and aim. The object was a young, not particularly "masculine" boy of seventeen, degraded, transient, dangerous; it was a composite of the girl with the penis (the phallic mother), plus the anal sadistic father, plus the ideal self-image as a sadistic, strong boy in control, plus as a masochistic weak girl (again the split ideal). The aim was merger, unification, identification with this object, plus masochistic submission, plus sadistic and, above all, narcissistic control and power: "It is, after all, *my* play!"

Again he was very clear about the split within himself: he is at the same time the older man, but subjugated, and the "young kid as I was then," but triumphant—simultaneously omnipotent and helpless, tormentor and victim, play acting and brutally real, father and mother, guilty about the underlying belligerence, ashamed about the submission and loss of control, transgressing and expiating.

The use of narcotics was above all a regressive gratification in form of a directly observable increase in self-esteem. When the therapist saw him before his daily methadone dose, he felt low, as if depleted of self-worth and interest in the world; when seen afterwards, he showed a stable, healthy level of self-regard, a realistically optimistic outlook on the future, an ability to put past and present in perspective. It was not an elation or an unrealistic overoptimism.

The narcotics clearly functioned as a regulator of self-esteem. Of course, the sadomasochistic gratifications were another very important source of such regressive gratification. The drugs played into this, as we have seen. The drugs as objects and symbols were a compromise formation: they were the badge of glory of a select, esoteric, feared in-group and conspiracy, plus a playing with fire (the excitement cited before), plus a revenge on the norms of society (externalizing by transgression) and against family, especially father, plus a stigma of shame, dependency, being an outcast, enslaved, alone. The drugs in regard to their pharmacological effect represented a compromise formation, too: boosting of self-esteem, plus denial of the archaic affects mentioned (especially shame and rage), plus a sense of power via action and magical substance (the particular mode of externalization), plus concretization of shameful dependency and guiltful triumph, plus a masturbation substitute and protection against shame-laden sexual impotence, plus a feeling of being freed up, "unfrozen," in his object relations. Finally, the drug use was a form of symbolic jail sentence and expiation for the murder.

His acts of violence—which, significantly enough, preceded the taking of drugs (except for considerable drinking and marijuana use)—especially the murder, were above all a vindication of his masculinity, a protest against the shame of being not quite a man, of being homosexual, weak, castrated. It was also a concrete crime as instrument to bring about real expiation in jail for his enormous and still enduring unconscious guilt, which in turn stemmed from the murderous events around father, mother and "crushed boy." Thirdly it was a suicide, an aggression turned back again from the self; as he felt: he could just as well have killed himself. Fourth, it was a sadistic counterattack and murder against the sneering, laughing, humiliating father in a condign substitute figure. And thus fifthly it was a direct defense against unconscious homosexual feelings within the Oedipal triangle against these two "disgusting" figures—after all he had had group sex, together with his victim to be. And finally, since the murdered person had been a murderer himself, one might wonder whether this was not itself a triumph: to kill the killer, to exact vengeance (in what has been termed irrationalization), revenge supposedly in behalf of society, but really in behalf of all the crushed victims, on the crushing assassins: the truck driver, father.

It seems useful to point to Andreas's archaic (oral) object dependency. There was an enormous psychological dependency on the "right dose" of methadone. His dependency on his therapist was also noteworthy; when Dr. Gerson went through a crisis, Andreas picked up on it more than most other patients and reacted much as an infant does to its mother's depression: by increased sullenness, withdrawal, sense of doom, a diffuse rage, reckless (homosexual) actions, and, eventually, leaving in fury his therapy. Obviously this dependency was itself very ambivalent, destructive, hateful, though the rage usually remained self-directed.

A few remarks have to be added here in regard to the narcissistic crisis. It had several steps: One was the death of the only ideal of his adolescence, his brother-in-law, combined with the neglect and lack of trust and structure at home; the second was the discovery in college that he was not such an excellent student anymore, the third of course was his dropping out and aimless drifting, then the humiliation by his enemy ("the spitting in the eye"), culminating in homicide and the year in jail. Any new imagined or real humiliation (verbal or slap in the face) was felt to be a massive crisis to be soothed only by drugs, by massive action or by flight.

While I do not find topographical considerations superseded by structural ones, there is little added to this case by taking a topographical view; obviously, given the archaic nature of the defenses, much material was preconscious rather than unconscious— and thus relatively easily accessible in therapy. The economic and adaptational models add little to what is already obvious in this case.

Once again we have to turn to the boundary metaphor and examine whether it adds anything beyond what we have already discovered. The answer is only partially positive; it does not lift any new data into awareness, but it allows us to connect under a different perspective much of what we have found. Most superficially, Andreas was continually venturing out—with fascination prowling at night, with scientific curiosity at work and in psychotherapy—beyond what was known, customary, licit. The very act of transgressing a limit was gratifying, was a crucial part of the externalization mentioned (drugs, violence, and homosexuality are the prime examples already noted). His plans were to travel into unknown lands—he was fascinated by Conrad's novels. Much of his past life gained worth and reality only when he followed the lure of excitement which always consisted in the violation of a socially set limit and rule. Of course fantasy and reality flowed into each other as well: Nothing could happen to him, he felt invulnerable when he did the forbidden. He was sure he could take drugs without getting addicted, and until late in treatment there was no realization that his nightly escapades could possibly hurt anyone or anything (his career, his family, his reputation): "Saturday evening I would become someone else, could take drugs, get drunk, etc; I thought it was completely separate from the rest of my life and would not affect it. Now I cannot hide it from you nor from myself that this was not true." Thus we see in these escapades several boundary phenomena: one is the artificial border and discontinuity (again also a kind of splitting) between one episode and the rest of life. Thus he set one boundary, in order to allow himself the pleasure of violating all others: the guilt boundary in the relationship to his family, the shame boundary, if he looked at his more mature aspirations, the limitations imposed by law as well as by the knowledge of his own past (for instance, the dangers of drinking).

Far more deeply we encountered the problem of claustrophobia, the pervasive fear of any limitation as a form of confinement which was to be broken at all costs! All external structures and lines become death traps. This was probably the most regressive boundary conflict in this patient.

Basically it was, as we have seen, a projection, a condensation and displacement of rage and excitement in regressed forms—somewhat in a mode like this: "I cannot stand being confined within myself with these bursting, intolerable feelings and desires." It referred to the horror about desires to merge with, and to devour, mother (with reversal) and about the whole gamut of his preoedipal aggressions. Even more specifically, much of the material points to what Arlow (1972) described in only children (and Andreas was functionally an only child): the fantasy of having "destroyed potential rivals by devouring them when he was inside the mother's body." In the claustrophobic symptoms observed by Arlow in these cases the child fears "an encounter with these adversaries [the murdered siblings] in the claustrum and being devoured from within by the rivals whom he had devoured and incorporated." It seems to me likely that this unconscious fantasy would tie together his early bug phobia, the wrenching out of the little man in the radio, the "crushed boy," his pervasive unconscious guilt, need for punishment and chronic, "haunting" depression, and, above all, of course, the severe claustrophobia.

Another form of particularly striking boundary dilemma was, as in Razit (case 18), the one between the guilty expansion of power in success versus the shameful collapse of power in humiliation. Again in both instances he used the metaphor of "invisible lines": when the Whelp or Sleazy violated his shame boundary he had to kill. In turn if the other was afraid, because Andreas himself had asserted his power too blatantly, or not given due honor to the enemy, he feared he would be killed. These lines of narcissism, of power, were terrifyingly real and concrete in this man's life. Lastly it was always the shame boundary which, if crossed by a foe, absolutely had to be defended by bloodiest violence. But before this occurred, there was a crash of self-esteem, a stunning, paralyzing sense of humiliation which could only be repaired by revenge, fueled by boundless rage. The prototype was his wish—at age eight—to kill his laughing, sneering father.

I am sure many more examples for the boundary conflicts in this man's life could be uncovered. The crucial one was, however, the ultimate border: the stifling, horrifying claustrum, the archaic mother who tempts and devours. Again drugs in many ways did away with boundaries, limits, claustra, and yet always led to even more confining ones.

In turn the structure of therapy, drug program, sentence, study plans—all of them kinds of "good" boundaries, giving him both security and freedom, firmness and flexibility—struck that balance between wish and dread which allowed him to mature.

Still there were pertinent aspects in the psychotherapeutic situation which raised profound dread. As he averred, he had to avoid his shame and hence eye contact by exchanging the couch for the face to face position. He also fled from the feared independence and unprotectedness without the narcotic into increased dependence upon his therapist. However this raised a much more profound anxiety, his claustrophobia: to be "close," intimate, dependent meant again to be confined and swallowed up, and had to be fought off with paranoid rage. In that sense the "structure of therapy" had also very regressive and antitherapeutic effects. This raises a critical question in therapy: If the sitting arrangement and nonintensive frequency mobilize unbearable shame conflicts, while couch and intensification allow dangerous regression—what is one to do? Some answers will be attempted in the later chapter about psychotherapy.

This metapsychological examination, as incomplete as it has to remain because of the only fragmentary understanding, can, perhaps with some justification, be enlarged by another perspective, by yet another metaphorical system which I have expounded in detail elsewhere (1973b, 1975b, 1975c): the notion of the "tragic character." Not a few compulsive drug users and a small number of other patients who are not using drugs as their mode of externalization belong to this character type. I consider this concept of the "tragic character" not as a separate nosological category, but as a psychodynamically meaningful cluster of character traits and symptoms, repetitive in main conflicts, major defense forms, and symptomatic manifestations; it is a dynamically rather than phenomenologically coherent grouping. This concept is deeper and dynamically more telling than surface manifestations, as symptoms like drug addiction or self-destructiveness. They are characters with symptomatic expression which change over time, maybe into classical neuroses or overt psychoses or "sociopathies."

The Nature of the "Tragic Character"

In a number of patients I was struck by a peculiarly "tragic impression" both patients and surroundings, including therapist, gained during treatment and going far beyond what Schafer so excellently described as part of all psychoanalyses (1970). Andreas himself felt that way: "I am living a tragedy," or: "Why does everything tragic appeal to me? Why do I always have this haunting feeling?" Other patients who did not use drugs felt the same way: "It is as if fate undid everything I tried in my life. I was, am and still remain a failure, haunted by disaster, disfigurement, rejection. Why do I continue living?" (case 7).

In some patients (in analysis or psychotherapy) the treatment itself becomes part of this "tragic fate," an unmasking of the intolerable truth and, like in Oedipus Rex, leading to a catastrophic deterioration, a "negative therapeutic reaction" (see Dolorosa, case 7, or Cassandra; case 17). In a separate study I hope to present case histories of such "tragic characters" and the literary and philosophical implications of this new metaphorical system. I reemphasize that it in no way replaces the customary metapsychological conceptualizations. It adds to them.

Yet what is so striking about this group is that with minor changes the entire description which follows was originally written in regard to another patient, one in analysis (Dolorosa, case 7), superficially a rather different case; and yet the commonality of this type is so strong that nearly every word remains applicable to Andreas and to a strikingly large number of parallel cases (Alexa, Cassandra, Katharina, Razit, Black Rose).

THE SUPEREGO AND SEVERE TRAUMATA

From the severe depressive forms of the fate neurosis or the transference neurosis and the subsidiary paranoid transformations of the self-reproaches in many, including Andreas, the questions arise: Whence this archaic, severely aggressive superego? Whence this flood of shame and guilt? Whence the inconsistency, even split, of the superego?

Certainly, on the face of it, there is little our patients could identify with in their parents to serve as models for a more solid conscience and ideal formation. Certainly also the intensity of their own aggressions against the surroundings (in revenge, jealousy, envy, direct sadistic impulses) and their scoptophilic, anal and phallic demands are reflected in the archaically lacerating, flagellating, biting and overscrutinizing functions of their superego; but it seems we have something here which goes beyond these well-known processes. I refer to the possible role of the multiple traumata which these patients had suffered; and I see flowing from this a particular form of identification with the aggressor, an archaic form of turning passive into active, but directed at the same time against the self. These traumata include "seduction" and "betrayal" by both parents, especially the multiple primal scenes, and many instances of violence (in Andreas's case the "crushed boy," the forced fellatio and perhaps even the sense of disfigurement; in Cassandra's the horrible mistreatment, etc.).

Thus I wonder whether the demonic superego and its tragic implications may not be a direct precipitate of the violent traumata themselves, based on the enigmatic process of introjection. Sabotage and punishment are continually expected to come from the outside. They clearly are those patients described by Fenichel: "These patients are 'traumatophilic' persons whose characters have the structure of a traumatic neurosis and who strive all their lives to evade the repetition of a severely painful childhood impression but simultaneously seek to experience it again and again in order finally to be able to master it by continual repetition" (1941, p. 94).

How eventually all traumata are sought and repeated in the outside again is the hallmark of fate neurosis (H. Deutsch 1930). It is hurt, pain, mutilation, being shortchanged and cheated, humiliated, dumped upon, which the "outside" seems to inflict on our poor victim again and again. One patient said: "I am such a loser. I am puzzled: what is so unlikeable, so awful about me? Why do *I* always have to suffer? Why am I always the victim of fate? What have I done to deserve this? Why do I have always to destroy what good happens? Why is good never good enough?" (case 7).

It is with these last questions which summarize so much of the catastrophic disasters in the lives of these patients that I introduce a feeling which accompanied me through most of the therapy or analysis of them: a sense of tragic suffering, the reminiscences of so many of the tragedies. I felt I dealt with a "tragic patient" without being able to specify what I meant, beyond such generalities as my own sense of despair and the technical notion of the "negative therapeutic reaction." Clearly not enough.

WHAT IS A TRAGIC CHARACTER?

The attempts herein will be to unite two apparently separate patterns: one is our clinical experience, the other a supposedly esthetic phenomenon. The first is a reaction to those patients who generate this "tragic" sense in us, patients who were followed for years in psycho-analysis or in often interrupted analytically oriented psychotherapy, or who killed themselves. It is also a reaction to some persons in our private lives whom we recognize as characters with a tragic fate. The second is our reaction to tragedy in literature—tragic figures or tragic constellations, and the philosophical reflection by some of the greatest thinkers of the Western world.

What is so deeply "engraved" in Andreas and in similar patients that gives us the tragic feel? In brief it is the combination of specific constellations of the masochistic and narcissistic character with the use of five specific defenses. The first three of these criteria in their specific characteristics are indeed less frequently met with in compulsive drug users than the other four.

The specific nature of narcissism: hybris in the pursuit of a value. In our tragic characters, and I believe throughout the tragic literature as well, one value (such as honor, pride, divine law, revenge, honesty) becomes so exaggerated and eventually ("tragically") self-defeating because it is a narcissistic value, an idea with which one's self has become totally, absolutely, radically identified—at the exclusion of all the other consciously maintained values. In Andreas, the leading value (to which he had dedicated life and much of analysis) had a triple formulation:

Above all he exaggerated the value of being respected as a man, of not being seen as weak, a freak, a failure, as a homosexual—and thus the continuous protection against shame.

A second value, many of these patients, including Andreas, proclaim to the utmost: "I want to be right, accepted and admired as the suffering hero." In Andreas's case this can be further specified: "By my suffering, I have atoned for the *guilt* of my Oedipal revenge and of the 'crushed boy'; but I have also undone the shame of my humiliation in the forced fellatio, of being not a man, identified with mother, by playing the part of the admired hero." His insistence was on the value of the masochistic triumph. Even his homicide was "ratiocinated" away as a service to society (to rid it of "such a vermin, a murderer, an obnoxious individual") and as preparatory act for expiation of a much more profound guilt.

In the last analysis, this excessively sought and destroyed value is derivative of the split parent image (all good and all bad). It is experienced and sought with extreme ambivalence: as the highest, loftiest goal, and as a totally destructive actuality. As another patient noted in the transference: "I have the right to trust you absolutely. I demand that you never betray me as my mother betrayed me." No such claim on absolute trust is ever fulfillable. The trauma of rejection and abandonment is continually provoked by the very insistence on this absolute trustworthiness—never to say anything wrong or be angry, never to misunderstand, never to respond sarcastically to the arrogant claims of these patients. In Andreas's case it was less trustworthiness, and more the wish to be respected, admired and adored, the derivative of the entitlement, which underlay the formation of such a split value: inspiring and fatal.

The sudden change from arrogant value pursuit to disastrous paralysis and devastation—truly the *peripéteia* in Aristotle's terms — comes when this heroic, vindictive, but self-defeating pride ("I will prove to you that I am right") suddenly collapses, and the patient is nothing but the wounded, helpless, confused little child again. Then eventually he gathers himself again in the image of the wounded hero who is going to be proven right.

All the tragic value conflicts are not merely archaic, they are basically narcissistic conflicts, specifically a pathology of excess idealization.

It is always a matter of ruthless persistence in pursuit of an overvalued goal, a violation of all bounds in the service of this mono-ideistic pursuit. And this is in fine a narcissistic phenomenon. The fanatical one-sidedness, the irresistible total exaggeration of a value is what leads to hybris, the outrageous overstepping; and the hybris leads both to inner guilt and shame and to outer Nemesis (retribution, humiliation). I concur with Kaufmann (1968): hybris is not pride as the Christian tradition wants us to believe; it is an "anarchical defiance of the bounds," a "wanton disregard for the rights of others." It means insolence, an arrogant breaking of the laws of nature or state, a self-righteous breach of norms accompanied by self-justification. Now we may perhaps understand *hybris* as aggression in the service of an ideal.

Thus we are dealing with variations of excessive idealization, of this event which is so inspiring and yet so catastrophic because of the poison of its inevitable betrayal. I believe it is mainly this that Aristotle meant with the *hamartia,* the fatal flaw of the tragic hero—neither moral nor intellectual as the critics meant, but on a different plane, on that of the compulsive onesidedness of narcissistic overvaluation; the loss of perspective in the service of this narcissistic aim. It lies on the plane of inner forces: it is a dynamic "flaw," a psychological taint.

Thus lastly the conflict is not between values as Hegel and Scheler presumed, but between the very excessiveness, the narcissism of value pursuit, and the personalized outside world: Fate, the Divine Law, Justice (*Dike*)—or then as Nemesis: as Fate's vindictively experienced response, the Furies or Erinyes, the externalized guilt or shame (Dodds 1951) for having transgressed the taboos in the service of that particular value. This has brought us already to the punishment for hybris and with that to the second characteristic.

The specific nature of the masochistic character: suffering as a "totemistic" sacrifice. In the case of a suicidally depressed woman (Dolorosa, case 7), there was the central childhood "myth" in form of a screen memory of delusional quality: "I am going to be killed by my parents—this night. There is no doubt about it. And there is a strange sense of calmness in this conviction." We heard a somewhat similar early childhood myth from Andreas: "I thought that the parents had spying machines in the rooms when they were not there, to spy on me"—a reversal of his own observing. And instead of killing father or boy, he identified with the victims, the mother and the crushed boy.

Most evident, however, it is not in form of a myth, but of a fantasy: to be tied to a pole and tormented to "show bravery" in martyrdom. There he was the heroic sacrificed victim.

In a sense the patients live out in life and often in the transference neurosis just this masochistic passion play: to be the victim, the martyr.

It reminds us of the core of the historical tragedy: either the passion play of Dionysos or of a single epic hero (the origin is controversial). In Else's view it "is not what the hero does but what he suffers ... death, loss, humiliation .... the whole development of Greek tragedy, from the beginning to the end of its life span, was a flowering from this single root, the hero's pathos" (1967, p. 65; see also Jaeger 1933, Cameron 1968). Others (Nietzsche, G. Murray, J. Harrison, G. Thomson, A. Lesky) saw and still recognize the dismemberment of Dionysos as its origin. This controversy is of little importance for us. The heroic pathos is the focus of tragedy.

But we are also reminded by it of parallel situations of pathos: It recalls the tragic vocation of Abraham, the so-called *aqeda,* the

330 THE HIDDEN DIMENSION

binding for slaughter of his son Isaak, and touches upon the myth of the suffering, scorned and sacrificed "servant of God," a myth which in itself became such a central symbol for the tragic fate of the Jewish people since the time of the prophets; and finally it recalls the passion of Jesus of Nazareth, the central tragic myth of Christianity.

What all four paradigms have in common is the sacrifice of the hero-child. If we take Freud's concept of the totem tradition seriously, "original sin and redemption by the sacrifice of a victim," "the son, who had taken the atonement on himself" is basically "the atonement for the crime committed" against God the Father (1939, pp. 135, 136), against the original father of the primal horde who had been killed, dismembered, and eaten and whose powers and prerogatives had been taken over by the happy, but guilty band of brothers.

If we apply this totem metaphor (and it is a symbol, not an historical "reality") to our concept of the tragic character we find that both the tragic patient and the tragic hero atone in their suffering, in their passion play and catastrophe for the crime they wanted to inflict originally on their crucial parent or on both parents. In Andreas's case he appeared in his own myth and acts as the innocent victim, instead of himself taking bloody, envious, jealous revenge on his treacherous parents (especially his father), a myth eventually belied by his act of homicide: here the totem victim became once again the parricide. Dolorosa was in her dreams either the spirit of revenge as an Erinys, actually repeatedly in form of the archaic snake symbol, or (as in external life) the victim of bloody laceration.

In short: the tragic character repeats the totem ritual in a masochistic version—externally and internally, heroically and totally, fully in accord with the leading defenses I shall describe. He atones for his oedipal (and preoedipal, especially narcissistic) wishes in such a masochistically exaggerated form because in his own history the oedipal drama had been a bloody chain of traumata.

I would think that this masochistic, totemistic self-sacrifice in a heroic (narcissistic) shine or halo is the cardinal, most specific hallmark of the tragic character, and its repetition is his fate. This presupposes, however, a peculiar defense:

Defense by exaggeration of a value. We examined this process first from the wish fulfillment (narcissistic) side; now it is its defensive aspect which we briefly inquire into. I cannot easily derive this defense from any better known mechanism in the analytic literature unless it is, as I believe, a peculiar form of reaction-formation: the heroic but self-defeating fight for a value. Often there is something brave and courageous about the insistence on some value which the patient exaggerates and fights for at every cost, at much personal suffering. An example: In many cases and despite (or probably precisely because of) their deep denials and sudden episodes of compulsive lying about which they feel profoundly ashamed (but do not correct) they emphasize a high standard of intellectual honesty.

We have already studied another central value some patients of this group pursue in this excessive fashion: the insistence on *human dignity* and *trustworthiness*—obviously not only sharpened by their own traumatic deprivations but by their deep wishes to demolish every value, to destroy every rival, to destroy every authority. The central value for which Andreas fought with fury and emphatic protest was his masculinity, protesting too much!

I would call all this the defense by heroism—a pursuit of a value to its extreme, to its excess, where the value itself and his defender become destructive and destroyed; another phrasing of the same is defense by exaggeration of a value. As already mentioned: what has been described up to now is not quite standard fare among compulsive drug users. "Tragic patients" share what follows with all toxicomanics.

Externalization by violation of sanctioned boundaries. There is an exaggerated concern for certain external, especially social boundaries, which then is supposed to justify the breaking of other boundaries which—for the rest of society—appear equally important. A consistent feature of Andreas was an insistence on being treated with respect, as a hero and superman, as a unique, special human being—and the rage inwardly as well as often outwardly if he felt "put down" in that assumed privilege, the paranoid wrangles he got into, and the "unforgivable sins" he saw others commit against him. He was so concerned about defending his narcissistic specialness that he fought back with a ruthless, murderous rage, disregarding the other's own sensitivities to a much larger extent than had been inflicted upon him.

I obviously refer to a different mode of externalization than that of finding inner solution in an external magical thing. It is the mode of transgression, as case 16, Shakran, so stressed. Just to violate barriers has not only a crucial instinctual valence as aggression and narcissistic overstepping, but it is a very important defense by action against inner conflict of whatever nature.

In Greek tragedy the tragic character is "the man who acts and declares himself in his own actions .... for such men, the world is inevitably tragic. For the heightened capacity for action does not enable the hero to escape tragedy, only to go further and further into it" (Cameron 1968, p. 144).

Totalization. This was already extensively described as part of the typical "heptad." I referred already there ahead to its traditional expression in form of "passio" or "páthos" and equated it with the affect-regression during the narcissistic crisis.

One of the most telling expressions of this "páthos" is Othello's "Fore my particular grief / Is of so floodgate and o'erbearing nature / That it engluts and swallows other sorrows, / And it is still itself." (Act I, Sc. iii, ll. 55-59)

In all our "tragic patients," as well as in all compulsive drug users, we encounter this type of pathos.

To be overwhelmed by affects like yearning and blind love, towering rage and abysmal shame, devastating loneliness and inner deadness, horrifying guilt and terror, is painful suffering to the extreme, and is terror in its own right. We know about the "traumatic experience" when the ego is overwhelmed by an unmanageable affect. I think this is directly a source of suffering, one we see clinically. Passion is indeed suffering; extreme passion is extreme pain, is traumatic pain and terror.

But suffering is also the result of these passions, of these affects which break through all order and measure. We remind ourselves of the towering rages of Oedipus and of Creon (in *Antigone*), of Lear and Kleist's Penthesilea. We think of the devouring greed and ambition of the Macbeths, of the lechery of *Troilus and Cressida*, where "appetite, a universal wolf ... must take perforce a universal prey and last eat up himself ..." (1.3, 121-124), or the Duke of Albany's comment about the brutal greed and pride of Lear's daughters: "Humanity must perforce prey on itself / Like monsters of the deep" (Act IV, Sc. ii, ll. 49-50). The same appears in the ruthless use of creativity in Ibsen's *When We Dead Awaken* and *Master Builder*, in the "murder of love for profit" and "soul murder" in his John Gabriel Borkman. All these rapacious affects cause suffering and death. They dictate the lives against the ego's better knowledge; they overwhelm rational decision and attempts at moderation. It is precisely the rapaciousness, the devouring global nature of these passions which cause suffering and disaster in these characters. It is this "passionate ignorance" and blindness—*Ate* throughout the Greek tradition (see Cameron 1968, p. 140, Dodds 1968, passim) which is crucial to all tragedy: "*ate* is a state of mind—a temporary clouding or bewildering of the normal consciousness" (Dodds 1951, p. 5).

It is typical for both the tragic character and the compulsive drug user that he is overwhelmed by such vehement affects, especially rage, love, terror, and greed. Disaster is an inevitable consequence of his unmanageable passion, since, as we already noted, it is an almost indispensable aspect of his suffering that it cannot remain internal. The propensity to provoke an external catastrophe is part of the tragic experience and of the fate of the tragic character.

Provocation of punishment. This is really a combination of externalization and of turning passive into active: the active provocation of punishment and rejection, the invitation of defeat, the turning of traumatically suffered insult, mutilation, humiliation and rejection into an active provoking of attacks on these patients in various, specifically meaningful forms. This provocation of rejection always ends up in the plaint: "Woe is me! I am the victim of cruel Fate. Why me?" It is eventually always their personal tragic fate which, no matter how hard they try and how well-meaning they are, catches up with them and leaves them as the defeated losers. Lastly, it becomes always an active pursuit of defeat, the search for a masochistic triumph, the quest for Nemesis.

Disjunction. Nothing has to be added here to what has already been studied in much detail in chapter 7.

To sum up then the tragic character: it is a combination of the narcissistic with the masochistic character and five indispensable forms of defenses:

1. The defense by *heroism,* the self-defeating fight for a value
2. *externalization* by violation of sanctioned boundaries
3. affect regression: the radicalization, generalization, *totalization* of affect

4. the *active provocation* of punishment, rejection and defeat
5. the defense by *disjunction*, dismemberment and fragmentation of
   meaning

These then are the seven criteria for the tragic character which all are necessary, constitutive elements. Historically all cases show massive traumatization in their childhood.

I end my thoughts by reemphasizing how the tragic character has a particular importance for nature and severity of the transference neurosis, because the latter is thus set up and so adamantly, pointedly sharpened toward defeat and catastrophe. The tragic character provokes a tragic form of countertransference: anger and despair in the analyst and thus indeed transgressions of boundaries on his side. Patients try to enlist the therapist as the secret ally of their punishment; they indeed can be invincible in forcing therapists and all of society to become their Nemesis. Obviously the specifications of the "tragic character" go far beyond those applicable to most toxicomanics, and at least one hallmark of the latter (the split in the superego) is not a sine qua non for the "tragic character." They are overlapping groupings.

THE ANTI-TRAGIC DEFENSES

All of what I have described up to now also entails defensive aspects against yet deeper layers—lastly against the "mortal wound," the core of traumatic injury to narcissism and trust. However, here I can only mention briefly that there is often a blanket spread over the entire problem of underlying tragic experience: cover symptoms, screen attitudes and character traits, pseudo-solutions with which these patients enter analysis or therapy or which the heroes start out with on stage. There are several forms of such antitragic defenses. They are all masks, forms of self-deception: "life lie," drug use, massive denial, mysticism, conformism, etc.

The Concept of "Sociopathy"

There are two crucial theoretical questions as well which are posed by this and by all other cases I had a chance to study more in-depth, and which certainly appear confirmed by the superficial clinical contacts with the several hundred compulsive drug users I have seen in these twelve years. These two theoretical aspects go far beyond the bland assertion: how severe the psychopathology in most, if not all, compulsive drug users really is. The first more specific point is the debunking of the concept of the sociopath or psychopath as a useful diagnostic category and its replacement by a more sophisticated understanding; the second is the nature of real massive traumatization in early childhood and often throughout their whole growing up which brought about a particular cluster of severe character pathology which is only now slowly being recognized in its overriding theoretical and practical importance.

I share the great uneasiness about the general categories of "sociopath," "psychopath," etc., which was expressed, I believe, originally by Phyllis Greenacre in her excellent article "Conscience in the Psychopath" (1945), repeated by B. Karpman in "The Myth of the Psychopathic Personality" (1947), and referred to by Elaine G. Karp (see Appendix A). To summarize my own findings, which correspond to those of Greenacre in particular: the so-called psychopathic character which most compulsive drug users evince is not that of a person without guilt or shame, but, as noted in detail for our group of compulsive drug users and now extended to all "sociopaths," of one with a particularly archaic form of massive guilt and shame anxieties, expected and provoked retribution and humiliation from the outside.

They are not persons without conscience, but persons with a conscience which is profoundly fragmented, externalized, particularly massive and archaic, more shame-than guilt-oriented, and projected into those whose violent retribution is constantly challenged and successfully brought about by the symptomatic actions of these patients. Only one of these symptomatic action sequences is the compulsive drug use and all the criminality preceding, accompanying and following this particular symptom. This archaic conscience is paired with an enormous amount of unbound, undirected anxiety, triggered to disastrous extent by minor frustration, and leading to equally primitive unbound, undirected forms of rage. As stated earlier, it would probably be much better to see in these patients—instead of the condemnatory tag of "psychopath" or "sociopath"—their truly severe pathetic pathologies.

The pathology of all so-called "sociopaths" can now be formulated in these terms:

They suffer from archaic narcissistic conflicts, conflicts about grandeur and abysmal disappointment in themselves and in others, again mainly in the realm of magical omnipotence.

They show concomitant severe structural defects: in reality testing, threshold of frustration and tolerance of it, cohesion of self and stability of defenses (Kohut 1959, 1971, 1976).

"Sociopaths" in general show particularly intense conflicts about outward aggression and masochism which are, often quite successfully, muted and covered up by their self-treatment with various licit and illicit drugs.

They all use denial and splitting and particularly externalization as preferred ways of coping with their usually overwhelming, prevalently narcissistically tinged affects. Whereas the compulsive drug user prefers that mode of externalization employing a magical substance, in other "sociopaths" it is power over people by speech and manipulation, or violence, sexual exploitation, the greedy acquisition of money (a kind of money addiction) or of prestige. As all these defenses, these various modes of externalization are utterly compulsive, unconscious, and disregard the needs of other people in their own rights and their own conflict solutions. By extension of the term all "sociopaths" could thus be viewed as kinds of addicts (money addicts, power addicts, sex addicts, violence addicts).

Very often it is assumed that such "naked" living out of narcissistic, sexual and destructive demands represents direct drive gratifications. The concepts just advanced and observations presented (especially those with Shakran and Andreas) allow quite a different conclusion, one stressed by Fenichel throughout (e.g., 1941): a consistent application of multiple layering, e.g., "threefold stratification" (instinct–defense–superficial instinctual attitude) is usually the correct one. Quite typically we encounter many forms of aggression as defenses against narcissistic conflicts; these (more specifically exorbitant narcissistic claims) clearly defend against deeper nonnarcissistic problems, as expressed in derivatives of the phobic core symptoms, that in turn cover conflicts about libido and aggression of disintegrating (traumatic) strength in dealing with realistically traumatizing situations. It is on that level that the confining structures which are to be broken represent a "bottling up" of drives; their violation figures as a primitive tension release, a bursting out. It seems equally fair to assume, in parallel fashion, depressive core symptoms in many, if not all such persons.

All show the split in the superego, the archaic, external nature of guilt and shame, and an array of defenses directed against the superego functions, not the id (Rangell 1974).

Concomitant with the debunking of the notion of the sociopath as a meaningful clinical concept in favor of a more precise diagnosis of character pathology goes the recognition of the severity of massive traumatization which at least many of these patients have gone through from early childhood on into early adolescence—all throughout their formative years. I have often felt overwhelmed by the severity of verified traumata these patients had suffered as little children. The symptomatic outcome from this massive traumatization may vary, particularly depending on the timing, intensity, and form it takes.

The practical consequences of these new insights, which are being developed by psychoanalytic pioneers of today (Greenacre, Kohut, Kernberg, Rangell, Beres), are difficult to predict except that the whole attitude in working with these patients radically changes if we move away from a moralizing, "reality oriented" preaching ("counseling") to a deeper understanding of this particularly taxing, provocative pathology which calls for a congeries of measures very different from the ones in neurotics or psychotics: e.g., strict limit setting, the importance of external structures and dependencies which, as Kohut correctly emphasizes, is not simply a catering to archaic dependency needs but a much needed "crutch" form of rehabilitation, a substitution of external structures for lacking internal ones–a lack which, in most cases, no psychotherapy will ever be able to fully repair.

A Practical Note

This brings us back to Andreas, who by all standards would have been adjudged, condemned and discarded either as a hopeless sociopath or an equally hopeless borderline, if not psychotic "acting-outer." The experiences with him show what grave injustice and inhumaneness lie in such labels. One may object: From a cost efficiency point of view it appears absurd to spend hundreds and hundreds of hours of a psychoanalyst's time on such a case. Or, as kind listeners to his history have asked: "But how many have the money?" Well, he had no money and his treatment was part of that program. But based on cost efficiency, would it not be far more expensive to society (to the "taxpayer") if patients like that go either untreated or insufficiently treated, wreak mayhem and death, or depredate society in other ways, than if they turn into real and potentially even great assets to the community? Many are less intelligent and gifted than Andreas, but still, when and if adequately treated, the relatively small costs, spent over a few years of intensive effort and perhaps many years of continued inexpensive supportive treatment, are vastly outweighed by the social gains (gainful employment, taxable income, avoidance of crimes, of court and jail-costs, welfare supports for families, etc.).

Here we only have to sum up what was innovative about the treatment of this very difficult, but also particularly promising patient whose complex basic diagnosis (instead of "sociopathy" or even "borderline") is that of a severe character disorder of combined narcissistic, masochistic, and paranoid nature. His self-treatment with narcotics or alcohol, his violence, his homosexual activities were merely symptoms. That the discrete EEG abnormalities add to the diagnosis is likely. What was crucial and innovative about the treatment of him (and other comparable cases) was the combination of a number of therapeutic measures: (1) intensive psychoanalytically oriented psychotherapy, with innovative measures in itself in order to stimulate his introspection (autobiographical write-ups, and other very active interventions) leading to gradual transition to the couch position, free associations, and more frequent sessions; (2) temporary methadone maintenance; (3) vocational retraining to the level appropriate to his intelligence; (4) counseling by a sensitive counselor, including court appearances: (5) work with his wife in times of crisis (in the early phases of therapy); and (6) antidepression medication gradually substituting for the narcotic.

What this paradigm should demonstrate is that we take our observations seriously: if indeed compulsive drug use is a coping mechanism, especially vis-à-vis rage and shame, then we can hope to wean a patient from it only if we help him most intensively in bringing his life in order, in resolving some of the underlying narcissistic and aggressive conflicts, if we attain in short an entire restructuring of his current life. Thus besides insight and emotional supports it involved a panoply of external structures and assistance and a continuous alertness about, and understanding of, the boundary problems outlined throughout. But more about this in chapter 16 and Appendix E.

The next two chapters deepen our comprehension of the predisposition. First we briefly examine some interactions between one group of drugs, the psychedelics, and the underlying personality; then we turn to a particular segment of the predisposition already outlined in broad strokes in chapter 8, but one that hitherto has been strikingly and massively neglected: the family. There is no contradiction nor competition between the crying need to study (and treat) the individual's psychopathology with the help of psychoanalytic knowledge and the equally crying need to develop different theoretical models and practical methods to study (and treat) the underlying, causally determining family problems.

Chapter 10

"FLEURS DU MAL":

EFFECTS OF PSYCHEDELICS

AND PSYCHODYNAMICS

Both De Quincey and Baudelaire sought in opium and hashish an escape from "melancholia," disgust with self and world, boredom and emptiness. De Quincey wrote about his *Confessions*: "The object of that work was to reveal something of the grandeur which belongs potentially to human dreams" (1845). In the same vein, Baudelaire entitled an essay in 1858, "About the artificial ideal: hashish," and identified himself with De Quincey in the motivation for his opium and hashish use: "L'horreur de la vie se mêlait déjà, dans ma première jeunesse, avec la douceur céleste de la vie." ("Already in my first youth the horror of life was mixed with the heavenly sweetness of life.") But in his collection of poems "Fleurs du Mal" (*Flowers of Evil*), he describes how he finds at the end of his inner, drug illuminated voyage only the "bitter knowledge": "une oasis d'horreur dans un désert d'ennui"—"an oasis of horror in a desert of ennui."

A survey of the drug effects causing (or imputed to cause) psychopathology is outside the scope of this book. There is by now an abundance of valuable literature (in regard to amphetamines see, e.g., Ellinwood 1971; to narcotics, Harms 1973a; to psychedelics in general, Tucher et. al. 1972, Keniston 1969, Culver and King 1974; in regard to cannabis especially Sassenrath 1975, S. Cohen 1975, and Hollister 1971).

Here a psychoanalytic evaluation of but two observations is included; the trigger function of a drug for serious psychopathology, and a self-experiment, both with some theoretical implications.

"Marijuana Psychosis"

There is no need here to rehash the literature about this hoary hobgoblin. Of interest, however, may be a series of observations tying dynamically the psychedelic experience with near or fully psychotic sequels. A number of such cases were observed by myself and Dr. Leon Levin (see our report, 1969); here only a brief account will be given, using mainly one concrete example.

What has struck me above all is that the *one time or sporadic* use of a drug, in this case, marijuana alone, can trigger in some susceptible individuals a chronic state of extreme self-consciousness, suspiciousness, a sense of loss of identity and finally a severe fright and depression. As stated earlier: a number of narcotic addicts were deadly afraid of psychedelics, including cannabis. What is equally interesting is that often such a serious state can be surprisingly quickly resolved in brief intensive psychotherapy. Before we consider how we may understand this paranoid depressive development, let us turn to a case.

CASE 20: SINCLAIR

All our previous notions about the essential harmlessness of marijuana were shaken when we evaluated in 1968 in a local clinic our first patient, a nineteen-year-old, very intelligent college student who, after a single experience with marijuana five months before, had become increasingly depersonalized and bewildered, unable to work in school or to concentrate on his homework and more and more seriously contemplating suicide. The *way* he expressed himself sounded even more ominous: "The main problem is that I perceive reality as if it never happened. Every word the teacher says—it's gone. I feel completely separated from reality. This fear—this separation from reality—drives me insane. I am afraid I am losing my mind. Sometimes

I am on the verge of killing myself ... When I took the drug, I fell into myself. When I say something I ask myself: Did I really say it? Who am I? Where am I going? Then I feel people can look into my self through my eyes. Or it's like light pouring into my mind, like through open windows. At night I have the sudden fear: What is in my mind? Why am I thinking? Before that, life was full and happy—now I feel separated, it is as if a black veil had been drawn over me."

Despite these severe symptoms and some statements, which reminded us of paranoid schizophrenia, the affectivity was warm and the train of thoughts coherent. It was clearly a typical, though severe state of acute depersonalization, accompanied by deepening depression.

A few relevant data from his life history: He was the third of four children; the other siblings were girls. His relationship with his parents was good, although both parents appeared to be rather strict.

A decisive event must be mentioned here: when he was one and a half months old, he was accidentally poisoned by an aunt who gave him a bleaching neutralizer instead of water. He barely survived the intoxication and had to be hospitalized a number of times through his childhood because of the ensuing nephrosis. He was, at the time of evaluation, somewhat hypertensive and under continuous medical surveillance, but not further handicapped.

After this evaluation session I saw him only in five sessions (one hour each) of intensive psychotherapy; the shortness of this therapy was not anticipated and actually quite surprising to me.

In the first stage of this focal therapy I started out with his core complaint: the separation from reality. He described how he had many times refused to smoke marijuana when invited by his friends. When he finally took it with several friends, he was scared to death. "After about a dozen drags—suddenly it echoed in me, I had a floating sensation and could not keep my thoughts. I felt extreme terror. I thought: suppose it does not go away? I had to keep talking to keep in contact with reality."

In the following days, he went around in a daze, convinced he had destroyed his mind, and felt completely separated from the outside world. This sense of not feeling a part of reality persisted henceforth. He doubted his perceptions. Whatever he saw, as soon as the visual image was gone, he asked himself if it had really happened. The sense of "separation" increased very much when he was away from home. I questioned this superficial layer consisting of his fear of losing his mind and of his sense of separation: "Is it really your mind you fear to lose? Do you have an idea what you may lose instead?"

His immediate answer was: "Perhaps love." He described how he feared and really experienced losing the approval of his mother after he confessed his adventure to her; in effect his using the drug was such a breach with his role of being a "good boy," such an attack upon his parents that guilt and self-punishment immediately set in. His mother told some relatives about it. "It hit me like a thunderbolt. I was so ashamed. When I got praise thereafter, I felt I did not deserve it. I could not study, my grades deteriorated, but I felt less guilty if I was not praised." It became clear that on this second layer the intake of marijuana was experienced both as an act of shame for having given in, and as an act of guilt for having committed something forbidden. It had to lead to rejection, to loss of acceptance by mother and society.

In the second hour he elaborated this theme: He had felt separated from mother and society before. As a child he often suffered separations when he had to be hospitalized. Now, with the marijuana, he had done it actively, instead of suffering it passively. But this was more specific than separation; it was a sense of rejection and exposure. This led to a new layer of feelings, his shame about a number of homosexual experiences. He felt separated from society because of it. "I felt I'd never grow up; my life is done. I felt this separation all along. Now I know it's not the drug, it's my shame and guilt for a lot of things, and I wanted to destroy myself because of this shame." Obviously his fear that marijuana had destroyed his brain reflected the dread that homosexuality (and, inferentially, masturbation) had destroyed his life as a man.

In the third session he returned to the change in perception and state: "I feel like the eyes are a mirror; all light comes in. How can I think? When my eyes are open and I look out, I wonder: how can I think if my thoughts come out? Thinking is dark, but then when all the light comes in it is as if people could see it."

I interpreted: "You want some thoughts to be concealed, and you are afraid; you are ashamed they would be exposed to others." He immediately returned to the experience with marijuana and his homosexual fantasies and memories but added: "I always felt like saying: I did it." "So you want to show it off?" He denied this but instead went into a description of his homosexual masturbation fantasies. Although he was quite attracted by some girls, he lost his erection when he thought of a girl in his fantasies.

Again more specifically: His fantasy stopped automatically when he thought of the girl undressing herself. He realized that it was a fright which blocked his fantasy at this point. In order to get more clarity about this, I suggested that he avoid his usual masturbation fantasies about boys, trying to think of girls instead and then to see what came to his mind. The topic disappeared for the moment. Instead, he started again at the surface, mentioning that in class he had had again a sense of unreality. When he had to say something he started doubting: "Did I really say it?" He himself was able to translate this feeling: "I felt detached from myself and society, because I felt ashamed for what I've done." The detachment was to assure him: "You have not exposed yourself at all—don't worry, don't feel ashamed—you have not said anything, nobody has seen you." I asked why he felt so frightened of exposing himself, of showing himself off. He related it to his severe acne during the previous few years, and how he was excluded as a sissy from some groups at school. He added he never exposed his body at home, and felt, especially in front of his father, ashamed when undressed. "I don't want him to look at me." Strangely enough (but fitting to his homosexual orientation) he felt no such compunction vis-à-vis his mother.

Why was he so afraid to expose himself? And why after all did he have to tell everybody about the event with marijuana? Why did he feel compelled to show people that he had committed this trespass? The answer, of course, was that he had strong and peculiarly conflicted exhibitionistic urges. This we explored more in the fourth hour. He stated that he felt very exposed in our therapy—just as if he were again under the effect of the drug.

But he also remembered how his chronic illness as a child made him very special and earned him a lot of attention. He noticed that he exploited his sufferance by bragging about it as a child. While discussing these exhibitionistic wishes suddenly a picture emerged: "I don't know, was it a dream or real. I was about six or seven. I went downstairs at night. I heard my father come out of his room. He was partly undressed. I did not understand what was going on, but I was very afraid he would see me. I stood against the wall until he went back in his room. I was more afraid of him seeing me (than of anything else). In the morning, I think I went in and I saw both of them partly undressed in their room; I was afraid they'd see me in there. I sneaked out very quietly." What was he afraid of? "That they would punish me for intruding in their privacy, that they would beat me up—although I know they would not have done it. But I was afraid of what they were doing—it was something dirty. I was confused and upset. When I recently heard in a health course about sex, I thought: My parents would not do that."

What he was ashamed of on this level was not so much his own exposure but the exposure of his parents in "doing something dirty," and his own active looking, perhaps spying. Of course we don't know whether this memory of the primal scene was rooted in a real occurrence or in a fantasy, or, most likely, in a combination of both in form of a telescoped screen memory; but what is certain is the central role, which looking, exposure and shame played in that memory, as in all the other layers. The threat involved in seeing the parental intercourse had not been spelled out—except in the fantasy of being beaten up, a derivative of castration anxiety and of feminine-masochistic identification. These truly unconscious conflicts were left untouched. Nor was the inference interpreted that his eyes, his ears and his mind also had to be punished for these infantile wishes, as reflected in his frightening feeling of unreality; the feeling as if it had not happened, as if he had not heard or seen, and as if his mind were destroyed.

But he did not get off so easily. The fear of exposure while singing or talking in class recurred and he went back to his observation of his father: "I had extreme fear of him seeing me: it was more powerful than if he had beaten me. I was so embarrassed for him. Now I remember, I was playing with boys already then—we were together, masturbating in our basement. I was ashamed of it, afraid that I might be caught."

After this very condensed review of his partly preconscious, partly really repressed conflicts about looking and being looked at, what they meant for his sense of identity and how the feelings of shame and guilt warded off these conflicts, we returned to the surface.

He concluded his therapy stating that he was again able to think with his eyes open, that he felt sure no one could look into his thoughts and he had not to fear exposure. "Vision is vision and has nothing to do with thinking." The derealization, the experience as if an event had not happened, had also disappeared after he recognized that it was he who wanted it not to have happened, especially that he had not exposed himself, and that in this symptom he had experienced his conflict about exhibition and shame. It helped because it was mainly he himself who had discovered all these connections. He was again able to concentrate and to study and also to expose himself without fear in school. A follow-up contact with him, eight months later, revealed that he had remained free of symptoms and advanced in his studies.

In summary: The experience with marijuana activated his conflicts centering around the wishes of being exposed and of looking, and around the punishment of being shamed, rejected and separated, and this to such a degree that a near psychotic state ensued. All his fears of passivity, femininity and homosexuality were accentuated on a perceptual level by the experience of "being opened up" by cannabis to the intruding looks of others, quite in line with Waelder's interpretation of paranoid states (Waelder 1951, Schafer 1968b).

The review of this central conflict—tracing it back from the marijuana adventure to his homosexual experiments, to his effeminacy and his acne, to the showing off of his suffering, to the primal scene and infantile masturbation—cleared up the symptomatology.

The technique employed in this very brief, but psychoanalytically focused therapy was mainly clarification of his feelings (Bibring 1954), of the connections of his experiences, supplemented by some suggestion and manipulation, and leading up to just one interpretation of a really unconscious aspect—namely that of his repressed exhibitionistic and scoptophilic wishes and their connection with the persistent, now crushing, shame anxiety and self-consciousness. It is this interpretation which is of further theoretical interest; we will return to it shortly.

This and similar cases show the mutual relationship between drug effect and psychopathology, the complex nature of this correlation, and the insufficiency of any unilinear cause-and-effect nexus. More specifically they illustrate how one pharmacogenic impact of any kind can trigger unpredictable psychodynamic (especially psychopathological) reverberations. It is in this context that Zinberg (1974) developed his trinitarian hypothesis of drug-set-setting. It is clear that he would stress in these cases the pathogenic impact of the setting, whereas I feel the personality at that moment and in its historical context ("set") has to be explored.

In particular, quite a few narcotics addicts expressed to me a deep fear of psychedelics, including the now so common street pot (a weak variety indeed!). Their being put together, their coping above all with paranoid fears of shame, is so tenuous that any drug deepening that type of regression is dreaded (e.g., Black Rose, case 2, the Prince, case 10, and Andreas).

For a more precise formulation in this case vignette we have to return to the concept of the several layers of etiology, as already used in chapter 5. The precondition can be found in the severe traumatization in childhood, particularly the poisoning and the frequent separations in childhood; the specific cause for the pathology is to be sought in the accumulation of exhibitionistic and voyeuristic experiences and conflicts, the problems around passive-feminine identification, his latent and manifest problems with homosexuality and the ensuing conscious feelings of guilt and shame. The concurrent cause can be sought in his family and their reaction and tradition, which was in conflict with the direct social ambiance, the peer group.

The marijuana experiment was nothing but the releasing event, a catalyst due to which all the elements of the other causes suddenly crystalized out in the lead symptoms of depersonalization, paranoid fears and depression.

Why and how this experience can function as such a trigger experience should now be studied.

No doubt, what S. Cohen and K. S. Ditman wrote about the LSD experience can be applied to the psychedelic experience with marijuana as well: "A single, or a series of, LSD treatments can produce a psychotic break presumably by releasing overwhelming conflictual material which cannot be handled by the patient's established defenses. It is possible that LSD disrupts psychic homeostatic mechanisms and permits reinforcement of latent delusional or paranoid ideas."(1963).

Our observations allow us now to become more specific about these dynamic implications of the psychedelic experience.

All these phenomena of psychodynamic relevance can be described as regression, and lifting of the various curtains of denial, repression and isolation, a process of a usually sudden, massive, often traumatic nature, while the process of splitting and fragmentation—of thinking, of object- and self-representation—increases massively. Let us now examine this piercing of the other defenses more in detail.

In the four cases of acute psychosis precipitated by a traumatic experience with marijuana observed by my coworker Leon Levin and myself (1969) the specific trauma appears to have been the sense of having been laid open and exposed to attack or derision (see Boroffka 1966). It was as if these patients had experienced a chemical rape. We have some evidence that this indeed may be one of the main psychological dangers of the use of psychedelic drugs. The psychedelic experience acts as a traumatic event eliminating the inner barrier against stimuli (Reizschutz); it allows the ego being overwhelmed with previously repressed infantile conflicts.

What is the impact upon *superego* functions? Since the psychedelic experience is not condoned by society and laden with legal sanctions, it evokes by itself strong feelings of guilt and shame. These conscious feelings are strongly reinforced by the regression.

In our investigation the response of shame with all its sequelae is much more typical as a reaction to the psychedelic experience than the guilt reaction. Why this is so becomes clear when we turn to the following aspects.

Several *ego* functions are changed regressively in a very specific way. First, the autonomous functions of thinking, seeing and hearing are flooded with instinctual qualities; they are not in the service of the ego anymore, but, as we will see in a moment, of the id. Second, the boundaries between inside and outside are dissolved. It is this which probably gives the sensation of the "chemical rape." The dissolution of these boundaries evokes profound fears of losing one's identity, especially of being exposed, intruded upon and overwhelmed, bare in the inmost thoughts to all eyes. One's own thoughts and perceptions, as well as those of the others, assume a magical, omnipotent, enormously destructive or merging quality.

Third, the synthetical function of the ego is affected probably most. The cohesion of thinking, perceiving and doing vanishes, and with that the sense of self-control disappears. Instead there is a vast tumble and jumble of fleeting thoughts, feelings and images. The coherence of the person, the continuity of time, and the unity of space start crumbling. This dissolution of inner structure can be, as we know from the psychotherapy with schizophrenics and "borderline" patients, one of the most frightening experiences known. It is equated with death, in its most primitive and frightening onslaught (see Frosch 1967). But it also can be a most gratifying, sought after experience—therefore the increasing and eventually compulsive use (see Wieder and Kaplan 1969).

From a theoretical point of view this third aspect may be the most promising and fascinating, although still profoundly puzzling. For one, it allows us to study a large range of phenomena of multiple meanings and functions on the one continuum of dissociation, a continuum of processes reaching, as we saw, from those which are highly differentiated and consciously employed to the most undifferentiated, regressed, predominantly unconsciously determined ones. Where on this particular continuum the reaction of the patient lies depends upon dosage, entire personality organization, and momentary mood and circumstance. What is particularly interesting, however, is that this continuum observably takes on its significance as a spectrum of defenses, of instinctual gratification, of cognition, and of motor activity.

Clinically it is more puzzling: why is this massive splitting, the dissolution of inner structures (as well as the dissolution of self-boundaries) sometimes most terrifying, sometimes most desirable—differing from person to person, even from time to time in the same individual? Certainly the external setting has some bearing, but not really all that much when we deal with the questions of preference or avoidance, of sudden breakdown or supreme bliss. This question is valid both for compulsive drug users (see cases 10 and 19) and those who commonly shun drugs (e.g., Sinclair, case 20).

The answer to this puzzle, derived from my observations, is still very tentative. I see the reaction determined at least by two sets of variables: The first is the severity, intensity, and even the nature of the conflicts dealt with precariously by any defense and mobilized by the psychedelic regression. But this is still rather unspecific, because I do not think the basic problems of narcissism, union, aggression and especially of exposure and shame were all that different between, e.g., the Bohemian and Andreas or the Prince.

But the preferred defenses show a difference; therefore, I presume they are the second set of variables.

Put very simply: Andreas or the Prince already had enough trouble with splitting and projections without psychedelics, whereas the Bohemian was extremely disturbed about his inhibitions, and the denial and repression of his feelings. Although he, too, used isolation, undoing and reaction-formation, the results of these latter mechanisms seemed to please, not to bother him.

Based on these observations I suggest the following solution to our quandary: If the prevalent defenses are already regressed forms of dissociation and boundary breaking (the latter especially by projection and introjection) and therefore helping already only most imperfectly against the underlying fears, any additional defense regression along the continua of dissociation and boundary dissolution would have to become extremely terrifying.

In the contrasting group, those who prefer psychedelics, we can observe how the major defenses are ranged on the avoidance continuum: massive denial and repression, to an extent that they give a deep sense of inauthenticity. Parallel we find of course disjunction and other processes on the dissociation continuum, but apparently of a far less regressive, frightening quality. We also noticed that secondarily denial and repression have led to such intense inhibitions in action, in social, deeper emotional and sexual relations, and to the use of isolation and reaction-formations, that the patients feel frozen into rigid boundaries. It is here that the psychedelics are experienced as a tremendous transient liberation, despite the deeper forms of splitting attained.

As stated this is a very provisional, very hypothetical answer.

Looked at in regard to the *id impulses* we have already noticed how in the process which is known as "topographic regression" (see Freud 1900, Modell 1968), perception (self-perception, seeing and hearing) is permeated with sensual qualities. Archaic scoptophilic wishes and fears are revived. The sense of being watched, stared at, looked into, means: the eyes of the others have total power to intrude into me, to merge with me and to annihilate me—and I want to do the same with the others (see Hesse's "Demian," Hoffmann's "Sandman," Ibsen's "Eyolf"). In many an increasing sense of detachment, of isolation from the others, of being out of touch and contact with the others, followed the acute or chronic use. Again it appears likely that the more intense and profound the fears of shameful exposure are, the more likely it is that the patient reacts with terror instead of pleasure.

This brings us to the cardinally important aspect of the tremendous intensification of *narcissistic* impulses. They reached megalomanic proportions only in those patients who also used LSD. In the marijuana users this upsurge of narcissism was reflected more in paranoid suspicions: everybody was looking at them—and in wishes to be admirable, grand, and have no limits. Finally it is: merger sought versus merger feared.

**An Experiment with Psilocybin—Some Additional Observations
About the Model: Drug-Set-Setting.**

In connection with these observations and the questions posed by
Zinberg (what the psychedelic induced "alternate" state of consciousness really consists of, the relative importance of the "setting" for the
effects) (1974, 1975) it might be interesting to reexamine a much older
observation of an intense psychedelic "trip" and check some of the
current claims, considerations, and conclusions against the experience
made in an era where this type of drug experience had nothing to do
with "drug culture," "consciousness expansion," etc.

In the late 1950s and early 1960s LSD and psilocybin were mainly
used in research to find out more about the mental processes in an
artificial psychosis and as a possible help to break through very rigid
pathological states (severe obsessive-compulsive neuroses, catatonia,
melancholia). I was invited to undergo such a psilocybin experiment in
early 1962. I had (and still have) an intense interest in working with
overtly psychotic patients in psychotherapy, and thus I felt particularly
motivated to learn to "emphathize" more (see Zinberg 1974, his
references to Kafka and Gaarder). In an extensive survey of
"theoretical and practical aspects of psychotherapy with schizophrenics" (Wurmser 1963), I included a detailed description of the various
phases of what is called in Europe an "acute exogenic reaction type,"
the psychosis induced by the experiment.

To use Zinberg's framework of drug-set-setting: The drug was six
mg of psilocybin by mouth. The properties and effects were not very
well known to me at the time. The setting was a quiet, friendly room in
the private section of the Psychiatric University Hospital in Basel; the
leader of the experiment (Dr. Gnirss) was a good personal friend of
mine. Except for his occasional checking on me, including brief
exploratory conversations, I was left alone, first lying on a couch, then
sitting in a comfortable armchair. I tried to take shorthand notes of all
that went on—an effort almost impossible in the beginning. At that
time I was an already fully trained psychiatrist and psychotherapist. I
translate from German my published report in a slightly expanded
form:

The experience is overwhelming because of the realization of the
elementary forces slumbering in us, and how irresistible and intense
they really can be. Half an hour after intake the first vegetative and

mental symptoms appeared: insecurity, dizziness, sleepiness, light nausea. A few minutes later consciousness clouded very rapidly. The flitting thoughts and the feelings could hardly be grasped any more. Perception of the external world and my body, of thoughts and feelings, was totally estranged (depersonalized and derealized). Restlessness shook like fire through the body. Waves of screaming heads of lions pushed on and on, elephants chased by with trunks raised. A fast musical rhythm sounded up and broke off again. In black rooms there was an empty gaiety. The feeling of loss of voluntary control, of powerlessness, helpless exposure and surrender slowly lost its sense of unpleasure. Anxiety, which had prevailed for a time, vanished. Everything danced, whirled, flitted by and was in jubilation.

I wrote down: "One haste—everything races, dims away, sinks down, is devoured and (drowned). The thoughts shove and push and flee, nothing can be held. The wildest associations chase by, uncontrolled, like dragons, then like snakes through the air. Every external perception, every single thought frees a cloud and whirling vortex of associations which cannot be articulated anymore. Japanese dragonheads and crocodiles tear open their mouths. A hitherto unknown greed to devour lets me eat everything which comes close (an offered sandwich is dropped, picked up from the floor and consumed). The need for help and clinging is great."

To sum up the experiences of this first phase: accompanied by total depersonalization and derealization and enormous reduction of clarity of consciousness (I estimated it to be perhaps reduced to one tenth!), an abundance of oral experience enters: a greed to devour, need to cling and to be taken care of, a hypomanic hilarity, unrestrained laughing, flight of thoughts; the time is shortened, it chases away, and at the same time there is a feeling as if eternities were passing.

In the second phase of the psychotic experience the estrangement of thoughts and feelings gradually decreases while that of outer perception and of the body, including the will power, continues unabated. Experiences of participation, of union and merger, become stronger while the oral wishes continue. These "participative" experiences are partly megalomanic, partly a most archaic fusion.

Again my own notes: "There is an esctasy among red masks. Waves which tower and break over each other, an inhuman elementary world of movement, animals, grimacing masks. One is in a sea of waves—and all that am I. The other person is remote, far, strange. I am the hungry child that cries for help. The defense breaks down; the structures are lifted. The casing of time is breaking in; there is no holding structure anymore. One drifts in a stream, one drowns without experiencing it as unpleasant. Just like the inner structures, the external boundaries fall away: when I write, this act does not go on anymore outside of myself. All boundaries are torn open; I flow into the surroundings. Imaginations immediately turn into images. Wishes, barely thought of, are satisfied in the fantasy. All are of extremely regressive nature: to lie, to laugh, to devour. An image of mother, of being nursed, emerges. It is the omnipotence of the infant: to have everything, to see all demands immediately fulfilled—an all-embracing, an all-merging, an all-devouring, an all-pleasure of most primitive force. Every reality appears plump and gross besides this ecstasy in which all yearnings for belonging and being protected (*Geborgenheit*) are fulfilled. The whole oedipal situation, castration anxiety, anything genital, anal, all guilt, shame, disgust—all that has ceased to exist. What exists is oral pleasure, reconciliation, harmony, happiness, peace, light, a pleasure pervading my whole body, a twilight of bodylessness, of comfort and motherliness—the mothers in the caves of yearning, of protectedness. Conscience has totally disappeared; only a small stump of the observing ego remains. It is the pure pleasure-self. No persons, no events, no conversations, only the rolling of the waves of an original (*urtumlich*) happiness, the thalassic feeling of pure being within oneself (*Innerlichkeit*), limitlessness and ecstasy."

At the end of this second phase, the estrangement can be broken through by an act of will, by a kind of start *(Ruck),* and the feeling of reality can be reestablished. At the same time, though, the happiness, too, the flooding of perceptions with sensuousness, can be brought back.

This enthusiasm, this fusion, is a satisfaction of pleasure never attainable in real life. It is like a present from another, archaic reality which is free of anxiety and guilt. It is this piece of real gratification whose conscious experiencing and after effect in a third phase might become therapeutically effective. This third phase which lasts several days is the conscious working through of the experience.

After the vanishing of ecstasy—about four hours after intake of the drug—there remains a slight depersonalization and mild depression at the reentrance into the gray, disappointing everyday world. What has a lasting impact is the conscious experiencing of a piece of most deeply repressed affectivity and drives, the presence of this feeling of blissful boundarylessness, of being connected and fused with all things. Everything external is in me, sensuous and animated; everything internal is world and reality.

I compared it with the experiences described by mystics: Ramakrishna, Vivekananda, Plotin, Ytzchaq Lurya. When I compared it with a schizophrenic psychosis, I noticed the same type of regression to earliest oral-narcissistic experiences, a disappearance of all the superego functions and most of the ego functions, the loss of limits and boundaries. The greatest difference, however, seemed to me at that time that I experienced the unleashing in archaic form ("deneutralization") of libidinous, participative forces, whereas the schizophrenic experiences that of aggressive destructive powers.

I agree with Zinberg that a small push in the "setting" one way or the other can, especially in the first phase, lead either to extreme pleasure (a *unio mystica)* or to equally extreme panic. I also would say that the fact that this was a fully legal, overt, acceptable event, did not, during the stage of utmost vulnerability, trigger a disaster of oral-narcissistic dimensions, but its opposite. My own personal stability had probably relatively little to do with the positive direction my "trip" took. But, in the framework of this book, this is not the only problem we are concerned with.

Of far greater interest—and, I believe, one which Zinberg throughout completely neglects—is the question asked by the British expert Ian Pierce James, as quoted by Judson ("Heroin Addiction In Britain," 1973): "The real question is, put it this way, why do all the people who have been exposed to alcohol not inevitably become alcoholics? Why don't we compare a group of addicts with a group who have 'failed' to become addicts?"

Zinberg stresses as answer to this question the "power of the social setting." For him it is the responses and expulsion by the environment, the view by others of the drug user as deviant, which impairs the ego's autonomy both from id and environment, thus pushes it into primary process and self-fragmentation and leads the person into compulsive drug use and addiction. Is it indeed the negative—or on the contrary, the positive—social setting which encourages the slipping into more and more frequent use? Or is it the "set," the personality? I can try to answer this for myself because, in the subsequent years, I had many invitations to repeat this "psychedelic" experience under both conditions—in settings which were totally positive, supportive, accepting, legal (as experiments and part of treatment programs)—but also within the broader cultural setting which was for me strongly negative: as part of the Leary fashion and counter culture.

Despite the intensely positive first and only drug experience I declined each and every such opportunity. The setting was totally irrelevant. I had other ways to fulfill whatever need the drug experience would have satisfied, without having to sacrifice the lucidity of my thinking. I found the large scale (or any partial) loss of consciousness a price higher than any gain in feelings and supposed insights. These latter I could also obtain in other ways—in smaller "dosages," it is true, and with arduous effort: in close human relations, in my own psychoanalysis, above all in creative working and in reliving the creativity of others: in the highest examples of novels, dramas, philosophy, and, strongest of all, in music and nature. The drug experience was uncontrolled regression, overwhelming, massive, a magical abolition of all inhibiting feelings of guilt, shame, revulsion, anxiety, anger; the other forms of experience were, if one wants to call them with Kris, "regressions in the service of the ego": they were controlled, used in their richness for inner growth and empathy into others, offering me meaning, richness in life, without the abdication of reason, that most noble instrument. Tertullian's "sacrificium intellectus" soon led to the literal self-castration by the other Father of the Church, Origen; we can do without both.

I have no questions that *it was the personality, not the setting* which prevented me from becoming a compulsive drug user and which in turn did *not* prevent the patients with whom I work.

I might add, too, that I can reply to Zinberg's added challenge when he states: "Almost none of them (the colleagues in the drug field)... had tried the drugs whose effects and whose users they were so assiduously studying. They were frightened." And he suggests "that my experimental capacity would have improved had I taken the drug with them," and includes heroin. This reminds us of what the seducer of Dorian Gray,

Lord Henry Wotton, thought: "There were poisons so subtle that to know their properties one had to sicken of them. There were maladies so strange that one had to pass through them if one sought to understand their nature" (Oscar Wilde). Is this indeed true?

Again I have to disagree with my esteemed colleague. I have used nearly all types of psychotropic drugs (except for narcotics), once or a few times and legally. I do not think these experiences have in any way enhanced my understanding of, and working with, compulsive drug users. The experience which counts stands on an entirely different level: it is the disciplined introspection of a long psychoanalysis, the supervision in my work, the empathy, the willingness and patience to listen, to hear, trying to understand the whole person, not just his career as a drug user, the respect for him and lastly for the suffering warded off with the help of the drug. It is the combination of all that which helped and taught me to work with these people.

And deeper down it is my conviction that Aeschylos' word "pathei mathos" (that learning comes by suffering), is one of the greatest maxims of wisdom. Joy teaches, but ordeal matures.

Chapter 11

FAMILY RESEARCH

I have already presented my own limited and merely clinical observations but several co-workers of mine (especially Cloe Madanes and H.T. Harbin) have now started a more careful, systematic and formalized study of the family pathology which should give us clearer and more specific answers to this problem. I am very grateful to them for their contribution.

The following section will be opened by a brief summary of the survey by H. Harbin and H.M. Maziar (1975), adding some new findings. Their major point (and with that the importance of this section for the entire book is: Briefly, that we cannot afford today to go on the basis of questionnaires or superficial examinations in order to assess the family patholoolgy. New methods have been developed over the past fifteen years which allow scientific family research on a much higher plane of sophistication—methods which need *now* to be applied to the background study, to the eventual exploration of the etiology, and to the application to prevention and treatment. Therefore the following chapter, also written by Dr. Harbin, presents a clinical case study of a family of a compulsive drug user in family therapy.

This will be followed by a direct application of a new stringent research method to the interaction in the same family. This part is written by Cloe Madanes who has developed this novel tool of investigation. This analysis is based upon (and excerpted from) a research interview (part of a larger project studying the family interaction of heroin addicts) that was done separately from the clinical-treatment context. Ms. Madanes makes some predictions about the family's behavior in treatment based solely on the research findings, and these are compared to the description given by H. Harbin in his chapter of the actual treatment.

If there is a particular need for innovative approaches it lies here: in the methodical, systematic, critical research in the family pathology (as to dynamics and cognition) of compulsive drug use—in black families and white families, in poor and rich, in users of narcotics versus those of other drugs and alcohol.

Family therapy is important, but I think at this stage as an instrument of exploration more than of actual treatment. We know far too little yet, but clinically we get more and more evidence that here an all-important trail is leading us towards a better understanding of compulsive drug use.

Summary of Pertinent Literature (H. Harbin)

The justification for a family approach to understanding the addictive process comes primarily from three sources; (1) clinical or empirical information, (2) formal research data about addicts' family patterns and characteristics and, (3) some preliminary data on the outcome of family therapy with addicts. A summary of the data collected thus far from the first two sources will be presented here and is based on two recent review articles (Harbin and Maziar 1975, Davis and Klagsbrun 1975). The first comprehensive review of the literature on families of drug addicts by Harbin and Maziar covers a period from the 1940s up to 1972. In this review the authors sectioned the various articles based upon the type of methodologies, with the most valid and reliable (yet restricted) studies being the ones that used control groups of non-addict families. The most consistent finding from this review was that family dynamics of compulsive drug users were invariably pathological. Family dynamics appear to be instrumental in the maintenance of pathological drug use. A frequent finding was the absence of one or both biological parents during the childhood of the addict. One of the most consistent family constellations, identified in many of the research articles with a variety of methodological approaches, was the combination of an overprotective, indulgent mother with an absent or emotionally distant father. Mothers were described as having "special" relationships with the sons and tended to be involved with their addictions. Some fathers were described as hostile and punitive rather than weak and ineffectual, but the end result seemed to be that drug addicts did not have a role figure with whom they could identify in a positive way.

A critical review of the entire literature led the authors to the following very important conclusions: A major difficulty is that in only a few of the studies were the actual family members other than the addict interviewed and the interactional patterns viewed directly. This method is of some value in understanding the perceptions and fantasies by the drug abuser of his family. This approach, however, limits a clear and objective appraisal of the actual family interactions, since the reality of family life is subject to distortion by any single family member. This distortion likewise is applicable to the few studies in which only the mother of the addict was interviewed. In the future, for a clearer understanding of families with a drug abusing member, there seems no longer a need for research involving only one family member. Another problem with many of these articles is that there is no specification of socioeconomic status, race, and sex among the experimental groups.

The most consistent family patterns identified in the literature about compulsive drug abusers, as just described, have been suggested for many different types of families where there is an identified psychiatric patient—homosexuals, school phobic children, and schizophrenics are some examples. The application of this pattern to such a wide variety of psychiatric syndromes is likewise seen in the frequent vague use of such terms as *narcissism, masochism,* and *aggression* throughout the articles mentioned in this study. The terminology used in the research thus far is particularly inapplicable to interpersonal transactions. At this point it might be asked whether it is presumptuous to assume that further specificity does exist for types of families with a drug abusing member. In view of past findings of more specific dynamics, for example the double bind in schizophrenia, it is reasonable to assume that, unless otherwise refuted, specifity may exist.

It seems useful to outline certain factors that need to be included in any future studies.

Exact criteria for the type of drug use and abuse is essential to the achievement of reliable research data. This includes the type of drug (whether amphetamines, barbiturates, cocaine, heroin, etc.). Also the frequency and duration of drug use is important in order to assess the compulsivity of use. The compulsive drug users are considered to have the most severe problem and are more likely to have disturbed family relations.

The sex of the drug user should be identified, as it is likely that there are different family dynamics for the male and female addict.

The socioeconomic background of the families studied should be similar so as to differentiate specific interactional dynamics for families of various cultures.

The entire family of origin should be directly involved in any research study. This can include any significant parental figures (such as grandparents) as well as siblings in order to assess all parts of the family's functioning, both pathological and healthy.

It is worthwhile to consider specific family styles that may be relevant to the development and maintenance of a drug abusing child. For example, a child's attitude may be determined by the parents' views toward the child's use of inanimate objects. The parents might constantly encourage the child to satisfy frustrations through relatedness to inanimate objects, i.e., pacifier, toys, medication, in place of interpersonal investments. The child would thus learn that the most consistent and safe way to satisfy internal needs and conflicts is to rely on nonhuman objects. With this set in later life, the individual may turn to drug abuse to resolve conflict.

Drug abuse as a symptom may be maintained by the individual to serve family functions. For example, an addicted adolescent may use his drug abuse as a means of maintaining involvement with the family. As long as he continues to use drugs, the family remains concerned about the addict's fate. Likewise the parents too may encourage continued drug abuse (e.g., giving money to the addict to purchase drugs) as a means of maintaining control of the addict.

A control group is essential in comparing the degree of pathology in drug using families.

Davis and Klagsburn (1975) focus more on articles published between 1972 and 1975, and they attempt to elaborate further on the "'symptoms' of individual (drug) abuse in the context of the family system." They see the individual drug use as being an adaptive behavior within the family. Frequently, drug use was seen as a way for an individual to protect himself and the family from a heightened awareness of painful affects. The frequent use of alcohol by the parents of drug addicts was reported. In one study the marital relationship of the parents of addicts was described as being emotionally distant until a drug taking episode took place which led to increased interaction between the parents around the issue of drug abuse. Again, a consistent finding was that the families of addicts manifest a great deal of psychopathology and are ultimately involved in maintaining the addicts' continued use of drugs.

Case 21: Sam the "Astrologer" and His Family

The identified patient is a nineteen-year-old white male, Sam, who was admitted to a psychiatric inpatient unit for three months because of drug abuse, depression and some allegedly "psychotic" behavior (looseness of associations, strong astrological beliefs). However the actual event that precipitated hospitalization was the discovery by the father of Sam's marijuana cache in the father's car and his subsequent attempt to destroy the marijuana. Sam, when confronted by his father about the drug, argued and attempted to wrestle the marijuana away from him; a physical confrontation ensued. The father was struck on the head, and Sam continued to be agitated and explosive for the rest of the evening so that the parents had to call the police and have their son put in jail. From jail, he was referred to the hospital for psychiatric treatment.

Sam has had a history of drug abuse for seven years. It had begun in the seventh grade when he started experimenting with a variety of drugs including marijuana, barbiturates, alcohol, amphetamines, LSD, and cocaine (this also included a "bad trip" on strychnine, followed by severe depression). He denied any use of morphine or heroin and did not use drugs intravenously. Sam stated that he began using drugs in response to the feelings of depression that ensued when a twenty-eight-year-old female teacher "left him" to get married. Sam had had a fantasized romantic relationship with his teacher and was personally crushed when she married someone else. His drug use increased over a time to where he was constantly "high." He managed successfully to complete high school at age seventeen but made it through only six months of college. During his last year of high school he became depressed after another "bad trip" and was sent to a psychiatrist. He denied any benefit from this experience and managed to hide his drug use from the psychiatrist as he had been able to do with his parents for approximately five years. He continued his frequent drug use (apparently mostly of psychedelics) in college and was increasingly depressed until he stopped because he felt that his peers there only furthered his drug use. He was able to obtain and hold onto a job as a manual laborer on a highway maintenance crew and used much of his salary to buy drugs. He continued to live at home but was becoming increasingly irresponsible. Drugs were taken by him before, during and after going to work. At times he took barbiturates specifically to calm himself down. His primary social activity was taking drugs with a group of peers and occasional visits to a "massage parlor." Often, his friends would steal money and belongings from him while he was high, and he related that he would often try to buy friends. One year prior to admission Sam's mother went back to her home in England for a visit, and during this time Sam stole a thousand dollars from her bank account by forging her name and then proceeded to spend the money on street drugs. The parents attempted to get psychiatric treatment for their son at this time but he refused help, and they accepted this. Several months prior to admission, Sam was arrested for disorderly conduct related to drug use.

The family consists of father (fifty years old), mother (fifty-three years old) and twin brothers (thirteen years old).

The father works as a machinist and is described by his son as "no fun, mean as a moose, and smokes a mile a minute." The father feels that his son's problem is "tearing me apart" and is interfering with his work performance. The father was an only child and his parents divorced when he was only three months old. He was raised mostly by his mother and her parents; his grandmother died of cancer when he was two years old. He described his mother as a "shrewd business woman" but as rarely at home. His mother's attitude was that children should be seen but not heard. His father was described as being pleasant, easy-going, and living a transient lifestyle as a jockey, frightened of his wife; their relationship was basically incompatible. Sam's father and mother have been married for twenty-one years; they had dated for six months prior to marriage. The father stated that his parents "couldn't care less" about his marriage and that he sees his mother approximately twice a year.

Sam's mother was described by him as a "typical, wacky, limey broad, but I still love her." She had two older brothers and one twin sister and was raised by both of her parents who resided in England at the time of her marriage. She described her own father as a "heavy drinker" who "denied the family and spent lavishly." She stated that she quarreled frequently with her father as she grew older. Mother said that she got along well with her mother and respected her for being a good disciplinarian even though sometimes she was "too strict." Her parents argued frequently and, at the time of hospitalization, were deceased. Neither father nor mother has any activities that they do together, but state that their family is normal with the exception of Sam's problems.

Family therapy was conducted on a weekly basis during the hospitalization and the father, mother and Sam were usually present. The very first session revealed some of the core dynamics that were present in this family. The father was somewhat intellectually detached, quiet, passive, and distant; while the mother was active, verbal, intrusive and domineering. Both parents were extremely anxious and felt guilty over the difficulties of their son. During this first session Sam was alternately very angry at his parents and very loving towards them. Mother and son seemed to be very emotionally sensitive to each other. At times Sam cursed at his mother, calling her a "limey bitch," and at other times manifested frankly incestuous motivations by patting his mother on the buttocks during the session. The mother's response to this sexual behavior was to look questioningly, but she did not say anything. Father, who observed the verbal disrespect, said nothing.

These few interactions pointed out the gross blurring of generational boundaries that has taken place in this family. Here is a son that can openly abuse his mother without comment from either parent. Yet, these are the same parents that have called the police on their son for hitting father. Yet again, these are parents who did not detect gross and frequent drug use in their son for five years and tolerated his stealing a thousand dollars from mother. They also complained about their son's use of drugs but continued to allow him to live with them for several years while he continued to abuse drugs. These same parents never identified as a problem that their son had no close peer relationships with either girls or boys (as therapy progressed, Sam's confused sexual identity emerged more clearly). The extreme acting out of ambivalent motivations (love and hate) towards his parents and himself on Sam's part is reflected in the equally extreme ambivalence of the parents in their defining of clear cut parent-child boundaries. Another corollary of these distortions was Sam's blurring of self-boundaries as manifested by his swinging from intense self-deprecation and doubt to the other extreme of grandiose views of self. Parallel to this split (and flipflop) in his self-image was a reverse split in his view of his parents: when he was grand, they were despised and degraded. As family sessions progressed, a profound sense of mistrust of parents to Sam and vice versa was revealed. Father did not trust the intentions of his son to change, having seen him lie and steal so often in the past. Sam did not trust his father to be a firm, consistent and nurturing figure to him. This pervasive sense of mistrust and doubt interfered greatly with the therapeutic attempts to create a sense of optimism which would motivate Sam to grow. His use of drugs as a response to his own confused ego boundaries and to assuage his inner pain is adaptive to a point. The cycle of drug abuse, however, further distances him from his parents, thereby increasing their mistrust of him. This also lessens his ability to learn an alternate way of resolving his painfully distorted interpersonal relationships within the family.

As he returns to drugs over and over again to solve his problems, he repeatedly rejects his parents and brothers as important people. His drug taking sends the message that he does not need them and that he can fulfill his own needs for love and acceptance through artificial and nonhuman means. This decreases temporarily the risk of being rejected by his father or of merging with mother, but it will eventually lead to his existence as an empty shell of a person. In the historical data, one sees that Sam began taking drugs after feeling rejected by his teacher, and his response is to reject others by denying any need for them. Obviously, he had not developed a secure sense of self prior to this fantasized love relationship or he would have been able to tolerate the rebuff from such an impossible love object. One has to look at the parents' relationship with each other, as well as their own families of origin, in order to understand how they might allow such gross disturbances to develop in their own role as parents. The father's background shows a great deal of rejection and emotional distancing by his father and his mother. He was left to be raised by his grandparents while his mother was a transient figure. His view of his parents was that they were relatively unconcerned; this father's behavior in the family therapy sessions to his wife was that he was likewise unconcerned, cool, and distant. Sam's mother came from a family marked by discord and a seemingly inadequate, alcoholic father. She was geographically cut off from her parents and had to depend on her husband's extended family for support, of which there was little. The history of alcoholism in the family background of a drug abuser is not surprising and has been observed repeatedly. Yet, Sam's parents were able to stay married for twenty-one years, and they showed some strengths in their ability to respond with emotional and financial support for their son. One does not observe in this family a repetition of the total emotional and physical abandonment that was present in the father's family. Instead, one sees a combination between over-closeness of mother and son and emotional distancing of father and son and husband and wife.

The initial goal of the therapist was to engage the parents and their son Sam in an empathetic manner. In addition, the boundaries of the therapeutic relationship must be firmly established and maintained by the therapist. In this family, the blurring of generational boundaries and the confusion of appropriate family roles have led to gross acting out behavior on one family member's part. The therapist must move quickly to restructure some of the confused communications in this family in order to create a situation in which mutual trust and further emotional growth can occur. One of the first tasks of the therapist with the family was to challenge the gross disrespect of son to mother. The therapist stated that the parents were the authority in the family and that they deserved respect for this by their children. The therapist specifically identified Sam's patting his mother's buttocks and his cursing behavior as disrespectful. The father subsequently agreed with the therapist that this was not correct, but the mother responded that this was one of the ways her son could show affection to her. The father and the therapist were able to convince the mother of the inappropriateness of the son's behavior in the future. This therapeutic intervention was a first step in helping the parents provide clear and definite limits for their son so that he could begin to disengage from an overly symbiotic relationship with his mother and to begin to see where his own behavior was an intrusion upon others. Many reinforcements of the generational boundaries were needed in the therapeutic work with the family. Another major focus of the family work was to increase the alliance between Sam and his father in order to foster an atmosphere in which more trust could develop. The increased trust led to Sam's beginning to identify more appropriately with his father. These clinical observations allow a glimpse into the macrodynamics of transactions within a disturbed family. However, it has become increasingly necessary for researchers to carry out a detailed analysis of the micro-communicational events that take place in families that produce a drug abuser.

Predicting Behavior in an Addict's Family:
A Communicational Approach

by Cloe Madanes

The aim of this section* is to describe the family relationships of a polydrug user and to show how behavior in therapy can be predicted** from the family interaction during an assessment procedure. This paper is part of an effort to develop a methodology to study families that is focussed on interaction, not on individual characteristics, and that is consistent with a family therapy approach that focuses on changing interaction.

The assessment technique used to study the family presented here is part of the research procedure used by the author in a study of family interaction of heroin addicts. On the basis of the family behavior in the assessment interview, predictions were made about the way the family would behave in therapy. The assessment procedure that was used produces behavior that is an exaggeration of the family's usual behavior and is therefore a good predictor. At the time the predictions were made all the author knew about the family was that the son was a polydrug user. The family presented above is the focus of the following inquiry.

* The preparation of this section was supported by National Institute of Drug Abuse Grant No. R01 DAO1141.
** The term *predict* is used in the sense that Margaret Singer (1974) uses it, following Benjamin (1959), that is, predicting from one set of data to another and not in the folk-sense of forecasting behavior yet to come. The procedure of predicting behavior in therapy from the family interaction during an assessment procedure has been used by Margaret Singer (1974).

ASSESSMENT TECHNIQUE

The assessment technique used to study the family consists of two parts: the Proverb Task and the Family Structure Task.

In the Proverb Task, the children are asked to wait outside of the interview room and the parents are given the following instructions: "I have here (on typewritten cards) a proverb which I am sure you know. I should like you to discuss the meaning of this proverb for not longer than five minutes. As soon as you have discussed the meaning, will you please call the young people in yourselves and teach them the meaning of this proverb. The proverb is 'A rolling stone gathers no moss.' The interviewer leaves the room and goes behind the one-way mirror. A detailed description of this task and of the results obtained from its use in a comparative study of families are presented elsewhere" (Sojit 1969, 1971).

The Family Structure Task consists of two stages and is designed to be used with a family of four. In the first stage, each family member is shown, individually, diagrams of eight different family structures and is asked to choose the one that most resembles the family relations of the four people who have come to the interview. The eight diagrams represent the different possible hierarchical relations between four people. In the second stage, the whole family is brought together and asked to agree on one diagram and on the distance between family members.

ASSESSMENT OF FAMILY INTERACTION

In what follows the family interaction during the two assessment procedures will be described in brief excerpts.

The Proverb Task: Text of Transcript

(After the preliminaries)

Mother: Okay. Well in other words a person who keeps moving around too much obviously is . . . not going to gather too much knowledge ...or... how do you feel about it? The meaning of this.

Comment: Mother gives one of the two possible interpretations of the proverb (that moving around is bad).

Father: Well, uh (laughs) that is obviously the meaning that if you move around too much you're not uh going to uh establish a base, a foundation, could be money, moss could be money I suppose, it's green.

Comment: Father agrees.

Mother: Mmm. Well, no, I wouldn't look at it that way....

Comment: Mother disagrees and it is not clear whether she disagrees with the father's interpretation (which is the same as hers) or with a detail or an item within the interpretation (PSEUDO-DISAGREEMENT*).

Father: In other words, there is another way to look at that. A stone that rests gathers no polish.

Comment: By saying "in other words," father defines his statement as a reframing of mother's and his own previous interpretation, that moving around too much is bad, but then he gives the opposite interpretation of the proverb, that *not* moving around is bad (INCONGRUITY). The mother's pseudo-disagreement is followed by a message by father that is incongruous (PSEUDO-DISAGREEMENT → INCONGRUITY).

Mother: Right. And, ah er um, it could be too that, um, the home has something to do with it that, um, a person who moves around too much, um, doesn't establish a stable home or for instance, if the father is gone away, he's not establishing a stable home, is he? He's moving around too much. Not in mm....

Comment: When father proposes a different interpretation from mother's, mother responds with a reference to the home that could be a subtle accusation of father (METAPHORIC ACCUSATION). She show no interest in father's interpretation and does not ask him to clarify it or expand it. She goes on with her own train of thought as if father had not spoken (UNRESPONSIVENESS). Mother responds to father's incongruous statement with a metaphoric accusation that is unresponsive towards what father has said (INCONGRUITY → METAPHORIC ACCUSATION AND UNRESPON-SIVENESS).

Father: Well I can't see where that would hold true in our situation.

Comment: Father takes mother's accusation literally and defends himself directly (METAPHORIC ACCUSATION → LITERAL DEFENSE).

Mother: No, no. For us I would say that uh a person who doesn't keep his ... mind on one particular goal in life isn't going to be too successful. You have to have one good goal in life; you have something to aim for rather than keep starting one thing and stopping and going on from one thing to another.

Comment: Mother agrees with father but adds an interpreta-tion about having a goal in life that may also be an indirect accusation of father (LITERAL DEFENSE →METAPHOR-IC ACCUSATION.

Father: M-hm.

Mother Okay?

Father: No, I don't like that either.

Comment: Father disagrees, he says he does not like it, but he does not expand or clarify why (METAPHORIC ACCUSATION→ WITHDRAWAL). By saying "M-hm" a few seconds before he probably led mother to believe that he was agreeing with her, but then immediately he says he disagrees. A repetitive pattern in this couple's relationship is probably that mother accuses father in indirect ways, father protests and then withdraws, mother criticizes him again indirectly and he withdraws more. Probably father interprets mother's indirect criticisms as unresponsiveness to him and mother interprets father's withdrawal as punishment. (META-PHORIC ACCUSATION AND UNRESPONSIVENESS → LITERAL DEFENSE AND WITHDRAWAL). Mother would probably like to see father more involved with the family, but when he does get involved she disagrees with him and criticizes him; so at this point it is not clear whether she wants his involvement any more.

Mother: You don't like that (laughs). Well in school I was taught, you know I saw a stone rolling down the hill and it didn't get into gathering moss and I was (laughs).

Father: Well, it's a very old saying.

Mother: It's very old, yeah. But, uh, we always were sort of taught....

Father: (sighs)

Mother: That it was better to remain fairly stable than to move around too much.

(Pause. They look at each other.)

Mother: Okay, let's go and get the children. (Laughs)

Father: All right, go ahead.

> *Comments:* Mother ends the conversation abruptly as if they had reached agreement when they had not and as if she had not heard father's objections to her interpretation (PSEUDO-AGREEMENT, UNRESPONSIVENESS).
>
> Father agrees with her about bringing in the children although he has disagreed with her about the proverb and has not explained his disagreement.
>
> Apparently mother wants to get over with the task, having had the last word about the proverb, and father is willing to go along with her, maybe to keep the peace. It is very important to

the couple to maintain an appearance of agreement but both of them undermine their own efforts, mother by making personal references which are indirectly critical of father and by ending the task abruptly in a way that leaves her with the last word and father by making it obvious that he is going along with her although there is no agreement. In this way, they communicate agreement and disagreement at the same time.

It seems extremely difficult for this couple to get together on anything. They would have great difficulty in making decisions or having a joint plan of action. If they did agree, one would immediately begin to undermine the other so that nothing would get accomplished. Probably they would do the same with respect to the therapist: agree with him and then undermine him by not carrying through with whatever has to get done and by proving him wrong by bringing up irrelevant or extraneous matters.

Their pseudo-agreement is also a comment on the interviewer and the interview situation. While apparently polite and cooperative, they are saying with their behavior that this is a silly game and that they will not abide by the rules. They will agree, not because they agree, but to keep the peace or to finish the task (PSEUDO-AGREEMENT FOR AN EXTRANE-OUS REASON). They probably challenge other social rules in a covert way. In this case they agree to finish the task, in other situations they might agree or disagree for another extraneous reason like the patient's behavior, the weather conditions, etc.

A brief excerpt from the evening interaction of the entire family:

Mother: That's all right. Now they want us to discuss this ah proverb here. Can you read that Sam?

Sam: A rolling stone gathers no moss.

Father: They want us to first find out what you think....

Mother: What do you think about that proverb? What does it mean?

Father: About that proverb.

Comment: Both parents distort the instructions. Mother changes them to "discuss" when the instructions were for the parents to discuss and then to *teach* the children. Father says that "they" want them to first find out what the children think which is something that has not been mentioned at all in the instructions. Both messages from the parents point to the difficulty in establishing a relationship with the children in which they, the parents, take the leadership and are in control (INAPPROPRIATE HIERARCHICAL RELATIONS). This difficulty is related to a pattern that very probably exists of going through the children to deal with their own differences. The father's distortion of the instructions is more masked and he refers to a vague "they" to support his statement that the children have to give their opinion first. This is another sign of the father's weak position in the family.

Sam: I am the rolling stone that gathers no moss.

Comment: The identified patient immediately takes the whole situation upon himself in an exaggerated way by making his first statement about the proverb, that he is the rolling stone (SELF-CENTRALIZATION). With this statement he offers himself as a subject of discussion rather than the proverb. It can be predicted that he will do this whenever there is conflict betweeen the parents. He will protect them by having their disagreements and conflicts be about him rather than about other issues that may be painful and difficult to the parents.

Mother: What do you think about it Jim?

Comment: The mother deals with Sam in the same way that she dealt before with father. She asks him about the proverb and, when he answers, she does not offer any comment or acknowledge his statement in any way. She just proceeds to something else, in this case to ask the younger brother what he thinks (UNRESPONSIVENESS).

Jim: I don't think anything.

THE FAMILY STRUCTURE TASK

In the first stage of the Family Structure Task, each family member is shown diagrams of eight different family structures and is asked to choose the one that most resembles the family relations of the four people who have come to the interview. After he has done so, the subject is asked to write down by each stick figure the name of the family member it represents and finally to move the figures to show how close and how distant family members are from each other.

The final product of the four family members was the following. The father represented family relations like this:

He, the father, is in charge of the mother and the younger brother. He tells them what to do, while the identified patient is at the same position in the hierarchy as he is, but he is distant and withdrawn from all family members, he is not in charge of anyone and nobody is in charge of him.

The mother represented relations in the family in this way:

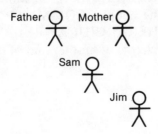

She, the mother, is in charge of the father and the two sons, although the father is somewhat marginal. The identified patient is in the middle between mother and father, he is closer to father than to mother.

The identified patient represented relations in the family like this:

Mother and father are in charge of the two sons and he puts himself under them but in the middle between them.

Jim, the younger brother, produced the following:

Father and Sam are in charge of the family, with mother and himself under them, although the father is more marginal and mother and himself are more directly under Sam than under father.

These choices reflect the power struggle between the parents. Mother's and father's diagrams are almost diametrically opposite. Father considers himself in charge of mother and mother considers herself in charge of father. A total lack of hierarchy, with parents at the same level in the hierarchy as children, or children in a superior position in the hierarchy with respect to parents, appears in all their diagrams, except the identified patient's (INAPPROPRIATE HIERARCHICAL RELATIONS). He puts the parents in charge with himself under them but in the middle between them. However, before moving the figures to end up with this arrangement, he had chosen a diagram that showed all family members in an equal position in the hierarchy, with nobody in charge of anyone. The diagram is the following:

It is interesting that Sam places himself in the middle between the parents (SELF-CENTRALIZATION), the mother also places him in the middle between the couple (COMMUNICATION VEHICLE, INAPPROPRIATE HIERARCHICAL RELATIONS), the younger brother places him in charge of mother and of herself (INAPPROP-

RIATE HIERARCHICAL RELATIONS), while the father puts him in the same position in the hierarchy as himself, but marginal and excluded from family relations (INAPPROPRIATE HIERARCHICAL RELATIONS). This is an indication that the father not only is in a severe power struggle with his wife, but also with his oldest son who is in a coalition with the wife. His position in the family with respect to his wife has probably been taken over to a great extent by the identified patient.

The identified patient's position as a mediator between the parents, where issues between the parents are dealt with through the son, is apparent in all the diagrams (COMMUNICATION VEHICLE). He places himself between the parents, the mother places him between the parents, the younger brother puts him directly in control of the mother, with father excluded, and the father does not place him between the parents, but puts him in the same position of the hierarchy as himself. This is an indicator that the oldest son is a communication vehicle between the parents. The power struggle between the parents makes it very difficult for them to deal directly with the issues between them, but they will deal with issues that are relevant to the son. His addiction and symptoms will keep them focussed on him rather than on the problems in their own relationship (SELF-CENTRALIZATION, COMMUNICATION VEHICLE).

In the second stage of the Family Structure Task, when the whole family has to agree on one diagram, the son's choices are quickly disqualified. The following is the conversation around the patient's choice. He had selected the diagram in which all family members are in an equal position in the hierarchy, with nobody in charge of anyone.

Mother: (pointing at the diagram that Sam had chosen) I cannot agree with this at all. Do you see that now?

Sam: Yes, I see that now.

Mother: So you don't agree with it either.

Sam: I don't agree with it.

Mother: Why did you say it in the first place?

Sam: Because I just did,that's all.

Mother: That was the way you felt...

Sam: The way I felt as soon as I came, as soon as I saw them, that's all.

Mother: You felt that we were four complete separates in the family and nobody was telling anything to anybody.

Sam: Yes. Yes. (superimposed with mother) Yes.

Mother: I'm sorry about that.

Father: No, he didn't realize that it is a chain of command.

Mother: So there is a chain of command, yeah, you looked at it from the arrows pointing from here to here to here....

Father: He was reading it from left to right.

Mother: You were reading it, in other words, from left to right and you were ignoring the arrows. To look at it the way you would look at it there would have to be an arrow sideways connecting them wouldn't there?

Sam: Uh-huh (nods affirmatively).

At the beginning of this interchange it seems that mother and son are going to disagree and argue, son immediately agrees with mother; but still she is not satisfied, and it seems there will be an argument. Then father comes to the rescue and distorts the son's choice by making up a new way of looking at the diagram by which there would be hierarchical relations between the figures going from left to right. This had clearly not been the son's interpretation when he chose the diagram, however mother considers that this is acceptable and the patient quickly agrees with her. In actuality, what has happened is that the patient has not been allowed or expected to take any responsibility for his choice. This is of course accomplished in collusion with the patient who is willing not to be responsible. One would expect that in most areas of life the patient will not take responsibility for his actions, thoughts, opinions, etc. (IRRESPONSIBILITY). Furthermore, this way of looking at the diagram is incongruous with the way they have been looking at the diagrams all through the interview (IN-CONGRUITY).

Soon after there is a struggle about whether father's or mother's diagram will prevail. Father's diagram is finally chosen and only modified by placing Sam closer to the family but in the same position in the hierarchy, next to father, with mother and Jim below them.

PREDICTIONS ABOUT THE FAMILY'S BEHAVIOR IN THERAPY

From the assessment results one would expect that father is probably quiet and withdrawn and mother would like to see him more involved with the family, but when he does get involved, she disagrees with him and criticizes him; so at this point it is not clear whether she wants his involvement any more.

It is very important to the parents to maintain an appearance of agreement, yet it seems extremely difficult for them to get together on anything. They would have great difficulty in making decisions or having a joint plan of action. If they did agree, one would immediately begin to undermine the other so that nothing would get accomplished. Probably they would do the same with respect to the therapist: agree with him and then undermine him by not carrying through with whatever has to get done and by proving him wrong by bringing up irrelevant or extraneous matters.

The parents are in a power struggle that is probably severe. They have difficulty in establishing a relationship with the children in which they, the parents, take the leadership and are in control. This difficulty is related to the pattern that very probably exists of going through the children to deal with their own differences.

The identified patient protects the parents by having their disagreements and conflicts be about him rather than about other issues that may be painful and difficult to the parents.

There is a coalition between the mother and the patient from which the father is excluded. Mother and father use the children as communication vehicles in their struggle with each other; arguments go through the children (particularly the patient) or are about the children rather than about the real issues between mother and father. They have difficulty in offering guidance to their children and give incongruous directives.

There are inappropriate hierarchical relations in the family and a confusion in generation lines. Because of the patient's position as a mediator between mother and father and because of his coalition with mother against father, he occupies a higher position in the hierarchy than is appropriate for a boy his age; his position is too central—he probably sometimes seems to be in control of the family. The father's position in the family with respect to his wife has probably been taken over to a great extent by the patient.

The patient is a mediator in the family and a communication vehicle between the parents. The power struggle between the parents makes it very difficult for them to deal directly with the issues between them; but they will deal with issues that are relevant to the son, and his addiction and symptoms will keep them focussed on him rather than on the problems in their own relationship. The patient's symptomatic behavior and his defiance of social rules is consistent with his position in the family and with the parents' behavior.

SUMMARY AND CONCLUSIONS

The following chart summarizes the results of the study of this family.

In the next two chapters, our critical probing extends to forms of outright pathology in dealing with compulsive drug use—the content for psychological factors (chapter 12) and the misuse of power (chapter 13).

	Parents Proverb	Family Proverb	Indiv. Family Structure	Joint Family Structure	Clinical Notes
Incongruity	x	x		x	
Accusation-Defense	x				x
Unresponsiveness	x	x			x
Pseudo-Agreement or Disagreement	x	x		x	x
Inappropriate Hierarchical Relations		x	x	x	x
Self-Centralization		x	x		x
Communication Vehicle		x	x		x
Inappropriate Use of Authority		x			x
Irresponsibility				x	

Chapter 12

DENIAL OF PSYCHOPATHOLOGY
AND ANTI-INTELLECTUALISM

"Rather, an't please you, it is the disease of not listening, the malady of not marking, that I am troubled withal."
—(*Henry IV, Part II,* Act I, Sc. ii)

Exposé

In this brief chapter the various strands woven in the main sections of this book converge once more. We encountered in the patients the complex interweaving of narcissistic conflicts, of emotions which cannot be tolerated and symbols which cannot be used; we noticed the lack of disciplined introspection which instead is either shunned or degenerates into fragmented dreaming and grandiose fantasizing; we found in them a denial of inner conflict, a falsifying of inner and outer reality, a host of externalizations. We shall see later on how these problems mirror some problems in our culture.

In this and the following chapter we turn to the same phenomena in the "drug abuse establishment." Perusing the literature and attending scientific meetings I have been impressed and distressed by the ignorance and outright *denial* of the problem of severe psychopathology as the core problem in many, if not all, compulsive drug users. On the one side there is an impressive sophistication devoted to pharmacological studies, to new drugs as antidotes to dependency causing drugs, to animal studies, to sociological and epidemiological inquiries, to battles about legal reclassifications of this or that substance, to refinements in the discovery of yet other traces in urine or other body fluids of some toxic substance, to broad gauged accounts of results with this or that modality alone or in combination. All these efforts are very important.

But they are not adding light there, where our ignorance is most massive.

Certainly even in the literature and scientific meetings there are exceptions—work done precisely in studying, exploring and treating in various forms the massive psychopathology I have been emphasizing. However, they are still scant, funded only peripherally or not at all, not carried out in a nationally organized, systematic way—and they are pitifully out of proportion, both as to the severity of the problems faced and to the efforts devoted to what I am convinced are less central aims.

Psychopathology among drug abusers has been brushed aside as of little relevance, precisely by many physicians, sociologists, psychologists and other well-trained professionals. In some a general aversion against psychological factors and clinical psychotherapy may have played a role, but I think it would be unfair to put all on such an aversion. Rather the problems we face in the psychopathology of drug abusers are of such complexity and magnitude, the instruments for their exploration and treatment of such intricate, difficult and often scientifically dubious nature, that it was natural to turn to the less difficult, more manageable fringe aspects first, and pragmatically to see how far simple measures can make a dent and to study then those simple lucid measures and avoid the murky shadows. But we cannot avoid them much longer.

In turn, as already mentioned, psychiatrists in private practice as well as in university departments have been loathe to approach drug abusers although they readily admit the severe psychopathology of most of these patients. They like to brush them aside, like their colleagues in the other fields, as not germane to their teaching or to their practice of psychiatry, as a primarily social or a criminal problem, or as far too difficult because of the mendacity, manipulativeness, of these patients and because of the general proclivity to deal pharmacologically, instead of psychotherapeutically, with inner problems.

How about the treatment personnel themselves? Has there been an equal avoidance and denial of psychopathology? I cannot speak in general, but in my own staff I observed that they are perhaps able to deny the existence of emotional problems among the first 30 per cent of patients I have described in earlier chapters, but that they feel awed and unprepared by the other 70 per cent and also by the rejects and dropouts, and devoutly wish they had good, solid, reliable, ever ready psychiatric assistance for those cases. This psychiatric assistance is, of course, only rarely available.

Some colleagues advise us to use reward and punishment, conditioning and deconditioning, to look with Skinner "beyond freedom and dignity." We are referred to the studies about rats and monkeys who get addicted and are taught by such a prominent researcher as Avram Goldstein: "Note that these addict monkeys did not suffer from unhappy childhoods or fatherless homes, nor were they alienated by oppressive conditions of life" (1972 Proceedings, 4th National Methadone Conference). But we know by now that reward and punishment, threats, cajoling, tempting do not work.

This antipsychiatric attitude in regard to drug users often takes off from the just cited pharmacological rationalization. A statement I have heard *ad nauseam* is: "Just as rats and other mammals, each one of us would get addicted if given an addicting drug. This is a purely physiologic phenomenon."

There are, of course, many arguments against this claim, but we have several natural experiments disproving what the animal experiments seem to prove; they all come down to the fallacious equation of physiological and psychological dependency.

One example consists of many surgical patients or patients with chronic painful diseases. As long as the painful state lasts they may be given narcotics, naturally in increasing dosages because of the developing tolerance. If this process continues they become clearly physically addicted—but they are not "addicts." Once the underlying illness is adequately dealt with, they can be withdrawn—with due regard for the physiologic withdrawal symptoms: gradually, in small steps. Only a small group stays behind and has become also psychologically dependent, developed a craving. The few medically induced narcotics (also barbiturates or Valium, etc.) addicts I have seen, remained "hooked"—not because of the drug, the doctor, the somatic illness, but solely because of the antecedent, underlying specific psychopathology.

The second example I witnessed still as a student, before the era of psychopharmacology in today's sense. Melancholic patients regularly were treated with slowly ascending and again descending dosages of an opium tincture, over a period of two to six months. It is dubious how helpful the drug was as an antidepressant, but decades of experiences taught the psychiatrists of yore that the physiological addiction never was followed by a psychological one. After gradual withdrawal no patient resorted to opiate abuse. Their psychopathology was not the one of the addictive personality. (What the difference might have been is still puzzling to me; I can speculate, but know merely this fact.)

The third concerns us directly: most, if not all of us, have been exposed to legal and illegal substances which create physiological or at least psychological dependency. We have drunk alcohol, smoked cigarettes, received sleeping medication or taken cannabis. Only a relatively few of us, even with free and unlimited access, become somatically or emotionally dependent on these substances—in contrast to the animal experiments.

Again, as Susanne Langer stressed, it is a treacherous exercise to draw inferences from artificial animal experiments (a) to a real animal psychology (without all the anthropomorphizations so common today) and (b) to human psychology (1972, pp. 66-67).

But it is this narrow focusing on the drugs which has led pharmacologists, sociologists and public speakers to all the proposals for public policy which neglect the profound psychopathology (whether in form of "mass inoculation" with a long acting antagonist, of ever more massive penalties, of "cost efficient" methadone programs, etc.) and therefore to eventual defeat and therapeutic nihilism.

Psychophobia, Its Reasons, and Some Philosophical Considerations

As stated there is a striking paucity of psychological inquiries into what the drug effect means in the life history of the individual patient and of his family.

If we look back over the history of psychiatry we find such initial omissions rather regularly. Hysteria was for two millennia declared an organic disease; schizophrenia and alcoholism were or are explained as metabolic disturbances. Again there is little doubt that such organic processes may somehow play a role, whether as primary cause or as secondary process we do not know. But what is usually overlooked is the fact that there is a huge gap between somatic basis and psychological experience, that there are many layers of causation one over the other, and that by discovering one element we cannot dispense with other causes. "Pars pro toto" dealing, "synecdoches" as they are now called, are surprisingly frequent scientific fallacies.

But how is it that the psychological causes and experiences are so consistently avoided? Why is the silence broken more by derision and angry rebuke than by a reasonable discourse? We know how this avoidance is partly a direct reflection of the denial and externalization by the patients themselves who are so prone to look for external solutions to internal problems, to seek quick magical answers to complex inner questions, and to aim for simple technical mastery over their profound feelings of despair, anxiety, and rage. Indeed the patients thus successfully enlist society at large in their own form of defense. It is a collusion of self-deception between compulsive drug users and society.

The longer these observations accumulate, the deeper the impression becomes that this avoidance of emotional problems, of psychological exploration, shared by patients and researchers, is a phobic response, appropriately called *psychophobia*. It is the other side of that craving for technical and chemical solutions for deep inner problems which has been called *chemophilia* (in A. L. Malcolm 1971, see also, Farber 1966), and the basic philosophy of which was ridiculed by H. J. Mueller in these words: "'Progress' is a debatable concept, and in popular discourse a very dubious one. It has inspired a naive, uncritical faith, in America a shameless boasting about a high standard of low living" (1958, p. 82).

What is this psychophobia all about? In both, patients and researchers, it protects the illusion of omnipotence; it allows, as we already saw, to preserve the fantasies of grandeur about oneself and the demanding insistence that society and the world fulfill the quest for meaning and value in a material way and through easy technical control.

388 THE HIDDEN DIMENSION

More important, I believe, is the reason given by Freud for any phobia: it is far easier to deal with an outer threat than with inner danger (1926). If we have to face the anxiety and pain of our inner conflicts, we are very inclined to ascribe their source to external factors and then to avoid those external forces. Obviously an endless and vain attempt of avoidance. In other words: drugs and scientific and social psychophobia are displacements from within to without in order to avoid the necessary working through and maturation.

A third aspect of this psychophobia is more of an epistemological nature; that psychology and psychoanalysis are not really scientific (e.g., Hilgard: "very bad science," R. Waelder 1960, p. 21), because their laws cannot be put into mathematical form.

I wonder very much whether this requirement does justice to the problems which are unique and relevant to the field of general psychology and whether the protestation in form of a mathematical purism is any different from the scholastic objections to the findings of Galilei and especially Kepler—namely that they did not obey the postulates of Aristotelian physics and metaphysics when they proceeded to a higher level of abstraction (see Wurmser 1977). Do we not need hypotheses and general laws of a nature peculiar to the field of psychology—namely laws of meaning instead of currently used mathematical formulae?

A fourth reason is the impetuous rush for action. The method of psychological understanding is most time consuming and basically contemplative; the urgency to find immediate solutions to intricate problems does not tolerate the patient in-depth work with individuals. This insistence on having grandiose answers right away to great problems demands apologies from psychotherapists who work only with a small number of patients. They are considered a luxury in a world of misery and viewed with envy and resentment.

Anna Freud referred to a similar situation in the treatment of children when she expressed "astonishment that in this field we proceed to action without inquiring into the quality of the material with which we deal. I wondered then" (40 or 45 years ago), "and I still wonder, what our position would be if we entered, for instance, the field of metal work or work with wood or leather merely on the basis of feelings—because we liked it or because we disliked it or because we wanted to alter its shape. We would not get very far" (1967, pp. 227-228).

So all in all we find psychology in its proper sense ground and riven between the two huge millstones of social and physiological sciences. The vast realm of introspection, of emotional reality, and of symbolic actuality and creativity is known to the public mainly in superficial vulgarizations and to so many scientists as an area of impractical and unscientific pursuits (see the outstanding exposés by Waelder 1960, 1962, 1967, 1970, 1973, and by Kohut 1973). This seems to be particularly glaring in the exploration of drug abuse.

Finally we may add the wholesale abdication of rational psychiatry, expounding the view that psychiatry and psychoanalysis are moribund, unjustified, unscientific, based on myths, and serve as tools of social suppression. Since I have dealt adequately with these obituaries in the *International Journal of Psychiatry*, 1972 (Vol. 10) we may bypass this beaten horse for this occasion.

As conclusion for this chapter: Denial and externalization of inner problems (in compulsive drug use in particular, as a theoretical field of study in general) are irrational defenses by patients and anti-psychiatrists alike. They are both part of what Hofstadter described as "anti-intellectualism in American life" (a parallel study could be written about the same attitude throughout human history and in all societies). It "is a resentment and suspicion of the life of the mind and of those who are considered to represent it; and a disposition constantly to minimize the value of that life" (1962, p. 7).

What Hofstadter's book tries to undertake, indeed what psychoanalysis endeavors as well, is to pursue the Socratic goal, "the ultimate value in existence of the act of comprehension" (p. 27). "The meaning of his intellectual life lies not in the possession of truth but in the quest for new uncertainties" (p. 30). For the anti-intellectual of many stripes "intellect *is* dangerous. Left free, there is nothing it will not reconsider, analyze, throw into question" (p. 45). The anti-intellectual "reveals a contempt for the reflective mind, for culture, and for the past" (p. 260). The compulsive drug user—in this sense—is a suffering anti-intellectual; his self-deception is an unwilling, unwitting betrayal of reason; that of the irrationalists in and against our field cannot be viewed that charitably. At least they *can* know when they violate what is our guiding value: "What a piece of work is man! How noble in reason! How infinite in faculty!" (*Hamlet,* Act II, Sc. ii).

CHAPTER 13

THE INSOLENCE OF OFFICE

The following chapter was the most difficult to write. If I followed my wish to lay out an unvarnished history of what I observed in errors and malfeasance in these twelve years of being deeply involved in a number of treatment programs, I would end up with several slander suits because it is absolutely incredible what abuse of power and position, fraud and intrigue, lying and deception, by the highest in political power and wealth as well as the lowest employee, is encountered in this work. Moreover, rumors, thick and fast, suspicions, heavy and dark, hang over many in the field: likely, but not provable. There is a matted mass in which unethical and illegal behavior of patients, families, staff, bureaucrats, and public officials are glued together and where wrong often cannot be teased out from right, where no action can be taken—a poisonous atmosphere pervading the treatment efforts.

In addition—and here of course I can be frank—this is the history of my own errors: lack of judgement, blind trust, rash actions, inability to see through the complex play of powers and interests which played with the program like six cats with one mouse, difficulties in finding my way through an administrative maze.

This aspect of overall pathology, a kind of microscopic social illness intertwined with the intrapsychic pathology, simply cannot be omitted in an honest examination of the theme posed by this inquiry: the hidden dimension in drug abuse.

The problems presented in this chapter point out the interweaving of the patients' defenses of externalization, projection and denial, of their ego and superego defects, but also of their eminent vulnerability as persecuted victims, with similar trends in many people attracted by this field. At times, the patients' actions directly provoke such pathology in the "healer," and often the reverse holds true.

Another aspect to be revealed is the fending off by "good society" (including the medical establishment) of such a tedious, "bad," "dirty," clientele, a profound ambivalence in institutions: the wish to "take affirmative action" in a most painful area of concern, countered by anxiety, disdain and disgust—efforts sabotaged and undone.

I am convinced that most physicians involved in drug abuse programs have undergone similar experiences, and an understanding by professional and educated lay public alike may make it easier to deal with our problems in the future. Remedial arrangements may be found which will reduce the likelihood of some of the frightful occurrences to be submitted now to your eyes.

It is also obvious that these professional hazards sooner or later befall many responsible for such programs and drive them out of the field. The tensions, vilifications and frustrations make both therapeutic and scientific work often almost impossible; most importantly, they affect the reputation and public standing of a professional to such an extent that it may be difficult ever to wipe out the stigma.

I shall give many examples; but they will remain anonymous as to place, time and person.

Corruption and Abuse of Power

Again a "case history," but this "case" is an entire program; its history reflects both individual case histories and systems pathology. In establishing one of the programs, I encountered incredible administrative problems. Because of a fight between the health department and the particular institution in which I worked, another hospital was given the grant and permitted to subcontract with us to run the program. That in-between hospital in turn was supervised by a community board. The money was available to treat two hundred narcotics addicts; but the budget in all line items had to be agreed upon by four independent powers: the state agency, the in-between hospital, its community board, and the eventual recipient, the host institution with its own rigid standards and rules. Eight months into the fiscal year the budget had not yet been agreed upon, although we had been compelled to start operating a large methadone program from one huge room which was largely unfurnished and either overheated or freezing. If we had waited, the grant would have been withdrawn. No employee got his first pay for the first two to four months. I, therefore, had to advance from my own pocket the pay check of everyone whom we had to hire. I had put in about nine revised, re-justified budgets. Conjoint sessions of the four parties involved were set up—yet usually only two or three attended. Agreement seemed impossible.

CASE 22: EDMUND

During those harsh months a lawyer with good credentials whose wife had contacted me a year before offered his services for free because he wanted to gain experience for leadership in another health organization. Edmund saw a few of our patients in legal counseling. Because of the excellence of his work we soon hired him as a part-time, paid consultant. As he became more deeply involved in the program and realized the crushing problems we faced, he offered to come on fulltime as administrator and requested, together with full salary, an academic appointment. Within perhaps four months, the whole mess was cleaned up: the budget (for the now almost past year) accepted, the hiring of employees facilitated. His method was a ruthless aggressiveness which literally bulldozed through the obstacles.

However, as soon as Edmund got his academic position and full salary he faded out, came less and less frequently to the program, did not put in the new budget, was utterly belligerent both towards the leadership of the program and the state officials when urged to bring the financial situation in order. With considerable skills he tried to incite part of the personnel against the leadership and thus caused endless bitterness and strife. Without official knowledge he set up an illegal separate fund into which patients had to pay small fines for various minor infractions and which was used in good faith by the directors of the program for recreational or emergency services for the patients. This secret fund was to assume yet another role a few years later.

In the meantime, his wife, a prominent, respected scientist, suggested that she develop a new method of psychological testing. Within part of a grant this project appeared feasible. All talk, little action! All in all few samples were tested over a period of about three months. She refused to write the summary of method or findings on the concluding account of the grant project or to share in writing any of the results. Her husband, in the meantime, put in a few hours of work a month in the institution, but remained fully paid. He was warned and threatened; then the affair was brought to the attention of superiors. No one was eager to take action and to bear the shame of having supported and promoted an "obvious troublemaker." Finally, about six months after the beginning of this eminently destructive course, a young substitute administrator discovered that bills were paid to Edmund's wife for the testing which were totally out of line with the work performed and the understanding achieved. Nearly seven thousand dollars had been paid into a dummy organization, run by the fabulous couple, over the forged signature of the head of the Division. Only at this point was it possible to fire Edmund and to launch a criminal investigation. The legal authorities and the police were ready to press charges against Edmund and wife, but, on higher orders, no action was taken. Today Edmund is a well known politician in another state who runs on a platform of "integrity and honest government!"

VAUTRIN (CASE 8, CONTINUED)

The few people in the program who knew about the hidden scandal would have had good reason to believe that crime pays. One of those was Vautrin. He had been an addict since the Korean War, was a very intelligent, gentle, kind person, married, with four children between ten and twenty. He had been in and out of jail, a "hustler" and pusher, until he entered one of the programs in town, became first a counselor, then a senior counselor. He then joined the program under discussion at its inception as coordinator of counseling. He was the soul of the program, apparently trusted by patients, staff and leadership alike. Very gradually and at his own request he even weaned himself off methadone.

Emotionally he was quite dependent on my approval and support which I gave him unstintingly. He worked day and night for the program. Eventually he was made its director. Shortly thereafter I developed a chronic illness which made my involvement in the program less intensive; there were weeks when I was seriously ill at home. Despite that, I had contact with Vautrin nearly daily, often several times a day. About eight months after his assumption of the directorship I had a feeling that a shadow was hanging over him, a slight sadness or distrust. I saw him come over to my office less often, less exuberantly. He kept asking me whether I really trusted him. Or he assured me that I could trust him absolutely. At first I ascribed this to the grave problems we had with community and institution in planning and setting up an in-patient facility, mainly for polydrug users. There had been perhaps a year or more of unsuccessful efforts in which Vautrin had spent many hours trying to convince politicians, community leaders and others. Though the money was available our plans never reached fruition because of the phalanx of resisting forces. Once everything seemed "all go" when a community group blasted the plan and finished it. Another time we had a building within the circumference of the hospital which needed no outside approval by community boards. On the evening after we had gotten the go ahead for definitive planning, the vacant building was burned down by arson.

Suddenly Vautrin disappeared. Five days later he called me, told me he had helped several members of his family and a co-worker in awful financial distress (after an accident, etc.), had accumulated such debts that he was on the verge of eviction and suicide. A colleague of mine and I spoke with him the next day; he still appeared in a state of severe depression with a paranoid tinge to it. The two of us advanced him the most urgently needed money and urged him at once to see a psychiatrist (he had insurance); I made the necessary referral.

A few days later a call came from the State agency inquiring why we permitted Vautrin to sign checks for the program. We looked into the matter, found out about the existence of the fund which had been illegally set up several years before by Edmund. Vautrin had started overdrawing it massively and thus its existence came to light. The same day that I found this out from the Health Department, Vautrin vanished for a second and final time, leaving in his wake an avalanche of bouncing checks, all under the name of our program, all cashed with his identification card as director. Four months and many thousands of wrongly cashed dollars later he was arrested, put on bail, continued charging the empty account, overdosed twice, jumped bail and disappeared for good. He is said to be a dealer and addict in another city and to have vowed he would rather kill himself than ever go back to jail.

After his disappearance, a variety of "ghosts" emerged from within the program. One counselor, Bardolph, told a ghastly story which had occurred about midway in Vautrin's tenure as director. A patient had claimed that Vautrin was in cahoots with the underworld and had promised him extra medication for certain shady services. Since Vautrin was trusted by everyone, the counselor discussed the story with him. A few days later, the patient was shot in the stomach and told by the unknown assailant that if he snitched again, he would be killed. A few months later, when we were told by the State to switch from methadone diskets to liquid methadone, suddenly nearly half of our patients complained about mild to severe withdrawal symptoms. We had a thorough investigation by FDA and DEA, besides the state's agency. No cause was detected. A few weeks later, after Vautrin's absconding, it was relayed that for some time he had brought extra medication to a number of our patients. The suspicion lingered on that the massive occurrence of withdrawal symptoms in patients was due to stealing and selling of methadone by our trusted director.

When I try to understand what happened to lead to Vautrin's decompensation, after about five years of greater and greater success, I came to the following conclusions:

He had remained dependent on me in form of an "idealizing transference"; when I fell sick and was largely unavailable, his support had fallen. It became known later on that he had always felt very insecure, frightened, threatened—under a facade of efficiency, eagerness, self-confidence and utter honesty.

His self-esteem depended on continuous success, recognition and admiration. When he partially failed, he felt a total failure and could not stand the collapse of his self-esteem.

In only seeming contradiction to the point just made, I also suspect that he was one "wrecked by success": that the burden of living up to ever increased responsibilities and positions became too heavy for him. The higher he climbed, the more he feared to fall low, ever threatened by any small slippage of control and power. Every minor failure confirmed his fear: "I cannot fulfill the tasks given to me. I do not deserve what I have attained."

He had been off methadone for about two years by the time of his disappearance. The question remains: would he have managed to deal with the enormous external and internal pressures with the help of this artificial booster of self-esteem?

Another incident then emerged: several counselors approached me after Vautrin's disappearance with accusations that Conrad, another ex-addict counselor, the special protégé of Vautrin, was not only involved with dealing in drugs, but had beaten and nearly killed the girlfriend of one of the counselors, that the girl, however, was scared for her life and thus feared to press charges. Moreover Conrad was said to have been deeply involved with Vautrin in underground activities. All these allegations were transmitted to the legal authorities, three times, with several months intervals and new suspicions added. Nothing could be proven. Firing, because of civil service restrictions, was impossible, although we considered Conrad both incompetent and very, very suspect. Only on the grounds of a great many instances of absence and lateness—all put in letter form every time—action appeared possible, about a year later and really on these relatively unimportant grounds, but once again dismissal was denied.

In the meantime Bardolph himself was accused by a female patient of sexual seduction; he denied it but admitted to me that he had engaged in sexual activities with other patients "in order to help them" and promised never to do it again. Bardolph, not an ex-addict, a rather simple man, was sufficient in his other functions. He could not be fired. Eventually he left on his own accord to take on a potentially more lucrative position in a penal institution. Other counselors were bribed by patients or they enticed money from their patients. Again firing proved impossible, although some of the stories made the newspapers.

What is the moral of this "case history of a program?" I think several conclusions have to be drawn from these experiences:

The setting up of such a program is fraught with political problems: with rivalries and conflicts between institutions and agencies, with power games by bureaucracies and community boards, overwhelmed at times by competitive forces. One expression of this is how fluid the budget is; one year there is greatest pressure to build up and to spend all the funds; the next year much is gone. Another expression is the passive, and at time active, resistance by hospitals against drug and alcoholism programs. No hard money is given—indeed after many years—even to the leaders of such a program.

The ordinary rules of hiring and firing should not be applicable to this type of program. The system of institutions, with their guidelines and regulations, result in the keeping on of incompetent staff, while we cannot keep the most competent people (it is impossible, almost as a routine, to change position and salary of somebody who proves especially qualified—so he leaves); the leadership is burdened with the silent knowledge of what is wrong.

Such programs attract—besides highly motivated and capable people—severely disruptive, "sociopathic" persons of varied social background: white middle class as well as black and poor, "squares" as well as ex-addicts.

Some staff cannot be trusted; the program atmosphere itself tempts weak characters to abuse their power.

Ex-addict counselors present a very severe problem; some of them prove to be indispensable, trustworthy and indeed able to find out what remains hidden from "straight" people. Yet, one has to be particularly on guard against excessive trust in some of these "helpers." There is much need, perhaps even as a mandatory requirement, for direct and regular psychotherapeutic support of these counselors themselves (if not of every counselor, ex-addict or not.)

The patients themselves are afraid to inform. The "street culture" with its code and menace reaches not only deep into the patient population (even after years of treatment), but far into the staff itself.

The power of the staff to discipline patients or grant favors has to be kept at the barest minimum.

Outside surveillance, not just auditing for misuse of money, but for abuse of power, for incompetence and dishonesty on whatever level of management, with the power to withdraw funds from the institution, should be mandatory. Grievance procedures help, but, in the light of the fear of informing mentioned above, may be a weak tool.

The problems encountered in chapter 6, mainly narcissistic conflicts, denial of inner problems, externalization, and, above all, the shakiness and splitting of the superego, plague not simply the patients and ex-addict counselors (who were once patients themselves), but tend to infect most who touch this population.

Despite the intra-institutional rigidity which makes efficient operation well nigh impossible, greatest value has to be given to the unreserved backing and support lent by the medical authorities within the hierarchy. Without their succor the many battles and scandals just described (and those omitted!) would have been insufferable—as the next "case history" will show. The program of this type develops so easily into a tar baby, sticking to its leaders, blackening their names, weighing them down into the mud. They see and hear and are powerless to change it.

I have noticed similar abuse of trust in other programs. The abuse of public funds, the severity of the condition we deal with, often the helplessness of the victims, the exploitation of the difficulty and complexness of starting off such programs thus makes it not merely a reason for personal grief, sorrow and outrage and a self-searching inquiry into one's own errors of judgment which hindsight always shows in a glaring light. Rather I think it is a general, widespread problem which has to have some public interest because of the large investment of funds and public trust in what has been called "the drug abuse industrial complex," and especially of therapeutic ethics which are involved (see also Wieder and Kaplan).

Still—despite the horrible events described—the benefit to society of such a program outweighs by far the social costs to be described in Appendix D. We are continually amazed how much a great number of patients really improve socially and emotionally, despite all these terrible events. The value of what is being done, of the overall structure, of the help rendered by the honest half of the personnel, seems to surpass by far all these evils. The split in the program is not unlike the one in an individual patient like Andreas: the horrors and tragic aspects do not wipe out the good, the honesty, the kindness, the generosity and helpfulness. It is scant consolation, but it should make us very humble!

The Conflict of Powers or the Six Ring Circus

Another briefer "case history" of a program should illustrate and probe in depth the first point already made.

Some years ago I was invited to start a drug abuse program at a very prestigious institution. Chairmen and deans assured me repeatedly before my assent to coming that such a drug treatment program was the highest priority of the hospital vis-à-vis the community and that I had their fullest support; an entire building was pledged. I agreed, secured within about three months various contracts and grants in the value of several hundreds of thousands of dollars and tried to start the operation. Instead of the building I was given two moderate sized rooms in a basement. As promised to granting agencies the functions had to start within ninety days. I hired about two dozen employees. But still no building—and more and more roadblocks. The patient fees which should have formed the basis for the matching funds, the building, other services which would also have helped to match the Federal funds, all were lacking. I was caught in a circle of which I found no way out: not enough patient income, not enough space, no Medicaid support, on the other side the promise of comprehensive services, broad teaching obligations and the task of "community education," a hired staff whose livelihood depended on the survival of the program, two competing community boards, both organized or used by fighting factions from within the institution, eventually the freezing of most expenditures by the institution because of insufficient outside funds. After about half a year I myself found in the vicinity a delapidated vacant building, although it was full of rats. Our staff rehabilitated it as best they could—painted it, poisoned the fauna, cleaned it, carried in the most pitiful furniture where they found it.

Only eight months after this nightmare had started I learned two facts which had been carefully concealed from me: (1) that the hospital itself was in such dire financial straights that it had allowed the program to come in only under one condition—that it would not cost it any money (but rather bring in more!). Therefore, at the emergence of the first financial shortfalls (which, with adequate support, could have been avoided) they froze us out. (2) That there was a mortal battle between dean and chairman of the department which brought me in. Our program was merely a pawn in that struggle.

When this became clear I was urged by all sides to get money wherever I could find it. However, the State's agency was at that time not interested in treatment. Most of its funds were to be given to "prevention" (school programs) or to urine testing! My first timid approach to the newspapers describing our plight was changed by the reporter into a vicious, paranoid attack on the drug abuse agency, supposedly launched by me. A correcting letter by me and my superior was not printed. One thing was sure: In a most difficult situation I had made the enemies I least needed.

But in the ensuing months the problem grew much worse. It became clearer and clearer, and some of the administrators told me outright: the institution wanted us to fold up.

But by this time we had over two hundred narcotics addicts in treatment, and a large and mostly quite competent staff. I contacted the Federal sponsors. They advised me to approach the political authorities for necessary funds and not to hesitate to put public pressure on the institution since the latter, not I personally, had given the promises to provide the required services. We addressed the legislature and went with a prominent politician to the chief executive of the State. The necessary funds were promised. Three weeks later there was no money. Further contacts remained fruitless. Then the supporting politician publicly reminded the executive of his promise which was promptly denied. Accusations of lies flew back and forth on TV and in the newspapers.

And only then did I learn a third fact: that the institution was engaged in most sensitive negotiations with the state government about much larger sums of money for another large scale health program. My own negotiations and the eventual massive and adverse publicity threatened their secret parleys. I felt that I was in a six ring circus: caught between Federal agency, State government, two warring factions within the institution, two hundred difficult patients, and an increasingly angry, rebellious, even openly fractious staff (some sought community support, others mobilized the media). But the signal of fire was given when the dean's right hand and emissary suddenly showed up at a staff meeting of the program and proclaimed that the staff better look for different employment since the funds were not available for continuance of the program. It was one of the most trying, traumatic experiences in my life. No matter what I could do, it appeared hopelessly bad. I decided to follow some of my employees and to use the media to put moral pressure on institution as well as

State government, as a last ditch measure to save program, staff and patients. I knew I was risking my own position.

It worked, and yet it did not work: suddenly all the money was available, suddenly the institution stood piously by its promises, suddenly new and better quarters and better furniture were found (for the new directors), but I was demoted. Because of the wide public support I could not be fired outright—immediately. The dean's men took over—political hacks, of little professional competence. The new chief issued the ukase that all patients not paying their fees would be discharged at once. "If they have no money, let them pawn, fence, steal—but bring the money." This man, untidy, habitually chewing his orange neck tie, was of shady reputation and even shadier acts in his brief tenure as chief. His deputy, an irascible, coarse professional, soon laid his hand on a particularly pretty female addict within the program whose husband was securely locked up in jail, and began living with her.

In the clinic building itself the rats came back; the house was declared a firetrap, but the clinic went on functioning there while the chiefs had a separate, luxuriously equipped building.

All the stuff was there for a Dickens' novel!

I got an honorific title, was kept on for the time, but stripped of responsibility or of the ability to do much meaningful work, and after about half a year I was bluntly told that I was persona non grata in the institution. Thus I left. Most of the old staff had been fired. Eventually the institution removed the program from under its aegis and gave it to the "community," thus getting rid of the "tar baby"!

In retrospect I can see many errors I made: no prior commitments in writing; a naive trust in the word of prominent people; ineptitude in playing the political game; perhaps ill-placed idealism: I should have quit before the conflicts reached unmanageable proportions. But I felt responsible toward the staff I had assembled, the patients we had taken on, and unable to leave them on a clearly sinking ship. And I learned that publicity and community support are double edged swords.

But I also was awed and terrified by the extent of cynical power games and hypocrisy, of duplicity and deception by omission and concealment, by ruthlessness and inhumanity of leading figures in medicine, hospital administration and politics. And I learned that the community primarily to be served was so splintered, so caught up in their own intrigues and in slogans (like being against "genocide"), that they were of no help at all.

I believe, in hindsight, that massive blunders were made by all concerned, including myself. I was not an innocent victim, but a naive physician whose therapeutic and scientific ambitions blinded him against early recognition of the true severity of what was going on, and who, once caught in the trap, reacted with unpolitic public anger against the authorities which threatened the program from all sides. Oedipal revenge in such a situation decidedly proved not very useful.

A Bright Counter-Example

As the dissolute Prince Hal took on the Crown as Henry V, he vowed: "to mock the expectation of the world, / To frustrate prophecies, and to raze out / Rotten opinion who hath writ me down / After my seeming...."

And turning to the advocate of "addiction," this "globe of sinful continents", Falstaff: "Presume not that I am the thing I was, / For God doth know, so shall the world perceive, / That I have turned away my former self, / So will I those that kept me company." (*Henry IV, Part II*, Act V, Sc. iii, ll. 126-129, and Sc. V, ll. 60-63).

These words can serve as motto for the next case history which not only illustrates again very many of the points I made throughout this book, but can serve as a positive, encouraging counterweight to the dark events I just described.

CASE 23: THE SEEKER

This is an ex-addict counselor working very successfully and for a number of years in a methadone program. He is now close to forty, but much younger looking. He is described by the director of the program in which he worked as a rare combination: having the intuition, empathy and understanding of a former addict, high intelligence and self-control, and undoubted integrity and honesty.

He was kind enough to give me the following oral autobiography, which, except for some abbreviations and condensation, appears here practically unaltered:

I come from a lower middle class family, father an alcoholic, with many extramarital relations, mother a naive country girl, eleven years younger than my father. I was their only child. From early years on there were many arguments, many fistfights between mother and father, grandfather and father. When I was about five, my father tried to kill himself with iodine. He told me what he had done; he really put a heavy responsibility on me. I told my grandfather, and my father was brought to the hospital. He was pale and clammy, and it took him a long time to convalesce. I did not know what death was, but I was very anxious.

Other early memories include: when I was three or four, I made a mudball around a stone and threw it at a car. I hit the driver in the head. As fate (or intention?) wanted to have it: it was the policeman who had locked up my father for drunkenness before. He chased me down, took me home, and asked my mother: "Is this your little dumpling? He sure is a chip off the old block." I remember, too, when I was five repeatedly seeing Father go to the bathroom half nude, with his erect penis, after sexual activities in the adjacent room. At least once I saw their intercourse; it was unclear to me what went on, but I was fascinated.

When I was six or seven, my parents separated for the first time, about a year or two later for the second and final time. Both events were traumatic. During the first separation, my mother had many boyfriends. We lived under very crowded circumstances. I slept in Mother's bed and was often awakened by her intercourse with men in the same bed. I felt bad about it, really jealous and rejected. Often my mother would leave me alone in the second-story apartment, to go out with one of her lovers. I remember how once they slammed the door and locked me in. I climbed out of the window and jumped onto the roof of the car, so they would not leave me alone. They gave me a beating and left me at home anyway. The second separation of my parents occurred while I was sent to relatives on the West Coast. I didn't hear from either parent for about four months until my mother picked me up and brought me, not to home, but to a strange apartment in another city and with a new boyfriend. Where we had lived before, the city looked glamorous; the new place was dilapidated, surrounded by junkyards, a rough area with many alcoholics and ruffians. It was really frightening. From that time on, my mother lived with my future stepfather, whom she married when I was eleven. He was a passive man given to drinking sprees of two or three weeks duration. We resented each other. Later, we would be physically aggressive against each other. He would challenge me.

Once he wanted to hit me with an axe. I injured him several times with my fists. I broke his nose when I was perhaps fifteen. In general, I was a hostile, nasty kid. I did not have much restraint placed on me and was often with a gang of kids, left to my own devices. In school I felt bored; I shouted at the teachers, and became truant more and more often. Even when I went to school I didn't do a thing. Eleven times they called me to juvenile court for truancy. The judge was actually more upset with my mother than with me. My mother told her in court: "Put him away; I cannot do anything with him!" I felt rejected again, as all along; she really did not care about me. I have more negative than positive feelings about her. Actually, action was never taken. Between twelve and fifteen I used to drink heavily. My mother was a drinker, too, and both fathers were. I did it although I had and have a profound antipathy against alcohol. I drank sporadically, usually with peers. It was a traumatic time in my life. At fourteen I started stealing cars, together with others, for joyrides. I picked fights, and was involved in vandalism. Then I became interested in girls. My only goals at fourteen were to have a car and an acquiescent female. Now—while I tell you this—I suddenly realize how similar all this is to my real father: the drinking, chasing women, the fondness for cars (he was a cabdriver), the violence. I identified more with him. I felt Mother had given him a raw deal as she had to me. We were both rejected.

Then, some of the kids with whom I was running around were into drugs, mainly marijuana, some amphetamines. At first, it was just a lark. It was like with alcohol: I would not have done it on my own, but I did it with the group I got involved with. Especially I had two close friends for whom I had a lot of respect, and they were smoking marijuana. That meant something special; it had an aura of belonging to a select group [this was in 1951!]. It went with good clothes and jazz. I was about fifteen by then. It was a symbol, something exotic, not the marijuana itself. It had been a bad year, but then I began to feel an identity: that I belonged to this group of people who used marijuana. It was like joining the Masons! The rituals and all. We had moved so often, and every time that we moved my identity would change. The only thread holding all that together had been my "acting out" (especially aggression)—much in order to get attention. But when I joined that little marijuana group, I stopped my "acting out." Aggression was taboo; it would have drawn attention to us. And then there was the concept of "coolness": you had to be more mature, not a child anymore, once you belonged to them.

At that time, at my insistence, I was in a vocational school; I had never gone to junior high school, and I went to that school not with any goal in mind, but that I could piddle around in the woodshop and have other physical action. I got a lot of attention because—to everybody's surprise—I scored very high in a citywide test, although I had never done any schoolwork. It was nice to get recognition. I was even invited to be the prompter in the drama club.

Then, in an assembly, a friend asked me for a quarter. When I handed it to him I was grabbed by a teacher. I got belligerent because she made an incident out of nothing. I was hauled to the principal; I became profane, and the principal told me: "Goodbye, and do not come back!" That was the end of my school life. I went home only to discover that the same day my mother had left my stepfather. He was drunk. It was a double rejection on the same day. One or two days later, I came home to find nothing there except for my clothes; my stepfather had also left. So I decided to find a job at once, and I started working as an electrician's helper, a job I found through one of my marijuana friends. I was working for three months, self-sufficient, engrossed in taking care of myself. I did not know where my mother, stepfather, or father were, and I felt no concern about them! Three months later my mother left her address for me. I thought: "She thinks she has hurt me. I want to show her how fine I am doing." I went to see her with my pouch of tools, as a badge of achievement. On the one side I wanted to let her know: "I don't need you anyway; I can do okay on my own." On the other side, I wanted to be close to her, but didn't want her to know that. She was pleased, but cool and formal. We both were uneasy. She asked me to move into the vicinity where she was now living, back together with my stepfather. It was on the other side of town. I continued working a little longer, but then there was a poolroom there. I spent a lot of time there. There were more marijuana smokers there. I felt at home with them, but they were very different from the first group. They were not working, as a sign of "slickness." They were pimping and selling marijuana. And there were hard drug dealers there, too. But the marijuana users were looking down on them. In our group there were older fellows who were always dressed nice, had big cars, prostitutes, always money. I emulated them. One of them was the main distributor of marijuana in the city; he took a liking to me. He was perhaps thirty-five. He said that I was a "sharp kid." He gave me, at discount price, large quantities of marijuana. I made a lot of money as a marijuana dealer. Also, I smoked it daily, three to five times, for one year, and without a break. I felt much better about myself. Everything lifted my self-esteem: the marijuana, the money, dressing well. And I got a lot of deference from others. I had power over people who were much older than I was. For the first time in my life I had power. It made me feel good. Then, one day, a shipment from Mexico didn't arrive. Suddenly everything was gone. It was a strange experience. I didn't feel right; something was lacking. I was seeking, but no one had marijuana. Then I ran into a junkie; he offered me dollar pills, heroin; I was seventeen. I was skeptical at first, but I knew: "To take it once was no problem. I have taken other drugs, I want to try it—just for the hell of it." I still remember the feeling when he injected it in my arm: it was a warm rush; I grew two or three feet, a tremendous feeling of power. I felt so much in control. It was almost like an orgasm, as if the whole body was pressed into a warm place, the comfort of a baby in the womb, such a well being. But still I had no particular desire to repeat it. My mother had left for the South. I did not go with her. I went with a friend who, when we were strolling once, suddenly discovered a doctor's bag on a back seat of a car. We went in through the closed window. It was in broad daylight. If you are well dressed, do not act furtively, but with self-confidence and as if you did something right, and people will ignore you. That became our specialty: to steal doctors' bags. We took only drugs and left the instruments behind. What use would I have for an opthalmoscope or a stethoscope? I would like to think of myself as a "considerate thief." Then, I was by now about eighteen, I suddenly got a telegram that my mother had died of a coronary in Florida. Since I had no money (I had lost my marijuana trade and group because of the hard drugs) I stole a couple of bottles of whiskey, sold them and took the train. I arrived just in the nick of time for the funeral; and I was in acute withdrawal, too. I felt bad that I couldn't even cry or really feel sad. But when I saw my stepfather's brother carting all my mother's belongings away, I became hostile, and we got into a fistfight. He took a hammer and chased me; then I pulled my pen knife and chased him. The police came and adjudged rights and belongings to the "uncle." When I came back north I felt extremely depressed and began using drugs really heavily. It was insulating me from feeling hurt. I had such a poor self-image. It was like with marijuana before. Both took away my emotional pain. Marijuana, in addition, had made me feel that I did belong. Heroin was an escape from hurting all the time, yet now I didn't feel like being close to anybody and was isolated. Heroin was much more powerful in that direction. It had also another function: I had a lot of guilt and it took that away. Despite everything, I had gotten from grandparents and parents strong notions of what was proper and what was improper. I am sure I had a lot of incestuous guilt. I had open, conscious fantasies of having sex with my mother, since much earlier. She had been seductive, sleeping with me in her thin nightgowns. And I also remember that when I was away, age five or six, I slept in the same bed with my mother's sister who resembled her a lot. She was about eighteen and played with me sexually.

But to come back to that time; I was about eighteen when I met my wife-to-be. We liked each other but didn't have sex. Then, later on, I was arrested, spent eight months in jail and in Lexington. I had nothing to come back to but my drug-using friend and that girl. She had just broken up a very painful relationship with a married man. We both were like two lost sheep and found each other. For a while I stayed with my friend and refrained from drugs. His parents were a kind of surrogate parents for me. I found a job in a steel mill. When I started having sex with my wife-to-be, I discovered that she had had a sexual affair with the man while I had been away. She always had seemed to me to be a "nice girl," in contrast to the tramps I had been involved with before. I was extremely disturbed: "Now you see how worthless women really are!" My mother had also always been unfaithful. I saw her like my mother. And I felt inadequate sexually; I felt I would come out on the short end, if compared with her other, older friend—like with my father. I suffered from premature ejaculation. My fear was that I was merely her second choice. I was extremely jealous and demanding. I believe I was setting her up to reject me, and I kept testing her. But she did not reject me. She is a wise woman. If there is one factor in my life to account for my eventual success: it was she who continued standing by me. We have a wonderful relationship, now with three children.

But to go back. I slowly fell back into taking drugs. I didn't like my job. I was one of the few contacts for white addicts in the black community; so I became a middle man, a "runner" more than a pusher. I made a little money and got my drugs. I still had my pain and had help from heroin; beyond that, the drugs gave me more sexual control, especially with the premature ejaculation. It made me feel powerful. When I was twenty, and just after having married, I was arrested for possession of heroin and got a ten-year sentence. Nearly six years later, I was paroled. I had remained drug free in jail—which was no mean feat! I continued staying clean for a year and a half more—altogether about seven years. I worked for a publishing company as a proofreader. However, I felt I owed my family a debt and put everything on acquiring things. Thus I started to publish illegal drivers' licenses for a night club owner. One night he showed me a huge layout of drugs and offered me some for free. I turned him down, drove home, but then remained sitting in my car and asked myself: "I would like to know what it was that caused me such problems; now I am strong enough. Out of curiosity, I want to try it again." It was a rationalization. I went back and got Dilaudid for free—but it cost me a great deal! Was it again the pain, or was it the euphoria? Certainly I was under severe financial pressures, felt confined, tied down. There was no excitement in my life; and I surely had led an exciting life, a thrill a minute. I soon got addicted again, lost my job, went steadily downhill. My wife noticed it, of course. Her hostility showed as passivity; she withdrew from me, and that made me feel even lower. During the eighteen months of freedom and abstention, my self-esteem had been pretty poor. I had disliked my job. And I had not been in control over my life. It didn't take long, about a year, that I was caught again and sentenced for another ten years for possession: it was for a spoon with traces of heroin on it! The head of the narcotics squad promised me a bullet in the head.

My specialty during that time was burglarizing drug stores; that gave me drugs and funds. Another way of getting drugs was to con physicians. I had read up on trigeminus neuralgia and kidney stones. So I went to them and described my pains in detail and said that in the past a drug like panope or so—purposely mispronouncing Pantopone—had helped me. At first I got a milder drug, Darvon. I went back two or three days later: "Doc, it really didn't help me at all. That other drug—that really did it!" So he prescribed a narcotic. And that "helped." After a while, he wanted to stop it. But then I had a threat over him: "You know, Doc, now you have addicted me! I will report you unless you give me the drug." Most of the times that was successful for a while, especially if done in parallel with several other doctors.

In the case of "kidney stones," I used to come in limping, holding my loins and crying about my pains. When he had me urinate, I pricked my finger with a needle and let some blood drop into the bottle. The physician found his suspicion confirmed, and I got what I wanted.

But now I was back in jail for ten years. On appeal that conviction was overturned, but ironically an undeserved conviction for larceny, which I had not committed, stood. I had not bothered even contesting it. After four years I was paroled to a program of compulsory abstinence. I did not want to be under supervision. I only wanted to be out on the street, a vacation from jail, before I'd finish the remaining eleven months. I had no intention of benefiting from the program. I was sent back to jail, came to a road camp, fled for the holidays, and spent twenty months on the street, working without taking drugs, was re-arrested while on a methadone program, paroled to a Naloxone (the currently leading narcotics antagonist) program. That I hated: although I had not taken drugs, I always felt in withdrawal when I took Naloxone and actually had to take drugs to feel better. Perhaps it was just psychogenic. When they wanted to ship me back to the pen, I persuaded the head of the parole board that—instead of going back for the remaining two months—I would be given a chance to be put on a methadone program. For about four years I was on methadone, went to college on a scholarship, and finally was employed as a counselor. About a year ago I was, after very gradual withdrawal, free of methadone. For a little while I got Valium legally to cope with withdrawal symptoms and with just feeling bad. I also took a sick leave and left with my car alone, to go to Florida. I called my wife from underway: "I've got it licked. I am free!"

Why did I succeed? I am older and have a wider perspective now. My self-esteem has been strongly lifted by school and work. For the first time I felt an investment in a social life; for the first time, too, I felt that my life was meaningful. I had some sexual relations with women on campus and felt more comfortable about that, too. But I think the main reason comes down to this: I felt a hell of a lot better about myself. But even now, when I am frustrated, I feel the violence welling up in me. Then I have to get away. It is then very important for me to go fishing. I build my own rods with my own designs with threads. I have a great satisfaction from that. It is something artistic, and it reminds me of my grandfather who was a fisherman. It is almost a religious experience: to stand far out in the water, in waders, totally alone, to be in communication with Nature and to step one pace back instead of being all wrapped up in myself and the day to day problems.

But still I would like to have a psychiatrist to talk to from time to time, to unwind—quasi therapy-as-needed.

The pseudonym (Seeker) was of his own choosing. He left the program after several years and works now happily and successfully as a craftsman, making fishing rods.

The last two chapters have been devoted to "knowledge spurned and power abused" in the treatment of compulsive drug use. Surveys of the approaches currently undertaken to deal with severe psychopathology are presented in Appendix B (various modalities), Appendix C (treatment of psychotics), and Appendix E (psychotherapeutic methods). Appendix D deals with the exorbitant costs to society of the untreated illness.

Here, however, we turn to a study of the broader cultural and philosophical implications of what has been found so far, before we delve into the thorny question of what should be done.

Chapter 14

CONFLICTS IN SOCIETY, CULTURE AND PHILOSOPHY AS CONCURRENT CAUSES OF DRUG ABUSE

Henry Kissinger concludes his essay on Bismarck (1968) with a quote from a letter of the Iron Chancellor to his wife: "that which is imposing here on earth ... has always something of the quality of the fallen angel who is beautiful but without peace, great in his conceptions and exertions but without success, proud and lonely."

When we start probing now into the depths, not of drug abuse as a sociopolitical problem, but of the underlying psychopathology extrapolated from the individual to the culture, this quote is an apt symbol.

Paideia

QUESTIONS

For a psychotherapist the perspective is the view from his own starting point: from the individual's wishes and fears, his history and his structure. Closest to his inner life is the interaction with the family: the mute expectations and clamorous demands, the hidden myths and the loud proclamations, the power struggles, secret loyalties and the succor within the family. But moving outward, peer group, social group, and the cultural and philosophical matrix become more and more important as life progresses. When we looked at these factors logically, namely in regard to their specificity as causes of deviance, especially of compulsive drug use, we had to assign them low specificity. They were merely "concurrent causes." This, however, does not mean they are unimportant and should be neglected. On the contrary, via family they affect the very development of the individual. The question of etiological specificity and with that of explanatory power has to be separated from that of general importance and relevance. In regard to what follows I deny the former and affirm the latter.

We are also faced with a paradox. On the one side we know that compulsive substance use as well as the underlying psychopathology to which the largest part of this book is devoted are ancient, reaching in one aspect or other as far back as there was historical and psychological self-consciousness. On the other side we have the undeniable, very massive upsurge in drug abuse in countless variants in the last two to three decades.

Our first answer to this paradox was that the only drug abuse which really should be a source of concern is the intensive one, meaning preponderantly compulsive; if there is not a very large variety of drugs easily accessible, the "addictive character" resorts either to the one drug always easily available (alcohol) or to other massive symptoms.

Still we might keep wondering: Is there not something more specific which might tie the prevalent massivity of this particular psychopathology to our culture? The following is then an attempt to look for such more specific links.

Already the concept of concurrent or auxiliary causes allows us to pose the questions which emerge from the complex picture gained so far, when we inquire into how cultural, societal and philosophical factors help to bring about the mass phenomenon of drug abuse.

The first questions can emerge from what we recognized as the constellation of "specific causes": How are decompensation in narcissistic crises, and their pseudo-resolution by denial and ego split, by various modes of externalization, especially involving sadomasochistic acts, and accompanied by splitting, externalizing or collapse of the superego, and the search for artificial boosting of self-esteem—how are all these processes supported by deeper factors in our civilization?

How do the predispositional causes, especially the difficulties dealing with intense affects, the prevalence of narcissistic conflicts in individual and family, the lacunae or breakdown of inner and outer structures, boundaries, limits, and generally of consistency, and the decay of symbolic processes, mirror more general problems?

How does the precipitating cause, the acceptance, accessibility, the availability of a great spectrum of chemical means to deny and to externalize fit into the mood of our age?

As a psychotherapist and analyst, my view of society (including politics), culture, and philosophy is necessarily different from that of professionals in those fields. No analysis of culture, civilization, and society in their philosophical dimensions has a place here. The implicit premises are easily found in Langer (1972, p. 355; 1967, pp. 87–90); Trilling (1971, pp. 26, 43, 125); Parsons (1967, pp. 8-9, 141); Jaeger (1933, Introduction). It is "dynamic" and dialectic—a view at conflicts on many layers, hierarchies of contradiction, countervailing forces, opposite values, contrary needs and demands, and a view at compromise solutions, reconciliations, of these conflicts.

Thus, if we start out from the crucial heptad of specificity, it is likely that narcissism and pleasure, denial, externalization with the help of magical means, the role of aggression, especially of masochism, and "compromise of integrity" will perforce be pivotal concepts which help us in this attempt to tackle this intricate, general, vague problem of the broad concurrent causes.

Society is the structure of the polity, its forces and conflicts. Culture is the structure of values pursued by education, legislation, and work, and their conflicts. Philosophy, as pertinent for this investigation, is the explicit pondering of value hierarchies and priorities; its epistemological and metaphysical concerns are of no relevance here.

"THE SIXTH CULTURE" AND ITS SPECTER

I add some reflections about where we stand with our culture today, thoughts which are not related as yet to such a relatively minor symptom of sociocultural pathology as the mass drug abuse (including alcoholism), but directed at the wide arches of human history.

As we saw in the most recent political history (here in the Johnson-Nixon era, in Europe during the twenties and thirties and maybe again now), the unreflective, unphilosophical rush to *surface values* like expediency, pragmatic success, power for its own sake, the precedence of strategies of power over considerations of value priorities, of limitations to force, of the price of deception, and of the weight of past history—all this leads dangerously downhill, and ends up in a cutting off of the very roots of the democratic system (see Laqueur 1974, 1975, 1976, Draper 1975, 1976, Moynihan 1969, 1975a, b, Nisbet 1975).

Not only has this, our own culture to live as an island in a sea of anti-democratic, anti-intellectual, anti-humanistic societies and powers, threatened from all sides by extinction from the outside. Even more importantly, all along, the Mephistophelean forces of negation, of saying No to these cultural values and to the free creating mind were on the loose from within. Resentment, ruthless ambition and force, value nihilism were worms gnawing at the roots of this culture. Under the guise of unmasking and honesty they expressed narcissistic self-aggrandizement and virulent aggression and destruction. The *heart of darkness,* the deep shadow of our culture, found its most horrifying expressions in the holocausts (fiery mass sacrifices!), instituted by the two forms of totalitarian rules which indeed were born by our very own culture: the various fascist and communist dictatorships. Both are scarcely distinguishable in their methods and doctrines, in their unleashing of absolute narcissism and unrestrained aggression, in their adulation of an external ego ideal and the virulent mass projections and exterminations. Together they form an enduring, even growing threat of two giant millstones grinding our modern Western culture between them (see Waelder 1967, Laqueur 1976). As symbols for their force I chose their extreme, most villainous, least masked, most massive forms, the death camps.

With that, I go beyond the American scene and the strict historical presence and encompass the entire culture of democratic, scientifically led, technologically shaped societies of the West, beginning around 1800.

(I tentatively call it here "the sixth culture," following the "collegium trilingue," as described by Momigliano (1975)—the Jewish, Greek, and Roman cultures—the Renaissance and the Enlightenment.) Rangell postulated the centrality of what he called the "Watergate complex" as a symbol for the current American version of the "compromise of integrity" (1976).

However, the "shadow" of the American experience did not surface only in Watergate, nor is it restricted to the U.S. We have to study it in the historical continuity of the six humanistic cultures which were all along accompanied by a deep "discontent" and most noticeably in our own, the sixth culture: a sense of foreboding, a tragic undercurrent, a "heart of darkness" in Conrad's metaphor, a denied, but omnipresent shadow of narcissism, guilt, shame, and outward sadistic aggression. In Conrad's novel, a powerful symbol for this cultural "heart of an immense darkness," lying in the "hollow core" of our great Western tradition, the feelings are uncovered: "It was as though a veil had been rent. I saw on that ivory face the expression of somber pride, of ruthless power, of craven terror—of an intense and hopeless despair." The final words of the dying invader and rapacious, but eloquent, conqueror were: "The horror! The horror!"

Therefore, if we look at this "heart of a conquering darkness" not merely as an episode from the colonial conquest of the Belgian Congo, if we explore it not just as an American phenomenon, i.e., as "Watergate complex," but as a cardinal phenomenon of the entire Western culture of the last hundred and fifty years, it might be more appropriate to oppose the high ideas of "paideia," "Bildung," "culture," to their betrayal in its ultimate horror and perhaps allude to it as the "death-camp complex." Even the words *Auschwitz* and *Gulag* immediately evoke revulsion, disgust, terror. We do not want to acknowledge, we have to deny, we shrink back from the feelings and images called back by the unbearable memory of this darkest side of our culture; and yet can we ever forget that they are the ultimate horror we have to live with? One may object and say: "No, that is past or mitigated; it is the threat of nuclear annihilation, or of exhaustion of resources, the problems of overpopulation and famine, or of ecological disaster that looms." Admittedly, these are all great threats, but they are pale possibilities of external catastrophes if compared with the shadow which concretely and in everyday presence is stalking our culture, our life, our personal sense of meaning from the inside. The two forms of holocaust comprised in this symbolic expression live on and threaten again and again in one form or another; they were preformed in many shapes, and as such have even accompanied all of human history. Yet they have appeared as a haunting specter in more and more explicit and traumatic forms in these last hundred and fifty or two hundred years—precisely when the human spirit soared to its highest attainments. Goethe's words have become terribly true: "Where there is a great deal of light, the shadows are deep" (Gotz, Act 1, Sc. 3). This specter emerges in novels, philosophies, ideologies, mythologies and finally systematized mass sadism and mass paranoia throughout the "sixth culture." We encounter the specter in Dickens's greatest novels, e.g., in *A Tale of Two Cities* ("echoing footsteps"!), *Bleak House* ("fog everywhere"), and *Little Dorrit*, in Dostoyevsky's *The Devils*, throughout Nietzsche's work, most prominently in Kafka's short stories and novels, in the omnipresence of child abuse and of impulsive or systematic individual and collective brutality.

This "heart of darkness" is more than just Rangell's excellent description of the "compromise of integrity," but it encompasses it as well. It is an entire syndrome: the higher the ideals, and the more binding, obligating and greater the "paideia," the deeper this particular shadow of systematized horror uniting indeed precisely the core features which we studied earlier: unbounded narcissism, denial of affect and split in judgment (high rationality and total irrationality side by side—the great fear of our case 19, Andreas), wildly driven action and externalization (though usually combined with very massive projection), action partly in form of sadomasochistic torment, partly in form of other magical, total solutions of aggressive portent and content, and finally the reexternalization, projection, radicalization and suspension of the superego, its splitting up in lofty ideals, personified in an omnipotent leader, and sanctioning all brutality. The similarity of this broad cultural syndrome, the "Auschwitz-Gulag complex," this nightmare of our culture, has some similarities to the heptad described in compulsive drug use.

This entire, basically tragic conflict between culture and the united forces of narcissism and aggression, is papered over, covered by many variations of denial—the anti-tragic defenses just briefly touched on in chapter 9. Freud's own view of culture was pessimistic, "tragic." He spoke about collective narcissism (including the "narcissism of small differences"), about the collective superego and need for punishment, and above all about "the fateful question for the human species": "whether and to what extent their cultural development will succeed in mastering the disturbance of their living-together by man's instinctual drive of aggression and self-destruction." (1930, p. 145). He ends this great philosophical essay (*Civilization and Its Discontents*) with the question: who can foresee success and result of the intercession by Eros in this battle?

At least equally pessimistic is Eissler's outlook, forty-five years later (1975):

> No remedy has obviously been found that could counteract the excess of aggression and narcissism that is a property of the species Homo sapiens .... It looks as if all that mankind creates must turn against it, become tainted and corrupted. [and this pertains even to psychoanalysis:] "Beneficial as it has proved to be in alleviating and even in curing many forms of psychopathology, it fails in any attempt to use it to solve the grave problems of the present. [pp. 640–641]

His concluding sentence entails deep darkness; after speaking of Atlas as the mythical bearer of "the burden of existential horror" (used by Heilbroner as symbol for mankind), Eissler states: "Indeed, it is possible that Atlas may be freed of his burden in the foreseeable future."

To return, however, now to the cardinal and *tragic conflict of culture versus narcissism and aggression* and the use of a plethora of *anti-tragic defenses:*

Besides "paideia," the general education and orientation of the culture towards central, meaning-giving values, there are other strong counterforces against this syndrome, this "heart of darkness." The most important one, as history shows, is a long national legislative, judicial, and philosophical tradition of civil liberty, independent thinking, and of the eventual supremacy of the Law over any individual or power aggregate (the Executive, corporations). Thus, Auschwitz and Gulag are unlikely to appear in their extreme form in a society where these democratic traditions are profound, strong, and ubiquitously manifested in many details: in the general family atmosphere, the liberal spirit in schools, the pervasive sense of fairness stemming from the important role of sports, the ancient tradition of town meetings or "Landsgemeinden." However, even in these favorable circumstances, this really means only that the specter is tamed, the demons chained; they have not disappeared.

The differences between this cultural syndrome and the individual heptad described in compulsive drug users are subtle: Most of the narcissism in the former is vested in the leader, the omnipotent, idealized, "archaic self-object" in Kohut's theory, in compulsive drug users rather in the nuclei of the grandiose self. Projection plays a much more ominous and powerful role in the cultural syndrome than in compulsive drug use; so do introjection, primitive possessiveness, acquisition and incorporation.

What will be outlined here cannot be limited to American society alone, but is largely applicable as well to all democratic, modern societies, and to a lesser extent even to the vast totalitarian, anti-democratic, anti-intellectual conglomerate and power blocks under which the majority of mankind now lives (see Laqueur 1976).

But beyond that, more specificity can be added even here.

The diverse ethnic groups, and in particular the various minorities, show slightly different forms of the cultural syndrome, of the shadow behind the shiny surface. Again here is not the place to expatiate on these various value conflicts.

In the following investigation, I selected a path parallel to the one followed in the individual, studying the major societal, cultural and philosophical correlates to the relevant dynamic phenomena in compulsive drug use and thus also some of the interactions between society at large and this group of "lepers," these representatives, delegates, from the dark shadows of our culture, the "invisible," demonized men and women.

Inevitably, there will be considerable overlapping between the various chapters.

Narcissism: Conflicts of Self-Esteem and Power

THE DESTRUCTION OF COMMUNITY

At the beginning, I put what I consider most important from a social point of view, a cardinal social conflict which I keep observing directly in its interweaving on the one side with drug abuse and its politics, and with value fragmentation on the other, philosophical, side: *the dissolution of community versus the wish to belong,* to be a part of a large cohesive group (see also Moynihan 1969).

Despite the clamor about community psychiatry, community boards, community programs, I came to see with profound regret that by and large communities in the true sense barely exist anymore. I think of organically grown, cohesively structured wholes, groups of individuals and families, who share common basic values and goals, who partake in each other's joys and griefs, where each knows the other by name, history, weakness and strength. It is a horizontal cohesion and a vertical continuity as community through the centuries, thus even decreasing the threat of death and the limitation to individual power and existence. The real community lives on and encompasses with meaning and enduring value the individual's brief existence.

The mobility and with that rootlessness of technological society prevents the growing of an "organic community." Rare exceptions are: small villages, some strong ethnic groupings and congregations, a few very cohesive professional guilds. Most are geographically scattered, but emotionally and intellectually bound together by a bond of sharing, honesty, and individual respect. It is only in such communities that something which I consider of outstanding importance grows: one's "name," a balanced acceptance of the value of the person, thus resolving most narcissistic conflicts. I can best express it in the words of a Swiss author of great stature, a poet, who—like so many others—has not gained his deserved recognition outside the German-speaking world, Jeremias Gotthelf. He wrote them in a novel more than a hundred years ago:

> Whatever we do (and however we behave) leads—without our knowing it—to a habit, which one cannot get rid of .... And just as one prepares by one's actions an inside habit, one creates for oneself a name on the outside. Everyone works on this name, on this reputation, on this respect among people from childhood to the grave; every small activity, indeed every word contributes to this name. This name opens or closes the hearts for us, makes us worthy or unworthy, sought out or rejected. No matter how small a person may be, he has a name; the eyes of the people around him look at him and judge what his worth is for them.

He thought above all that we have to work on our name for honesty and integrity, for reliability and competence.

It is today's destruction of community and with that the loss of one's "name," of one's individual right for recognized identity and respect, for a stable place with its duties and dignity, with its holding solidarity and belonging, which has a host of consequences: regressive forms of belonging, for instance, the "communes" and "therapeutic communities," drug using groups and fraternities, individual and gang violence, the chaos in values and goals, the sense of "alienation," the loss of tradition on all levels (humanities, religious ceremonies, family herit-

_ ιeverence for cultural knowledge) (see also Forrest 1973).

κ. Hofstadter (1967) ascribes to this collapse of community the perversion of language, the fierce power struggles, the paranoid aggression, in a shifting population. "This has become a country in which so many people do not know who they are or what they are or what they belong to or what belongs to them." Hofstadter puts forth the hypothesis that pseudo-conservatism, the right-wing extremism, is "in good part a product of the rootlessness and heterogeneity of American life and, above all, of its peculiar search for secure identity." It would not appear farfetched to ascribe all political radicalism of this paranoid nature to the loss of roots in an organic community. The grown community is sought after, but is not found in the perversion of community.

One of the ways to create such a pseudo-community, to find a way out of the alienation and to achieve a sense of one's identity, is that propagandized by many drug devoted groups.

Accessibility and spread of drugs (including alcohol) always seemed to have accompanied crowding, urbanization, uprooting. One among several examples is the prevalence of narcotics addiction in "slums." In that connection a lot has been said about the sinister role the "pushers" play. It largely belongs in the realm of mythology. "Contrary to widely held beliefs," writes Jaffe, "the 'peddler' or 'pusher' does not play a major role in enticing nonusers to try either opiates or marijuana .... The pusher feels safe only when selling to a known addict. Furthermore, solicitation is unnecessary. Illicit drug traffic is a seller's market" (1965, p. 291). Social misery and early seduction, usually by slightly older playmates (the "dominant influence of deviant peer group associations"), are the main precipitating causes of addiction in the slum dwellers. Similarly, M. Partridge writes, "the best way to become an addict is to know one. Addiction is almost a contagious disease" (1967).

Quite typically, addicts' families are uprooted, have broken with their traditions of rural life or lost their spiritual background. Thus, it was observed that the same most blighted areas in Chicago, which showed the highest prevalence of narcotics addiction in the thirties, still showed the highest incidence in the fifties. Yet, twenty years before it was inhabited by immigrants from Eastern Europe, and now by Blacks from the deep South: "The old and new residents of these areas of high drug use had one thing in common: social and economic deprivation" (Mental Health Monograph, No. 2, HEW; no date).

Most addicts are unskilled laborers, coming from broken homes.

Meers and Gordon (1972) in their psychoanalytic studies of children raised in the ghetto remind us of the enormous intensity of raw violence, of undisguised sexuality, and of the lack of a structured environment in which these children grow up from earliest childhood on, in an unremitting uninterrupted stream of traumata.

Thus poverty and social degradation, overcrowding and overload in stimuli (especially noise and violence), absence of outer and inner structures, a pervasive lack of trust, lead to the socially important role of the drug using peer group as a substitute for a lacking family and social structure. Moreover the narcotics and sedatives are not merely the glue, holding some of these groups together; they directly substitute for what is missing: warmth ("the drug gives me a glow, a sense of warmth"), of belonging; they shut out the pain caused by noise and outer violence; they dampen anxiety and violent rage inside, and thus are both prop and surrogate for inner structure and control (see Kohut). Finally their rule as economic equalizer has already been mentioned (see Appendix D).

Mutatis mutandis, much the same can be said about the shiftless quicksand society of "upward mobility" in the middle and upper classes. It is true: naked aggression, open sexuality, and deafening noise may not be evident; violence is hidden behind curtains of civility. But the breakdown of extended and nuclear family (including, as we saw, of intergenerational boundaries and even of incest taboos on a grand scale!), the orientation towards success at all costs, in form of prestige, money, positions in sorority, clubs and institutions, etc., the actual absence of working or otherwise busy mothers—the constant din of social events without deeper communal bonds, the general "anomie"—all have very similar consequences: the child is lonely, neglected, trustless, "it does not belong." The only forms of belonging are a hectic busyness (scholastically, in business, socially) or the nightly gatherings of drug using groups in the clubrooms of indulgent (neglectful) parents, in fraternity meets, barrooms, and especially in the various hangouts on shopping plazas.

Concretely, I have heard a number of drug users from the suburbs complain that there are no places to go where they feel at home. When a girl I treated intensively for three years (not presented in this book) started staying away from drugs and from her friends with whom she had shared in drug use she had nowhere to go nor social contacts, nor did her friends: "The kids do not know what to do. They sit and take

drugs the whole weekend because they are bored." She wished there
were places in the suburbs where she could stay on the weekend with
interesting shows, movies, art, and rock music, discussions where she
could meet people of her age. She did not want to go to the center of the
city where crime is rampant and intelligent discourse is hard to find.
And at home there was no communication—only an endless chain of
demand, rage, and self-centered monologue.

Much drug use is derived from the search for intimate groups in
opposition to the "value-empty" surroundings (see Goode 1969).

Thus drug use becomes an important symbol of this conflict.
Especially in the ghetto and in many schools the use of particular drugs
(heroin in the first, psychedelics in the second instance) has grown into
a powerful symbol of group solidarity against the prestigious authority
of the establishment. It has become a kind of point of honor for the
outsiders and outcasts forming the contingents of the "counter
culture." Thus it boils down to the conflict between esoteric group and
ruling society, the alternative between belonging to a meaningful
though risky community and adhering to abstract, propagated, though
deeply questioned, principles of legality and authenticated authority.

As noted in Appendix D, this forming of a pseudo-community is by
no means so very different from the reigning entrepreneurial pseudo-
community, that of the "rat race," the preoccupation with and the
sharing of superficial goals: primarily by equating happiness and
fulfillment with material success, and accumulation of wealth and
titles. Both formations are largely artificial, based on facade values.

Still we are left with the breakdown of community, "name" and
shared value hierarchies of a higher order.

I know we cannot turn back the wheel of time. The nostalgia for the
small cohesive stable communities of yore will not recreate the
destroyed communities in the desert of modern life.

OUTER POWER VERSUS INNER CONTROL

Many of the following conflicts and paradoxes can be viewed as
expressions of this one cardinal contradiction in our technological
culture: The fantastic expansion of *outer control* which fulfills most of
the ancient dreams of mankind is not being matched by a similar
expansion of *inner control*. If anything, the extent of self-mastery may
have decreased. Outer power, unhinged from its inner moorings,
becomes arrogant and evil.

In 1868 the great historian and philosopher Jacob Burckhardt gave a series of lectures at the University of Basel. After his death they appeared as a small but monumental work, *Contemplations About World History*. There he wrote: "And now power in and by itself is evil, no matter who uses it. It has no stability, but is a greed eo ipso unfulfillable, therefore unhappy in itself and thus has to make others unhappy as well." (1963, p. 97). Similarly, Albert Schweitzer's words: "A dangerous world: Man dominates nature, before he has learned to dominate himself".

Power, control, mastery, greatness—all are aims sought and fulfilled on the outside; they are culturally sanctioned and promoted forms of externalization, and thus easily may serve the denial of internal conflict, of deeper yearnings and archaic sanction, limitations and threats. Thus most of the ancient magical fantasies of mankind about outer control have been fulfilled whereas most of the techniques used in the past to gain an (albeit often spurious) sense of inner mastery and control have been discarded.

In our culture of abundance the cycle of growing production and growing wants moved into the center of the official value philosophies of the Western world (Galbraith 1958). In a society of "economic abundance, automation and greatly increased leisure time a value system which demands that pleasure be earned through work would be obsolete" (McGlothlin and West 1968). Out of this achievement of affluence and technological mastery a whole new set of problems, questions, of forms of excessive pursuit (i.e., once more of hybris and nemesis), of tragic conflicts, arises.

The first question is raised by everyone who is disturbed about the chasm between affluence and opportunity with all their temptations available to many, and the poverty, hopeless degradation, lack of work and opportunity, the want of appropriate health care (including psychiatric help), the rootlessness, not-belonging and violence besetting the substantial rest of the population: How can we narrow this gap and give real help to the economically, culturally, psychologically, legally, medically deprived? The second question is a kind of counterpoint to the first. It has been posed very poignantly and convincingly by Nisbet (1975) when he rightly observes:

What has in fact happened during the past half century is that the bulk of power in our society, as it affects our intellectual, economic, social, and cultural existences, has become largely invisible, a function of the vast infragovernment composed of bureaucracy's commissions, agencies, and departments in a myriad of areas. And the reason this power is so commonly invisible to the eye is that it lies concealed under the humane purposes which have brought it into existence.

One origin and consequence of this new power shift is the demand for a new equality—not an equality before the law and of opportunity, but also (and lastly, instead) an equality of condition and result, and in that, surreptitiously "the affinity between centralization of power and mass egalitarianism" as Tocqueville long ago observed.

The extreme of this combined process of leveling and concomitant accretion of power to the state is reached by the authoritarian states.

The outcome of this process in the huge sweep of history in the past two centuries is the deep sense of alienation and estrangement, of not-belonging, of living in an empty meaningless world which philosophers, writers, sociologists—and our patients—so vividly describe, and which most of us have faced ourselves.

On this level the conflict is clearly between *liberty and equality*. If one is pursued to its extreme, the other is so massively violated that it leads to the destruction of both values in the end—a conflict of tragic meaning and dimensions not so different from the tragic conflicts described in chapter 9 in the individual. Is it not lastly once again Antigone versus Creon? Or in our case 4, Patpet, the ruthless pursuit of unrestrained freedom versus the compulsive need to bring about archaic forms of restraint and constraint, of limitation, structure, and punishment from the outside with its deprivation of his individuality? Or in most of our cases: the driven, restless, "exciting" transgression of all conceivable boundaries versus the yearning for the protection by a claustrum, even were it the cell of a jail, of a prison, or the encasement in the drug dependency?

Besides the enormous outer controls there are similar powers now over our body, again following Nisbet: "I am inclined to think that the advances of humanitarianism during the past century or two, together with advances in technology which have made possible a liberation, through drugs and machinery, from the incidence of pain our ancestors knew, have combined to give people a very different attitude toward the visible infliction of cruelty and brutality .... It is difficult, in our age of pain-preventives and pain liberators, to realize the extent to which the physical pain was once common place...."

The power of drugs and other medical means to prevent or at least relieve suffering is again of magical extent, compared with mankind's history of agonized suffering.

Immediately the question arises whether the same expectations can not also be fulfilled in regard to our inner life: Why not find a material shortcut to happiness, and instant way to self-recognition and a sense of personal omnipotence and Godlike self-esteem? And it is on that level that the drugs provide a sense of magical domination and manipulation over one's inner life analogous to the one that science and technique appear to give towards outside world and body.

The reverse of this pursuit of the value of *pain relief to its extreme* in form of the illusion of omnipotence over body and mind is the positing of, and search for, another value: the recognition that there are painful limitations to all our lives, that particularly no emotional problems yield to chemical or other material solutions, that the artificial boosting of self-esteem and power is followed by anguish and self-destruction, that lastly again we are faced with Aeschylus' "pathei mathos," learning through pain.

The extreme of this value pursuit is indeed despair, an almost *numbed sense of resignation,* as expressed by Ecclesiastes: Wisdom too is "merely a grabbing of air, because in the plenty of wisdom is a plenty of discontent, and who increases knowledge, increases pain" (Eccles. 1:17–18).

This conflict is thus once again magical power and "self-infatuation" (as Patpet called it) versus the inevitability of anxiety, grief, and pain when faced with loss after loss (and it is "when," not "if"!), with boundary after boundary, limit after limit.

Thus we are on a social, cultural and philosophical level once again faced with what emerged at the beginning of the book in that one individual case as the metaphor of the "quadrangle of fire."

To some of these points we shall return in due course.

THE DEMAND FOR PLEASURE VERSUS SELF-DISCIPLINE

On the one side we live in a society which puts a supreme value on material gratification, on easy pleasure and quick relief. It is almost a puritanism in reverse: "I claim the right for immediate happiness and for avoidance of frustration." And yet the same society expects utter discipline in its pursuits of scientific standards, delay of gratification in the learning of skills, and throughout a high degree of rationality in the operation of the instruments of technology.

The paradoxes go farther (reaching into factors of projection and the inconsistency in superego representatives). One example is the conflict between easy pleasure, immediate material gratification, and indulgence versus the often bizarre harshness of the responses by representatives of punitive and often corrupt authority (e.g., the death penalty for some small drug sales, sentences of twenty-five years for the giving away of one marijuana cigarette, entrapment and degradation of drug users by law enforcement officials). We shall come back to that aspect when we study the superego conflicts in the culture.

But as to the "omnipotence of pleasure": In our culture, the trivialization of sexuality, the noisy, shameless exhibition and din and deafness of intimacy, the boasting of anality in a modern version of Dickens' "bully of humility"—all these have become widespread, well nigh standards, to such an extent, that, as Lowenfeld described in his excellent, short article "Notes on Shamelessness" (1976), the very failure in this vaunted shamelessness is felt as a disgrace: "A young girl, who in other times might have been ashamed of offending moral standards if she had lost her virginity, may today feel ashamed if she is still a virgin; shame permits her to hide this failure" (p. 70). Pleasure, metaphorically speaking, has become the wild monotonous beat of solo drums, unleashed, driven and driving, instead of the full symphony in which all instruments participate. Intimacy, closeness, relationships have become what Walter Muschg (1956) in German called *zerschwatzt,*—"talked to pieces," "chattered asunder." As with our patient Patpet, there is incessant talk; there is a constant musical dribble, a stream of disconnected noise and imagery, a hectic running after gratifications—and yet such a profound sense of emptiness and lack of stability, dearth of substance, want of solidity!

Just as with drugs, so much of our social and cultural life is spent in an "expensive search for cheap pleasure."

And yet there is again a profound split in this. This enormous dome dedicated to pleasure and technological power stands on the rock of scientific discipline, of extreme controls over our machines, of systems within systems of repairing or building reliably these means of power and pleasure, and of the tyrannical force of time schedules. This paradox is profound and runs through most of our lives.

Implicit in this is the conflict of two basic patterns of life, of two value systems, and with that, of two types of morality. The first pattern is that dictated by immediate gratification of our main wishes, regardless of the rules, laws, and limitations of outside reality. These main wishes are those of self-aggrandizement and power, demands to be loved and admired, to show off, to possess, the drives of hunger and sexuality, and, very importantly, the expression of rage, anger, and the desire for revenge.

The second way is to adjust our impulses and wishes to the basic laws of nature, to allow delay and detours in our satisfaction, to permit changes in our aims, and to renounce many gratifications which are not compatible with an adult way of life in a complex, technologically highly sophisticated society.

Shakespeare summarized this polarity of the two ways of life in "Troilus and Cressida": "for pleasure and revenge / Have ears more deaf than adders to the voice / Of any true decision. Nature craves / All dues be rendered to their own." Who gives in to the demands of pleasure and revenge has to pay the price imposed by Nature (we would call it reality in our jargon today) on this way of life.

Of course we immediately recognize this first form of value priority as part of the "pleasure-unpleasure principle" (Freud 1911).

But what we also might add now is that this relentless search for primeval gratification and avoidance of pain—regardless of "Nature's dues"—is an eminently narcissistic orientation, disregarding boundaries and limits of cognition and ethics.

NARCISSISTIC CONQUEST VERSUS NARCISSISTIC RETREAT

Still another version of narcissistic conflicts lies in the observation that on the one side we belong to a culture and society where achievement and material success, the cynical striving for conquest, power, and fame, are considered more important than integrity and honesty, where fraud and tax avoidance are condoned or even legislated, as deception was in the Homeric epics. On the other side we also have the Christian credo emphasizing humility and renunciation, ferociously combating pride, but also the central precepts of responsibility, integrity, and self-limitation in Judaism. This contradiction indeed goes back far beyond our present culture.

Looking back over these four narcissistic conflicts we recognize that the mass abuse of drugs, especially of psychedelics, fits rather well into these vast antitheses: It emphasizes belonging (against homelessness), introspective power (against conquest of Nature), subjective pleasure (against impersonal, dehumanizing reality), abdication of worldliness and a neo-romantic quest for peaceful giving up of individuality by a dreamed union with the Universe (against non-reflective activism, pragmatism, competition). Thus it pitches one syndrome of narcissism against another: retreat into the self against virulent expansion of power. As usual, the very defense against a wish comes more and more to fulfill just this wish, in barely disguised form.

Even the counter culture, of which the drug culture is just a part, is pervaded not only by the same anti-intellectualism as its antagonists, but by similar conflicts. The one trend in our counter culture is toward drug induced passivity, the other toward drug shunning political radicalism and fanaticism. The Janus face of the counter culture thus apes the Janus face of technological society (see also Kristol 1972).

OMNIPOTENCE AND DEGRADATION OF THE PHYSICIAN

Szasz rightly pointed out how the physicians have acquired enormous power in reality, how they have become kind of high priests of a religion of health, if not material immortality, and that their holy water and rituals consist in most powerful drugs and procedures. For the first time in history medicine has indeed succeeded in mastering a great number of ailments and alleviating or removing a vast amount of suffering and pain. Medicine is one of the triumphs of rationality, of the combined use of scientific knowledge, technical instruments, and practical skills. Each single physician is, even more than a king of the past, master over life and death, every day, in a most real sense.

This puts him into a curious dialectic. On the one side he feels—quite realistically—very powerful, awed by the fulfillment of his own wild fantasies of magical omnipotence, chastened as he may be by failure, constant need for vigilance and often superhuman strain and stress. Still his power is enormous. And so are the temptations of power: The patients who do not improve are reminders of the boundaries, become an insult to his illusion of omnipotence and thus a source of rage.

Or what is not subject to his technical, scientific control, especially the emotional problems of his patients, need still to be subjugated by technical means: by drugs or surgery, instead of appropriate interventions (counseling, psychotherapy, analysis). They medicate themselves, their children and spouses in a way mindful of what Eugen Bleuler half a century ago called the "autistic-undisciplined thinking in medicine," totally disregarding the co-mingling of the inevitable emotional ambivalence in their family relationships, all the transference implications, with their magical powers and hence the unavoidable clouding of judgment.

The reverse side of the coin—showing this image of the *all-healer*—is the deprecated, misused, distrusted *sorcerer's apprentice* who cannot tame the spirits he magically called forth. He is hounded by demanding patients and malpractice suits, by unscrupulous lawyers and newsgreedy reporters, and sneered at by despotic bureaucrats, administrators, and politicians. Just like the teacher he has lost his dignity and intangible authority. He drowns in insurance forms, grants and chatty meetings. The hours of his work and responsibility have no limit; he neglects his family and is haunted by guilt, reproach, and remorse. His prestige is precarious and bought at a price which some legal, emotional, or family catastrophe suddenly comes to demand from him.

And more: lasting health and immortality are mere illusions. The doctor always must end up as the defeated magician. The expectations put on him always outpace, nay outrun his performance. He is only human but is blamed for it!

A second antithesis affects his relationship to money. It is true, many physicians are mercenary and overcharge, are in medicine primarily for the financial security and gilded base. Many others, perhaps the majority, have relatively modest incomes, if measured against the gigantic costs of training, their continued education, the time spent at work, the sheer costs of practicing (overhead, insurance), the weight of responsibility, the skills and gifts needed. On most physicians there is put this double image: that of a *greedy Shylock,* and that of the selfless, humanitarian helper, indeed often of an utterly exploited peon.

In both antitheses it is not easy to find a middle way: to reconcile power and disillusionment, to balance the need for a commensurate income and for help to the needy without recompensation.

The doctors and their main tool, medication, play a very important role in the problem we explore. A disproportionately high number of physicians (5–7 percent) are themselves drug abusers or drug addicts, including abusers of alcohol—unnoticed or condoned. More important: it is *their* technology, it is *their* power which is usurped by the illegal drug user. Not rarely it is the doctor who has started it all, who promoted it by injudicious prescribing and who is conned and manipulated into giving drugs. Every drug pusher is in a sense a pseudo-doctor, both a counterfeit entrepreneur and a counterfeit healer-magician (see Szasz 1973).

This entire problem of narcissistic antitheses leads us over without clear delimitation into our next topic.

Denial, Splitting, and Externalization

In this section we examine the possible collective correlates of the two leading defenses and the process of splitting, which we uncovered in the individual who is compulsively using drugs and in his immediate family.

DRUG USE AND DRUG TRAFFIC IN THE GHETTO

As an important social problem we have to recognize the meaning of narcotics in the ghetto. In a life of extreme resentment and profound hopelessness as it exists in our slums, drug use, besides individual and mass violence, becomes a central, though again multidetermined symptom.

For many the hustling and dealing is their only meaning in life, the only way to achieve status and money (Preble and Casey 1969). To some the drug high gives the only fast escape from rage and boredom. As long as this demoralization and degradation is the lot of the youth in the slums, such symptoms as narcotics use, indiscriminate, all pervasive violence, stealing, "fencing," and looting will continue to exist.

One aspect of this fact is treated with curious nonchalance: its economic impact. In Appendix D details of this side of the problem are presented. Here I need only mention several paradoxes. One is the discrepancy between the damage suffered and the niggardliness towards treatment programs. Another is the fact that comparatively little is being done to tackle this problem. Yet there is one aspect which is particularly hushed up: the equalizing economic effect. The drug related criminality in the form of shoplifting, pilferage, burglary, car theft, flim flam, etc., is one channel through which a quite massive stream of goods flows from the affluent society into the slums, a kind of internal Marshall Plan. This collusion in denial is one aspect of the complex social conflict, the conflict which we might well call the one between the arrogance of the affluent establishment and the despair and shiftlessness of the poor.

DECEPTION AND SELF-DECEPTION

Self-deception lies at the core of drug use; deception is a universal phenomenon, cultivated and sophisticated in our commercial society and culture—contradicting the great leading ideals of honesty and genuineness. Thus, we partake in a culture and society where for every interpersonal and inner problem an advertisement promises an easy and often fraudulent cure with drugs or other material means; in the words of Edwin Schur (1969): "Any sensitive observer of the American scene recognizes that modern mass advertising at its heart represents a kind of institutionalization of deception and misrepresentation." And yet, it is a society making a cult of frankness, openness and sincerity.

Even more generally, the search is for universal relief. Today we just have to listen to our commercials on radio and television. For all types of problems and unhappiness either a drug or another remedy on the material level is offered (see Farber 1964).

What the use of all these substances has in common is that they allow us to lie to ourselves. They deceive us either about the outside world or about ourselves. They put up an appearance of something which is not there. They either let the world appear more interesting, cheerful, and rich, or they make us feel more vigorous, free of disappointment, insecurity, dissatisfaction, and weakness. So we may vary Farber's statement ("Ours is the addicted society") into: "Ours is the lying society."

Yet, in every society there is a credibility gap; in every society there are institutions of hypocrisy to deal with the gap between ideal and reality (Keniston 1968). What is specific for our society is that we have two technological institutions which allow each individual to escape from reality into the world of mere appearance. One consists in the mass media, especially television; the other is the mass production and mass availability of drugs which change thought, memory, perception, and, in particular, emotion and mood.

This element of self-deception, with the help of a drug is basically again a deception about the limits of power, one's own boundaries. This problem of deception and truth becomes particularly important in the use of psychedelics, from marijuana to LSD and to the very dangerous, usually camouflaged, animal tranquilizer, phencyclidine.

Both casual and compulsive users try to break through to truth, to authenticity. In regard to the "heads" Keniston specifically writes: "they feel compelled to root out any 'defense' that might prevent awareness of inner life; self-deception, lack of self-awareness or 'phoniness' are cardinal sins" (1969).

But as it occurs throughout psychopathology: the symptom expresses not only the fight against a "sin," but turns into this "sin" itself. Drug use becomes self-deception in the extreme, the very sin which it seeks to eradicate, comparable to obsessive symptoms which first are formed to defend against masturbation or aggression, and more and more come to resemble these impulses themselves in an only thinly disguised shape. The deception is well put by McCracken (1971): these drugs are "theomimetic," a doctrine of "ersatz divinity," based on "the nasty assumption that man is not good enough."

TELEVISION

We live in a society where passive trends and denial are extensively furthered, particularly with the enormous stimulation of passive receptivity and dehumanization from early childhood on with the TV culture's emphasis on magical gratification, in content: of what is presented, as well as in the form of "turning on" (McCracken 1971). This stands in sharpest contrast to our dominant social value, which is activism, boyish independence, and a kind of free-roaming, almost gypsy-like mobility.

Specifically, we might wonder how much the shallowness of, and presentation of shortcuts to, gratification by television, viewed for many hours daily from early childhood on and thus substituting a passive form of presentation for the development of an active fantasy life may contribute to this search for easy stimulation (see Grotjahn 1971).

Television, this tool of highest potential value, has very often become a degrader of sublimation, a reducer of symbolic processes, a destroyer of art and personal closeness. Grotjahn rightly states that, while "art experience ... aims at working through of unconscious conflict," television "aims to distract from conflicts and not to solve them. Television may tease unconscious conflicts and play with them but will not lead to solution ... Commercial television has succeeded in perverting the symbol to a slogan.... It communicates almost nothing that is worth being communicated.... Children view television for passive pleasures.... It helps withdrawal from the real world.... It prostitutes the symbol of art and puts it to work as slogan on the marketplace. Art experience leads to mastery. Television leads to consumption of goods.... Television entertains, where dramatic art educates." And as to the role of the parents in all this: "The more driving and ambitious the parents are, the more time is devoted by their children to escaping them. Television may not spoil children, but spoiled children may turn to television ... the less trouble in the family, the less viewing...." It is "a reliable babysitter and is always available." It does not directly cause delinquent behavior, but it "seems to feed malignant impulses that already exist."

Thus TV is indeed one of the most powerful enforcers of externalization in our culture (in contrast to a first rate novel or drama or music)—and yet it could indeed become a mediator of culture, especially of the high art forms of film and drama (see Langer 1953). Rudiments of high cultural value which are intrinsic and specific for television exist: documentaries of all kinds, political debates and commentaries, and scientific and historical presentations not easily possible in other media.

It is speculative but inescapable to sense a close connection between TV addiction in childhood and compulsive drug use in later years, between the general alienation from one's feelings, induced (or just expressed) by TV in society at large, and the ever-expanding denial of inner conflict, the rush into external manipulation, the role of "psychophobia" in social and scientific life.

LEISURE AND CREATIVITY

So many of the drug users I have met—not just compulsive ones, but also the social/recreational ones—fill the emptiness of their lives with drug effects and drug based companionship. In all societies and cultures, from the earliest prehistoric times on, creativity in its widest sense was a central constituent of human life in community. Following Cassirer and Langer we may define *creativity* as all those activities which give symbolic expression to man's inner life—to his fantasies, feelings, thoughts—in a form which can be shared with others, re-created, relived, rethought by others. And now we suddenly discover that we encounter here the non-compulsive, "normal" healthy counterpart to the pathologic defense which I moved onto center stage in chapter 6 : *externalization*.

In most human communities of the past, when and if the battle for sheer survival against famine, illness and enemies receded into the background, there was much space and time given to creative activity: to carving, painting, molding, decorating, cutting with scissors, sculpting, to writing and story telling, to singing, playing instruments and to dancing. Besides life's immediate necessities, as eating, sleeping, sexuality, childrearing, working, mutual caring and helping, external living consisted in essence making all these activities, especially work, symbolically profoundly meaningful (e.g., in form of myths and rituals) and of creating or re-creating.

Not so today. Instead of creativity we have leisure and recreation, very often an empty time filled with pure physical action: driving, sports, jogging—or with passive entertainment, not re-creation—with externalization without the sharing of symbolic forms. I do not downplay the value of recreation as such; it is indeed a very helpful counterpoise to the tensions of a technical world. But it does not fill the crucial void left by the vanishing of creative activity.

SPLITTING AND ESTRANGEMENT

So far we have mainly contemplated the correlates of denial (of inner conflicts and of limitations to narcissistic expansion) and of externalization, as encountered in the public realm, and therefore in the popular function of drugs and equivalents as to these two defenses.

Here we turn to some very brief thoughts about the philosophical and hence sociocultural substratum or accompaniments of splitting and estrangement.

Throughout our present culture runs what Hegel described as the "hiatus irrationalis," the gap between outer reality and inner truth, between mere appearance and inner essential necessity, between the absolute ideals and sheer chancy contingency, of "colorful rind" and "inner pulse" (Lowith 1941 pp. 49, 60). One may object: what has this hoary philosopher of German idealism and political absolutism to do with our current philosophical and cultural dilemmas?

The answer is multiple: Hegel felt himself to be the spokesman for his moment of history and, with Goethe, was shocked by the "new barbarism" of the democratic revolution of 1830, of the violent overthrow of what he considered absolute values. Delving much deeper, he sought, through a ceaseless negation and estrangement, for the absolute truth, which he posited in brittle bridges: he saw in his own philosophy the reconciliation of reason and faith, of Christianity and the political state. But, as the outstanding thinker Lowith once said in an offhand comment: "Originally the (philosophical) fraud (or deceit) started already with Hegel" (personal communication). This leads to the second reason why we have to look back to Hegel. It was from him that much of Western philosophy took a new beginning, and it was through his direct philosophical successors that an enormous movement and fermentation went through our culture. What all the still influential thinkers of the nineteenth century have in common is well put by Lowith: For Kierkegaard, Marx, Bauer, Feuerbach, etc., "reality did not remain in the light of the freedom of being at one with oneself, but in the shadow of man's self-estrangement" (1941, p. 64); each one tried to break through to authentic existence: Kierkegaard saw it in the ethical-religious existence of the "single" person, Feuerbach in sensual feeling and passion, Marx in the economic existence of the masses (pp. 156–157). Nietzsche went more radically, through power and value nihilism, to a "will for Nothingness *and* eternity," to the timelessness of eternal and cyclical returning. "Nietzsche's real philosophy is a system of thinking at whose inception stands the *Death of God,* in whose middle *nihilism,* and at whose end the self-transcending of nihilism to the *eternal return.*" (pp. 210–211). This was possible "only by estranging himself from the present and current reality, by being six thousand feet removed from Man and Time." He saw himself as the philosopher of the future, of modernity. If we re-read him—just in the brief quotes given—we seen how his transformation of Hegel's inheritance has become a groundswell of deep motivation and reason for our modern generations, just as Marx's very different version has become a lodestone for large segments of mankind.

Thirdly, the yearning to "return home to oneself," to overcome relativism, not-belonging, estrangement, homelessness, is not only a steady preoccupation of the leading value philosophers of this century (e.g., Heidegger, Jaspers, Scheler, Buber, Marcel, Sartre), but a deep feeling of sensitive youth, protesting against the shallowness of external power (technology, material success, political and economic power), a longing perhaps best symbolized in Hesse's writings, which are again so popular today. The youth cultures, employing psychedelics, try to use these drugs to transcend a sham reality, by making it totally unreal, by negating it altogether, and thus to break through to the authentic core, to absolute values, and to a deep sense of meaning, of being at home in a cosmic reality beyond the cold here-and-now.

Unfortunately this abyss of alienation, which was first opened up to thinking man's view by Hegel, was neither overcome by Hegel himself, nor by Marx, Kierkegaard, or Nietzsche, neither by Buber nor by Jaspers nor Sartre, neither by the "Bohemians" nor the "Liars and Transgressors" of today.

We are resigned to the insight that this split, this estrangement from self and world, will remain with us as part of the human condition. No fraud will succeed in building bridges of paper and proclamations, of dreams and drugs, of fire and death, over this profound split. I believe the process of coping with this split—in society as in the individual— lies in the acceptance of the gap between ideal and real, between the yearning for something absolute and the actual living within limitations. This inner reconciliation and acceptance, often in form of the irony of wisdom, will reduce, though never entirely abolish, split and estrangement. The integration by psychoanalytic working through remains an asymptotic ideal, a value beyond full reach—for individuals as for society. This last value still brings us closer to an authentic experience than either mysticism or violence or the phantasmagories of psychedelics.

Yet one step beyond: We saw how depersonalization in the individual is not only rooted in separateness and split identification, but profoundly in shame. The question immediately poses itself: Is the current air of shamelessness so eloquently described by Lowenfeld (1976)—parallel to the apparent guiltlessness (Rangell's "compromise of integrity")—not a sham? Are not both—the abrogation of shame and the abdication of guilt—illusions, hiding a much deeper and more archaic sense of being relentlessly exposed, discarded, dehumanized, really shamed to the core, and analogously concealing a deep, externalized sense of "not knowing what to do," of being guilty for an attitude of hybris whose real nature remains unacceptable, of never being innocent again, as Arthur Miller put it? Is not excess pursuit of the values of power—as ruthless liberty and as ruthless equality, as violence by State or wealth, by bureaucracy or machine—itself a form of hybris, whose nemesis lies in this deep sense of shame and guilt, covered over by estrangement and despair?

We have to abandon these philosophical questions for the moment and return to more superficial concerns, concerns, though, which have to be seen against this background of profound problems.

Projection and Aggression

Parallel to the "compromise of integrity" and the splits and archaic versions of the superego in the individual, parallel to the inconsistencies in the families of compulsive drug users and the secret structure of our culture, we have a host of more superficial social conflicts and inconsistencies: in the exertion of authority in the service of values, and in the rebellion against such vindictive or inconsistent authority.

DRUG USE AS A "SEXUAL" VICE

Most superficially seen, society looks at drug abuse in moralistic terms. It is condemned with as much indignation as masturbation or premarital sex were only a few decades ago. The drug abuser is seen as indulging in a vice which evokes the secret jealousy and the overt hateful persecutory zeal of the moralist.

The obverse side of the same coin is that youth who always had to break away from the parental generation can now use drugs as a valuable symbol of rebellion. Precisely because it is frowned upon as morally bad, it becomes a sign of brave revolt to break the taboo of the elders—just as free love, anarchy, communism and other revolutionary youth movements served for the last hundred years as symbolic separation from the parental authority (see Laqueur 1969). Thus, this social problem can be seen as the conflict between moralists and rebels. It has strong sexual implications: It is the forbidden lust which is sought and fought.

Underlying this conflict is the shift in sexual mores already hinted at: Early sexual experimentation is accepted; the passionate sexual pursuit against all obstacles of rigid authority as well as its use as a vehicle for protest and rebellion have become vestiges of a romantic past. For so many, easily accessible sexuality is a source not of anxiety, despair and commitment, but of tedium and routine. The denied, split off emotions involved in sexual yearnings are sought instead on other avenues, particularly with the help of pharmaca.

WEAKNESS AND MANLINESS

At a deeper level there is an irrational equation of weakness, femininity and drug dependence (just as there is an equally prejudicial equation of alcohol tolerance and masculinity), which may explain the widespread scorn and distaste shown by some law enforcement officials as well as lay public and some very strident voices in the media. Yet, at the same time, we can not fail to notice the secret admiration for murderers in many of the same vociferous defenders of maleness. It is a classical match between sadistic and masochistic partners. However, there is also a deep cultural meaning in this overvaluation of masculine aggression and the self-righteous scorn for passive dependency (and homosexuality!)—in striking contrast to many oriental cultures. This overemphasis on competitive aggression is opposed by a form of neo-romanticism whose dreaminess can assume precisely that trend to oriental passivity and retreat into mysticism which runs counter to the virility of the supermen (Roszak 1968, 1973, 1975).

This conflict raises a host of questions and opens at the same time new avenues of understanding.

What does it mean morally that alcohol is legal though it is addicting, releases aggression, liberates coarseness, numbs us or exhilarates us, whereas other drugs with more or less the same stupefying effects are forbidden and under sanctions exceeding those of crimes of violence, even of manslaughter? What does it mean if a law—and I refer to the marijuana laws—is broken untold times and only those few are punished, and then often most severely that are caught? Our youngsters ask us none too rarely: what does it mean morally to allow violence in the service of a political goal, but to punish by imprisonment the self-contained methods of escape? Perhaps we can understand this conflict best by the deep strand of irrational and anti-intellectual tradition which has been described so cogently by Hofstadter (1962, 1967).

In pursuit of this thought we realize that one particular group of people, their values and their sickness, are changed into something abysmally evil and demonic, whereas the preoccupations and values of the popular majority which are basically not different from the despised minority have the ring of virtue. The decisive mark of difference between these two poles appears to lie in the predominant features of the two types of dependency.

How can we understand this type of Manichean split? It is conspicuous that alcohol, which in smaller dose stimulates aggression and activity and the use of which has often been extolled as a mark of virility, is accepted in general in Western culture, whereas opium and cannabis, which induce a state of peaceful harmony, satiation and passivity, are derogated into fiends of mankind. In the Islamic East the value emphasis is exactly reversed: opium and cannabis are at least tolerated, alcohol decried.

We can infer (and it is just a speculative inference) that a culture which gives irrational accolade to activity and aggressivity is inclined to praise a drug like alcohol with the same irrationality as it deprecates symptoms of passivity like opiate abuse or homosexuality. For the old sedentary races inhabiting the Middle East which antedate the advent of Islam by millenia and which have preserved some of the basic characteristics of the pre-Arab cultures (Carmichael 1967) an opposite kind of irrational value orientation can be observed; so far all the modern reversals (in form of fanatical nationalisms and pseudo-modernization) seem to affect but the surface of this basic passive attitude and to effect no real transformation.

Here we also have to refer back to a point made in chapter 4—the striking antithetical relationship of compulsive drug use to phobic neurosis. It was noted there that the phobic-neurotic *avoids* the symbol of his anxiety in projected and condensed form whereas the drug abuser equally compusively seeks the pathognomonic object as a similarly projected and condensed symbol of protection against uncontrollable, overwhelming affects and moods. Now we may add: drug abuse and drugs function correspondingly for society as phobic objects. Like witches, criminals and other objects of projection, this set of taboos is both alluring and abhorrent, fascinating and frightening, titillating and disgusting. Such a thrill-fear mix is, of course, typical for the content of phobias.

CONFORMISM AND SELF-ASSERTION

More divorced from the drug scene and far more veiled as a form of sadomasochistic conflict we find one which I described in concrete examples in chapter 13 ("The Insolence of Office"). Here we scan it most briefly as a general problem of a society where submission and conformity to institutions is demanded and where any violation of the code and any act of "civil courage" is quickly punished and with a vengeance—and yet again where the virtues of pioneer independence, of "rugged individualism," and of rebellion against traditional authority are extolled.

All too often the tyranny of conformism, of undemocratic manipulation of power and justice, and, most recently, of the "New Egalitarianism" (see Kristol 1972, Seabury 1972, Frankel 1973, Nisbet 1975) overrule competence, right, and independence of thinking. Who does not conform, who reveals massive breaches of publicly given promises or civil rights, or beatings in a school for the retarded, or noncompliance with public trust, is typically called a "troublemaker." This label has indeed become a badge of honor of those who act, like Socrates, as gadflies or who, like Freud, shake the world in its sleep. One may almost say: it is the "troublemakers" who keep democracy alive. The very foundation of democracy, both in the United States and the few other model democracies, is just the imperative "to speak one's mind," to form one's own opinion and stand in pride to it (in the town meetings literally: "to stand up and to be counted").

And yet no democracy has been free of these forms of massive abuse of entrusted power: Athens had her despicable destroyers, like the infamous Alcibiades and Plato's uncle, Critias; the great old democracies of Iceland, the Netherlands, and Switzerland have known perversion of justice and abuse of power. Democracy is indeed the dialectic between demand for conformity and defiant self-assertion.

Value Conflicts and Cultural "Superego Splits"

INCONSISTENCIES AND ABSURDITIES OF THE LAW

An ominous and most dangerous conflict is created by the inconsistency and ensuing unenforceability of the law. In this context, I would like to insert a few grotesque examples. First a quote from the *New York Times* (15 November 1970):

Marijuana Ruled a Narcotic: Dallas, November 14. United States District Judge William M. Taylor, Jr. ruled yesterday that the State of Texas has the right to classify marijuana as a narcotic drug, although he acknowledged that this "may or may not be wise or desirable." Judge Taylor entered an order refusing to free Luke Joseph Rener, sentenced to 30 years for possession of one marijuana cigarette. Rener contended that he had been illegally convicted because the Texas law making marijuana a narcotic was unconsititutional.

Approximately at the same time, another story appeared in the same newspaper which may serve as counterpoint: a political leader on the West Coast was challenged in his party position after he had under the influence of alcohol driven a car without lights, crashed head-on with another car, and killed its driver. There was no word of any punishment although presumably some legal action was taken.

Another example, an editorial in the *New York Times,* 22 January 1972:

> State Supreme Court Justice Paul A. Fino, in embarking on a personal "crusade" against narcotics pushers, is apparently determined to use antitank howitzers to kill mosquitoes. In the process he seems prepared to mow down anyone who considers objectionable this method of judicial overkill—one manifested in a maximum sentence of 30 years in prison imposed on a small-time addict for selling a few grains of heroin to an undercover police agent.
>
> The penalty was so grossly excessive that Bronx District Attorney Burton B. Roberts, the prosecutor, is joining with the Legal Aid Society in seeking a reduced sentence. Mr. Roberts calls it "unconscionable" to make a sick, indigent 23-year-old hooked on drugs "the fall guy for all the ills of society."
>
> That protest brought from Justice Fino the demagogic suggestion that the District Attorney has "gone soft on crime and become another bleeding heart." The reality is that Mr. Roberts has won wide praise for diligence in going after major suppliers and distributors of heroin. If anything, the Bronx prosecutor tends to take an overly hard line on such issues as the "prompt trial rule" recommended by the state's judges—a rule he feels might degenerate into legalized jailbreak.
>
> The Roberts approach of letting the punishment fit the crime offers better assurance of rebuilding respect of law than the vengeful, indiscriminate scourge Justice Fino has applied.

Once more, the New York Times (19 February 1972):

Addicted Ex-G.I. Sentenced, Fort Lauderdale, Fla. March 18 (UPI).A young Vietnam veteran who resorted to heroin to kill the pain in his mine-shattered leg has been sentenced to three years in prison for a holdup staged to support his $80-dollar-a-day drug habit. Officials said Thursday that Tom Murray, 23 years old of New York City, had agreed to undergo an operation at Raiford Prison to have the leg, which has become cancerous, removed.

I could go on and on. I have a whole file of such grotesques, including personal letters asking me for help.

Once I testified for an addict who had an arrest record for possession. For the theft of two bottles of whiskey he was sent to a prison institution as a defective delinquent. He had been there for seven years with no hope for release.

On the other side I refer back to chapter 13 and the example of Edmund. The same type of bizarre inconsistency is found in the public attitude towards illicit drugs versus alcohol (or, for that matter, smoking and particularly guns).

In the same week, almost side by side, I found two items of news, illustrating this point. President Ford said in his Law Day address in Dallas, Texas, April 9, 1976: "Frankly, despite all the rhetoric of recent years I do not believe that we have yet succeeded in making it tough enough for drug traffickers. As far as I am concerned, the people who traffic in hard drugs are nothing less than merchants of death and should be put behind bars for a long, long time.... Those who live off the misery of others must pay the price—and the higher the price the better." Estimating the national costs of drug abuse at seventeen billion dollars he vowed: "I will spare no effort to crush the menace of drug abuse" (*New York Times,* 10 April 1976).

Although I certainly have no sympathy for high level pushers they exist largely because of an irrational system of approaches to the problem.

But the real split comes to the fore when I quote from an article by Dr. E. Braun in the *Schweizerische Aerztezeitung,* 3 March 1976, about alcoholism. He quoted a number of investigations from around the globe, especially C & EN, a journal of the American Chemical Society; under the title "Fetal alcoholism is more serious than the thalidomide disaster" it is reported that one third of the infants born to chronically alcoholized mothers show brain damage. Bierich (Budapest) is cited as calling alcohol the most frequent teratogenic noxa.

Who calls alcohol producers or advertisers "merchants of death"? Or gun dealers?

The point I am trying to make is: If laws are as inconsistent as ours, their very flouting may become a symbol for self-respect and integrity. Comparable to the civil disobedience of the followers of Gandhi or Martin Luther King or the dissidents in a totalitarian society, the breaking of laws considered unjust, one-sided, can become a matter of positive ethical decision.

"COLLECTIVE SOCIOPATHY"

There is a deeper lawlessness rampant. If we look back to chapter 13, "The Insolence of Office," we faced, among other gross examples, an instance where several counselors massively abused their trust. In one case all evidence was there that one employee had made a patient pregnant, had taken financial advantage of her, and had even performed sexual acts on the premises. The counselor was fired. He appealed. However, the personnel department of that institution found the evidence was not strong enough! He was reinstated with full back pay. The tremendous impact this has on staff and patients is evident: no boundary has to be respected, provided some petty bureaucratic rules can be adduced to cover over the violation. One has to multiply that thousands of times to recognize what damage this does.

In turn highly qualified personnel who in greatest integrity and honesty devote all their efforts to their tasks are kept at low salaries; again for a number of bureaucratic reasons their positions and their salaries cannot be upgraded. Eventually they leave.

This can work as a principle of negative selection: The program may be left with more and more incompetent people who cannot be discharged, while losing all or most capable personnel.

This is part of a kind of "collective sociopathy."

No patient whom I got to know better—drug user or not—has not had many experiences of that kind. One of the counselors leaves our employ to take a salary cut as a prison guard. Everyone knows his secret income will by far outpace what the reduction in his official salary amounts to: some prison guards are partners in smuggling in drugs and thus improve their income.

Many patients assert the same about magistrates and judges: a poor black is stuck in jail whereas the white youngsters from middle or upper class background are bought free.

From employees and patients I hear another version—not monetary or sexual bribing—but a collapse of work ethic: sick days are there to be used. When an employee of any kind (counselor, teacher, etc.) does not feel like working, he takes off "as a sick day"—for a trip, for entertainment, regardless for what. It goes so far that they may go to work when they really are sick in order to take off when the weather is nice—"as mental health days."

Yet another facet of this is the indoctrination in many families: "Everybody is out to screw you; and you have got to do it to them before they do it to you. Get away with as much as you can, do as little as you can." Thus, cheating is elevated almost to a general moral principle!

I think our society cannot function without bureaucratic structures. But indeed—do we have to live with this gnawing rot of "bureaucratic sociopathy," where systems, rules and structures count, but not human reality, human needs, ethical conduct? Is this decay indeed an inevitable price? I do not know the answer. I only know that each drug abuser's problems interdigitate with this general inhumanity and lawlessness pervading our culture. The individual "sociopathy" feeds on this collective lack of superego. As one former dealer said: "Here I was a poor black kid, from a rat-infested house, a horrible family, in my teens. There was this kingpin pusher offering me an income of $500 each time I ran a packet full of narcotics across town. Soon I had a car, I had women, I was rich and respected, I could have whatever I wanted. I had beaten the white man. Only then I started taking drugs myself. I was rich, but miserable and frightened."

Not that this explains all; I maintain that these social aspects are merely concurrent causes; but they count, they weigh heavily on all of us.

And yet an observation: the cynicism. When I reproached one of our fabulous cheats (Edmund, in chapter 13) for having neglected imperative duties of accountability and responsibility, he answered with biting sarcasm: "Were you born yesterday?"

THE SURFEIT OF LEGALISM AND OSTENTATIOUSNESS VERSUS THE NEED FOR GUILT AND SHAME

Taking up the earlier thoughts once again: the current shamelessness and compromise of integrity are symptoms both of an excess of power and much deeper meanings of guilt and shame.

The prominent philosopher of law, Thomas Ehrlich (1976), rightly talks about "legal pollution." "Much of the problem is rooted in the public expectations that adjudication is the answer to every dispute and that a statute or regulation is the solution to every unmet need. Legal pollution is largely a result of political processes that put a premium on rhetoric, and of legislatures and agencies that pass laws and rules without adequate regard for problems of implementation...." We need ways to "de-lawyer" problems. One consequence is particularly ominous: "Poor people are most oppressed by the growing weight of legal pollution because they have no effective access to the legal system." Ehrlich concludes with a quote from Learned Hand: "To keep our democracy, there must be one commandment: Thou shalt not ration justice."

We had a chance in many earlier passages to recognize the excess of bureaucratic regulations as well as of legislation, and to observe the result: too many laws mean lawlessness, too many lawyers mean injustice. The wealthy wrongdoer (many of the cases presented) gets away with massive criminality. So does the violator protected by union rules and bureaucratic regimentation. So does the unscrupulous shyster and power broker. The poor populate jails and prisons for the same or much smaller law violations, jails indeed which are so overcrowded that mattresses are hung over urinals; imprisoning destroys all chances for rehabilitation instead of bringing it about.

And yet there is a deep sense abroad of what is right and wrong, a yearning for simple fairness and justice and the real order which only can survive in a climate of such deeper justice.

All the shysters and excessive laws have not eliminated the depth of the superego, the deep need for boundaries, limits, structures and hierarchy (socially and value philosophically). Where there is no outer clarity about what goes, where one "can get away with murder," we find a profound, gnawing sense of guilt, a need for atonement and expiation. Andreas (case 19) was a particularly paradigmatic instance.

The same holds true for its counterpart: public exhibition. Sexual shamelessness cannot eliminate a profound need for privacy, of being master over one's intimate life, a dread of being constantly exposed.

The omnipotence and radicalism of the demand for pleasure, the promiscuous living out of all impulses, of all archaic wishes, the baring of the innermost soul to every stranger in encounter groups, all the "primal screams" and obscene or cruel versions of "honesty"—all this surfeit of ostentation and exhibition is sham!

More archaic forms of shame, forms of narcissistic mortification and rage about being humiliated and dehumanized, are seen not just in patients, but can be found in all of us. There is a profound revulsion in us against the pervasive invasions of privacy by all layers of society. This intrusion is obviously far more horribly visible in the totalitarian state than in Western democracy. Our form of shamelessness is still far less profound than the one exercised by the dictatorships of the Right and the Left, but it is a threat to our dignity nevertheless.

We need the protection by guilt and shame, especially in today's lawless and shameless society, by rational forms of these two powerful socializing affects.

THE PROBLEM OF MEANING
AND THE DECLINE OF THE HUMANITIES

With these last problems we have already been led into a philosophical area. As we saw in the clinical section, the emotional and even more the physical dependency on a drug is the pathological counterpart (almost a caricature) of the commitment to life-determining values or meanings ("a chemical mythology"). The choice of a guiding value, the decision for our inner and outer priorities, is lastly a philosophical choice—implicitly or explicitly. We see how some patients can suddenly seize on a cause, on an ideal—the civil rights movement, the Black Muslims, or Synanon. Such a total reorientation of life, a kind of religious conversion, can have surprising curative effect, but it occurs rarely, and we are unable to predict it. But the conscious contemplation of the problem of meaning, of value priority in one's life, is actually an essential part of any psychotherapy.

Faithful to our times, our drug-using youth seek synthetic values when family, job, and culture cannot provide them with a genuine meaning of life. The drug mysticism not less than the thoughtless pragmatism of our society, the fanatical ideologies not less than the power hungry cynicism of much of our public life, reflect that profound betrayal of philosophy, the abandonment of philosophical questioning.

We find this disregard for philosophical questioning particularly striking and ominous in our education. Few in our schools have been confronted with the tragic dilemma of Socrates, with the depth of feeling and thought in the Greek tragedians or Shakespeare, or taught to listen to Mozart or Beethoven. The value blindness of the educators is mirrored by the yawning boredom of the educated. There has been little consideration of the impact of a shallow, technically and pragmatically oriented, but vastly protracted education. Schooling, devoid of most tradition and humanistic values and carried by teachers vastly underpaid, undereducated, and held in low esteem, cannot provide those values and ideals which could give most of us a badly needed structure in times of crisis—whether in the developmental crisis of adolescence or the historical crisis of demythicization and devaluation in which we are stuck.

Hand in hand with this goes the general wilting of authority and limitations, and with that of challenge, expectation and aspiration. The shallow hue and cry about the permissiveness of our society may have a shred of reasonableness if we look at this last point. One of many examples is my own profession. In the words of Ashley Montagu: "What is not generally recognized is that the doctor is one of our most poorly educated citizens. ... there is usually too little time for anything other than the preparation for and the practice of his profession. In this way many a promising mind has been arrested and the student, doctor, family, and the community are losers."

In the *American Scholar* (1974), the late Lionel Trilling wrote in an article full of important thoughts: "our society will tend increasingly to alienate itself from the humanistic educational ideal"; the latter is the ideal "that the best citizen is the person who has learned from the great minds and souls of the past how beautiful reason and virtue are and how difficult to attain." He refers to the importance of what is called in German *Bildung* ("being fashioned, being formed, being shaped"); I would add the relevance of Allgemeinbildung, the providing of the youngsters between ten and twenty-two (when they are most open and avid to gain a sense for values) with a general humanistic and scientific education (instead of specialized, technical skills). Trilling stresses "that humanistic educational traditions of the past were grounded in strenuous effort and that the idea of ordeal was essential to them." In contrast many Americans (and, I might add, modern Europeans as well—not to speak of all the antihumanistic "cultures") feel "that being taught or required to learn is an arbitrary denial of autonomy." We are losing the old "idea of a conceived and executed life ... the idea of making a self, a good self" and have replaced it with that of a "personal fluidity, a self without the old confinements," a "limitlessness in our personal perspective."

I have expressed similar thoughts in terms of the conflict between emotional dependency on material gratification and breaking through boundaries and limits versus the search for meaning-giving values and commitment to a philosophical ideal. More specifically it is the conflict between the prevalent orientation towards the value of quantity versus the potential dominance of the value of quality. The question posed is: Do we live to have more in form of possession and technical power—or do we live to be inwardly richer and wiser? Do we live for the efficient life—or do we life for the "good" life?

THE BETRAYAL OF PHILOSOPHY

In the famous autobiographical "Seventh Letter," Plato lets his friend and disciple Dion reproach his teacher, who hesitated to join him in Sicily: "But philosophy—whose praises you are always singing, while you say she is held in dishonour by the rest of mankind—must we not say that philosophy along with me has now been betrayed, so far as your action was concerned?" Hence the title of this section. What I refer to here is a general deprecation and disregard for philosophy and more specifically the lack in intellectual and political leaders of a careful weighing, especially of questions of value priorities. We face the possibility that it might be this general lack of explicit philosophizing about values—outside of the professional circles of philosophers, sociologists and anthropologists and some other comprehensive minds—which has something to do with the present rush to drugs. How this betrayal of philosophy contributes to the causation of drug abuse and how it reflects itself in conflicting popular attitudes and contradictory laws will have to be one aim of this part of the study. I submit further that it is the lack of philosophical contemplation in general which in society at large is conducive to an "addictive life style" and to other compulsive routes of escape from meaninglessness and value blindness. We live in a society faced with a multitude of philosophical questions as never before, a culture brimming with restlessness, a spirit of search to find answers to these questions. But we also live in a society where philosophical contemplativeness is taboo, even ridiculed as an empty, scholastic enterprise, where questions about meaning and value appear obsolete, where metaphysics is almost a curse word, and where a thoughtless, unreflective activism is praised. To be called a "philosopher" means pejoratively to be a dreamer, impractical, a fantast.

Most political leaders and the entrepreneurs financing them are blind to the problems of value philosophy. The "philosopher-king" in Plato's postulate is very rare. Moreover we find, as Eissler remarked, "in leading positions, in democratic societies as in others, more frequently than not personages the core of whose personalities is aggressive-narcissistic" (1975, p. 628). Even the intellectuals, fending off the repeated tides of anti-intellectualism, are scientists and merely scientists, not also philosophers in a reflective sense. We live in a society of "two cultures," as C.P. Snow put it, the culture of the sober scientists and technocrats on the one side, and, separated by an abyss from them, the culture of literati, artists and romanticists on the other side. Neither of the two cultures, however, attempts a reconciliation between doing and viewing on a more basic plane of philosophical inquest.

The poets are "engages"—committed in their protest against alienation and fiercely recommending this or that remedy: revolution, drugs, mysticism. But what most fail to be engaged in is to *ask* in a pensive mood. Rather they scoff at the questions pondered by the best minds of the past. They propose easy solutions for easy questions of their own making. I confess I prefer the honest work of great art, which conceals in the profundity of its ambiguousness the depth of mystical experience, or the original profound mystical works, by far over this trivial trial to "transcend self-conscious selfhood" (Huxley 1963).

In contrast, we scientists of all stripes are enmeshed in the staggering complexity of developing the questions in our fields of inquiry, of devising the methods how to answer them, of delineating our fields, and of tabulating our results. What we forget is to stand back several steps and look at the place of science in human history, its position within human potentiality, its basic value within an encompassing hierarchy of values. Is scientific truth the apex of the pyramid of values? We fail to ask this question because we leave philosophy to the philosophers and, if we ask ourselves honestly, are often rather inclined to send it to the dump pit of history.

The tragedy of philosophy is manifold. It is its betrayal by those who do not ask its questions. It is its state of being bypassed and overcome by science. It is degraded into a nihilistic skepticism and radical empiricism or into semantic-obsessional ruminations. It is shouted down into silence by ideologists and dogmatists. And finally, it is simply forgotten in the world of affluence.

In many forms of betrayal, one value system is considered absolute, dogmatic and unquestioned—it allegedly obviates further question about meaning and value. Such an unquestioned pseudo-philosophy may be overt or concealed—but it determines all major decisions of a group, a science or an individual.

The result of these many forms of betrayal of philosophy can be put in Yeats's words:

"Things fall apart; the centre cannot hold;
Mere anarchy is loosed upon the world."

The anarchy I am thinking about (the same "anomia" mentioned in the individual) is the *fragmentation of values* and *disintegration of value hierarchies*, entirely parallel to the destruction of community and the striking at the roots of democratic life mentioned before.

The betrayal of philosophy I refer to is this lack of standing back—not only to evaluate what one has done and accomplished, but also to evaluate the values upon which the doing was based, and to see these values in the broader context of ideas and the their history. It is this "standing back" which is entirely incommensurate to the amount of the "doing"—regardless of the topic: sex education, building of highways, the free reign to advertisement, national policy. There is a frenzy of action and decision, and absence of contemplation, of "the generous and reflective use of leisure" in Butler's words, as quoted by Trilling (1974, p. 55). It is by no means the question of which philosophy should reign or be taught but the aim is to learn to philosophize, to ask the basic questions, and to ponder them in every concrete life situation. It is here that the old Socratic method meets the new psychoanalytic method.

Yet, in a world without philosophy, drugs (among other things) are used to fill the gap of meaning.

We come then to the conclusion that the "addictive society" is the one whose steady restless search is for meaning in material goods and technical control, whose day-to-day happiness depends upon succeeding in this search, and, if this search fails, whose ultimate grasp for meaning and Huxley's "selfhood" is the intake of drugs. We cannot enter here into a more thorough value philosophical contemplation. Instead a few psychoanalytic comments are offered.

Immediately the objection may be raised: What right does psychoanalysis have to ponder problems of values? I answer with Rangell (1976):

> What I am advocating is a scientific, not a moralistic, attitude toward morals—the same attitude psychoanalysis always has—but one which includes a more complete range of psychic forces. The superego is involved in intrapsychic conflict. To neglect its role is to render one third of patients' problems incomplete.... The psychoanalyst is not without a value system, a misunderstanding which has led to a great deal of confusion among analysts and public alike. Freud separated himself from transient, culture bound neurosogenic values, not from the timeless values of civilized man. [And most important]: Analysis has values intrinsic to its task, such as rationality, the search for truth, freedom from neurosis. Neutrality does not include an abandonment of values nor of the role they play in the determination of final pathways in mental behavior. [p. 57]

Value is a quality an outside object or sets of objects or an inner idea have which evokes strong positive feelings, affects of active interest, aspiration, striving, joy in us. Value *systems* and value *philosophies* are abstract constructs representing such qualities on a higher symbolic level. Psychoanalytically, values ultimately derive from inner and outer ideals, and with that from idealized persons and their qualities, or from the archaic, idealized self. They take on a life of their own, become symbolic, abstract ideas, instead of concrete feelings and images attached to persons, actions, situations. In the energy metaphor: they change their libidinous or aggressive cathexis into neutralized energy.

All values have a kind of specific negatives, *countervalues,* which evoke the opposite affects. Value theory and affect theory belong together as two poles of one phenomenon.

Many pyramids of values, value hierarchies, are possible; exploration and choice of the priority of values is lastly a philosophical question, but one which concerns psychoanalysis very centrally. From all the possible value preferences I select here only three. The first is the one which puts external power, power by concrete outer means or by prestige, fame and honor, on the top of the pyramid. This is a basically narcissistic (and implicitly aggressive) value orientation. A second one subordinates every other value to love, to "altruistic surrender," squashing our own needs, denying our own nature, in order not to hurt the other. Whereas the first value orientation heaps shame on its "countervalues" (of defeat, ignominy, "bassesse" and dishonor, in de Gaulle's instance), the second loads guilt on the representatives of its "countervalues" (of sin, tort, injury, hurt). There is an implicit value philosophy also in psychoanalysis, as alluded to (but not carried through to its philosophical end) in chapter 4 and taken up in the quotes from Rangell's paper: At first blush, the top value in our science and practice is freedom from inner compulsion, is rational self-control, inner mastery, as far as it is possible, within the limits each of us has to live with: within the limits of the personal constitution and the inalterable scars left by our own life history. But this entails far more. It is a synthesis in the dialectic of narcissistic-aggressive and object libidinal (and often masochistic) value priorities and encompasses both. When we go out from Polonius's famous words, "To thine own self be true, And it must follow, as the night the day, Thou canst not then be false to any man" (*Hamlet,* I. iii), it is clear (see Trilling 1971) that this statement reconciles both: inner honesty and sincerity within oneself, trustworthiness and integrity towards the other. It entails a balance of self-respect and respect for the other's need and value. We can go beyond and suggest that this value combines self-love and deep feeling for the "next" (see also Aristotle's reconciliation of "philautia," self-love, as a high value, with "philia," friendship or love, in the *Nicomachean Ethics*).

This central Biblical word alluded to just now asks not for love toward mankind as an abstract, but for the rea which, in Hebrew, means not just everyone, but "fellow, friend" and, secondarily, "the other, the neighbor"—an injunction which is put in direct opposition to narcissistic revenge in the first part of the sentence ("do not take vengance and hold grudges"). Obviously it also reconciles self-love with object-love: "love the other like yourself" (Lev. 19: 18).

Thus we find so far the following components of the value complex central to psychoanalysis: (1) freedom from compulsiveness and drivenness, a prevalence of conscious controls; (2) inner and outer honesty, integrity, sincerity; (3) a balance between self-love and love of the other, between narcissistic and object libido. To this we can add (4) a use of aggression for constructive purposes, aggression under rational control. But most important, it entails (5) a deep insight and acknowledgment of the inner stratification, an integration of the conflicting parts of ourselves in an ongoing, dynamic, dialectic process. Implicit in all this is (6) the recognition of boundaries and limits, internally, externally, of "degree, priority and place." I believe that all six parts form *one value,* as seen in various perspectives.

If we return to our topic proper, we found externalization as the cardinal defense in compulsive drug users, an extension of magical, technical control, a forcing power, an overwhelming clobbering via the outside means of drugs (and other instruments) over the inner life, much like the calling in of foreign forces to squash an indigenous rebellion.

It is a special form of power philosophy, an adoration of force.

Thus, the use of drugs is a particular segment of technological control and as such, like all technique, a piece of magic become true. Drugs of any kind serve to "master" those problems which pertain to parts of ourselves, not to the whole of our personality. However, whenever global controls of any of the varieties of power are applied to us as persons we feel exploited. Therefore, when this control from the outside is exerted through drugs it is not farfetched to regard it also as a kind of exploitation. It is not less distasteful as the one by naked force, economic power or hypnotic fascination—notwithstanding the sense of dependency on, and protection by, the magically healing substance which may stand in the foreground of consciousness.

But is this really so, since, after all, we try to exert these controls ourselves? After all, it is ourselves who employ technological means like drugs in order to give meaning to our life—whether this meaning consists in the inner change itself brought about by the drug, or in the sense of power felt because of this apparent capability of changing ourselves, or just simply in the feeding ourselves with such a powerful agent.

With this, we are faced with a basic philosophical and an equally basic psychological question: Is technological control and power through physical manipulation acceptable as a supreme value? Can the search for a deeper meaning of one's (personal) life not merely through material, non-personal means, but by the supremacy of power, exploitation, manipulation,and with that by profound self-deception (the pharmacogenic denial), not be considered a kind of philosophical perversion, on the one side not entirely different from a dogmatic, absolute ideology—on the other from perversion in psychopathology?

The answer lies not only on the level of exploitation, but of dependency. If we use the value of power in form of drugs, or of cars, or over other people, or by sexuality, as the central meaning of our life, we notice right away the constricted and narrow nature and the compulsiveness of such a life style. We are back to the psychoanalytic insight in the individual: The supremacy of these values is a betrayal of our inner life. It uses externalization as a defense against overwhelming conflicts and thus assumes this peculiarly driven, compulsive quality. The problem boils down to the compromise solution of a very archaic power conflict. The wish is: "I want to be omnipotent and control my whole life; I want what I want and when I want it." This wish is countered by the realization: "I am helpless; since I cannot have *all* power, I have *no* control whatsoever, I am entirely dependent." The drug use combines these two ideas into one: "I am all powerful, but I am absolutely dependent."

Psychodynamically, the potential of aggression once this compromise solution is broken up is very high: "I am furious if my demand for power is not fulfilled."

Other values may enter the drug orientation. One was mentioned: the opposition, the countervalue to an aggressive, overweaning work ethic, for which the "indulgence" with opiates or cannabis are fulcra of sinful indolence. Another value, already described, is "community," belonging; drugs may mean both symbols of belonging and help to attain a sense of union and merger, dissolving the limits between inside and outside, self and mother, to overcome painful separateness and aloneness. They release inhibitions and allow touching, huddling together, the fusion into an archaic intimacy.

We can only hint here that, in contrast to any psychopathology (not only as it pertains to compulsive drug use), the "good life" is the one where the whole symphony of values, its fullest and richest unfolding, its leading melodies and their many variations, lend to value philosophy its full actuality. Constriction to a few leading values is impoverishment. By the same token, awareness and conscious choice of a few leading values and subordination of the others to these give direction and meaning to our life. This is actually identical with Aristotle's definition of "the good life" or "happiness" of man as "the active exercise of his soul's faculties in conformity with excellence" (with their highest potential and values) (*Nicomachean Ethics,* I. VII).

A Synopsis

Let us look back to the original set of problems from which we started out: What are the "concurrent causes" of drug abuse? What is the morality of the addictive society? And what are the psychological, sociocultural, and value philosophical implications of this question? What we have found should provide us with a theoretical basis to tackle the intricate cultural problems of drug abuse and addiction.

We live in a time of fantastic triumphs of science and technology, but also in a time where the voice of the philosophical quest is muted. We do not witness the end of philosophy, but a crisis of philosophical inquiry. Poor and rejected, but not dead—philosophy was perhaps at all times a stranger without a home, remote, betrayed; yet it has survived, has indeed been the parent to all sciences and humanities.

The rejection of philosophy is part of an intense anti-intellectual strand which is very strong not only in American tradition but in all societies at all times.

We have discovered the value philosophical factors possibly leading to an addicted life:

If we do not have any central meaning to our life we may take to material means, especially drugs, to fill the philosophical emptiness with a pseudomysticism.

If we chose implicitly or explicitly a value philosophy of power and control, drugs give us the illusion that we can master our own mind and body with the same magical swiftness and elegance as we master a car or the electromagnetic waves.

If we chose implicitly or explicitly a value philosophy of pleasure, drugs provide us with the illusion to have pleasure under our control and in steady easy grasp, oblivious of the price we have to pay.

If we declare the value philosophies of technical efficiency and success at all costs, of affluence and status, as the leading principles of a society, but have at the same time a considerable portion of the populace excluded from ever attaining these values, we open up the alternatives of failure with violence versus failure with retreat into the artificial paradise, the gates of which are opened by drugs.

If we have vacillating, muddled value convictions, if a society is filled with value conflicts and permeated by an air of hypocrisy, and if this hypocrisy is expressed in an extreme discrepancy of laws pertaining to violence and alcohol on the one side, most of the drugs on the other side, of surfeit of laws versus lawlessness, all forms of rebellion against authority can equate its use of drugs with a protest against this hypocrisy. We know that the ascetic Protestant ethics which fathered the laws of Prohibition and against drugs is a carrier of hidden resentment and revenge and evokes precisely the same affects in those who are attacked by representatives of these ethics. This contradiction is ever sharpened by the excess of legalism at the detriment of justice.

If we have a shameless society, dignity, privacy, self-respect are overwhelmed by the clamor of exhibition and of noisy self revelation. The excess of equality leads to the tyranny of exposure, to the despotism of impersonal power over private, personal needs. The boundaries become blurred between public and private, between private and intimate, between intimate and, finally, being alone and honest with oneself; none of these boundaries holds anymore. Hence the value of authenticity, of being just oneself without sham, but also without promiscuous exposure, is deeply yearned for. Drugs are a form of lying which pretends to offer the truth, the rightness and revelation of the most private self—yet in fact they just lead into more falseness and hence yet deeper shame and exposure.

If we look at it from the value principle inherent in psychoanalysis which is the philosophy represented here, we see clearly that the use of drugs leads to a betrayal of the central value of rationality and inner freedom. To succumb to our compulsions, to submit to our infantile wishes for omnipotence and destruction, for greediness and limitless gratification, is in my view a form of failure, a violation of this one leading value.

The implications of these findings will be recognized in chapter 18 of this book when we turn to recommendations.

Chapter 15

MISPLACED EMPHASIS

IN LARGE SCALE PLANNING

I am in agreement with Kaplan and Wieder when they write that "drug abuse and addiction will be with us until the day all mental health problems are solved" (1974, p. 176).

I agree, too, that any attempt to launch a concerted effort of treating the serious forms of drug use (mainly compulsive drug use) poses a mass problem to psychiatry—to the psychiatric profession in universities, private practice, in the drug programs, and in research facilities.

In the light of my personal experiences in trying to bridge the gap between perceived need for intensive reconstructive and propping up work to be carried out with these patients whose ego pathology, whose character disorder, whose neurotic or psychotic symptomatology, whose family disturbances, are all so profound and massive—versus the actually available resources, skills, funds, even just interested and sufficiently trained people, I offer some very sharp, almost cynical observations and criticisms about the frivolous lack of focus that goes on in the treatment of this problem. I, too, have shared in some of these frivolities; some I have opposed from the beginning; some may be of parochial nature; but I think they are paradigms for some of the more general problems.

Exaggeration of the Urine Rituals

Urine testing has its place as a subordinate, truly ancillary checking mechanism in mass programs and occasionally in the more individualized treatment. Its origin was in that time when compulsory forms of abstinence were in vogue and when the only two mechanisms to keep the patient in treatment were the threat of his return to jail if he "violated" his abstinence and the verification of such violation by foolproof urine testing. A third ingredient: active help, supervision, the benevolent, but, lastly, punitive or threatening authority, mainly the parole officer, occasionally a psychiatrist or psychologist, who kept looking over the shoulder of the patient, was of dubious weight in holding the patient "on track."

Now we have a bureaucratic structure set up for all programs, especially for methadone maintenance programs, which has instituted a rigid pursuit and enormously costly system (costly in time, effort, attention, energy, and money) to make sure that patients do not take drugs.

The focus is totally misplaced. Urine tests can be valuable as confirmations of clinical suspicions; they can be important clues. At best, what a good program does with the results is that it treats it as a signal that something has gone awry with the patient—not as a signal for discharge from the program, but as a red flag alerting us: "the patient goes through a crisis, the help rendered is not sufficient."

A good clinical program will by and by pick up such danger signals anyway, will not treat them as "violations," but as symptoms, and try to work with the exacerbation of the psychopathology.

The overemphasis on the urine rituals detracts so massively from the real issues, the attention to the real, enormous problems, that the devotion of time with which we had to solve these riddles appears to me often rather frivolous. Quite besides this, we encounter in this misfocusing another example of social complicity with individual pathology: the dictate of urine rituals directly plays into the addicts' archaic shame conflicts.

Again the statement by Kaplan and Wieder in their book's title is what has to be kept in mind: "People Take Drugs, Drugs Don't Take People." *The focus must be on personalities, not on urine.*

Cost Efficiency

I quoted Khantzian and co-workers as to the nemesis of that emphasis: *patients are rehabilitated as to drugs and are failures as to treatment.* Methadone, because of its cost effectiveness, has been oversold. Those portions most important in helping patients must be sacrificed or, are at best, considered "ancillary." The numbers of slots filled count, not the actual work done in most time-consuming crisis interventions. In turn, a program may run smoothly, finally really cost-efficiently, because, as several critics noticed, it has become "silted-up"—it is filled with the less problematic, less difficult, though often stagnant patients. The others have been originally rejected, have dropped out or were administratively dismissed. All slots are filled. Everyone becomes complacent; and to add unnecessary burdens would mean rocking the boat of the cost-efficient, "rational," "well-run program."

This irony again reaches frivolous proportions if we consider what is covered up within the program itself in psychopathology—and who is turned away as not treatable.

Frivolity and Tragic Misperceptions Due to Punitiveness

I might refer to the tendency of vindictiveness within programs as outlined in Appendix E.

But punitiveness is not a problem restricted to treatment programs; it is a political, legal reality on an international scale.

The focus is on deterrence, police action, tightening the laws to excess. As with all victimless crimes I am convinced that the reliance on law enforcement is counterproductive in many ways: (a) it detracts a vastly understaffed police, prosecutorial, judicial and penal system from the persecution and treatment of the really serious forms of criminality; (b) it creates an enormous amount of secondary criminality (including the hierarchy of the underworld with its huge profits); (c) it uses funds better spent in rehabilitation; (d) it misses again the focus: we deal lastly with severely disturbed patients who are not treatable with punishment, but with more appropriate (including at times compulsory) measures, lastly of a psychiatric nature.

In other words: The view of compulsive drug use as a sin which is to be purged by punishment is untenable. The results of punishment have been poor; at best a symptom exchange may have occurred—opiate use to suicidal depression, or to alcoholism.

The antipsychiatric and antipsychoanalytic prejudices lend strong helpful hands to an overdrawn, irrational emphasis on responsibility where most of the ability to act responsibly, ethically, is overwhelmed by compelling, unconscious forces (not because of "addiction," but underlying, preceding psychopathology) (see Fingarette 1975).

Inertia of Institutions

Hospitals and universities have not been hospitable to the starting up of drug programs—often for very good reasons: the patients might be a menace to the rest of the hospital, the politicization of the problem, including pressures from prominent figures to get fast results, regardless of clinical soundness, the breaking of precedents in hiring and firing, the often very uncertain funding pattern, etc.

But there is more to it: As we saw in chapter 13, every institution is a system of power distribution; every change in such a system evokes massive resistance and plays part in an often precarious equilibrium between power blocs. Such a new program, especially if introduced under the intense pressures of state and federal authorities as well as the lay public (and therefore forced to build up very fast), disturbs the balance of powers within institutions, thus arousing fear and rage and calls for attempts to stifle and destroy such an emerging troublemaker.

How to deal with this series of problems of power and hierarchy would deserve a separate extensive consideration; here I might say that to deal with it requires of the program leaders above all three qualities; (1) a lot of political know-how, a science of power distribution—particularly delicate if one does not want to violate one's own integrity; (2) a deep ability of seeing through the mask of people, their public appearance, to separate the wheat from the chaff at once; (3) specific self-control, on the one side of the feelings of exasperation, helplessness and anxiety—on the other side of the feelings of anger about impervious authority and of despair about the bureaucratic maze. As we saw: To try to ram one's protests through the walls of power evokes only more resistance and that in its more insidious forms. Protest is a sword that turns in one's hand.

Deluge of Bureaucratic Requirements

Partly as a consequence of the previous problems, though far less pernicious, is the build-up of a costly bureaucratic apparatus, swallowing up large portions of funds and proving their own worthiness and need to exist by their zeal to drown the working therapists under a tide of paper. The protocols for grants and necessary permits, the forms to be filled out on each patient, the evaluative reports, swallow huge chunks of time of professionals and paraprofessionals. Much is reduplication: city, state and various federal agencies demand mostly overlapping data, but on different sheets, often with a dozen or hundreds of questions—sometimes every two weeks!

It takes at least one fulltime person, and usually some time of everyone else, just to cope with this paper work.

One has to view this aspect, however, with sympathy and understanding. Suddenly huge sums of public money are channeled into treatment approaches; systems of grants administration have to be developed ab ovo if a responsible accounting of how the moneys are spent is to be done. And particularly in light of what I said before (the entrance of many unscrupulous opportunists in the field), such a painstaking accounting is imperative, not to speak of the measures needed to prevent diversion of drugs from the programs; yet still much streamlining could be done.

Here I can quote from a paper presented recently by P. G. Goldsmith:

Although the treatment directors are sincere and concerned in their efforts to improve their programs, almost all can be fairly described as having little management training or experience. One of the results is poor utilization of staff resources, and organization of treatment efforts. A substantial proportion, 40 to 50 percent, of treatment program staff effort goes into management and supervisory activities ... and the number of patient/health professional contacts is very low .... Both physicians (including psychiatrists) and nurses were found to be performing administra-

tive and supervisory functions during large percentages of their time.
[1974]

This leads not only to wasting of most valuable skills and time, but
faces the clinician with the dilemma: either he continues this line of
work, often at the detriment of his best qualities, desperately trying to
work in ways he is least capable and trained, or he leaves this field
altogether.

One-Track Mentality

Nearly every write-up about treatment programs speaks about
modalities, and usually vaunts a multi-modality program, meaning
that a patient can enter either methadone maintenance or psychotherapy, a residential facility or be placed on narcotics antagonists. Only
rarely is there a timid attempt to combine methods.

And yet, my observations with all types of drug use has been that a
great number of patients do not fall into the treatment modalities
which currently exist and are eligible for funding. The strictures on
methadone maintenance: the conditions of eligibility and the low level
of funding (one to two thousand dollars per patient a year), make it
very hard (possible, but neither cost-efficient nor "looking well"
statistically) to accept patients for the only form of ambulatory
detoxification which makes any sense, namely protracted withdrawal
over two to six months, combined with intense counseling and other
avenues of rehabilitation, especially psychotherapy. Nor can the
intensity of work to be done with this large category be afforded in a
fundable program. Or: The vast number of patients with multi-
habituations, with combined forms of compulsive drug use (narcotics
and alcohol and cocaine, for example), as well as patients with
compulsive barbiturate, amphetamine and psychedelic use alone,
cannot be successfully treated with currently funded methods;
moreover even those very intensive and expensive in-patient treatment
methods which are used, though not covered in regular programs, have
up to now been only rarely successful.

Or: Many patients clearly eligible (and accepted) on methadone
maintenance are failures, continue using other drugs or engaging in
nefarious activities, or they develop serious psychiatric problems. The

intensive efforts required (individual psychotherapy or a residential sojourn combined with methadone) are outside of the pale of funding.

In other words: the either-or approach which is so popular today may be justified in basic research, but not in treatment. We may draw on very similar analogies in the therapy of schizophrenia, leukemia, and tuberculosis: we have to combine two, three, and more agents, "modalities," for one given patient—often simultaneously. Such combinations of treatment are absolutely needed—instead of the one-track model so welcome to intellectual laziness.

Thus the desolate problem of how to treat compulsive drug use becomes part and parcel of the much more encompassing logistical problems: how to treat emotional disorder on a large systematic scale and with appropriate means—with well-trained personnel, a rich combination of methods, a profound sensitivity to the complexity of each individual's psychopathology and the delicacy its treatment requires.

I repeat what Kaplan and Wieder so eloquently stated: "In truth, drug abuse and addiction will be with us until the day all mental health problems are solved."

"Street Wise and Treatment Foolish"

In chapter 13 in particular I have commented about direct observations of severe malfeasance by staff, malfeasance moreover not amenable to disciplinary action.

I have listened to a number of friends working all over the country in this field, and the examples I have given were by no means unique. The Vautrins and their ilk are at least frequent occurrences.

Yet there has been for many years a pressure from the funding sources to employ ex-addicts as counselors and, in general, use only people at such meager pay that their qualifications perforce are at best questionable. Some turn out to be outstanding (ex-addicts or not), but underpaid. Others are and remain a millstone weighing the entire program down, into some forms of malpractice, into fraud, into an unethical, if not a criminal malaise, into public scandals, thus once again discrediting the entire field (treatment as well as patients).

This does not invalidate the great usefulness of "streetworkers" and ex-addicts in programs, as shown in the contrasting studies of

O'Malley et al. (1972) versus Renner and Rubin (1973), presented in Appendix E. Especially at intake and in recurrent evaluations their services can be invaluable. It is simply necessary to keep in mind, (a) that the "Peter Principle" applies here, too, and (b) that street wisdom and former drug use do not wipe out nor always outweigh the frequent massivity of their underlying problems nor do they eliminate the crucial need for professional skills of the highest order.

In short: As in many bureaucracies the focus lies on trivial details, on quantity, on often rather unreasonable rules, on cost-efficiency while the grave problems are neglected ("fiddling while Rome burns"). Sapienti Sat!

Summary

I gave a brief outline of what I consider misplaced emphasis, missed focus: the exaggeration of the urine rituals, the over-trust in "helpers" and the need for much psychotherapeutic and professional support for the paraprofessionals, the counselors (whose help is invaluable but only in conjunction with that of professionals), the fetish of cost efficiency which has done much harm in missing the crucial values in programs, the misperceptions due to vindictiveness and punitiveness, the inertia of institutions (especially hospitals and universities), the overabundance of bureaucratic hinderances, and the bane of the "one-track mentality."

A brief study of the literature in regard to the use of psychodynamic considerations in treatment of toxicomanics and a presentation of how we try to apply such insights in our own program is enclosed as Appendix E.

Chapter 16

INTENSIVE PSYCHOTHERAPY

Precious little is known about the underlying psychopathology; but the systematic development of a psychotherapeutic method for compulsive drug users is, as far as I can detect, nil.

Premises

The following is a first attempt to use some of the deeper insights gained and to describe how psychotherapy can be conducted with this most difficult category of patients.

When we look back to chapter 6, we can conclude that the drug has an adaptive, self-controlling function; no punitive action can fully replace the need for this function. The question arises: How can transference, countertransference, working alliance, and restructuring of the entire life situation help or impede the resolution of the conflicts hitherto coped with pharmacologically.

At the same time the acute drug effect and often the chronic effect as well interfere with meaningful psychotherapy to the point of making it totally useless. There are, however, a few exceptions which are noteworthy: some are patients on stable doses of narcotics (concretely: methadone), others who were maintained on amphetamines, and a third group strongly helped by minor tranquilizers (Valium, Serax, Librium), despite the potential for abuse of such pharmacological support, if not most carefully handled.

The chief propensity of these patients is to act as a defense, to externalize, instead of looking into themselves at their feelings and conflicting parts. The other two leading defenses (and dangers!) we observed were denial and dissociation. Idealization, projection, and symbiotic identification were still other forms of defense which were frequently encountered. If the patients do not use drugs for these defensive purposes, they surely use alternate means which have to be examined equally seriously.

All compulsive drug users have most massive problems of self-esteem. They are very brittle and need even more tact than most other types of patients although they know precisely how to evoke tactlessness, the anger of frustration, in the therapist (as countertransference). Allied with this form of narcissistic problem are the conflicts of power, the difficulties observing boundaries, limits, degree.

Although they are the most devious, manipulative, controlling, lying, unreliable group of patients I know, they have to be treated with utmost honesty and thus can become treatable.

Since the drugs provide not only enormous relief, but also huge pleasures, they have to suffer first from the consequences of their illness before they are motivated for treatment. Often they have to reach despair, rock bottom, a kind of sociolegal Thermophylae, before they become treatable.

Since their problems are intertwined with those of their families, the focus has often to shift. Sometimes the family has to participate directly—at least in severe crises; more often the family pathology as viewed by and mirrored in the patient has to take a high priority in the problems dealt with. There is often an easy way out for patients and therapists which turns out to be a blind alley: to blame. To blame the parents (or society) just supports the already preponderant propensity to externalize and project. It has to be stressed to patients and families alike that to understand, to examine, to question does not mean to condemn, to humiliate and to assign faults.

As noted also in regard to program strategy, external structures are needed to make treatment possible, since there is such a lack of internal ones. Conditions for continued treatment, or court commitment and probation, may be very necessary. A kind of curious split in the superego functions has to be built into the therapy: on the one side we need a partial suspension of the usual watchdog functions of the conscience during the therapy session; but, while we can trust in neurotic patients that they continue to function as far as outside actions are concerned (Paul Gray, personal communication), we cannot presume this with toxicomanics. On the contrary, the therapist has actually to take on some of these functions himself. *He is an auxiliary external structure, a guardian of boundaries and limits.* But this leads from previous findings into a more careful description of the methods used—an application of our novel psychodynamic insights.

The last three points above already carry their implications for the treatment method with them.

Dynamic Considerations:
Transference and Defense Interpretations

The type of drug abused is really not all that important as to the conduct of psychotherapy—provided that the direct pharmacotoxic effect or its legal complications do not interfere with any meaningful conversation.

TRANSFERENCE, COUNTERTRANSFERENCE, AND WORKING ALLIANCE

One cannot do "business as usual" with this type of patient. In many ways they resemble psychotic patients. Despite the usually dismal prognosis it is important to state that I have seen a number of very severe chronic drug abusers successfully in long-term therapy. I think in particular of several patients who had been dependent for ten to twenty years on very high doses of amphetamines (one hundred mg and more) or similar stimulants or of narcotics (with dosages of one- to eight hundred mg of methadone daily) whom I saw for one or several years. I was unfortunately not permitted—at the patients' explicit demand—to present some of the most striking examples here, even in disguised form. But if I look back over these experiences one precondition of treatment particularly sticks in my mind: the readiness on both sides for very intensive, analytically oriented work, sticking it out no matter what. By "very intensive" I mean—in times of crises—six or seven sessions a week (sometimes much longer than one hour), plus telephone availability in times of lesser urgency. I have had cases who decompensated repeatedly and necessitated brief hospitalizations (e.g., for suicidality in the case of amphetamine abstinence—often many months after withdrawal), but were able in such very intensive psychotherapy to work out their problems sufficiently to be not only capable of assuming highly responsible positions, but also able to enter psychoanalysis proper with colleagues of mine.

Obviously this would not have been advisable with myself—for the idealizing as well as hostile transference had found far too much basis in the external reality relationship with me for it to remain analyzable by myself. Given the severely regressive nature of the entire personality organization it gradually became clear to me that the treatment situation has to encompass the following built-in transference elements:

It has to have strongly nurturing, supportive elements without, however, feeding into the often overwhelming fears in the toxicomanic patient of engulfment. The therapist has to be far more *active*, warm, interested, personally involved, yet again without becoming *intrusive,* as very often the mother was.

In all instances the exact counterpart has to be observed as well: to maintain distance, to be very patient, not pressuring, almost detached, without, however, supporting the profound sense of abandonment and despair so deep in these patients. One has to create a clear boundary of separateness, an atmosphere of non-symbiosis and respect for individuality while still allowing symbiotic conflicts to be expressed, to become interpretable, and not having the patient feel exploited and treated as a nonhuman object, no matter how much he tries to do that himself.

Clinical experience appears to indicate that there may be indeed two basic types of compulsive drug users, one far more afraid of engulfment (a preponderantly claustrophobic type), the other fearing much more isolation and loneliness (in whom claustrophilic needs prevail; see also Stierlin 1974).

In the first type more distance needs to be preserved for a longer period of time for trust to arise; whereas in the second type far more direct support is needed, making up for a traumatic sense of object loss.

In most cases, though, a delicate balance needs to be found, a constant empathetic weighing of whether more nurturing or more distance is needed at the given moment.

Limit setting, external structure, is crucial. Time and again the patient needs to be faced with the alternative of curtailing some particularly noxious form of acting out or of forfeiting any true benefit from therapy and even the gains already attained. Each time of such an intervention is a crisis for the therapy. The patient may concur and work on the intense anger this limit setting evokes, with additional gain in self-control and with that in the ability to observe himself and in the working alliance. Or he may bolt, revolt, vanish, seeing the guardianship of the therapist over boundaries and limits yet as a new form of entrapment, of intrusion, of enclosure. Therefore, such interventions have to be used very sparingly and without any moralistic implication: transgression of ethical or of any other boundaries has to be treated strictly as a symptom with severe self-destructive potential, the compulsiveness of which is the sole concern, not its antisocial (or socially positive) valence!

This leads naturally over to problems of countertransference. Outrageous disregard of limits is often enacted precisely to provoke rage, punishment and scorn from the therapist, and thus to reconfirm the masochistic triumph: "No one can ever be trusted. I am suffering betrayal and degradation again, and thus I prove the basic unworth of human relationships; I can rely only on my actions and on nonhuman substances."

Or in turn the therapist becomes a masochistic partner, forced by the ostentatious suffering of the patient into endless giving and giving-in, or into going along with and thus once again indulging the severest, most pernicious regressions.

Again the therapist has to find a golden mean: to set limits actively, but without anger, sadism, shaming, and vindictiveness, and yet to be very flexible, patient, always oriented not toward ethical values in a narrow sense, but toward the central psychoanalytic value outlined in chapter 14.

This demand for giving and indulgence may in some cases be overwhelming, especially in massively spoiled or severely neglected patients. The transference-countertransference bind may turn into a sadomasochistic nightmare, a severe negative therapeutic reaction and hence into defeat (e.g., Cassandra, case 17): rage, pain, hopelessness alternating with insatiable demands. Here the dilution of the dyadic therapy relationship may save both treatment and life (see case 24, Toni, below; also Patpet, case 4). In a number of cases the splitting up of the therapeutic approaches into a combination of individual, family and group therapy, carried out by different therapists, proved far superior to individual psychotherapy alone. This is again an approach directly contravening the one-track mentality already duly pilloried in chapter 15. (I owe a clearer recognition of such combination treatment mostly to Drs. Richard Anderson, Edward J. Khantzian and Ellen McDaniel.)

Whereas the just mentioned type of transference-countertransference constellation is a kind of perversion of intimacy, the next is a type of distancing which can reach extreme proportions. In many patients it may take a real therapeutic moratorium of months, even years, of passive drifting, boredom, interrupted treatment, apparent endless stagnation, of a deep gloom of despair and hopelessness in the patient and at times effectively transmitted to the therapist until a solid basis of trust has grown to start therapy in earnest. Andreas was a good example of that.

This moratorium of passivity might be necessary not only because of the deep fear of intimacy, of the claustrum, and thus the devouring, engulfing mother, but also as the dread of the murderous aggression unleashed in the submission to the power of the stronger "other." (This may also account for the fact that nearly all drug abuse patients treated in psychotherapy abruptly broke it off, very often after having gained sufficient self-mastery to be superficially "adjusted," but not enough to satisfy criteria for successful termination.)

In order to tolerate both lengthy moratoria and break ups the therapist has not only to be patient and rather at peace with his own narcissistic needs, but also in need of two additional traits. For one he has to see in the patient strongly redeeming features. In this feeling of respect and esteem for the patient, there is, of course, a lot of *hope* which outweighs the massive despair. Secondly, as Freud stressed, he has to subordinate his therapeutic zeal to scientific curiosity: to understand and to help to understand must take precedence over the wish to heal, to mold according to one's own value priorities. Waiting may mean building trust and showing caring; but then stepping in and setting the right limits at the right moment may be critically important.

The working alliance was defined by Greenson (1967) as "the relatively nonneurotic, rational rapport which the patient has with his analyst." I believe this concept to be equally applicable to the analytically oriented psychotherapy commonly chosen with these patients. In most instances these patients are too sick, too self-destructive, too demanding, to leave much room for such rational cooperation. At first it merely consists of a gut reaction: "I have suffered enough; I want to start anew. I am unwilling to pay the price I paid in the past again in the future." Thus it is not so much the value of rationality which attracts them, but the fear of further pain and suffering which pushes them from behind. But as the time passes (again often years) an identification with the value of inner freedom, of self-mastery, of non-condemning exploration and knowledge, as represented by the therapist, may replace the more archaic ego ideals, and gradually lend more and more force to rationality and thus to the working alliance. Hence, shame and guilt may become associated with such a standard of reason instead of the grandiose self-image which had ruled supreme.

DEFENSE INTERPRETATIONS

As Kernberg (1975) emphasizes, the consistent interpretation of the negative transference in the "here and now" perforce leads to an interpretation of the leading, archaic defenses, especially splitting. I usually find a hierarchical layering of lines of defense. The first line of defense consists of shame and/or guilt. The second line are the defenses already described as the Alpha and Omega in these patients: denial/split and externalization, the latter often combined with projection. The third line is the magical transformation of inner and outer reality by conscious lying and manipulating (carried though by intense unconscious narcissistic demands). The fourth line of defense is mainly the grandiosity which hides the deep and repeated traumata, the suffering underneath, and, withal, the phobic and depressive core constellations.

Passivity as defense against aggression, idealization as defense against haughty, arrogant dismissal of the other, may enter here or there along the line.

In addition the utmost reliability, honesty and consistency on the side of the therapist has a crucial effect over the years—in light of the "anomia" described. It is so utterly easy to fall into the innumerable manipulations, seductions, urgencies as traps, that the postulate just made remains an ideal, never completely reached. Nor is it easy to bridge this polarity (the therapist's attitude of consistency and honesty against the patient's often utter unreliability) with clear, lucid defense interpretations. And yet it needs to be done as far as feasible.

The deeper work is mainly directed at grandiose expectations of themselves and of others, at this regressive splitting between all-good and all-bad, the generalization and "totalization." It focuses on reliving much of the often very traumatic events from early childhood and the hurt, rage, loneliness, and terror going with them, and the rekindling of these feelings by present disappointments and frustrations. The latter include the particularly complex therapeutic relationship where real relationship and transference aspects inevitably mingle. Very importantly it deals with fury, anger, and the anxiety about this rage against others and the self. In nearly every such case it is sporadically important to make the patient aware of how he has tried to provoke (or indeed succeeded in provoking) anger or hurt in me—and thus to bring the tremendous, usually unconscious or preconscious aggression under the microscope of psychotherapeutic exploration.

A great deal of direct support to narcissistic wishes or needs is necessary, especially at the beginning. In general, the issue of drug taking very soon takes a back seat in the psychotherapeutic work.

SPLITTING OF TRANSFERENCE

The case presented below as an illustration for the need to split up quite concretely the therapeutic relationships and thus the transference has been graciously contributed by Dr. Ellen McDaniel.

CASE 24, TONI

Toni sought psychiatric help following a conflict at work with her department chairman. Her complaints were vague: insomnia, intense recurring headaches, and nervousness. She gave a perfunctory sketch of her family background and, although seemingly eager to get into treatment, could not clearly describe what was the nature of her distress. She spoke in a coherent and well organized manner, had no evidence of any thought disturbances, hallucinations, delusions, impairment of intellectual functioning (in fact she was felt to be very bright) or obvious indications of a mood disturbance. If anything, her affect seemed flat. The fine trembling of her hands and some slight tearing (which the patient blinked away almost before the therapist could be certain that they were tears) were the only indications of feelings. Toni denied feeling anything in particular other than being nervous at seeing a psychiatrist. Twice a week visits were agreed upon. Just as the hour was ending, Toni told the therapist that she had been taking barbiturates for some time. She had no idea how much she took but felt that it was at least three hundred mgs of phenobarbital each night. She refused to discuss hospitalization for detoxification and declared that she would withdraw herself. The therapist remembered a feeling of sadness after the patient left. Toni seemed to be reaching out but was so denying of feelings that the therapist was left wondering if the patient was not suffering very much; however, at that point the picture was not clear.

The early years of this woman were characterized by massive and unremitting traumata. Toni was the youngest of six children. Both parents worked and neither were home during the time between dinner and bedtime. The father was home during dinner. The four daughters were expected to make the meals for the family. Two older brothers (eight and ten years older than Toni) were responsible for the after dinner care of the four younger girls from at least the time that Toni was in kindergarten. Cloudy memories of preschool years included being shifted among the neighbors for temporary supervision. Predictably, much physical abuse (and on a few occasions sexual abuse) by these older brothers occurred over the ensuing years. When father was home, he was even more violent and unpredictable than Toni's siblings. However, he did acknowledge Toni's existence by his criticism and anger, unlike the mother who was described as very withdrawn and uncommunicative. When father would beat the children, mother would "go to another room and cry. She never did anything! Father at least cared about what we did."

Toni began stealing in first grade, initially from parents, later from anyone available. From her description, the stealing had a compulsive quality to it, both aggressive and erotic in tone. She described this activity as follows, "I would plan how to take the money. It would be very exciting. All of my interest was on the plan, which became more skillful the older I was. I'd get the money and hide it and then feel terrible. I felt like I was the scum of the earth. I was so ashamed of myself and thought that I didn't deserve to have any friends. I'd pray to

God all the time to help me stop but at the first opportunity, I'd be back at it again."

Because of her intellectual ability and her quite appealing way of engaging people's interest, Toni did very well in school, both academically and socially. She pursued graduate training in medicine and, at the time of beginning treatment, was considered to be a very competent radiologist at a well-known medical center. She was not married. Later the therapist was to learn that Toni had become involved in a very conflictual sexual relationship a short time before seeking treatment.

Therapy proved to be very stormy. The patient was silent and expressionless for many of the hours during the first two years of treatment. When she talked she would give limited content descriptions of what was going on at work and in her relationships with her colleagues. She quit therapy after the first six months and returned three months later. She again stopped on the day of her first psychiatric hospitalization. The therapist was very concerned about her inability to make contact with Toni. She realized that Toni was depressed but believed (because the patient seemed able to maintain her professional and social commitments, and because the patient seemed well defended against experiencing the full brunt of her melancholy) that the best therapeutic approach was a quiet acceptance of the patient as she presented herself until greater security in the therapeutic relationship could be established. This then would enable Toni slowly to get in touch with her feelings of emptiness and estrangement. However, this approach proved to be devastating to Toni. Later she would describe how the therapist's inactivity was experienced as disinterest and the failure of the therapist to realize the worsening depression was the failure of "my last chance. After you didn't understand me, I had no one at all."

The following is an example of the therapeutic miscommunication as well as an illustration of the extreme degree that splitting (of objects into "all-good" and "all-bad") was used defensively by Toni. When the patient discussed her sexual partner at a time when she was angry with him, she referred to the person by the last name (which was the kind of name that could also be a first name) and described him as her roommate. When Toni was discussing this person in a more positive sense, the first name was used and the setting was as a colleague at work. The therapist did not realize until the second year of treatment that these "people" were the same person. In the transference, this particular mental mechanism contributed to the disintegration of treatment. The therapist was all-good when therapy began but after the failure of the therapist to perceive empathically the despair that was increasing within the patient, the therapist became all-bad. Toni's attempt to integrate the two objects into the person of the therapist led to a most unfortunate fragmentation.

During those first two years of treatment, the patient was on increasing doses of amphetamines. The primary drug of choice was the barbiturate which initially permitted the patient to sleep and "forget everything." The amphetamines were then introduced to offset the barbiturates so that Toni could continue her productivity at work. At the time the therapist did not know about the amphetamine abuse. Attempts by both parties to examine the faltering relationship failed. Toni announced one day that she was stopping. That night she was admitted to a hospital (with which the therapist had no affiliation) after overdosing and cutting her wrists. She was in respiratory distress upon admission and was psychotic for the next twenty-four hours. The psychosis cleared completely after that first day (probably an amphetamine psychosis), but Toni remained profoundly depressed. The hospital insisted on electroconvulsive therapy because of the concern about another suicide attempt. The hospital viewed the therapist very negatively because of the differences in treatment approach between the two, and she was prohibited from visiting the patient. Toni later would describe making a massive effort to appear healthy so as to end the shock therapy. She was discharged after six weeks and decided, without the hospital's support, to return to her previous therapist. She recalled years later, "I had to make it work"— restore the "goodness" of the therapist (and herself).

During the next phase in treatment the therapist (who by this time had knowledge about the patient's nonverbal communication as well as her critical life events to venture more educated guesses about what might be going on with Toni) became much more active in the hours. Feedback was given on how Toni was coming across, how the therapist felt, why any particular question was asked and what the reality options were. Whatever interpretations about behavior that could be made were made.

Soon after discharge, Toni shifted from amphetamines and barbiturates to codeine, demerol, and large quantities of darvon. The compulsive stealing continued. She frequently came to sessions nodding and two years later would sadly tell the therapist, "I have lost a year of my life." The drugs allowed her not to feel; to steal without remorse, to lessen the anguish of responsibility and concern that she felt for friends involved with her; to decrease her relentless headaches and rages. She described watching herself go through the motions of living without any particular awareness that the person that she was watching was herself. This extreme depersonalization made therapy very difficult. It was like talking to a person who was not really there. During this third year of treatment, meetings were scheduled four times a week; two fifty minute sessions and two half hour sessions. The therapist expressed concern that therapy might be more upsetting than beneficial, in view of the obvious increasing drug abuse. Toni emphatically responded that these nearly daily treatment hours were the only times that she felt safe and together.

Almost one year after the first hospitalization, Toni's abuse of Demerol was so great that losing her license to practice medicine was becoming a very real danger. Both therapist and patient agreed to an elective psychiatric hospitalization for Toni at the hospital where the therapist did consultation work. During that hospitalization Toni became acquainted with an alcohol counselor who conducted group therapy for alcoholics. This counselor suggested that Toni might benefit from group therapy since so many of the problems of drug and alcohol abusers were shared. The therapist agreed but primarily for another reason. She felt that Toni's inability to integrate ambivalent feelings made it impossible for her to withstand the disappointment and rage that she felt towards the therapist without fragmenting. The therapist hoped that if Toni had another therapist, the transference could be usefully split until such time when tolerance for experiencing ambivalence would be achieved. The individual sessions were reduced to three times a week and group therapy took place weekly. Also of interest was the use of a major tranquilizer at nighttime during this third year. The tranquilizer seemed to diminish the "realness" of dreams and allowed the patient to sleep through the night. The drug was also experienced by the patient as something concrete that the therapist gave her.

During the fourth year of work, the narcotic and Darvon abuse continued. Perhaps the big difference now was that Toni discussed it more openly than before. The group gave her a sense of belonging and made it possible for her to share her drug problem with others without feeling overwhelming shame. The stealing continued but was also more openly discussed. Shortly before the patient's third hospital admission, the stealing had escalated to the point where Toni was afraid to leave her home for fear of the temptation. She felt desparate. The only two choices that seemed even possible to pursue for the removal of this specific symptom were behavior therapy and hypnosis. Toni chose the latter. After a few sessions with a psychiatrist specializing in that technique (not the therapist), the stealing did stop. Toni never believed that the hypnosis was responsible for the symptom removal but did clearly associate the ending of her stealing with seeing that hypnotist. Soon after that problem was resolved the group began applying supportive pressure on Toni to assume greater responsibility for her drug abuse. The group had made a recent commitment that each member contribute more to the progress of the whole. This touched on an important aspect of Toni's character structure. Toni strongly felt that she had made a commitment to the group's well-being when she joined and it became a matter of self-esteem to keep that commitment. Hospitalization was arranged in a general community hospital for detoxification. If it had not been for that group, this detoxification would have been tragically delayed.

Following that last brief hospitalization the patient remained drug free. Individual and group therapies progressed to working on many previously unapproachable subjects and feelings—dynamic understanding of the symptomatic behavior expanded.

The stealing represented the outcome of a multitude of conflicts coming together in a problematic compromise. The stealing was an aggressive assault on important objects towards whom negative feelings were not intrapsychically permitted. It symbolized security during a time when father threatened to desert the family. "I used to panic at the idea of my father leaving. How would we be able to live? I knew mother couldn't handle the family so I learned how to steal. That I could do no matter what happened!" The stealing could not have occurred without the extreme use of denial, depersonalization, and externalization. "I never felt it was me stealing until it (the individual act) was over. Then I'd feel horrible." The drugs helped to maintain the use of these defense mechanisms so as to keep the patient from fragmenting when her all-good objects (friends, family, teachers, colleagues and, of course, the therapist) would be unable to maintain their exalted positions. The patient then would feel shame, rejection, and despair and would attempt to maintain her own self-esteem by making these people all-bad or by blaming herself for their downfalls. This left her feeling utter dejection and hatred for herself. She said of her first hospitalization, "How could I blame you if I wouldn't talk? I couldn't be angry with you. You were my last chance. It had to be I that was the failure."

The patient continued to have areas of difficulty. Sexual conflicts and fantasy material continued to be only infrequently mentioned. Splitting and denial continued to be used but to a lesser degree. The dynamics of splitting were not clear but probably involved (1) a childhood need to preserve parental objects as loving figures during frequent periods of disruption, (2) a split in the patients's self-images, and (3) a contradictory communication from parents and siblings between what was demanded (obedient, quiet, nonaggressive and nonsexual behavior) and what actually took place.

In summary, this patient made use of a multi-therapy approach (in-patient, out-patient, group, individual, medication, and hypnosis) to assist her in dealing with her psychological difficulties for which she had previously used drugs and primitive defense mechanisms in an attempt to hold onto life.

Besides the demonstration of the problem now under discussion—the handling of a severe negative therapeutic reaction, probably dictated by overwhelming shame—this patient also lends independent confirmation to many of the concepts presented earlier (e.g., the importance of depersonalization and other forms of denial and splitting, of externalization, the use of drugs as an affect defense, the severe traumatization). It is particularly important to stress that Dr. McDaniel arrived at these formulations independently of my own work.

The same could be observed in Cassandra (case 17). Dr. Phillips adds to his case description:

Regarding the treatment, it gradually became clear that Cassandra's feelings of despair and rage were intolerable to her, and that twice weekly, analytically-oriented therapy was inadequate to support her ability to tolerate these feelings. In addition, she was inconsistent in taking the purely administrative steps necessary to have her insurance pay the majority of the clinic fee. Therefore it was felt that she required a combination treatment after discharge from her latest hospitalization: this should include neurological support for her anticonvulsant therapy, individual therapy for continuing efforts at integration of past traumata with present reality, and group therapy. This last modality was felt to be particularly important. In a group of substance abusers, meeting weekly, the patient could obtain a sense of community support and caring never experienced in her abusive and neglectful family experience. Her inclination alternately to idealize and degrade the therapist while simultaneously acting out her rage and shame intolerance by drinking, might be diluted in the group setting.

Concrete Recommendations

When I take on a patient in intensive, analytically oriented psychotherapy I usually insist on seeing him or her at least three hours a week. Some I have seen, at the beginning at least, for four or five hours, schedule permitting. Some patients I see privately at usual fees; others I have seen for free. There has been no difference whatsoever in results. One thing is important: if a patient who can afford private fees (now around forty dollars per hour) is allowed to get away with no or minimal payments, a basic principle of his pathology is condoned and confirmed by the therapist: "I can have what I want and when I want it without having to pay a price for it. I want to get away with a transgression without penalty. I want something for nothing." This is quite generally a problem in oral, narcissistic characters, not just in drug abusers.

To come back to the frequency: unless we are satisfied with superficial manipulation, with counseling, we have to treat these patients intensively. The pathology is too severe to leave vast stretches of life and time outside of constant examination and "microscopic" scrutiny. I try to make myself available for extra appointments, if needed, and—again, in crises—for telephone contacts, although I try to avoid carrying out telephone therapy. The latter feeds too much into the magical expectations of the patients. I restrict the telephone contacts to brief crisis intervention or call-backs after a particular dangerous period.

At the inception I set up a verbal contract with the patient which entails his and my obligations. I usually present it in the following manner: "We are engaging in a very difficult task together, and we both have to observe some conditions if you want to get my help in helping yourself. One of these conditions, really the most important and perhaps most difficult one, is that you do not hide anything from me, that you do not lie by omission or commission. If you want to con me, this is the easiest thing to do. I am not a detective. As a therapist I can only help you to understand how you deceive yourself unconsciously, and that is difficult enough for both of us; but if we have to deal with two curtains of lies—conscious and unconscious ones—the task becomes impossible. You and I would waste our time. I know it will be at times almost impossible for you to be open with me, but try anyway.

"A second point: if you take drugs, please tell me; I am not going to 'kick you out' of treatment for it. I have no moralistic attitude about it; I see it as a symptom, not as a sin—as something whose meaning we have to try to understand together. But at the same time if you keep taking drugs it undoes the very effort which you make by coming here, and we would have to wonder whether you are not wasting your time and mine. I would like to make that very clear: most of these drugs interfere so severely with psychotherapy that nothing whatsoever can be accomplished in hours where you are 'high.'

"The third point is a mutual agreement to keep the hours and (where applicable) to pay on a monthly basis."

In some instances where I was very leery about the reliability of patient and family, I requested that during the first two or three months the patient pay at the end of each hour.

I continue: "Only if we meet frequently do we have a chance to achieve a deeper change. And it is a difficult, at times very painful, task.

"A fourth point: whatever you tell me remains confidential. I won't have any communications pertaining to you without your being involved. If your parents call I shall tell them that I would prefer them to say it with you on the other line; if that is not possible I would ask them to come in to your next appointment (if it is a grave issue) or that I shall repeat our entire conversation to you, but that in turn I cannot relay anything from the therapy to them.

"However there is one important limit to this confidentiality: when there is an acute crisis, a severe threat to your life or the lives of others. For me life is a higher value than confidentiality—but this is the only instance where confidentiality has not first priority. Without this reliance you could not be honest toward me."

Of course I do not give that as a set speech, but I explain and discuss these points, and, as we saw in one instance, I had a patient himself draft his own version of this mutual understanding.

A constant focus of therapeutic work has to be the tendency to veer from inner problems, especially feelings, to externals; denial and externalization as the most important defenses have to be interpreted innumerable times: the flight from tension, disappointment, anger into action, from inner insecurity to outer flamboyance and bragging, from a vague sense of guilt and shame to overt actions of self-degradation or provoked violence—in whatever form it appears. It is interesting that after consistent work on this defense the talk about drugs disappears almost completely from therapy whereas at the beginning it dominates the hours.

In patients where denial is extreme (e.g., Patpet) I felt at times motivated to state: "When I put myself into what you just have told me—the worries, the problems—I myself feel a burden, a sense of depression and anxiety." I feel it, not the patient. In that case I encouraged the patient to note down whenever an uncomfortable feeling was actually emerging and before it was smothered by the all-pervasive, unconscious process of denial. The jotting down lends it a sense of concrete reality which counteracts its evanescence.

Since narcissism is obviously the crucial overt as well as covert area of problems, it needs very much attention, but in a way, as Kohut described: It has to be dealt with with utmost tact, seriousness, respect. Any sarcastic or ironic treatment of it increases the need for it. It is best to pose it as a problem, how we can understand that they are so easily injured in their self-esteem. Again: one has to return to this problem of "wanting to be so great because of feeling so low," or the pervasive sense of shame, humiliation, embarrassment, self-consciousness, time and again; however, to "attack" the narcissism as an original wish is ill-advised.

It cannot be stressed too much how valuable in this context the technical recommendations and theoretical concepts of Kohut, Kernberg, Greenacre and Beres are—even if there are contradictions in some of the theoretical understandings. It appears crucial to me not to "destroy" narcissism, not to put it down, not to emphasize reality and deride fantasies—on the contrary to listen and accept these wishes and dreams of grandeur as an inner reality of utmost importance to the patient. What can be added, however, is: how important these fantasies are as a defense—against disappointment and hurt. Again it pays to go this way from externalization to narcissism to disappointment, hurt, anger, loneliness untold times, down to the many concrete details of the last few days. In this context it is particularly valuable to keep the theoretical model of manifold stratification in mind. Roughly we may discern, in analogy to Fenichel's threefold layering, the levels of superficial narcissism—phobic depressive syndrome—basic narcissistic conflicts and traumatization. This is oversimplified though. A more careful inquiry reveals the following rather typical structure: Manifest grandiosity, ruthless overstepping of boundaries, and violence are quite typically not the "real" narcissism and aggression, but substitute forms, defensive counterfeits. The second layer is formed by defenses proper, particularly externalization, denial, projection. Much deeper, after a series of repeated layerings of what has just been described, we encounter the phobic and depressive constellations. They hide, in turn, conflicts about the original archaic drives, including archaic forms of narcissism, and the original traumata.

In contrast, what is relatively easily accessible in this regard and can barely be called transference but an automatic repetition in all human relationships, is the distrust, the lying, the looking at me as a dangerous, conniving manipulator, as a convenient, impersonal thing, or (as we saw) as a judge, meting out humiliation and punishment—that indeed is accessible early and often needs to be treated as initial resistance to treatment.

Most of the patients whom I have offered treatment dropped out after the first two or three months—usually in a flurry of drug taking, criminality, or in simple disappearance. I believe that this drop-out rate can be cut down if this initial resistance is tackled openly and honestly.

I try to "analyze," to understand the history of, and need for, this lead symptom of deviousness from the very beginning. I focus on how they circumvent my questions, how hard it is to tell me about some incidents (not just regarding drugs), except after a lapse of time. What hinders them to talk about them right away? It is the old, but so difficult analytic adage I try to apply to these circumstances: to analyze the defenses.

In this context and particularly since human beings are in this process of externalization so easily altered into "things," another aspect of the honesty has to be brought up. In contrast to patients in analysis I feel I have to be far more "real"—not simply a mirror. I am very active with these patients—asking, nodding, repeating or rephrasing, supportive, and even at times an auxiliary superego, not just an auxiliary ego. This entails the superego's three main functions: warning, observation, ideal; it is, however, an auxiliary superego of less archaic, fragmented nature.

"Dangerous Drugs" as Life Savers

This section cannot be concluded without giving passing thought to the use of some of these forbidden drugs by the physician.

We have had ample evidence how these drugs were taken by patients as a form of self-treatment. Quite a few mentioned that life without them became unbearable, that the drugs saved them from suicide or murder.

I myself have only used methadone as a stabilizing drug with narcotics addicts, and through periods of crises prescribed Valium besides or instead (the latter after detoxification), but usually only for a few weeks and with all due precautions against abuse. Occasionally I found Thorazine helpful as a non-addictive medication for insomnia.

In the following I present, however, vignettes from two contrasting case descriptions which Dr. M.M. Kayce in Belmont, Massachusetts put together for this book and very generously allowed me to publish.

The first case (once more an instance of the "archaic shame syndrome" depicted in chapter 7) stopped her self-treatment with amphetamines, and was not given any by her physician—with tragic consequences. In the second instance amphetamine maintenance was tried with dramatically opposite effect. The latter course took a lot of courage because it goes against prevailing regulations.

CASE 25: SILVIA

A sixteen-year-old girl, adopted in her first weeks of life, was raised in a sophisticated, urban setting by a depressed, emotionally detached mother, and an often absent father. The mother could easily shift from an interested involvement to angry remonstrances when her daughter frustrated her, while the father stressed compulsive orderliness more than love.

When she was four a natural son was born to the family and the parents were patently pleased and excited. It was at that time that she was told that she was an adopted child. This remained a very traumatic memory.

She was bright and made good academic progress, was well liked; although inwardly she was jealous and destructive of authority controls, she covered it well by a sweet veneer till her aggression reemerged with the sexuality of early adolescence. By thirteen she had allowed circumstances to lead to forcible and promiscuous sexual encounters, fighting with other girls, flight from her home and open drug use. The background of this fairly sudden emergence of provocative counter culture identification was a highly pathological splitting of objects into good (controllable, giving) figures and bad (dangerous, controlling, needed) ones. The upsurge of sexuality evoked a lot of body shame and self-consciousness. The latter were partly denied by acting out in hetero- and homosexual object choices with a gradual preference for feminized males, following fearful exposures to abusive street toughs, including rape. Her shame increased to body preoccupations of near delusional proportions. She thought that her slender body was large, fat, dumpy, that her eyes looked dull, strange, were sadistic "blank eyes." She had severe blushing and an erythrophobia. These intense feelings of shame were checked in depersonalizing numbness "till I had to cut myself." Her regressive orality resulted in alternating bulimia and fasts.

The turmoil of her faltering attempts at separations from parental supplies without any cohesive identity was assuaged by early (age twelve) use of sedatives, marijuana and gradually generalized poly-toxicomania just short of heroin. Cocaine and "speed" seemed to be the most successful anti-depressants, allowing "me to feel beautiful and together like I wanted to be."

"Acid" often produced terrorizing flashback images, "but they fascinated me, dead faces singing." Dr. Kayce thought they got close to the enticing of the witch mother that cast her out originally. The conviction: "I didn't feel I belonged anywhere" turned into fugue state and gross acts of self-mutilation (slashing herself) and antisocial behavior (mainly stealing—once even a cow!). This physically acted out sadomasochism defended her from open depression and total self-annihilation, and finally elicited attempts to hospitalize her.

It is of major significance that during the hospital course, when she took unprescribed amphetamines, this seemed to allow some distancing from her sullen, angry, frightened, absorbing self, so that some "good mother" transference could take form. When she escaped from the hospital, after some argument with a staff member, she was unable to maintain a cohesive self-image. She took recourse to speed, as a source of strength, and to LSD, as the key to fantasy fusion with a good mother.

The separation-loss experience seemed to potentiate the rabid, destructive, images which had been freed by psychedelics.

She hid in the vicinity for several weeks, repeatedly calling Dr. Kayce. She kept taking small dosages of speed, but then ran out of them; instead she took marijuana, some LSD and a lot of alcohol. Within hours thereafter she killed herself by a form of self-immolation. In her diary and a note left behind she described her overwhelming loneliness and the wish to "rejoin something better," to find her (unknown) true mother. This occurred very shortly after she had persuaded another boy to return to the hospital, thus once again being the good protective mother to others, the bad, rejecting, murderous one against herself.

Thus she enacted the fantasies she had revealed in therapy and her diary: on the one side to destroy the bad girl; her insufficient adoptive mother, and her rejecting natural mother; and on the other side to find and merge with the image of her good, sweet, natural mother, while saving the good image of her adoptive mother from the pain she inflicted, and atoning for her savage, deadly anger toward her brother.

It is nearly certain that the psychedelics released the "bad" images whereas the stimulants supported the "good" ones.

CASE 26: XENIA

This was a twenty-eight-year-old single female of lower middle class origins. At nine she had moved to an affluent suburb where she was unable to adapt socially and experienced gradually increasing anxiety and depression. At the onset of adolescence she had already crystalized a depersonalizing defense orientation, which was accompanied by a rigid reaction formation: that of a pseudo-involved "good girl." Toward the outside she presented, in her words, "my sweet and noxious self," a phoney facade. Underneath she always felt semi-involved, more depersonalized than derealized: she felt she was not there; her feelings had an "as if" quality.

During her late teens, when she had been most dissatisfied with her body image (acne, subjectively but not objectively real obesity; the feeling that she looked angry, ogrous, sick, horrible), she discovered a restitutive awareness of herself when she took *anorexiant drugs*. Later she at times abused them to obtain an "alive sensation" which was described as an excited erotic state. The only times she felt real and living, at least modestly so, was on amphetamines. After considerable therapy she had some incipient arousal at the beginning of a date, but these feelings vanished after a few minutes and she just acted "the nice good date," fighting off by depersonalization both angry and sexual wishes, not because of guilt, but once again because of shame.

She continued to take amphetamines (fifteen mg over the day), was well stabilized, and felt halfway normal on them.

Once again marijuana and other psychedelics were shunned because of the deepening of depression and estrangement.

Without stimulants she was unable to work: incapable of facing people.

During a period of transference anger at the promising, disappointing, powerful mother, which emerged as Dr. Kayce enforced the requirement that she again hold a job and attempt the involvements needed, Dr. Kayce decided to prescribe amphetamines in order to give her something tangible, directly internalizable from him; and in order to stimulate more alertness and perhaps a durable sense of mastery. The effort was modestly successful.

Dr. Kayce has observed that in both patients the buoyancy effect of amphetamines assisted in the denial of painful affects and the sense of helplessness. In Silvia it was depression, loneliness, radical isolation and profound shame; in Xenia mainly shame about anger and sexual desires (about not living up to her mothers expectations). It also helped counter some symptoms which resulted from the splitting of the body ego. In both there was a rapid alternation between an ugly, aggressive, mostly shame-laden part and another one which is temporarily acceptable, not that fat, disgusting and grotesque. There seemed to be less need for intense structural regression toward projective splitting in form of primitive destructive fantasies and paranoid changes of the transference.

It is also good to remember that the accepted psychotropic drugs (major tranquilizers as well as antidepressants) may have severe paradoxical effects, as in these two cases, and lead in many toxicomanics and other severe character disorders to an aggravation instead of an amelioration of the psychopathology, especially of most massive depersonalization. We observed the same in Andreas (case 19) and Alexa (case 13). It is possible that in some these serious reactions are due to minimal brain damage which in contrast is well compensated, even in adults, by some of the "dangerous substances"—in some by amphetamines, in others by narcotics, in a few even by barbiturates or minor tranquilizers. This is not proven in the two just described cases.

The use of these drugs in a medically supervised, specifically and individually adjusted way can indeed be life saving and may yet become an indispensable adjunct to psychoanalytically oriented psychotherapy.

Chapter 17

SYSTEMATIC RECOMMENDATIONS
FOR INNOVATIVE TECHNIQUES

Obviously, by shifting the focus entirely to the personality of the compulsive drug taker and away from the drug taking, drug possessing and drug selling, many new vistas open up.

Treatment

I have indicated how I consider many of the current techniques (encounter, behavior modification, emphasis on antagonists or compulsory abstinence) as ill-suited, if not disastrous, for those vast contingents amongst the compulsive drug users whose psychopathology is very severe, even if the latter does not reach psychotic proportions. I mentioned that I estimate that 70 percent in a stable methadone maintenance program like ours would fall in this category of serious psychopathology, and that the percentages among the drop outs, the rejects, the "untreatable" poly-toxicomanics probably is yet far higher. I outlined a network of services for those latter unfortunates (Appendices B, C).

But the focus of recommendations lies in this one point: to take the psychopathology of compulsive drug use very seriously and treat it with the vast know-how we psychotherapists and psychoanalysts have accumulated, in combination with the help we get from psychopharmacology (especially long lasting narcotics substitutes like LAAM, antidepressants, antianxiety agents, antiepileptic drugs, perhaps even amphetamine maintenance). Above all we have to design for each individual patient the treatment combination best suited for him. We cannot afford to fall into the current faddish shortcuts; they do massive harm just at that critical time when the patients seek help for their overwhelming problems. I strongly feel that pseudo solutions are even worse than no solutions. I am very concerned, in what I have seen, among patients and psychiatric residents alike, that much of what is fashionable now, is an avoidance of the difficult harsh truths of clinical reality: that no severe psychopathology can be easily resolved and that its treatment very much needs professional skill and training.

At first we survey the findings presented in Appendices B and C .

PSYCHOTIC PATIENTS

Floridly schizophrenic patients who are routinely excluded from drug programs should be accepted. They prove, by and large, to be "good," well-treatable patients on methadone, provided a psychiatrist is available to diagnose and appropriately treat their disorder. The combination of methadone with major tranquilizers, the stable program structure and the sensitive, sympathetic treatment by the staff of the combined disorder makes hospitalization in many cases unnecessary.

Other forms of treatment (antagonists, compulsory abstinence, therapeutic community of the traditional type, detoxification, group therapy, "behavior modification") have either proven to be destructive and countertherapeutic or must be presumed to be so (both on the grounds of general clinical knowledge and the telling lack of evidence to the contrary throughout the literature).

Paroxysmal, epileptic and "minimally brain damaged" patients are very dangerous types of cases, unless recognized, and adequately treated. Because of their psychotic rages they are usually discharged or end up in jail, instead of being properly diagnosed with the help of EEG and treated with antiepileptic medication. In some cases amphetamine maintenance is suggested as a pilot research study, parallel to the experiences with MBD children. This entire category of patients is rarely thought of, scarcely diagnosed, and infrequently treated with appropriate measures. In contrast, in many cases the usual antipsychotic or antidepressant medications elicit a paradoxical response: a severe deterioration of psychopathology (including transient psychoses) and some sort of seizures. Again the regular, almost daily presence of a well trained psychiatrist, particularly with a background in neurology, is indispensable to deal with this entire group.

Suicidal depressions respond usually not to antidepressant medication specifically, but properly belong into the next category of severe, but non-psychotic psychopathology.

SEVERE, NON-PSYCHOTIC PSYCHOPATHOLOGY

It is estimated that in a stable population of a methadone maintenance program about 60 percent belong into this category (after deduction of the 10 percent psychotics), showing severe character disorders with massive depressions, rages, anxiety, and mood swings of tension and empty drivenness and of boredom and sadness. They are treatable with a flexible combination of treatment methods, an individually designed treatment strategy, employing, if possible, intensive psychoanalytically oriented psychotherapy, major or minor tranquilizers, occasionally antidepressant medication, intensive vocational retraining, work with the families, a non-punitive modulation of the maintenance dosage and, not too rarely, eventually slow, gradual detoxification. The same combination of seven or eight treatment methods in an individually fitting strategy holds true for patients who are not on methadone, especially for poly-drug users. Encounter methods, group therapy, behavior modification have by and large had more negative than positive results with this vast category of severely disturbed, compulsive drug users (narcotics addicts and multihabituated drug users alike); they may be more appropriate for that minority of less severely ill cases of compulsive drug use (30 percent) and for those patients of less intensive drug use.

Here, the newly accruing knowledge of severe character pathology, especially of narcissistic and aggressive-masochistic personality disorders, and the relationship to perversions is both theoretically and practically of cardinal importance, instead of the earlier fall back on the pejorative, clinically meaningless "catchall" classifications of psychopath, sociopath, or even borderline patient. The new broad

insights gained by researchers like Greenacre, Kohut, Beres and
Kernberg will have to be applied methodically and systematically to
the treatment of this pathology and should be deepened and further
specified.

THE USE OF SKILLED PSYCHOTHERAPISTS

In view of the breadth and depth of psychopathology observed
among compulsive drug users, an innovative revamping of all
programs dealing with compulsive drug users is recommended.

Much more psychiatrists' time should be allocated to all types of
treatment programs. They should play, as especially Kaplan and
Wieder have persuasively argued, a determining role in helping to set
up the treatment strategy in the evaluation of each individual case.
More specifically, as demonstrated in our program, there is a dire need
for much direct psychiatric help in form of psychotherapy, psychopharmacological intervention, proper diagnosing of the type of
pathology, psychodynamically informed advice to counselors, etc.
Undoubtedly a great many patients could profit very much from direct
intensive, psychoanalytically oriented psychotherapy, now that so
many other supportive elements are functioning (program structure,
narcotics maintenance, vocational retraining). The psychotherapeutic
pessimism of the past is outdated now, as some of my own experiences
with psychotherapy combined with temporary or unlimited maintenance and also with abstinent patients have shown.

The impact recommended here should go farther though:

The use of paraprofessionals in staffing and even directing of drug
programs should not be diminished; many of them have proven their
unique qualifications, such as most professionals sorely lack. But they
should be far better trained, as part of their in-service training or in
their preparation, in the basics of psychopathology, psychotherapy
and family pathology. These added tasks may require an upgrading of
the intellectual level of at least some of the staff, and also be reflected in
their salaries. In other words: they (or many of them) should become
able to be "assistant psychotherapists." They are this often today, but
in an unsystematic and untrained way. In many, less psychiatrically
oriented programs a spirit of antipsychiatric, vindictive rigor prevails.
The participation of psychiatrists or psychotherapists with adequate
training should become mandatory for all programs dealing with
compulsive drug users. And this should be not just pro forma!

Based on my own disappointing experiences and the knowledge of severe psychopathology in all compulsive drug users it should be seriously considered whether not all ex-addict counselors employed in responsible and particularly in leading positions in drug treatment programs should be in psychotherapy, or whether at least the opportunity for this should be offered as part of program and funding. There is often, as I can see, such a pairing of high quality, ability and sensitivity on the one side, such a pathology in crucial ego (and superego) functions (the "anomia" described) on the other side, that to forgo their help would be regrettable, but to trust their stability may be a folly which I wish I had had the wisdom to avoid.

Still under the same heading, I have to repeat the emphasis on professional skills. The current climate for shortcuts in psychiatric training, as in all education, is inimical to the severity of the pathology we deal with. Many of the so-called innovative techniques of the day (encounter, group, marathon, sensitivity, behavior modification) may be valuable for the lighter forms of pathology; they are very destructive for the severity of psychopathology encountered in the vast majority of compulsive drug users. There is no substitute for psychiatric knowledge and psychotherapeutic tact, empathy, skill and know-how. Psychotherapy is one of the most difficult arts to learn, and compulsive drug users are among the most difficult patients to treat. Specialized, psychoanalytically oriented training programs for psychotherapy (not just restricted to psychiatrists, or even physicians) should be set up to train junior psychotherapists who would work under the supervision of experienced psychoanalysts specifically with these patients.

I am sure that this idea will sound outrageous to most; it goes against too many taboos on too many sides. Despite the resistance I expect from all sides, I see it as mandatory, if we want to make headway in this vast category of severe psychopathology, to enlist the active interest and help of the psychoanalytic societies and institutes, of the American Psychoanalytic Association as an organized body of training and research, as well as of individual psychoanalysts, for leadership roles in coping with this mass problem. Specifically, I would suggest to have Federal and State funds available to enlist this most highly qualified professional skill and acumen for help in such programs. I stress again that this does not entail psychoanalytic treatment of these patients. What it means is that the vast knowledge about character pathology and how to approach it with appropriate tact which competent analysts have, has up to now been nearly totally neglected, untapped, even derided, at the detriment of these patients. Psychotherapy and management of these patients have to utilize this knowledge if we are really serious about evolving innovative and beneficial techniques for them.

FAMILY RESEARCH AND FAMILY TREATMENT

Of no lesser weight is the need for concentrated work in the family field:

This is practically a barren field: no serious, sophisticated research has been done which is on the level of family research in other types of pathology. Before treatment can advance, systematic research into the pathology has to be undertaken. Again there is ample clinical evidence that the family background of compulsive drug users is as disturbed as that of psychotics and that there is a causal link between pathology in the family and in the children, but systematic studies to bear this out and refine these impressions are urgently needed. Therefore I would assign also very high priority in funding to methodologically sound research in the field of dynamics and cognitive disturbances in the families of compulsive drug users.

Clinically there is overwhelming evidence that compulsive drug use (probably not the other forms) grows out of a background of severe family pathology. Funding should be specifically made available to treat the families of juvenile compulsive drug users with good, sophisticated family therapy and to enlarge by training the pool of available family therapists. Nothing of this is done now! Although our knowledge is very scanty and haphazard, a beginning should be done to allocate to each drug abuse program which deals with patients under twenty-five years of age, a part-time, trained family therapist or to set up state-wide training programs in family therapy (not family counseling) if not enough therapists are available.

A NETWORK OF PROGRAMS FOR
MULTIHABITUATED DRUG USERS

This is the most neglected area where very severe psychopathology (both as underlying cause and as consequence) is practically coextensive with severe drug use, and where nearly no "modalities," no programs exist. I described how the many contact points with this "refuse" population should be used to channel them into intensive treatment facilities where again only the combination of methods will have any chance of success. The following are some of the possibilities which I, as a clinician, can envision as promising leads:

Psychiatric inpatient facilities specifically set up or at least geared for adolescent and adult compulsive drug users, with individualized treatment plans, would be of great help, particularly to deal with the desperately complex, self-destructive forms of polytoxicomania. Many forms of such inpatient facilities can be conceived of: therapeutic communities with much psychiatric input, rationally led facilities with sophisticated structures, communities with strong emphasis on the development of creative abilities (literary, artistic, musical, dramatic), facilities centered around family therapy. Use of psychotropic drugs may be a helpful adjunct, but not more.

There is need for innovative techniques in the psychiatric work with these patients. I personally think that a combination in the same person or at least in the team setting up such novel programs may be needed, consisting of (a) psychoanalytic in-depth understanding and sensitivity, (b) flexibility and an outgoing attitude in the approach, (c) firm limit setting, built into the structure of the program, (d) ample use of new avenues of creativity, and (e) features of outright compulsion.

As stated, there are no treatment programs which focus at present on the massive character pathology, the severe neurotic symptoms, and relatively frequent underlying (or drug induced) psychoses of multihabituated drug users. I do not see any stringent need to set up completely separate programs for that purpose but it would be very desirable if every federally funded psychiatric in- and out-patient program would be compelled or invited to entail specific, well-structured, thought-through services, paying a lot of individual attention to this sadly neglected patient category.

There have also been a number of reports indicating that it would be better to have separate wards (within existing facilities) for heavy drug users rather than to throw them together with the rest of the psychiatric patients. More research into this question is probably needed.

One other educational aspect should be added:

University programs, training medical students, psychiatric residents, social work and nursing students, should not simply have courses in drug abuse and alcoholism, but there should be actual training for, and an increased acceptance of, the work with the severe psychopathology underlying drug abuse and masked by drug abuse.

The programs to be set up for polydrug users could be particularly instructive places for such training, because of the unusual severity of psychiatric, somatic, social and familial problems and the special need for a comprehensive team approach outlined above.

FEDERAL AND STATE-WIDE FACILITATORS

Against the background of the severe psychopathology which demands all the professional and paraprofessional attention available, it is deplorable to be faced with the problems outlined in chapter 13 and 15—particularly the difficulties with several bureaucratic juggernauts at once (including the institutions themselves within which many programs try to survive), the managerial problems; and lastly the constant threat of unscrupulous personnel within these programs.

Here are a few suggestions of less specific nature than the other five recommendations (and moving already somewhat outside of the purview of this chapter) of how to deal with some of these administrative problems:

Only the close surveillance of the program from inside and outside by ethically reliable persons will prevent the invasion of the team by persons of gross superego defects and the exploitation of a particularly vulnerable population and program by such individuals; close auditing of all programs by clinically sensitive and administratively schooled statewide "facilitators" would probably be more helpful than much of the current paper-oriented bureaucracy which misses both outstanding value and outstanding misuse of facilities.

More generally, it would be very good if both the state and federal agencies would act more as direct assistance and advisers to programs than as devisers of forms and regulations. These agencies should be paired down as to quantity, and their staff rather selected as to their combination of clinical perceptiveness and administrative know-how than as to their bureaucratic rigidity and conformism. I even recommend that they come to much more frequent visits of programs and offer much more direct help in resolving snags which arise in the setting up of new program branches, help in changing the direction of emphasis and especially assist in locating available resources. In short, I would like to see State and Federal agencies as facilitators of the very difficult clinical tasks of programs, instead, as so often has happened, as obstacle courses, making difficult tasks even more difficult or impossible. But again: their focus, too, will have to shift from drugs, "violations," "discharging," "cost efficiency" to the severe psychopathology of these personalities and their families and how to employ more well-tested psychiatric, especially psychotherapeutic techniques, in the treatment of this particularly severely ill population.

These outside facilitators with the power to cut off funds would be a necessary counterpoise against foot dragging and nonsensical requirements and rules within those institutions that are suffocated by their own bureaucratic weight.

Here, too, we need a system of visible checks and balances rather than the "new despotism" elucidated by Nisbet (1975): the invisible powers of bureaucracies which rule by regulations instead of quality controls, which esteem numbers and uniformity but squash creativity and rights and needs of individuals.

Immediately the objection is heard that all six proposals would *cost* far too much. I would doubt that very much, as already stated in connection with the psychotherapy of Andreas (chapter 9) and with the socioeconomic costs of ineffectively treated or untreated drug abuse (Appendix D). In the long run society ("the taxpayer") has to pay far more dearly if this personally and socially very noxious symptom is not dealt with in depth, wherever possible by more than palliative means. Very often a short-term, intensive, costly investment in appropriate treatment is far less than the long-term, non-intensive, unskilled treatment followed or accompanied by severe setbacks. The latter weigh not merely heavily in financial but, really more importantly, in human terms.

We are confronted by a severe chronic illness. We can ill afford to view it as an acute problem ("they just need withdrawal from the drug!"), as simply a pharmacological issue ("The injection of a long term antagonist deposit will suffice as answer!"), or as primarily a problem of ethical value and legal responsibility ("We have to increase their willpower by negative reinforcement," by deterrence, punishment, deconditioning). All these partial answers, although not always entirely incorrect or useless, miss the severity and chronicity of this condition.

Research

There are various areas within the purview of this book where research is urgently needed.

Of relative low priority, I consider a first group which I have covered from a clinical point of view. I refer to systematic research into (a) the extent of moderate, severe and very severe psychopathology in existing drug programs; (b) among the rejects and drop-outs from such programs; (c) among the poly drug users seen in emergency rooms, adolescent and adult clinics of hospitals and outpatient facilities; in shelters and "crash pads"; (d) inquiries in the observations of social agencies and drug counseling centers.

Such an epidemiologic-psychodiagnostic study should be undertaken with relatively modest means. Its purpose is less to find some new startling results (though this cannot be precluded either), but rather to verify the very strong clinical impressions presented throughout this book and by the many (quoted) observers.

Far more important, it appears to me, is the carrying out of systematic research into the psychological background of various types of drug abusers (types as to intensity and as to drug category), correlating severity of psychopathology with severity of drug use. Such a postdictive study, if carried out by highly sophisticated examiners, could try to distinguish between psychopathology preceding drug abuse and that caused by it, and would be preliminary to true predictive research.

As already mentioned, I would assign particular importance to systematic family research.

Summary

Heavy (compulsive) drug use is coextensive with moderate to severe psychopathology underlying the drug use, not caused by it. The crisis in the treatment of these patients which are either rejected or inadequately treated by the currently existing programs is also coextensive with the crisis in the treatment of emotionally disturbed or outright mentally ill patients in general. Innovative facilities should be created along the lines described above, employing the gamut of already known psychiatric techniques to this class of patients; it appears imperative to develop and implement innovative psychothera-peutic techniques specifically for this type of pathology—combining in-depth dynamic (psychoanalytic) understanding and leadership, structure building and limit setting, family treatment, vocational retraining (or new training), opening up of creative or recreational avenues of gratification, and the flexible use of psychopharmacologi-cal agents. In other words: instead of one track-modalities we need combinations of four to seven methods for each individual patient in a methodical specific way.

It calls for the avoidance of many of the current faddish short-cuts and fashionable new "simplistic" techniques because of their destructive potential with these severely ill patients. It requests a deeper involvement in the positions of leadership by psychiatrists and psychoanalysts in dealing with the majority of the problems of compulsive drug use. The current debunking of a thorough training in psychiatry and especially in intensive individual psychotherapy, and with that the nearly total lack of understanding for the psychodynam-ics of these patients and their families has been devastating for psychiatry in general; but it has left the field of treatment of these patients almost entirely to paraprofessionals and to specialists from other fields who are naive as to the gravity and nature of the psychopathology in the majority of these cases and as to measures how to devise rational treatment strategies for each individual case.

Most specifically, it calls for a deeper involvement of psychoanalysis in such a leadership role, not as a treatment method, but as the only accredited institution which has set itself the goals of a deeper systematic understanding of the human mind and of a methodical, thorough, well-structured and supervised training of its practitioners. Despite its current external and even internal crisis, its factual contribution to the huge problem at hand could perhaps be the most innovative suggestion this book can make—as old-fashioned as it may sound to many of its readers.

This leads us on to broader considerations of a sociopolitical and lastly philosophical nature and to perhaps rather revolutionary recommendations.

Chapter 18

CONCLUSIONS AS TO PUBLIC POLICY

> The voice of the intellect is a soft one, but it
> does not rest till it has gained a hearing.
> Finally, after a countless succession of rebuffs,
> it succeeds.—Freud, (1927)

> Tantae molis erat se ipsam cognoscere men-
> tem. (It required such an effort of the mind to
> get to know itself.)—Hegel (Lowith 1941)

"Nemesis of Psychiatry"

Much furor has been raised by my putting an article about drug
abuse under this heading.

Originally "nemesis" meant "reproach," "blame." It came to mean
retribution both in form of shaming (humiliation), and in form of guilt
oriented punishment. It assumed mythical grandeur as a godly force. It
still has this deep meaning: an awe inspiring, almost uncanny form of
punishment for transgressions of society's and nature's bounds, a
haunting, stalking specter, ready to exact punishment in a tragically
massive form for sins of omission or commission, for neglect, haughty

disdain, or for violent disregard of rights and needs of persons, groups, nations. It is a powerful metaphor for a part of the "tragic experience."

When I talk about the nemesis of psychiatry I mean it in a double sense. For one, our society's vast neglect of the importance of emotionally noxious experiences, the undervaluation of psychotherapy and psychoanalysis, except in their most superficial vulgarizations and misinterpretations, comes now to haunt us. I suspect that, as a society and as a culture, we have a psychiatric mass problem before our eyes which we could have reduced if we had been far more keen about the insights given to us by eighty years of experience in psychotherapy and psychoanalysis.

With that I mean precisely the opposite of what some of the most pungent attacks on my article stated. They cite the misapplications of psychoanalytic knowlefge in the past and refer to the same vulgarizations. I implied, namely those of "licentiousness," "permissiveness," sanctioned by references to the early analytic theory which saw the origin of neurosis in "frustration" (Freud 1916–1917, p. 350); such an application obviously completely disregarded everything else in the analytic models and in the enormous development of psychoanalysis in the intervening sixty years, above all the focusing on defenses, on the need for such inner structures, corrupt conscience, a need for values and ideals. It is precisely there that the grossest deficiencies in our culture can be found. There is an enormous emphasis on the one side on external conflict solution, with concomitant disregard for internal conflicts and needs, on manipulation, on giving in to demands and not only on gratifying all needs, but incesantly creating new desires. With that goes a wholesale dismantling of visible, respected authority and hierarchy, a lifting of restraints and erasing of limits and boundaries. The intergenerational boundaries and necessary sexual taboos (particularly incest taboos) are disregarded. Perhaps most importantly the cohension of the family is dissolved. Traditional value systems have been replaced by a cynical orientation towards solely utilitarian, lastly exclusively hedonistic aims. It is the abolition of superego standards on a large scale. Many patients state just that: "I come to therapy in order to get rid of guilt and shame"—instead of: to grow free of irrational, archaic, both paralyzingly strong and destructively weak superego forces.

On the other side authority is—even in our democratic society— often exerted in an arbitrary, vindictive, archaic way. Moreover it has become depersonalized, bureaucratized, and often functions totally in disregard of all other values outside of its own special forms of power and control. This problem of sagging value consciousness by authority cannot be dealt with on the level of the currently so attractive slogans, attacking centralized government per se, "blaming Washington," etc. These are themselves externalizations in the service of denying the deeper philosophical problems.

This double emphasis on externalization denial and scapegoating in our society is what I mean with this first form of nemesis: it is the disregard for an enormous wealth of theoretical and practical insight gained in the clinical laboratory of the psychoanalytic and psychotherapeutic situation. I hold that the lack of rational prevention and treatment and with that spread and social noxiousness of drug abuse and other forms of addictive behavior are the price paid for this general neglect.

On the other hand, drug abuse is the nemesis to haunt psychiatry itself. The enormity of emotional problems dwarfs both our skills and indeed our insight and knowledge, although we understand still far more than we can actually influence—comparable to the knowledge about infectious diseases, which, before the advent of antibiotics in somatic medicine, far outpaced the ability to intervene.

Analogously I feel both society in general and our profession in particular faces now the task which somatic medicine faced up to eighty years ago: the need for a tremendous expansion in breadth and depth, in energy and manpower, a need not solely to tackle drug abuse, but the powers unmasked and unleashed by this symptom. With that I mean a vast recruitment of physicians and non-physicians, like teachers, social workers, and nurses, for psychotherapeutic tasks, a deepening of our training, a development of new methods of treatment through research, an application of our knowledge, gained in psychotherapy, to the culture at large, especially to education, television, and legislation. Just as the pollution of air and water has been recognized as a self-suffocating factor only in our culture because of the tremendous expansion of technology, we have to learn how our culture and society far more potently than earlier cultures can attain or destroy those values which hold individual, family and society together: inner integration and self-discipline, integrity and honesty, beauty and a mature form of love, hierarchies and boundaries. Right now it appears to me that our culture interferes far more with this potential than it uses it, but I may be too pessimistic about this. Certainly, this form of emotional "pollution" is by no means novel. Yet it is also so much more devastating in our crowded and technically pervasive society; the means of escape from maturity and rationality are far more sophisticated; the safeguards in form of respect for tradition and authority have been removed to a far higher degree than in the old small communities with similar problems.

When I try to be more specific I have to restrict myself to a few explicating ideas, some practical suggestions, some questions.

I think above all of the need for much better funding on a state and federal level for psychiatric treatment, training, and research programs. The enormity of the extent of emotional disturbances is not matched by an awareness of needs, let alone by budgets. I believe that the victims of inner conflict and stunted inner development need as much attention in research and assistance as the victims of all somatic illnesses from caries to cancer: in money, in personnel, in varied methods. One just has to compare our state hospital system with health care delivery in general; or put side by side widespread neurotic misery, which practically never can be treated with our current resources, with the dental hygiene system; or just juxtapose the early treatment of severe emotional family disorders, which could be a potent form of true prevention, with pre- and post-natal care of physical problems. Not that the second part of the comparison is anywhere sufficient or even equitable, but the first part is minuscule still in comparison.

My suggestions, as explained more in greater detail in the previous 17, are: (a) massive increase of funding for treatment; (b) development of large scale research to tackle the problems beyond the naivete of so many community mental health programs; (c) thorough and long term training of paraprofessionals by clinically mature psychiatrists, above all by supervision; (d) training of teachers and ministers to spot early enough grossly disordered families and youngsters and to help them to get into treatment, or even to become "assistant psychotherapists" themselves; (e) relief of well-trained psychiatrists from administrative tasks so that they can apply most of their skills to research, treatment and training instead of to the scrounging for matching funds and to the battles with bureaucrats (I point to the excellent thoughts of Kubie and Bandler 1970–1971); (f) influence of our profession on making legislation a primary instrument of ordering interpersonal relations, not private lives and public vengeance; and (g) an influence on the mass media in support of acceptance of limitations and the role of our inner life against the overemphasis on material gratification; (h) but most importantly, yet least specifically and least tangibly, I foresee, nay, I hope for a decisive role of thinkers emerging from our midst who could assist in a value-philosophical reorientation of our culture. Again, as stated before: psychoanalysis can and should be a cultural force par excellence.

Obviously, in all these suggestions we skirt or enter the area of ethics. Yet why should we on the basis of our clinical experience not add our voice to the basic discussions about such value-philosophical problems? Why should we not be heard in what we know about the disastrous effects if reason is betrayed?

The Aim of Laws

Currently the laws in all civilized societies form a patchwork quilt of rational measures to protect the rights and integrity of the individual and of the state as a whole, mixed with arbitrary, vindictive, irrational legislation, used to demonize and exorcize in a mythical and magical fashion what does not fit in with some leading values.

Next I try to fit the current laws and attitudes vis-à-vis drug abuse into a value philosophical framework.

DRUG ABUSE LAWS AND VALUE PHILOSOPHY

Taking up the threads from our earlier value-philosophical musings and the contemplation about society and culture, we arrive at five antitheses reflecting society's stand vis-à-vis drug abuse.

The value philosophy of the Western world places very high (and sometimes the highest) emphasis upon outwardly demonstrated self-control and independence, upon activity and self-assertion. The countervalues which assume a metaphysically demonic quality are seen in "enslavement," dependency, loss of control and passive abandon. The carriers of such countervalues are looked at with contempt and often furious scorn. Often much pleasure is imagined to be associated with this countervalue. Drugs inducing such counter-values are condemned as "killers," as "devils," as abhorent poisons.

Drug users are despised as emasculated, enucleated, dehumanized robots, monsters, demons, the "living dead."

A very large portion of American life is dedicated to financial success and technological power almost at any price; the excess of advertisement represents the extreme value put on selling and on winning money. Yet this economic religion is, as we saw, a teasing fata morgana: to the poor it shows what they do not have but could have; to the rich youngster it is a hollow promise, a value without substance, a cold golden calf. It shows them what they have (material gratification) as if it were something that they actually do not have (emotional fulfillment). The value of economic victory is at crass variance with the value of independence, at least if we think of it as inner freedom. The pleasures of possession and financial power are bought at the price of an enslavement to material goods which has rarely been witnessed before. The luxuries of Sybaris, of the late Roman Empire, of France of the eighteenth century, and of Baghdad before the Mongol invasion come to mind—images which evoke in us certainly not a sense of freedom and self-control. The countervalue is seen in being a business failure, in losing, in being poor. The addiction to financial and sociopolitical success is one side of the coin; the addiction to drugs is the other side. As we noted earlier: drug use, too, is a form of perverted use of technological power, an illusory form of mastery. Thus, in fine, the dependency on one socially excessively praised good leads to the rebellion in form of a defiant dependency upon another material object, one, however, which is socially excessively despised. Neither of these two antitheses can be resolved by their own inner dialectic; they need to be transcended by other values—as expounded in detail earlier.

The philosophy of freedom, "the idea of liberty under law," as developed mainly in the England of the seventeenth and in North America during the eighteenth century (Kohn 1955), sees a cardinal value in privacy. Only those actions which interfere with the rights of others are subject to legal sanction. Based on this legal philosophy there is, as Bazelon indicated, no justification for the prosecution of drug users qua drug users. The legal aims devoted to this value are respect for, and protection of, privacy and the rights of the individual, including his right to harm himself; above all there should be no attempt to legislate values. The countervalue in this philosophy is the intrusion into the private sphere and the dictation of what private pleasures the citizen may or may not have, of what he has to think, to feel, to strive for, and to believe.

Yet, the drug laws as they stand today are a break with the value of privacy and contradict the legal philosophy reigning in most of the Western world. On the basis of this value philosophy, it certainly would make sense to prosecute *actions* induced by drugs which are detrimental to society: violence and stealing, disorderly conduct and depredations in order to support himself. How about the seduction of others into using drugs? the contagion? One would have to conclude that the punishment for such proselytizing actions should correspond with the punishments meted out for inducement of similar nature: to violence, promiscuity, to the use of alcohol and cigarettes.

The most problematic area of conflict of these two values is that between this right for self-determination versus the protection against self-destruction with the help of treatment, if the latter is compulsory. Here I feel constrained to disagree with many extreme civil libertarians of today who put liberty above all other values, including life. Too often I have treated patients who were hopeless victims to their inner compulsions and had tried to destroy themselves, who were literally saved from death and their own self-directed rage by compulsory treatment and have grown into very functional, respected and self-respecting members of human society. This antithesis can be resolved in a dialectic balance between the respect for the other's privacy and the responsibility for the other's safety—even against his own, most destructive compulsions. This synthesis is a most delicate one. Most despotisms of the past have justified ("irrationalized") their sadism by the claim of the second value: that they merely acted on behalf of the good of the victim or at least in behest of the rest of society. However, abuse does not invalidate use and importance of a value.

A fourth and fifth value orientation relevant to the present discussion are encompassed by what was called by Philip Rieff "the triumph of the therapeutic."

This double antithesis is suffering versus complete comfort, individuality versus conformism (a derivative of equality). The courageous facing of discomfort, pain, tension, disappointment for one, the often not less brave standing up against the majority, being eccentric, not conforming, secondly: all these are "bad," are countervalues. The values are happiness, well-being, comfort and conformity, conventionality, "adjustment." They redound to the demand never to suffer or to have "problems." Whatever drug can promote this value is good, regardless of its "enslaving" quality. It is contrasted with the richness of life, the depth of its true problems, the value of individuality. Conformism, adaptation as lead value, painlessness—all cover over the deep, painful, but enriching conflicts. As I called them earlier—they are part of the vast array of antitragic defenses. How to find a balance in this dialectic?

Every psychiatrist knows that his chronically schizophrenic patient has to take his Thorazine, often for a lifetime. His insistence rests on the conviction that a lifelong dependency is far superior to the wild fluctuations of mood and delusional panics and rages, the restless demands, the nagging suspicions and accusations, the bizarre gyrations of the untreated schizophrenic. Equally, most compulsive drug users are not able to function without the crutch of a drug. Responsible representatives of such a value synthesis defend the need for these patients to use these addictive drugs (for instance methadone or amphetamines)—as long as necessary—provided they do not cause direct psychological or social harm (as alcohol, LSD, or cocaine do), and that they are given under such precautions that their use is not contagious (or only minimally so). A regulation of the source and a dispensation by qualified professionals (physicians) would replace the punishment of the user. Yet, if unhinged from this balance, the therapeutic value orientation may very easily, as Szasz and others ("Aristedes" 1976) proclaim, clash with dignity, right of freedom, and privacy of the individual, or "trivialize" life, deprive it of its depth and richness.

LAWS: SOME HERETICAL RECOMMENDATIONS BY A PSYCHOTHERAPIST

How we may reconcile practically these five antitheses partly depends on our own value philosophy and thus ultimately comes down to personal decisions. However, one thing is immediately clear: a rational approach based on the insights given by psychoanalysis would not exclude any of the five posited theses (the values of self-control, power, privacy, happiness, and adjustment, as important aims), but would put them into a hierarchical order and subordinate them to the value outlined in the philosophical section.

I proceed now to a brief presentation of my personal stand. If we take up where we left off there we may wonder if the the reigning value chosen on the plane of individual psychology and psychotherapy may not have some practical applicability on a social level. The value of rational authority, of maximum inner freedom with a minimum of compulsion, combining self-love and object-love, inner honesty and outward sincerity, recognition of boundaries, limits and priorities internally and externally, can perhaps be translated into a common, social value: a combination of clear limit setting in education and polity, of hierarchical authority structure and order, with maximum gratification of the emotional and material needs of all and with cultivation of creativity for many, a compromise between the extreme versions of liberty and equality. This would be a policy avoiding several most powerful countervalues: those of rigidity and vindictive punitiveness, the demands for permissiveness and licentiousness, the strivings for anarchy and inconsistency, the use of public deception and hypocrisy, the pursuit of the tyranny of any absolutism with its concomitant persecutions.

A political system based on such rational authority is ideally flexible enough to adapt to changing social conditions. It avoids falling into the anarchy of a corrupt system based on the premises: "Quod licet Iovi, non licet bovi" (what is permitted to the mighty, is forbidden to the powerless). But it also shuns the "rigor mortis" of the totalitarian state. Economically and socially the application of this value would not exclude but subordinate the lower level values of self-reliance, power, economic success, equality and material gratifications. However, it would absolutely exclude ruthless exploitation and, most importantly, the vast economic discrepancies—unmeasured wealth, widespread poverty—within one state and between nations. What is happening to the poor and the sick in our rich society is a profound betrayal of justice and integrity in the service of narcissism pure and reckless. The social value of rational authority as proposed is incompatible with this.

In fact, whether such a value can truly assert itself against the overwhelming forces of narcissism, aggression, oral greed and flight from sublimation, no one can say.

In the following, however, I try to make some concrete recommendations, at least in regard to drug laws.

Persons disturbed enough to suffer or to make others suffer should have the right to receive any treatment alleviating their problems in the most lasting way. If this means the chronic use of a drug, so be it—regardless of its "enslaving" nature (a partial legalization as in Great

Britain). What we know now speaks, however, loudly for a much broader right for treatment: the right to receive all possible help to resolve the inner and outer problems of the compulsive drug user (and of every other emotionally disturbed person). This right for appropriate, effective treatment where such is known should be respected, as it is, at least as postulate, in somatic medicine.

This would entail also an examination of the psychological, social and philosophical void underlying all chronic drug abuse and the development of an appropriate strategy of psychological treatment (of individual and family), of socioeconomic rehabilitation and renewal, and a much deeper education toward the truly democratic values outlined before, an education essentially based on inner freedom and integration, on rational authority and order.

Concretely, I suggest that instead of the alternative between prohibition and legalization, a new system of *regulation* should be found. No use or possession of any drug should be punishable—only large scale illicit selling would be a crime. The less dangerous forms, as wine, cigarettes and marijuana, should be sold, but put under high taxation. These taxes should be exorbitant for more dangerous drugs such as liquor and hashish. This levy should be high enough both to discourage intensive use and to support extensive treatment facilities for compulsive users. Of course, no advertisement of any kind for any of the regulated substances (including alcohol) would be permissible. Narcotics, especially in the form of methadone, should be rather liberally given, though under strict medical supervision and, in a manner similar to the revised British system, in special treatment centers. LSD, barbiturates, amphetamines, and cocaine should be used only for very specific medical (including psychiatric) indications. The illicit use of these drugs again should not lead to penalties, but to hospitalization or out-patient treatment, perhaps even on a compulsory basis, and should be combined with a guardianship of a type already well-known on the European continent. (Logically, a parallel system would apply to weapons: only a system of strict, nationwide registration and regulation can curb the horrendous extent of violence.)

The penalties for large scale illicit traffic would have to be consistent with other laws against assault and injury—selling guns, selling or driving unsafe cars or driving in an intoxicated state. However, I believe illegal selling would become so unprofitable if this system of regulation were introduced that I predict a nearly complete disappearance of the black market. This is the only way I see to destroy the unholy alliance between organized crime and those segments of society which are in complicity with it.

The laws as they exist now precisely prepare the ground for what the former Chief Justice Warren described: "Organized crime can never exist to any marked degree in any large community unless one or more of the law enforcement agencies have been corrupted....The narcotics traffic of today, which is destroying the equilibrium of our society, could never be as pervasive and open as it is unless there was connivance between authorities and criminals" (*Washington Post*, 14 November 1970).

The use of drugs which affect driving should be treated with the same rules as appropriate for alcohol use: driving a vehicle in a state of reduced perception and judgment represents a grave social menace. All measures preventing this (breathalyzer tests, revocation of license) have to be employed with utmost consistency and severity for alcohol, and not differently for other drugs (except for the method of proof). Here any leniency is destroying the rights of all others. As our case 4 (Patpet) showed, the general lack of enforcement of these laws and with that a terrible inconsistency are simply astonishing. That a wealthy man can have a dozen serious car accidents within four months without loosing his license whereas others go to jail for ten, twenty, thirty years for the possession of minute amounts of drugs, is not only astounding, but precisely an expression of inequality before the law which is well-hidden by the current hue and cry for equality of result.

Campaigns of information about the effects of drugs would give people the opportunity to chose between pleasures of a certain kind with specific risks and abstinence; they would avoid the alluring equation of "drug use equals rebellion." The penalties for violations of these rules and regulations would be strictly commensurate with those for comparable violations. Again, there should be an unmistakable, explicit and clear-cut proportion of social harm and penalty, without demonization and vindictiveness. *The only relevant moral issue is direct social damage, not the use of drugs as such.*

Although I am not completely satisfied with such a revised legal system, I think it still is the lesser of the two evils.

Certainly this does not take care of the cases of compulsive behavior;

for that, again, a compromise between the values of the rights of others, of their security, and the value of dealing rationally with emotional illness needs to be worked out. Obviously someone who injures others or threatens to do so must be sequestered. But is jail indeed the right place?

The question may also be raised whether such a "licentiousness" toward drugs would not rot the pith of our society, sap it of its rugged strength, just as it is said to have emasculated the Orient.

I am of the opinion that a strict regulatory system as outlined would accomplish exactly the opposite: it would take out of the drug scene the sting of revenge and revolt; it would limit the use in a rational way, and it would make it available for the large number of disturbed individuals that either already take it and are pushed, because of their "need" (whatever this consists of), into the ranks of the criminals—or should take it because they are sociable only under the influence of this type of tranquilizer. And it would cut out the immense black market with its horrendous profiteering and the equally enormous economic damage the illegal procurement of drugs entails.

By the same token it certainly holds true that any official advertisement and encouragement of the "easy way out," of quick relief and freely available self-gratification, is propaganda for neurotic acting out and may very well lead to a national state of languidity, effeteness, and self-indulgence. Something similar holds for irrational punitiveness, which very often is indeed more enticing than deterring. Regulation of the type I advocate is as far removed from licentiousness as it is from demonization. Thus it tries to strike a balance in the alternative between unrestricted liberty and necessary or desirable limits and restraints.

Edwin Schur (1965) has convincingly pointed to the hopeless and self-defeating prosecution of the so-called "crime without victims." We have seen how ineffectual, inconsistent, and inhumane the punitive approach to the problem of drug abuse is; this is the approach which has been pursued with zeal for the past sixty years—and yet where are we today?

John Stuart Mill's words of 1859 are still apropos to the point I try to make:

There is a limit to the legitimate interference of collective opinion with individual independence: and to find that limit, and maintain it against encroachment, is as indispensable to a good condition of human affairs, as protection against political depotism.

[That principle is]that the only purpose for which power can be rightfully exercised over any member of a civilized community against his will, is to prevent harm to others. His own good, either physical or moral, is not a sufficient warrant.... Over himself, over his own body and mind, the individual is sovereign.

Besides the one exception from this maxim in regard to which I disagree with Mill, I think it a valid postulate. I have become convinced that the present drug laws transgress this limit unduely and disastrously and that therefore the costs far outweigh the benefits (as John Kaplan eloquently argues in regard to marijuana in his book *Marijuana—The New Prohibition,* 1970).

A similar legal-philosophical question was raised by Judge Bazelon (1969):"Is the criminal law the best tool available for controlling the harm that flows from the use of drugs?" He answers:

If we agree to confine—by civil commitment or criminal process— only those drug users who are dangerous to others, we are left with the vast numbers of drug users who harm only themselves. For these people, the criminal laws against drug use interfere with essentially private conduct. Like laws against suicide, or laws against riding a motorcycle without a helmet, they limit one man's liberty without protecting anyone else. Putting a man in jail is a rather primitive way of protecting him. In other areas we have developed regulatory mechanisms to protect people from harmful products....The regulatory model imposes sanctions on manufacturers and distributors, not consumers. The consumer is regarded as a victim, not a criminal.

Society is neither obligated nor able to legislate any value orientations; it *has* to legislate about actions, and solely about actions, not about attitudes and values.

In the argument so far it has been taken for granted that drug use necessarily is eo ipso harmful. The material submitted in this book casts much doubt on this automatic assumption. If and when it is a form of self-treatment, it may indeed be quite a lesser evil.

What I have submitted may be looked at as utopian or moralizing. I cannot agree with that. It is merely an attempt to change the usual vantage point under which such human activities as drug addiction, psychotherapy, and modern industrial society are viewed and to suggest a new approach to some of the problems involved. It is correct, though, that I think these problems have their roots in an area which is beyond the realm of science, but not beyond rational inquiry.

Questions About Eduction

Sir William Osler said: "One of the first duties of the physician is to educate the masses not to take medicine" (G. Byrd 1970, p. 20). This would for our purposes have to be modified into: "One of the foremost tasks of a psychiatrist is to educate the masses not to seek the solutions for the basic problems of human existence in drugs and technology." The question is: How?

"DRUG ABUSE EDUCATION"—SOLD AS PREVENTION

Drug abuse education has a value for the public at large, especially for physicians, social workers, and teachers, as instruction but not as deterrent, for potential or actual experimenters and social users. The prospective compulsive drug user in particular is not influenced by such superficial cognitive means. Not even the overdose deaths of his closest friends serve as a lesson!

There is no evidence for, and considerable evidence against, the usefulness of education as prevention of the really menacing forms of drug abuse, namely the compulsive types. The hue and cry for drug abuse education as prevention is by and large as naive and carried by similar magical expectations as drug use itself.

This clinical observation and inference was confirmed when the *New York Times* (12 January 1972) printed the results of a study at the University of Michigan. In summary, the findings were that six hundred junior high school students who were exposed to a drug education program sharply increased their experimentation with drugs, in contrast to a control group of three hundred fifty other students. Dr. Richard B. Stuart called these programs "a false panacea." The tragedy was, as I alluded in chapter 13, that due to this false emphasis crucial treatment programs were sacrificed or severely curtailed.

Often the comparison with smoking is adduced. To begin with, the comparison with the efficacy of education in regard to smoking is fallacious. Since smoking is not illegal, it is motivated much less often and much less strongly by pathologic and with that compulsive determinants. This implies that it is in many more people accessible to cognitive persuasion. Even so, most truly compulsive smokers will not give up smoking simply because they learn about its life threatening effects. And it is this category we must compare with the category of compulsive drug users that we are concerned with. In fact, aside from this, it appears even dubious today whether any lasting curtailment of mass smoking was attained by this huge propaganda!

But there are two areas in regard to drug abuse where education could be of truly preventive value.

REBELLION AND SICKNESS: OPPOSITE EDUCATIONAL MODELS

One of the fallacies of "drug abuse education" lies in the need to set up villains, to exorcise demons.

Instead— if we look back over our findings—we can demonstrate that drug taking is not so much an act of heroism and courage, but more often stems from, and if pursued, leads to, weakness and failure. Any intoxication is a transient sickness, with some drugs and for some people a mild and harmless one, and with some and for some a very dangerous sickness. Thus we are able to change the public image of drug abuse; it does not have to remain a symbol for an honest and valiant stand against the inconsistencies, a rebellion against hypocritical attitudes in our community. Instead it becomes—what it truly reflects much more appropriately—a symbol of weakness and self-destruction.

The value philosophy and the correlated affects in these two approaches are radically different: the use of drugs and addiction should be treated not as being fraught with guilt (as today's laws and society's views do), but as a sign of illness. Today it is officially guiltful, it is a sin to be a drug user or an addict. Yet the other side of the same coin is that it is precisely for that reason shameful in many circles *not* to belong to the group using it. The non-user, the non-violator of the widely proclaimed taboo is derided as a square, a punk, an outsider, just as the non-user of alcohol is scoffed at as an unmanly teetotaler.

The non-user of drugs "betrays" the rebellion of his peers against authority; and this betrayal, as every form of treason, is fraught with shame. In other words: as long as society treats drug use as guilt, all rebellion uses the violation of this taboo as its symbol, the violators as its heroes, and the non-violators as its antiheroes, as shameful weaklings or at least as derided outsiders.

Such a rebellion is particularly appealing to adolescents if it can point, moreover with self-righteous indignation, to the absolutely irrational tolerance of the same society and the same authorities toward alcohol and guns, and to the disequilibrium in the system of justice. Though two wrongs do not make a right and the indulgence in alcohol and violence does not justify the abuse of psychedelics or narcotics, respect for authority can be reestablished only if there is far more consistency and less hypocrisy.

But does preventive education really make sense if it emphasizes the shame-evoking weakness and illness symbolized by drugs, instead of the lurid dangerousness of the forbidden? This throws us right back to the controversy at the beginning of this book: that "illness" is socially considered bad; especially, emotional illness still is commonly a badge of shame, of dishonor.

In fact, any illness (somatic or emotional) is indeed a form of weakness and with that tends to evoke in deeper layers of everyone a host of feelings: wishes to be taken care of, self-pity, severe plummetting of self-esteem, and with that shame. In the onlooker it is a mixture of the wish to help, of sympathy, pity and, well nigh inevitably, though strongly suppressed in ethically very conscientious persons: of contempt, condescension, and smugness.

No matter how careful we are, the equation of drug abuse with illness and severe inner problems thus has two social side effects. The scientific stance is: to understand, to help, instead of condemning and detesting, a stance represented by the quote from Spinoza put at the head of chapter 1. Society at large, especially the young, will tend to react with shame (vis-à-vis themselves) or contempt (vis-à-vis others) to this equation which now suddenly emerges: drug abuse=weakness= moral failure=shame. Although such a demotion from its status symbol for rebellion could have more deterrent value than all the laws, since the shame sanction is usually far more powerful than the guilt sanction, this results in replacing the revenge by anger with a more hidden, though more pervasive type of revenge, that by contempt and shaming. This cannot be the goal of education; it may perhaps prevent the symptom, but, if anything, worsens the underlying problems. A success attained by Machiavellian means is not a triumph by reason.

This deepens our problem—really opens an antinomy—perhaps beyond currently possible grasp. An attempt to answer part of it is entailed in what follows.

THE VALUE OF A HUMANISTIC EDUCATION

We saw the basic inconsistencies in family, society and culture as principal contributors to drug abuse—the vacillation between, on the one side, permissiveness and licentiousness, easy gratification and giving in to most demands, on the other side the angry, vengeful imposition of punishment and the elevation of temper tantrums and vendetta to an alleged tool of education and social policy. The outcomes are the myriads of youth who have learned very little self-discipline, who are outraged by every limitation and who take every no as an insult.

A major task of education today should rather be to teach adults, youth and children alike to accept limitations, to learn self-control and self-discipline, to shun vindictive anger as well as giving-in to all wishes. The mass media could play a crucial role in this reeducation and reorientation toward higher values instead of being diligent masters in the present miseducation.

Here lies the true task of education and prevention, not in a sanctimonious faith in the magic effects of drug education. For example, the aforementioned drug oriented propaganda in the news media has to be eliminated. I am afraid I am Utopian in expecting any change but I think all pills belong in the hands of the physician; they should not be sold over the counter nor should they be advertised. All pills which are effective are potentially dangerous—even fatal, particularly all pain relievers. But more importantly they convey the message: "If you have problems, take pills." But this is really still quite superficial.

I think much of general education has to be thought through anew. I share fully the wish of Lionel Trilling (1974): a rich education is humanistic in nature and gives us, who are uprooted from "community" in a true sense, a new deeper and lasting continuity and meaning—a meaningfulness no pragmatic orientation, no training for power and specialized techniques can provide. The basis of education is rather "a general consciousness of the values which govern human life." If we want to survive as what I called the sixth culture, a humanistic culture and civilization, it depends on education as "the deliberate pursuit of an idea" (Jaeger 1933, p. xiv).

The goal of a humanistic education entails, I believe, above all the imperative of a basic philosophical reorientation in the value priorities of our whole society, away from the emphasis on outer power and prestige, on commercial success and unreflective activism, on unrestrained externalization, and a reorientation toward the values of inner integration and rational control and toward those values which are embodied in the humanities, mainly in art and philosophy. Science and more generally intellectual pursuits cannot be restricted to subserving the first (external, practical) group of values; our reason has an even nobler task in inquiring into those vast areas represented by the second group of values.

Indeed we have to become philosophers in the Socratic tradition.

Thus education cannot sustain our culture if it is pervaded by the abandonment of a philosophical orientation as I described it before, when it seeks the easy way out from the basic problems of human existence: the questions of value and of meaning. The quest for "the meaning of it all" is relevant for many of our most intelligent youngsters.

As mentioned, I do not mean that we should simply teach philosophical systems, but we should help them—by our own honesty and integrity—towards a contemplative searching and rational questioning of the basic premises of life, work, society and science. Again: we cannot really solely teach that but we can live it ourselves and can be much more responsive to the questions we are asked.

Such contemplation is an expression of the conviction that "the unexamined life is not worth living." It means to look at the whole, not as the sum of its parts, but at the meaning, or lack of meaning, of the whole: of human life, of human relationship, of human cognition, and—perhaps most of all—of human limitation.

BOREDOM

In chapter 14 I mentioned the conflict between creativity and leisure. Our culture and education do not systematically support creativity, but show the easy way out in form of externalizations devoid of deeper symbolic significance. This leads to a vast sense of emptiness, boredom, idleness, to a passive drifting or a blind active driving. I do not think the boring, superficial, empty stretches of much education "cause" drug abuse, but I believe that undertrained, underpaid teachers do not offer a counterforce against the weights so many adolescents carry with them. They do not give them the values which their families had failed to transmit to them and which would make the leisure time really rich, filled with meaning and creative activity, a center of the whole of their lives, instead of a barren stretch of empty time. I concede, I have also witnessed much to the opposite: excellent stimulating teaching of youngsters. I am afraid though these are exceptions; I am impressed (and depressed) by the overall low quality of education of those between ten and twenty (the most important age for education), and the resulting shallowness of amiable, but bored and boring adults.

CONCRETE RECOMMENDATIONS FOR EDUCATION

The schools are one of the five central institutions which our form of culture and society absolutely needs for its survival and vitality. These are: (1) the three branches of government and its bureaucratic apparatus, (2) the four major branches of the healing arts (medicine, surgery, obstetrics, and psychiatry), (3) the scientific establishment, (4) the structures of national defense, and (5) the educational system with its center of gravity from age fifteen to eighteen.

Other cultures may be able to survive without some of these five; democracy cannot. The current devaluation of schools (in favor of highways, etc.), the low respect and deplorable training of teachers is a bad omen and both sign and source of cultural stunting and decline. High school teachers who cannot read Shakespeare and have no real access to the great novels, physicians who lack basic literary or historical knowledge, academicians who cannot read another language—what a sign of cultural impoverishment! I find the loss of the humanistic tradition a national tragedy for any democratic society.

We need to bring up all teachers in standing, pay and training roughly to those of lawyers, physicians, psychologists, officers, administrators and politicians. They should be *authorities* in the original, profound meaning of the word. "Auctor" and "auctoritas"

mean someone (or something) which furthers and increases believabili-
ty, trust, truth. He testifies for validity and thus is a warrant for value;
he is a model, an example—by what he is and by what he transmits.
Concomitant with the decay of values and tradition, the term *authority*
itself has become most ambiguous, meaning simply power, even (in
"authoritarian") the abuse of power. In line with what I just stated, the
bearers of our five central institutions should be seen and respected as
"authorities" in this best sense. For that they need to be selected and
educated with greatest care and salaried correspondingly.

The humanities have to be taught in a rich, deep, challenging form—
besides the now so highly valued sciences, mathematics, technical
skills, and physical education. History, literature, music, philosophy,
languages, and even the principles of psychoanalysis belong in a basic
curriculum—thus opening up to the gifted, interested, questioning
majority of middle school students the main areas of symbolic forms.
The pervasive problems of hyposymbolization, deficient ideal and
value formation and the precipitous rush into externals, so important
in the more serious types of drug abuse, would find here not a true
prophylaxis, but at least a force counteracting those symptoms. This
force is: the stimulation of all available forms of creativity, to
encourage, teach, enlarge creativity corresponding to the gifts of each
individual student.

The important role of psychoanalytic insights—not as therapy, not
only as a subject to be taught, but as a key to open up the feeling for the
inner life, as a counterpoise against the enormous stress on practical
values, on action, achievement, competition—cannot be overemphas-
ized.

It will sound outrageous to many that psychoanalysis as a crucial
of symbolic forms should be taught to youngsters. Still I think we
simply cannot afford not to transmit the tremendous insights in a
disciplined, careful, profound way. Examples for required reading
might be Anna Freud's *Psychoanalysis for Teachers and Parents*,
Freud's two series of *Introductory Lectures*, Kohut's *Psychoanalysis in
a Troubled World* and his article about narcissistic rage, and, very
importantly, some of Erikson's and Rangell's outstanding works.

*

I am aware of the limited value these recommendations have as far as
drug abuse is concerned; I think the influence they could have on the

culture as a whole though would be considerable. The problem at hand (the hidden dimension of drug abuse) helps reveal the rot in our cultural and societal fabric; other approaches would lead us to the same results.

This rot is *anti-intellectualism,* one of the great dangers to our scientific, democratic society. Its allies or subgroups are bigotry, racism, totalitarian ideologies of all shades, the substitution of creativity by blind pragmatism, action for action's sake, the degradation of the great symbolic forms. One of its most glaring products are the drug cults and drug cultures.

Anti-intellectualism is thus the social companion piece to denial and pathologic externalization in the individual; it is another expression of the disavowal of inner conflict, of the avoidance of one's inner life and its Socratic scrutiny.

"Prevention"

Finally a few words about specific prevention.

Prevention in the most meaningful sense centers on the family. We have seen how the deepest roots of drug abuse are found in the family. Ideally we should attempt to step into those families which are known to be seedbeds for deviancy and work with them very early. This presupposes also that the disturbed youngster is spotted early enough, preferably even before he starts taking drugs and participating in or forming antisocial peergroups. Obviously his own treatment is important, but I wonder how much can be attained without deeply involving also his family. He is just the bellwether of a broader pathology.

A second, more superficial level of prevention may lie in the forming of positive peer groups in school, best around an inspiring teacher who is able to transmit a sense of commitment and solidarity, and around projects emphasizing creativity and social solidarity.

Ideally again, this would lead to the building up of "countergroups," groups in the schools which foster solidarity and stand for values without resorting to drugs. Drugs gather a pseudo-community where there is no community, where there is no genuine sense of purpose and deeper meaning in one's school group. We might find a new approach to prevention if we succeed in replacing such a pseudo-community with a true sharing and with a true belonging to group and family.

Beyond this we have to reverse the adage and say: *treatment is the best prevention.* Only in this limited sense the metaphor of drug abuse as a contagious disease is valid. Group processes, "chemical mythology," play a role. One way of preventing the spread of drug abuse is by treating the drug abuser and the peergroups which he influences.

A last line of prevention lies on the social, general end: we may be able to organize the community into constructive self-help groups with the purpose of abolishing some of the worst roots of social and economic distress. Any other prevention remains superficial, costly and ineffective. The sequelae of this very last point lie in "social reconstruction"—a task which I can only sketch in a few sentences; it belongs under the aegis of experts in social policy.

As long as there is the present screaming injustice, especially in law enforcement, economic possibilities and in health care, the rampant drug use in the ghetto will remain a festering sore. We live with the horrible inheritance of centuries of degradation, inhumanity and enslavement.

Again the focus is usually on the direct consequence of racial discrimination, and once more I feel the really difficult, but decisive issue is shunned.

Of course, instead of the illegal flow of goods we should have a massive plan for reconstruction of the slums. However, the economic side of this, including the building of decent housing, as huge as it is, is dwarfed by the task of human rehabilitation of desperate, undisciplined, and angry children, youths and adults. The building of inner structures necessitates an entire social strategy of rebuilding destroyed external structures, supports, limits. The inner "anomia" and lack of structures and cohesiveness and the social phenomenon of "anomie" are to some extent (but only partially) related. I do not know how such a large scale rehabilitation can be undertaken. One model for this huge and again partly psychiatric task may be found in those therapeutic communities which served a somewhat comparable task for another ghetto population: the Kibbutzim in Israel.

Chapter 19

SOME CONCLUDING
THEORETICAL THOUGHTS

It befits the theme of this book as well as my own personal preference that I do not end this book with practical recommendations, with the values of the "vita activa," but with those of the "vita contemplativa," with the values of "viewing and asking."

The Fashion Aspect—Some Questions

I am puzzled about the fashion aspect of psychopathology. Shearn and Fitzgibbons call massive drug use one currently popular manifestation of psychosocial deviance. Certainly it has been for the last decade at least one of the leading and noisiest manifestations, both of emotional disturbance (where the compulsive aspects are prominent) and of social protest, rebellion, and disagreement. (*Deviance* has a pejorative connotation; yet it really means: to walk off the well-trodden way, and thus, certainly for a philosophically minded person, could reassume a thoroughly positive meaning of nonconformity, of going one's own, independent way, to achieve one's own opinion and value priority.)

If we look back over history and literature there have been fluctuations in what attains psychiatric prominence (whether this is a fact of reality or only of perception I do not know). There is a varying historical emphasis on certain emotional illnesses and—presumptively—with that, on certain defenses. In the latter part of the nineteenth century and the beginning of this century the major was on hysteria. The leading defense was repression. In the middle of this century we witnessed the huge sweep of mass paranoia and with that the prevalence of projection. Then there was a brief period where depersonalization, estrangement, alienation—both culturally and in psychopathology—took much of the limelight, and with that the defense by denial of internal and external perceptions. Now we see what was called (misleadingly) "the epidemic of drug abuse," in reality the tendency of much psychopathology to take on the garb of compulsive drug use and thus to employ this particular form of the defense by externalization—besides other less frequent modes, as violence, pseudo mystical union, hectic driving (in many meanings), and manipulation "beyond dignity and freedom."

It might be a most fascinating enterprise of psychohistory to study not so much the fashion aspect of symptomatology, but that of the changing prevalence in perceived, treated and usually negatively valued forms of defenses. What we might find out is that precisely what shows up in a historical period as a leading defense form in psychopathology, may be at the same time a defense which, with slight alteration in mode, may be shared by much of the surrounding culture and cherished as value. We studied in chapter 14 the correspondence of externalization in our culture, in the modes of unrestricted action, of the use of impersonal agents like food, television, money, of lying and manipulation, and by aimless violence—as sought after solutions for internal problems on the one side—with the externalization by use of a magically powerful, meaning giving, at times even pseudo-religious drug experience on the other side. Two parts of this polarity in externalization: the culturally accepted ceremonial versus the demonized phobically heated use of drugs ("communions, holy and unholy"), and the admired, nearly omnipotent medical use of drugs (by the guardians over life and death, the physicians) versus the abuse of these drugs by illegitimate "healers" (pushers) are well described by Szasz (1973).

Whether the same can be applied throughout observable human history I do not know.

I pose it as an intriguing, tentative question.

And, is there also a similar historicity and periodicity in drive conflicts? Was the "time of hysteria" marked by concerns about archaic object libido, the "time of paranoia" by conflicts about primitive aggressions, the "time of depersonalization and drug abuse" by conflicts about narcissism?

Posed in this way these questions strike me as intolerable oversimplifications, as onesided illicit generalizations. Yet still, they may point the way to a more careful study of both: change in presenting symptoms in patients and change in the cultural atmosphere.

In contrast to the two sets of questions posed before (in regard to *defenses* and *drives* as historically more or less prominent) I feel persuaded that there has been—in education, philosophy, cultural atmosphere and thus in psychopathology—indeed such a gradual revolution in regard to the superego, as depicted by Rangell and the Lowenfelds. It needs no elaboration anymore how their findings interdigitate with what I have presented throughout this book.

THE NEED FOR NEW METAPHORS

David Beres, in an unpublished paper (1974), disagrees with the notion of "borderline" personalities. He considers it a catchall term for severely ill patients, and suggests instead the use of specific character disorders—narcissistic, masochistic, etc. I agree very much with him. Like "sociopathy," it becomes a verdict, putting them beyond the pale of intensive, meaningful, insight oriented psychotherapy or analysis; it may increase the perceived distance from ordinary, less severe neurosis and blur the radical difference from real psychoses.

I would go a step farther: Compulsive drug abusers form—together with other such severe character disorders (and perhaps also with various psychoses)—a contingent of patients for which we need a deepening and rejuvenation of psychoanalytic theory as well as better and new modes of finding access to and ability to alter the profound structural defects and archaic conflicts of these patients. One way to achieve this is to look for novel metaphorical systems which could help us to conceptualize and order the baffling and now largely untreatable phenomenona.

Elsewhere in a series of philosophical inquiries I stressed the legitimacy and fruitfulness of using metaphors in theory formation

(1975a, c, 1977); and in yet other studies I explored the concept of "tragic experience and tragic character" as an entire broad metaphorical system.

Only deepened, lengthy, very intensive psychoanalytically guided psychotherapy with compulsive drug users and with "sociopaths" in general will give us a new range of metaphors which will help us to understand and help these patients; they cannot be imposed from the "outside"—either from the experience with ordinary neurotics or from superficial observations in our treatment clinics, jails, drug cultures, communes, or by the autocratic powers who lead a campaign of scapegoating and vendetta against them.

I have no good, extensive models to offer as yet. The concepts of the "tragic character" and the "anti-tragic defenses," the closer scrutiny of the theoretical meaning of inner and outer boundaries, limits and limitations in regard to narcissism and aggression, the more detailed and subcategorizing efforts in regard to broad defenses, like denial, and externalization, greater specification as to the nature of aggression: all these may help us a small stretch on our way. I hope so, but I am not certain.

The quadrangle of fire, comprising the extremes of freedom, structures, self-infatuation, and self-destruction as superficial phenomena, may yet turn out to be a helpful construct for a deeper understanding, above all of the most prominent forms of externalization (and transference) and of the response by the surroundings to them (including countertransference).

Then we have observed the "feeding on itself," the "Antony metaphor"—"other women cloy/The appetites they feed, but she makes hungry/where most she satisfies" (*Antony and cleopatra*, Act) II, sc. ii); the same in *Hamlet (Act I, sc. ii): "As if increase of appetite had grown/By what it fed on"*—it is found not solely in drug abuse patients but throughout psychopathology. One analytic patient stated: "I am angry at myself for not tempering my anger." Another patient, following her associations in analysis, found them ridiculous, absurd, but then turned around, immediately condemning this inner judge also as absurd and ridiculous—obviously a self-condemnation of infinite regress, "feeding on itself." Andreas, to whom we can be deeply grateful already for so many excellent formulations and expressions of what is commonly hidden, stated: "Success goes with success, failure with failure, shame leads to more shame." Several analytic patients mentioned this "vicious spiral," typically in regard to shame: "I cannot talk because I am embarrassed to say what I just think, and then I become even more embarrassed about my silence, and the shame becomes worse and worse. I can only think in snatches and cannot say anything." This "feeding on itself" is a most powerful metaphor which *needs a thorough theoretical examination.*

Here I break off. All these questions lead over to new concepts, to other inquiries, to fresh perspectives. They will be taken up in other books. It may turn out that, to use yet another metaphor, "the stone which the builders rejected has become the cornerstone" (Psalm 118, line 22): that those who do not fit our theoretical model will provide us the cornerstone of an enlarged and broadened theory.

APPENDIX A

Extent and Nature of Severe Psychopathology in Compulsive Drug Users: Phenominological and Psychodiagnostic Assessments

There is convincing evidence that heavy ("dependent," "compulsive") drug use is coextensive with severe psychopathology, usually of a nonpsychotic nature. It encompasses severe character and affect pathology, often designated with pejorative, circular labels ("psychopathy," "deviancy," "inadequate personality," "narcissism," "borderline" personality, etc.). In-depth studies of the last twenty years, however, have allowed us in chapter 3 to proceed beyond such phenomenological or pseudo-psychiatric terms, and to study the deeper dynamics of these various forms of psychopathology.

The circularity often enters in two ways (and we had to guard against same in our chapters on psychodynamics). One is: all drug addicts are socially very deviant ipso facto (by their very syndrome), therefore they are sociopaths; and because they are sociopaths they became addicts. There is, of course, a way to break out of this circle: if we have independent standards of defining a "sociopathic personality" and some or all compulsive drug users fit these extraneous criteria, we would have justification to use the term. But still a profound uneasiness remains. I have worked a lot with such so called "sociopaths"; once a patient becomes better known in psychotherapy this diagnosis begins to appear to be a thin veneer hiding most profound neurotic, "borderline," sometimes psychotic conflicts and defects and above all very severe character problems with abysmal unhappiness, pain, and anxiety lurking under the varnish of glibness and "acting out" (whatever that overextended term may come to mean).

A second circularity enters when traits which may be secondary are assumed to be underlying personality characteristics: much depression, much mendacity, much rage may be caused by the dismal situation which gradually was created by prolonged severe drug use with its host of criminality, self-sabotage, exploitation of family and friends, the non-development of professional skills or the loss of professional standing. Again careful in-depth and longitudinal studies, anamnestic data from before drug use, data from periods of long-term stabilization (methadone maintenance or abstinence) support the data gained by the more superficial, cross-sectional methods now presented.

Phenomenological Studies

One of the few serious explorers not only of the physiologic problems but also the personalities of drug abusers, at that time particularly of narcotics addicts (and the political and legal mishandling of the problem of drug abuse), was L.S. Kolb (1962). His book remains very stimulating—and depressing—reading. Although the terms he uses to point to the psychopathology of his patients (mostly patients in the U.S. Public Health Service Hospital in Lexington, Kentucky) appear faded, unsatisfactory, almost quaint, the message is still clear: addicts he studied were very disturbed people, ill a priori, before the onset of their drug dependency. Kolb writes: "The present-day addict combines a number of traits which add up to his being an immature, hedonistic, socially inadequate personality" (1962, pp. 5-6). More in detail: "Emotional disorders affected 86 percent of the addicts, of whom 13 percent were criminal psychopaths, 13.5 percent psychoneurotics, 21.5 percent inebriates, and 38 percent hedonistic, unstable types" (pp. 39-40). These archaic categories fit in no modern nomenclature; he describes these types in greater detail (pp. 40-49). I forgo further quotes because later studies appear to me to have superseded Kolb's concepts and classifications (which essentially go back to 1925); however, his book is still a goldmine of information about the medical and social aspects of drug abuse.

Ausubel (1958) defends, I believe rightly, the crucial relevance of personality factors as disposition for compulsive drug use (especially narcotics addiction) against the one-sided sociological-physiological theory of Lindesmith (1947, 1965). He distinguishes, with R. H. Williams, between "primary addiction, in which opiates have specific adjustive value for particular personality defects; symptomatic addiction, in which the use of opiates has no particular adjustive value and is only an incidental symptom of behavior disorder; and reactive addiction in which drug use is a transitory developmental phenomenon in essentially normal individuals influenced by distorted peer group norms" (p. 39). I confess I cannot make much sense out of his second and third categories. However, it seems to me that his first group coincides with the type we are mainly concerned with, the compulsive user.

What J.H. Jaffe wrote in 1965 is, from a descriptive point of view, a good, still acceptable summary:

> Older views that compulsive users of opiates or alcohol were morally weak persons who simply over-indulged themselves have been largely replaced by the realization that such individuals are emotionally disturbed. It is also felt that the emotional disturbance would have manifested itself even in the absence of drug use, and the use of drugs may be an attempt to cope with this disturbance.

Although it had been suggested that individuals with widely differing problems use pharamacological agents for different reasons, Jaffe comes to the conclusion that there is

> a growing tendency to see in compulsive drug users a constellation of common characteristics that cuts across the diversity of clinical diagnoses and that may be thought of as the "addict" or "alcoholic" personality. Thus, alcoholics are often schizoid, depressed, dependent, hostile, and sexually immature ... Although most narcotic addicts show a constellation of common features similar to that seen in alcoholics, they also exhibit striking differences. Alcoholics tend to solve conflicts about aggression, dependency, and sexuality by "acting out" in a "pseudomasculine" fashion;

narcotic addicts prefer to handle such anxieties and conflicts passively, by avoidance rather than by aggressive acts.

Psychodiagnostic and Biographical Studies

Various personality tests again confirm the severity of pathology, mostly in the direction of depression, paranoid and outright schizophrenic symptomatology—besides the very frequent psychopathic deviancy.

S.A. Sola and W.F. Wieland reported in 1971 elevated D and Pd scales in the MMPI, indicating the presence of depression and psychopathic deviancy. The findings of depression were born out in several self-rating tests, and this despite the fact that they were in treatment with methadone and counseling.

The BDI revealed that irritability was the predominant factor, followed by disorders of appetite, weight, and sleep, and performance difficulties.... These findings present objective evidence that opiate dependent patients under treatment in a methadone program tend to continue to experience dysphoria. It is more severe than normals but less severe than neurotics or psychotics. Furthermore, the nature of the dysphoria differs qualitatively from neurotics and psychotics in that opiate addicts experience more irritability, performance difficulties, and negative outlook as the important constituent factors of their depressions whereas neurotics and psychotics tend to experience a predominance of deeper depressive mood.

The motivation to use heroin was related to these feelings of dysphoria, worries, nervousness, depression, coping with anger, relating to other people and self-blame.

Heller and Mordkoff compare the MMPI findings in narcotics addicts with those in nonaddicted, multi-habituated adolescents (1972). They postulate two general types of "drug abusing personalities." The first, associated with heroin addiction, seems to show "a psychopathic type of personality with little evidence of overt reports of anxiety, guilt, insecurity, or depression, and dominating antisocial tendencies." The other set of studies, probably of less severe forms of multiple drug abuse, "seems to indicate a personality marked by antisocial tendencies but also evidencing overt signs of the anxiety and depression lacking in the first type" (p. 71).

Interestingly (in regard to what was presented in chapter 6), another recent MMPI study (Henriques et al. 1972) finds no correlation of MMPI findings of various types of drug abusers with "drug of choice."

On the other side, a New York team reported in 1967 they succeeded in selecting a fifty-seven item "heroin scale" (He) from the MMPI with an accuracy of 75 percent for adults and 67 percent for adolescent addicts. In the latter category, "false positives" turned out to have some predictive valence: a number of non-using, but test positive adolescents were seen to have turned to heroin one year later (Cavior, Kurtzberg, Lipton).

Independent from the MMPI, Haertzen and Panton (1967) developed an Addiction Research Center Inventory (ARCI) with five-hundred and fifty structured questions, containing a scale of seventy-four items permitting the differentiation of "psychopathic" from "non-psychopathic" groups of patients. According to this scale "criminals and addicts were most socially deviant, alcoholics were intermediate, and normal subjects were the least deviant."

Schoof, Ebner, Lowy, and Hersch (1973) compare the MMPI profiles of black inner city addicts with those of suburban heroin addicts. In the former group, the major elevation is on the Pd scale (psychopathic deviate), reflecting alienation from social groups, dissatisfaction with and bitterness toward parents, and a dysphoric and resentful subjective state; in the latter there is the same Pd peak, but in addition the so-called neurotic constellation (hypochondriasis [Hs], depression [D] and hysteria [Hy]). Both groups show also Sc-elevation [Schizophrenia], indicating feelings of alienation, social isolation, and idiosyncratic, unrealistic thinking. On the basis of the MMPI, Rorschach, TAT and clinical findings, the authors delineate two groups of heroin addicts who are psychologically quite different: "The suburban addicts can be described as more verbal individuals, who experience greater feelings of anxiety, futility and hopelessness. They experience alienation from accepted social conventions, and anger towards their parents and peers... these individuals use heroin to alleviate their anxiety and to avoid reality. The inner city group, in contrast, appear to be less neurotic and to experience minimal anxiety. These individuals can be described as impulsive, using little mediation between the initiation of a thought and its transference into action, relying minimally upon an internalized set of standards, living in the here-and-now, having more unrealistic self-concepts and using denial as a major means of coping. In short, this group appears to be less mature and to rely upon others for limit setting and directions in everyday living." A very important, albeit tentative conclusion is drawn by these authors: for addicts falling "into the neurotic classification, heroin usage represent a symptomatic expression of individual psychodynamic conflict and an attempt to alleviate subjective distress or to 'act out' in relation to parents and other significant emotional figures. In contrast, for those addicts falling into the 'character disorder' classification, heroin usage may be more closely related to socio-psychological environmental factors than to individual psychodynamic conflict, in that these latter subjects evidence fewer signs of internal psychological struggle." They emphasize that there is not a complete congruence between neurotic and suburban versus character disorder and inner city but a higher respective incidence. The last conclusion of course pertains to the clinical, not the social groups.

Critically one would have to wonder why the accumulation of social alienation, bitterness towards parents and resentment in the inner city group would necessarily speak more for environmental factors. It indicates certainly a shift in the main weight of psychopathology from more neurotic to more characterological disorders, but we have to be careful here not to omit the intermediary link: that we simply have indications for a different set of grave conflicts and perhaps graver structural deficiencies in the inner make-up which then in turn can be explained by the differences in sociocultural mores, economics, family structure and pathology. This comment does not at all detract from the great value of the findings of Schoof and his group.

Based on a newly developed "biographical personality assessment test" and on psychiatric observations, the much quoted study of Clara Torda (1968, pp. 144–145) comes to the conclusion that there exists regularly a symbiotic bond between heroin addict and an overweaning impervious mother, who fed him before he could feel his own needs, always rewarding passivity and stifling any activity, self-assertion and hostility; the father was usually weak or absent. This combination was seen as promoting a mixture of masochism, passive dependency, and narcissism, and as leading to a near constant state of irritable, helpless depression.

Another recent and important study by C.J. Frederick, H. Resnick and B. Wittlin (1973) from the NIMH again emphasizes the central role of depression and self-destruction in heroin addicts. They refer to older studies (e.g., O'Donnell 1964) which indicate that the suicide rate among heroin addicts is nearly five times that found in the general population. With a short form of the "self-rating depression scale" developed by Zung, they examined ninety-eight hardcore addicts who had been in a methadone treatment program less than three months or in an abstinence program and compared them with several large control groups (entire population of the study: two-hundred and sixty-eight subjects).

The addict groups had unequivocally higher depression scores. Particularly interesting is the finding that "in the methadone group nearly 40 percent of the sample scored in the depression range, mild to moderate or higher, while 60 percent of the abstinence group revealed clearcut depression scores in the mild to moderate range or above."

The actual suicide attempt rate in this group is "remarkably excessive, surpassing the suicide-attempt rate expected for age-adjusted averages nationally by 18 and 16 times, respectively" (methadone and abstinence group). The authors come to the following central and very interesting conclusions:

1. "Addicts in general are more depressed than nonaddicts in young age groups whether on methadone or abstaining...." Remarks disclosing evidence of disgust, despair and hoplessness were evident.

2. "Addicts are more self-destructive than nonaddicts. It is clear from personal report through the questions asked in this survey that past behavior discloses a significantly greater number of suicide attempts among addicts than most of the other control groups."

3. "Addicts have more aberrant attitudes toward life and death than nonaddicts. In general there are attitudinal differences on morbidity which differ between addicts and nonaddicts, although the significance is not firmly established. There are at least some differences between the abstinence group and the controls. Suicide has been considered, projected, and even verbalized, especially among abstaining addicts...."

4. "Being black adds to the problem of addiction. Throughout the results a greater difference appears between addicted groups and white controls than among black controls.... It may be that blacks seek identity and conformity through addiction and then find themselves much more alone than they had anticipated."

5. "Methadone appeared to act as a palliative, not as a cure. Methadone reduces depression and attitudes towards violence, aggression, and morbidity. It is an aid to holding aberrant throughts in abeyance."

Another type of drug abuse, namely those who combined amphetamines with alcohol, were studied by A. Kipperman and E.W. Fine (1974) with the help of several psychological tests. Here, too, there was prevalence of moderate depression and increased anxiety.

Several studies report correlations between psycho-pathology and treatment outcome (Levine et al. 1972, Kaplan and Meyerowitz 1969).

Most interesting is E.G. Karp's study (1973) of various groups of narcotics addicts in methadone maintenance which tries to correlate (besides other factors) dropout rate with type of test diagnostic (MMPI) pathology. For our purposes the two following passages are of particular direct interest:

1. The fact that patients with prominent "psychopathic" traits did not respond poorly to psychotherapy and methadone maintenance lets her question—with Karpman—the meaningfulness of the whole concept of psychopathy. It "may be a catchall term, including many types of persons who have little in common other than some form of legal difficulty. In labelling psychopaths one often describes the symptoms rather than the dynamics, and Karpman believes that this symptomatology may mask neurotic or psychotic dynamics." It appears that heroin addicts fit into a type of psychopath that "might more usefully be characterized as suffering from some other form of psychic disturbance than be characterized as psychopaths."

2. "Some measures of pathology were found to be significant negative predictors of outcome for addicts. These measures...are generally considered to assess psychotic-like processes, rather than neurotic ones. Thus, subjects who tended to have had unusual experiences, paranoid, suspicious ideation, flatness of affect, difficulty in interpersonal relationships, inadequate testing of reality or thought disturbances were relatively likely to drop out of therapy. On the basis of these results one might speculate that two factors exist which discriminate between remainers and drop outs. The first might be called psychoticism vs. ego strength. The second factor might be a character disturbance factor highly loaded on authority conflicts."

Her findings do not directly contradict my assertion—elaborated in this book—that psychotic patients can be "good" patients. The proviso is: if they get the whole fulcrum of care their doubly massive psychopathology warrants—which they did not receive in the populations studied in the most valuable work by E.G. Karp.

A study from Phoenix House, a therapeutic community, by DeLeon, Shodol and Rosenthal (1971), again underlines the severity of psychopathology among the heroin addict population. In one of their "schizophrenic scales" they rate even higher than two schizophrenic control groups! The Beck Test again showed moderate depression. Interestingly some of the psychopathology (especially depression, anxiety, suspicion, and anger) gradually decreased during the stay in the program, whereas the dropouts scored consistently in the direction of more severe psychopathology.

Of a more general nature are the observations made in the Armed Forces. J.F. Greden, D.W. Morgan and S.O. Frenkel (1974) report: "Heroin users in all three samples were impressively characterized by their long-standing histories of social and psychological conflicts. When compared with nonusers, a much higher percentage reported conflicts in civilian life with parents, school officials, and legal authorities. Their marital and job histories were dramatically chaotic. A number had entered the military to avoid jail."

A study devoted to the personalities of marijuana users should also be mentioned. The findings of D.J. Kupfer et al. (1973) in regard to the "amotivational syndrome" are of great interest. In contrast to the usual assumption, namely that is the heavy marijuana use which leads to this well-known psychopathology, they found in a comparison of light with heavy users (with the help of a standardized psychiatric evaluation form) the amotivational personality type in both groups. Heavy marijuana smokers showed, however, significantly higher scores for depression and organicity, and lower ones for anxiety.

Finally there is a most interesting, but still unpublished study by Harvey Milkman and William Frosch ("The Drug of Choice")which uses a psychoanalytically relevant test, the Bellak-Hurvich Interview and Rating Scale for Ego Functioning. One finding is of particular interest; "Amphetamine users were found to have greater overall ego strength than heroin users, and both groups seemed to decrease in ego functioning capacity in the intoxicated condition."

Before concluding this section I would like to present two pilot studies undertaken within our drug abuse program at University of Maryland Hospital, one by a psychologist, Lucy Kirkman, the other by a psychiatric resident, Dr. Rochelle Herman (using a test developed by Dr. Walter Weintraub and co-workers).

Although methodological questions may be raised, both pilot studies are presented, although in abbreviated form. It appears to me that the results can claim considerable, though in parts still provisional, validity.

The study by Lucy Kirkman (1976) is remarkable in its breadth and extent—the sheer number of patients examined, the combination of an array of experimental tools, and the large collection of histories:*

The following is a preliminary evaluation of the results of 252 Minnesota Multiphasic Personality Inventories (MMPI), 232 Bender Gestalt Visual Motor Tests (Bender), 234 partial Wechsler Adult Intelligence Scales (WAIS), 38 California Personality Inventories (CPI), 38 Szondi Tests, 12 Rorschachs and 159 Social Histories obtained over a three year period from narcotic addicts in a methadone maintenance treatment facility.

MMPI

Although widely used in clinical settings and research, in this setting the MMPI proved to be limited in delineating possible underlying dynamics and predicting overt behavior, appropriate treatment or success. The most characteristic feature was that only a very small number of profiles were normal. It is interesting to note that in these cases the other test results did not usually confirm the MMPI but indicated at least some degree of pathology. Approximately 50 percent of the profiles were in line with other reported MMPI results— elevation of the Psychopathic Deviate Scale and/ or the Mania Scale. Of the remaining 50 percent nearly half showed elevation of all or nearly all scales indicating massive pathology. The remaining profiles were elevated on various neurotic scales in addition to the Psychopathic Deviate and Mania Scales. In interpreting the results, the most common features occuring to varying degrees were: irresponsibility, immaturity, egocentricity, defensiveness, impulsiveness, childishness, restlessness, dependency, emotional instability and sexual maladjustment or confusion about sexual identity. The second group of profiles,

*I quote directly from her dissertation from this point through p. 544.

in addition to the above, were characterized by bizarre, confused, erratic thoughts, often entailing excessive resentment and suspiciousness of others. Consistent in the third group of profiles in which neurotic indices were elevated was a marked concern about bodily functions and/or depression. In general the patients comprising these three groups did not manifest consistently any distinguishable patterns, let alone the predicted ones. Rather the behavior of an individual patient varied nearly to the degree and in the manner as did the entire sample of profiles.

BENDER

This test can be used to measure organicity, be interpreted as a projective test and includes a recall test as a measure of memory (as well as estimate of intellectual functioning). Of the 232 Benders, under 5 percent had gross distortions of the gestalts indicating organic dysfunction and under 15 percent showed slight distortions not allowing dismissal of CNS involvement as a possibililty. Over 60 percent of the Bender recalls indicated average memory functioning and nearly half of the remaining 40 percent indicated above average memory. Interpreted as a projective tool the most frequently occurring patterns were problems with sexuality and in relating to authority figures. In the case of the former this often involved indications of confused sexual identity and desertion-attachment-dependency problems resulting in difficulty forming close heterosexual relationships and often avoidance. In relating to authority figures the patients most frequently showed signs of submissiveness and overcompliance to win security, approval and to manipulate in a fashion characteristic of passive dependent and/or passive aggressive behavior. Impulsiveness, erratic affect (often hysterical in nature), depression (or denial thereof) and hostility were also typical indications. Anxiety, fear of social disapproval, self-centeredness, overextension of life-space, guarded, often withdrawn, poor self-concept, compulsivity, denial and rigidity were found in various combinations.

WAIS

The distribution of prorated full scale IQ scores obtained from 234 partial WAIS approximates that of the normal population. The individual Verbal IQ scores were consistently higher, often significantly, than the Performance IQ scores. The patients typically scored highest on tasks measuring abstract reasoning ability, auditory short-term memory and grasp of social conventions. They often scored low on tasks involving practical ability to plan in a social context and ability to separate relevant from irrelevant material.

CPI

This is a self-report inventory measuring various parameters of social adjustment. The patients generally scored average or low on measures of poise, ascendancy, self-assurance and interpersonal adequacy but generally average or above on self-acceptance. Over half scored unusually low on measures of socialization, maturity, responsibility, intrapersonal structuring of values and sense of well-being. The remainder generally scored in the average range on these dimensions with a low score in one or the other area. Over 70 percent scored below average or low in measures of achievement potential and intellectual efficiency. A frequent finding was elevated femininity scores for men and depressed femininity scores—though to a lesser degree—for women.

SZONDI TEST

The 38 Szondi Test Profiles were remarkably similar. The findings indicate extraordinary lability of ego defenses and an apparent breakdown of ego patterns. In a preliminary statistical analysis of 30 Szondi Tests 25 had highly labile and fragmented ego functions. Of the 5 profiles with consistent ego patterns three were neurotic-hypochondriacal and two were infantile-narcissistic. The various types of ego patterns in the labile profiles were most frequently infantile (archaic) ego functioning patterns. An inflated, omnipotent ego with little concern for reality is one example. Another is an ego which is functioning at the level of introjection of material objects to replace the lost object. A third type of infantile ego functioning is the autistic, undisciplined one which is possessive and projective at the same time.

Occurring over 80 percent of the time were indications of constant fear of abandonment, refusal to look for a new object and desperate clinging to old objects—stuck in the need to be accepted. In over 70 percent of the profiles there are reactions indicating extreme passivity and a tendency toward self-defeating, self-destructive behavior. The fourth most frequently occurring characteristic is a need to be good, a preponderance of shame, and desire to hide what is not acceptable. Orality, hedonism, conflicts about values and neurotic defenses, such as inhibition, denial, repression, depersonalization, compulsivity (and to a lesser extent both everyday adapting and psychotic-like projection of blame), are commonly seen in the profiles. There is some indication of sexual inversion in that the males are more typically unusually passive and the females are often unusually aggressive.

RORSCHACH

These are given on referral and usually to the more severely disturbed patients. The only consistent finding in the limited and biased sample was disturbed cognitive processes, often schizoid-like, and adolescent or unrestrained sexual responses.

SOCIAL HISTORIES

Characteristic features include lower or lower middle socioeconomic backgrounds; broken homes with the father figure usually absent or ineffectual; large numbers of siblings and half-siblings; reports of extremely close knit families or great difficulty relating to a parent or other significant figure corporal, often erratic discipline and alcohol or drug abuse among relatives. Among the 15 percent to 25 percent from a middle class (or above) background parental overprotectiveness and indulgence is characteristic. Many reported that the reason for their continued use of narcotics was due to increased feelings of power and control over themselves and their environment. A little over 25 percent of the patient population are females and of these approximately one third reported sexual abuse by one parent or the other.

CONCLUSIONS

Although couched in different terms the preliminary results of these various tests do consistently point to several problem areas. In general the pathology appears to be widespread and often seems to affect all three levels (id, ego, superego) of personality structure: The most striking sign is the overall lability and fluctuating, shifting nature of ego functions, including defenses.

The difficulties in gratifying excessive needs adaptively, the preponderance of shame over guilt, and a generally low self-esteem are remarkable if compared with other populations. Another frequent finding consists in difficulties with their interpersonal relationships, particularly maternal, heterosexual and authority. Often poor relationships are at least in part due to their great needs for approval and use of passive-dependent and passive-aggressive behavior as a means of getting these and other needs fulfilled. The test findings often indicate a strange combination of psychotic (frequently schizoid), neurotic and antisocial (psychopathic) personality patterns within one individual; many terms used above are reminiscent of one of more of these types. However, this sample as a whole seems to be markedly different from any of these types.

Whereas schizophrenics are typically detached from reality and withdrawn from contact with others, for this group of narcotic addicts reality is out of focus—they are often unrelaxed, anxious and insecure in their rapport with reality. In contrast also is the addict's dependency on a significant other, great need for affiliation, approval and acceptance. Schizophrenics share with this sample the lability of ego functioning, but they have a more extensive breakdown in their self-boundaries, with lability among more primitive and regressive patterns. Among the narcotic addicts the lability of control patterns—in particular of defenses used—is far more extensive, but involves less regressive levels of ego patterns; there is a wild shifting around among various infantile, narcissistic, adolescent, neurotic and at times psychotic-like patterns. Moreover there appears to be a wide variety of boundary problems, of fuzziness and blurring which does not reach psychotic proportions but evidences unique fluidity in limits of the field of action and self-boundaries.

The major difference between this sample and other neurotics is the labile ego patterns and functioning versus consistent albeit maladaptive and/or rigid patterns. A greater frequency of self-denial and excessive self-criticism is also found in the neurotic. A lesser degree of ego conflict, guilt and attachment need is generally thought to be present in those diagnosed as antisocial personalities than is found in this sample of narcotic addicts. It appears that if this sample is representative of the narcotic addict population, they not only may suffer from a variety of different problems but may also have some behaviors and pathology in common, distinguishing them from other psychopathologies.

The second study is that of Rochelle Herman (1976); it is a pilot study, pointing in a new direction—one of the important attempts to bridge the gap between psychological laboratory and psychoanalytic-clinical experience.

Dr. Herman's is one of several studies relating characteristics of speech to behavior. In previously published papers the speech of obese, delusional, compulsive, depressed, and impulsive patients was found to differ significantly from that of normals along eleven objectively scored categories. These variables appear to be related to psychological defense mechanisms observed by psychoanalysts.*

METHODS

The experiment was conducted according to the method described by Weintraub and Aronson (1963). The group of subjects consisted of twelve men and six women. They were all patients of an inner city methadone maintenance program from the University of Maryland. The subjects volunteered to sit in a room with a silent observer and speak freely into a tape-recorder for ten minutes. The following categories of speech were scored.

1. Number of words.
2. Silence; all pauses longer than 5 seconds.
3. Rate: the number of words per time speaking.
4. Non-personal reference: All clauses with a subject and a verb were counted, then divided into personal and non-personal; personal referred to when the subject was the speaker or someone known to the speaker.
5. Negators: all negatives scored, i.e., not, never.
6. Qualifiers: all clauses, phrases, or words which indicate vagueness or uncertainty, modifiers of the forcefulness of a statement, i.e., I suppose, it's more or less, I did what one might call....
7. Retractors: anything detracting from the preceding statement such conjunctions as although, however, etc.
8. Explaining: words like *because, as a result* of; reasons:"My purpose was"; participi al phrases: "having gone."
9. Direct references: any reference to the experimenter, the situation, the surroundings, or the equipment.
10. Expressions of feelings: "I enjoy," "I was shocked" (the referent must be the speaker).

*I quote directly from Dr Herman up to the last paragraph of p.548.

11. Evaluators: all value judgments (good/bad, useful/useless, propriety/impropriety, pleasant/unpleasant).

RESULTS

Addicts scored significantly higher in seven out of eleven categories, and lower in one. They used fewer words and were more silent, while speaking at a normal rate. They used more negators, qualifiers, retractors, explainers, direct references, expressions of feeling, and evaluators.

TABLE I

	normal males	normal females	addicts	depressed	impulsive	delusional	compulsive	obese
WORDS			*	*				
SILENCE			*	*				
RATE				*				
N-P				*				*
NEG			*	*	*	*	*	*
QUAL								
RET	*		*		*		*	*
EXP			*			*	*	
D.R.			*	*	*	*		
FEEL			*	*	*	*		*
EVAL	*		*	*	*	*	*	

* denotes significant difference from normal males (higher except for words)

DISCUSSION

It can be readily seen that addicts have a markedly aberrant speech pattern when compared to normal control groups using this method. In sheer number of significant differences, they most resemble the depressed patients, sharing six of their categories.

In previous papers, several defense mechanisms have been postulated to coincide with six of the verbal behavior categories. Negators seem to indicate denial and negation. Qualifiers, although they have only been found higher in a group of sociopathic prisoners studied by Eichler, may indicate "undoing before the fact." Retractors are like "undoing after the fact," and may indicate a certain amount of impulsivity whereas the qualifier could indicate caution. Explainers seem to measure rationalization. Direct references are high with a high degree of anxiety, lack of frustration tolerance, impulse control and the subject's need to manipulate the environment. Evaluators may be measuring an aspect of the superego, as was postulated for the impulsive patients who were thought to have harsh though inconsistent superegos.

In the drug addicts, the decreased quantity of speech and increased silence can only be partially explained by depression, since the depressives spoke at a decreased rate. Perhaps this corresponds to "hyposymbolization," the inability to articulate feelings. Yet they scored higher on feelings. This probably reflects the overwhelming nature of affects against which the drug is used as a defense, albeit not completely successfully.

Chein et al. (1964) describe the defenses of the addict as a "melange of projection, rationalization and denial," and the high incidence of negators and explainers may help to confirm this.

Another prominent defense as described in the literature is said to be externalization which may account partially for the psychopathic behavior commonly observed; correspondingly the reliance on others outside the self or on drugs as the cause of their discomfort is striking indeed in the content of their speech: "Drugs turn my whole life around." "It controls you." "My whole life revolves around this program."

Perhaps the high direct reference score is indirectly tapping some of the externalization as well as the very low frustration tolerance and desperate attempts to manipulate others whom they see as causing their discomfort. In two speech samples, the subjects saw the experimenter as an extension of the clinic despite prior clarification of his status. One subject tried to manipulate the experimenter to grant more privileges on the program in return for his "cooperation" with the experiment. Another bitterly complained that the money she assumed the *clinic* spent on the tape recorder should have been spent on a gym for her to lose weight in because she was sure that methadone was "making people fat."

The high incidence of evaluators may be addilional evidence for the recent investigative efforts of some authors into superego pathology: i.e., that addicts are not devoid of conscience, but possess an archaic form as also hypothesized for the impulsive patients. This is anecdotally known about addicts, who do not necessarily adhere to the values and morals of normative society, but who operate by the "law of the talion."

The category of non-personal references might have been predicted to be low, indicating a preoccupation with self. Addicts in fact spent most of the time talking about themselves, but with the subject of the clause being methadone, drugs, etc. "The methadone enables me to function normally." "People don't seem to like my personality." The idiosyncratic expression "you know" was also counted as a non-personal reference.

Concerning the nature of object relations, the combination of feelings, negators, evaluators and direct references can be applied to addicts as they were to depressives shown in the diagram, confirming suggestions that one of the unconscious motivations of drug use was the need to replace a *lost* object.

In summary, the speech of drug addicts most closely resembles a combination of that seen in depressed and impulsive patients with one additional category, explainers (indicating rationalization), which was seen in delusional and compulsive subjects."

Rochelle Herman tries then to correlale in the following diagram the clinical observations (left column), based on the literature about narcotics addiction, with the speech patterns directly observed. The arrow in front of a term denotes "lower than normal," the reverse arrow the opposite.

TABLE 2

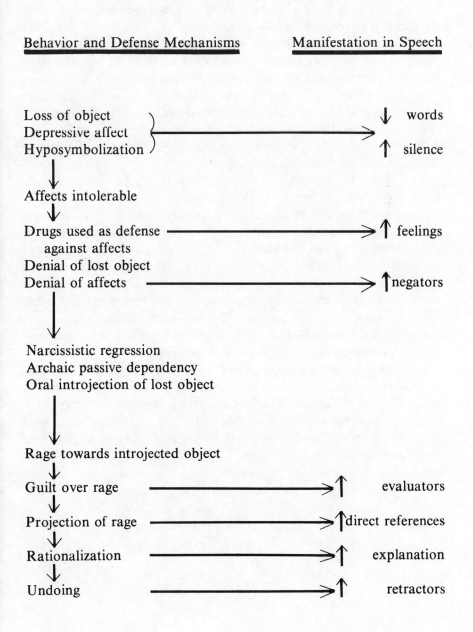

Behavior and Defense Mechanisms	Manifestation in Speech

Loss of object
Depressive affect → ↓ words
Hyposymbolization → ↑ silence

Affects intolerable

Drugs used as defense → ↑ feelings
against affects
Denial of lost object
Denial of affects → ↑ negators

Narcissistic regression
Archaic passive dependency
Oral introjection of lost object

Rage towards introjected object
Guilt over rage → ↑ evaluators
Projection of rage → ↑ direct references
Rationalization → ↑ explanation
Undoing → ↑ retractors

Summary

If we now look back over the findings of this appendix, we arrive at the following conclusions:

1. We encounter an almost complete consensus that those few categories of intensive or compulsive drug users which actually were studied with the help of tests were replete with severe psychopathology, that severe drug use is nearly co-extensive with such deep disturbances whereby severe character or personality disorders represent that vast majority, neurosis a minority, and psychosis a rarity.

2. The extent of depression for all categories and particularly for narcotics addicts is strikingly massive.

3. There is no attempt to distinguish the psychopathology among various types of abusers as to the class of drugs they prefer.

4. In a few inquiries the particular fluidity and lability of defenses used, the lack of inner structure and the blurring of various forms of boundaries are at least alluded to.

5. With a few exceptions (and those in pilot studies, as in the last two projects) the findings are crude and, for a clinician who would like to set up improved treatment forms based on a better psychological understanding of these patients, by and large uninformative and disappointing, except—that he is grateful to find independent confirmations for some of his clinical experiences.

6. Thus it becomes obvious which examines in a relable, objective, probably quantitative method what is relevant from a psychodynamic point of view, what has been found with astonishing convergence in psychoanalytically informed studies of these patients, and thus what needs experimental and theoretical deepending from an angle which satisfies more the scientific needs for clarity and replicability.

APPENDIX B

"And Reason panders will"
—Shakespeare. *Hamlet* Act III, Sc. iv.

How do the major treatment modalities deal generally with the problem of severe psychopathology? It will quickly become apparent how vast the gaps are between the extent of psychopathology and what is being done.

First, however, the major modalities have to be presented and examined as to relevance for our purposes.

"Modalities" and "Unspecific Ancillary Services"

The years 1969–1973 in particular have witnessed an efficient, systematic and—despite many shortcomings—well-organized development of treatment programs all over the nation (and indeed internationally as well), devoted to a very few "modalities"—(a) methadone maintenance, (b) rapid detoxification, (c) compulsory abstinence, (d) therapeutic communities, (e) narcotics antagonists, (f) hospitalization or involuntary commitment. Usually these "modalities" employ a number of "ancillary" or "auxiliary" methods, viewed by and large as subservient and subordinate to the "modality" and unspecific in nature. These so called ancillary methods which are ubiquitous to a major or lesser extent in nearly all the programs, regardless of "modality," are the following:

1. *Counseling*—a supportive, reality oriented activity, mainly directed toward solving external problems, with some encouragement to express affects and "change attitudes".

2. *Educational* activities—reschooling, vocational rehabilitation (especially in order to achieve a better fit between intellectual abilities and actual useable skills); tutoring in reading, writing, job applications.

3. Counseling with *families,* especially spouses and parents; occasionally whole families are members of a program (we often have husband and wife, or father and several sons as patients on our methadone program).

4. *Group counseling,* often called group therapy—again largely oriented towards solving of external problems, much vaunted in the literature, in my personal experience of rather limited value.

5. *Encounter and sensitivity groups or training*—the evidence about their usefulness is very contradictory. Many authors describe their destructiveness, especially toward more seriously sick patients (e.g., Kqantzian).I have no personal experience with this "ancillary" method. Khantzian writes that "the encounter approach often succeeds in breaking down the massive denial and sense of entitlement that is present in many addicts"—thus leading to often dramatic improvement and temporary compliance. But he adds that "many of these encounter approaches grossly underestimate many addicts' limited capacity to deal with intense affect, particularly aggressive feelings" (1974, p. 68).

6. *Arts and crafts*—occasionally mentioned in the literature as an adjunct.

7. *Recreational activities*—rarely mentioned, this aspect is felt to be very helpful in our own program.

8. The *structure* of the program: rules, regulations, "contracts," consistent enforcement of policies, limit setting to violations, explicit discipline, such as emphasis on keeping appointments and working, incorruptibility, consistent and prompt medical and psychiatric care

where needed, support in court if warranted, close surveillance of the entire staff, etc., non-vindictive, but psychotherapeutically oriented evaluation of infractions (absences, "positive urines", etc.)—all these form a therapeutically powerful ingredient of any program.

How important all these "ancillary" measures (especially the eighth) are is clear when we review in our mind what we have studied up to now—especially the complex boundary and "structure" problems, which in turn were based on deep conflicts of narcissism (omnipotence) and aggression.

Specific Adjunct Therapies

Among the just mentioned unspecific "ancillary" methods there appear two which are so prevalent and have become a feature of nearly all "modalities" and programs that they may just as well be counted again under these more specific, perhaps indispensable forms of therapies: focused *skilled counseling* and *specific vocational retraining and rehabilitation.* In addition, in a very few programs the following specific therapeutic interventions are available and commonly used:

1. *Intensive psychotherapy:* Much is called with this label which, by rights, falls under unspecific once or twice a week counseling. Under intensive psychotherapy the patient works with a well trained therapist at least once, hopefully twice or more times a week for a 30–50 minute session (or more), with the goal of resolving some of his inner problems. The methods used are clarification of underlying affects, elucidation of the conflicts between prevailing attitude and leading wishes or values as life goals, some work on the more accessible unconscious determinants of these conflicts and honing in on the major defenses. In other words, some (albeit rather superficial) work on the massive character pathology underlying the severe external conflicts as well as some of the prevailing symptoms and affects (especially anxiety, rage, and depression) can be done, if the program is oriented toward more psychotherapeutic aims.

2. *Psychopharmacological intervention* is often used in many programs to cope with gross psychopathology: antidepressant, antipsychotic and antianxiety agents being the most prevalent ones. We use it relatively sparingly.

3. *Family therapy* of a sophisticated nature is a very "rare bird," indeed, in the field, but there is a crying need for a vast involvement of families where existent.

4. *Hospitalization* in cases of suicidal or homicidal decompensation—very difficult, very rare (perhaps 1–2 percent of the patients in our program and others I have been in contact with). None of the underlying problems are usually solved since most are of such chronic and severe nature that the short term hospitalization, often in a state hospital, is at best of very transient value.

5. *Various forms of behavior modification, desensitization, etc.*— there has been little regard for severe psychopathology in the use of these specific adjuncts to the modalities. I admit my own lack of specific knowledge in this area beyond what I read in the literature which seems irrelevant to the problem area which we study. There is a fair amount of literature about the various forms of behavioral treatment of "drug addiction" (see, e.g., the interesting "review and analysis" by D.C. Droppa 1973), but the interest is exclusively focused on combating the one symptom (most frequently smoking, some cases of alcohol or narcotics use). There is no reference made as to how deeply disordered and disturbed the rest of life and personality of such patients might be. I suspect that this method works with those drug users who either are not of the "compulsive" category, or, if they are, that they belong to that part of the spectrum which shows only moderate pathology (see chapter 3).

6. *Group pressure, group inspiration, solidarity*—an important specific therapeutic adjunct which plays a large role in many programs, both positively and destructively (contratherapeutically), but is of a central role in therapeutic communities (in both directions—very helpful, at times very destructive, as repeatedly observed).

Methadone Maintenance and Severe Psychopathology

SUCCESS

The most successful "modality" has been the maintenance on higher (80 mg) or lower (20–40 mg) dosages of methadone over months and years, time limited or unlimited. This "modality" actually was initiated in Vancouver, B.C., by Paulus and Halliday in 1959, but applied systematically and with far more aplomb and methodological clarity by Dole and Nyswander since 1964. The result rate varies between 60 and 90 percent, dependent on the selection of patients and probably many other factors, like the unspecific "ancillary" methods described above ("structure", waiting periods, missionary zeal, etc.).

The experience is convincing that vast numbers of otherwise unsuccessfully treated, both inveterate and relatively recently enrolled, addicts who averred to be dependent on heroin and other narcotics could be treated in large numbers, at convenient cost ratios, and with relatively simple and easily standardized procedures in methadone maintenance programs. Side effects were minimal, social and medical complications negligible, the result rate as to abstinence from other drugs (to be found in frequent randomized urine-testing) fair to excellent (in our program 75-95 percent) and the result rate as to social rehabilitation (work, retraining) splendid (in our program 75 – 80 percent during good economic times; this has slumped very much during the current severe recession).

RETENTION AND DROPOUT RATE

The retention rate, however, varies much. Due to the high rate of preplanned slow detoxification (over a period between six months and three years) we ourselves had for years a retention rate between 50 and 60 percent, which is quite low. Other programs retain 70 - 80 percent. Currently, due to the gradual self-selection of who stayed, the retention rate is perhaps close to 90 percent in our program.

It has been observed by a number of sympathetic as well as critical evaluators that the excellent results with methadone maintenance may be deceptive though (see Perkins 1972, Maddux and Bowden 1972, and Corman et al. 1973); all comment about the superficial nature of rehabilitation and the "sitting up process" in programs (their being filled up by chronic stagnant cases).

Yet, despite these and under more radical criticisms, the results of methadone maintenance remain impressive. However, the real reasons which could explain these bright results remain unknown gaps in understanding which at best are filled with narrowly based psychodynamic hypotheses, or farflung, if not fanciful, metabolic speculations! The only justification for the existence of methadone maintenance is that it is the lesser of two evils, or better, the least dismal of several terrible options.

Before we leave the topic of methadone maintenance we have once more to turn our attention back to two problems already touched upon: The first one refers to the many rejects prior to admission and the dropouts from methadone maintenance. The reasons are usually, again, severe signs of emotional disturbance: multiple drug dependence, "lack of motivation", threats of violence, severe symptomatic acting out (running away, homicide, other crimes, etc.). Again, the same categories of severe character pathology as described for problems *within* the program can be discerned, especially categories (c) and (d) (see chapter 3).

The second question is that of the nature of the methadone effect: narcotics, including methadone, mute various overwhelming affects, and their absence brings forth a "craving" which very often can be understood as a breakthrough of those archaic feelings and a rapid narcissistic decompensation.

A very important practical (and also eventually theoretical) issue emerges: that of the compensation level, a notion so far not accepted by the vast majority of workers in the field.

A curious threshold phenomenon, mentioned by Dole and by Jaffe (1969) during the second National Methadone Conference (see Proceedings), was seen here too: as soon as the dosage threshold of 20 - 30 mg per day of methadone was passed, psychological de- or recompensation occurred (dependent whether this line was passed on the way up or down), and regardless whether the patient knew the dosage or not, regardless too of the fact that the "detoxification" occurred usually at the wish of the patient. I do not think that this is a magic line; I assume from other, less well-observed cases that this threshold is individually quite different, but fairly specific for a given person. In most cases it is far below the so called "blockade" level (more appropriately: tolerance level). I call this crucially important threshold the *compensation level.*

These experiences are very comparable to those made with psychotics. In a number of chronic schizophrenics who were seen in intensive psychotherapy both with and without phenothiazines, it was striking how a certain threshold of the tranquilizer was needed to help them to be, or keep them, compensated—socially and in psychotherapy. The reduction, e.g., from 10 to 8 mg of Stelazine, was in several cases accompanied by overwhelming, mostly undirected rage and fragmentation, leading to social withdrawal, complete uncooperativeness and disintegration in therapy: the increase to the former dose was equally prompt in its effect of recompensation. This forces us to very important theroretical considerations:

We do not know as yet how methadone, or for that matter the other narcotics, work, But we have some indications now. Practically, we all are very familiar with the phenomenon of cross-tolerance which explains the "blockade" effect if methadone is given in a high enough dosage. This is, of course, a strictly physiologic event.

However, what has by no means been satisfactorily explained up to now is the observation that the "narcotics hunger" or "craving" can be diminished or even eliminated with methadone, even at doses at far below the blockade level. In observations presented in chapter 7 we saw a direct effect on basic affective states (rage, shame, hurt), in the form of an artificial affect defense. The effect of methadone (and other narcotics) is merely a mitigation of these affects and hence a partial resocialization of the patients.

Dole suggested that the effect of methadone may lie in the correction of a metabolic error. I doubt this very much. If we take into account the long history of severe pathology antedating the use of narcotics, the often observed wild shopping around for the appropriate drug and the final settling down to narcotics, we would have to assume that the specific disorder is not caused, but calmed by narcotics, including methadone, and must have pre-existed during most of the life of the patient. In other words, if such a metabolic error exists, it would have to be (a) antedating the use of narcotics, and (b) a specific predisposition for massive narcissistic disturbances.

For the sake of explanatory parsimony and logical coherence we are better off to watch the psychopathological phenomena in their breadth and depth without speculating about the mythical aberrant enzyme. The crux is that narcotics, including methadone, work, above the specific compensation level, as a bona fide psychotropic agent. This effect on the "craving" appears to be also entirely independent from the "high" (euphoria).

From all this it becomes abundantly clear that far more research into the nature of action of methadone and of its dosage, its interaction with psychopathology, overall structure of program, and "ancillary" services is urgently needed.

I profoundly deplore the widespread dogmatism, zealousness (pro and con) and rigidity in regard to these, in my opinion, barely touched questions.

Therapeutic Communities and Severe Psychopathology

In these residential facilities, most of which operate with intensely effective forms of religious indoctrination and cohesion, a certain type of patient—again usually a narcotic user, sometimes a polydrug user, more often from a higher socioeconomic background than the methadone maintained patient, also more often white—can remain successful. The support lent by such *parareligious* communities consists in a strong emphasis on *authority-child-relationship,* a hammering in of an amply providing dependency, quite reminiscent of the experience of a two–six year old child in an emotionally archaic, austere, and harsh farm family.

However, this also implies the massive reliance on instruments of chastisement in form of verbal "confrontation" (a form of vituperative scolding) and outright vindictive measures using direct shaming (shaving of the head, hanging of a sign around the neck with some self-deprecatory slogan, days of sitting silently in the corner) and atonement by doing most menial tasks. This double barreled approach of appealing to infantile dependence and of taking over by the outside of archaic superego functions by direct, concrete, primitive punishment has a tremendous protective effect: suddenly there is a firm hierarchical structure, an intensely shown solidarity and belonging, a clear line between right and wrong, and an ideologically sanctioned channel for vindictive aggression. Again, patients with a certain character pathology (infantile, passive, dependent above all) are helped: they recompensate as to their leading symptomatology while under the shelter of such a protective environment. Despite the severe confinement and degradation we see how this modality can be very tolerable if we reflect about the psychopathology of compulsive drug users: above all it plays right into the cardinal defense of externalization, although in a different mode than that of "using the magical thing," and establishes rigid external boundaries, limits, structure.

The other side of the coin is not so different from the one just described as to methadone maintenance: The number of rejects and dropouts is very large (according to last reports only about 5 percent of applicants "make it"). Many of the dropouts are said to come out yet more shipwrecked and broken because of the insensitive, brutal assaults on their brittle defenses, although, again, numbers are not available. Research into these aspects alone—how many patients are rejected a priori, drop out in the first three months of treatment in such a facility, or leave at any time with a deepened psychopathology— should not be all that difficult, but does not exist.

An article in *Science* ("Drug Abuse: Methadone Becomes the Solution and the Problem," (179, 2/23/73, p: 773) quotes from the Ford Foundation's study "Dealing with Drug Abuse"; "it would be surprising if careful evaluation showed that more than five percent of those who came in contact with [therapeutic communities] are enabled to lead a reasonable drug-free socially productive life."

Equally, a *New York Times* editorial of 25 June 1971 states: "An unpublished review of the City's Phoenix House therapeutic community program asserts a success rate of only 3.7 percent and, deplorably low as this figure is, it may even prove inflated" (see also E.M. Brecher 1972, *Licit and Illicit Drugs*, pp. 81–82).

It would be quite expectable from all the evidence already garnered that the "brutal confrontations" employed would lead in a majority of patients to an exacerbation of their severe psychopathology unless they ran away in time.

Peter G. Bourne and Ann S. Ramsay appropriately comment: "A troubled adolescent may be unprepared for the confrontational attack methods used in many therapeutic communities. If he has been admitted without proper psychiatric screening, or professional staff are not present during therapy, serious emotional injuries may result. A psychiatrist in a southern state reports that he sees two to three young people a week in a psychotic or suicidal state after participating in the very large therapeutic community program in his city."

Here I might quote once again from Wieder and Kaplan's critical assessment in their excellent book *Drugs Don't Take People, People Take Drugs* (1974):

Most therapeutic communities are directed by ex-addicts, and many reject all psychiatric knowledge. They account for drug abuse and addiction in a closeminded and inflexible way which is not only dogmatic but superficial and incorrect as well. Their graduates are limited by this rigid viewpoint, by their own personality difficulties and by their lack of training.

A balanced view is expressed by Robert L. DuPont (1973): "It is now generally recognized that therapeutic communities are valuable but that they should be restricted only to patients who voluntarily join them and that, in any event, they will only be attractive to, and effective with, a small percentage of the heroin addicts needing and wanting help."

On the other side, there seem indeed to be far more supportive forms of residential facilities which work mostly with inspirational and added psychotherapeutic methods (even some methadone support) and thus avoid the serious threats to severely ill patients, e.g., The Vitam Program in Norwark, Conn., run by W.X. Lehman and formerly G.G. De Angelis (1973, 1974) and the *Holy Cross Program* in Rhinecliff, New York (A.J. Coghlan et al. 1973).

In sum, I concur fully with Bourne and Ramsay when they recommend "an interfacing of local mental health delivery systems with well-run, professionally staffed therapeutic communities, especially to serve troubled adolescents." Instead of sending these severely disturbed drug-using or high risk adolescents to state hospitals or correctional facilities, they should be sent to professionally led therapeutic communities "that would offer short-term but more intensive treatment....Use of supportive group techniques, rather than the severe confrontational methods used for the heroin addict, might offer the troubled adolescent a constructive surrounding in which to work out his problem."

Narcotics Antagonists

All the papers dealing with this modality which I have reviewed shun the question of serious psychopathology. Again the selection of success seems to preclude that vast contigent which we are concerned about. The most relevant reference I was able to find is the 1971 survey article in *Science* "Narcotic Antagonists: New Methods to Treat Heroin Addiction":

Most of the treatment programs using narcotic antagonists...are restricted to patients who appear to be highly motivated to stop using drugs. But even with these patients a wide variety of problems are often encountered, including high dropout rates during the early stages of treatment and the use of other drugs. One of the chief causes appear to be that patients are compelled to face their problems and to deal with the realities of their social situations, however impossible. This may well be beyond the capability of large numbers of addicts, many of whom presumably use narcotics to avoid just those situations.... The relaxed jovial atmosphere of a methadone ward contrasts sharply with the tension, frustration and anxiety that characterize a cyclazocine ward, according to one psychiatrist who has worked in both.

From all clinical knowledge it appears contraindicated to put psychotic narcotic addicts or all those (circa 60 percent) with severe character pathology on antagonists, unless a very intensive substitution therapy for the severe inner structural defects and massive emotional needs of these patients, on a level of highest professional (psychiatric-psychotherapeutic) skill and around the clock coverage (preferably at the beginning on an in-patient basis), can be guaranteed.

Insofar as antagonist medication is basically a form of compulsory absinence, viz., that the prohibition is of a chemical nature instead of the external threats built in the traditional compulsory abstinence programs (parole or probation, daily urine tests), similar conclusions will have to be reached in regard to the next modality.

Compulsory Abstinence

On the basis of my own four-year participation (1964–1968) in the Baltimore Narcotics Clinic (see Kurland et al. 1966a, b, 1967, 1969), a program combining parole status, daily urine testing, weekly group therapy sessions, individual psychiatric counseling, and the threat of return to jail if the patient kept "violating," either in regard to verified illicit drug taking or noncooperation with clinic and parole officer, I have come to the following conclusions as relevant to the topic of severe psychopathology:

1. The success rates with the several hundred patients treated by now is roughly thus: 25–30 percent "make it" on the program—do not show any or only very infrequent violations (mainly in regard to urines); about 20 percent abscond; and the rest: 50–55 percent, have to be returned to jail.

2. I was impressed by the switch in "symptom choice" in most of those 25 to 30 percent who were the *"successes"* of the program: moderate to massive *alcohol abuse,* or of nondetectable other drugs, severe, nearly or fully suicidal depression (see case 5, Shaky), severe rages, including homicidal outbursts (several nearly successful—see case 6, Breadth of Morpheus), or other forms of compulsive acting, such as gambling, overeating, suicidal car racing. My conclusion was: The more successful a patient was in changing from compulsive narcotics use to another, usually equally or more self-destructive or socially dangerous form of symptomatic action, the more likely he was to survive in the program for prolonged periods. The other 70–75 percent simply tried to cope with their moderate to severe psychopathology (of a nature entirely, quantitatively and qualitatively, comparable to the one I described as from within our own methadone maintenance program) by the only means they knew: occasional and increasing use of narcotics or barbiturates, sporadically of cocaine or amphetamines; and disappeared or ended up being handcuffed in the back room of the clinic and transported back to jail.

3. Increase and refinement of a system of reward and punishment (reduction in frequency of urine specimens to four times a week, etc.) had a great impact on morale and motivation and certainly improved the success rate. It had no positive effect whatsoever on the overall psychopathology—quite to the contrary. The more punitive and deterrent we became, the less psychotherapeutic work on the severe problems of these patients was possible, the more rage and anxiety prevailed, the more other symptomatic actions appeared. The observations can be likened to those with the narcotics antagonists: the whole rationale of behavior modification by reward and punishment falters once the overall severe character pathology and the rest of the massive symptomatology is considered; the overall pathology increases!

4. I tried once or twice weekly psychotherapy with several patients on compulsory abstinence who seemed to be particularly promising candidates for this added method. In contrast to my later experience with voluntarily abstinent patients or with those on methadone maintenance, intensive psychotherapy proved completely unsuccessful—despite (or because of) the massivity of the external structures supposedly supporting it. The only benefit, I believe, was on my side: I became convinced that here we deal with a type of patient

whose pathology rivals in depth and severity that of psychotics with whom I had had by that time about eight years of intensive psychotherapeutic experience—and more success.

5. There is a small group, perhaps altogether 5–10 percent, where this gloomy assessment does not hold: they remain abstinent, do not show other severe psychopathology and thus do not switch to other "symptom exits." These exceptions are the *true successes,* at least while on the program. Later, after expiration of parole, even some of them may turn to failures, as I unhappily noticed in several instances.

The overall conclusion again is: compulsory abstinence, even when successful as to abstinence, does not improve at all the severity of psychopathology present in the very vast majority of these patients (I estimate that 80–90 percent of my patients in that program were emotionally very sick), but indeed adds to their pathology by a switch to other severely destructive forms of symptomatology.

My later experiences in the modified system of civil commitment first, compulsory ambulatory abstinence second, under titles NARA I, II, and III, which I participated in, did not principally change the above conclusions.

The Untreated Polydrug Users

There are innumerable polydrug users with severest psychopathology, refused as too frustrating, if not untreatable in office practice by most psychiatrists, refused, as described, by the rigidly set up methadone programs, unable to make it in therapeutic communities, thrown out by most psychiatric facilities after the first inevitable episode of acting out or turned away even before admission. Some, though it is impossible to know how many, run afoul of the law and end up in jail on some related or unrelated felony conviction. Often they are involved in bizarre car accidents, etc. But they are not recognized as what they are: patients with very massive and very self-destructive character pathology, not too rarely floridly psychotic, who resort in an unsystematic, uncoordinated, in itself very self-sabotaging way to using, buying, trading, selling, and stealing of intoxicating substances—usually a mixture of the most accessible drugs: sedatives, alcohol, stimulants, psychedelics, with some predilection, dependent on their pathology.

What unites this huge mass of "untreatables" whose number no one knows, nor even counts, is that they have fallen between the cracks of the bureaucratically set up drug and alcoholism programs (whose own vested interest lies in preserving the status quo, their own limited know how and the smooth running according to federal and state guidelines). They are outcasts as far as all the federally acceptable protocols are concerned which are solely designed to deal with a few select groups. They are outcasts as far as hospitals are concerned: many of the physicians in the hospitals turn them away as patients because "we are fed up with them," "they cannot be helped anyway." Other physicians, nurses, and social workers genuinely try to engage them in treatment but are overwhelmed by the severity of their pathology, the chaotic, horrible situations in their families, the horrifying climate of deprivation, licentiousness, violence and overstimulation surrounding them in the apartment "project." The sheer mass of individual, family, and social pathology, of conflict and misery, the enormity of the noxious, destructive chaos surrounding, e.g., the thirteen-year-old glue sniffer, the fourteen-year-old heroin addict with hepatitis, the fifteen-year-old comatose patient who had taken an unknown sedative, make therapy in so very many cases appear hopeless. There are no places to send these youths. And the same holds true for adults: no facilities, no programs, no plans for how to approach this monstrous interweaving of most pernicious character pathology, family pathology and social compliance.

It is easy to fall into apocalyptic and strident words simply because no one knows the dimensions of this problem, but many of us are faced day in and day out by the appearance in emergency rooms, waiting rooms, agencies and jails of these "hopeless," "untreatable" cases, the refuse, the ones turned away callously or helplessly. Are there hundreds or thousands in any large city? My own feeling is that in a city of one million inhabitants (like Baltimore) there may be several tens of thousands of such "untreatable" polydrug users with devastating psychopathology. They are to be found on all socioeconomic levels. Actually, the latest figures given by Maryland's drug abuse administration state that the number of narcotics addicts or users is about 20,000, mostly in and around Baltimore, of "polydrug abusers" about 135,000, and of alcoholics about 200,000—out of a population of close to 4,000,000. This equals about 9 percent of the population!

APPENDIX C

Extent and Treatment of Psychoses Among Heavy Drug Users

Unhappily, this appendix has to be rudimentary. My own clinical experience in various "modalities" as well as the few references in the literature point to a small number of outright psychotics, probably around 10 percent—schizophrenia, psychotic rages and very severe paranoid states, epileptic twilight states or rages, hysterical psychoses and the very severe depressions.

However, most paranoid or depressive states, including even those of homicidal and suicidal dimensions, which are by no means rare, are not of psychotic dimensions. They are very severe forms of character pathology, usually dubbed "borderline cases," very difficult to treat, but therapeutically accessible with an innovative combination of methods.

There is simply no literature dealing specifically with the treatment of psychotic drug users—except for occasional oblique references; the usual comment is rather that psychotic patients were excluded from treatment. Again personal experience will have to fill in where the literature leaves a large void.

Schizophrenics

Against current beliefs and common expectations, most floridly psychotic (schizophrenic) narcotics addicts are not too difficult to treat. They are, of course, preferably maintained on methadone. No dosage reduction is recommended while they are in the acute phase. In addition, the usual treatment with neuroleptica (e.g., Thorazine, Stelazine) has been, in my own experience, successful; even massively psychotic patients did not have to be hospitalized. The combination of (a) the daily visit to the clinic itself, (b) the tranquilizing effect of the narcotic, (c) the specific efficacy of the major tranquilizer, (d) the weekly or biweekly visit to the program psychiatrist, (e) the continued supportive, often daily visit with the counselor, has such a structuring, calming, antifragmentary effect on most psychotic patients that, as I said, hospitalization can be averted, and often they can continue even at their work. In some cases, transient hospitalization could not be avoided and met little resistance both on the side of patients and on that of the psychiatric institutions. In this regard, I can offer no innovative technique but an important piece of advice: Schizophrenic symptoms or history are in no way a contraindication to the acceptance of a patient on methadone maintenance.

In contrast, any other modality (therapeutic community of the traditional, Synanon patterned structure, narcotics antagonists, sensitivity and encounter groups, behavior modification, compulsory abstinence) is usually countertherapeutic. The narcotic (illegal or legal) is in these cases the last barrier between at least partial compensation and a full psychotic breakdown. Its effect is comparable to that of the major tranquilizers—again I have several clinical paradigms in mind which I witnessed personally.

In brief: schizophrenics are typically "good" methadone patients, provided there is sufficient psychiatric coverage—a point that I return to time and again. My findings with about two dozen overtly schizophrenic addicts are thus consonant with those described by Wellisch, Gay, Wesson and Smith (1971). What about the psychotic compulsive drug user who is not a narcotic addict? That answer has to be deferred.

Paroxysmal Disorders

Although by no means all patients with severe EEG pathology show either an epileptic psychosis or even manifest seizures, it is appropriate—because of the potential seriousness of these disorders—to consider them here (R. R. Monroe 1970, Dietrich Blumer 1971, 1974). I think this is a nearly totally neglected, overlooked category of compulsive drug users who present most massive problems. We surprisingly often discover severe EEG pathology in our patients. In some, this hidden pathology is expressed in explosive, murderous, psychotic rage, especially under the influence of alcohol or after minor frustrations or provocations at home, in a bar, or in the program. Here the presence of a knowledgeable psychiatrist on the program is again indispensable for diagnosis and treatment. Such patients are not candidates for humilation or dismissal from the program or for return to jail, but for appropriate antiepileptic medication given best in the clinic itself (Dilantin, Mysoline, etc.). There is also increasing evidence that many if not all compulsive drugs users show a characteristic CNS instability, as shown up in the Alpha-Choralose provocation text as Delta wave abnormality (G. Balis, personal commication). Research in this field is urgently needed and may be of great practical consequence. These findings, by the way, do not invalidate the psychodynamic views.

These disorders may have predated compulsive drug use, and the drugs (barbiturates, narcotics) were chosen by the patients precisely to cope with the rages and suicidal terrors evoked by these paroxysmal disturbances. However, in some, this pathology may already be the consequence of drug use, i.e., of earlier overdoses, head traumata, vascular incidents.

What is innovative here is: (a) to think of such disorders and (b) to *treat* them accordingly—together with the compulsive drug use—instead of punishing the "violent" patient!

A particular caveat: *avoid alcohol!* These can be patients who show "pathological intoxications": small amounts of alcohol lead to homicidal rages with amnesia afterwards. Also antipsychotic drugs, like Thorazine, often prove dangerous with serious epileptic disorders. Psychotherapy itself is not enough; understanding of the organic nature of this illness is crucial.

Again, these are good candidates for methadone maintenance (even low dosage 30–40 mg), very poor candidates for all other modalities (because of the emotional strain placed on them). LAAM seems to be particularly beneficial, because of its even higher stabilization effect than methadone proper. In most cases, antiepileptic medication is a must (see Karp et al. 1975).

Psychotic Polydrug Users Out On the Street

This is the most worrisome category. They are not acceptable to the usual drug programs; they are a "pest" for the usual psychiatric facility, for emergency rooms, for drug counseling centers, for social agencies. They combine two very severe, very serious forms of psychopathology and are usually shunned by the facilities set up for either one. Again, we need good psychiatric diagnosticians at the contact points and then establish a network of innovative programs specifically for the psychotic or near-psychotic, paroxysmal or suicidally depressed polydrug user—a treatment network which is nearly totally lacking now.

What I envision is an inpatient facility combining, (a) very much emotional support, (b) a firm structure with clear limit setting, (c) a psychiatrically trained and psychoanalytically sensitive team, (d) a program to develop the creative skills of many of these patients, (e) intensive family therapy, (f) vocational training or retraining, (g) pharmacotherapy with major and minor tranquilizers. (After three years of working on establishing just such a facility we had to give up because of the resistance from all sides.)

All that I say here about the psychotic polydrug user is directly applicable to the non-psychotic multihabituated patients, except for the choice of the psychopharmacon.

I mentioned contact points: I think not solely of the aforementioned psychiatric and social facilities, but emphasize particularly: (a) the intake offices of the drug programs (who routinely turn away such patients with a helpless shrug); (b) the emergency rooms which "kick them out"; (c) the police stations and jails which allow these patients to go into life-threatening withdrawal (epileptic seizures, delirious psychoses) or to hurt kill themselves.

Minimal Brain Damage and Amphetamines

Here is another, little known clinical entity which belongs on the border between this section about psychotics and the earlier sections about severe psychopathology. There are few papers written about this syndrome, which is well known in children, but probably exists among adults as well (see Hartocollis 1968, Conners 1967). I have treated a few stimulant abusers where I indeed suspected a connection between this entity as underlying pathology and their drug use as attempted self-medication.

Thus we are faced with the following paradox: On the one side we know that in contrast to narcotics, stimulants (amphetamines, methylphenidate, cocaine) have in most users a directly potentiating effect on aggression. This, coupled with the mobilization of vague paranoid feelings, if not of specific delusions, puts them among the most dangerous drugs. The threat lies mostly in outward directed murderous rage (see Ellinwood 1971, Griffith 1968).

On the opposite side, there are a fair number of cases where we find that these stimulants suppress massive outward and (more importantly) inward directed rage and allow the patients to function and feel normally. In some of these (adult) patients, minimal brain damage can be found in the EEG, so that one hypothesis is that they actually need the stimulants in order to correct an organic damage, in the same way as minimal brain damaged children do. In others, a strictly psychological explanation—increase of self-esteem leading to decrease of rage and depression—seems warranted. But the crucial alternative has to be kept in mind: that the organic damage of the brain may be a consequence of, not a reason for, the chronic amphetamine use (see Lemere 1966, perhaps related to the periarteriitis described by Citron 1970).

Unfortunately, I cannot present new findings in this area, nor any study about the types of patients who react—positively or adversely—to stimulants and about the possible mechanism of this reaction. Attempts at defining such criteria have been made in regard to children (see Fish 1971, Conner 1967), but an exploration of this problem in adults has barely started (see Arnold et al. 1972).

However, on the basis of some of these clinical findings, the question has to be raised in all seriousness whether we do not need more careful and systematic research to prove or refute this hypothesis—namely that, in some cases of minimal brain damage, amphetamine maintenance may have a corrective, directly violence=reducing effect similar to its effect on hyperkinetic children. This is an innovative suggestion which bears testing in a pilot study (Lion 1976, personal communication).

As background to chapter 14, about society and culture, the consequences of compulsive drug use to society need to be cursorily examined. What follows will be chilling indeed. The entire problem of socioeconomic costs is fraught with the most massive problems. In the most recent report available to me (thanks to the help of Dr. Seif), put together by Paul V. Lemkau, Zili Amsel et al. at Johns Hopkins University, which will serve as a kind of foil to the following study, it is written: "Given the balance of known and unknown factors, and the stigma and illegality associated with drug abuse, we believe that no such determination (of social and economic costs of drug abuse) is possible."

In the following I use first some general statistical information available to me. In a second part I present a small-scale study within one program which shows a striking discrepancy from general epidemiological data. Although some of the data were gathered three to seven years before completion of this manuscript (1978), details may be outdated, but the idea supported by the data is not.

Socioeconomic Impact of Compulsive Drug Use

I quote first a news release by *Managerial Research,* 18 August 1971: "Recent test results show that almost 10 percent of a company's job applicants may be using drugs of one type or another. The effects of drug use—inattention, increased absenteeism, psychotic behavior in some instances—coupled with the fact that 'hard' drugs users nearly always turn to criminal activity to pay for their drugs, makes drug abuse a serious problem for industry."

A careful study of the *New York Times* (21 June 1971) states "that almost every major company had a drug problem, but many do not know it or will not acknowledge it." In the same article a New York laboratory testing the urine of applicants for a large number of local companies, gives the following numbers: with four to five hundred urinalyses a day "the tests showed the presence of drugs in the following percentages: 6.5 percent heroin, 1.8 percent barbiturates and 0.7 percent amphetamines. Urine tests will not reveal the use of marijuana or the hallucinogens such as LSD." Still the extent of alcohol problems is about five times that of drug abuse: an insurance company is quoted as saying that, "out of one hundred people referred for rehabilitation, from forty to forty-five were for alcoholism, against eight to fifteen for drug problems."

In the reports at my disposal the estimates of the extent and costs of alcoholism in industry and business vary somewhat, but an article, again in the *New York Times,* quotes Dr. N.A. Pace, Medical Director of the General Motors New York headquarters: "5 percent of the average work force suffers from alcoholism, and the national loss of industry from alcoholism is estimated at eight to ten billion dollars annually" (23 January 1973). The *Hospital Tribune* (23 July 1973) adds to this that "the medical professional in general, and company doctors in particular, tend to cover up cases of alcoholism, durg abuse, and emotional illness."

Just as background here are some numbers for the population at large, all gleaned from the Shafer report (2nd Report, National Commission on Marijuana and Drug Abuse): In 1971 the retail sales of alcohol in the U. S. totalled $23.8 billion. There are at least nine million alcohol dependent persons in the U. S. Fifty percent of traffic accidents, 64 percent of violent crimes involve alcohol. On the other side the drug arrests were estimated at five hundred thousand a year.

Nationwide there were in 1972 about five hundred sixty thousand
active narcotics addicts. The report by Lemkau et al. (1975) puts the
number of arrests for violations of the drug laws in 1973 at 628,000.
They estimated the number of narcotics abusers within twenty-nine
metropolitan areas at slightly above five hundred thousand.

The conclusions as to overall costs of drug misuse in various
categories were that, all in all, drug abuse costs society nearly eleven
billion dollars a year, with the prudent caution that "the estimates
given tend to err on the side of underrepresentation." A few items out
of their list: law enforcement close to three and a half billion, judicial
process close to six hundred million, incarceration and probation over
two billion, stolen property (a category we shall explore more
carefully) over a billion, loss of productivity over three billion, drug
abuse treatment four hundred forty million. A not yet published
compilation of newest and preliminary statistical results (spring 1978),
kindly provided by the Office of Program Development and Analysis
of NIDA (Dr. Richard Lindblad and F. Goldman), estimates the
overall costs of all compulsive drug use at \$14.5 billion per year, about
half of it in direct costs (e.g., criminality not related to drug laws, law
enforcement, prevention, treatment), and half in indirect costs
(mortality, unemployment, incarceration). In regard to property
crimes the costs used were not those given by the victims (the "mark
up"), but their yield to the drug abuser; they are put at \$1,360,075,000
(per year).

It is considered too difficult now to achieve an estimate of the
average level of narcotics habit per user or addict. Due to a number of
factors (large scale methadone treatment, "chipping", and especially
the broad movement into polydrug use), the fluctuations are so great
that a single number is not considered sufficient anymore, as it still
perhaps was at the time of the inquiry presented in condensed form
below.

The Costs of Untreated Narcotics Addiction

If we talk about treatment of narcotics addicts we are often asked to
justify costs and methods used; therefore, in 1969, when we started
building up a comprehensive drug abuse center in Baltimore, it was
decided to come up with more reliable data about the actual costs
inflicted to society by untreated narcotics use. During the few periods

when our intake was open in winter 1969–70 and again in early summer 1970 we filled out a questionaire with our patients when they were admitted. The flaws in objectivity and exactness of this method are obvious: I will comment about them after presenting the findings. (Some of the data presented here have been published by O'Connor et al. 1971.)

Despite these limitations I believe the findings are worth reporting. Not only did they serve us as a provisional guide in our practical dealings with the social and political powers, but—more importantly—we now have a better idea of what to recommend and why it is imperative not to sweep this problem under the rug. Most importantly these findings should serve as a stimulus to launch a large-scale inquiry in other cities to get reliable data about the consequences, not so much of narcotics addiction, but of the present legal methods of *dealing* with narcotics addiction.

There have been a few previous scientific studies of this aspect. I refer to Chein et al. (1964) and Preble and Casey (1969).

METHOD

Approximately two thirds of the patients in the program came from poverty areas in the inner city of Baltimore, although there were many patients from other parts of the city and even from the suburbs. About half of the patients were black. Although we did not study the correlation between our findings and social and racial background, it should be obvious that there is no striking difference in regard to the extent of costs of addiction between the races and social classes.

Almost all patients were heroin addicts, a few just heroin users; most sought help voluntarily. The main treatment modalities we offered were short term detoxification (four to six weeks), limited methadone maintenance (six months), and unlimited maintenance. A few patients came on as abstinence cases. All were assigned to individual or group counseling or to individual or group psychotherapy.

At the intake or shortly after admission all our patients were asked to fill out a questionnaire about their criminal activities; very often this was done in the presence of the interviewer—either a psychiatrist or a social worker, a drug abuse counselor or a volunteer. The patients were told that their replies would be anonymous, that we were bound by our confidentiality not to bring any information they might give us to police authorities, but that we undertook this inquiry in order to know what the costs of narcotics addiction to society really were. We tried to match the data received against the extent of the "tracks" (scarred veins) of the patients, the withdrawal symptoms observed when they turned to us for help, the amount of methadone needed to cope with, or prevent, these symptoms without inducing overdose. Moreover, at that time we had an ex-addict counselor who talked with most of these patients and checked the data.

No noticeable benefit ensued for the patient if he over- or under-estimated the purported amount of drugs and costs.

Another approach for validation taken in only a small number of cases (about 15 percent) was intensive individual psychotherapy over a prolonged period of time during which the veracity of at least a few of the data could be reassessed and confirmed. We considered the non-threatening, non-punitive, factual approach in a treatment setting a great asset.

FINDINGS

Over a period of about six months we gathered one hundred fifteen replies: an original batch of sixty replies and a few months later a second batch of fifty-five. Incidentally, the findings in both groups were practically identical. Their difference merely consisted in their time of admission to the program. This stability in our findings was somewhat surprising and can serve as one partial confirmation.

The average habit of these patients before entering the program was forty-eight dollars a day, with a few as low as ten dollars twice weekly, and a few as high as two hundred fifty to three hundred dollars a day.

To support this habit nearly all had to resort to illegal activities: seventy-three reported engaging in shoplifting; sixty, in selling drugs; forty, in burglary; twenty-one, in robbery and mugging; eighteen, in gambling; nine, in forging checks and other cons; six, in borrowing and stealing from family; six, in prostitution. Of course, these are overlapping statistics. We noticed the preponderance of shoplifting and selling drugs as a source of income, but the extent of violent crimes in form of robbery was rather surprising.

The proportion between the value the stolen goods obtain on the black market and the original store value is estimated as follows: forty-two reported getting one third of store value; twenty-five, one half; twelve, one quarter; only three, over three quarters.

Based on these two sets of data it appeared justified in 1970 to estimate the average cost to society caused by one untreated addict at around fifty thousand dollars a year. One source of error with this number, namely the extent of dealing, will be discussed later on.

Accordingly we find a large number of arrests. In eight replies out of the one hundred fifteen we find no usable statement about their arrest record; two of these simply reported "many." Among the remaining one hundred seven responses fifteen indicated they had no arrests. Most were quite precise, but some said: at least fifteen arrests, or more than forty, or about fifty. A total of six hundred sixty-two arrests was reported among these one hundred seven patients; this means an average of over six arrests per patient. These were spread over a very variable period of years: between half a year and thirty-five years duration of addiction, an average of almost six years. Despite the vast number of arrests (with the corresponding enormous burden on the entire legal system), the discrepancy between extent of crime and actual arrest rate was nothing short of fantastic. It appears likely that *only one in several hundred criminal acts committed by these subjects leads to arrest* (one arrest per patient per year). (The following numbers as to costs of narcotics are probably too low for today's market, although clinical evidence from current patients at intake give roughly similar data as to cost level of drug use ($50 to $150 per diem). In quite a few cases this level apparently does not even suffice to establish actual physiological addiction.)

To give a better grasp I quote a few examples. One patient with an eighty to one hundred dollar a day habit stole the preceding day, a Sunday, from a drug store 30 watches (each $9) and 60–70 packs of razor blades (each $2)—altogether at a store value of $400. He sold them for $110. He estimates that he shoplifted in 1 year goods in the value of a few hundred thousand dollars. (He was by the way one of the many heroin addicts we see whose first drug was heroin.) His activities ranged over the department stores and shopping centers of downtown Baltimore.

Another example is a twenty-two-year-old heroin and Dilaudid addict. He started out on cough syrup, was addicted only for half a year and had a habit of $65 a day. His specialty were tape decks from cars. He had stolen about 200 tape decks in these 6 months. In addition he had taken 40–50 leather coats, 50 TV sets, about half of them color TV's, 30–40 radios, one mink stole the week prior to admission, and a few hundred dollars of money from private houses. Besides cars and dwellings he depredated department stores.

Another one with a $70 a day habit shoplifted only in department stores—in one typical day: 2 coats and 1 suit in the store value of $300. Another one in one day: 11 suits, 3 women's coats, a carton with knit shirts.

And a last case: a thirty-one-year-old heroin addict with a habit between 15 and 50 bags, or $75 to $250 a day engaged in mugging three nights a week which netted him about $150 a night. A few years ago he switched to drug selling. He gets about 150 bags a day, sells 100–130 and uses the rest himself. He got arrested about 50 times.

The reader can be assured that most of the remaining 111 case surveys are equally graphic. If he wants to peruse the original findings, he may turn to the aforementioned paper by O'Connor et al. (1971).

INTERPRETATION

It is hazardous to venture too far flung conclusions at this relatively provisional date of inquiry. But the following statements can be made with some assuredness:

The economic drain to private and public property caused by narcotics use in a city like Baltimore is extremely high. We may carry out a brief calculation. If we take a $48 a day habit and multiply it three times and for one year, we arrive at an average amount of property damage caused by one narcotics addict per year of about $50,000 (today's estimate is $100,000 to $120,000).

According to the state's case registry six thousand narcotics addicts were know to diverse agencies in Maryland, the vast majority of them in Baltimore City. Today's estimate (1976) based on a number of much more reliable data, is between sixteen and twenty thousand (the latter figure by the State's Drug Abuse Administration, the former by Lemkau et al. 1975). For sixteen thousand narcotics abusers the estimate of property damage, based on current (1976) and the older (1970) findings would amount to over one and a half billion dollars. However, these numbers are likely to be too high because many addicts feed from other users through dealing, a factor I will come back to shortly. There are many other sources of error: overestimate by user both of bought "drugs" (whatever they contained) and daily costs. Some observers, including patients, claim that such costs are inflated because they solely give the peak, not average use, or serve boasting. Still I think that there is such an enormous underreporting and underarresting that I am inclined to reduce the first computation only to about one fourth—perhaps three to five hundred million dollars of property damage for this city and quite possibly much higher!

This is an enormous loss to the economy—not to speak of all the human misery involved. The large stores and, with that, the casualty insurance companies bear the brunt of that onslaught. But their losses are, of course, passed on to the consumers.

We saw also what a cardinal criminological and penological problem drug addiction involves. Again if we take sixteen to twenty thousand narcotics abusers in the city we could extrapolate that they would show an estimated annual arrest rate of twenty thousand arrests for any crime (again, just for the Baltimore metropolitan area). It seems safe to say that property crimes and robbing due to narcotics addiction represent a central problem, if indeed not *the* central problem, of the recurrent concerns for "law and order."

There is considerable complicity and collusion in the non-addict society. As has been noted by several authors (e.g., E. M. Schur 1965, and Preble and Casey 1969) this traffic in money and stolen goods represents one broad avenue through which goods flow down from the affluent society into the indigent strata. A great number of persons knowingly sell and buy stolen goods at vastly reduced prices, goods which otherwise would not be available to the poor. Many steal on order or specialize in business-like activities: e.g., driving around in a truck and stealing copper wares and wires wherever they can find them. Some reported direct links to police officials and politicians. There is a deep irony that our society needs such a system to bring about (in an extremely insufficient way) some social justice and retribution. Again, I know from reliable sources that this "fencing" is by no means restricted to poor people, but extends to most prominent and affluent personalities!

Again as Schur, Preble and Casey so convincingly described, the narcotics traffic presupposes an extended and highly developed business establishment to organize and steer this illicit traffic. All the small and big "employees" and "entrepreneurs" partake in the central business ethos with its own profits, rules and penalties. They are a kind of only slightly perverted representatives of the American value system, involving competitive bidding, well-established forms of transactions (laws of demands and supply, inflation), and even the ensuing prestige and respectability. There are many levels in the trade; Preble and Casey differentiate eight layers from the lowest street peddler up to the large-scale drug entrepreneur.

We have had some conversations both with dealers and with buyers in which this value orientation was expressed. On the other side there must be considerable complicity on the side of the establishment, albeit partly unwittingly and unwillingly: the extent of this problem is hushed up, attempts to deal with it effectively are disparaged and impeded, the funds made available to cope with this social disease are incomparably smaller than the funds lost. Last but not least, the laws themselves are largely responsible for the criminal aspect of drug addiction. A more rational legal approach would vastly reduce the extent of narcotics related crime and corruption.

CRITICISM

We must add that there are several possible objections to the findings. They are: (1) that we do not know the actual number of narcotics addicts in Baltimore; (2) that perhaps an even larger portion of the habit than we assumed might be supported by dealing and other unknown factors, not by actual depredation of the environment, e.g., since the really weighty habits of one–to six hundred dollars a day which push the overall average high up are supported mainly by selling drugs; (3) that we can not really gauge the actual severity of the individual's habit since he may exaggerate it in order to receive higher methadone doses; and (4) that our sample of one hundred fifteen patients seeking help for their addiction may be not representative of the whole population of narcotics users or addicts.

Some of my own patients (e.g., Andreas), who are probably better informed than all of us "experts," suspect that it may be the addicts with the worst habits who have sought help in programs, that those 90 percent of addicts (e.g., here in Baltimore) who are not currently enrolled in treatment may have lesser problems. This would support the fourth objection—that the sample is not representative.

An anecdote adds to the second criticism: A female addict was said to have put a piece of liver up her rectum, gone to a well-known physician telling him that she was dying of cancer and requesting

Dilaudid. He fell for it. I am told that she went to fifty physicians once a week and got their well-meant help (in some instances paid for by fenced valuables). She used part of the Dilaudid and sold the rest on the black market. If true, this is a good example how even a large habit could be supported at little or no fiscal cost to anyone.

On the other side, however, it has been claimed that in the year 1975 alone illegal narcotics of half a billion dollars' worth in street value have been confiscated by the various agencies. In view of the tremendous extent of actual illegal narcotics use it seems highly unlikely that such an amount represented more than 50 percent of the opiate reaching these shores (as the admittedly very conservative estimate by Lemkau et al. (1975) of over a billion dollars of property crimes due to narcotics addiction would allow us to assume). In view of the renewed upsurge and spread this amount can safely be multiplied many times which again would put us closer to my own estimate.

Thus neither objections nor supports can adduce proofs. We deal, as with much of criminality, with enormous uncertainties, the so-called dark numbers *(Dunkelziffern* of German criminology). In some categories only a very few percent of all crimes are actually cleared up (or even reported). Therefore, I still believe that my own assumptions put into the question by the aforementioned doubts retain a fair amount of probability, though eventually new methods must be devised to refute (or confirm) the objections raised.

Therefore, these findings are submitted only as preliminary approximations and as rough estimates.

CONCLUSIONS

One conclusion remains certain: that the economic damages inflicted by narcotics addiction upon society are enormous and that it costs very many times more (in our estimate ten to forty times, in some cases over a hundred times more) to leave an addict untreated on the street than to have him treated.

Secondly, we can conclude that the main type of crime still consists in shoplifting, but that the extent of robbing and mugging, though lagging far behind, should not be neglected. Even a small percentage represents a huge number.

Thirdly, the broad social and cultural implications of the drug traffic have deeper cultural and political significance (as are taken up in chapters 14 and 17): I refer in particular to the economically equalizing effects the addict's life style (his "hustling") as an often most artful, skilled "shadow-profession," and the hierarchy of the business enterprise, forming an eight-layered pyramid of the wholesale, detail, and retail sale and buying of drugs (see Preble and Casey 1969).

SOME AFTERTHOUGHTS

If the Shafer Report is correct in estimating the number of narcotics addicts in the U.S. at 560,000, a simple calculation will result in the costs in property crimes alone of over fifty billion dollars. However, due to dealing, jailing, prescriptions, prostitution and other falsifying factors, this number must be exaggerated—by how much, though, is totally unknown. But even if it is only one fourth or one eigth of that amount (which I presume) it still represents a giant drain on the economy. Even the most expensive treatment modalities, if responsibly led, would cost a small fraction (one tenth to one fiftieth) of each addict's depredation.

But this is not the whole story: If 50 to 75 percent of the jail population consists of narcotic addicts a whole new staggering sum is added. If we add yet to this the costs of arrests and police, courts and defenders, the support for the families of addicts and victims of violence—the sums are astronomical, as the Lemkau study showed (an additional ten billion dollars).

Then we need to go outside of narcotics users and just take the arrests for marijuana possession alone. NORML's figures show that in 1973 there were nationally nearly 430,000 marijuana arrests, costing about six hundred million dollars; 93 percent of the arrests were for possession, not sale!

When I have presented some of these findings some in the audience have wondered aloud whether the alleged Chinese solution (to shoot all addicts) might not eventually be the answer. I for one believe that we cannot live in a democratic society and condone such "final solutions," violating all basic humane tenets and civil rights. Despite all I have presented here I still find it a small price to pay for a civil and free society.

My reasoning takes a different tack altogether: If we consider the enormous costs just outlined, along with what we have found in the rest of this book—the severe psychopathology of compulsive drug users—

we must ask ourselves whether there might not be indeed more rational approaches to this huge problem, approaches which treat the sick and abolish the web of crime, underworld corruption, and astronomical costs to society. The question is posed. I have attempted to answer it in my final chapter (19).

Literature Survey

It should by now have become clear that the severity of psychopathology besetting at least a large proportion of compulsive drug users can be adequately treated only if a much more comprehensive, much more psychotherapeutically informed treatment strategy is taken. I again quote from or paraphrase those authors with which I am most in agreement.

The suggestions made by E. H. Kaplan and H. Wieder in their already extensively quoted book *Drugs Don't Take People, People Take Drugs* (1974) have to be taken with particular seriousness. They are perhaps the two psychotherapists who have collected most experience in the treatment of the disorders in which we are interested. Their recommendations are radical, perhaps shocking; however, I agree with them to a very large extent. I can present only a few very scanty excerpts. The reader is urged to consult their outstanding book itself.

Therapeutic goals must be individualized, based on the unique combination of assets and liabilities of each personality. And modification or elimination of drug use is only one of the goals to be determined in a comprehensive treatment plan. [pp. 155–156]

Drug use is symptomatic behavior, and the psychological reasons for the behavior must be diagnosed for each user since the reasons vary from one individual to the next. The fallacy that lumps together all drug abuse as a unitary illness seriously hampers the rational approach to treatment, the approach through diagnosis. [p. 157]

...the dangling bodies of addicts who have hung themselves in jail cells tell us that abstinence can be as fatal as an overdose. More precisely, enforced abstinence with no help in coping with the painful ego state that drove them to addiction in the first place can result in death by suicide. Thrown back on their own resources, it becomes abundantly clear that they have none. [p. 154]

A patient is not "well" simply because he is drug free. Until and unless the processes of healing and maturing affect his personality, he will feel the need for regression. [p. 155]

This means relapse back to his drug of choice. I have described my own experiences with compulsory abstinence.

Their conclusions are grim: "One of our aims is to dispel these pipe dreams of magic cures for abuse and addiction, in order to clear the way for more rational productive lines of approach...."

They rightly postulate that "research must come before the development of mass treatment programs, not as an afterthought. Research must be designed for integration into the entire sequence of diagnosis, disposition and treatment" (pp. 177–178).

In their earlier quoted paper (1974) Khantzian et al. go on and write: write:

Specifically, we believe that psychotherapy must be of an educational variety in which the therapist actively pursues with the patient the ways in which he has used drugs to avoid life's inevitable pain and vicissitudes. In order to do this the therapist must be willing to make significant aspects of his own personality available to the patient and to share with him some alternative ways to bear disappointment and endure distress. In such a process the therapist provides opportunities for the patient to identify with the healthier qualities of the therapist, who more successfully adapts to and masters his or her own conflicts and life through other means. [p. 164]

Report after report emphasizes the need for additional ("ancillary"!) services to cope with these problems.

Ramer et al. (1971) recommend a combined program of methadone, crisis intervention, various psychotherapists and counseling, dental care and legal aid.

Based on their important study of the self-destructive aspects of hard core addiction, which was reported earlier, Frederick, Resnik and Wittlin (1973) reached the following treatment recommendations for hard core addicts:

> When the addict abstains from methadone, depression tends to recur and attitudes toward violent death are more manifest. Specifically designed psychotherapy should be forthcoming as well as other aspects of rehabilitation. A new job to enhance self-reliance, new friends, new successes so as to build self-confidence and independence in place of the dependent, impulsive behavior patterns integral to the addict are required. This must be done in segments with each success building upon its reinforced predecessor. [p. 585]

Many other comparable works could be cited (Cohen et al. 1971, Proskauer and Roland 1973). E. Harms (1973b) raises a cautionary note about group therapy; although he does not discount the value of group therapy, he stresses:

> I have witnessed great harm done by a vulgar response of ridicule to a display of deeply felt emotion. A group with a therapeutic purpose must be carefully assembled and should never have any but an experienced group leader in charge. Only a limited number of presently conducted groups have trained, experienced leaders. Others are presided over by former presumably cured addicts, a practice borrowed from Alcoholics Anonymous! There is no insight into the basic difference between drug abuse and alcoholism. [p. 219]

A rather dark picture about an addict self-help program is painted by E. Kaufman (1972). Although his description of "Reality House" is highly laudatory, it is evident that, again, precisely those patients who drop out or who are excluded need help most, despite the use of psychiatrists at the advanced levels of treatment.

The high dropout rate (82 percent) in the first two stages of the program warrants discussion. These stages represent a two-month screening process that eliminates those addicts who are not motivated or suitable for this type of program. This method of screening is in some ways less selective than methods utilized by other treatment centers of addiction. On the other side: "That 25.5 percent of those who have entered the doors of Reality House are drug-free eighteen months months later is in itself quite impressive. There is much less use of harsh, devastating confrontations or denigrating terms [than in therapeutic communities], and the individual is not stripped rapidly to the level of a helpless infant."

The absence of this brutality may be related to the personal style of the directors of Reality House.... There is more emphasis on an ego reconstruction, utilizing the past when necessary. This is done by using psychiatrists at advanced levels of the program. The frequent use of psychiatrists as therapists and supervisors is in contrast to many other programs where there has been a tendency to dispense with the psychiatrist... [pp. 850–851]

Of major interest for the specialist are the very conflicting results obtained in a walk-in clinic for narcotics addicts. The addition of ten street workers and of a well-structured aftercare program changed a disheartening failure into a successful treatment program (O'Malley et al. 1972 versus Renner and Rubin 1973).

REPORTS ABOUT IN-PATIENT TREATMENT

There are now quite a number of papers dealing with the need for hospital psychiatrists to be alert to drug problems on their wards (Crowley et al. 1974: over one third of their patients in a university hospital had drug problems), with the combination of methadone maintenance and inpatient treatment (Brill 1972, 1973), the necessity of adding intensive direct help, group and individual therapy, vocational assistance (Tomin and Glenn 1968, Gertler 1973, Hughley 1973).

I select for quotation only three papers because they focus on important areas in the in-patient treatment:

P. Hughes et al. report that on an in-patient basis the changeover from the traditional "matriarchal, psychiatric-nurse-dominated milieu to one in which nurses and ex-addicts had separate areas of responsibility and dominance" led to a dramatic decline in the drop-out rate (discharge against medical advice from sixty to ten percent). M. Hattersley (1973) moves entirely away from individual psychotherapy and emphatically questions the treatment of addicts in a general psychiatric hospital:

> We must consider if treatment of addicts within the conventional psychiatric structure may not actually be creating more addicts than it is curing...
>
> But an increasing weight of evidence indicates that addiction, as a distinctive and alloplastic illness, responds best in an institutional situation where users are isolated from other patients and peer groups are employed as the primary therapeutic tool... [pp. 438–439]

Finally, R. Ketai (1973) suggests in a stimulating brief paper a special type of psychotheraphy for hospitalized narcotics addicts: peer observation.

> The method advocated here involves individual psychotheraphy sessions conducted before observing addict peers. These sessions were immediately followed by a period of observer-participant interaction. Empirical observations indicate active involvement and interest on the part of these addicts, evidenced by sincere affective displays, high levels of participation, and increased group cohesiveness. [p. 51]
>
> By observing these conflicts being examined in depth they have the opportunity to gain greater cognitive understanding of such conflicts. This type of extensive exploration is usually not possible in a traditional group because it would exclude other members for great length of time. [p. 52]

A few conclusions about what we felt to be particularly important in our own methadone program at University of Maryland Hospital follow; they can be adjusted without undue alterations to other types of treatment programs and to other forms of compulsive drug use.

Discipline or Revenge? The Need for Structure
in a Drug Abuse Treatment Program

1. We have become convinced that our patients need more than just a mixture of Tang with a narcotic; methadone maintenance cannot be defended in the long run just as a juice dispensation. We are faced with massive social and psychological problems in each individual case. These patients need treatment as whole persons. It has to include their family, their scholastic and vocational deficiencies, their history, and their inner life. Methadone maintenance is not just one modality, but like any competent treatment program, a bundle of available treatment forms.

2. Our program structure is precise, clear and rather paternalistic, and thus may foster dependency and reliance on others. By and large it works rather well. We realize that in any psychotherapeutic program, patients with such severe problems need outside support and assistance for a long time. We have accumulated our own experiences the hard way, namely through innumerable disappointments, and have concluded that the program structure is, as much as methadone medication itself, a needed crutch without which most patients could not climb up the steps towards social reintegration and emotional recompensation. With these structures we responded to the dire need for boundaries and limits commented upon in the sections about psychodynamics.

3. Condoning, indulgence, weakness, inconsistency are features to be avoided. If patients (and staff) can get away with things, there is no support, no trust, no reliability and no respect. As soon as there is a collusion of illicit activity between patients and staff, or as soon as the patients can get away with major infractions (dealing on the premises, "fencing"), the program is bound to crumble.

On the other side of the ledger, however, no rule should be absolutely rigid. There are always reasonable exceptions to any rule. To walk a tightrope between flexibility and weakness is an art which cannot easily be put into words or mastered!

4. The obverse side of the same coin is the very important factor of vindictiveness: We have observed in several programs and in our own structure how some employees use rules to "kick out" patients. The reason may be personal disappointment about the inability to control

the situation; or they may feel threatened by a given patient. In particular, they fear for their own illusion of omnipotence—that they cannot play the savior and thus feed into the very sickness of the patients.

If patients are "kicked out" simply because of relapses and because of arousing the ire of someone on the staff, a spirit of arbitrariness and fear starts pervading the organization; it is almost needless to add that such a fear of vindictive retaliation (so much a part of the drug user's psychopathology anyway) is countertherapeutic. Again, the line between firmness and vindictiveness is fine and very difficult to draw.

This is also the reason why we have been cautious so far with the institution of self- government and self-policing by a patient group. Unless done with much tact and prudence, this again opens the door to power conflicts and acts of revenge.

5. Role reversal and chumminess are dangerous. For instance, a counselor may inappropriately reverse roles and confide some of his problems to a patient, thereby losing the minimum amount of respect. A patient placed prematurely into the role of a counselor or in the always impossible role of savior will not learn to cope with his own problems and is bound to become a treatment failure.

6. We have also seen how staff accepted or protected patients under the condition of sexual obedience or of remuneration. This is devastating to the responsibility of the entire program vis-à-vis patients and community. This aspect is part of the large problem of misuse of power: if patients are accepted on the basis of sexual compliance or of financial gratuity or just plain like and dislike, the goal of helping the patients toward a more rational, honest and responsible existence is corrupted. With such acts, one upholds, even reinforces, the worst part of their illness: the belief that everybody is crooked and morally corrupt and that to manage life equals to lie. Moreover, the "straight" staff has then greatest difficulties to maintain a rational, structured therapeutic environment with their patients.

7. Closely related to this point is: never to lie to patients. To lie, especially about dosage, is a breach of trust and countertherapeutic to the extreme. If we do, we set the stage for continued dishonesty between patient and life. Moreover, one lie quickly drags along other lies and finally, an entire world of fantasies, delusion and deceit. Again the overall duplicity described before has a disastrous impact on the morale of patients and staff alike.

8. Regarding the selection of personnel we have noticed that many people highly qualified in other professions and interested in joining are unable to work with addicts. Others are attracted by the quick glory into this work and turn out to be more devious, corrupt, and destructive than the patients themselves. In contrast, we found people who have little training of any kind but may have just the necessary combination of firmness and sympathy to become pivotal in a program. It is those who have access to the street people and their language, and yet the knack for the essentials. Above all they have the ability to see through the deceptions and manipulations, paired with an inner restraint against reacting with vengeful threats and punishment to the inevitable and often very severe frustrations of the job. They are few; many decompensate as the years pass by. It appears the inevitable course—that many fail, and only a few remain firm, strong, and committed.

In view of these paradoxes, the turnover of employees in such programs would be, indeed should be, high, were it not for the artificial constraints which make it so hard to get rid of the least capable, most harmful, often outright unethical staff.

To sum up: We need (a) *firmness* without rigidity—the setting of unequivocal limits in a program, clearly spelled out expectations of patients and staff alike, and a basic structure of discipline, consistency and clarity; (b) *honesty*—a refusal to play games of any kind, particularly manipulation and deception of patients; (c) a basic *respect* for the patients and the realness and magnitude of their inner and outer problems; (d) the emotional *support* when necessary to help the patients through the long chain of crises they inevitably have to pass through on the way toward a more integrated life.

However, the longer I work with such programs the more I feel convinced that the entire program should be yet far more psychotherapeutically and neuropsychiatrically oriented: there should be much more psychiatric time dedicated to staff and patients alike!

Looking at this appendix in a broader, national scope, I have to share the discouraged feeling expressed by John C. Ball (1972): "To date, attempts at program evaluation and coordination among facilities have been most disappointing. On the basis of both state and national surveys of drug treatment facilities, we have found that the quality of scientific resources and the intellectual effort devoted to contrasting, comparing, and evaluating the outcome of treatment is minimal."

But I should go a step farther: there is widespread recognition that the treatment of intensive and compulsive drug abuse should pay central attention to the depth of psychiatric disturbances in these patients. The efforts carried out, however, to deal with the seriousness of this problem are contradictory, sparse, often superficial and untrained. Psychiatry has shunned getting deeply involved. Sectarian, dogmatic, self-righteous treatment approaches have abounded.

The field is, partly dictated by the conditions of sponsor agencies on state and federal level, filled with untrained or ill-trained paraprofessionals, whose background in clinical ethics, knowledge, and ability is often deplorable and for the patient-victim devastating. Much more stringent conditions for the participation of well-trained psychotherapists, psychiatrists and psychoanalysts in the running of all types of programs for heavy drug users (obviously not for the peripheral groups) is widely recognized, but in the famous expression, "it is a custom more honored in the breach than the observance."

REFERENCES

Albright, W.F. (1973). From the patriarchs to Moses. *Biblical Archaeologist* 36:5–33, 48–76.

Altschul, S. (1968). Denial and ego arrest. *Journal of the American Psychoanalytic Association* 16:301–318.

Arlow, J.A. (1966). Depersonalization and derealization. In *Psychoanalysis—A General Psychology: Essays in Honor of Heinz Hartmann,* ed. R.M. Loewenstein, L.M. Newman, M. Schur, and A.J. Solnit. New York: International Universities Press.

——— (1969a). Unconscious fantasy and disturbances of conscious experience. *Psychoanalytic Quarterly* 38:1–27.

——— (1969b). Fantasy, memory, and reality testing. *Psychoanalytic Quarterly* 38: 28–51.

———(1972). The only child. *Psychoanalytic Quarterly 4:507–536.*

"Aristides" (1976). Incidental meditations. American Scholar 45:173–179.

Arnold, L.E., Strobl, D., and Weisenberg, A. (1972). Hyperkinetic adult: study of the "paradoxical" amphetamine response. *Journal of the American Medical Association* 222:693–694 (November 6).

Ausubel, D.P. (1958). *Drug Addiction: Physiological, Psychological, and Sociological Aspects.* New York: Random House.

Ball, J.C. (1972). Editor's notebook. *American Journal of Psychiatry* 128:873–874.

Bandler, B. (1970/71). A generation in jeopardy. *International Journal of Psychiatry* 9:714–718.

Battegay, R., Ladewig, D., Muhlemann, R., and Weidmann, M. (1976). The culture of youth and drug abuse in some European countries. *International Journal of the Addictions* 11:245–262.

Baudelaire, C. (1947). *Les Fleurs du Mal; Spleen de Paris; Les Paradis Artificiels; Journaux Intimes.* 2 vols. Lausanne: La Guilde du Livre.

Bazelon, D.L. (1969). Drugs that turn on the law. Address at the Ditchley Foundation, November 9.

Becker, H.S., (1967). History, culture and subjective experience: an exploration of the social bases of drug-induced experiences. *Journal of Health and Social Behavior* 8:163–176.

Bendix, R. (1970). *Embattled Reason.* New York: Oxford University Press.

Benjamin, J.D. (1959). Prediction and psychopathological theory. In *Dynamic Psychopathology in Childhood,* ed. L. Jessner and E. Pavenstedt. New York: Grune and Stratton.

Beres, D. (1965a). Symbol and object. *Bulletin of the Menninger Clinic* 29:2–28.

——— (1965b). Psychoanalysis, science and romanticism. In *Drives, Affects, Behavior,* Vol. 2, ed. Max Schur, pp. 397–417. New York: International Universities Press.

——— (1965c). Structure and function in psycho-analysis. *International Journal of Psycho-Analysis* 46:53–63.

——— (1968). The humanness of human beings: psychoanalytic considerations. *Psychoanalytic Quarterly* 37:487–522.

——— (1974). Character pathology and the "borderline" syndrome. Unpublished manuscript presented at Baltimore–District of Columbia Society of Psychoanalysis.

Beres, D., and Arlow, J.A. (1974). Fantasy and identification in empathy. *Psychoanalytic Quarterly* 43:26–50.

———, and Joseph, E.D. (1970). The concept of mental representation. *International Journal of Psycho-Analysis* 51:1–9.

Berman, Leon E. A. (1972). The role of amphetamine in a case of hysteria. *Journal of the American Psychoanalytic Association* 20:325–340.

Bibring, E. (1954). Psychoanalysis and the dynamic psychotherapies. *Journal of the American Psychoanalytic Association* 2:745-770.

Bing, J.F., McLaughlin, F., and Marburg, R. (1959). The metapsychology of narcissism. *Psychoanalytic Study of the Child* 14:9-28.

Binswanger, L. (1957). Der Fall Ellen West. In L. Binswanger, *Schizophrenie*, pp. 57-188. Pfullingen: Neske.

Blos, P. (1971). Adolescent concretization: a contribution to the theory of delinquency. In *Currents in Psychoanalysis*, ed. I.M. Marcus. New York: International Universities Press.

Blum, R.H., et al. (1969a). *Society and Drugs*. San Francisco: Jossey-Bass.

――― (1969b). *Students and Drugs*. San Francisco: Jossey-Bass.

――― (1972). *Horatio Alger's Children*. San Francisco: Jossey-Bass.

Blumer, D. (1971). Neuropsychiatric aspects of psychomotor and other forms of epilepsy. In *Comprehensive Management of Epilepsy in Infancy, Childhood and Adolescence*, ed. S. Livingston. Springfield, Ill.: Charles C Thomas.

――― (1974). Organic personality disorders. In *Personality Disorders*, ed. J.R. Lion, pp. 203-222. Baltimore: Williams and Wilkins.

Blumer, D., and Benson, D.F., eds. (1975). *Psychiatric Aspects of Neurological Disease*. New York: Grune and Stratton.

Boroffka, A. (1966). Mental illness and Indian hemp in Lagos. *East African Medical Journal* 43 (9):377-384.

Bourne, P.G., and Ramsay, A.S. (1964). The therapeutic community phenomenon. Unpublished manuscript.

Bradlow, P.A. (1973). Depersonalization, ego splitting, non-human fantasy and shame. *International Journal of Psycho-Analysis* 54:487-492.

Brecher, E.M. (1972). *Licit and Illicit Drugs*. Mount Vernon. N.Y.: Consumers Union.

Brill, L. (1972). *The De-Addiction Process*. Springfield, Ill.: Charles C Thomas.

――― (1973). Review of innovative programs and techniques. In *Methadone: Experiences and Issues*, ed. C.D. Chambers and L. Brill, pp. 269-289. New York. Behavioral Publications.

―――, ed. (1972). *Major Modalities in the Treatment of Drug Abuse*. New York: Behavioral Publications.

Brill, L., and Lieberman, L. (1969). *Authority and Addiction.* Boston: Little, Brown.

Brill, N.Q., and Christie, R.L. (1974). Marijuana use and social adaptation. *Archives of General Psychiatry* 31:713-719.

Bromberg, W. (1939). Marijuana: a psychiatric study. *Journal of the American Medical Association* 113:4-12.

Brown, B.S., Kozel, N.J., Meyers, M.B., and Dupont, R.L. (1973). Use of alcohol by addict and non-addict populations. *American Journal of Psychiatry* 130:599-601.

Burckhardt, J. (1868). *Weltgeschichtliche Betrachtungen.* Stuttgart: A. Kroner, 1963.

Bychowski, G. (1968). *Evil in Man: The Anatomy of Hate and Violence.* New York: Grune and Stratton.

Byrd, O.E. (1970). *Medical Readings on Drug Abuse.* Reading, Mass.: Addison-Wesley.

Carmichael, J. (1967). *The Shapicg of the Arabs.* New York: Macmillan.

Cassirer, E. (1906, 1907, 1920). *Das Erkenntnisproblem in der Philosophie und Wissenschaft der neueren Zeit.,* Vols. I-II. Hildesheim: Georg Olvs Verlag, 1971.

—— (1910). *Substance and Function.* Transl. W.C. Swabey and M.C. Swabey, pp. 3-346. New York: Dover, 1953.

——(1921). *Einstein's Theory of Relativity Considered From the Epistemological Standpoint.* Transl. W.C. Swabey and M.C. Swabey, pp. 349-460. New York: Dover, 1953.

—— (1923a). *Philosophie der symbolischen Formen,* Vol. I. Darmstadt: Wissenschaftliche Buchgesellsehaft, 1956.

—— (1923b). *Philosophie der symbolischen Formen,* Vol. II. Darmstadt: Wissenschftliche Buchgesellschaft, 1958

—— (1927). *The Individual and the Cosmos in Renaissance Philosophy.* Transl. M. Domandi. New York: Harper and Row, 1963.

—— (1929). *Philosophie der symbolischen Formen,* Vol. III. Darmstadt: Wissenschaftliche Buchgesellschaft, 1959.

—— (1932a). *The Question of Jean Jacques Rousseau.* Transl., ed. P. Gay. Bloomington: Indiana University Press, 1967

—— (1932b). *The Philosophy of the Enlightenment.* Transl. F.C.A. Koelln and J.P. Pettegrove. Princeton: Princeton University Press, 1951.

————(1937). Wahrheitsbegriff und Wahrheitsproblem bei Galilei. In *Philosophie und exakte Wissenschaft,* pp. 90–114. Frankfurt a.M.: Vittorio Klostermann, 1969.

————(1939). Descartes' Wahrheilsbegriff. In *Philosophie und exakte Wissenschaft,* pp. 62–89. Frankfurt a.M.: Vittorio Klostermann, 1969.

————(1940a). Mathematische Mystik und mathematische Naturwissenschaft. In *Philosophie und exakte Wissenschaft,* pp. 39–61. Frankfurt a.M.: Vittorio Klostermann, 1969.

———— (1940b). *The Problem of Knowledge,* Vol. IV: *Philosophy, Science, and History since Hegel.* Transl. W.H. Woglom and C.W. Hendel. New Haven: Yale University Press, 1969.

———— (1942). *The Logic of the Humanities.* Transl. C.S. Howe. New Haven: Yale University Press, 1961.

———— (1944). *An Essay on Man: An Introduction to a Philosophy of Human Culture.* New Haven: Yale University Press, 1962.

———— (1945). *Rousseau, Kant, Goethe.* Transl. by J. Gutmann, P.O. Kristeller, and J.H. Randall. Princeton: Princeton University Press, 1970.

———— (1946). *The Myth of the State.* New Haven: Yale University

Cavior, N., Kurtzberg, R., and Lipton, D. (1967). The development and validation of a heroin addiction scale. *International Journal of the Addictions* 2:129–138.

Cameron, A. (1968). *The Identity of Oedipus the King.* New York: New York University Press.

Casswell, S., and Marks, D.F. (1972). Cannabis and temporal disintegration in experienced and naive subjects. *Science* 179:803–805.

Cheek, F.E. (1973). Methadone plus a behavior modification training program in self-control for addicts on methadone maintenance. *International Journal of the Addictions* 8:969–996.

Chein, I., Gerard, D.L., Lee, R.S., and Rosenfeld, E. (1964). *The Road to H.* New York: Basic Books.

Citron, B.P. (1970). Study cites fatality risk in methamphetamine use. *Psychiatric News,* December 16; *New York Times,* November 6.

Clark, L.D., and Nakashpma, E.N. (1968). Experimental studies of marijuana. *American Journal of Psychiatry* 125:379–384.

Coghlan, A.J., Dohrenwend, E.F., Gold, S.R., and Zimmermann, R.S. (1973). A psychobehavioral residential drug abuse program: a new adventure in adolescent psychiatry. *International Journal of the Addictions* 8:767–777.

Cohen, C.P., White, E.H., and Scholaar, J.C. (1971). Interpersonal patterns of personality for drug abusing patients and their therapeutic implications. *Archives of General Psychiatry* 24:353–358.

Cohen, M., and Klein, D.M. (1974). Posthospital adjustment of psychiatrically hospitalized drug users. *Archives of General Psychiatry* 31:221–227.

Cohen, S. (1964). *The Beyond Within: The LSD Story.* New York: Atheneum, 1968.

—— (1975). Marijuana today. *Drug Abuse and Alcoholism Newsletter* 4:1.

Cohen, S., and Ditman, K.S. (1962). Complications associated with lysergic acid diethylamide (LSD–25). *Journal of the American Medical Association* 181:161–162, July 14.

—— (1963). Prolonged adverse reactions to lysergic acid diethylamide. *Archives of General Psychiatry* 8:475–480.

Coles, R., Brenner, J.H., and Meagher, D. (1970). *Drugs and Youth: Medical, Psychiatric and Legal Facts.* New York: Liveright.

Conners, C.K. (1967). The syndrome of minimal brain dysfunction: psychological aspects. *Pediatric Clinics of North America* 14:749–766.

Conrad, J. (1900). *Lord Jim.* London and Paris: The Albatross, 1947.

—— (1902). *Heart of Darkness.* In *The Shaping of Fiction.* New York: Washington Square Press, 1970.

Corman, A.G., Johnson, B., Khantzian, E.J., and Long, J. (1973). Rehabilitation of narcotic addicts with methadone: the public health approach v. the individual perspective. *Contemporary Drug Problems* (Winter Issue), pp. 565–578.

Culver, C.M., and King, F.M. (1974). Neuropsychological assessment of undergraduate marijuana and LSD users. *Archives of General Psychiatry* 31:707–711.

Crowlay, R.M. (1939). Psychoanalytic literature of drug addiction and alcoholism. *Psychoanalytic Review 26:39–54.*

Crowley, T.J., Chesluk, D., Dilts, S., and Hart, R. (1974). Drug and alcohol abuse among psychiatric admissions. *Archives of General Psychiatry* 30:13–20.

Curtis, H.C. (1939). Psychosis following the use of marijuana with report of cases. *Journal of the Kansas Medical Sociaty*, pp. 515–526.

Davis, D., and Klagsburn, M. (1975). Substance abuse and family interaction: a review of the literature and recommendations for future research. Paper presented at the Symposium on Family and Drug Abuse, Columbia, Md.

De Leon, G., Skodol, A., and Rosenthal, M.S. (1971). Phoenix House: changes in psychopathological signs of resident drug addicts. *Archives of General Psychiatry* 28:131–135.

Deutsch, H. (1930). Hysterical fate neurosis. In *Neuroses and Character Types,* pp. 14–28. New York: International Universities Press, 1965.

Dodds, E.R. (1951). *The Greeks and the Irrational.* Berkeley: University of California Press. 1968.

Dole, V. P. (1969). Research on methadone maintenance. *Proceedings of the 2nd National Conference on Methadone Maintenance,* pp. 359–370.

Dole, V.P., Nyswander, M.E., and Warner, A. (1968). Successful treatment of 750 criminal addicts. *Journal of the American Medical Association* 206:2710–2711.

Dole, V.P., Nyswander, M.E., and Warner, A. (1968). Successful treatment of 750 criminal addicts. *Journal of the American Medical Association* 206:2710–2711.

Draper, T. (1975). The United States and Israel. *Commentary* 59:29–45.

——— (1976). Appeasement and détente. *Commentary* 61:27–38.

Droppa, D.C. (1973). Behavioral treatment of drug addiction: a review and analysis. *International Journal of the Addictions* 8:143–161.

DuPont, R.L. (1973). The treatment of heroin addicts: a historical and personal review. *Career Directions* 3(3):20.

Edwards, G. (1968). The problem of cannabis dependence. *Practitioner* 200:226–233.

Ehrlich, T. (1976). Legal pollution. *New York Times Magazine,* February 8.

Eisnitz, A.J. (1974). On the metapsychology of narcissistic pathology. *Journal of the American Psychoanalytic Association* 22:279–291.

Eissler, K.R. (1950). Ego-psychological implications of the psychoanalytic treatment of delinquents. *Psychoanalytic Study of the Child* 5:97–121.

———— (1959). On isolation. *Psychoanalytic Study of the Child* 14:29–60.

———— (1969). Irreverent remarks about the present and the future of psychoanalysis. *International Journal of Psycho-Analysis* 50:461–471.

———— (1971). Death drive, ambivalence, and narcissism. *Psychoanalytic Study of the Child* 26:25–78.

———— (1975). The fall of man. *Psychoanalytic Study of the Child* 30:589-646.

Ellinwood, E.H. (1971). Assault and homicide associated with amphetamine abuse. *American Journaliof Psychiatry* 127:1170–1175.

Else, G.F. (1967). *The Origin and Early Form of Greek Tragedy.* Cambridge: Harvard University Press.

Erikson, E.H. (1950). *Childhood and Society,* New York. Norton.

———— (1959). Identity and the life cycle. *Psychological Issues* I.

———— (1964). *Insight and Responsibility.* New York: Norton.

———— (1968). *Identity, Youth and Crisis.* New York: Norton.

Esman, A.H. (1967). Drug use by adolescents: some valuative and technical implications. *Psychoanalytic Forum* 2(4):340–353.

Fairlie, H. (1975). Anti-americanism at home and abroad. *Commentary* 60:29–39.

Farber, L. (1966). Ours is the addicted society. *New York Times Magazine,* December 11.

Farnsworth, D.L., and Oliver, H.K. (1968). The drug problem among young people. *Rhode Island Medical Journal* 51:179–182.

Federn, P. (1952). *Ego Psychology and the Psychoses.* New York: Basic Books.

Fenichel, O. (1934). Defense against anxiety, particularly by libidinization. In The Collected Papers of Otto Fenichel, Vol. 1, pp. 303–317. New York: Norton, 1953.

———— (1941). *Problems of Psychoanalytic Technique.* New York: Psychoanalytic Quarterly.

———— (1945). *The Psychoanalytic Theory of Neurosis.* New York: Norton.

Fingarette, H. (1975). Addiction and criminal responsibility. *Yale Law Journal* 84:413–444.

————(1976). Disabilities of mind and criminal responsibility: a unitary doctrine. *Columbia Law Review* 76:236–267.

Fish, B. (1971). The "one child, one drug" myth of stimulants in hyperkinesis: importance of diagnostic categories in stimulating treatment. *Archives of General Psychiatry* 25:193–203.

Forrest, D.V. (1973). On one's own onymy. *Psychiatry* 36:266–290.

Frankel, C. (1973). The new egalitarianism and the old. *Commentary* 56:54–61.

Frederick, C.J., Resnick, H.L.P., and Wittlin, B. (1973). Self-destructive aspects of hard core addiction. *Archives of General Psychiatry* 28:579–585.

Freud, A. (1936). The ego and the mechanisms of defense. *The Writings of Anna Freud,* Vol. II. New York: International Universities Press, 1971.

——— (1963). The concept of developmental lines. *Psychoanalytic Study of the Child* 18:245–265.

——— (1965). Normality and pathology in childhood: assessments of development. *The Writings of Anna Freud,* Vol. VI. New York: International Universities Press.

——— (1967). Residential vs. foster care. *The Writings of Anna Freud,* Vol. VII. New York: International Universities Press, 1971.

Freud, S. (1895). A reply to criticisms of my paper on anxiety neurosis. *Standard Edition* 3:121–139.

——— (1900). The interpretation of dreams. *Standard Edilion* 4/5.

———(1905a). Three essays on sexuality. *Standard Edition* 7:123–243.

——— (1905b). Jokes and their relation to the unconscious. *Standard Edition* 8.

——— (1911). Formulations on the two principles of mental functioning. *Standard Edition* 12:213–226.

——— (1912a). The dynamics of transference. *Standard Edition* 12:97–108.

——— (1912b). On the universal tendency to debasement in the sphere of love. *Standard Edition* 11:179–190.

——— (1914). On narcissism: an introduction. *Standard Edition* 14:69–102.

——— (1915). Instincts and their vicissitudes. *Standard Edition* 14:109–140.

——— (1916/1917). Introductory lectures. *Standard Edition* 15/16.

——— (1919). A child is being beaten. *Standard Edition* 17:175–204.

—–— (1920). Beyond the pleasure principle. *Standard Edition* 18:3–66.

—–— (1923). The ego and the id. *Standard Edition* 19:3–68.

—–— (1924). The economic problem of masochism. *Standard Edition* 19:157–172.

—–— (1926). Inhibitions, symptoms, and anxiety. *Standard Edition* 20:75–174.

—–— (1927). The future of an illusion. *Standard Edition* 21:3–56.

—–— (1930). Civilization and its discontents. *Standard Edition* 21:57–145.

—–— (1938a). An outlice of psychoanalysis. *Standard Edition* 23:139–207.

—–— (1938b). Splitting of the ego in the process of defense. *Standard Edition* 23:271–278.

—–— (1939). Moses and monotheism. *Standard Edilion* 23:3–137.

Freund, P.A. (1975). The great diuorder of speech. *American Scholar* 44:541–559.

Frontiers of Hospital Psychiatry (1968). *Roche Report,* Vol. 5, April 15.

Frosch, J. (1967). Delusional fixity, sense of conviction and the psychotic conflict. *International Journal of Psycho-Analysis* 48:475–495.

Frosch, W.A., Robbins, E.S., and Stern, M. (1965). Untoward reactions to lysergic acid diethylamide (LSD) resulting in hospitalization. *New England Journal of Medicine* 273:1235–1239.

Galbraith, J.K. (1958). *The Affluent Society.* New York: Mentor Book.

Gertler, R. (1973). Some aspects of general psychiatric ward management of drug addicts. *Drug Forum* 2:395–402.

Gill, M.M. (1963). Topography and systems in psychoanalytic theory. *Psychological Issues* Monograph 10. New York: International Universities Press.

Gilman, R.D. (1965). Brief psychotherapy: A psychoanalytic view. *American Journal of Psychiatry* 122:601–611.

Glasscote, R., Sussex, J.N., Jaffe, J.H., Ball, J., and Brill, L. (1972). *The Treatment of Drug Abuse: Programs, Problems, Prospects.* Washington, D.C.: Joint Information Service, APA and NIMH.

Glover, E. (1932). On the etiology of drug addiction. In *On the Early*

Development of Mind, pp. 187–215. New York: International Universities Press, 1970.

Goethe, J.W.v. (1968). *Gesamtausgabe*, DTV. München.

Goldsmith, P.G. (1974). Evaluation of treatment programs for drug abusers. 5th International Institute on Prevention and Treatment of Drug Dependence, Copenhagen.

Goode, E. (1969a). Multiple drug use among marijuana smokers. *Social Problems* 17:48–64.

——— (1969b). Marijuana and the politics of reality. *Journal of Health and Social Behavior* 10:83–94.

Gordis, R. (1968). *Kohelet, the Man and His World: A Study of Ecclesiastes.* New York: Schocken, 1973.

Gotthelf, J. (1840). Ulideknecht. In *Birkhäuser Ausgabe*, Vol. 4. Basel, 1948.

Gray, P. (1973). Psychoanalytic technique and the ego's capacity for viewing intrapsychic activity. *Journal of the American Psychoanalytic Association* 21:474–494.

Greden, J.F., Morgan, D.W., and Frenkel, S. (1974). The changing drug scene: 1970–1972. *American Journal of Psychiatry* 131:77–81.

Greenacre, P. (1945). Conscience in the psychopath. In P. Greenacre, *Trauma, Growth and Personality,* pp. 165–187. New York: International Universities Press, 1969.

——— (1960). Further notes on fetishism. In P. Greenacre, *Emotional Growth*, pp. 182–198. New York: International Universities Press, 1971.

——— (1963). Problems of acting out in the transference relationship. In P. Greenacre, *Emotional Growth*, pp. 695–712. New York: International Universities Press, 1971.

——— (1970). Notes on the influence and contribution of ego psychology to the practice of psychoanalysis. In P. Greenacre, *Emotional Growth*, pp. 776–806. New York: Internaional Universities Press, 1971.

Greenson, R.R. (1967). *The Technique and Practice of Psychoanalysis.* New York: International Universities Press.

Griffith, J. (1968). Psychiatric implications of amphetamine abuse. In *Amphetamine Abuse*, ed. J.R. Russo, pp. 15–31. Springfield, Ill.: Charles C Thomas.

Grinker, R. (1955). Growth inertia and shame. *International Journal of Psycho-Analysis* 36:242–253.

Grinspoon, L. (1971). *Marijuana Reconsidered.* Harvard University Press.

Grotjahn, M. (1971). *The Voice of the Symbol.* Los Angeles: Mara Books.

Haertzen, C., and Panton, J. (1967). Development of a "psychopathic" scale for the Addiction Research Center Inventory (ARCI).*International Journal of the Addictions* 2:115-128.

Halikas, J.A., and Rimmer, J.D. (1974): Predictors of multiple drug abuse. *Archives of General Psychiatry* 31:414-418.

Halliday, R. (1963): *British Columbia Medical Journal* 5:412.

———(1964). Treatment of patients addicted to narcotic drugs. *Canadian Medical Journal* 90:937-938.

Harms, E. (1973a). Psychopathology in the juvenile drug addict. In *Drugs and Youth: The Challenge of Today,* pp. 120-130. New York: Pergamon Press.

———(1973b). Psychotherapy with the juvenile drug addict. In *Drug and Youth: The Challenge of Today,* pp. 206-221. New York: Pergamon Press.

Harbin, H. and Maziar, M. (1975). The families of drug abusers: a literature review. *Family Process* 14:411-431.

Hartmann, D. (1969). A study of drug taking adolescents. *Psychoanalytic Study of the Child* 24:384-398.

Hartmann, H. (1922). Ein Fall von Depersonalisation. *Zeitschrift f.d. Gesamte Neurologie und Psychiatrie* 74:593-601.

———(1939). Psychoanalysis and the concept of health. In H. Hartmann, *Essays on Ego Psychology.* pp. 3-18. New York: International Universities Press, 1964.

———(1947). On rational and irrational action. In H. Hartmann, *Essays on Ego Psychology,* pp. 37-68. New York: International Universities Press, 1964.

———(1951). Technical implications of ego psychology. In H. Hartmann, *Essays on Ego Psychology,* pp. 142-154. New York: International Universities Press, 1964.

———(1955). Notes on the theory of sublimation. IN H. Hartmann, *Essays on Ego Psychology,* pp. 215-240. New York: International Universities Press, 1964.

Hartmann, H., Kris, E., and Loewenstein, R.M. (1946). Comments on the formation of psychic structure. *Psychoanalytic Study of the Child* 2:11-38.

—— (1947). Notes on the theory of aggression. *Psychoanalytic Study of the Child* 3/4: 9–36.

Hartocollis, P. (1968). The syndrome of minimal brain disfunction in young adult patients. *Bulletin of the Menninger Clinic* 32:102–114.

Hattersely, M. (1973). Heroin addiction and the psychiatric hospital. *Drug Forum* 2:431–440.

Heller, M.E., and Mordkoff, A.M. (1972). Personality attributes of the young, non-addicted drug abuuer. *International Journal of the Addictions* 7:65–72.

Hendin, H. (1974). Students on heroin. *Journal of Nervous and Mental Diseases* 158:240–255; Students on amphetamines. *Journal of Nervous and Mental Diseases*, 158:255–267.

Henriques, E., Arsenian, J., Cutter, H., and Samaraweera, A.B. (1972). Personality characteristics and drug of choice. *International Journal of the Addicligns* 7:73–76.

Herman, Rochelle (1976). Application of verbal behavior analysis to the study of psychological defense mechanisms: speech pattern associated with heroin addiction. Unpublished manuscript.

Hoffer, A. (1965). Dlysergic acid diethylamide (LSD): a review of its present status. *Clinical Pharmacology and Therapeutics* 6(2):183–255.

Hoffman, S., and Hoffman, I. (1968). The will to grandeur: de Gaulle as political artist. *Daedalus* 97:829–887.

Hofstadter, R. (1948). *The American Political Tradition*. New York: Vintage Books.

—— (1962). *Anti-Intellectualism in American Life*. New York: Vintage Books.

—— (1967). *The Paranoid Style in American Politics and Other Essays*. New York: Vintage Books.

Hollister, L. (1971). Marijuana in man: three years later. *Science* 172:21–29.

—— (1973). *Clinical Use of Psychotherapeutic Drugs*. Springfield, Ill.: Charles C Thomas.

Hughes, P., Chappel, J., Senay, E., and Jaffe, J. (1971). Developing inpatient services for community based treatment of narcotic addiction. *Archives of General Psychiatry* 25:278–283.

Hughley, E.J. (1973). Vocational and social adjustment of the treated juvenile addict. In *Drugs and Youth,* ed. E. Harms, pp. 164–169. New York: Pergamon Press.

Huxley, A. (1963). *The Doors of Perception* and *Heaven and Hell.* New York: Harper Colophon.

Jacobson, E. (1957). Denial and repression. *Journal of the American Psychoanalytic Association* 5:61–92.

——— (1959). Depersonalization. *Journal of the American Psychoanalytic Association* 7:531–610.

——— (1964). *The Self and the Object World.* New York: International Universities Press.

Jaeger, W. (1933). *Paideia: The Ideals of Greek Culture.* Vol. I Trans. G. Highet. Oxford: Blackwell, 1965.

——— (1943a). *Paideia: The Ideals of Greek Culture.* Vol. II. Trans. G. Highet. New York: Oxford University Press, 1969.

——— (1943b). *Paideia: The Ideals of Greek Culture.* Vol. III. Trans. G. Highet. New York: Oxford University Press, 1969.

Jaffe, J. H. (1965). Narcotic analgesics. In *A Pharmacological Basis of Therapeutics,* 3rd ed., ed. L.S. Goodman and A. Gilman, pp. 247–311. New York: Macmillan.

——— (1969). Pharmacological approaches to the treatment of compulsive opiate use: their rationale and current status. In *Drugs and the Brain,* ed. P. Black. Baltimore: Johns Hopkins Press.

Jaspers, K. (1949). *Einfuhrüng in die Philosophie.* Zürich: Artemis Verlag, 1950.

——— (1957). *Die grossen Philosophen.* Munich: R. Piper.

Jorgensen, F. (1967). Psykoser 1 Tilslutning TilCannabis. *Ugeskrift for Laeger* 129:1648–1656.

Jones, E. (1929). Fear, guilt and hate. In E. Jones, *Papers on Psychoanalysis,* pp. 304–319. Boston: Beacon Press, 1967.

Judson, H.F. (1973). *Heroin Addiction in Britain.* New York: Harcourt Brace Jovanovich.

Kaplan, E.H., and Wieder, H. (1974). *Drugs Don't Take People, People Take Drugs.* Secaucus, N.J.: Lyle Stuart.

Kaplan, H.S., and Meyerowitz, J.J. (1969). Psychosocial predictors of post-institutional adustment among male drug addcits. *Archives of General Psychiatry* 20:278–284.

Kaplan, J. (1970). *Marijuana: The New Prohibition.* Cleveland: World.

Karp, E.G. (1973). Narcotic addicts: personality, treatment, and outcome. Unpublished disertation.

Karp, E.C., Wurmser, L., and Savage, C. (1975). Therapeutic effects of methadone and LAAM (two case reports). *American Journal of Psychiatry* 133 (1976):955–957.

Karpman, B. (1947). The myth of the psychopathic personality.

Katan, M. (1964). Fetishism, splitting of the ego, and denial. *International Journal of Psycho-Analysis* 45:237–245.

Kaufman, E. (1972). A psychiatrist views an addict self-help program. *American Journal of Psychiatry* 128:846–852.

Kaufmann, W. (1968). *Tragedy and Philosophy*. New York: Doubleday Anchor, 1969.

Kazin, A. (1976). "The giant killer": drick and the American writer. *Commentary* 61:44–50.

Keeler, M.H. (1967). Adverse reaction to marijuana. *American Journal of Psychiatry* 124:674–677.

Keeler, M.H., Reifler, C.B., and Liptzin, M.B. (1968). Spontaneous recurrence of marijuana effect. *American Journal of Psychiatry* 125:384–386.

Keniston, K. (1960). *The Uncommitted: Alienated Youth in American Society*. New York: Dell, 1967.

——— (1968). Youth, change and violence. *American Scholar* 37:227–245.

——— (1969). Heads and seekers: drugs on campus, counter-cultures and American society. *American Scholar* 38:97–112.

Kernberg, O.F. (1967). Borderline personality organization. *Journal of the American Psychoanalytic Associalion* 15:641–685.

——— (1970a). Factors in the psychoanalytic treatment of narcissistic personalities. *Journal of the American Psychoanalytic Association* 18:51–85.

———(1970b). A psychoanalytic classification of character pathology. *Journal of the American Psychoanalytic Association* 18:800–822.

———(1971). Prognostic considerations regarding borderline personality organization. *Journal of the American Psychoanalytic Association* 19:595–635.

——— (1974). Contrasting viewpoints regarding the nature and psychoanalytic treatment of narcissistic personalities: a preliminary communication. *Journal of the American Psychoanalytic Association* 22:255–267.

———— (1975). *Borderline Conditions and Pathological Narcissism.*
New York: Jason Aronson.

Ketai, R. (1973). Peer observed psychotherapy with institutionalized
narcotic addicts. *Archives of General Psychiatry* 29:51–53.

Khantzian, E.J. (1972a). A preliminary dynamic formulation of the
psychopharmacologic action of methadone. Proceedings of 4th
National Conference on Methadone.

———— (1972b). Narcotic addiction and dynamic psychiatry. In *Career
Directions* 3(3):26–37.

———— (1973). Opiate addiction: a critique of theory and some
implications for treatment. *American Journal of Psychotherapy*
28:59–70.

————(1975). Self-selection and progression in drug dependence.
36:19–22.

————(1976). The ego, the self, and opiate addiction: theoretical
considerations and implications for treatment. NIDA, Technical
Review, Psychodynamic Aspects of Narcotics Addiction.

Khantzian, E.J. Mack, J.E., and Schatzberg, A.F. (1974). Heroin use
as an attempt to cope: clinical observations. *American Journal of
Psychiatry* 131:160–164.

Kielholz, P., and Battegay, R. (1963). The treatment of drug addicts in
Switzerland. *Comprehensive Psychiatry* 4:225–235.

Kipperman, A., and Fine, E.W. (1974). The combined abuse of alcohol
and amphetamines. *American Journal of Psychiatry* 131:1277–
1288.

Kirkman, Lucy (1976). Preliminary findings with a test battery
obtained from narcotics addicts upon admission to treatment.
Unpublished manuscript.

Kissinger, H.A. (1968). The white revolutionary: reflections on
Bismarck. *Daedalus* 97:888–924.

Kleber, H.D. (1967). Prolonged adverse reactions from unsupervised
use of hallucinogenic drugs. *Journal of Nervous and Mental
Diseases* 144:308–319

Kohn, H. (1955). *Nationalism.* Princeton, N.J.: Van Nostrand, 1965.

Kohut, H. (1959). Introspection, empathy and psychoanalysis.
Journal of the American Psychoanalytic Association 7:459–483.

————(1966). Forms and transformations of narcissism. *Jorunal of
the American Psychoanalytic Association* 14:243–272.

————(1968). The psychoanalytic treatment of narcissistic personality disorders. *Psychoanalytic Study of the Child* 23:86–113.

————(1971). *The Analysis of the Self.* New York: International Universities Press.

————(1972). Thoughts on narcissims and narcissistic rage. *Psychoanalytic Study of the Child* 27:360–400.

————(1973). Psychoanalysis in a troubled world. *Annual of Psychoanalysis* 1:3–25.

Kolansky, H., and Moore, W.T. (1972). Toxic effects of chronic marijuana use. *Journal of the American Medical Association* 222:35–41.

Kolb, L. (1962). *Drug Addiction: A Medical Problem.* Springfield, Ill.: Charles C Thomas.

Kramer, R.A. (1974). Adolescent drug abuse: a problem or a solution? Reported to the 5th International Institute on Prevention and Treatment of Drug Dependence. Copenhagen.

Kristol, I. (1972). About equality. *Commentary* 54:41–47.

Krystal, H. (1974). The genetic development of affects and affect regression. *Annual of Psychoanalysis:* 2:93–126.

————(1975). Affect tolerance. *Annual of Psychoanalysis* 3:179–219.

Krystal, H. and Raskin, H.A. (1970). *Drug Dependence: Aspects of Ego Functions.* Detroit: Wayne State University Press.

Kubie, L.S. (1934). Body symbolization and the development of language. *Psychoanalytic Quarterly* 3:1–15.

————(1947). The fallacious use of quantitative concepts in dynamic psychology. *Psychoanalytic Quarterly* 16:507–518.

————(1953a). The distortion of the symbolic process in neurosis and psychosis. *Journal of the American Psychoanalytic Association* 1:59–86.

————(1953b). The central representation of the symbolic process in psychosomatic disorders. *Psychosomatic Medicine* 15:1–7.

————(1954). The fundamental nature of the distinction between normality and neurosis. *Psychoanalytic Quarterly* 23:167–204.

————(1956). Influence of symbolic processes on the role of instincts in human behavior. *Psychosomatic Medicine* 18:189–208.

————(1970–1971). The retreat from patients. *International Journal of Psychiatry* 9:693–711.

Kuhn, T.S. (1970). *The Structure of Scientific Revolutions.* 2nd ed. Chicago: University of Chicago Press.

————(1970b). Logic of discovery or psychology of research. In *Criticism and the Growth of Knowledge,* ed. I. Lakatos and A. Musgrave, pp. 1–23. Cambridge: Cambridge University Press.

Kupfer, D.J., Detre, T., Koral, J., and Fajans, P. (1973). A comment on the amotivational syndrome in marijuana smokers. *American Journal of Psychiatry* 130:1319–1322.

Kurland, A.A., Krantz, J.C., Henderson, J.M., and Kerman, F. (1973). Naloxone and the narcotic abuser: a low dose maintenance program. *International Journal of the Addictions* 8:127–142.

Kurland, A.A., Wurmser, L., Kerman, F., and Kokoski, R. (1966a). Urine detection tests in the management of the narcotic addict. *American Journal of Psychiatry* 122:727–742.

————(1966b). Laboratory control in the treatment of the narcotic addict. *Current Psychiatric Therapies* 6:243–246.

————(1967). The deterrent effect of daily urine analysis for opiates in a narcotic out-patient facility: a two and one-half year study. Reported to the Committee on Problems of Drug Dependence, National Academy of Sciences, National Research Council, Published in proceedings.

————(1969). Intermittent patterns of narcotics usage. In *Drug Abuse: Social Pharmacological Aspects*, ed. J.O. Cole and J.R. Wittenborn, pp. 129–145. Springfield, Ill.: Charles C Thomas.

Lakatos, I. (1970). Falsification and the methodology of scientific research programmes. In *Criticism and the Growth of Knowledge,* ed. I. Lakatos and A. Musgrave, pp. 91–196. Cambridge: Cambridge University Press.

Langer, S.K. (1942). *Philosophy in a New Key.* New York: Mentor Book, 1962.

————(1953). *Feeling and Form.* London: Routledge and Kegan Paul, 1973.

————(1956). *Philosophical Sketches.* New York: Mentor Book, 1964.

————(1967). *Mind: An Essay on Human Feeling.* Vol. I. Baltimore: Johns Hopkins Press, 1970.

————(1972). *Mind: An Essay on Human Feeling.* Vol. II. Baltimore: Johns Hopkins Press, 1974.

Laqueur, W. (1969). Reflections on youth movements. *Commentary* 47:33–41.

————(1974). The gathering storm. *Commentary* 58:23–33.

————(1975). The west in retreat. *Commentary* 60:44–52.

————(1976). Fascism–the second coming. *Commentary* 61:57–62.

Lehman, W.X. (1974). A unique method of therapy for the adolescent drug abuser. Presented at 5th International Institute on Prevention and Treatment of Drug Dependence, Copenhagen.

Lehman, W.X. and De Angelis, G.G. (1973). Adolescents and short term, low dose methadone maintenance. *International Journal of the Addictions* 8:853–863.

Lemere, F. (1966). The danger of amphetamine dependency. *American Journal of Psychiatry* 123:569–572.

————(1968). *Hospital Tribune,* January 29; *New York Times,* April 29.

Lemkau, P.V., Amsel, Z., Sanders, B., Amsel, J., and Seif, T.F. (1975). Social and economic costs of drug abuse. Unpublished Report.

Lesky, A. (1972). Die Tragische Dichtung der Hellenen. Göttingen: Vandenhoeck und Ruprecht.

Levin, S. (1971). The psychoanalysis of shame. *International Journal of Psycho-Analysis* 52:355–362.

———— (1972). Some metapsychological considerations on the differentiation between shame and guilt. *International Journal of Psycho-Analysis* 48:267–276.

Levine, D.G., Levin, D.B., Sloan, J.H. and Chappel, J.N. (1972). Personality correlates of success in a methadone maintenance program. *American Journal of Psychiatry* 129:456–460.

Levy, L. (1925). The psychology of the effect produced by morphia. *International Journal of Psycho-Analysis* 6:313–316.

Lichtenberg, J.D. (1975). The development of the sense of self. *Journal of the American Psychoanalytic Association* 23:453–484.

Lichtenberg, J.D., and Slap, J.W. (1971). On the defensive organization. *International Journal of Psycho-Analysis* 52:451–457.

————(1972). On the defense mechanism: a survey and synthesis. *Journal of the American Psychoanalytic Association* 20:776–792.

————(1973). Notes on the concept of splitting and the defense mechanism of the splitting of representations. *Journal of the American Psychoanalytic Association* 21:772–787.

Lindesmith, A.R. (1947). *Addiction and Opiates.* Chicago: Aldine, 1968.

————(1965). *The Addict and the Law.* New York: Vintage Books.

————(1960). *Heidegger, Denker in dürftiger Zeit.* Göttingen: Vandenhoeck und Ruprecht.

Lowenfeld, H. (1976). Notes on shamelessness. *Psychoanalytic Quarterly* 55:62–72.

Lowenfeld, H., and Lowenfeld, Y. (1970). Our permissive society and the superego: some current thoughts about Freud's cultural concepts. *Psychoanalytic Quarterly* 39:590–608.

Löwith, K. (1941). *Von Hegel zu Nietzsche.* Stuttgart: W. Kohlhammer, 1958.

Lynd, H.M. (1961). *On Shame and the Search for Identity.* New York: Science Editions.

Maddux, J.F., and Bowden, C.L. (1972). Methadone maintenance: myth and reality. And: Critique of success with methadone maintenance. *American Journal of Psychiatry* 129:435–446.

Malcolm, A.I. (1971). *The Pursuit of Intoxication.* Toronto: Alcohol and Drug Addiction Research Foundation.

Marcovitz, E. (1969). On the nature of addiction to cigarettes. *Journal of the American Psychoanalytic Association* 17:1074–1096.

Maurer, D.W., and Vogel, V.H. (1954). *Narcotics and Narcotic Addiction.* Springfield, Ill.: Charles C Thomas, 1968.

McCracken, S. (1971). The drugs of habit and the drugs of belief. *Commentary* 51:43–52.

McGlothlin, W.H., and West, L.J. (1968). The marijuana problem: an overview. *American Journal of Psychiatry* 125:370–378.

Meers, D.R., and Gordon, G. (1972). Aggression and ghetto—reared American Negro children: structural aspects of the theory of fusion–defusion. *Psychoanalytic Quarterly* 41:585–607.

Mendenhall, G.E. (1973). *The Tenth Generation: The Origins of the Biblical Tradition.* Baltimore: Johns Hopkins Press.

Menninger, K. (1968). *The Crime of Punishment.* New York: Viking.

Mettler, E. (1976). Schiefer europäischer Blick auf Amerika (Editorial). *Neue Zürcher Zeitung,* January 3, 4.

Milkman, H., and Frosch, W.A. (1973). On the preferential abuse of heroin and amphetamine. *Journal of Nervous and Mental Diseases* 156:242–248.

Modell, A.H. (1965). On having the right to a life: an aspect of the superego's development. *International Journal of Psycho-Analysis* 46:323–331.

———(1968). *Object Love and Reality.* New York: International Universities Press.

Momigliano, A. (1975). The fault of the Greeks. *Daedalus* 104:9–19.

Monroe, J.J., Ross, W.F., and Berzins, J.I. (1971). The decline of the addict as "psychopath": implications for community care. *International Journal of the Addictions* 6:601–608.

Monroe, R.R. (1970). *Episodic Behavioral Disorders: A Psychodynamic and Neurophysiologic Analysis.* Cambridge, Mass.: Harvard University Press.

Moore, B.E., and Fine, D., eds. (1967). *A Glossary of Psychoanalytic Terms and Concepts.* New York: American Psychoanalytic Association.

Moynihan, D.P. (1969). *Maximum Feasible Misunderstanding.* New York: The Free Press.

———(1975a). The United States in opposition. *Commentary* 59:31–44.

———(1975b). Presenting the American case. *American Scholar* 44:564–583.

Mueller, H.J. (1958). *The Loom of History.* New York: Mentor Books, 1961.

———(1970). *The Children of Frankenstein.* Bloomington, Ind.: Indiana University Press.

Murphy, J. (1976). Psychiatric labelling in cross-cultural perspective. *Science* 191:1019–1028.

Murray, J.M. (1964). Narcissism and the ego ideal. *Journal of the American Psychoanalytic Association* 12:477–511.

Muschg, W. (1948). *Tragische Literaturgeschichte.* Bern: Francke Verlag, 1969.

———(1956). *Die Zerstörung der deutschen Literatur.* Bern: Francke Verlag, 1958.

Musto, D.F. (1973). *The American Disease.* New Haven: Yale University Press.

Nesbitt, M. (1940). Psychosis due to exogenous toxins—marijuana. *Illinois Medical Journal,* pp. 278–282.

Nilsson, M.P. (1925). *A History of Greek Religion.* London: Oxford University Press, 1972.

———(1932). *The Mycenaean Origin of Greek Mythology.* Berkeley: University of California Press, 1972.

Nisbet, R.A. (1975). The new despotism. *Commentary* 59:31–43.

Nowlis, H.H. (1969). *Drugs on the College Campus.* Garden City, New York: Anchor Books.

O'Connor, G., Wurmser, L., Brown, T.C., and Smith, J. (1971). The drug addiction business. *Drug Forum* 1:3–12.

Offer, D., and Sabshin, M. (1966). *Normality: Theoretical and Clinical Concepts of Mental Health.* New York: Basic Books, 1974.

O'Malley, J.E., Anderson, W.H., and Lazare, A. (1972). Failure of outpatient treatment of drug abuse: I. heroin; II. amphetamines, barbituates, and hallucinogens. *American Journal of Psychiatry* 128:865–868, 1572–1576.

Parsons, T. (1967). *Sociological Theory and Modern Society.* New York: The Free Press.

Partridge, M. (1963). Drug addiction in Great Britain. *Comprehensive Psychiatry* 4:210.

———(1967). Drug addiction: a brief review. *International Journal of the Addictions* 2:207–220.

Paulus, I., and Halliday, R. (1967). Rehabilitation and the narcotic addict: results of a comparative methadone withdrawal program. *Canadian Medical Association Journal* 96:655–659.

Perkins, M.E. (1972). Editor's notebook. *American Journal of Psychiatry* 129:461–462.

Piers, G., and Singer, M.B. (1953). *Shame and Guilt.* Springfield, Ill.: Charles C Thomas.

Pittel, S.M. (1971). Psychological aspects of heroin and other drug dependence. *Journal of Psychedelic Drugs* 4:44.

Popper, K.R. (1962). *Conjectures and Refutations: The Growth of Scientific Knowledge.* New York: Harper and Row, 1965.

———(1970): Normal science and its dangers. In *Criticism and the Growth of Knowledge,* ed. I. Lakatos and A. Musgrave, pp. 51–58. Cambridge: Cambridge University Press.

Powell, D.H. (1973). A pilot study of occasional heroin users. *Archives of General Psychiatry* 28:586–594.

Poze, R.S. (1972). Heroin addicts in a community mental health inpatient unit. *American Journal of Psychiatry* 129:206–210.

Preble, E., and Casey, J.J. (1969). Taking care of business: the heroin user's life on the street. *International Journal of the Addictions* 4:1–24.

Proskauer, S., and Rolland, R.S. (1973). Youth who use drugs: psychodynamic diagnosis and treatment planning. *Journal of the American Academy of Child Psychiatry* 12:32–47.

Pulver, S.E. (1970). Narcissism: the term and the concept. *Journal of the American Psychoanalytic Association* 18:319–341.

Pumpian-Mindlin, E. (1969). Vicissitudes of infantile omnipotence. *Psychoanalytic Study of the Child* 24:213–226.

Quitkin, F.M., Rifkin, A., Kaplan, J., and Klein, D.F. (1972). Phobic anxiety syndrome complicated by drug dependence and addiction. *Archives of General Psychiatry* 27:159–162.

Radford, P., Wiseberg, S., Yorke, C. (1972). A study of "main line" heroin addiction: a preliminary report. *Psychoanalytic Study of the Child* 27:156–180.

Radó, S. (1926). The psychic effects of intoxicants: an attempt to evolve a psycho-analytical theory of morbid cravings. *International Journal of Psycho-Analysis* 7:396–413.

———(1933). The psychoanalysis of pharmacothymia (drug addiction). *Psychoanalytic Quarterly* 2:1–23.

———(1963). Fighting narcotic bondage and other forms of narcotic disorders. *Comprehensive Psychiatry* 4:160–167.

Ramer, B.S., Zaslove, M.O., and Langan, J. (1971). Is methadone enough? The use of ancillary treatment during methadone maintenance. *American Journal of Psychiatry* 127:1040–1044.

Rangell, L. (1972). Aggression, Oedipus, and historical perspective. *International Journal of Psycho-Analysis* 53:3–11

———(1974). A psychoanalytic perspective leading currently to the syndrome of the compromise of integrity. *International Journal of Psycho-Analysis* 55:3–12.

———(1976). Lessons from Watergate: a derivative for psychoanalysis. *Psychoanalytic Quarterly* 45:37–61.

Rapaport, D. (1953). On the psychoanalytic theory of affects. In *The Collected Papers of David Rapaport,* ed. M.M. Gill, pp. 476–512. New York: Basic Books, 1967.

Ray, O.S. (1972). *Drugs, Society, and Human Behavior.* St. Louis: C.V. Mosby.

Renner, J.A., and Rubin, M.L. (1973). Engaging heroin addicts in treatment. *American Journal of Psychiatry* 130:976–980.

Robitscher, J. (1969). Morality, marijuana and the law. *Medical Opinion Review,* September.

Rochlin, G. (1973). *Man's Aggression: The Defense of the Self.* Boston: Gambil.

Rosenfeld, H.A. (1960). On drug addiction. In H. Rosenfeld, *Psychotic States,* pp. 128-143. New York: International Universities Press, 1965.

———(1964). The psychopathology of drug addiction and alcoholism: a critical survey of the psycho-analytic literature. In H. Rosenfeld, *Psychotic States,* pp. 217-242. New York: International Universities Press.

Rosenthal, S.H. (1964). Persistent hallucinosis following repeated administration of hallucinogenic drugs. *American Journal of Psychiatry* 121:238-244.

Roszak, T. (1968). *The Making of a Counter Culture.* Garden City, N.Y.: Doubleday.

———(1973). Some thoughts on the other side of this life. *New York Times,* April 12.

———(1975). Gnosis and reductionism. *Science* 187:790-792.

Sandler, J. (1974). Psychological conflict and the structural model: some clinical and theoretical implications. *International Journal of Psycho-Analysis* 55:53-62.

Sandler, J., Holder, A., and Meers, D. (1963). The ego ideal and the ideal self. *Psychoanalytic Study of the Child* 18:139-158.

Sassenrath, E.N. (1975). Test monkeys display "marijuana syndrome." *Journal of the American Medical Association* 233:1251-1255.

Schafer, R. (1968a). *Aspects of Internalization.* New York: International Universities Press.

———(1968b). The mechanisms of defense. International Journal of Psycho-Analysis 49:49-62.

———(1970). The psychoanalytic vision of reality. *International Journal of Psycho-Analysis* 51:279-297.

——— (1972). Internalization: process or fantasy? *Psychoanalytic Study of the Child* 27:411-436.

———(1973a). The idea of resistance. *International Journal of Psycho-Analysis* 44:259-286.

———(1973b). Action: its place in psychoanalytic interpretation and theory. *Annual of Psychoanalysis* 1:159-196.

———(1975). Psychoanalysis without psychodynamics. *International Journal of Psycho-Analysis* 46:41-56.

Scheler, M. (1915). *Vom Umsturz der Werte.* Bern: Francke Verlag, 1955.

————(1916). *Der Formalismus in der Ethik und die materiale Wertethik*. Bern: Francke Verlag, 1954.

Scholem, G.S. (1941). *Major Trends in Jewish Mysticism*. New York: Schocken Books, 1954.

————(1973). *Sabbatai Sevi*. Princeton, N.J.: Princeton University Press.

Schoof, Ebner, Lowy, and Hersch (1973). Personal communication, presented at APA Meeting.

Schur, E.M. (1965). *Crimes Without Victims: Deviant Behavior and Public Policy*. Englewood Cliffs, N.J.: Prentice-Hall.

————(1969). *Our Criminal Society*. Englewood Cliffs, N.J.: Prentice-Hall.

Schur, M. (1953). The ego in anxiety. In *Drives, Affects, Behavior,* ed. R. Loewenstein, pp. 67–104. New York: International Universities Press.

————(1966). *The Id and the Regulatory Principles of Mental Functioning*. New York: International Universities Press.

Seabury, P. (1972). HEW and the universities: how Washington enforces new forms of discrimination in the name of equal opportunity. *Commentary* 53:38–44.

Searles, H.F. (1960). *The Nonhuman Environment in Normal Development and in Schizophrenia*. New York: International Universities Press.

Shafer, R.P. (1972–1973). Marijuana: a signal of misunderstanding; Drug use in America: problem in perspective. First and Second Reports of the National Commission on Marijuana and Drug Abuse, R.P. Shafer, chairman. Washington, D.C.: U.S. Government Printing Office.

Shearn, C.R., and Fitzgibbons, D.J. (1972). Patterns of drug use in a population of youthful psychiatric patients. *American Journal of Psychiatry* 128:1381–1387.

————(1973). Survey of reasons for illicit drug use in a population of youthful psychiatric in-patients. *International Journal of the Addictions* 8:623–633.

Sherwood, M. (1969). *The Logic of Explanation in Psychoanalysis*. New York: Academic Press.

————(1973). Another look at the logic of explanation in psychoanalysis. In *Psychoanalysis and Contemporary Science,* Vol. 2, ed. B.B. Rubinstein, pp. 359–368. New York: Macmillan.

Siegman, A.J. (1970). A note on the complexity surrounding a temporary use of denial. *Journal of the American Psychoanalytic Association* 18:372–378.

Sifneos, P.E. (1974). A reconsideration of psychodynamic mechanisms in psychosomatic symptom formation in view of recent clinical observations. *Psychotherapy and Psychosomatics* 24:151–155.

Simmel, E. (1929). Psycho-analytic treatment in a sanatorium. *International Journal of Psycho-Analysis* 10:70–89.

Simon, B. (1973). Plato and Freud: the mind in conflict and the mind in dialogue. *Psychoanalytic Quarterly* 42:91–122.

Singer, M.T. (1974). Impact versus diagnosis: a new approach to assessment techniques in family research and therapy. Paper presented at the Nathan W. Ackerman Memorial Conference, Cumana, Venezuela, February, 1974.

Singer, M.T., and Wynne, L.C. (1966). Principles for scoring communication defects and deviances in parents of schizophrenics: Rorschach and TAT scoring manuals. *Psychiatry* 29:260–288.

Sisk, J.P. (1973). On intoxication. *Commentary* 53:56–61.

Slap, J.W. (1974). On waking screens. *Journal of the American Psychoanalytic Association* 22:844–853.

Smith, K.L. (1977). Organizational aspects of health care social organization. In *Psychiatric Foundations of Medicine,* ed. G. Balis, L. Wurmser, and E. McDaniel. Reading, Mass.: Butterworth, 1978.

Snow, C.P. (1963). *The Two Cultures* and *A Second Look.* Cambridge: Cambridge University Press.

Sojit, C.M. (1969). Dyadic interaction in a double bind situation. *Family Process* 8:235–259.

———(1971). The double bind hypothesis and the parents of schizophrenics. *Family Process* 10:53–74.

Sola, S.A., and Wieland, W.F. (1971). The psychopathology of narcotic dependent individuals. Committee on Problems of Drug Dependence, National Research Council.

Spruiell, V. (1974). Theories of the treatment of narcissistic personalities. *Journal of the American Psychoanalytic Association* 22:268–278.

———(1975). Three strands of narcissism. *Psychoanalytic Quarterly* 44:577–595.

Stanton, D.M., and Todd, T.C. (1976). Structural family therapy with heroin addicts: some outcome data. Unpublished manuscript.

Stewart, W.A. (1970). The split in the ego and the mechanism of disavowal. *Psychoanalytic Quarterly* 39:1–16.

Stierlin, H. (1969). *Conflict and Reconciliation*. New York: Anchor Books.

————(1974). *Separating Parents and Adolescents*. New York: Quadrangle.

Stolorow, R.D. (1975a). Addendum to a partial analysis of a perversion involving bugs: an illustration of the narcissistic function of perverse activity. *International Journal of Psycho-Analysis* 56:361–364.

————(1975b). The narcissistic function of masochism (and sadism). *International Journal of Psycho-Analysis* 56:441–448.

Stolorow, R.D., and Grand, H.T. (1973). A partial analysis of a perversion involving bugs. *International Journal of Psycho-Analysis* 54:349–350.

Van Stone, W.W. (1974). Treating the drug dependent veteran: perspectives from a Veterans Administration hospital. *International Journal of the Addictions* 9:593–604.

Szasz, T.S. (1957). The problem of psychiatric nosology. *American Journal of Psychiatry* 114:405.

————(1961). *The Myth of Mental Illness*. New York: Hoeber-Harper.

————(1973). *Ceremonial Chemistry*. Garden City, N.Y.: Anchor Books, 1975.

Tarachow, S. (1963). *An Introduction to Psychotherapy*. New York: International Universities Press.

Tomin, B., and Glenn, A. (1968). Psychotherapy with drug abusers in a male admitting service. *Psychiatric Quarterly* 42:144–155.

Torda, C. (1968). Comments on the character structure and psychodynamic processes of heroin addicts. *Perceptual and Motor Skills* 27:143–146.

Treece, H. (1962). *The Crusades*. New York: Mentor Books, 1964.

Trevor-Roper, H.R. (1956). *The European Witch-Craze*. New York: Harper and Row, 1969.

Trilling, L. (1971). *Sincerity and Authenticity*. Cambridge, Mass.: Harvard University Press, 1974.

————(1974). The uncertain future of humanistic education. *American Scholar* 44:52–67.

Trunnell, E.E., and Holt, W.E. (1974). The concept of denial or disavowal. *Journal of the American Psychoanalytic Association* 22:769–784.

Tucker, G.J., Quinlan, D., and Harrow, M. (1972). Chronic hallucinogenic use and throught disturbance. *Archives of General Psychiatry* 27:443–447.

Tylden, E. (1967). A case for cannabis? *British Medical Journal* 3:556 (August 26).

de Unamuno, M. (1921). *The Tragic Sense of Life*. New York: Dover, 1954.

Ungerleider, Y.T., Fisher, D.D., and Fuller, M. (1966). The danger of LSD. *Journal of the American Medical Association* 197 (6): 389–392.

Vaillant, G.E. (1966). A 12 year follow-up of New York narcotic addicts. I. The relation of treatment to outcome. *American Journal of Psychiatry* 122:727–737; II. The natural history of a chronic disease. *New England Journal of Medicine* 275:1282–1288; III. Some social and psychiatric characteristics. *Archives of General Psychiatry* 15:599–609.

Vaillant, G.E., and Rasor, R.W. (1966). The role of compulsory supervision in the treatment of addiction. *Federal Probation* 30:53–59.

Vierth, G. (1967). Psychopathologische Syndrome nach Haschisch—Genuss. *Munch. Med. Wschr.* 109:522–526.

Waelder, R. (1930). The principle of multiple functioning. *Psychoanalytic Quarterly* 5:45–62.

————(1936). The problem of freedom in psychoanalysis and the problem of reality-testing. *International Journal of Psycho-Analysis* 18:89–108.

————(1951). The structure of paranoid ideas. *International Journal of Psycho-Analysis* 32:167–177.

————(1960). *Basic Theory of Psychoanalysis*. New York: International Universities Press.

————(1962). Psychoanalysis, scientific method and philosophy. *Journal of the American Psychoanalytic Association* 10:617–637.

————(1967). *Progress and Revolution*. New York: International Universities Press, 1970.

————(1970). Observation, historical reconstruction and experiment: an epistemological study. In *Psychoanalysis and Philosophy,* ed. C. Hanly and M. Lazerowitz. New York: International Universities Press.

————(1973). Sigmund Freud centennial lecture. *Annual of Psychoanalysis* 1 26–35.

Wallerstein, R.S. (1963). The problem of the assessment of change in psychotherapy. *International Journal of Psycho-Analysis* 44:31–41.

————(1964). The role of prediction in theory building in psychoanalysis. *Journal of the American Psychoanalytic Association* 12:675–691.

————(1974). Psychoanalysis as a science: its present status and its future task. Presented at the Meeting of the American Psychoanalytic Association, May 1974, Denver.

Wallerstein, R.S., and Sampson, H. (1971). Issues in research in the psychoanalytic process. *International Journal of Psycho-Analysis* 52:11–50.

Washburn, S.L. (1965). Conflict in Primate Society. In *Conflict in Society: Ciba Foundation Symposium,* ed. A. de Reuck and J. Knight. Boston: Little, Brown, 1968.

Weeks, K.R. (1976). Book review: La Médecine égyptienne au temps des pharaons, by A.P. Leca. *Journal of Near Eastern Studies* 35:43–46.

Weil, A.T., Zinberg, N.E., and Nelsen, J.M. (1968). Clinical and psychological effects of marijuana in man. *Science* 162:1234–1242.

Weil, E. (1975). What is a breakthrough in history? *Daedalus* 104 (2): 21–36.

Weiss, E. (1960). *The Structure and Dynamics of The Human Mind.* New York: Grune and Stratton.

Wellisch, D.K., Gay, G.R., Wesson, D.R., and Smith, D.E. (1971). The psychotic heroin addict. *Journal of Psychedelic Drugs* 4:46–49.

Werner, H. (1948). *Comparative Psychology of Mental Development.* New York: International Universities Press, 1964.

Wieder, H., and Kaplan, E.H. (1969). Drug use in adolescents: psychodynamic meaning and pharmacogenic effect. *Psychoanalytic Study of the Child* 24:399–431.

Wiesel, E. (1974). Ominous signs and unspeakable thoughts. New York Times, December 28.

Wilde, O. (1962). *The Picture of Dorian Gray.* New York: New American Library.

Wilder, T. (1967). *The Eighth Day*. Toronto: Popular Library.

Wishnie, H. (1971). Opioid addiction: a masked depression. In *Masked Depression*, ed. S. Lesse. New York: Jason Aronson, 1974.

Wittenborn, J.R., Brill, H., Smith, J.P., and Wittenborn, S.A. (1969). *Drugs and Youth: Proceedings of the Rutgers Symposium on Drug Abuse*. Springfield, Ill.: Charles C Thomas.

Wurmser, L. (1959). Raubmörder und Räuber. *Kriminalistik* (Hamburg).

————(1962). Ueber die Entfremdung (About estrangement). In *Beiträge zur Diagnostik, Prognostik und Therapie des Schicksals*, ed. L. Szondi. Bern: Hans Huber.

————(1963). Theoretische und praktische Aspekte der Schizophrenie-Psychotherapie (Theoretical and practical aspects of the psychotherapy of schizophrenics). *Schweizer Archiv für Neurologie, Neurochirurgie und Psychiatrie* 92:437–488.

————(1965). Rauschgiftsucht: Verbrechen oder Krankheit? (Drug addiction: crime or disease?). *Kriminalistik* (Hamburg) 19:356–359.

————(1966a). Depersonalization and shame: a clinical contribution to the study of estrangement. Unpublished manuscript.

————(1966b). The compromise character of estrangement. Unpublished manuscript presented at the Fall Meeting of the American Psychoanalytic Association.

————(1968a). Drug addiction and drug abuse: a synopsis. *Maryland State Medical Journal* 17:68–80.

————(1968b). The phenomenology of shame psychosis. *Sinai Hospital Journal* 14:88–103.

————(1968c). Structure and function of shame. Unpublished manuscript presented at the Spring Meeting of the American Psychoanalytic Association.

————(1968d). Two types of boundaries and the development of aggression. Unpublished manuscript presented at the Fall Meeting of the American Psychoanalytic Association.

————(1968e). Magical eye and shame. Unpublished manuscript.

————(1970a). Myths and facts about marijuana. *Johns Hopkins Hospital Alumnae Magazine*, March.

———— (1970b). The program of the Johns Hopkins Hospital Drug Abuse Center. *Johns Hopkins Hospital Alumnae Magazine*, March.

————(1970c). Principles of prevention of drug abuse. Presented to U.S. Senate, Committee on D.C., (Sen. Tydings), April 15. In *Crime in the National Capital.* Washington, D.C.: U.S. Government Printing Office.

————(1970d). Why people take drugs: escape and search. *Maryland State Medical Journal* 19:62–64.

————(1970e). Observations about the effects of marijuana use. Presented at International Symposium on Drug Abuse, August, Jerusalem.

————(1970f). Some psychological comments on prejudice against methadone maintenance. In *Proceedings of the 3rd National Methadone Conference, New York, 1970.* Washington, D.C.: National Institute of Mental Health. Excerpt published in *Psychiatric News,* June 1971.

————(1972a). Drug abuse: the nemesis of psychiatry. *American Scholar* 41:393–407.

————(1972b). Methadone and the craving for narcotics: observations of patients on methadone maintenance in psychotherapy. *Proceedings, 4th National Conference on Methadone Treatment, 1972,* pp. 525–528.

————(1972c). Author's reply. *International Journal of Psychiatry* 10:117–128.

————(1973a). Unpolitic thoughts about the politics of drug abuse treatment. *Journal of Drug Issues* 3:178–185.

————(1973b). "Tragic patients": psychoanalytic thoughts about the tragic experience. Presented at the Fall Meeting of the American Psychoanalytic Association.

————(1974a). Psychoanalytic considerations of the etiology of compulsive drug use. *Journal of the American Psychoanalytic Association* 22:820–843.

————(1974b). Personality disorders and drug dependency. In *Personality Disorders* ed. J.R. Lion. Baltimore: Williams and Wilkins.

————(1975a). A defense of the use of metaphor in psychoanalytic theory formation. *Psychoanalytic Quarterly* 46 (1976): 466–498.

————(1975b). A clinical study about the tragic character. Lewis B. Hill Award Presentation, Baltimore–D.C. Society for Psychoanalysis. Unpublished manuscript.

————(1975c). Tragic character, metaphor, and the problem of knowledge in psychoanalysis. Unpublished manuscript.

Wurmser, L., Levin, L., and Lewis, A. (1969). Chronic paranoid and depressive symptoms in users of marijuana and LSD as observed in psychotherapy. Presented at the 31st Annual Meeting of the Committee on Problems of Drug Dependence, National Research Council (Published in Proceedings).

Wurmser, L., and Spiro, H. (1969). Factors in recognition and management of sociopathy and the addictions. In *Modern Treatment,* vol. 6, ed. E.T. Lisansky and B. R. Schochet, pp. 704–719. New York: Hoeber.

Wynne, L.C., and Singer, M.T. (1963). Thought disorder and family relations of schizophrenics. *Archives of General Psychiatry* 9:191–206.

———(1966). Schizophrenic impairments of shared focal attention. 10th Annual Bertram Roberts Memorial Lecture, Yale University.

Yorke, C. (1970). A critical review of some psychoanalytic literature on drug addiction. *British Journal of Medical Psychology* 43:141–159.

Zilboorg, G. (1941). *A History of Medical Psychology.* New York: W.W. Norton.

Zinberg, N.E. (1974). *"High" States: A Beginning Study.* Washington, D.C.: The Drug Abuse Council.

———(1975). Addiction and ego function. *Psychoanalytic Study of the Child* 30:567–588.

INDEX

modes of, 152–54
nature of, 150–52
splitting and denial and, 432–39
deception and self-deception, 433–34
drug use and drug traffic in ghetto, 423–33
estrangement and, 436–39
leisure and creativity, 435–36
television, 434–35

facilitators, federal and state-wide, in treatment, 498–99
family
as part of predisposition, 276–78
research and treatment of, as innovative technique in treatment, 496
family interaction, addict's assessment of, 369–79
family research, 359–81
case history, 363–68
predicting behavior in addict's family, 368–81
assessment of family interaction, 369–79
summary and conclusions, 380–81
in therapy, 379–80
summary of literature, work of H. Harbin and, 360–63
Farber, L., 387, 433
Federn, P., 250
Fenichel, O., 46, 48, 50, 127, 128, 259, 336
Feuerbach, L., 437
Fine, B.D., 150
Fine, D., 115
Fingarette, H., 94, 462
Fino, P.A., 443
Fitzgibbons, D.J., 61, 526
Forrest, D.V., 421
fragmentation and disjunction, partial splitting by, 139–42
Frankel, C., 442
Frederick, C.J., 61
Freud, A., 51, 110, 127, 128, 147, 151, 239, 388
Freud, S., 22, 44, 47, 80, 86, 89, 90, 91, 103, 104, 105, 114, 115, 116, 117, 124, 129, 130, 131, 136, 138, 141, 145, 150, 161, 194, 235, 236, 247, 249, 268, 330, 351, 388, 418, 429, 442, 472, 503, 504
Frosch, J., 349

Galbraith, J., 425
Galileo, 23, 84, 98, 388

Gautier, Théophile, 24
Gerard, D.L., 52
Gerson, A., 285, 310, 313, 317, 318, 321
ghetto, drug use and drug traffic in, 432–33
Gill, M.M., 128
Glasscote, R., 69–70, 101, 102
Glover, E., 15, 43, 45, 46, 47, 49
Goethe, Johann W. von, 23, 155, 417, 436
Goldsmith, P.G., 463–64
Goldstein, A., 385
Goode, E., 424
Gordon, G., 423
Gotthelf, J., 421
Gray, P., 149, 469
Greenacre, P., 51, 65, 140, 335, 337, 483, 494
Greenson, R., 473
Grinker, R., 259
Grotjahn, M., 434
guilt, shame and boundaries of, 259–62
dilemma of narcissism and, 253–55
need for, vs. surfeit of legalism and ostentatiousness, 447–48

Halikas, J.A., 62
Hamill, P., 221
Hand, Learned, 447
Harbin, H.T., 359, 360–63
Harms, E., 61, 341
Harrison, J., 329
Hardy, Thomas, 160
Hartmann, D., 56, 160
Hartmann, H., 80, 86, 128, 132, 194, 271
Hawthorne, Nathaniel, 260
Hegel, G.W., 436, 437, 438, 503
Heidegger, M., 437
Heilbroner, R., 419
Hendin, H., 59, 60
Hesse, H., 351, 437
hierarchy, etiological structure of, 102–105
causes of, 103–105
phenomenological distinction, 102–103
Hilgard, E.R., 388
Hoffman, I., 274
Hoffman, S., 273, 274
Hoffmann, E.T.A., 144
Hofstadter, R., 389, 422, 440
Hollister, L., 342
Holt, W.E., 110, 130, 135, 194
Homer, 109
Hugo, Victor, 260